THE
BICYCLING BOOK

"BICYCLING – the best thing man has ever done".

THE BICYCLING BOOK

☆ TRANSPORTATION ☆ RECREATION ☆ SPORT ☆

DESIGNED & EDITED BY

John Krausz & Vera van der Reis Krausz

Paul Harris, M.D. Medical Editor

The Dial Press
New York

This book owes much to Lou Maltese's and Fred Hamel's knowledge of bicycling and of human nature, and to Howard Marder's editorial, Bill Knight's legal, and Bob Perl's financial advice. It would never have read as well without Mel Bernstine's and Ed Dimenberg's editorial assistance, or looked as beautiful without the help of Ms. Kerman and Ms. Constantin of the Netherlands Information Services, nor Nancy Hunt-Webber's cleaning up of the mechanicals.

In the course of preparing this book, the following have also, for the good of cycling, most graciously allowed us to impose on their time: Torchy Peden, Keith Kingbay, Cecil Behringer, Roy Stetina, Eddy Van Guyse, Miji Reoch, Paul Cornish, John Marino, James Fulton III of the League of American Wheelmen, Alan Parker of Australia, Stuart Parker of Scotland, Dr. Gabe Mirkin, Rich Hammen, Connie Orentlicher, Peter Cummings, Amy McClellan, Ron Friedel of Wisconsin, Dr. Ken Phifer of Maryland, Jim Reynolds of New Jersey, Captain Jack Smith of Florida, Ralph Sinclair of Ohio, Philip Smith of Arizona, Barry Zalph of North Carolina, Willie the Gypsy, Harold Hill of the New York City Board of Education, Philip Burke of the Bicycle Manufacturers Association of America, Grey Siple of TOSRV-Bikecentennial, Ray Caparros of the Schwinn Bicycle Company, George O'Connell, director of the Bicycle Safety Program for the State of Illinois, G. Donald Adams of the Henry Ford Museum, and William Gillum of the American Railbike Association.

We also thank the following for their courtesy and help: Ms. Buch of the Danish Information Office, Geoffrey Wood of the British Trade Association, Georges Henri of the French Information Service, Jim Smith of the Bicycle Commuters of New York, Rosalind Heinz of the Long Wharf Theatre, Dottie Saling of the USCF, Ned Levine and Dixon Newbold of Rhode Gear, Barbara and Robert George of *Velo-News,* Jim Konski, Ralph Hirsch, Peter Stevens, Ron Skarin, Sue Novara, Ron Shepherd, Leslie Moore Nitz, Joan Marshall, Mark Wierzba, Jackie Simes III, and Heinz Walter.

Page 1: "Bicycling, the Health Giver," by Jean-Pierre de Mondenard, M.D., translated from the French by Vera van der Reis Krausz, originally appeared in *Caducycle* (10 place Peyron, 95641 Marines, France), the magazine of the Amicale Cycliste du Corps de Sante (Friends of Cycling in the Health Professions), Vol. V, No. 17, 1977. Reprinted with permission of the author. Pages 3, 6, 20-21, and 265 all have excerpts from *Albina et la bicyclette,* by Jacques Faizant, copyright © 1968 by Calmann-Levy, reprinted by permission of Calmann-Levy, Ltd., Paris, translated by Vera van der Reis Krausz. Page 7: "Better Bike Riding," by John Forester, appeared in a slightly different version in *The Complete Guide to the Bicycle,* Petersen Publishing Co., Los Angeles, California, 1975. Copyright has reverted to John Forester. Reprinted with permission of the author. Page 37: "Effective Cycling—A Model Adult Training Program," by Edward B. Deuerlein, reprinted with permission from *The Midwest Bicycle Review,* is excerpted from articles from May through August, 1979, based on *Effective Cycling,* copyright © 1978 by John Forester, Custom Cycle Fitments, 726 Madrone, Sunnyvale, CA 94086. Page 75: "The Way the Wind Blows" originally appeared as part of the chapter "Getting on with the Elements" in *Bike Tripping,* by Tom Cuthbertson, copyright © 1972 by Tom Cuthbertson and Philip Wood. Distributed to the bike trade by Ten Speed Press, Box 4310, Berkeley CA 94704, and to the book trade by Random House; in Canada by Random House of Canada, Ltd. Page 78: "Tips on Touring," by Hartley Alley, is reprinted with permission of the author from the catalog of the Touring Cycle Shop, Boulder, Colorado. Page 107: "Winter Cycling in Finland," by Alan Robson, appeared in a slightly different version in *Freewheeling,* 14 Picardy Place, Edinburgh 1, Scotland, January and February 1980. Reprinted with permission; copyright © 1980 by Freewheeling Ltd. Page 112: "American Bicycle Polo," by Walter K. Ezell, appeared in a slightly different form in *The American Wheelman,* September 1978, reprinted with permission; copyright © 1978 by League of American Wheelmen. Page 128: "Come Ride With Me," by Michael Roeder, is reprinted from *Double Talk,* the bulletin of the Tandem Club of America, Vol. 2, No. 1, with permission of the author. Page 130: "Tandem People," by Ruth Rapp, is reprinted from the "Bicycle People" columns in *The Bicycle Paper,* copyright © 1978 and 1979 with permission of the author. Page 158: "The Tour de France," by Nicolas Freeling, first appeared in a slightly longer version as "The Last Gasp to the Last Lap," in *The Daily Telegraph Magazine,* issue 552; reprinted with permission from Woodfin Camp & Associates, New York City, American representatives of DTM. Page 183: "Advice from a Sports Physiologist," by Edmund R. Burke, Ph.D., includes "If you need help, go to an athlete doctor," from *Inside the Cyclist,* copyright © 1979, reprinted by permission of *Velo-News,* Box 1257, Brattleboro, VT 05301. Pages 184-187: "Cyclists, Control Your Own Physical Condition," "Diet for Cyclists, Whether Racers or Not," "Carbohydrate Loading," and "A Myth to Dispel—Driest is Fastest," are all by Jean-Pierre de Mondenard, M.D., translated by Vera van der Reis Krausz, excerpted and reprinted from *Caducycle* (op. cit.), April-June 1978 and July-September 1979, with permission of the author. Page 218: "The Uniped Theory," by George Gipe, is reprinted from *Great American Sports Book,* copyright © 1974, 1975, 1976, 1977, 1978 by Time, Inc. Portions of this book first appeared in a slightly different form in *Sports Illustrated.* From *Great American Sports Book* by George Gipe. Reprinted by permission of Doubleday & Co., Inc. Page 220: "Women and Exercise," by Dorothy Harris, is abstracted from articles previously published in *Womensports* magazine, copyright © 1977 and 1978, reprinted with permission from the author and from Womensports Publishing Co., by Charter Sports, New York, New York. Pages 236, 240, and 255: "Frames," "Wheels and Wheel Building," and "Component Wear" are by Donald Taylor, and previously appeared in *Freewheeling,* (op. cit) © 1979 and 1980. All are reprinted with permission of the author. Page 257: "Obstacles to Human-Powered Transport," by David Gordon Wilson, is reprinted from *Technology Review,* copyright © 1979 by the Alumni Association of the Massachusetts Institute of Technology, with permission. Page 267: "Profession: Cyclist," by Bertil Lundquist, reprinted by permission from *International Cycling Guide 1980,* copyright © 1980 by A.S. Barnes & Co., Inc. of San Diego, and The Tantivy Press of London. Page 269: "Yes, Those Were the Days," by Rex Coley, reprinted with permission from the December 16, 1978 issue of *Cycling,* I.P.C. Business Press, Ltd., 1 Throwley Way, Sutton, Surrey, SM1 4QQ England.

Published by
The Dial Press
1 Dag Hammarskjold Plaza
New York, New York 10017
Copyright © 1982 by John Krausz and Vera van der Reis Krausz
All rights reserved.
Manufactured in the United States of America
First printing

Library of Congress Cataloging in Publication Data
Main entry under title:

The bicycling book.

Includes index.
1. Cycling—Addresses, essays, lectures.   I. Krausz,
John.   II. Krausz, Vera van der Reis.   III. Harris,
Paul, 1936–
GV1041.B526   1982   796.6   81-15082
ISBN 0-385-27666-4 (pbk.)   AACR2

Bicycling, the Best Thing Man Has Ever Done

The bicycle is the most recent invention that everyone can understand, and the only thing that bridges the green technology of handicrafts and gardening and the gray technology of applied science and factories.

Biking is about four times more efficient than walking or running. The bicycle provides door-to-door transport; it is the perfect urban vehicle, making all but the most sprawling city man-sized.

The bicycle is the best thing man has ever done because it is almost as if man was designed to ride a bicycle. His agile brain gives a moment by moment report of states of balance and rates of change in angles and speeds, then dictates the minute adjustments that need to be made; his clever hands steer, work gear-change mechanisms and brake levers, ring bells and honk horns; his powerful legs—designed for climbing, running, and kicking—now freed from the need to support his body by the exoskeleton of the bike, move him faster than the swiftest horse.

The modern bicycle is of such terrifying efficiency that it allows almost anyone to outrun and outlast the finest runner, and yet can give people with physical limitations the mobility they desire. World-class cyclists are the most fit of all athletes, yet no sport can boast of as many active septuagenarians and octogenarians (and to them this book is dedicated). They are one of the great resources of our sport, and we have learned much from them.

And bicycling is SUCH FUN. Almost everyone is capable of going 15 miles an hour, as if he had legs twenty feet long, and with some practice can keep this up hour after hour. Long after the marathon runner has hung up his shoes the cyclist continues. . .

Someone once said about bicycling that it's like rolling your childhood into a ball, putting the ball in your pocket, and riding with it the rest of your life.

By becoming a cyclist and not just an owner or occasional user, you join a vast fraternity. Even if you're walking, other cyclists will recognize you as one of their own because you look at their bikes and not at them. But be warned—you might become one of the bands of young men who spend their entire youth roaming the country looking for another bicycle race to compete in or another mountain to climb. Drenched to the skin and blue with cold, you'll have the time of your life. You might become fifty-five percent bicycle, like the postman in Flann O'Brien's The Third Policeman, one of those who "get their personalities mixed up with the personalities of their bicycles as a result of the interchanging of atoms of each of them." Or you might become like Hemingway, always regretting that you don't write in French, because French is the only language in which you can really write about cycling.

If you become a cyclist you will make friends with people you wouldn't have dreamed of knowing. You'll want to do things you wouldn't have dreamed of doing, like racing little old ladies to a traffic light, pretending you're in the Tour de France, or, having finally completed your first century (100 miles in less than a day), planning your route across the country. You'll find you can do without a car, but must have another bicycle.

That's because bicycling is fun. This is so self-evident that cyclists writing about cycling usually don't mention it.

The problem here in America is that the stream of cycling tradition was all but broken by post-war affluence, which brought with it—among other things—all the cars; people moved out of the cities and into the suburbs, which resulted in more cars; and ultimately the attitude developed that the bicycle was a child's toy—or at best an antiquated mode of transportation—and so, as soon as possible, people got cars and left the bikes to the kids. Aside from a handful of hardcore cyclists, the only people who continued to cycle in the '50's were college students on large campuses or school children who biked out of necessity. And parents who didn't cycle themselves could only tell their children to "watch out for the cars!"

Children learned the liberation that the bicycle gives you, but the bicycle, if mentioned at all in school programs, was considered as a pre-car or sub-car form of transportation and was certainly treated as such by traffic planners and road builders during the massive highway construction that followed the Second World War.

In the early '50's Dr. Paul Dudley White introduced the idea that cycling was good for you. This is a fine and true thought, but to anyone who has experienced the joy and the almost hidden vice of being on a bike, that's almost beside the point. Biking lets you express an exuberance of motion, a sort of secret orgy of delight that no one knows you're experiencing. To others you are only riding a bike—only riding a bike!

Only the racers hadn't forgotten that biking was fun, but in their emphasizing speed and competition, they never thought to tell the rest of us the secret. But they more than made up for this by helping to introduce people to the joys and techniques of riding 10-speed bicycles. Unfortunately, unless you were a racer or a "friend of the sport," there weren't enough experienced cyclists around to act as role models, and a lot of people had to learn the hard way.

During the bicycle's eclipse, many people were introduced to bicycle touring by the few remaining clubs and the American Youth Hostels. But the tradition of being able to count on having a club to back you up and teach you the hows and whys of cycling, was lost.

Just as every happy family is alike, every really practiced cyclist recreates that tradition for himself, learning what constitutes the behavior of a two-

wheeled vehicle, and the validity of the social agreement that's called traffic. Bicycling is a combination of craft and art; bike-handling ability and road-craft. As Jerome K. Jerome said in 1900, there are two ways to get exercise from a bicycle: to fix it or to ride it. Like him, we have decided in this book to concentrate on riding a bike with the greatest pleasure and the least pain, and to try to present technical insights not covered elsewhere – all with a minimum of shoptalk. We have corresponded with cyclists in Great Britain, where the tradition has never died, and the Continent, where it is a living thing, as well as with pockets of enthusiasts in Australia, Malaysia, and Japan.

We decided that no riding of a wheel should be closed to us – unicycle, bicycle, tricycle, or tandem – off-road or on, in mountain passes or heavy urban traffic.

Considering how much cyclists love to argue, it is amazing how much agreement we found among the almost three hundred cyclists with whom we discussed various aspects of this book. Agreement about traffic and the laws and what cycling was all about, agreement about almost everything. There was disagreement about some important issues of cycling, like how to gear your bike, or who makes the best rims, or what a new frame should look like. But on the simple life-and-death issues – that half of all accidents are self-inflicted, and that the bicycle must be designed back into the traffic mix with the rights and responsibilities of any other vehicle – everyone we spoke to was more or less in agreement on these subjects.

The most striking thing about talking with cyclists was how intense their feelings toward the sport were, how willing they were to share their experiences and expertise, and how concerned they were for other cyclists.

Our editing this book gave us a chance to reprint things we are particularly fond of, such as an essay by G. H. Stancer, one of our heroes when we were fledgling cyclists. It gave us the opportunity to get questions answered by racers we admire like John Allis, Beryl Burton, and Laurence Malone. It permitted us to interview experts in many fields, and to suggest topics to engineers like Alex Moulton, Fred DeLong, and David Gordon Wilson. It gave us the delight of discovering that our favorite mystery story writer was a devoted follower and chronicler of the Tour de France.

Editing this book has been an education for us – above all in bike handling, for we seemed to learn something applicable to everyday riding from each of our specialists – but also in engineering, medicine, and the psychology of perception. We have edited it to please and entertain. If it does not succeed in pleasing or entertaining you, do not blame the other contributors, blame us.

John Krausz
Vera van der Reis Krausz

About the Editors

John Krausz *has been cycling since his childhood on Long Island, and still misses his blue Columbia dual top tube with the 28-inch wheels and the New Departure brake. He finds his greatest pleasure fixed wheeling in traffic, which he calls "urban cyclocross." He is a photographer and graphic designer; he designed the* Gardener's Catalogue *series of large-format paperbacks, and both designed and edited* How to Buy an Elephant (things you never knew you wanted to know).

Vera van der Reis Krausz *grew up in Holland, where bicycles are an accepted part of transportation. She worked for ten years as an editor and copywriter before becoming a teacher of French and Linguistics in the New York City school system. She has slightly wider bicycling interests than her husband, because besides commuting to work on a fixed wheel, she has been known to use a 10-speed for more extensive trips.*

The Krauszes own about ten bicycles between them.

Dr. Paul Harris *is a pediatrician and a veteran bike racer. He has been an avid cyclist all his life, and is the father of a young man who has successively been Midget, Intermediate, and Junior champion of the state of Connecticut. Dr. Harris is an active member and club physician for the Century Road Club Association and he continues to compete in USCF open events (Veteran Class) as well as club races. He has ridden both road and track events, and does cross-country skiing in the winter time. He is director of the Pediatric Primary Care Center at Jacobi Hospital, and assistant professor of pediatrics at the Albert Einstein College of Medicine in New York City.*

Barbara Remington, *whose drawings and charts enliven these pages, is an illustrator and lifelong cyclist. Cycling has a history old enough that the newest ideas have been tried before – manpowered aircraft before the first world war, and aerodynamic construction in the early thirties. This drawing, which was lovingly reconstructed from a faded newspaper clipping, shows a very early full-fairing bike.*

Bernard Thompson *has been photographing the British cycling scene for over twenty-five years. His photographs show much more than a journalist's grasp of the subject. Anyone who reads* Cycling, *the British weekly, is familiar with his work. We are pleased to have this book introduce his work to an American audience. This photograph hit a responsive note in every cyclist we showed it to.*

TABLE of CONTENTS

It is better,
for the joy of the world,
to write about cycling
than about ethics.

Men taste
enough bitterness in life
so that, from time to time,
one should teach them
where the sweet is hidden.

L. Baudry de Saunier, 1891

ELEMENTS OF BICYCLING

Bicycling, the Health Giver

Jean-Pierre de Mondenard, M.D.

Translated from the French by Vera van der Reis Krausz

Doctor de Mondenard is a passionate cyclist and also a physician who treats racers both during and after competition. For more of his advice on how best to use cycling to build your health, see the Fitness and Training section.

Benefits of Cycling for Health

The bicycle is one of the least known yet best and safest medicines that exists. There is no more agreeable means of building one's health than bicycling.

Respiration is improved because the pulmonary capacity is enlarged considerably. The champions' oxygen capacity is double that of ordinary people (6 to 8 liters).

The Circulation of the Blood becomes more dynamic. A blood richer in oxygen flows into the deepest reaches of every tissue. And oxygen is the source of all life for cells.

The Heart becomes larger, stronger, and slower; it reacts to effort with a moderate acceleration, which it can sustain for a long time without tiring. After effort it rapidly returns to the resting state. Therefore, it does more work with less effort, and the amount of blood carrying oxygen throughout the organism at each contraction is greater.

Digestion becomes easier, appetite is better, and you get more nourishment out of what you eat because the body absorbs more completely the nutritive elements drawn from food. Furthermore, constipation is less frequent than in sedentary people.

The Elimination of Wastes is faster and more complete. During effort you perspire abundantly and your sweat and urine contain more toxic products than when resting.

Muscles that work grow larger, suppler, faster, and stronger. The more regularly they work the more strength they gain. Besides those of the lower body, muscles used in biking include the paravertebral— those on each side of the vertebral column that keep it straight. The muscles of the thorax and upper body are used less, but develop somewhat. Those least developed by cycling are the abdominal muscles; they should be built up by supplementary exercises because they play an important part in breathing and in supporting the vertebral column.

The Joints of the hip, knee, and ankle are so benefited by bicycling that it is the basic exercise used for rehabilitation of rheumatics and those with leg injuries. (Pedaling is good for you!)

The Press and Cultural Section of the Consulate General of the Netherlands

Sleep comes more readily. A good evening ride relaxes the muscles of the body, which have a tendency to tighten up after the activities of the day. It causes an agreeable sense of physical tiredness and helps eliminate the consequences of mental strain and the small troubles that prevent a deep and restoring sleep.

Control of Obesity is made easier. The bicycle presents a way of losing weight without too much trouble. Fat professional cyclists are very rare, even after they've stopped racing; on the contrary, they keep the thinness of young men for many years.

All the Organs work more economically, permitting us to better fight fatigue. But to reap all these benefits one has to take the medicine regularly, and not just once or twice a month.

Press and Cultural Section of the Consulate General of the Netherlands

Who Should Cycle?

If biking is excellent medicine for the healthy person, it is equally good for the sickly. It has a beneficial influence on the majority of organs, so it is especially good for:

Cardiac Patients. Cardiologists are prescribing cycling more and more after heart attacks and in cases of angina. Rest used to be considered the best remedy, but nowadays training is begun the thirtieth day after a heart attack, and by the end of the second month the patient is in good physical shape; regular work is usually resumed after three months.

Hypertensives. High blood pressure, which afflicts about fifteen percent of the active population, very frequently benefits from prudent and progressive practice of a sport like cycling.

Arthritics. People who have arthritis of the hip can benefit from rehabilitative treatment by cycling, either after surgical intervention, or in the inoperable patient to strengthen the musculature, smooth the articulative play, and thus diminish pain.

Insulin-dependent Diabetics. Recent experiments have shown that daily bicycling can be an important means of treatment, which spectacularly betters the insulin balance of the diabetic, if effort is pushed far enough.

Children who love nature and adventure; children who don't like exercise (the bicycle will get them used to physical effort gradually), and children without willpower. Bicycling is a school for willpower from the moment that training is regular enough to permit long and interesting trips without fatigue.

Who Shouldn't Cycle?

Using steady pedaling seated on an upright frame, no one.

Intense and difficult trips, especially racing, are formally forbidden to children with weak hearts (murmurs, problems of cardiac rhythm, excitability), those with respiratory deficiencies, and those with spinal column illnesses. It is very important to have all postural abnormalities evaluated before letting a child bicycle, or chronic back pain is a definite risk.

Cycling is also not recommended for those who hear badly, because it makes safety difficult, because cyclists depend on their hearing to know what's happening behind them. A hearing aid may be enough to permit cycling, thus we give no formal interdiction for the hard of hearing.

Cycling Risks.

Falls. These are the main danger. The most frequent region hurt is the shoulder, with the possibility of breaking the collarbone. Legs are very rarely broken.

Bad Position or Errors in Materiel. A bent pedal, a badly adjusted cleat, a saddle or handlebar set too low or too high are enough to cause backaches, cramps, muscle strains, tendonitis.

Excess Effort. Impassioned children don't know how to measure their strength. Youngsters who dream of becoming racers are capable of using up all their energy reserves, and going beyond them. The only solution: Enroll them in a serious club where a competent trainer will take them in hand.

Precautions to Take.

Proper hygiene is indispensable in avoiding boils and saddle sores, major inconveniences of a seated sport.

Practitioners of this open-air sport are also advised to learn to clean their eyes properly, as these are often exposed to foreign bodies such as tar, dust, and insects.

Dietary precautions are necessary. Water and glucose are indispensable during effort. That way you can avoid "fringale" (depleted blood sugar) and the symptoms that accompany it—lightheadedness, visual problems, legs like lead.

Make sure the bike fits the cyclist to avoid vicious positions that generate cramps and back pain. From the beginning get used to sitting correctly, leaning toward the handlebar with the back straight and not arched.

Weight Control (with Calorie/mph Chart)

Vera van der Reis Krausz

Albina appears at the door of the hotel dining room. Her expression is serious and her eye sad. She is dismayed.

– I gained two pounds! she says. If in a week of cycling I gain two pounds, that's four pounds in two weeks and eight pounds a month.

– And a hundred pounds a year, I said, and a thousand pounds every ten years. After that, we'll put you in a sideshow.

– Oh, that's really very funny. But you, who told me everything about the bicycle, carefully omitted telling me it makes you gain weight.

– If the bicycle made people gain weight, Albina, most cyclists would be obese. You gained a pound, you'll lose it. The bike makes fat people get thin and thin people get a little fatter.

– Why does it make thin people gain weight?

– Because it gives them a good appetite.

– Okay, says Albina. To begin with, I won't eat supper.

Jacques Faizant, Albina et la bicyclette
Translated from the French by Vera van der Reis Krausz

Many people run or cycle so they can eat. It really isn't news that exercise is good for the heart and also helps you lose weight. It accomplishes the latter by increasing the rate at which energy (and fat is stored energy) is used. Dr. Dorothy Harris notes in "Women and Exercise" that this increased metabolic rate doesn't stop when you finish exercising. Studies have shown that you are still burning more calories four – perhaps even six – hours later than you would have if you hadn't exercised. Furthermore, the onset of obesity is related to inactivity

in nearly 70 percent of the cases . . . in only 3.2 percent was increased food intake the cause!

It is not nearly as easy to figure out how many calories you use when you are bicycling as when you are running. Then again, cardiologists make it clear that the 100 calories expended per running mile is just an approximation. It assumes a body weight of about 150 pounds; if you weigh 200 pounds, you're using about 110 calories; if you weigh 100 pounds, only 90. The more fit you are, the more efficiently you run and the less calories you burn.

In both bicycling and running, road surface, wind velocity and direction, and degree of hilliness also affect how much energy you need to cover a certain distance. Which means those charts giving energy-calorie equivalents are vast oversimplifications. The type of bicycle makes a big difference, too. For a technical discussion of calorie consumption comparing 3-speeds, ordinary 10-speeds, and racing bicycles, see David Gordon Wilson's "Calories and Power."

It would be nice if the charts that show 600 calories consumed in an hour of cycling ten miles were true for every bicycle. This is the correct rate for a 3-speed. On most ordinary 10-speeds you would have to cover 16 miles an hour, on a racing bike about 20 miles an hour.

Our chart assumes that you're on a racing bike and in an efficient (aerodynamic) position. Air resistance becomes the major factor as you go faster because it goes up geometrically as you increase speed.

While you will lose weight from diet alone, it isn't nearly as easy or good for your heart as combining diet with exercise . . . Try to work up to expending a total of 2,000 calories a week through strenuous exercise spaced at least three times during a week, and you will also gain protection from heart attacks. For more good advice on the cardiological aspects of cycling, see our training section.

We won't get into the whole fat percentage controversy, but realize that muscle weighs more than fat, and that exercise builds muscle. Some people get discouraged when they don't lose a lot of weight, but the way their clothes fit should give them a clue that they've replaced fat with muscle.

For some athletes, and some recreational riders, too, losing weight can get to be a kick – to such an extent that some athletes have symptoms much like the teenage girls' *anorexia nervosa*. Some have lost as much as five pounds a day by combining starvation with high energy expenditure. This is dangerous. It can hurt both your health and your athletic performance. Three pounds a week is the *outside* limit for most people to lose weight safely.

It's not difficult to lose that much weight through bicycling if you just don't gorge yourself, because you can cycle for so much longer than you can do practically any other sport.

EXAMPLE

If your bicycle has—

    48 tooth Crank Sprocket
    13 tooth Rear Sprocket
    27 inch Dia. Rear Wheel

Then—

$$\text{"Gear"} = \frac{48}{13} \times 27 = 100$$

For Pedal RPM of 72 Read from Graphs—

    Speed   = 21.5 MPH
    Horsepower   = .28
    Calories/Minute = 11.5

Chart courtesy of Racer-Mate, the Wind-Load Simulator

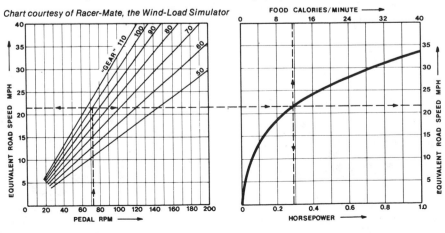

3

Balancing Ain't Bike Riding

John Allis

Balancing ain't bike riding, but a good bike rider uses balance in ways unimaginable by the rookie. The rookie steers to keep his balance, the bike rider balances to steer. Being able to balance on a bike is what you "learn as a child and never forget." But balancing on a bike and bike riding are very different.

Good bike riders don't self-destruct by braking incorrectly or by running into curbs or mailboxes, but last year a half million Americans went to hospital emergency rooms because of bike accidents, and over half of these accidents involved nothing more than the bike, the rider, a moment of fear, or an immovable object.

Most people learn to ride a bike as a child, and that's the way too many still do it, improvising from moment to moment, hugging the curb, or going the wrong way in traffic because someone once told them that was the way to do it. Going the wrong way in traffic vastly increases the chances of an intersection accident—the most common type, twenty times more common than the overtaking one wrong-way riders

fear. It also angers motorists and frightens pedestrians, as neither expect anything to come from that direction.

Making up your own rules is a difficult way to learn. In several years or about 10,000 miles of riding, a cyclist can discover almost everything about road craft and bike handling. But there is no need to discover everything by yourself.

In this book experienced cyclists explain what there is to know about many types of cycling both on and off road—for errands, recreation, touring, racing, and commuting. They answer most questions you might have ... how to buy a second bike, how to climb a hill, how to pack for a tour, how to be safe in traffic.

As John Allis says later in this article, nobody tries to fake driving a car, but a shockingly large number of people pretend to know how to ride a bicycle. John shares insights gained from a lifetime of cycling that includes being a member of three Olympic teams. He still holds the record for the climb up Mount Washington—the highest peak in New England.

Cycling under any circumstances is a fairly logical procedure with certain rules that are violated at the cyclist's peril, particularly in traffic. This is emphasized by a recent Consumer Product Safety Commission (CPSC) report, which indicated that despite zero maintenance on many bikes, only 13 percent of all cycling accidents are due to mechanical causes.

Even that percentage is worth thinking about, and the best first move is to have a bike professionally assembled—or if you do it yourself, to have it checked out by an expert. Brakes, reflectors, and lights are the obvious safety items, but simple failure of the gears can get you in trouble, because you'll find you can't move. Mobility is an essential aspect of safety; make sure your derailleur or Sturmey-Archer works. Make

sure the whole bike works—it's a vehicle, not a toy.

And to the extent that you can arrange it, make sure your body works. It's very common for a thirty-year-old to buy a bike and head out for a ride he could have done easily when he was fifteen. No good. Such a rider will be unable to keep a reasonable pace for the distance, will fall apart on climbs, and/or will become uncoordinated and erratic when he runs out of glucose in the blood—on which the brain is very dependent. (It doesn't hurt to take along a candy bar and a filled water bottle.) A certain degree of physical ability is essential to confidence and assertiveness, which in turn are necessary for safe riding. The way to develop this ability is to exercise in a methodical way several days a week, preferably on the bike. Five

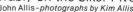

John Allis—photographs by Kim Allis

or ten miles may feel like a lot the first day, but a month later twenty or thirty miles may not seem hard at all.

Several things are basic on the road. Like the airplane, the bicycle has a certain safe-speed range, usually estimated at a minimum of 8 mph for a 3-speed, and 15 mph for a 10-speed. The bicycle is easily controlled at this speed, and can become part of the traffic flow on most roads and streets. You should be riding in the same direction as the rest of the traffic, and not be obsessed with the fear of being overtaken and hit from behind, except in low-light situations.

The CPSC does not deal with lights, but experienced cyclists do—emphatically. The traditional leg-light with fresh batteries is acceptable (in terms of being visible from the rear) if worn on the left leg. But no matter how many reflectors, lights, reflective hoops, horns, or mirrors you have, you must always be conscious that you are part of a traffic flow and are relatively unprotected. You must keep your speed up, not only because the bike is more stable this way, but because it reduces the closing speed of cars approaching from the rear. Many more accidents occur to riders who ride against traffic. Riding with traffic is also required by law in most states. Because it is a vehicle, the bicycle has all the rights and duties of one in most states.

One general principle is not to keep to the extreme right, but to be prepared to yield space very quickly when necessary. If you do stay on the extreme right, you will be weaving in and out around parked cars, broken bottles, and sewer grates. This weaving motion is not compatible with the basically straight-line motion of the automobile, and it makes you unpredictable. Predictability is another basic principle, so you want to ride as straight a line as possible, which is not easy at low speeds. Despite all precautions, however, you will have to be ready to make sudden moves from time to time.

Stills from Bicycling Safely on the Road, *Iowa State University Film Production Unit*

Because most of these things are obvious, it becomes clear that stupidity and lack of concentration are the greatest dangers. After these comes the automobile (partly because drivers aren't trained to notice cyclists). Other hazards are making left turns, and encountering a dog.

Making a left turn in traffic is a basic test of whether you belong in traffic. Here again, riding on the extreme right is asking for trouble because a left turn from the gutter, entering and cutting across one or more lines of traffic is unexpected by other road users. Except in unusual circumstances, you should be in the traffic flow, working your way into the left lane before you reach the corner. And you should be sufficiently in control of your bike to signal clearly with your left hand well in advance of changing lanes. You should also be handling the bike well enough that you can glance back to see if the road is clear and if your signal is understood without wandering all over the road. Looking back is a way to let drivers know you are aware of their presence.

Much of the above implies that practice would be a very good idea: Practice maintaining a cruising speed to begin with, but also practice keeping a straight line at every speed, when stopping (applying both brakes at once), when turning at different angles and speeds, when glancing back while moving forward, and when shying away at short notice. All of this is common sense, all easily practiced in some empty area such as a parking lot that is unused on weekends. This is the cyclist's equivalent of driver training, and while it can be done alone, it is done more effectively with an experienced cyclist. Just as defensive driving courses are becoming popular with motorists, on-road training for adults is becoming available to cyclists in many parts of the country.

Common sense will also tell you that practice may also make you cocky, which is to be avoided. But the benefits of practice are real beyond technique. Lack of fitness and technique erode the physical confidence that makes execution easy and natural. The tired and inexperienced cyclist is an erratic rider—a fact every racing cyclist knows and allows for.

Just as for the automobile, city and country present different problems. Traffic tends to be constantly present in urban situations, but is intermittent and moving faster on country roads. Because the ambient sound level is much lower in the country, the ear becomes an accurate safety device for most people. It is possible to hear and gauge the speed of an approaching car, enabling you to yield ground when it

Distributed by Iowa State University Research Foundation, Ames, Iowa 50011

sounds excessively fast or close. Distance-fatigue demands are greater, though, and dogs must be dealt with. (Sometimes dogs and cars must be dealt with together.)

Despite all this, cycling is not nearly as dangerous as many would have you believe, and what danger there is, is reduced enormously for those who learn how to ride. Riding a bike on the road is about as difficult to learn as driving a car. Nobody fakes driving a car, but it's surprising how many people do exactly that on a bicycle.

5

3-Speed Good, 10-Speed Different

John Allis & Bjarne Rostaing

I explained to Albina that going by bike and knowing how to ride a bike were two completely different things, and that all cycling misery comes from the fact that everyone believes he has perfect mastery of it, an arrogance whose vanity is exposed by the first outing of any length. . . .

I begged Albina to pedal continuously and to undo as quickly as possible the bad habit she had of freewheeling for a hundred feet whenever she had pushed the pedals three times. She thought I was very irritating.

I taught her to change position on the saddle and on the handlebars according to circumstances, and to brake with both brakes at the same time, because she had the popular superstition that the front brake is just there to look pretty and to give some symmetry to the ensemble.

I forced myself to teach her to shift gears by lessening the pressure of her foot on the pedal during the fraction of a second the operation requires.

This was an extremely painful moment for anyone with sensitive ears. A veteran cyclist who passed us sent us the suspicious look one normally reserves for child molesters, vivisectionists, beginning violinists, and other sadistic torturers. . . .

I then taught Albina to look behind her while riding without wavering like one intoxicated, to lift her pedal on turns, and to watch for treacheries of the road surface. All of this did not proceed without argument, because Albina had theories about everything, and particularly about things she didn't know how to do and that she wished were done some other way.

Jacques Faizant, Albina et la bicyclette
Translated from the French by Vera van der Reis Krausz

In purchasing a 10-speed to replace a 3-speed, people think that simply by adding more speeds they will have easier riding. This is not always the way things work out because the two types of bicycles present very different problems.

Unquestionably the 3-speed is slower, but it is also easier to fit and less demanding. Almost anyone can get on a 3-speed and ride off in some semblance of comfort and control. The properly designed 10-speed is a very different beast; it requires not only a radically different position and careful fitting, but also the use of different muscle groups.

Pedal action is different too; a 10-speed should have toeclips, and the ankling that is useful on a 3-speed is no longer appropriate. The 3-speed rider can relax and pedal along in comfort at his own speed, but the 10-speed position, which brings the rider's trunk to a more horizontal position, makes different demands.

To ride a 3-speed, you sit upright, pretty much as on a chair at a table, pushing the pedals alternately. Comfort and visibility are good for most people in this upright position. For the 10-speed position, the imaginary table is taken away, and the individual leans forward, as if to get out of the chair. The chair (saddle) has become more a balancing point, with the dropped handlebars also supporting considerable weight. The rider's arms and shoulders take additional strain, and the neck is bent slightly. On a 3-speed, practically all the rider's weight is supported on the seat, whereas a good 10-speed position is often defined as placing about 45 percent of the rider's weight on the front wheel. (This varies with racing and touring positions, but anything less than 40 percent on the front wheel is definitely less efficient). The cyclist's back is stretched forward to achieve this, and the back muscles are involved in driving the pedals. This is, in short, a *learned* position. But while the description is not attractive, many people come to prefer the 10-speed because of its grace and efficiency once it is mastered.

Different positions are accommodated by different frame designs. Top-tube lengths and frame angles can vary widely on 10-speeds, and 10-speed frames are made in almost an infinity of sizes from about 19 to 26 inches, with custom variations going even beyond this range. (These sizes refer to seat-tube lengths.) The 3-speed market basically relies on three sizes (19, 21, 23), to which almost anyone can be fitted. The appeal of the 3-speed lies in its low cost, easy maintenance, comfort, and durability. On the other hand, the 10-speed is designed for efficiency. Wind resistance is greatly reduced.

One reason why "fit" on a 10-speed is so important is that more is demanded of the rider, specifically the suppleness and strength to maintain the position dictated by dropped handlebars. The arms must be strong enough to bear considerable weight, and the back muscles must adjust not only to the position, but to working in this position.

In addition, the 10-speed saddle takes some getting used to. The 3-speed mattress saddle is no problem for most people, but the narrower, firmer, 10-speed model can be, especially if the rider does not have some weight forward on the bars. Until recently, it was particularly uncomfortable for women because there were no saddles specifically designed for them.

While the narrow saddle is not comfortable in the upright position, (it isn't designed for that position), it is necessary to the "forward" position. It does not chafe the legs and, in fact, is as much a fulcrum as a seat. Like the 10-speed, you must learn to use it, and small variations in the seat and its position can make a big difference.

Why bother? Because the 10-speed becomes more and more natural in its operation as you go more and more miles. It is just about impossible for a 3-speed to approach the speeds and distances it can handle. And if your friends are all on 10-speeds, it will be very difficult to keep up with them on a 3-speed for any length of time. Not only is the pedaling position less efficient on a 3-speed, but wind resistance is much greater. At ten to twelve miles an hour this is not such a big thing, but semi-fit 10-speed riders can usually double that speed for fairly long periods of time, and to double speed is to multiply wind resistance by four. Wind resistance becomes the most important factor at higher speeds.

But there is an alternative for those who don't feel like making the transition to the 10-speed bike. There are upright design (3-speed type) bikes with 5- and 10-speed derailleur systems. Such an arrangement offers the best of both worlds: the increased gear capacity of a 10-speed and the comfortable 3-speed position.

John Allis is the author of the preceding "Balancing Ain't Bike Riding," and Bjarne Rostaing is the American editor of the annual International Cycling Guide. *They also collaborated on "Advice to a Beginning Racer" in the racing section, which covers many areas of advanced bike handling.*

Better Bike Riding

John Forester

Your bike supports you at three places — saddle, handlebars, and pedals. You will be most comfortable and least tired if you position yourself so that part of your weight rests on each support. Your bike has five adjustments to help you achieve a comfortable and efficient posture. Start out by adjusting your bike to suit yourself according to these instructions, but remember that everybody is different and the most important thing is your comfort.

The basic adjustments to your bike are made by sliding the seat post and handlebar stem into or out of the bicycle frame. You must always leave at least 2½ inches of seat post inside the frame. Pull the whole seat post out and measure it so that you know whether you have left enough inside. Pull the handlebar stem out until you see a slot or cut. You must push it in so that you leave at least an inch of handlebar stem above the slot inside the frame.

The basic adjustment for comfort is saddle height. Sit on the saddle with your heels on the pedals, and rotate the cranks. The adjustment is correct if you can keep your heels on the pedals all the way around without rocking your hips. To adjust the seat post height, loosen the clamp bolt, slide the post up or down, and then retighten the bolt.

Okay, now to the handlebars. Adjust the handlebar so that its top (or the grips of flat or raised bars) is level or one inch below the saddle top. To adjust handlebar height, loosen the stem clamp bolt one or two turns and tap it downward with a block of wood and a hammer. That should loosen it enough so you can twist and slide it up or down. Then retighten the clamp bolt.

Now go back again to the saddle for adjustment of the position and angle. Loosening the saddle clamp permits you to tilt the saddle and to slide it forward or backward. Set it level, and then tilt it either way until you feel comfortable when reaching for the top of the handlebars. For easy pedaling you must lean forward with part of your weight on your hands. How much you lean depends on how fast you ride. Even if you ride slowly, lean forward somewhat, otherwise you will expend unnecessary effort by holding yourself forward when you pedal.

Next, tilt the handlebars in the handlebar stem so that the angle of the lower grips is comfortable for your hands. For most people, the tops of the handlebars are also level, but some people prefer the front to be a little higher.

John Forester *is a traffic engineer, fourth generation cyclist, and developer of the League of American Wheelmen's famous Effective Cycling Course.*

Still from Bicycling Safely on the Road,
Courtesy of Iowa State University Film Production Unit

After you have ridden a while you should experiment by making small changes — particularly if you experience aches or pains. The most important thing is to be comfortable for the kind of riding you choose. Don't try to look like a racer if you don't race — just be comfortable.

When you are properly positioned on your bike and have developed a smooth pedaling action, you should look like this: legs almost (but not quite) straight at the bottom of the pedal stroke; body leaning forward from the hips, with only a little curve in the back; arms reaching forward and down for the handlebars, with elbows almost straight and wrists at a comfortable angle; head held high enough so you can easily look ahead, level with the road.

EASY PEDALING

Easy pedaling requires using the whole leg. Don't push the pedals down, but twirl them around and around.

To start, place your foot carefully on the pedal so that the ball of the foot is exactly over the pedal pivot. Don't let your foot slip forward so that you are pedaling with your instep. As your pedal rises, bring your toe up first, so that as the pedal reaches the top you are ready to push it forward. Then think about pushing forward, then downward, and finally backward. When your pedal is almost at the bottom, your toes should be positioned down so you can push backward as much as possible. Then when the pedal starts up, you quickly bring your toes from down to up, so you are ready again to push forward. Now, repeat this for your other foot and synchronize the two into a smooth rhythm.

This divides up the work between thigh muscles and calf muscles, so you can go farther before feeling tired. It also keeps the calf muscles moving so they don't get stiff.

Always keep thinking: "Twirl the pedals around and around," and practice it every time you can until the action becomes automatic. The hallmark of the stylish cyclist is a steady flow of power all around the pedal circle. Toeclips and straps are the best encouragement to efficient pedaling. As soon as you have become comfortable on your bike, learn to use them.

Putting your foot in the first toeclip is easy. Once you are moving and can't reach down with your hand, you must learn to flip the pedal with your toe to get your foot into the clip. This is a knack that is best learned in a parking lot away from traffic. If the straps are just tight enough so you can put your foot in, you can also pull your foot out. Just don't forget. Once you have learned to use them, you will never ride without them.

USE YOUR GEARS

Don't save your gears just to climb hills. Use the gears to match your body's best performance with the conditions so you can keep pedaling fast. High gear on most bikes is too high for easy riding on the level, but you see many people straining in their highest gear through traffic at low speed. That's both slow and tiring. You can do better. Here's how.

Start out your riding program by riding on the level in middle gears. Concentrate on twirling the pedals around and around. If you have a watch with a sweep second hand, count your pedal revolutions and work up to turning the pedals 60 to 80 times per minute.

Once you have developed your pedal speed, you can then change to higher gears on the level in order to ride faster, or to lower gears in order to climb hills or fight headwinds. Whenever the conditions are against you— hills, wind, or just plain tiredness —change to the next lower gear to keep your pedal speed up. If the conditions are so difficult your pedal speed drops more, change down again to maintain your pedal speed.

Pushing too high a gear for your strength makes you stronger but slower—it stiffens your muscles and your leg action. Spinning the pedals in gears lower than necessary slows you down for the moment but improves your leg action and endurance. It is better to exercise in too low a gear than too high a gear.

QUICK, SAFE STOPS

Your brakes will stop you plenty fast if you use them correctly. However, most cyclists don't use their brakes properly because they haven't been taught how. You should learn by following these instructions and practicing until hard braking becomes automatic whenever you need it.

You must first be sure that your brakes are in proper working order —and learn to keep them that way. The basic brake test is to squeeze the brake levers as hard as you can (unless you have extremely strong hands). The brake levers must stop before reaching the handlebars —that means the brake systems are transmitting all your force to the brake blocks.

If either lever can be forced to touch the handlebars, you need a brake adjustment. Loosen the locknut of the brake adjusting barrel, unscrew the barrel to tighten the brake cable, and retighten the locknut. The brakes should be kept adjusted so the brake blocks barely clear the wheel rim as it rotates. If the barrel unscrews out of its support, you must screw it all the way in and tighten the cable at its anchor instead. Get a friend to hold the brake clamped on the rim, or tie it tightly with string in the clamped position. Then loosen the brake wire clamp bolt, pull the wire tight, and retighten the clamp. Then make a fine adjustment, if necessary, with the adjustment barrel.

Check two other points. If you have center-pull brakes, make sure that the cable hook that connects the brake inner wire to the bridge wire just above the brake does not move up to touch the cable housing stop when you apply the brakes hard. If it does, you need new brake blocks or a bit of modifi-

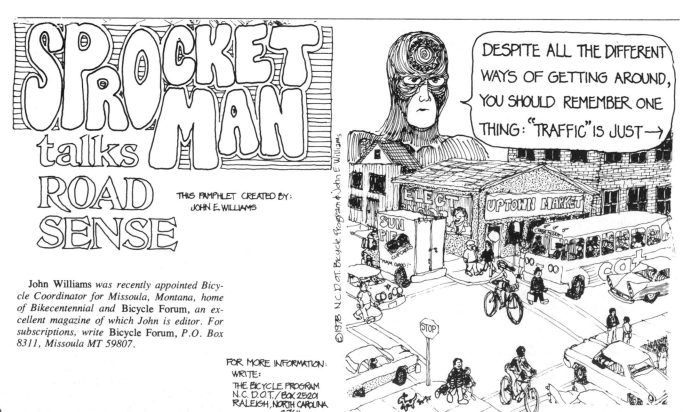

THIS PAMPHLET CREATED BY:
JOHN E. WILLIAMS

John Williams was recently appointed Bicycle Coordinator for Missoula, Montana, home of Bikecentennial and Bicycle Forum, an excellent magazine of which John is editor. For subscriptions, write Bicycle Forum, P.O. Box 8311, Missoula MT 59807.

FOR MORE INFORMATION:
WRITE:
THE BICYCLE PROGRAM
N.C. D.O.T./ BOX 25201
RALEIGH, NORTH CAROLINA
27611

cation from your bike shop. Second, make sure the brake blocks have at least an eighth of an inch of rubber left over their shoes, and are pressed squarely against the side of the rim without touching the tire or being worn into a shelf under the rim. Reposition them if they are not correctly positioned.

The front brake can provide two and a half times the braking force of the rear brake, but it can also somersault you onto your head. Most cyclists are so cautious to avoid somersaulting that they don't use the front brake as hard as it can be used. But there is a safe way.

First, practice using your rear brake alone, harder and harder. You should be able to lock the rear wheel, then release the brake just a little so the rear wheel rolls but you are still slowing down. Don't keep skidding along on a locked wheel — you'll wear out your tire and won't learn anything. Stopping like this with the rear brake alone takes more than double the distance of a proper stop.

Second, learn to apply both brakes until the rear wheel locks, and then immediately to release a little until it rolls again. This gets you down to only one and a half times the proper stopping distance.

Third, the really skillful part, learn to use the front brake three times harder than the rear brake. Increase the force on both levers until the rear wheel locks, then immediately ease off both levers until it rolls again. That rear wheel locking is your signal that you must not use more force or the front brake will somersault you. As long as you have some braking force at the rear wheel, it will always lock before you start to somersault. Once you feel the signal, ease off just enough to let the rear wheel roll again. This is normally your quickest stop when done correctly.

You could stop a little bit quicker using the front brake alone, but you must release it the moment your rear wheel lifts as you start to somersault. It takes a lot of practice to do this, and it's just too dangerous for most people to do. It's fine for demonstrating proper braking technique, but not too safe when you're concerned about avoiding a car or a dog. So, try to always use the rear brake with the front, only with much less force.

In wet weather, your brakes won't grip until the brake blocks have wiped the water off the rims. This is okay on hills, but bad for sudden stops. When riding in the rain, keep an extra safety distance ahead of you. If you intend to ride in all types of weather, buy aluminum alloy rims, because they dry off in a few feet and then work well, while chrome-plated steel rims take a hundred feet or so to dry, and then don't work well at all. Besides, alloy rims are lighter, where weight really counts.

STEERING AND MANEUVERING

When you first started to ride a bike you learned three things of great importance without realizing it. Probably nobody ever taught you. You just kept falling down until you learned; and when you learned, you stayed up. The first thing you learned was that leaning over meant turning. Whenever you leaned over you fell down, unless you turned. The second thing you learned was that turning required leaning. If you turned the handlebars without leaning, you fell down. So you learned to lean before you turned. The third thing you learned was to let the bike steer itself — to just relax and let the bike do it.

When you want to ride straight, you can't do it without a little wobble, but as you wobble your bike corrects itself. If you lean over to the right a bit by accident, the bike steers just enough to the right to get its wheels underneath you again. If you want to turn right instead of going straight, you wait until it leans a bit right and prevent it from correcting itself until you are leaning over far enough for the turn. Then you let it steer itself into the turn to match the lean. This is fine for gentle maneuvers and easy riding, but it is not quick enough to get you out of the way of a car. To make a fast turn you must outsmart your bike and force it to lean quickly.

Here's how to make instant turns. You need to use the instant right turn to get away from turning cars more than you need the instant left turn. To make a right turn you must first

9

lean right. But you don't want to wait until your bike accidentally starts to lean right. So, how do you force yourself to lean right? You steer the wheels left. If the wheels go to the left you are leaning right. But if you don't steer right when you are leaning right, you'll fall over — hard. So the moment you start leaning over the correct amount, snap your front wheel to the right, and you're in a sharp right turn.

The motion of steering left is almost like hitting the handlebars — just a very sudden sharp wiggle to the left followed by an immediate snap to the right. The greater the leftward wiggle, the more you lean, and the sharper the right turn must be to keep you balanced.

You cannot do this on the first try. It takes practice at an empty parking lot. Don't practice on the street when you don't need it — you'll tangle up traffic and may get hit because you turn faster than the cars. Make a marker of a ball of crumpled newspaper or a piece of sponge. Place this in the middle of an open space. Ride directly toward it, and just before you reach it, wiggle the front wheel going left around it. This will make you lean right, so catch yourself by steering right. Start doing this slowly and gently. As you get the feel of it, make the wiggle more forceful and the resulting turn will be sharper. Practice left turns the opposite way. The reason for choosing newspaper or sponge is so you can hit it by accident without hurting yourself, but when you've got the right feel you should swing around it in a 90-degree turn without hitting it.

OBSTRUCTIONS AND DANGERS

Sharp edges and corners — Never ride fast over sharp edges — they'll split your tires, dent your rims, fold your wheels, and bend your forks. The most frequent sharp raised edge is a curb; next, chuckholes in the street. It's not the drop that gets you, but the raised edge on the far side where you try to climb out of the hole. Other sharp edges include out-of-level grates, manhole covers, and railroad tracks. When your front tire reaches the raised edge, it's just like hitting the tire with the corner of a two-by-four with all your weight

and speed behind it. It squeezes the tire flat and dents the rim, and in bad cases can fold the wheel rim right in or bend your forks backward. If you must ride over a sharp edge, do it slowly (so it will be less like a hammerblow) and raise up off your saddle with your knees flexible so your bike can bounce without having to lift you also.

Slots and ridges — These include anything that can grab your front wheel and either stop it or swing it sideways. Either way you fall — on your face if you're going fast, on your side if going slow. Drain grates with the slots going the same way as you are are the most obvious danger. Another bad obstruction is the railroad track that crosses the road diagonally. It's not the bump that gets you, but the slot between the rail and the road surface. In some places they have storm drain "ditches" along the road, just wide enough for your tire to fall into and just deep enough so you can't get it out. In all of these, the slot or ridge turns your front wheel so that your bike steers to one side when you haven't leaned over first. The result is that the wheels go one way and you go straight on, wishing you could fly because now there's no bike underneath to hold you up.

Cross all of these at as close to a right angle as you can, even if it means zigzagging in front of traffic. It's much better to be up and moving so you can dodge later than to be dumped in front of cars and not be able to get out of the way. If one of these slots catches you unaware, stiffen your arms and hold the front wheel straight as the slot grabs it. Try to jump the front wheel up over the ridge. If you get the front wheel across you're almost safe, because if the ridge shoves the rear wheel sideways you can compensate by steering the front wheel.

Slippery places — Oil, gravel, ice, water, mud, and similar surfaces offer minimal traction. These are not dangerous to ride on unless you are turning or braking. If you find a slippery spot halfway through a turn, straighten up for a few feet when you cross it, then turn again. This move is basically two instant turns back to back: one to straighten out, the second

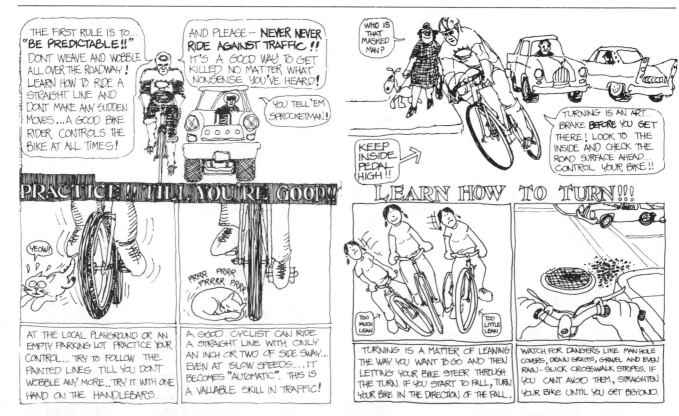

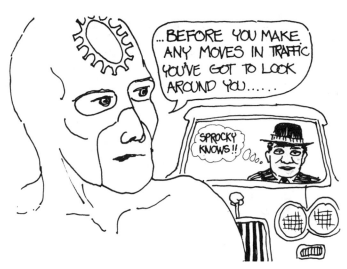

LOOK WITHOUT SWERVING

MOST UNSKILLED RIDERS SWERVE WHEN THEY LOOK AROUND FOR TRAFFIC. THIS SENDS THEM INTO THE PATH OF APPROACHING CARS. GO BACK TO THE PLAYGROUND AND PRACTICE LOOKING..

A GOOD CYCLIST CAN LOOK OVER HIS SHOULDER AND RIDE STRAIGHT. DO IT IN ORDER TO SEE WHAT'S BEHIND YOU... NOT JUST FOR SHOW! LOOK OTHER DRIVERS IN THE EYE!

HAND BRAKES FOOT BRAKES

- USE BOTH BRAKES TO STOP. ONE IS NOT ENOUGH!
- KEEP THEM IN GOOD SHAPE! THEY ARE YOUR BEST FRIENDS!
- IF YOU HAVE TO STOP IN A HURRY, SHIFT YOUR WEIGHT BACK AND LOW SO YOU WON'T FLIP OVER THE HANDLEBARS.
- DO IT LIKE SPROCKETMAN!

- A FOOTBRAKE WON'T STOP YOU AS QUICKLY AS GOOD HANDBRAKES SO DON'T RIDE TOO FAST OR CLOSE TO ANYONE.
- THEY ARE EASIER TO MAINTAIN AND ARE WEATHERPROOF.
- OIL THE REAR HUB OFTEN.
- CHECK YOUR CHAIN FOR SIDE PLAY AND EXCESS WEAR...

DRIVEWAYS:

LOTS OF BICYCLISTS USE THEIR DRIVEWAYS AS LAUNCHING PADS. THEY DON'T STOP OR LOOK...AND THEY GET HIT. STOP AND WAIT FOR TRAFFIC BEFORE RIDING INTO THE STREET!

NOTE: MOTORISTS SHOULD ALWAYS WATCH FOR BICYCLISTS-ESPECIALLY YOUNG KIDS-DARTING OUT OF DRIVEWAYS! GO SLOW ON NEIGHBORHOOD STREETS!

---

to turn again. If you are braking, ease off and then reapply. It's almost always better to stay up and in control than to slide on your side.

Pillars, posts, and barricades—Of course you won't ride into the barricades set up around a hole in the street—but there are lots of others around. There are the posts to keep cars out of pedestrian areas, and these are hard to see in the dark. Some places put up posts along bike paths to protect you from the cars, but the danger of the posts is far greater than the danger from the cars. There is no way to handle these posts and barricades except to watch for them and avoid them.

Moving obstructions—Dogs, balls, and children can all be considered "moving" obstructions. The danger of dogs is not in being bitten but in being thrown. There's no set rule for this situation. Just keep your eyes open and ride smart. One theory says slow down and talk to dogs. Another says threaten them by steering toward them and shouting aggressively before they can get close enough to upset you. Cans of spray don't protect—they'll drive dogs away, but you haven't time to get to them if the dog is going for your wheel. At that moment you need both hands to steer and sprint.

SHARING THE ROAD

So far we've discussed how to train yourself to make your bike go at its best, but we haven't said anything yet about where to steer it. Now we're going to tell you to share the road with the motorists. This is what all good cyclists have learned in a century of cycling. This traffic technique contradicts what you have probably been told before. This is because the bike-safety publicity is written by motorists who worship the car. Most Americans believe that car-bike collisions are caused by cyclists slowing down motorists, so they instruct cyclists to ride as close to the curb as possible to guarantee a clear path for motorists. They've written this principle into law. They've told you since you were a child that it's sinful to get in front of a car, and they've impressed upon you that "the wages of sin are death."

This is just superstition to cover up motorists' dislike of being slowed down. Look at it this way—if motorists drove along without looking where they were going, they'd be stopped by something solid long before reaching a cyclist. Look at the car-bike collision facts. Car-bike collisions are caused by turning and crossing maneuvers. That means when the car turns at you, or you turn suddenly across its path, or you both meet at an intersection or driveway, somebody makes a mistake. For your own safety obey the same traffic laws that motorists obey, and watch out for the times they disobey them. Obeying those two principles will reduce your chance of being hit by more than 50 percent, while trying to hug the curb will increase your chances of being hit or driven off the road. Worrying about delaying motorists should be the last of your worries because it is a matter of politeness, not safety. Because it is a matter of politeness, you should give them extra room to overtake you whenever it is safe for you to do so, but not otherwise.

Because of this motorist-influenced superstition we have two kinds of bad bike riders on the roads. First we have the ''sinful kid,'' who darts in and out of traffic, rides on the left-hand side when he feels like it, and runs through stop signs and traffic signals. These are dangerous maneuvers. Dodging out into traffic from the curb is the number one cause of car-bike collisions. Wrong-way riding is the second leading cause (not head-on crashes, but intersection crashes because the motorist is looking the other way for danger).

The other kind of bad bike rider is the ''prude.'' He rides as close to the curb as he can, dodges in and out between every parked car, makes left turns from the curb across all the lanes of traffic and crosses intersections in the pedestrian crosswalk. This behavior causes car-bike collisions, but because this rider pretends to clear the way for motorists, the car worshipers praise his riding behavior as the safe and responsible way to ride.

LET YOURSELF BE SEEN

Here's what you should do to be a real cyclist. First, realize that motorists and cyclists have equal rights. That's the law. Equality refers to status, not strength. Some men are stronger than others, but all are equal in legal status. Motor-ists must not unjustifiably slow you down, just as you must not unjustifiably slow them down. But neither can require the other to endanger himself for convenience.

Second, ride to the right of the cars if there's room for you there. Don't follow the curb, the gutter, and the drain grates, ride as straight as you can three feet to the right of the moving cars. Cars move straight on the road because roads have been built that way. They don't dodge in and out between parked cars because the street has a straight stripe to mark the traffic lane. You should ride straight, too. Generally there's just enough room to do so. If there's more room to your right, don't go over to the curb. That's asking to be hit by turning cars and cars from the side streets. Ride where the motorist expects traffic, and you have the best chance of not being hit.

Riding like this allows the cars to overtake you all the time. Fine! You should ride so they can overtake you if it is safe to do so. What do you do when there isn't enough room for them to overtake you in the same lane? Take the whole lane by riding near its center so the motorist has to move into the next lane to overtake you. If you ride really close to the curb because there is little room, you encourage motorists to squeeze by when there isn't enough room for mistakes. This can result in you being run off the road as they go past because they get suddenly anxious about being sideswiped by other cars in the next lane.

Ride as an equal among equals and obey the traffic laws just like a motorist. This riding behavior should keep you and your bike safe.

MOTORISTS' MISTAKES

Learning not to put yourself into a dangerous position is only half the battle. You must also learn how to get out of dangers that others create.

Motorist left turn — The most frequent motorist mistake that causes car-bike collisions is the left turn that hits the cyclist coming from the opposite direction. Your first move is prevention. Ride as close to traffic as practicable — not over by the curb. That gives the left-turning motorist the best chance of seeing you. Your second move is evasion, dodging him if he turns anyway. Be especially aware as you approach intersections, so you can see him start the turn. If you are too close to stop before you reach him, make an instant right turn and go up the side street ahead of him, or across his front into the crosswalk where you can stop on the far side of the road.

Motorist right turn — The second most frequent motorist mistake causing car-bike collisions is the motorist right turn. Avoid approaching an intersection alongside the rear of a car where the driver can't see you. Either speed up and get ahead, or slow down and get behind. Always assume, signal or no signal, that he will turn right. Stop if you can, or make an instant right turn inside his turn if you are too close.

Motorist at stop sign — This is the motorist who creeps out after stopping at a stop sign or at a red light where he's allowed to turn right. If you think he hasn't seen you and is coming out regardless of traffic, brake and make an instant right turn to get behind him.

Now you know why it is so important to ride with the cars and practice instant right turns. You must make these habits practically instinctive if you want to do the right thing in an emergency.

CARRYING LOADS

Often you'll want to use your bike to help you carry things around. A lightweight backpack is okay for short trips around town, but uncomfortable on longer trips or with a heavy load. Its best use is as a supplementary pack to carry goods home when your other bags are full. For any serious carrying, you want the load to be on the bike, not on you.

For heavier or bulkier loads, fit a carrier rack on your bike. The aluminum racks from Pletscher and Schwinn are the best that are easily available and work quite well. But make sure that the front end is both clamped to the bike frame and held up. The easiest way is to wrap wire around the seat post and the front of the carrier. A more elegant way is to fix a metal strap between the carrier clamp bolt and the rear brake bolt. Otherwise the carrier will slip down and prevent your rear brake from working. The better racks do not fold flat for shipping, so they won't slide down in front when in use. However, they are hard to find.

13

You can carry things either on top of a carrier or hanging from the sides in baskets or pannier bags. Both ways work well, but remember that everything must be strapped down tight to prevent it from bouncing and swaying.

Whenever you carry anything, make sure that nothing can get caught in the spokes or between the brake block and the rim. Load pannier bags so the rear corner cannot fold into the rear wheel. Secure all strap ends by doubling them under buckles or tying the ends together.

Any heavy load will make your bike sway more, and the swaying makes it steer erratically. Adopt a careful, easy pedaling motion to prevent the swaying from starting. Also, be a bit stronger on the steering to prevent the swaying from steering the bike on a wobbly course. People have carried enormous loads on bikes, but twenty pounds is about all that most bikes will take and still handle acceptably.

LIGHTS AT NIGHT

You can ride at night safely if you follow these rules. You must have sufficient light both to see by and to be seen by. Even if the street lighting is so bright that you can see the road, you need a light so the motorists will see you. The lamp lens should be made so that its light can be seen from the sides as well as from the front. The combined generator and lamp unit that clamps on the left front fork blade is excellent. The Raleigh #66 and the Sanyo are the best, the Union next, and the Soubitez after that. Battery lamps are easier to install, but they are more expensive to operate.

Always carry a spare bulb. Wrap one in paper, then adhesive tape to protect it and hide it behind the reflector inside the lamp housing—there's usually room.

At the rear you must have a red reflector, positioned so your loads don't cover it up. If you sometimes use a carrier, have a second reflector mounted on the rear of the carrier itself so the light can't be obscured. The reflector must be the three-inch diameter type sold for trailers and such. Bolt it to a piece of spoke or a metal strap, which is in turn bolted to your bike. The best place is to the left rear mudguard eye. You must have the reflector even though you also may use a red rear lamp, because when rear lamps go out you may not know it.

Never enter an intersection unless you can keep going all the way across without stopping. Motorists cannot see bikes stopped crosswise in an intersection at night—too many dazzling headlamps in their eyes, for one thing.

No matter what the government says, don't rely just on front, side, or pedal reflectors or reflectorized tires. Motorists' headlamps don't shine on them until it is too late to avoid a collision.

FIND THE 12 HAZARDS:

THERE ARE TWELVE HAZARDS FACING THE CYCLIST AT THE BOTTOM OF THIS PICTURE. IDENTIFY EACH ONE AND THINK OF THE BEST WAY TO AVOID ITS DANGER. ALWAYS RIDE WITH A PLAN FOR EMERGENCIES. THOSE WHO HAVE A PLAN ARE MORE LIKELY TO AVOID HAZARDS.

SPROCKETMAN IS A CHARACTER CREATED BY THE URBAN BIKEWAY DESIGN COLLABORATIVE

THE ANSWERS:

1. **MOTORIST PASSING UNSAFELY:** YOU SHOULD SLOW A BIT AND BE READY TO BRAKE WHEN PASSED.
2. **OPEN CAR DOOR:** YOU OUGHT TO RIDE AT LEAST 3 FEET FROM PARKED CARS.
3. **CRACK ON ROAD:** AVOID IT OR YOU MAY BE SORRY!!
4. **PEDESTRIAN:** WATCH HIM! HE'S NOT WATCHING YOU!! BE PREPARED TO STOP.
5. **POT HOLE:** AVOID IT! YOU MAY NOT BE ABLE TO TELL HOW DEEP IT IS.
6. **LEAVES:** AVOID THEM! THEY CAN BE SLIPPERY ESPECIALLY ON A TURN!!
7. **RAILROAD TRACKS:** DON'T CROSS AT ANGLE, CROSS THEM PERPENDICULARLY (STRAIGHT ON!!)
8. **DOG:** WATCH HIM! YELL "GO HOME!". IF THAT DOESN'T WORK GET OFF BIKE ON OPPOSITE SIDE AND WALK. DON'T KICK HIM!!
9. **TRAIN:** STOP AND WAIT.
10. **DRAINAGE GRATE:** AVOID IT!!
11. **WRONG WAY BICYCLIST:** WATCH HIM!! PASS CAREFULLY ON LEFT. TELL HIM "GET OVER, TURKEY!!"
12. **CAR BACKING OUT OF DRIVEWAY:** WATCH HIM! BE READY TO YELL "HEY! WATCH IT!!" IF HE DOESN'T STOP, HE IS SUPPOSED TO WAIT FOR YOU.

Basics: Roadworthiness
Braking Technique
Gearing
The Dog Problem
Bike Fit

The Editors

ROADWORTHINESS

Many people think bike maintenance is beyond them, but according to the Consumer Product Safety Commission, 13 percent of all bike accidents are caused by mechanical failure. Even people who don't plan to work on their bikes themselves still have the responsibility of making sure they're operating correctly. A bike is a simple machine, and anyone can understand it. There are some very experienced riders who don't do their own work, but they all know how a bike is supposed to function, and when they do have repair work done, they are very careful when they inspect the finished job to see that everything works the way it should.

Many accidents can be prevented by checking to see that everything is on tight. Vibration and jarring can loosen nuts and bolts. A screwdriver, pliers, and an adjustable wrench are all the tools you need to ensure that nothing comes off on the road. Reflectors, lamps, baskets, racks, bells, pump holders, toeclips, bottle cages, and chainwheel bolts all need to be firmly fastened on. You don't lose your amateur standing by tightening your fender to keep it from rattling. You should also make a habit of checking to see that the stem and the seat clamp are tight, so that neither the handlebars nor the seat loosen when you're out riding.

Emergency room nurses call accidents caused by open handlebar ends "apple core" wounds, so replace lost plugs or grips immediately. Handlebar tape is not just there to look official, but to help absorb sweat—and road shock. Ride a 10-speed without it and your hands will probably feel numb because of the pressure on the ulnar nerve. Keep it up day after day, and you can damage the nerve permanently, and even suffer paralysis. There are a lot of padded handlebar tapes: If you don't like the feel of them, cover them with ordinary cloth handlebar tape. And if you don't want to keep changing it, choose a navy or black to begin with.

If the bike has been left unattended, or if the wheel has been removed for any reason, check to see that the wheels are in tight and straight. This is particularly important with the front wheel because it could come off at the first pothole. It's easy to get a rear wheel in crooked enough to rub against the frame and act like a brake when you don't want it to, so check that it's correctly centered in the dropouts.

After changing a flat or putting on a new tire, check to see that the tire is on right—that it fits snugly and evenly into the rim all the way around on both sides. If it doesn't, it could start to come off while you're riding. You might be warned that this is happening by a pounding noise that is hard to identify. And, of course, check the pressure in the tires each time you go out.

Check that the brake is properly attached by making sure it doesn't rock back and forth. On a center-pull brake, the cable must be seated properly on both sides of the groove. Pull the brake levers: They should not come nearer to the handlebar than half an inch. If they do, the cable has to be shortened. Brake tension adjusters do this to some extent. It's an easy but frustrating adjustment, but can be much helped by a gadget called a "third hand."

Besides checking the brake levers, you'll have to inspect all four brake blocks periodically; the pads get worn and can work their way loose. Make sure there is at least an eighth of an inch of rubber above the metal sides. If the blocks have an open and a closed end so that the rubber pads can be easily replaced, make sure the closed end faces the front of the bike, or else the rubber can be forced out by the turning of the wheel. Now see that the whole surface of the block is angled so that the pad touches the rim, *not* the tire. Then check to make sure that the bolt holding the block in place is on tight. Do this after each adjustment. Check this bolt periodically, especially after riding over a rough surface. If even one of these brake blocks falls off, the whole brake is useless: It takes both to restrain the wheel.

Brake action can be checked by walking next to the bike and applying each brake hard, then releasing it quickly. The front brake should make the rear wheel lift off the ground. The back brake should make the back wheel skid.

A minute spent with a spray lubricant will ensure that your chain is clean and moves freely. Aim the spray onto the surface that touches the chainwheel and the cogs, then wipe the excess off the outside of the chain.

A teaspoon of oil in a 3-speed hub can keep it going smoothly for months and make the whole bike feel as if it's geared lower. Your bike store should

be happy to sell you the oil and show you how to use it.

Headset, cranks, pedals, and wheels should move freely but without excess play from side to side. A lesson from the bike store or, better yet, hands-on experience in a repair course, can be very helpful in learning to know when any of these parts needs to be adjusted. You can ruin a set of alloy cranks by riding when they are loose.

BRAKING TECHNIQUE

Many braking accidents result from overbraking. Before riding a bike you are unfamiliar with, or whenever any changes have been made to the brakes of your bike (replacement of rubber or cables, or any adjustment) check the braking action carefully so you know just how much pressure it takes to stop without shooting over the handlebars. Test the brakes while riding at a low speed; apply the brakes very gently, then more firmly, until you get the rear wheel to lift a bit. If the rear wheel lifts when gentle pressure is applied, the brake needs to be readjusted or it will catapult you onto the street at a higher speed. Move back on the seat and try again.

Sitting back on the seat is always the safest position to brake from, because applying either brake lightens the load on the rear wheel and increases it on the front. When you apply the rear brake hard, the wheel skids because it has become too light to hold the road properly. The rear brake is only one third as powerful as the front brake, so you'll need both when you want to come to a full stop.

If you hit the brakes too hard, they can lock onto the wheel. Practice "feathering"—rapidly and rhythmically pulling and releasing, pumping them. Doing this is particularly important to dry the rims when it's raining, and to keep rims from overheating (and blowing your tires) on a long downhill. Also, on a downhill your back wheel is higher than your front wheel, and therefore even more likely to upend you if the brakes are applied suddenly. *Always* get way back on the seat when going down a hill, in order to get as much weight as possible on the rear wheel.

Braking is particularly tricky when a steep descent is combined with a series of turns. You can't turn hard and brake at the same time on a bike, any more than you can in a car. Tires have only so much grip on the road, and it can be used either to turn or to slow you down. (If you've completed a driver education course, this won't be a surprise.) Always slow down before you enter a turn.

CHANGING BALANCE POINTS
"G" is Center of Gravity

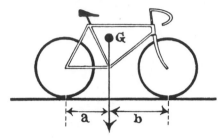

At uniform speed both wheels have a good grip of the road.

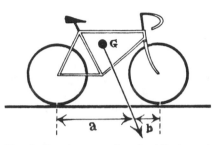

When braking the center of gravity shifts forward. The rear wheel can lose its grip of the road.

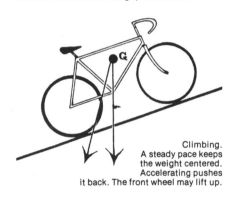

Climbing. A steady pace keeps the weight centered. Accelerating pushes it back. The front wheel may lift up.

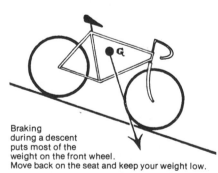

Braking during a descent puts most of the weight on the front wheel. Move back on the seat and keep your weight low.

GEARING

Gearing is not an absolute concept, but a relative one that depends on the weather, hilliness, and how you feel. As you get into shape, you'll be able to spin a higher and higher gear; illness, extra weight (on you or on the bike), or wind in your face, all can force you to a lower gear.

Standard 3-speeds are geared much too high for anything more than a slight

incline, unless you are a super athlete. So there's nothing wrong with you if you can't roll up a hill as quickly as someone on a 10-speed. Even most 10-speeds are set up for super athletes —like the guys who work in the bike stores.

Your foot is meant to *spin* the wheel around in a smooth steady motion that you can keep up for hours without strain. It is not meant to *push* the pedal around against a great deal of resistance. Doing that can hurt your knees, perhaps permanently. On a 10-speed, the smaller the chainwheel in the front and the larger the freewheel sprocket in the rear, the lower the gear—therefore the less pressure you need to spin the pedal around. Also the less distance the wheel travels with each pedal stroke, so you want to spin as high a gear as you comfortably can— and no higher. Ideally, you should keep a steady pedal stroke—or cadence—of about 80 revolutions a minute, under all conditions.

Spinning in Low Gears

"Learn to spin" and "Use a lower gear" are perhaps the two most often heard pieces of advice in cycling.

Spinning takes practice, and until the skill is developed, most people's pedaling speed is limited to their fast walking speed.

But unless you practice spinning, and this means using the lowest bearable instead of the highest possible gear, riding in a low gear is clumsy. When you push the pedal the bike lurches forward and steering becomes squirrely. Since a low gear offers little resistance, the temptation is to spin like mad, get tired, and then coast— even uphill. This is caused by the desire to preserve road speed, to go as fast uphill or against the wind. But the idea of multigeared bikes is to preserve pedal rate, not road speed. Coasting is fun, but it denies you the opportunity of practicing spinning. Until you have gone from the beginner's 50-60 to the experienced cyclist's 70-80, you shouldn't miss a chance to practice increasing your pedaling rate. The experienced cyclist seldom coasts unless safety demands it.

The higher your pedaling rate, the faster you go and the better your acceleration. This makes you safer riding in traffic. One of the reasons racers pedal at between 80 and 100 revolutions a minute is that it enables them to act quickly to start a breakaway or to catch one. For this they are willing to give up a little efficiency.

You go just as far pushing a 90-inch gear once as spinning a 45-inch gear twice, and the latter is much easier on your knees. The "Cycling Injury" chapter makes it quite clear that just as beginning runners tend to overstride, beginning cyclists tend to push too high a gear – and the result in both cases is often leg injury.

Until pedaling rate can be increased, the temptation is to push a higher gear in order to go faster, but this is self-defeating. While it may make you stronger and give you the feeling that you're really exercising, in most cases it will limit the distance you can ride because it is very tiring to push too high a gear. Pushing high gears often cuts cycling longevity, so if you want cycling to be a lifelong activity rather than something you used to do, learn to spin.

BIKE FIT

When the pedals are horizontal – at 3 and 9 o'clock – a plumb line should pass from the front of the knee through the axle of the pedal. Any variation that puts the knee in front of the axle should be avoided.

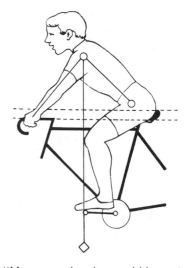

THE DOG PROBLEM

Unleashed dogs cause about eight percent of all bicycle accidents. The problem isn't being bitten, it's being knocked down.

Experienced cyclists point out that traffic is more dangerous than dogs, if fighting a dog makes you lose control of the bike. Cyclists have been killed by losing control while swinging pumps at dogs. If you can't scare one off by yelling, and you don't think you can outrun it (which may mean outrunning a large, muscular dog), get off the bike and use it as a fence between you and the dog – then use an animal repellent, squirt a water bottle, or throw something at the animal. Often just getting off the bike is enough to make the dog lose interest.

Cyclists in Eastern Europe used to carry whips, and in some places small guns or special water pistols filled with ammonia have been popular. These tactics are not advised unless you are also prepared to deal with an irate dog owner.

Phil Smith of Arizona reminds us that dogs are territorial, and once you've left their territory, they have no more reason to chase you. "They always stop in amazement when I reach down a hand for them and whistle or call in a friendly manner . . . frequently I slow down hoping to lure

one on and run him to exhaustion. I have yet to have one pursue me for even half a block."

Barry Zalph of the Department of Mechanical Engineering at Duke University suggests the following steps: 1. Speak calmly in a friendly voice ("You don't have to chase me, I'm a friend.") 2. Shout "Go Home!" 3. Bark back (effective if your bark is convincing). 4. Reverse roles by chasing the dog. Few animals will continue to attack a larger one if the latter stands unafraid.

In this country rabies has been practically eradicated in dogs, but that doesn't mean a dog bite can't be serious. If you are bitten, stop cycling, clean the wound, ice it, and immobilize it. Carry Deferens as an antiseptic. If you continue cycling you will pump bacteria into your bloodstream. A nurse reported that a man had a gross infection with a fever of 106° because he continued to cycle hard after he had been bitten.

It is important as a public health measure to report a dog bite. The police or health department will usually help you track down the dog, as they want to check if it has had rabies shots and if it has a history of attacking people. This means take a good look at both the animal and the location; you'll need to describe them later.

"Many people who would be astonished if you were to suggest they go for a hike wearing their little cousin's shoes, jump joyfully onto the first bike that comes along, and after riding twenty miserable miles, declare that the bicycle is an abominable machine."

When Jacques Faizant, well-known humorist and cyclotourist, notes this in *Albina et la bicyclette,* he brings up two important points about bike fit. The first is that since people think of the bike as a freedom machine, they approach it as if anything were possible. And so it is – for a short while. A lot of people end up with bikes that don't fit them because they think that trying one out for five minutes will tell them if it's the one they want. Unfortunately, it's much more exhilarating to jump on a bike and ride off than to wait around and have all the changes made that would make it fit you. 10-speeds are particularly exciting to take out for a short distance.

The main causes of orthopedic problems in beginners are gross errors in bike fit: seats over an inch too high, too low, or too far forward . . . plus doing crazy things like going for a fifty-mile ride when the farthest they'd ever ridden before at one time was fifteen miles.

Experienced cyclists can cause problems for themselves in an attempt to fit some ideal position based on a formula rather than their own body build. For example, many develop knee trouble by fixing cleats in a straight-ahead or toed-in position when their natural stance is turned out.

The ideal position has to do with wind resistance, not comfort. A study of the riders who participated in the 1979 Tour de France showed that only about 60 percent are anywhere near approaching the "ideal" (eyes over the handlebars when in the dropped position). Two thirds had a better aerodynamic position when their hands were on the rubber tops of the brake handles.

BK

No matter what kind of bike you ride, your seat should be high enough to fully extend the leg – with your heel on the pedal. It should not be so high that you cannot stay on the seat without shifting your hips from side to side. You should have almost full extension, but without the knee locked, when you pedal the way you should – with the ball of your foot on the pedal. Bicycles can be accelerated faster than cars, and this is an important safety feature. If you pedal with your instep, or your seat is too low, you give up a lot of power and safety. You should wear stiff-soled shoes; the better a shoe is for running, the worse it is for cycling. On a 3-speed you should be able to reach the handlebars from a comfortable upright position, elbow bent but not squashed against the body. Touring position on a 10-speed should let you reach the handlebars with about a forty-five degree forward lean. Wom-

Photograph by John Krausz

en's handlebars should be level with the seat, men's about two inches below. You must be able to straddle any men's frame with a half-inch – but no more than two inches – clearance. The "Cycling Injury" chapter of our orthopedic section makes the reasons for all this perfectly clear. The "Cycle Fit" section of that chapter explains all the necessary adjustments in greater detail.

Eddie Merckx, perhaps this generation's greatest racer, said that it took him five years after his most successful season (1969) to perfect his position and get comfortable on the bike.

Very minor adjustments can make major differences when you are riding a hundred miles a day. So even the formulas in our orthopedic section are only a starting point. Once you have approximated the correct position, give it at least a week before changing anything. Change gradually, perhaps as little as a millimeter at a time.

It's too bad toeclips have become associated with the idea of going fast, because they are really a safety device – the safest, easiest way to keep your feet in the proper position and you on the bike when the road surface is rough.

Generally speaking it's safer to ride a bike a shade too small than a shade too large, although an extra long seat post can put you so far over the rear wheel you do unplanned wheelies. Too big a bike can hurt if you stop suddenly and land on the top bar; if you push your seat too far forward it's really bad for your knees and tilting the seat forward puts all your weight on your hands; both adjustments increase the rear wheel's tendency to send you over the handlebars when you brake. Too long a top tube makes some people tilt the handlebars back toward them so they're riding with their hands on the brake handles, which means they can brake inadvertently or put so much pressure on the brakes that they lock the wheels.

There are one-armed bike riders, one-legged bike riders, riders with one arm shorter than the other, and people who can't walk but can ride. The handlebar shown here was made for someone with a large difference in arm length. It is only a small example of what someone with mechanical ingenuity can accomplish in fitting a

bicycle to a particular person.

If you have a special problem getting a bike that fits, you can often find help at a bike club. If your bike store can't recommend one, write to the League of American Wheelmen for the name of a club near you (LAW – P.O. Box 988, Baltimore, MD 21203).

Bicycles are sold in varying seat-tube lengths – 21 and 23 inch are the most popular – which is nice for the stock room, but not much help in choosing a frame that fits, since that does not tell you how far the top tube is from the ground. Let us hope that this method changes as bicycling becomes more popular. Manufacturers are already expanding the range from 18 to 27 inches – we show here a "Piccolo" as an example of a small good quality frame you needn't get from a custom builder. Periodicals like *Bicycling* magazine regularly research and review bicycles for short people and for tall people, giving top tube as well as seat tube dimension (too far a lean can cause just as much trouble as too high a seat, and top-tube length can vary as much as four inches for the same size seat tube!) Magazines also periodically list custom builders.

The Piccolo has an 18" frame, 19½" top tube, 38" wheel base. This is made possible by the use of Mafac cantilever brakes. Picture courtesy of The Flying Dutchman, Ltd., 340 Holly, Denver, CO 80220.

TOURING AND RACING POSITION

Cycling instructor Myrna Meyer, one of the teachers interviewed in the "On-Road Training" chapter, says:

Comfort on the bike can make all the difference between whether someone

Racing Position Minimizes Wind Resistance

becomes a cylist or gives it up. Touring position is different from racing position. You rarely ride on the drops, only in a head wind or something like that. Racers just have to watch the pack around them, but on the road you have to be able to pick up your head and look around. Having your arms too low causes tremendous pain in your

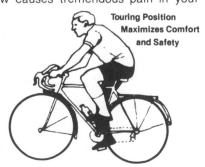

Touring Position Maximizes Comfort and Safety

shoulder blades.

Too many bike stores set bikes up racing style, with too long a stem for general riding; then the stores just push the saddle forward to compensate. That puts the knee in front of the pedal instead of over it, which causes knee problems. You get the same effect if your toeclips are too long. Regular toeclips come in different lengths, but the new mini ones only come in one size, and for many women they're too big, and put the foot in the wrong place on the pedal. It's much smarter to buy the right size toeclip and leave the strap off until you're used to it. Racing style also sets the stem too low for general riding. It should be level with the saddle or at the most an inch below; sometimes an inch above is more comfortable.

Weather and the Cyclist

Vera van der Reis Krausz

That cyclists should be particularly careful to protect themselves from the weather was made clear to us when every doctor we spoke to wanted assurance that the subject would be thoroughly treated in this book. Only in wartime are people exposed to the weather for as long a time as cyclists, therefore much of our information came from medical advice for doctors in the armed services. Our medical editor checked the section out to make sure we hadn't forgotten anything.

Cycling can be continued far longer than any other activity. Even people in moderate condition can stay on a bike for hours in weather that would keep most other athletes from participating in sports. However, the effects of temperature extremes are almost imperceptibly cumulative, and are influenced by duration of exposure. Therefore, cyclists are in more danger of both hypothermia and hyperthermia than most people. Cycling reaches levels of intensity and duration unequaled by any other sport, and the racer's combination of heat, dehydration, and mountain climbing has resulted in deaths from heat stroke. In the winter, the combination of sweat, hunger, fatigue, and cold is equally dangerous. Any cyclist can also be put in danger from exposure by an unexpected breakdown, either physical or mechanical. Many also inadvertently put themselves into a racing-type situation by pushing themselves beyond their own physiological limits either by trying to do a certain number of miles in a certain time or by trying to keep up with people who are better trained.

Clothes are one way to avoid these dangers; cycling technique is another. Understanding what forces cause the hazards will help you understand the reasons for the solutions offered.

The laws of physics treat your body like any other object, so you lose or gain heat by convection, conduction, radiation, and evaporation. Heat only flows from a hot place to a cold one. The air that touches you warms up, which makes it lighter; it rises and is replaced by cold air. This is convection, and one of the most important ways your body loses heat. On a bike it happens faster because the wind blows the warm air around you away more quickly.

If something hot touches something cold, heat is conducted from one to the other. A hot object also loses heat to a distant object that's colder by radiation – which is how the sun heats you. Human skin is a good radiator and also absorbs radiation well. Skin color makes no difference in absorption, but lighter skin reflects more. Wear light clothes in summer, and darker (but still bright, please) clothes in the winter.

Your body provides the heat that turns water into vapor, which cools you by evaporation. Besides sweat, a certain amount of water vapor is continuously and imperceptibly leaving your body through both your skin and the air you breathe out. Unfortunately, your body cannot sense water loss as well as it can some other things, so when you're riding you must force yourself to drink at regular intervals.

Dress to suit your physiology. There is a tremendous variation among people as to what temperature is comfortable. No wonder: 98.6 degrees is just an average; in any fifty grown-ups at rest, temperature will range from 97 to 99 degrees. And while everybody's temperature rises with exercise, some people produce twice as much heat as others, which explains why some athletes win races in cold weather, and others do best in the heat. What feels good one day may not the next. If you're healthy and fit, neither heat nor cold bother you as much. Doctors have discovered that soldiers who are hungry, frightened, or tired are more susceptible to cold: Time of day and age also make a difference; body temperature rises during the day; cold bothers elderly people more.

Acclimatization is not just imagination; your cardiovascular system gets used to heat and cold and sends more blood where it's needed to keep your body at a constant temperature. That's why the first hot or cold day hits us so hard. When you travel where the weather or altitude is radically different from what you are accustomed to, take it easy on your system by dressing appropriately and by not exercising fiercely at first.

You might consider acclimatizing yourself to heat before your trip; an hour a day at the elevated temperature is enough to train the sweat glands. You may be doing it already if you use rollers or a stationary bicycle. It doesn't matter whether you exercise or not; what matters is that you sweat.

Cycling in the Heat

Getting used to the heat means getting used to sweating. All other conditions being the same, a person working for four hours at 90 degrees Fahrenheit for the first time will have a temperature of 103 degrees, a pulse rate of 180, and two liters of sweat loss. Four weeks later the temperature will have dropped to 99.5, the pulse to 130, but the quantity of

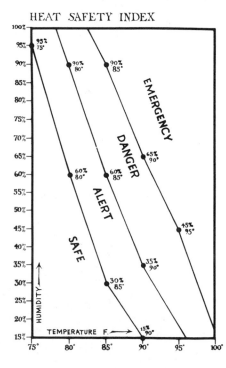

HEAT SAFETY INDEX

sweat will have doubled! If you are out on an all-day trip on a bike, you could be working under similar conditions. If you're not used to it, you could be in danger. Most people tend to reduce their work level when they are hot or uncomfortable; this is a built-in safety mechanism. You may have a hill to climb, or a long way to go in the sun, or may be riding with people who are more fit than you, and thus may not feel free to slack off. Once again, you may be in danger.

As the humidity goes up, less and less of the water on you can evaporate, so it's harder and harder to stay cool; that means you should avoid all the hills you can – and if you must climb them, do it slowly. If possible, don't bike at all in the heat of the day.

Man can live and work in the heat better than any other animal because his capacity for sweating is greater; but dehydration decreases this ability. With dehydration your body temperature rises. This can happen imperceptibly because the wind dries your sweat, and you forget to replace the water you've lost. Once it starts to rise, the heat increases the rate of metabolic processes – which creates more heat; at 106 degrees there is usually irreversible damage, especially to the brain; at 108 degrees, death occurs. So you have to monitor yourself and your fellow riders closely in the heat.

The first sign of distress is often muscle cramps, caused by lack of minerals. Then heat prostration follows, which is very close to shock; the person is pale, clammy, feels slightly weak and sometimes nauseated. In either case provide rest and sips of salty water or orange juice diluted with water. A true medical emergency is heat stroke, where the person is flushed and dry; they must be cooled as soon as possible – inside and out – or death may result.

Dressing for Heat

Starting at the top: Cover your head! A white helmet or bike hat reflects the heat and keeps sun out of your eyes. A thin white shirt with roll-up sleeves protects you from the sun and keeps you cooler than you'd be with bare skin. Or you can sew pockets onto the back of a strong T-shirt and have the convenience of a bike shirt at minimal cost. Bike mitts soak up the sweat so your hands don't slide on the grips. Make sure shorts or bathing suit don't chafe. Ride around the block in them before you go on an all-day trip. Leather shoes are cooler than sneakers. Bike shoes are perforated and lightweight and can be worn without socks, though I think a thin fabric liner keeps you drier. Floppy sandals are dangerous: They can get caught in the works.

Sunburn significantly decreases your body's ability to deal with heat. The ultraviolet rays of the sun, which cause sunburn, are filtered by the depth of the atmosphere and by pollution, so going to the mountains, the desert, or the seashore can increase exposure tremendously.

Day-long riding can also expose you to burns in unexpected places – behind the knees, inside the ears, and even under the knit portion of cycling gloves. One person on a long tour actually had to go to the hospital to have his bike gloves taken off, so even someone who tans easily may need the protection of sunscreen.

Sunscreens have come a long way since the days when mountain-climbers and lifeguards smeared their noses and necks with zinc oxide. Today's sunscreens, most of which use PABA (a vitamin derivative) as their active ingredient, are calibrated by the number of times they increase an individual's resistance to sunburn -- from three to fifteen. Use a low number to permit tanning, a higher one to maximize protection. They're available both in small tubes and in lotion bottles, so it's not much trouble to carry two or three for different parts of the body.

A cool morning start may make you forget to protect all skin newly bared to sun with sunscreen or suntan lotion: that includes the tops of your thighs and the back of the neck and ears. Be careful that sunscreens don't block the pores completely and prevent sweating.

Don't forget the principle of the first refrigerators: Water cools by evaporation. Pour some on yourself – hat and cotton shirt included – and let the breeze from your biking do the rest. And don't forget to pour some down your throat at regular intervals, whether you're thirsty or not.

Wind

The wind-chill factor is intensified on a bike. In fact, add your speed to the wind to figure out how much heat you're losing. If you're tempted to forget taking a Windbreaker, remember that traveling at fifteen miles per hours into a ten mile per hour head wind gives you an effective wind force of twenty-five miles per hour. That brings fifty degrees Fahrenheit down to a below-freezing wind-chill factor . . . don't even ask what it does for thirty degrees! Just look at our chart. Paper is a good insulator and weighs almost nothing. A piece between shirt and sweater can prevent shivering.

Rain

With proper equipment, rain should not be an excuse to stop rid-

---

Intemperance is the lot of the cyclist as it is that of the sailor, the mountain climber, and all those who choose to play their game in nature and the open air.

On the subject of winds, the cyclist is only beaten by navigators and millers. On the subject of rain, by nobody. To hear him talk, he spends half his cycling life in the rain. He knows every type, and can make an audience of frogs thrill with the recital of outings when it rained so much there was water up to his inner tubes. (Albina says that rain is good for the complexion.)

Sometimes it happens that the cyclist has the wind at his back. This is an intoxicating sensation which has to be distrusted because it leads to vanity, and nothing is more dangerous on a bicycle than vanity. The cyclist pushed by the wind thinks he is a great champion, and his morale, which has flown too high, is going to sink like a brick when he turns a corner and realizes that he's only been sailing.

Wind demands patience. One has to nibble the road like a mouse nibbles a cheese, and accept all its inconveniences,

ing, although it does make flat tires more likely, braking less sure, and also cuts drivers' visibility. Capillary action almost glues a piece of glass to the tire that in dry weather would have just fallen off, making tire savers a good idea; and, of course, you must ride slower and brake sooner, squeezing and releasing the handle several times to dry the rim so the rubber holds it properly.

You might not consider fenders part of clothing, but that's why they're there. On tour you can always tell who doesn't have them because of the muddy stripe down that rider's back and the dappled effect in the front. Fenders also protect the brake mechanism, the headset, and the bottom of the saddle. They don't work completely, but they help. If your seat post is open at the top, it should be stopped with a cork, or covered with tape to protect the bottom bracket.

Fenders come as standard equipment on 3-speeds, and on a commuting bike they should be left on, or put back on. They can be made to work perfectly by adding mudguards (rubber aprons that send the slush back onto the road where it belongs). Because the modern 10-speed is derived from the racing bike, and because fenders do create more wind resistance and slow down tire changes, they're hard to find on American bikes. They are standard equipment on European touring bikes, and they are one of the requirements for entering the World Series of endurance riding – Paris-Brest-Paris (750 miles in less than 90 hours) – because they help keep mud from flying up from your wheel into the face of the person behind you. Join a club ride without fenders and you often have to stay in the back.

Danger of Freezing Exposed Flesh for Healthy, Properly Dressed People; one minute at -25° to -75°; within thirty seconds below that temperature.

WIND-CHILL FACTOR

AIR SPEED	Dry or Wet	\textbf{AIR TEMPERATURE (FAHRENHEIT)}							
		50°	40°	30°	20°	10°	0°	-10°	-20°
CALM	Dry	50°	40°	30°	20°	10°	0°	-10°	-20°
	Wet	45°	34°	26°	14°	3°	-6°	-16°	-27°
5 MPH	Dry	48°	37°	27°	16°	6°	-5°	-15°	-26°
	Wet	44°	33°	24°	12°	2°	-10°	-20°	-32°
10 MPH	Dry	40°	28°	16°	4°	-9°	-24°	-33°	-46°
	Wet	30°	16°	2°	-12°	-28°	-48°	-56°	-72°
15 MPH	Dry	36°	22°	9°	-5°	-18°	-32°	-45°	-58°
	Wet	22°	4°	-12°	-30°	-46°	-64°	-80°	-96°
20 MPH	Dry	32°	18°	4°	-10°	-25°	-39°	-53°	-67°
	Wet	14°	-4°	-22°	-40°	-60°	-78°	-96°	-114°
25 MPH	Dry	30°	16°	0°	-15°	-29°	-44°	-59°	-74°
	Wet	10°	-8°	-30°	-50°	-68°	-88°	-108°	-128°
30 MPH	Dry	28°	13°	-2°	-18°	-33°	-48°	-63°	-79°
	Wet	6°	-14°	-34°	-56°	-76°	-96°	-116°	-138°
35 MPH	Dry	27°	11°	-4°	-20°	-35°	-51°	-67°	-82°
	Wet	4°	-18°	-38°	-60°	-80°	-102°	-124°	-144°
40 MPH	Dry	26°	10°	-6°	-21°	-37°	-53°	-69°	-85°
	Wet	2°	-20°	-42°	-62°	-84°	-106°	-128°	-150°

The concept of "Wind-Chill" depends upon many factors, including absolute humidity, relative humidity, air pressure, and temperature. Slight discrepancies are due to the difficulty of making precise measurements under totally controlled conditions.

If the only fenders you remember are the heavy metal ones, there are now plastic, short aluminum, and removable plastic back ones that add little weight to your machine. They should be put on with Loctite and/or serrated washers. Like everything else in cycling, they are not without their own disadvantages and even dangers. Mud can build up in fenders and come loose just when you put on your brake . . . so check fenders for clearance. Snow presents similar dangers, but the buildup can happen so fast, it's probably not a good idea to ride with fenders in the snow.

---

such as having to pedal in the descents, which is rather discouraging. . . .

– Did you see the temperature? Eight below zero!

– That's an ideal temperature, I said. Don't let figures drive you wild. In Fahrenheit it's even more imposing.

I had convinced Albina that the winter and its rigors didn't stop bike outings. It's ridiculous to say it's too cold to go biking when there are people on line at the railroad station to go to the four corners of the world to ski. Skiing is an interesting sport. But between being

pulled up a slope on a rope and climbing it by the force of your calves are degrees. And these are precisely the ones that see to it you don't feel cold while biking.

– Well, said Albina, I'm cold.

– That's because you're standing there talking about skiing. Let's go! A cap down over your ears, your collar pulled up to your nose, goggles, furry gloves, and wool everywhere – you can't feel cold unless you have a poor attitude.

– I don't have a poor attitude, says Albina. I have poor circulation.

– Precisely. The bike cures that, too.

Albina is very surprised by the number of cyclists we pass (nothing surprises noncyclists so much as cyclists). Alone or in groups, well bundled up, they wave hello and pedal happily, making their blood circulate and their hearts and lungs work.

– Cold, Albina?

– No, not anymore. Under the wool it's like a steam bath.

Jacques Faizant, Albina et la bicyclette, 1968

Translated from the French by Vera van der Reis Krausz

Dressing for Rain

Water is an excellent conductor; it makes the air effectively six to sixty degrees colder depending on wind velocity. Since any clothes impervious to rain also let moisture condense on the inside, if it's really hot out, get wet and enjoy it. Don't try to avoid getting wet. You might use a racer's trick and put Vaseline on your knees to keep them dry. You must protect yourself from cold rain, because the breeze that kept you cool in the summer is still cooling you by evaporation. Frostbite, trench foot, and hypothermia (dangerously low body temperature) have occurred when rain was combined with air temperatures as high as sixty degrees Fahrenheit. So always carry a Windbreaker that can protect you from the rain as well. If it's not too cold, a rain cape is sufficient cover. Capes for rain use were developed in Britain, where if you stayed indoors every time it rained, you'd never get to ride. Perhaps you can convert a poncho into one from this description: They are cut tight so they don't tangle with spokes or cranks, but with enough of a tail to sit on. In the front they cover the handlebars (elastic loops hold them in place) so you can work the brakes under them and keep your hands dry. They are open at the sides for ventilation. Team one with a southwester hat that will keep rain off your neck and out of your eyes. Avoid hoods; they cut peripheral vision, and when you turn your head to see what's behind you – you only get to see the inside of your hood!

Instead of a rain cape, any rain jacket will do if it's long enough in the back to cover your kidneys and the exposed part between your shirt and pants – and if it is ventilated under the arms. "Breathable" rainwear is an improvement; one is less hot and sticky, but not completely dry and comfortable by any means. If it rains a lot where you live, the relatively high price might be worth it. Whatever you get, make sure it's bright – even garish! Drivers can't see as well in the rain, so choose a vibrant orange or yellow rather than camouflage khaki.

Cover your feet with something waterproof – even a plastic bag will do – toes chill fast. In the Northwest, where it rains all winter long, people team ponchos with gaiters that protect the leg from knee to ankle; farther south they use chaps, which are open at the back. Whatever rain pants you wear, make sure they cover your boots and are secured out of the way of the chain.

Riding in the Cold

Bikes aren't stable on snow or ice, but a ride on a cold day is quite exhilarating. Melted rock salt is bad for tires and metal – rinse it off carefully. Watch out for corners and dark patches; both of them often mean ice – and no traction. In Finland they cycle in temperatures as low as -22°C and live to tell the tale; the advice is do everything smoothly – accelerate, turn, and brake. In fact, if on ice or snow, *steer* rather than brake, even if it means steering into a ditch to avoid a car. Bikes get a little cranky in the cold; they don't shift or brake as smoothly as normal. Metal gets brittle, lubrication doesn't work as well. All this adds to the chances of unplanned roadside stops. And it's when you have to stop suddenly that you are in danger of getting chilled, especially if you've been sweating. So carry an extra sweater for emergency stops. Handlebar bags are good in winter because they block the wind and carry emergency equipment – which should include tools, food, and perhaps a Thermos of warm soup. Be careful not to touch your bike with bare hands; skin can freeze to metal! If at all possible, get yourself and your bike to shelter, or at least out of the wind. You might even consider walking to a nearby house or stopping a motorist for a lift.

Walking rather than stopping short also gives you a chance to cool down without chilling and to restore feeling to your toes.

Eat well: Fats and proteins stay with you longest. Carry emergency rations, and don't overdo it – being tired or hungry increases your chances of cold injury – either frostbite or hypothermia – which can creep up on you without notice. Extremities start to get numb, as the body saves the blood to keep the core warm.

In hypothermia, core temperature is what's important. The core is about an inch in; if the body's warm, painful cold is not felt in the extremities unless they're at under 59 degrees; but they can get clumsy at higher temperatures than that and make handling a bike difficult.

As body temperature slowly drops, you feel sleepy and woozy; judgment is impaired. If it goes below 90 degrees, unconsciousness results. If you think this is happening to either you or to a companion, cut the trip short, stop for something warm to drink (unbreakable vacuum bottles are great for winter outings), try to get help. Avoid both alcohol and smoking; they impair circulation. If first aid is needed, don't rub hands and feet, but warm the body – or the cold blood from the extremities may rush in and cause heart failure. If you suspect frostbite (the skin is gray or white), get to a hospital rather than trying to treat it at home. Pour warm water over frozen clothes to loosen them, but never use extremes of heat or ice to thaw frozen flesh – and never rub it; you can cause further damage. Don't even try to thaw it if it will be frozen again later – that causes wastes to form that can poison the whole system. It takes a long time to know how much damage has been done, and great care must be taken to prevent permanent damage.

Dressing for the Cold

The easiest way to regulate temperature is with a hat; forty percent of your body heat escapes from your head. Next easiest, the zippers on your Windbreaker. Truly super ones have two-way zips, or zip-through pockets that let air cool under your arms. Cover your knees when it is under sixty degrees because the body, in preserving the core temperature, cuts down the supply of blood to the legs, which limits chemical transfer to the muscles and makes your feet feel cold and the joints more prone to injury. Winterize your helmet by covering the holes with tape from the inside, but first see if wearing a hat under your helmet is enough. Try a wool or acrylic "baclava" that covers your ears and neck as well. In extreme cold you can pull up the bottom and cover your nose, chin, and mouth. No face masks – they restrict vision. Goggles keep eyes from watering in intense cold. (Safety goggles used around machinery are cheap and good.) Antifog solution (or saliva) keeps them from steaming up.

Cross-country skiing is similar to biking in its effect on the body, so if your bike store doesn't have the clothing you want and you can't wait to order it from a catalog, try a ski store, but make sure all tops are cut long enough to cover your wrists and kidneys if you're stretched out with your hands on the bottom of the handlebars.

You warm up fast when you're riding; what's comfortable upon setting out may feel like a steam bath ten minutes later. And perspiration gets you just as wet as rain, with just as much danger of hypothermia and frostbite. That's why all cold-weather experts recommend starting with a layer that wicks the moisture away from your skin, like wool or silk (a thin layer of cotton will wick to wool – the idea behind the two-ply ski underwear which many cyclists wear in the winter). Add wool layers on top of that, and end with a Windbreaker that lets some moisture out while preventing wind from entering. (Test fabric for breathability by blowing through it; you should be able to feel your breath on your hand.) Buy your Windbreaker in yellow or orange; white doesn't show up well against snow. Winter days are often overcast, so it's important to wear something bright.

As you ride, your body warms the air around you; the layers trap the warmth and prevent it from escaping; you insulate yourself as you would a house. How much insulation a fabric provides depends on its thickness; wool is very elastic, so it stays fluffy; cotton compresses. Some people bike in down parkas; I find they get too hot and are too bulky, and even though I've never fallen in the winter, the idea of a dog crossing

my path and my leaving all those feathers on the ground has never appealed to me; too much like a cartoon. Instead, I wear up to six layers, some of which I remove once I'm warmed up.

Legs don't get nearly as cold as the upper body, so thermal underwear (you can sew a chamois crotch inside) with one other layer is usually sufficient. The other layer can be tights, sweat pants, ski pants, or warm-up pants. Be sure there's enough room for your knees to move freely; do a few knee bends to test pants you plan to bike in.

Hands and Feet

How long you stay out will ultimately depend on how cold your toes are. Your feet are moving faster than any other part of your body, so they're effectively exposed to a lower temperature. To counteract that, there is nothing that hasn't been tried by bikers desperate for a spin, including battery-operated socks and fur-lined toeclip covers (they slip on and off with an elastic). Fleece-lined shoes or low boots are adequate for short hops, but for longer rides most people go the layered route, which means getting shoes at least two full sizes larger than normal. In either case, you may need wider pedals and larger toeclips (you can add washers to these).

Start with a sock liner of cotton or silk; then one or two layers of wool to wick perspiration away from the body, and possibly a ski-type sock on top. You might just use the toe for the middle layer; it gives warmth where it's especially needed, without

taking up space where it isn't. Your winter cycling shoe must fit loosely over all that; you defeat the whole purpose if there is constriction, because tight shoes cut circulation and cause numbing. Bowling shoes, athletic shoes with the cleats sawed off, or cheap sneakers with stiff soles all can do the job. Some people cover the whole shoe or toeclip with another thick sock. Others use plastic bags between socks, or over the shoe; but they make my feet feel clammy. Plastic toeclip covers, on the other hand, do protect the foot from the wind.

Heat loss depends on diameter as well as surface temperature – so you'll need thicker insulation on your hands as well. A thin layer of cotton or silk, then wool, then either a leather-palm ski glove or mitten. Some wear wool gloves covered with a thin leather work mitten (the kind you can get in a hardware or variety store). I prefer thick mittens; they let the fingers keep each other warm, but make shifting a bit more difficult; you'll have to decide which is most important to you.

Since the body keeps the core warm by lessening circulation to the extremities, pressure on handlebars and pedals increases the problem and can numb fingers and toes. Keep flexing these, and keep both hands and feet moving: Change hand positions frequently and don't coast. If your fingers get numb, shake your hand and slap it against your thigh to restore circulation. If your toes get numb, run next to the bike for a minute or two.

Clothing: What to Wear Riding

Vera van der Reis Krausz

Always a Good Idea

1. *Identification.* Name, date of birth, address. Serial number of bike. Medical information: blood type, date of last tetanus booster, heart rate if exceptionally low, presence of dentures, contact lenses, allergies, medication. Any special medical condition such as seizure disorder or diabetes. Work and home number of person to notify in case of accident. A plastic cover to keep all ID dry.

2. *Visibility Item.* (Can be tucked away until needed.) Bike accidents not caused by biker error are caused by not being noticed. Wear a fluorescent vest with a large reflective X, or a light yellow or white Windbreaker with a reflective band. If it's too hot for this, wear white; remember, red is invisible at night. Fluorescent arm or leg bands take up almost no room and use Velcro for closing.

3. *Audibility Item.* A horn or bell to announce your presence. Whistles are illegal in most states.

4. *Helmet.* Head injuries are the most serious of all bike injuries, so more and more experienced riders are wearing helmets—though some say they can lull you into being careless. Helmets are not a substitute for good bike handling!

The best helmets are built like a coconut: a smooth, hard outer layer and a compressible styrene liner (hard to the touch), foam pads for sizing. These are designed to survive one crash. Both MSR and Bell claim, on the basis of helmets returned to them for inspection, to have saved a lot of heads from fractured skulls and concussions. Less protection is given by plastic helmets with foam rubber linings, often cut out for coolness. They're okay for secondary impact, as is the traditional racer's helmet: strips of foam-filled leather or plastic attached at front and back. Hockey helmets are a good choice for children, because they are adjustable; the new smaller bicycle helmets may be hard to find. A light-colored helmet reflects the heat. Holes or scoops send the wind whistling through, which takes some getting used to, because it sounds as if cars are following you when they aren't. All helmets keep hair out of eyes.

5. *Energy Insurance.* Tuck a few hard candies into a pocket. The exhilaration of cycling sometimes makes you use all your glucose reserves without noticing until you feel faint.

6. *Gloves.* Any glove gives protection in case you fall; bike gloves and handball gloves also provide padding against road shock; the latter have full fingers. Cross-country ski gloves with knit backs and padded palms are fine until freezing weather forces you to ski mittens.

Photography by Paul Boyer

7. *Shoes.* It may be better to ride a bike barefoot than to walk barefoot, but you're taking a lot of chances. Stiff-soled shoes are more efficient, but bike shoes are hard to walk in. A court shoe is better than a running shoe. Our solution: Get the least-expensive leather bike shoes, add a thin-ribbed rubber sole to the front, and a small rubber heel to the rear.

No matter what distance you ride a bike, the ball of your foot is what belongs on the pedal, not the instep, and certainly not the heel. This is always true, whether commuting, shopping, or touring; and with whatever kind of shoe you're wearing, including high heels. Never put the pedal between the front of the shoe and the heel; it can act as a wedge and cause the heel to break off; the sudden loss of restraint is liable to make you fall.

8 *Batten it all down!* Nasty accidents are caused by things falling into wheels, because they make the bike stop suddenly, and the rider keeps going. So—no long scarves, floppy coats, or long ponchos. Make sure nothing dangles. Tuck pants legs into socks, or secure with garter or pin. Best of all are the new

reflective fabric clips. Long flowing skirts are not a good idea (why do you think bloomers were invented?). An A-line is okay. Be careful how you knot your jacket around your waist; a sleeve can get caught in the wheel. Tie shoelaces in double knots; they've been known to get caught in the chain or between the pedal and the crank.

Make sure tie-downs are tied down; check them if you've removed something from the bike. A tip: Put extra rubber bands on handlebars. They make grips less slippery in the rain, and are wonderful for folding things small, holding things together in an emergency. So is a little extra tape.

Utility Riding

If you ride in an upright position and have a chain guard and a basket or rack to help carry bundles, you can dress for cycling as you would dress for work.

Commuting Run

What you wear on a commuting ride depends on the length and purpose of your commute and the nature of your job. There's no reason to look grungy, or to arrive disheveled. Your bike should be set up with a basket, bag, or rack for extra clothes. Remember, exercise is warming, but if you don't want to shiver the first ten minutes of your ride, you will need an extra layer you can stow away.

For the least annoyance, wear things that button or zip rather than those that have to be pulled over the head. If you ride in traffic wearing dark-colored business clothes, you may be putting yourself in danger.

If you have a really long distance to commute, you might consider the Clark Kent–Superman routine. Superman rides the bike, in proper, comfortable bike clothes, and turns into Clark Kent at the office.

Long Distance Touring

Bike-racing clothes were designed for long hours in the saddle. If they look too freaky for you, at least get the gloves and the shoes. People vary in how much they're bothered by seams in pants. A chamois can be sewn into regular pants or shorts. Sweat pants are a comfortable and inexpensive solution, and can be worn over thermal underwear in the winter, cut off in the summer. If you're riding a 10-speed, make sure your shirts are long enough to cover your kidneys when you're on the drops. Button-front shirts are cut longer, and also give you a choice of sleeve length.

Why Bike Racing Clothes Look So Funny

The racer's uniform was developed in response to the needs of this most taxing sport, which can have the athlete in the saddle, burning as many as a thousand calories an hour, for hour after hour, day after day. Provision has to be made to replace these calories on the go, to absorb and evaporate sweat, to protect pressure points, to minimize wind resistance, and to maximize pedaling efficiency. To make the spectacle more spectacular and to assure the racer good visibility for on-the-road training, bright colors were added to the tops.

Early racing pictures show clothes borrowed from running: singlet, shorts. Shorts creep up from knee length, and in 1905 the first pockets appear on the jerseys; by 1920 the back of the pack looks very modern; 1930's pictures seem to show all the present-day features. New fabrics have been assimilated; when nylon

came in it was snapped up for Windbreakers; now Damart is being tried for cold-weather underwear.

When you consider what a multimillion-dollar sport bike racing is in Europe and how few changes have been made since the 1930's, you realize that the clothes must be doing their job very well indeed. For comfort and convenience, bike clothes can't be beat, whether racing, touring long-distance, or taking any trip over an hour long.

Racers do not tend to be fat. People whose proportions don't match the racing standard might have to have their biking clothes custom made. This is not much more expensive than buying ready-made. Cycling clothes are about as expensive as skiing clothes, and you pay for quality (which usually means wool).

Photograph by Paul Boyer

Let's start with the important accessories first.

1. *Shoes.* Cycling shoes have a stiff sole, so that none of the power transmitted to the pedal is lost. Sometimes the sole is double, with a piece of metal between the two layers. Plastic soles are the stiffest of all, but tend to heat up. The leather tops and the soles are perforated for air conditioning and to drain water in case of rain or slush. Also, shoes are "revolving weight," so racers like them as light as possible. Cycling shoes are worn barefoot or with a thin wool or silk sock, and are bought a tiny bit tight, as the leather stretches. They lace low over the instep to keep the foot from sliding forward and to keep the toes from pressing against the front. Racers add a cleat that keeps the ball of the foot positioned absolutely properly and pull their toeclip straps tight, which permits them to pull up on the pedal with one foot, while they push down with the other. Winter shoes have no holes. There are also fur-lined booties, and overshoes with Velcro backs and holes for the cleat.

2. *Gloves.* Well, mitts, really. These have padded leather palms to protect you from road shock, let you wipe your tire after going through glass or gravel, and are faster and less painful to replace than skin if you take a tumble. The backs are loosely knit cotton and double as handkerchiefs for a quick wipe of forehead or nose.

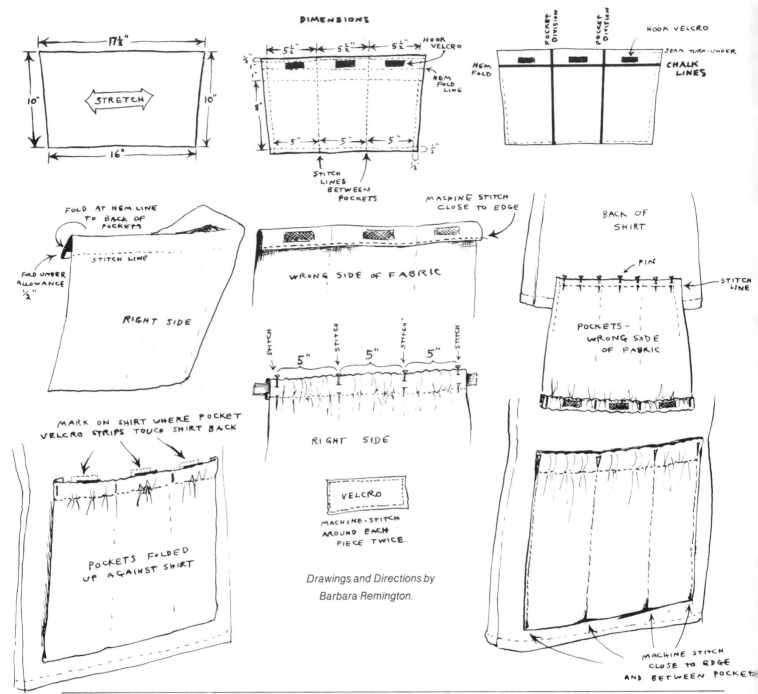

Drawings and Directions by Barbara Remington.

Turning a T-Shirt into a Cycling Jersey

Start with a ready-made T-shirt or jersey, or make your own from a pattern. Be sure it is plenty long. It should extend about 9 to 10 inches below your waistline.

Use the same or contrasting color jersey for the pockets.

The stretch of the fabric should be from side to side rather than vertical, and should be one-way stretch.

Cut piece 17½'' wide at top, 16'' wide at bottom, 10'' high (see illustration). Draw chalk lines along the stitch lines between the three pockets and along the top hem fold line.

Sew a 2''-long strip of hook Velcro tape to center of each pocket, as indicated. (Use Velcro that is ½ to ¾'' wide.) Machine stitch around each piece twice (see illustration).

Fold hemline to back of pockets and fold under allowance ½'', showing wrong side of fabric. Machine stitch close to edge.

Insert 16''-long piece of elastic (up to ¾'' wide) in hem tube. (Use safety pin close to one end to pull it through.) Adjust and pin top of pockets so that each section between the chalk marks and to within ½'' of each side is 5'' wide, or just *slightly* less.

Hand or machine tack at each pin to anchor elastic. Cut off excess elastic at each end.

Measure back of shirt to determine location of pockets. Top of pockets should be just at, or below, waist level and bottoms 1 to 2'' from bottom hem of shirt.

Place and pin pockets upside down as shown. Machine stitch bottom ½'' from edge. Leave ½'' seam allowance on each side—backstitch at each end. Turn in and pin ½'' side hems.

Turn pocket section up toward waist. Carefully mark on shirt with pins or chalk where pocket Velcro strips touch shirt back. Sew 2'' long strips of Velcro pile to each spot. Machine stitch around each strip twice.

Hold pockets in place with Velcro at top, and with pins along turn-under side seams and along chalk marks between pockets. Machine stitch close to side edges and along chalk lines. Back stitch at bottom; reinforce tops of pockets with triangles.

3. *Cap.* Low-cost way to a lot of efficiency. White cotton to reflect the heat, with a brim to keep sun and rain out of the eyes, and protect the back of the neck. Drench it with water in the heat; (racers used to put cabbage leaves under them). Too bad they only come in one size . . . if too small, a small slit and tacking widens it. In winter this is replaced by a wool hat, two layers thick, with a visor and an extra flap that looks perky turned up, and comes down to protect the ears.

4. *Shorts.* An unobtrusive black that doesn't show dirt or saddle oil, they have a lovely surprise inside: a soft, thick, absorbent chamois insert that keeps you dry and protects your bottom from friction and pressure. Designed to be worn without underwear, the seams are flat, so none dig in no matter how many hours on the road. The fabric is usually tightly knit and long lasting: nylon or cotton for those with deli-

Photograph by Bernard Thompson

cate skin; wool for everyone else, because it "wicks" perspiration away from your skin, keeping you warmer in the winter, cooler in the summer. The best shorts have buttons for suspenders. It's important not to constrict your breathing, and when you exert yourself, your stomach moves in and out. (Many racers take the elastic out of the waist completely.)

5. *Jerseys.* If comfort is the feature of the shorts, convenience is what these super sweaters are all about. Good ones have five pockets: two in the front, three large deep ones in the back, which means you can carry your lunch and extra clothes, plus a newspaper, wallet, keys, extra tire, tools, and have nothing rattling around on the bike. Not only that, you can reach a lot of it while you're riding . . . like food to replace those hundreds of calories you're burning up! All those pockets are neatly finished with buttonholes, buttons, and elastic at the top to keep everything safe. Bike shirts are cut long, so that your back is completely covered even when you have your hands on the bottom of the handlebars. Shirts should fit the form neatly without binding, have a nylon zipper at the neck for easy on and off (metal ones scratch your nose and rust from sweat) and some adjustment for heat and cold.

Bike jerseys aren't exactly unobtrusive. A looser knit than the shorts, they are usually in a bright, deep color, with lighter stripes or a lighter-colored band across the chest. The darker background allows you to get a bit dirty changing a tire or wiping a chain without looking too messy. World champion shirts are pure white, with a rainbow-colored band. If you're a world champion you have a mechanic to do

the dirty work for you. (By the way, don't wear one of these in Europe; it's considered impudence, and you may get knocked down!)

Wool is still first choice, cotton second; acrylic is faster-drying, softer and cheaper, but that doesn't make up for its lack of wicking ability.

6. *Arm and Leg Warmers.* Like all athletes, bike racers are extra aware of joints and muscles, and they know that keeping muscles warm from the outside until they are warmed up from exercise is very important to avoid injury. Furthermore, there can be forty degrees temperature difference going up and coming down a mountain, or at dawn and noon on a spring day. This led to the use of arm and leg warmers. Usually made of wool, they hug the arm or leg, tuck into sleeve or short leg, and can be rolled up and fit into a back pocket when no longer needed. Only dancers are more finicky about keeping warm—so a dance store is a good place to find these.

7. *Cold Weather Gear.* When it's very cold, long-sleeved jerseys are teamed with tights, sometimes on top of the shorts, sometimes chamois-lined ones instead of the shorts. As an alternative to the tights, some racers find knickers give their knees more freedom, and they match them up with natty wool knee socks. They make sure neither the socks nor the knickers constrict the calf. Thermal underwear under it all, a windshirt or cycling jacket over it although generally speaking, racers prefer more and more layers of wool that wicks to waterproof Windbreakers in which water condenses, so they often wear thick cycling sweaters similar to the French fisherman's ones, some with zippered crew necks, some with turtlenecks, all cut very long.

Care of Bike Clothing

1. *Fabrics.* Wool and cotton are absorbent, but fade in the sun and shrink unless washed in cold water, so polyester is often added to make a stronger, cheaper, machine-washable blend. Anything not clearly labeled machine washable probably isn't. Polyester and acrylic blends can be machine washed and dried (not too hot). Nylon, ditto—very cool!

2. *Wool Jerseys and Warm-up Suits.* Empty pockets thoroughly, then treat as you would a good sweater: cold water wash with Woolite or equivalent, several rinsings. Lay flat on a towel and carefully roll the towel up, pressing down on it, but not wringing; this gets most of the water out, and means that the shirt will be dry eight hours later in most climates.

3. *Shorts.* You can't go wrong following Beryl Burton's technique for riding or for clothing care: "When I wash my shorts, I always wash them by hand, with a soap powder, not detergent. I give them a good spin, hang them outdoors to dry. When they're dry I rub the chamois together with my hands, and it comes lovely and soft. If it stays a bit hard, I usually put a spot or two of olive oil on."

4. *Gloves* can be washed with soap, right on the hands; a soft brush helps get the dirt out. Dry away from heat.

5. *Bike Shoes.* Polish them! If they get wet, fill with wadded newspaper to keep their shape, and dry away from heat to prevent cracking.

The Bike Seat — The New Rider's Main Complaint

Vera van der Reis Krausz

Your bottom hurts. Why?

Dr. Wayne Leadbetter, orthopedist, says: "The measurements of men's and women's pelvises are different. However, that's a statistical thing. There are some men with seat bones as far apart as some women's, and some women with as little distance between them as some men's. You have to be aware that if you are not fitting on the seat you've chosen, this is one of the variables to consider. Decide whether you need a wider seat, even though you're a man, or a narrower seat, even though you're a woman."

About sling and thickly padded saddles, he says, "If it works, do it. Far better that you have something to sit on and go off and cycle than not to cycle at all."

The big mattress saddles with springs and padded seats have to be checked to make sure they don't have a thick metal plate on the bottom – which negates any softening the cushioning might give!

Spring saddles are okay for 3-speed or upright position, but are not the proper shape if you're riding with dropped handlebars. The springs absorb some of the road shock, but they also absorb some of the energy you put into pedaling, making you work harder for less results.

If you need this kind of saddle in the beginning or after a long layoff, that doesn't mean you have to stay with it. After a month of regular cycling, see if a more efficient saddle wouldn't work for you – it's surprising how little time it takes to condition yourself to riding.

Are you wearing the right clothes? On a 3-speed it doesn't matter too much, but in the dropped position, the seams in jeans can really dig into you. Most serious cyclists wear special chamois-lined shorts. Racers usually wear shorts without underpants and change them after one wearing. Less fanatic long-distance tourers use bikini-stretch underwear with soft seams. All riders recommend that shorts be kept scrupulously clean, and that they fit properly, with no bunching, and with legs long enough to protect the thighs from chafing.

The seat's just too hard? In Europe, where nothing's too good for the bike racer, there are people who specialize in breaking in seats. According to seasoned cyclotourist Jacques Faizant, one of the best uses a combination of red wine and olive oil! It's often one of the jobs assigned to the newest team member. Ideale saddles are broken in at the factory. One solution is to buy a used bike seat, one a racer has decided is too soft to propel him without loss of speed; they're cheap, and many bike stores have several lying around.

You have a beautiful Brooks saddle, and want to break it in? Winter's a good time, either outside, or on your Exercycle. Takes too long? Tradition suggests warmed neats-foot-oil top and bottom. (No wonder riders wear black shorts!) More radical (and much more work), ingenious cyclist Nat Wilkes' solution: Immerse seat in shoe-stretching liquid, slip a piece of wood through the metal supports so you can fasten it with a clamp to a firm surface – and then attack it with a rolling pin for half an hour while it's still wet. Dale Brown, in *American Wheelmen,* says this is overkill, because all you want to soften is the part that hits your seat bones. These should be on the wide part of the saddle. Once you've figured out the right position for you (perhaps with the help of a friend), locate exactly where the pressure points are and mark the underside of the saddle. Remove the saddle from the bike, turn it upside down, and put a "silver-dollar-size dollop of Proofide" on those points. Put your saddle on an old cookie sheet and slip it into a two hundred-degree oven until the Proofide melts and penetrates the part you want to soften. Put the saddle back on the bike, take a ball-peen hammer, and lightly but firmly tap the pressure points. Don't overdo it! Ride the saddle around, and if it needs more work, give it a little more tapping. (According to Brown, a ball-peen hammer is the only way; it makes a small, controllable impression – make sure the "peen" end is smooth so it won't scar leather.) He adds:

"A non-oily conditioner like Lexo (available at leather shops) may be preferable for routine top maintenance. Black or dark brown saddles will always give stains by nature of their dyed surface; use a plastic cover on dress-up days."

When you ride a bike after a long layoff, be sure to get out of the seat every so often, and change your position a bit. Once you've gotten used to it again, most problems should go away.

If you should decide to get a new saddle, allow at least two weeks before you give up on it. And once you have a saddle that's properly broken in, treasure it and move it from bike to bike as long as it keeps its shape; if it starts to go, start breaking in a new one immediately on short trips, or on your Exercycle.

And For Women

Women are built differently from men, and in no place is this more apparent than in the parts that meet the saddle. What is less well-known is that there is also a tremendous variance in proportions among women: distance from front to back and from side to side. Martha Jack is doing a study and has found ten centimeters (four inches!) difference in width between seat bones in just sixty-one women! That explains why some women can use men's saddles, some can use women's, and some haven't found a comfortable one yet.

There's nothing wrong with you if your bottom hurts after you've been riding a while, but there may be something wrong with your bike. Before you change the saddle you have now, check certain other things: Is your stem short enough? Most women's arms are shorter proportionately than men's, and so the handlebars may make you lean too far forward, which means you have to bend over too far. This pushes the front of the saddle right onto your most sensitive area.

No? Okay, maybe the saddle is tilted up too much. All the books tell about how to set up a man's bike – and that's tilted up. A woman's saddle should be absolutely level (not tilted down, or you start to slide off, which puts too much pressure on your hands). You may have to get a micro-adjusting seat post, because a tiny adjustment may make all the difference.

Maybe the handlebars are set too low. Men's are always set one or two inches below the saddle height. Handlebars on women's bikes, according to Dr. Francois Piednoir, should be set level with the seat. This does make you less aerodynamic, but you can cheat a bit by getting handlebars slightly wider than your shoulders (you should anyway, if you're busty). Unfortunately, many good stems are simply not long enough to do this safely. If that's the case, raise them as high as possible, leaving at least 1-½ inches inside the tube for safety. And request them from your bike store! The manufacturers have to know you want them.

You still have a problem with pressure in the front? You may have to go the drastic route worked out by John Forester and described in *Effective Cycling:* Basically, start with a plastic saddle and cut out the part that causes pressure (back to the anatomical models of the 1890's!).

If the front's okay now, but the back isn't, and it starts hurting after an hour or so on the road, maybe the seat's too narrow, and doesn't support your sitting bones properly. A woman's saddle may be what you need.

Visibility — Day and Night

Fred DeLong

All too often in this country, motorists are just not tuned in to anticipate or to expect bicyclists in their traffic path. They do search for large, heavy, moving objects that can inflict pain and damage to them. But even though brightly colored, a cyclist's body seen from the side is small compared to the body of an auto or truck. Bicycle frames and wheels are virtually transparent even when brightly colored. From straight ahead or at small angles, the disparity is even greater. To the motorist, a bicyclist can look like just another tree or pole in the background. Then again, since a bicyclist can be temporarily hidden by a light pole, a windshield, a pillar, or a rearview mirror when the driver scans in our direction, we can go unnoticed.

Extensive Accident Studies

Some excellent research has been done in Europe on day and night bicycle visibility and accident protection. One study, entitled "A Visible Bicycle," was made by R.E. Groot (Visual Research), and M. Stoovelaar of the Traffic Department of the ANWB—the Royal Dutch Wheelmen's Association—which represents both bicyclists and motorists, effectively combining the work of an AAA and a LAW. The International Study Group for Road Accident Prevention has reported on "Prevention of Two-Wheeled Accidents in Darkness."

The latter study, confirming part of the Dutch research, was done in darkness, in dry weather, and also in drizzling rain. It showed that side-flank collisions were common both in daytime and at night. Wheel reflectors provide a measure of protection when the wheel is rotating. Reflective tires positively give recognition of a bicyclist entering the traffic zone, moving or not, because of

Fred De Long *is an engineer and author of* Chilton's Guide to Bicycles and Bicycling *and technical editor of* Bicycling *magazine. He here reports on the whys and hows of solving the visibility problems that face every cyclist. He reports on future trends later in this book.*

their circular or (at angles) oval shape. With these reflective devices, distance to the bicycle can be estimated with greater certainty, and dangerous instinctive reactions are reduced. The motorist has a bit more time to brake or to take evasive maneuvers. Reflective tires are recognized earlier than reflectors. This is particularly true for the left-turning cyclist.

These same findings were reported by Albert Burg and Jinx Beers in California; all too often the spoke reflectors were seen too late.

Dr. Kenneth Cross, in his monumental report for the United States Department of Transportation, "A Study of Bicycle-Motor Vehicle Accidents—Identification of Problem Types and Counter-Measure Approaches," forcefully discusses the importance of bicyclist noticeability.

Brightness, contrast, movement, and size must all be utilized, Cross states. To require all cyclists to use bright clothing is difficult, but the multidirectional strobe is feasible, although it is costly and requires maintenance.

Half of the nighttime accidents Cross studied involved bicycles equipped with rear lighting that met current lighting standards. It is clear that these standards are inadequate, and existing regulations governing them should be rewritten.

Since the mandated equipment now available is better than none at all, Cross recommends existing laws on bicycle lighting equipment be stringently enforced. Cross's research shows that the operator of the overtaking vehicle often fails to see the bicycle until the motorist is so close that successful evasive action cannot be taken. Sixty-three percent of the nonfatal and seventy percent of the fatal overtaking accidents in his study occur in darkness.

Half of the cyclists struck in front were equipped with operating headlamps. Because of the inefficiency of many bicycle headlights, cyclists are unable to detect and dodge road defects and debris at the edge of the road.

Therefore, at night they ride farther to the left into the highway than they do in the daytime.

Cross also maintains that adequate equipment must ensure detection by motorists who are drowsy, intoxicated, fatigued, or not anticipating a cyclist.

Motorists' Perception Problems

Sunglare or glare from artificial lighting (and headlamps) are found to cause accidents by blinding the motorist.

Stoovelaar and Groot's study points out that all too often visual research applied to traffic problems overemphasizes quantitative factors—brightness or luminescence. Insufficient attention is placed on pattern recognition. The eye is incorrectly considered a simple detector cell.

The visual system recognizes not images, but things. A configuration incorrectly chosen, therefore, may lead to perceiving the wrong thing; this can trigger the wrong reaction. Thus, items that have a natural or historic affinity with the bicycle will promote more rapid, correct detection and proper evasive action on the part of the driver.

There's a definite difference between a cyclist's and a motorist's interaction with his surroundings. A cyclist can feel himself moving. The motorist, in contrast, is at rest within a vehicle that surrounds him. To him it's the outside world that moves, projected, as it were, on the windows through which he looks. Movement of bright objects draws his attention to the object on this screen.

Flags, strobes, and moving lights are therefore more easily perceived than the largest steadily moving object.

A good number of motorists, pedestrians, and bicyclists report their attention is drawn by the cycloidal motion of yellow wheel reflectors while approaching intersections in daylight, even when looking against the sun. The effect was far greater than the motion of the rider's legs. This colorful motion is detected much farther from the intersection in daylight than at night because of the 29 more limited beam spread of auto headlights. With the sun coming from head-on, the effect is even more dramatic. Reflective tires, while effective at nighttime when in the headlamp beams, are ineffective in daylight.

A recent development for city riding, made by Everybody's Bicycle Shop in Needham, Massachusetts, has not received the attention its effectiveness deserves. Its name, "Halo Hoop," perhaps is too much associated with the Hula Hoop, a children's plaything. A lightweight, translucent, bright orange tube spirally wrapped with reflective tape, it is threaded inside the spokes near the rim. Its motion, color, and reflectivity attract the attention of other road users both day and night.

Form helps in recognition at night. Early Warning fabric is best, otherwise using large areas of white, or bands of two-inch wide reflective tape on the rider's helmet and jacket, draws attention in headlamp beams.

The Dutch study found a vertical pattern to have greater recognizability than a horizontal band which "appears to hover in the air." A retro-reflective yellow vertical stripe on the rear fender, about 33 centimeters (13 inches) in height, with the taillamp and rear reflector in its center, was found considerably effective. Likewise, the bright electric front headlight, supplemented by a retro-reflective reflector above or below it, causes more instant recognition by motorists.

Reflectors

The cube corner reflector has been considerably improved in recent years. It gathers light from the motor vehicle headlamp beam and directs it back intensely. Reflectors are designed as if the motorist's eye were in the center of

the headlamp. However, their effectiveness is greatly reduced because the eye is actually both above and to one side of it. At a considerable distance, when the angle between the headlight beam and the line of sight from eye to reflector is very small, efficiency is quite good. Nearer to the cyclist, the observation angle increases, and the intensity of the illumination is cut to almost nothing.

The comparison between the three-inch diameter Consumer Product Safety Commission-type, wide-angle rear bicycle reflector and the Society of Automotive Engineers class-A, non-wide-angle reflector of equal diameter has been misinterpreted.

On straight roads, with headlamps on high beam, and the bicycle well out in the road or a long distance ahead, either type will suffice. But if the road curves, if the approaching vehicle is rounding a street corner, and if the cyclist is closer to the road edge, the CPSC type can give far better protection.

If both types were amber instead of red, they would be two and a half times as light reflective at all angles.

Lights Versus Reflectors

Taillights are much brighter than reflectors except at close distances and direct angles; the greater the distance, the greater the difference. The light received at the driver's eye varies for electric taillights as the inverse square of the distance (i.e., at double the distance, the light received is one fourth that at the original distance). But for reflectors, since the light from headlamps falls off as the inverse square also, the reflector beam falls off to the fourth power. Therefore, at double distance, the signal returned to the driver is only one sixteenth as great.

Extra Hazards

If atmospheric haze, smoke, or fog is present, the above effects are amplified. Taillamp light is partially absorbed, and the signal received is lessened. If the windshield is dirty or coated with raindrops, a further loss occurs, and if it is raining, the raindrops are illuminated by the headlamp and provide inbetween light that masks the taillight or reflector signal, making it appear less intense.

Opposing streetlights, illuminated signs and storefronts, and headlamps and taillamps of other vehicles further reduce the apparent contrast of the cyclist's safety lighting. After passing these obstacles, it takes a period of time before the driver's eye becomes readjusted to darkness.

Drivers may have impaired vision, or be color blind. The driver's attention can be distracted, and though a rider or signal light or reflector may indeed be visible, it may not be seen.

Eye movement studies have shown that on curves, the eye moves in a series of successive fixation points. In a left-hand curve, the eye tends to track the road centerline; on a right curve, it tracks the road edge. If the cyclist is between the eye fixation points, he may be "jumped over."

If the driver is not expecting a cyclist or pedestrian in his path of travel, it takes a considerably longer period to detect, recognize, react, and act than if he is consciously or unconsciously searching for one. Researchers have indicated that the time needed to detect, recognize, react, and act may be from two to five seconds—far above the often quoted three quarters of a second reaction time. At 55 miles per hour, this means 160 to 400 feet. An additional 160 feet of travel are required for the

RECOMMENDATIONS

Use the best amber reflectors you can get; but know their limitations.

Wear a light, bright Windbreaker or shirt; light cars are statistically in fewer accidents than dark ones.

Add vertical bands of reflective material to your bike, helmet, and Windbreaker.

Configure bicycle: Draw attention to the wheels with reflectors, Halo Hoop, or reflective tires.

Make your bike appear larger than it is: Foldaway flags have been made mandatory in Scandinavia. In hilly country a tall flag will keep you visible longer.

Motion attracts attention: Use flags or lights on flexible rods. Legs go up and down: Take advantage of that with eye-catching reflective pants-restrainers or lights attached below the knee; pedal reflectors unfortunately are often hidden by heels.

In rain, darkness, or fog (or on Saturday night) be extra careful, and add lights to the system; multidirectional strobe lights combine motion as well. Carry extra bulbs as well as batteries—but don't wrap them in adhesive tape, it sticks.

Never assume you have been perceived; horn or bell can supplement visual information.

vehicle to stop if its brakes and tires are in good condition, more if they are not. Thus, from 380 to 500 feet are needed to attract attention.

Recent research has indicated that for reliable detection, the signal strength received at the driver's eye should be 1,000 times the visual threshold (the light-level an eye adjusted to darkness can see on a dark night).

Obviously the cyclist cannot pick the age, visual acuity, vehicle condition, alertness, or reaction time of the drivers and vehicles approaching him from front, side, or rear. Because of his small size and the possibility of being in a blind spot when the driver scans, it behooves him to take every precaution to enhance his safety. I've learned from several painful personal experiences that days in a hospital bed and months of recuperation make knowledge that the driver was incompetent or negligent a matter of little comfort!

Children and Bicycles

Paul Harris, M.D.

Children love to ride bikes and eagerly anticipate the time when they can manage a two-wheeler on their own. Frequently in pediatrics we measure a child's developmental status by acquisition of new skills, and most normal children can master riding a bike by the age of seven. However, there are many preconditions that must be met and caveats for safety and motivation that must be borne in mind by parents, teachers, and the kids themselves.

Paul Harris - *Photograph by Julian Harris*

Dr. Paul Harris, *our medical editor, is director of the Pediatric Primary Care Center at Jacobi Hospital, attending pediatrician at the Bronx Municipal Hospital Center, and assistant professor of pediatrics at the Albert Einstein College of Medicine in New York City. He is a fellow of the American Academy of Pediatrics, the Ambulatory Pediatric Association, and the American Public Health Association.*

Unfortunately, bike riding in this country is potentially quite dangerous and accounts for an extremely high proportion of injuries and deaths in children of all ages. The risk of accident is second only to skateboarding and trampoline. And accidents cause far greater disability in the pediatric range than do illnesses.

That training children is effective in reducing accidents has been proven in England. Road accidents to children under the age of fifteen have decreased by more than forty percent since 1958, in spite of the fact that motor traffic has more than doubled and the number of children riding bicycles has increased by at least twenty percent. This is principally due to the Cycling Proficiency Program backed by the Royal Society for the Prevention of Accidents. Six hours of instruction in schools and local road safety programs, spread over at least two weeks, seems to be sufficient to prepare children nine years and up for the National Cycling Proficiency Certificate and Badge.

The official test is very similar to what we require for a driver's license and covers three areas: roadcraft, knowledge of the Highway Code (including signs and signals), and bike maintenance. Children must show that they can adjust their bikes to a good riding position and keep the brakes, lights, chains, tires, handlebars, and seat in good condition. To pass the road test candidates must cross intersections safely, make right and left turns, and demonstrate correct pedaling and braking techniques. Automatic failure results if the candidate forgets to look behind or to signal before moving into traf-

Photograph by Paul Boyer for The Bicycle Paper

fic or changing lanes.

Parents should monitor what is happening in the schools about bicycle education and encourage a program like the one described above.

The tetanus immunization status should be current in all school-age children, and bike riders are no exception. For the healthy child there are virtually no medical contraindications to riding a bicycle, and chronic conditions may limit only the degree of activity, such as competition. Of course, no acutely ill person belongs on a bike, and conditions such as hemophilia, diabetes, or severe visual handicaps would require medical clearance.

Asthma in and of itself is not a contraindication to bicycling. Cycling is an especially good choice for the asthmatic child because it is possible to control the level of exertion. On the other hand, some children who have asthma don't know enough to limit their activity, in 31 which case parents will need to supervise them and prevent excessive exertion. Of course all medical management of child asthmatics should be carried out by their physicians.

Children with exercise-induced asthma, in which the symptoms often don't appear until after exercise has ceased, may be able to take Cromolyn as a preventive measure before they participate in strenuous activity. Cromolyn is difficult to self-administer, however, and children will probably be about ten years old before they can manage this form of treatment. Cromolyn administration prior to exercise may not only make it possible for children to cycle, but may also enable them to participate in organized sports activities in school.

Sometimes "vulnerable" children—those with innocent or functional heart murmurs or mild asthma—are overprotected by their parents and are not permitted to exercise at all. Or the child may refuse to participate in any physical activity. This is not a desirable state of affairs; exercise is important for children's social and psychological development as well as for their physical development, so it is important for such families not to go beyond their doctor's recommendations.

Timing

A natural progression from tricycle to two-wheel scooter to bicycle is desirable. And although it may seem obvious, children do not learn these skills unless introduced to them with supervision at appropriate ages. Neither premature introduction nor delayed presentation of opportunities will result in a successful, competent cyclist. Two- to five-year-olds should be exposed to tricycle use and become adept before moving on. Six-year-olds under supervision can be expected to handle two-wheelers. If your child does not, however, don't push it; some children need a little longer to get this kind of coordination. In Europe children ride balloon-tire scooters from age six to about eight. An eight-year-old can be taught to ride a two-wheeler in a few days; but don't wait much after that. Although children often learn biking from their friends at a later age, they are often not as steady on a bike, and therefore not as safe.

Remember to have braking practiced almost as soon as forward motion! Tell the child that pedaling backward will slow, then stop the bike—and have them do it on command.

Equipment

The bike should be simple, sturdy, and of the correct size. It is dangerous and an unnecessary handicap to introduce kids to equipment that is too large or too small. Of course, expense is a consideration, but it will pay to buy used, properly sized bikes and pass them along in the family or neighborhood rather than presenting children with something new that they have to "grow into."

For correct frame size: When the child straddles the bicycle with both feet flat on the ground there should be from one to three inches of clearance between the top tube and the crotch. Seat height is correct if the child can pedal a full revolution with both heels on the pedals without the pelvis or upper body swaying from side to side. This way, when the ball of the foot is on the pedal, the knee is not quite locked at the bottom of the pedal stroke. The child should look and feel comfortable on the bike and be able to reach the brakes easily and quickly.

When the bike is too large or the seat is too high, it is hard to stop without falling; when the seat is too low, it will prevent full rotation of the pedal cranks and cause lack of power. Too small a frame makes the bike hard to steer and will result in the knees hitting the handlebar.

Photograph courtesy of the British Cycling Bureau

Setting up the handlebar properly is very important, especially if the bike has hand brakes. Since you may have to signal while braking, the rear hand brake should be on the right, as it's the safer one to use. The bell or horn should also be within easy reach of the right hand.

Unfortunately most of the bikes made for small children weigh as much as the children do themselves and are very shabbily made, with sleeve bearings rather than decent headsets. Check that steering and braking are not too difficult, and that there are no sharp protruding objects, especially between the seat and handlebars. Children under seven often cannot operate a hand brake and should be able to touch the ground with their feet.

Although the banana chopper and BMX bike have significant appeal to young riders, they are hard to steer. They do have application for off-road use if well constructed, and knobby tires are very good for dirt roads, but are less maneuverable on smooth surfaces. A lightweight single-speed coaster-brake bike with short upright handlebars is best to begin with.

Training wheels do not help balancing and provide a false sense of security.

I am not really in favor of adjustable folding-type bicycles for children learning to ride because the levers protrude and children cannot get used to a specific seat or handlebar height unless it remains the same all the time. They must get used to one bike of the correct size in order to concentrate on learning new skills, and a folding bike that is too adjustable will be different each time it's put together. A bike of this type also tends to come undone easily or to have parts taken since they come off so easily.

Bikes with gears and dropped handlebars should only be considered for children who have mastered balance and bike handling on a simpler bicycle. There is no question that dropped handlebars are superior because of decreased wind resistance and better distribution of weight on the bike, but they involve learning new braking techniques to avoid somersaulting off. Moving back on the seat while riding and practicing sudden stops away from traffic are essential to safe use. Also, the narrower tires of most 10-speeds can get caught in gratings that a balloon-tire bike would traverse safely.

Toeclips are safer at speed when you don't want the foot to fly off the pedal and allow pulling up on the cranks as well as pushing down.

A horn or bell is also necessary so that young cyclists can announce their presence.

It is dangerous to carry things in the hand, on the handlebars, or over the shoulder while riding, so a basket or rack is handy even if seldom used.

Teach the child to make sure nothing is dangling that can get caught in the spokes or the chain. This means no tying jackets around the waist, and making sure shoelaces aren't dangling.

A word about helmets for the young cyclist. Although soft racing helmets are better than no helmet at all, they have been shown to be ineffective in preventing injury in serious crashes. Hard helmets (Bell, MSR, hockey, Skid-lids) are better but quite uncomfortable and even they have not prevented serious injury. Nevertheless, helmet-wearing should be encouraged, insisted upon if possible, if for no other reason than to remind the rider of the dangers involved in cycling.

Add reflectors and reflectorized tape when independent journeys may have children out at dusk or later. Bright clothing should be worn in traffic situations. Generator lighting is not a bad idea by the teenage years. In fact, you must forbid riding at night without lights.

Maintenance

Equipment must function perfectly, so check the bike regularly. When a child is learning, the bike falls over frequently, and this loosens nuts and bolts. Even after the child has learned to ride well, the bike should be checked at least once a week to see that the brakes work properly and to make sure that all nuts and bolts are tight—including those for reflectors, racks, and basket. Handlebars and saddles should be raised as needed, because being cramped makes for poor

Courtesy of the Danish Tourist Board

steering and knee trouble.

Children should become familiar with their own equipment and should learn to maintain and care for it. They can do this by being responsible for the whereabouts, functioning, and maintenance of their own machines. It is not unreasonable to expect a ten-year-old to check for correct tire inflation pressure, and for a twelve-year-old to be able to change a wheel and repair a flat tire. Cleaning and lubrication can be learned by the age of nine; checking brakes, bearing play, and derailleur adjustment can be mastered by the early teens.

Family Involvement

Riding a bike is the perfect opportunity for parents to interact with their children in a supportive manner that encourages and guides the child as well as providing needed physical and emotional contact. The sense of accomplishment for both parents and children can be most rewarding. However, patience and common sense must be exercised. Daylight, off-street riding at times when neither party is overtired or overexcited should be stressed.

Teaching your six- or seven-year-old to ride a two-wheeler certainly takes patience and physical stamina, but the rewards of seeing new confidence emerge in your child are exciting. By the time children are ten or eleven they can keep up with adults on trips, and by the early teens they should be racing their parents and even participating in organized tours.

Carrying Children

Under no circumstances should children ride on the handlebar or frame of a bike or on the shoulders of a rider, as this is much too dangerous.

Children up to three years old are better off carried on a carrier in the front of the bike, where you can keep an eye on them and make sure they don't fall asleep. Older ones should ride in the back, as their extra weight in front would interfere with steering.

Bike-mounted carriers should be strong and should be screwed to eyelets rather than clamped on. Sufficiently high back and side restraints and a sturdy adjustable strap are needed for comfort and safety. Adjustable footrests will prevent ankle fracture by keeping the feet out of the spokes. Make sure nothing is protruding from you or the bike that can hurt a child and dress children warmly enough; exercise may be warming you, but they will be sitting still and exposed to wind.

Tandem bikes, while more difficult to handle, can be used by two people of dif-

ferent abilities and sizes.

Riding Sites and Safety Rules

Most severe accidents involve automobiles, nighttime riding, or more than one child on a bike. Under no circumstances should children ride barefoot; and while learning, riding should be for prescribed times and places – not for transportation. Level surfaces and traffic-free areas, not trails, are preferable.

Courtesy of the Consulate General of the Netherlands

Although the bicycle is an excellent means of transportation, I do not feel that children should ride for this purpose until they have had many years of experience in bike handling under ideal ''play'' or ''sport'' conditions. Riding at night, under adverse weather conditions, in traffic, with loads, or on an errand adds other dimensions to the skills of bike-riding, which may, in children too young, result in accident and subsequent injury.

The young rider, after learning balance on level ground, must be able to stop in an appropriate distance without falling, shooting over the handlebars, or skidding. The child should learn to apply both hand brakes simultaneously and never the front one alone. Negotiating hills (both up and down) and handling the bike on different surfaces will be the next challenge. Avoid steep downhills until they can control the bike on less steep ones.

A good exercise in handling intersections is for the child to stop and look before leaving the driveway for the sidewalk. And until taught how to ride in traffic, the child should get off the bike at the corner, look in both directions, and walk the bike across the street.

BMX and cyclocross-type activities are great for sharpening bike handling skills away from traffic. If your child is adven- 33 turous, this is a good outlet; but make it clear that the road is no place for stunts.

Parks, Bikeways, and Group Rides

If there is a recreational, traffic-free environment to ride on, certain things must be practiced and emphasized there as well. A bikeway, because of the mixed recreational traffic, with loose dogs, skaters, and runners, all capable of sudden erratic moves, is very dangerous indeed. Another frequent cause of accidents is bike-bike collisions, and children should not count on everyone else being a good rider. Hopefully you can accompany children and teach them to ride safely. Tell them:
- Ride straight, on the right-hand side.
- Look around and signal before changing their line to move right or left.
- Try not to stop abruptly.
- Observe other road users for sudden moves. On a bikeway or mass ride someone stopping suddenly to pick up something can cause a freeway-type pileup.
- Slow down when approaching a corner and be particularly careful if you can't see around it.
- Don't brake or turn suddenly on oil, sand, wet leaves, or mud.
- Don't ride through puddles as you can't tell how deep they are. It's bad for the bike and the puddle may hide something that can catch the wheel.

Riding in Traffic

One reason so many children get hurt in traffic is that they don't understand the rules because no one has tried to explain them. They don't know that you can often tell what a driver is planning to do by studying the signal lights of a car – that when a winking light is on, the driver is

34
Courtesy of the Consulate General of the Netherlands

planning to go in that direction, either to change lanes or to turn; that when the red brake lights are on, the car is going to stop. And cars can stop faster than bicycles, so it's not wise to ride too close to them.

It's not a bad idea to get one of the driver training books that most states give out with learner's permits, so the child can learn to recognize the meanings of the signs and markings on and along the road; reading the signs gives them more time to plan. Explain that triangles show dangers to watch out for, like railroad crossings, animals, falling rocks, intersections, narrowing lanes; that a double line on a road means cars shouldn't cross it, but a broken one means they can; that arrows indicate what direction they can turn in, or whether to go straight ahead.

Show the child how to communicate with drivers by giving hand signals – the left hand straight up for right turns, out for left turns, and down to indicate slowing or stopping. Signals have to be given clearly, in plenty of time, and should be held for a few seconds, as you can't count on someone watching every moment. They should be practiced off-road;

Photograph by Paul Boyer

first looking over the shoulder without swerving, as many people swerve when they look behind them or signal. Have the child practice signaling before stopping, and practice slowing down and stopping at pedestrian crossings.

Tell the children to ride with traffic and obey the traffic regulations; to stop when the light is changing, rather than trying to push through, and not to hug the curb or ride so close to parked cars that an open door could hit them.

Teach them to scan both sides of the road to look for things that might force them to stop suddenly, like a car leaving a driveway, a loose dog, or small children playing, and to trust their own eyes and ears rather than obeying someone who can't see what they do.

As children gain maturity with increasing age and responsibility, so will biking skills increase, allowing for more independence from parents and eventually biking for the purpose of transportation. I think that adolescents must learn the value of ownership – including cost plus maintenance – of their bicycles, as well as being thoroughly familiar with traffic rules and regulations, before being given complete freedom to roam on their own.

RESPONSIBLE CYCLING

Responsible Cycling

G. H. Stancer, O.B.E.

Cyclists in this country are rediscovering some very old truths indeed – truths that G. H. Stancer made clear to the British consciousness for over three generations . . . right until 1961 when he died at the age of eighty-four. For over fifty years he had fought to preserve the cyclist's position as a legitimate user of the public thoroughfare.

G. H. Stancer, O.B.E., perhaps cycling's strongest and most eloquent defender, knew that cycling was an art and a craft, and that cyclists got into trouble and caused accidents precisely when they ignored their rights and responsibilities to behave – not like vehicles – but as vehicles.

The last of the great Victorian cyclists, George Herbert Stancer was born in Yorkshire in 1878. He and the bicycle grew up together. He rode and raced and wrote about it, joining the staff of Cycling in 1906, and becoming its editor four years later. He held this post until 1920, when he became secretary of the Cyclists Touring Club. He then took control of the CTC Gazette and transformed it into a weapon for cyclists'

rights. As president, member of the council, and committeeman, he became the ultimate authority on politics, highway law, and the history of cycling.

Stancer saw the cycle relegated in Europe to side-paths that were then neglected. He knew that for the bicycle to survive, it had to have the right to the road. His public writings gave support to the CTC's campaign against reckless road users and those who encourage them by not enforcing traffic laws. Together with the Pedestrians Association, he helped organize the public demonstration against such officials.

He loved both the sport and the pastime of cycling. His main active interest was in time trialing and road records, but he also toured and led tours on his tricycle well past the age of seventy.

Stancer's writing is part of every cyclist's heritage. The following paper was read during the 1931 National Safety Congress at a special session arranged by the British Cycle and Motor Cycle Manufacturers and Traders Union.

To suggest to a cyclist that he should adopt the motto of "Safety First" is not to appeal so much to his generous impulses as to his instinct of self-preservation, for he bestrides the frailest of all road vehicles, and in a collision with any other road user – not excepting the pedestrian – he is always likely to be the chief sufferer.

Nevertheless, safe bicycling implies two considerations – avoiding injury to other people, and taking care of yourself – and from every moral standpoint the first of these is the more important. We shall never attain a high degree of road safety by seeking to lay the blame on those who are unable to get out of our way with sufficient quickness and agility; and a cyclist's first duty is to avoid running down anyone else on the road, even when that person is manifestly at fault.

One becomes a little tired of hearing accidents explained away by throwing all the responsibility upon the weaker vessel. I have even seen statistics which show that children of five are usually to blame when they are knocked down, and I can well believe this to be the case. But the true test of roadmanship is the ability to avoid collisions even when the other fellow is entirely and hopelessly in the wrong. The competent cyclist, like the competent motorist, usually manages to keep clear of accidents, and does not have to justify himself before any tribunal.

The hazards of cycling were once of an entirely different character from those of today. No longer have we to mark our hills "dangerous" owing to the deficiencies or nonexistence of brakes. Seldom are we troubled by the unfriendly attentions of stray dogs; and even indignant old gentlemen do not now thrust 35 their walking sticks into our wheels. Moreover, the ruthless repression of our so-called "scorching" exploits – that is to say, our speeds of 10, 12, or 15 miles an hour – is a thing of the past, and in the press of modern traffic we are almost unnoticed.

Today the risks attached to cycling – which, after all, are still very slight – are almost entirely due to the fact that we share the road with numerous vehicles of far greater weight and speed, controlled by men and women of widely varying degrees of skill, experience, and judgment, and used under conditions of weather which frequently have a detrimental influence upon the recognized factors of safety.

G.H. Stancer, *courtesy of the Cyclists Touring Club*

If mankind could have foreseen what the introduction of motor traffic upon ordinary roads was going to mean in terms of life and limb, it is inconceivable that such an innovation would ever have been permitted.

The safety hints for cyclists, as issued by the National Safety First Association, constitute an admirable code of conduct, which I would commend in every detail to my fellow cyclists.

I do not propose to recapitulate the hints to which I have referred. It is unnecessary here to emphasize the importance of observing the rule of the road, of crossing streetcar lines – those murderous anachronisms – at a wide angle, of looking out for pedestrians who step suddenly off the pavement, of taking special care when roads are greasy, and of not being so foolish as to hold on to other vehicles in motion. But there are still a few ideas which may be enlarged upon with advantage. For example, the purpose of hand signaling is much misunderstood. A cyclist will sometimes fling out his right arm and almost simultaneously make

a turn to the right, across two lines of traffic, thinking no doubt that his signal is sufficient to bring all other adjacent vehicles to a halt. That notion should be dispelled, for a signal is merely an indication of the desire to change direction, and possesses none of the authority of a policeman's uplifted arm. The proper course is to take a glance behind in order to ascertain whether the premeditated maneuver can be safely and conveniently performed. If it cannot, then it is wisest to dismount and wait for a suitable opportunity.

It is difficult to deal with cycling at night without alluding to a controversy in which I have been personally engaged for more than twenty-five years, but I propose to say nothing about the merits of rear lights or reflectors except that the latter are now widely used for all kinds of road warnings and are recognized by motoring authorities as being quite efficacious. It has frequently been alleged that cyclists are not complying with the law that requires them to fit properly certified reflectors to their machines, but the available evidence is all to the contrary. Many months ago Major H.R. Watling, of the Manufacturers' Union, assured me that sufficient approved and certified reflectors had been made to satisfy the requirements of the whole cycling community, and I happen to know that Major Watling estimates the number of British cyclists at a figure some millions higher than my own estimate, so there cannot be any doubt about the demand having been fully met. If these reflectors are not in use, therefore, where are they and what purpose are they serving? I am much more impressed by the statement of a prominent cycling journalist that on a recent motor run by night from London to Birmingham he took a census of cyclists to discover the proportion of lawbreakers, and found that *only* 3 out of 534 were without visible reflectors.

So much has been said in various quarters about cyclists' rear lights that the importance of the front lamp has been somewhat discounted. Nevertheless, it is highly desirable that all cyclists should use headlamps of sufficient power to illuminate the road ahead for a distance within which they are capable of coming to a standstill. That is a sound rule for all traffic, and cyclists should not consider themselves exempt from it. Far too many riders are content to use headlamps that merely comply with the law, whereas the provision of a reasonably powerful lamp would greatly increase their enjoyment of night riding, as well as adding to their safety and that of the pedestrian, who is often compelled under present conditions to walk in the road.

Finally, I would quote that admonition of the Safety First Association which contains the essence of roadmanship: "Always extend the same courtesy toward other road users that you expect to receive from them." In other words, do just what you would wish the other man to do if the positions were reversed. If that principle governed everybody's actions on the road, the terrible toll of casualties would soon be reduced, and we should all live much more happily together.

Effective Cycling — A Model Adult Training Program

Edward B. Deuerlein

Effective Cycling is the first complete compilation of cycling knowledge that we are aware of. It's the collective common sense of thousands of cyclists.

John Forester wrote the book in 1975 ...and in 1976, EC was adopted by the League of American Wheelmen as its educational and training standard for cycling education. LAW certified instructors to teach the course across the nation.

Teaching the course in a variety of settings, the instructors have begun to show how bicyclists and motorists can share the same roadway. Let's look at some of the reasons why people don't ride bicycles: the scares and near misses that give cycling a bad name.

You'll see how Effective Cycling can eliminate many of these problems.

AN ACCIDENT AND A SOLUTION

A twenty-four-year old nurse was riding through a small shopping district when she was caught in a squeeze between a parked car and a vehicle trying to turn into a store parking lot.

The woman was not injured because she was able to stop quickly, but her pedals did put scrapes in the sides of both the parked car and the moving vehicle.

THE DETAILS

The lane is about 21 feet wide at this particular point: 8 feet for a parking lane along each curb, and 13 feet for moving traffic. The speed limit is 35 mph, but traffic rarely moves even that fast, because of congestion. The parking lot entrance is narrow, just wide enough for a single car to enter or exit. A traffic light is located at the end of the block, several hundred feet away.

Ed Deuerlein *made* The Midwest Bicycle Review *one of the best magazines we came across thanks to his broad interest in cycling and his trenchant editorial style. He permitted us to reprint his summation of traffic strategy from the* LAW's Effective Cycling Course.

The motorist passed the young lady, then forgot about her and turned right, pinning the bike against a parked car.

It's not an unusual type of accident, but it could have been much more serious. It is the type of accident that scares many people out of using a bicycle for short-distance shopping and into using a car, even for just a few blocks.

If the cyclist had been taking a wider share of the road, she would have clearly communicated several things to passing traffic.

• I am a legitimate road user.
• I'm traveling in a predictable direction and at a predictable speed.
• There is no reason why a motorist should try to pass me.

In a low-speed situation like this, there is really only one possible response for the motorist: to wait a few extra seconds behind the cyclist, until he has an unobstructed line to the parking lot entrance. The motorist would only be delayed a few seconds.

STARTS AND STOPS IN TRAFFIC

Many city bikers like to head for a curb or step when starting out. That's because correct bike setup requires the saddle to be positioned high, with almost full extension of the leg. That means, of course, that the cyclist's feet won't reach the ground except on tiptoe on a cambered road.

Imagine you're riding down a street on the right side, with a line of cars parked along the curb. You come to a traffic-light intersection (the light is red), and there are no cars parked right at the corner. You plan to continue biking straight ahead when the light changes.

Now, you go for the curb in order to reach old terra firma during the red traffic light. But that move—toward the curb—has actually put you into position for a right turn.

Cars will now pull into position on your left, and will possibly make right turns, even while the light is red (this is

legal in many states). There you have it: You're at the curb and don't have any way to "claim" the right to go straight ahead. How do you solve it?

The cyclist stops in the traffic lane during the red-light period, and waits comfortably as long as necessary. Sure, traffic might back up behind you... just as if you were driving a car. (This is the classic right-on-red conflict, when everyone wants to turn except the person in front.) Simply hold your ground. It's the only way to get "your piece" of the road. With the curbside technique, it's impossible to do so.

HOW TO RIDE ON A WIDE LANE

On a wide road, or a road with a wide curb lane, cyclists should ride just outside the normal traffic lane, about three feet to the right of passing motorized traffic (not right next to the curb). This position places the cyclist within the motorist's field of vision, but well out of his or her path. If the curb lane is at least 14 to 15 feet wide there should be no problem.

Parked cars are a slightly different matter. Whenever you pass a parked car, imagine the door wide open, and keep your distance. A suddenly opened car door is dangerous. Even if you don't hit it, you might be tempted to swerve left—into the path of overtaking traffic.

Most motorists aren't attuned to the additional hazards of riding a bicycle. But they don't travel close to parked cars, so they don't worry about a door suddenly opening in their path. You shouldn't ride close to parked cars and therefore worry about suddenly opened doors either.

WHY NOT RIDE CLOSE TO THE CURB WHEN YOU CAN?

A cyclist riding along a curb in a gap between a line of parked cars is out of the motorist's line of vision. Overtaking motorists may not even know there's a bicyclist on the street. They certainly won't be expecting one.

NARROW LANE
RIDE IN CENTER

WIDE LANE   STAND'D WIDE
RIDE JUST TO THE RIGHT OF THE CARS,
EVEN WHEN CURB IS FURTHER RIGHT

Drawings by Barbara Remington

Like the small child chasing a ball into the street, the bicyclist will appear very suddenly. In effect, he or she will dart out from behind a parked car. Even on a wide lane, there may not then be room for both the cyclist and the motorist.

How many people can make a left turn and never overshoot the available space? If the biker swings even a small amount wide, he or she may be moving into the path of overtaking traffic.

Legitimate road users act in predictable, logical patterns. When a motorist moves into the right lane, it's usually to park or to make a right turn. When a bicyclist pulls over to the curb, other road users expect him or her to be making a stop. Body language is a well-developed form of communication between cyclists and motorists. Use it properly.

THE LAW

Except when preparing to make a turn, bicyclists shall operate as close as practicable to the unobstructed, traveled edge of the roadway.

Memorize that sentence, exactly. It's part of the Uniform Vehicle Code, a nationwide guideline for traffic laws and ordinances. It's on the book in many states.

Notice that it does not say: *A bike rider shall ride as close as possible to the curb.*

The difference will become more crucial when we discuss narrow roads.

Notice the word traveled. That means that a cyclist does not have to ride in a parking lane. There's your legal justification for not swinging in and out between parked cars.

The law also says, as close as practicable to that unobstructed, traveled edge of the roadway. That permits the cyclist to keep a healthy car door's length away from parked cars. While it is *possible* to ride close to a parked car, it certainly isn't a reasonable, healthy practice.

Also notice the word *unobstructed*. Obviously you don't ride over parked cars and roadside barricades. But what about broken glass, loose gravel, and sewer grates? All of these are obstructions for a bicyclist. Passing motorists may not react to a patch of gravel. They can barely see it. Their vehicle is so wide and heavy that gravel is not a hazard. But a cyclist has a different set of obstruction criteria. And who is the better judge of what a bicycle can handle; the cyclist or the motorist? Obviously, the cyclist.

DEALING WITH NARROW STREETS AND NARROW LANES

The Effective Cycling recommendation is simple, but forceful. When the lane width is inadequate for bicycle and motorized traffic, the cyclist simply occupies the full lane, forcing passing drivers to make proper vehicle-code passing maneuvers.

Takes guts? Certainly. But which would you rather do? Have each passing car squeeze past you on a narrow lane, or take charge of the issue by establishing your rights as a legitimate road user?

Many cyclists choose the first solution. They try to ride along as innocently as possible, cowering on the edge of the roadway, praying the passing traffic will give them safe clearance. It doesn't happen.

A car passing a cyclist in this situation will usually straddle the lane lines. *No one* has safe space to operate. The cyclist has voluntarily ridden into the hazards of the right edge of the road. The motorist is blocking two lanes of traffic.

For many cyclists, taking a lane is a step toward militancy. It seems so brazen to hog the road. It runs against all they've been taught about bicycle riding. But let's look at what they've been taught.

HUGGING THE CURB: *The cyclist is out of the traffic mix, but must merge into traffic to avoid obstructions and road hazards.*

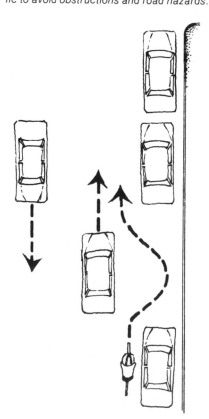

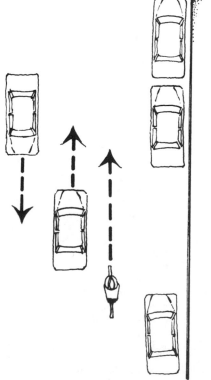

PREDICTABLE AND SAFE: *The cyclist takes adequate road space to allow for common traffic hazards. His path is straight and predictable.*

"I shouldn't slow down traffic."

As noted above, even the curb hugger reduces the flow of motorized traffic, unless hot-shot drivers cut things too close. And where in the constitution of any state does it give people the inalienable rights to life, liberty, and unobstructed speed on the roadway?

"I'm more likely to be struck from behind if I ride in the middle of the lane."

No. The incidence of accidents where a motorist overtakes and hits a bicyclist from the rear are rare, except at night when the bicyclist isn't using adequate lights or reflectors. (That's another problem entirely.) A recent study of accident types found that this sort of incident accounted for only 4.5 percent of all accidents.

Actually, a cyclist in the middle of the lane is more likely to be seen by overtaking traffic. The cyclist is in the center of the driver's field of vision and probably has a solid background, the road. Curb huggers tend to blend into the camouflage of sidewalk traffic, parked cars, and visually "busy" backgrounds.

The only real increased risk of a cyclist being struck from behind comes from impatient, irrational drivers who demand every lane to be open. They often use their vehicles as weapons to force their own way. In this sort of situation, *don't risk it.* Pull over and stop. But resume your place on the road when the driver has passed.

"I feel 'exposed' when riding in the middle of a lane."

Not surprising. This is a bold step. Like anything else, it takes practice. Bicyclists have been drilled with a variety of scare tactics for years. Most bicycle training is directed toward primary-grade children by police officers.

For adults, that sort of training just doesn't make it. It restricts the bicycle to recreational uses and very low speeds. Face it. To get from here to there, sometimes the best (or only) route is down a busy street. With gas over a dollar a gallon, are you going to let advice designed for third graders dominate your life?

"But can't I get a ticket for obstructing traffic?"

Maybe. But not if you use some reasonable judgment. It would be a difficult case to prosecute in court.

One note of caution. Some folks think, "If a little is good, then more will be better." So they ride in the center of right-hand lanes, even if the lane is wide. Not good.

A bicycle is only two feet wide. Any cyclist who tries to maintain control of a 14- to 16-foot lane by riding in the center of it, will only invite traffic to pass on the cyclist's right.

CHANGING LANES AT SLOW SPEEDS

In slow-speed traffic, when motorists are moving at about the same speed as the bicyclist, it's easy. You just ride about two feet from the line of cars, match their speed, and start looking over your shoulder. As you alternate your glance from the road to the line of cars, any passing driver will understand what you are trying to do. It's a form of body language. The driver has to see you; there's only eight feet between the two of you. This way you ask, "Will you let me in?"

The driver will answer by backing off and allowing you a space (or by gunning the engine to cut you off). If he or she drops back, you can swing out another foot, just to verify the question, give an arm signal, check one last time, and move over if the spot is still open.

You are following Effective Cycling strategy and being predictable. If a driver understands what you want to do, he'll probably cooperate. If you do find a driver who doesn't want to let you in, fine. Drop back and follow him. Better for you to follow him, than for him to be following you.

RESPECT IS THE KEY

And that, for starters, is Effective Cycling. It is respect for your body, your bike, and for the cyclist.

Sure, there are "common sense" rules of physiology, balance, and perception that will do just as well. But many people learn them only after their first ten thousand miles on a bike. People can learn much more quickly and safely by following the rules of Effective Cycling.

The ideas in this article are based on the principles of Effective Cycling, *by John Forester, copyright 1975 and 1978, used with permission of the author.* Effective Cycling *is available from Custom Cycle Fitments, 726 Madrone, Sunnyvale CA 94086.*

ACCIDENT IN THE MAKING: *The biker is hugging a line of parked cars, tempting the moving vehicle to "sneak" by and proceed with its turn into the parking lot. Biker gets caught in the squeeze when the driver "forgets" the two-wheeler.*

EFFECTIVE CYCLING TECHNIQUE: *The rider takes up a bit more of the lane, forcing the car to wait until the bike clears the upcoming driveway before the vehicle makes its turn.*

On-Road Training — Three Teachers Speak: John Pixton, Myrna Meyer, Bonita Dostal Neff

John Forester called Myrna Meyer his most qualified applicant because she not only knew how to bicycle, she knew how to teach—having taught math, swimming, canoeing, horseback riding, and led a lot of rides for three local clubs, including the Country Cycle Club in Westchester, New York, of which she is now president.

The stumbling block with most bike safety programs is the reluctance to assume responsibility for taking students out on the road. Can you imagine all the driver training being given only in the classroom or only on make-believe, traffic-free roads? It's absurd.

The LAW's Effective Cycling Course has been set up so well that no matter what level riders come in at, they go out at a higher level. It increases their confidence in traffic and their understanding of the bicycle's role as a vehicle. After the course they use their bikes more often, and for more things.

The course takes thirty-six hours—that's ten three-hour sessions and one all-day session. The ten or twelve hours spent on mechanics teaches most people all they need to know to be self-sufficient on the bike.

The course is not for beginners. You have to be able to do ten miles before you come into the class, and be bicycling several times a week. That's the minimum; I've had everything from that to people who are interested in racing.

The first session is strictly fitting the bike to the individual, or putting bikes back together. Some people come in with brakes hanging loose and machines that have been sitting in a garage for years.

Many students start with new 10-speeds equipped with racing gears, which are completely unsuitable for them. By changing to a wide-range rear cluster and perhaps smaller front chain rings, hill climbing is no longer an impossible struggle, and cycling becomes the pleasurable activity it is supposed to be.

Some strong young men who sell bicycles don't understand how anyone can need different gears from what they use.

Then again, I get some extremely strong cyclists who have bikes with touring clusters, and who are using only the three top gears. I switch them over to a much tighter cluster, and they pick up speed. The ones who commute tell me it takes them half the time. So I'm really individualizing the course in every way.

I follow Forester's outline pretty closely, and include physiology, mechanics, and safety education. Two thirds of the time is spent on the road. I teach panic stops, rock dodging, in-stant turns, watching for motorist error, changing lanes, intersection maneuvers, overtaking. We practice riding in heavy traffic and in the rain. We prepare for commuting, touring, and riding in the dark.

All riders must know how to change a flat tire and adjust their derailleurs. They're forced into it; if they break down on the road, they hold up the whole class, and people feel terrible about that. We've got everything here that we could possibly need to repair a bike. I have a dozen old pedals that I make the students take apart and I check each one to make sure they know how to adjust the bearings. In every class we also do a headset or a bottom bracket; usually someone's bike needs it done.

Comfort on the bike can make all the difference between whether someone becomes a cyclist or gives it up. Touring position is different from racing position. You rarely ride on the drops, only in a head wind or something like that. Racers just have to watch the pack around them, but on the road you have to be able to pick up your head and look around. Having your arms too low causes tremendous pain in your shoulder blades.

For panic stops I make students put their weight so far back on the seat

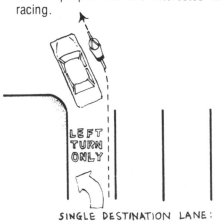

SINGLE DESTINATION LANE: RIDE ON THE RIGHT SIDE

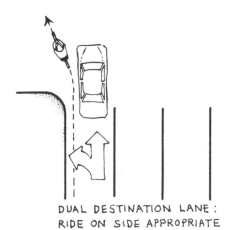

DUAL DESTINATION LANE: RIDE ON SIDE APPROPRIATE FOR DESTINATION

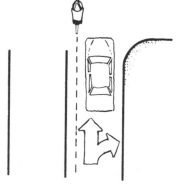

WITH SIGNIFICANT RIGHT TURN TRAFFIC THIS IS A DUAL DESTINATION LANE

they're practically sitting on the rear wheel—the important thing is not to go over the handlebars when you put on the brakes.

There's a big difference between stopping short and slowing down to control a bike on a long downhill. That should be done primarily with the rear brake. The front rim will heat up more rapidly than the rear because it has more weight on it when you're braking. But longer cable length sets up much more friction, so to get the same amount of force on the rim you have to sqeeze the rear brake lever more firmly than the front one.

Teaching people to handle hills starts inside, with the bike on a stand, showing them how the derailleur moves the chain. I show them that in close to the center of the frame are the gears for climbing the hills (you can't make a rule about levers; bikes aren't all set up the same way). Use the sprockets next to the frame to make it easier to climb, out away from the frame for more speed. I teach them to look down and see what gear they're in (they're always fascinated to know that's possible to do without falling off). They're taught to shift down before they get to a hill. They've been told you have to keep pedaling when you change gears, but if they do that they rip their derailleurs apart, so they have to be reassured that they can ease up for a second before shifting.

When I find someone who's pushing too high a gear, I say, "Make believe there's an egg between your foot and the pedal. Get a fast, comfortable spin going with very light pressure; shift your gears to always keep that pressure, never let it get so hard that you would crush that egg!" That's how you get people to think about it. And

they begin to feel and to pay attention.

I try to get them to spin at least seventy rpms, but some people can't; everyone has to find a cadence that's comfortable for them. To help them spin smoothly I ask them to pretend that their feet are hands holding onto the pedals, pushing them around in complete circles and pulling them up in the back of the stroke. You can watch someone who's only been pushing through a quarter of the circle, and after you tell them that, all of a sudden their ride looks smooth!

Here in Westchester we have a network of narrow, winding backroads that were built before the thruway. You have to take the whole lane on a road like that and control the traffic. You don't permit cars to pass you unless it's safe—even a police car. Drivers will understand that as long as you signal constantly. I watch the road; I keep a mirror in close to my eye and can see six whole lanes. I also look back often, and make my students practice holding a steady line as they look back over their left shoulders—I won't take them out in traffic until they can do that.

One morning when traffic is heavy and moving at forty miles an hour I take the class to Mamaroneck Avenue and we do thirty left turns. This is after I've checked out every student and am sure they are ready to do it. They're always amazed at how easily it can be done.

The final day of the course I evaluate their performance. They're given a direction sheet for a course they've never been on before. They're not always going to ride on roads where they know what the dangers are, and I want to know they're prepared to do so before they graduate. I deliberately choose a difficult route, with steep hills, rough roads, and heavy traffic. I tell them, "To pass the course you have to survive this." They know I'm joking, but they're careful after that. Since they don't know when the hard part is coming, it's a good test of whether they can think quickly on a bike.

I give an abbreviated course, where I go over what I consider the most important things; I leave out much of the mechanical part. I don't give certification for that, because a partial course is not certified by the LAW. This last session people said, "I want to learn, I don't need a certificate to hang on a wall."

Besides teaching history, John Pixton teaches bicycling at Penn State's Ogontz campus. Phys. Ed. 5 has as its aim to make "the student into a competent, independent cyclist on the existing roadways." Pixton teaches a shorter commuting and recreational course evenings from six to eight for the Philadelphia YWCA. The eight sessions include seven rides. Riding in traffic, commuting strategy, bike maintenance, and safety are taught. Visibility is stressed.

"Riding at night is a whole different ball game. You need everything in the world going for you. A minimum is to have generator illumination, light colored clothing, and reflectors. Using batteries takes a lot of planning—they run out when least expected. Rechargeable ones are all right for commuting."

All Pixton's students have to obey five survival rules:

1. *Ride right with traffic.*
2. *Obey traffic laws.*
3. *Use hand signals.*
4. *Be visible.*
5. *Keep your bike roadworthy.*

Pixton thinks that cyclists should ride in threes and fours, rather than strung out all along the road. "When you're riding in a group you should all handle traffic situations in the same way, or you'll frustrate and annoy the motorist. So do what the guy up ahead is doing, even if you don't think it's the right thing. Stay with him, stay closed up, so cars can pass after your bunch goes by.

"Classes are limited to twenty-four students. I have an assistant who's a scout leader and good cyclist. We identify a couple of more skilled riders and I'll appoint them to lead the smaller groups. All students fill out a bike data sheet called "Know Your Bike," which we recommend to all cyclists as a way to eliminate a lot of the misery of part replacement and maintenance. It includes gearing, spoke type, diameter and length, and what size wrenches are needed for repairs.

"We spend two or three weeks getting the bikes in shape. We have twelve maintenance exercises they all should know how to do, plus fitting yourself to the bike and knowing when a bike fits and when it doesn't. The rollers are helpful here."

A special feature of the college course is learning to ride on rollers, both for cardiovascular fitness and to improve dynamic skills. Students learn to shift, brake, and signal with either hand 41

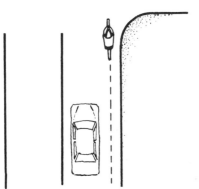

WITH RARE RIGHT TURN TRAFFIC
THIS IS A SINGLE DESTINATION LANE

while looking over their shoulders. "If you can do that on the rollers you can do it on anything," says Pixton. "It teaches you to hold your line with assurance, make your movements brisk. Everybody thinks they know how to ride a bike, but that doesn't mean they know how to do it in traffic, so it's important to teach them that they still have something to learn...and riding no-hands on a roller or doing a track stand on a unicycle gives them something to try for."

He shows safety films, like the Automobile Club of America's "Only One Road" and the McDonald's Bill Cosby film, both of which he thinks are quite good. "We stop the film and discuss the problems it brings up. Very few drivers really want to kill you, but they might out of ignorance or carelessness. Sometimes it's safer to get right out in the middle of the lane and prevent a car from coming around you rather than ride onto litter or other hazards.

"People have to be encouraged that it is simple to ride a bike. I want to overcome the tendency of people to say, 'I'd love to ride my bike but I'm afraid of traffic,' or 'I only want to ride on a bikepath.' We want to go to the Pennsylvania Department of Transportation and say, 'This is a good road for cyclists but it has these problems,' and have it corrected as routine maintenance of the roadway rather than some heroic thing that requires special funds."

Bonnie Dostal Neff is bicycle safety coordinator for the state of Michigan and national education director for LAW. She teaches bicycling on a grand scale—whole cities are being trained in effective cycling techniques through the national network of instructors she has taught and certified. At present there are over three hundred instructors in Michigan, and she's moving into Ohio. Grand Rapids and Oakland County have been trained, as well as thousands in two sites near Detroit. She also teaches a fifteen-hour course for decision makers—police officers, engineers, etc.

Bonnie Neff feels there are two major problems in getting bicyclists to commute safely: teaching them to communicate their intentions to cars, and teaching them to know where they are on the road—"cognitive mapping." And that fear prevents both kinds of learning from taking place.

We're finding out that people really don't know what commuting is all about. We do a pretest and look at all the external situations and equipment necessary. There is only four hours of actual contact with the instructor, two sessions of two hours each. They have reading assignments for homework – a guide for commuters that includes what I think is critical.

It's always thrilling to see the difference those few hours make. In the beginning, cyclists are hugging the curb, obviously tremendously afraid.

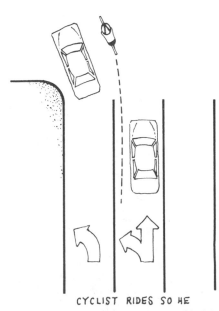

CYCLIST RIDES SO HE DOES NOT CROSS TRAFFIC INSIDE THE INTERSECTION.

CYCLIST RIDES SO HE DOES NOT CROSS TRAFFIC INSIDE THE INTERSECTION

The diagrams of how to turn a corner have been adapted from John Forester's *Effective Cycling*.

Four hours later they confidently take their place on the road, and casually wave on cars. Their whole posture changes as they overcome their trauma and start to look at their environment, and communicate with it. Having them analyze their panic and deal with it makes the difference between someone who commutes and someone who wouldn't.

One day we were on a three-lane road; two cars came up; some cyclists dashed to one side of the road, while the rest hugged the opposite curb. I yelled to the motorist, "Go right on through. Obviously no one is moving." The motorist smiled, waved, and went on. You could see a shock going through the cyclists' bodies when they realized that in that car was a human being who was willing to cooperate with them.

In driver education you develop a sense of the width and length of a car and its relationship to traffic; but that hasn't been done on the bicycle, and we're finding out that people don't know how much of the road they're taking up, or how to judge distance as they're moving. There's a difference between pushing down on an accelerator and gauging your own speed and reaction time; and you're much more affected by wind, road conditions, and hills.

So we have to get people comfortable on a bike and have them learn what they can and can't do, and how long it takes. It varies from person to person. The first step is getting you to know what gear to start off in and how much time and space it takes for you to get up to the right speed, or to brake. Once you know what your individual capacity is, you have to get a sense of what your relationship is to other things in the environment—how long and wide you and your bike or packages are, what possible dangers are present. It's simply driver ed. skills applied to the bicycle, but the trauma of being out there, so exposed, shuts off the learning experience.

When you first take people around the block to see where they're at, before they've had any instruction, they don't scan an intersection, all they do is bury their heads between their elbows and kind of hope they won't get hit. We used to think that because someone looked behind them, they saw the road. But some people are so frightened that even though they turn around, they don't see anything. So now we have cards with shapes on them–a bicycle, a car, a figure–and we make them yell out what they see to definitely show us that they're receiving information. That has made an incredible difference. We do it both in an off-traffic situation and on the road; sometimes on the road we hold up a hand and they have to tell us how many fingers they see. At first they don't see anything, that's how traumatized they are. But adults who have had driver ed. can get over that in four hours.

Everyone says youngsters shouldn't be on the road, but the trouble is, they haven't had driver ed., and though they know what the flow of traffic is, it's a totally new idea for them to stay on the right side of the road. We teach school children and senior citizens; a fifteen-hour course for people who have never ridden a bike or didn't have driver's ed. or are really inept and need that review.

We train employees of companies to commute to work. I trained five hundred people–thirty people to every two instructors–at Dow Chemical. I have to admit that's a very unique case : Ninety-five percent of the employees live within five miles of the factory, and there's another five miles within the plant complex. So we had two types of training: on the road, and inside the plant, where the roads were not designed as well (they thought all you had to do was lay down concrete). I went over the course to identify the hazards, then to show the instructors what the problems were. Sight lines are poor, so cyclists have to take curves more slowly, because the radiuses weren't designed properly. There are pieces of pipe sticking out of the ground that are hard to see from a bike. So we taught hazard recognition.

It's going to be an ongoing thing; we're training instructors inside the plant so new employees have to go through the course before they are allowed to bike on plant grounds. They get a little permit, which they have to show at the gate to prove they've been through the course. It's called the Dow Permit. It has a bicycle, their number and picture on it.

Since some commuting is bound to be in darkness, we tell people that they definitely have to have reflectors, and we strongly recommend that they go beyond that to beacons, leg lights, and reflective materials on helmets; it's a combination of all those things that makes it effective.

We have to show wrong-way riders the national statistics proving that riding the wrong way is one of the major causes of accidents. And even that isn't always enough; there are some pretty tough people out there who think that if they can see what's coming they'll be all right. They don't realize there's more to it than that, so we have to go to the second line of argument, based on driver ed. principles, and explain that you won't be scanned because you're not expected when you go against the flow of traffic.

The commuter has to become an advocate for cycling, and not just "put up" with conditions. This is a critical aspect of the course. When motorists start to be issued citations for assaulting cyclists, cooperative behavior will start. If road hazards are a daily problem, contact your local traffic engineer and change the environment. A commuter on a bicycle is more susceptible to bone shock, a chronic soreness of the joints, and rough road surfaces cannot be tolerated.

Commuting – Bringing It All Together

The Editors

The commuting cyclist travels during the twilight rush hour, the most dangerous time of day, under the most crowded road conditions, yet has the lowest accident rate per mile of any category of cyclist. That is because commuting traffic is much more purposeful than shopping or weekend traffic. Almost everyone, whether in a car or on a bike, knows where he is going, so the danger of someone stopping or making a turn on impulse is not very great. Also, once the cyclist establishes his route to and from work, he becomes a "pro" for the ride. A cyclist in good condition can handle a commute of twenty to thirty miles a day.

According to the United States government, about 500,000 people biked to work in 1977. Many more would probably do so were it not for worries about traffic and parking.

Bike commuting can be as simple as going to the store or as complicated as touring.

If your run is more than a couple of miles to work or to the train or bus, there are some problems to consider, such as choosing the best route, wearing suitable clothing, carrying tools and equipment, and avoiding theft. Doubtless, trade-offs will have to be made. Perhaps you'll have to give up the scenic route for a faster one, or the better road for one that has fewer hills or traffic. The more you ride to work, the more you'll realize that some of your initial apprehensions, such as breathing car exhausts (bikers actually have less contact with gases than motorists) or finding a place to leave your bike (it will probably cost you a tenth of what it costs to park a car), are quickly calmed and dismissed. Even biking to a carpool or a bus or railroad station can save you money. A year's insurance premium on a second car costs the same as a good commuting bike.

So, let's assume that you have decided to try commuting. Unless the distance to cover is very short, get a map and try out a few different routes on weekends. What are you looking for besides the shortest distance between two points? For the most part, wide, clean smooth roads with few intersections and as few steep hills as possible. They are busier, but are a lot safer than pretty residential areas, where each driveway is a potential intersection, and where children or dogs may dart out unexpectedly.

Be cautious your first few times out. That's when accidents are most likely to happen because you are unfamiliar with how the motorists react, where a lot of left turns are made, where to expect pedestrians, and the duration of traffic-light intervals. Allow a third more time for your first real trip to give yourself a chance to observe and remember actual traffic patterns. The physical surface–lanes, drains, cracks, landmarks–can be mastered on a nonwork day, but it's amazing how different everything seems in workday traffic, when people in a hurry may cross right in front of you.

Once you've chosen a route, check it out for wrong-way sewer gratings, tunnels, railroad crossings, and other obstacles. Make sure you can maneuver around or over them before you also have to be concerned with traffic. Try to make one trial run with your bike packed the way it would be on Monday morning, as bikes sometimes handle differently with weight added. If it has been raining, good–you can check to see if any parts of the road get dangerously deep or if the water hides objects that should be avoided. You should also practice wet-braking technique at a time when you're not worrying about being late.

When you begin commuting in earnest, you will discover that experience with a set route over a long period of time will help you become a better cyclist. By riding the same route daily, you'll learn about the problems and bottlenecks, and what to do about them. You'll be ready for the narrow lanes; you'll anticipate the turnoffs; you'll learn when to ride with traffic and when to ride to the right of it. However, don't ever become so relaxed that you are not ready for emergencies. Ride wide enough to avoid an unexpected car door opening. On a corner, be ready to turn with a car if it starts to cut you off.

You will probably be leaving earlier than most cars, so you won't encounter the heaviest traffic until you are near your destination. Mark down the time you leave. If you've enjoyed your trip, leave at exactly the same time the next day. If it's a little too hectic, leave five or ten minutes earlier; if too deserted, start out a little later.

Of course, if you've been commuting by car, you already know that most people keep regular schedules. Meeting the same drivers every morning gives you added safety. They will soon be expecting you. But remember, your behavior is being judged and evaluated. If you are courteous and obey the traffic laws, you can expect courteous treatment in return. Signal your intentions, turn your head to see if they're understood (if possible, make eye contact). If you wave cars on when there's no reason to interfere with them, avoid cutting in and out of lanes and jumping lights, and smile thanks when given the right of way, don't be surprised by

the offer of a lift when you have a flat or there's a cloudburst.

If you must stop for emergency repairs en route, signal right, and get onto the shoulder or sidewalk, well off the road.

The striking thing about cycle commuting is that you stop seeing "cars," and start seeing the people operating the vehicles. You can't talk to a car, but you can make a social agreement with a motorist. Eventually, you may have to confront some antibike nut, but control the temptation to tell him off. A smile is a good answer to a shout. With no rude remarks to give him further ammunition, he may give up harassing you–just as you have thought up a really good deflating rejoinder!

As your confidence grows, so will your skill. You may want to change your route. Commuters become selective. They tend to pick the most direct line possible, and use only those bike paths that don't take them out of their way. As you gain experience, you may discover that the slower pace used on bikeways, with their unpredictable traffic, breaks up the rhythm of the ride. Sidepaths can be a vacation from traffic when they parallel a river or wind through a park, but commuters generally stay with the busy thoroughfares.

Troubles with drains at intersections and with doors of parked cars opening into you disappear if you accept your responsibility as a vehicle operator and don't ride too close to the curb. Look out for badly designed drains and try to have them replaced, because you could still be forced into having to ride over them. But when someone says you must ride as near as twelve inches to the curb, he is either talking about extreme circumstances, or he has allowed himself to be intimidated by cars.

Exploring alternative routes on the way home can give you enjoyable variation, and help you find detours to use when you have weather or traffic problems. Tunnels and underpasses can become treacherous in the rain. Coworkers may possibly offer you a ride home if the weather turns bad, but don't depend on them. Have your "escape route" ready.

Carry bike tools and a spare, but keep some extra equipment at work, too. With a little ingenuity, you can make your workplace a home base. A desk or locker can hold office shoes and an extra shirt or jersey, soap and a washcloth, as well as brake blocks and spare tubes to avoid the hassle of re-

pairing a flat before you go home.

How you have to dress for work will determine how much extra clothing you must carry. If your ride to work is short, if you have a shower at work, or if you're in very good physical condition, sweating won't present a problem. Most experienced bike commuters who don't have these advantages count on resting about ten minutes before washing up. This cooling-down period minimizes excess perspiration. As you get into better shape, you will perspire less. The same ride that left you drenched at first after several months will be completed with much less effort as your body adapts to the regular exercise. At the most, you may want to change your shirt or blouse. Using a deodorant may help you feel fresher and more secure about your welcome.

If you are cycling in part for cardiovascular training, you know that perspiration is a sign that you're working hard enough. Dr. Sam Fox, the cardiologist whom we interviewed for our fitness section, counts on cycle-commuting to help him keep fit and commutes fourteen miles a day over four good hills. Dr. Fox says, ''It usually takes six to ten minutes to generate a sweat except in very hot weather. Keep it up for ten good minutes.'' By that time, you should be well on the way to work! He also reminds us to be sure to cool down afterward and to drink plenty of liquids to replace the water lost through perspiring, particularly in hot weather.

Dark-colored cars are involved in more accidents than light-colored ones. For safety's sake, it is important to make yourself as visible as possible. But being visible means being conspicuous. A lot of people who don't mind decorating themselves to be safe on a pleasure trip are too shy to do it commuting. You should wear bright yellow, orange, or white, especially on overcast rainy days. And get a helmet, both to protect your head and to make you look more competent and serious. Of course, you don't have to walk into your office building in your safety attire. Stop a few blocks away, remove the bright Windbreaker, the fluorescent pants clips, the bike gloves, and any other attention-getting items. Put them inside your helmet, which itself can go into a nondescript bag. Wipe your face, comb your hair, and walk the last bit. It is an excellent opportunity to cool off and relax.

Preventive measures differ with the seasons. For example, you can't count on reflectors to protect you once the days grow long because cars won't have their headlights on to shine on them. You really need front and rear lights, especially at twilight. If you use rechargeable batteries, have one set charging during the day and ride with the other. Carry extra bulbs and batteries and keep a supply at home and at work.

Year-round cyclists try for a Christmas tree effect: a duplication, even a multiplication of lights, reflectors, and reflective clothing. For rear visibility, use two flashing beacons or two leg lights and reflective pedals (moving lights are more easily noticed than steady ones). Studies have shown that foldaway rods with flags on the ends cause drivers to allow more room for the bicycle. How motorists react is a check of how visible you are. By monitoring your shadow, you'll be able to see if cars have to swing out at the last moment—which should make you modify your appearance.

You need a headlight to see with. Put it on the helmet, on the handlebars, or on the bike bag. Unfortunately, if your bike has to be left outside unwatched, the lighting units had better be on you or on a removable pack.

Even if you're brightly dressed, not all drivers are aware of bicyclists, and a car may start to back right into you. That's when you have to be audible, and fast! No problem if your lungs are strong and it's summer—but a horn can be heard even through rolled-up windows that might muffle a bell or a cry. It's polite to alert a truck to your presence if you pedal up past their signal lights—they really don't want to turn into you. A horn also assures you a crossing if traffic lights are changing and a driver is tempted to jump the light. Remember that a pedestrian's sense of traffic is cued to the noise of cars. Many blind people are frightened of bikes because of their fast, silent approach. The features that make bikes ideal for guerrilla warfare are the very ones you must overcome in order to cycle safely.

Successful commuting takes a bit of planning, but then so does every kind of travel. What you take with you and where you put it are twin problems all bike commuters have, from the stockbroker who puts his attaché case on his rack with shock cords to the all-weather, all-year-round twenty-miler who may be carrying more than any experienced touring rider would even consider. Rack requirements, then, can range from the rack that came with the bike to a full touring setup. Any sliding problem can be corrected with a mounting plate or by brazing a special support to hold the rack to the chain stays. Alloy rims, plastic seats or seat covers, mudguards and fenders, and track nuts rather than nuts and washers help make the bike safe and easy to maintain.

Gearing should be somewhat wider than the route would seem to indicate. Wind, rain, and fatigue all call for lower gears.

Visit the bike store Thursday or Friday evening when there's still time to have a repair made or get parts for your bike. Monday morning is too late to replenish your supplies.

Cyclists are very stubborn people and often try to make do with one bike. If space limits you, you're stuck. But many experienced bike commuters have a special machine to use for work. Even at today's inflated prices, it is possible to own an inexpensive bike that can be left at railroad stations in any kind of weather. Sometimes it can be put together from parts bought at garage sales. The performance of an old 3-speed can be so improved that rides up to ten miles long can be accomplished. (See the chapter, ''Improving a 3-Speed.'') That's a feat only a very strong rider would consider on a 3-speed with standard equipment. Renewed interest in utility cycling means that bikes built specially for commuting are beginning to be offered on the American market. You're replacing the use of a car or dispensing with a second car, so don't settle with what you have (if it isn't acceptable) unless you lack money, manual skill, or access to a bike store that can make the necessary changes.

Parking conditions will influence what kind of bike you use and its appearance. A bike locked at a train station or at a deserted spot outside work should probably be made unattractive. In New York, that has become a form of art. Use inexpensive or old-fashioned equipment, dirt, tape wrapped around the frame, and a sloppy paint job. Mudguards make a bike look awkward and bulky, not to mention out of style, and can be kept drab and battered. If you ride a folder to work, take the seat inside with you; the bike then looks like a child's. But keep a replacement for the quick release in your desk drawer with your spare tube.

Photograph by John Krausz

Photograph courtesy of the British Cycling Bureau

Photograph by John Krausz

A bike stored at your office, on the other hand, might require plastic sheeting to protect the wall from scuffmarks and the floor from dirty water or oil. Become friendly with the maintenance man or elevator operator where you work. He may know about some places you could put your bike and even have wash-up facilities. A garage owner might let you lock up a bike against his wall for a small fee. A bike bag that doesn't say BIKE could insure your entrance into an elevator that would otherwise ban you.

If you live in an urban area and have both a commuting bike and a better bike, it's a good idea to lock your bike up at home if the house is left unattended. Both wheels should be secured when locking any bike.

Where to leave the bike and how to lock it is a problem that most beginning commuters have. A well-traveled place is usually best. The newest storage lockers and racks require that you only carry a padlock; chains and locks can sometimes be left in place (it takes a very determined thief to steal a chain). Kryptonite and Citadel locks discourage theft.

Assuming that you and your bike are roadworthy and that you have found places for tools and spare parts, you should carry the following items on your person: phone money, a description of your bike, identification, and the phone number of the police on your route (they're well-trained in all sorts of emergency procedures). In addition, you should list such basic medical information as your blood type, allergies, use of dentures, contact lenses, and so forth. Everyone, biking or not, should be so equipped. If you are in really good condition, the information should include your heart rate. Racers have been given shots to "overcome" their resting heart rates of fifty to sixty because this seemed too low to the people who were giving medical aid.

One development you might not expect when you start commuting is fellow workers who will tell you that they, too, would commute if there were a "safe way to do it." If you are not yet convinced of your own ability, they can add to your feelings of uneasiness. It's a great source of comfort to some novice commuters to know that some bike clubs and bike activist groups have buddy systems to encourage people to try biking to work. They will also help you choose a route. Often, a riding partner can be found in the neighborhood or through the local bike shop. He may not share your exact working hours, but he usually is willing to help you get started by biking with you a few times. Who knows? After such a good experience starting to commute, you may someday help other bike commuters in the same way!

Common problems often have common solutions: two people who want to bring their bike inside an office building may be refused, but if four or five people have the same request, they might all be admitted. If you get together with lunch-hour exercisers, you may be able to share wash-up and storage facilities.

THE RIGHT TO THE ROAD

The Bicycle and the Law, Including Insurance

Edward F. Kearney

This chapter will tell you what the law in your state, county, or city *probably* is. But it is the responsibility of each cyclist to know the law in the places where he or she rides.

Bicyclists should obtain copies of their state vehicle codes and determine what they provide with respect to the ownership and operation of bicycles. Most state departments of motor vehicles have pamphlet versions of the state vehicle code. Once you have a copy of your state vehicle code, you should check these points:

How does the state vehicle code define "vehicle"? Does the definition include or exclude devices moved by human power?

How does the state vehicle code define "bicycle"?

What special rules of the road have been adopted for bicycle operation?

A few departments of motor vehicles now provide safety brochures for bicyclists. Ask whether your state has one. If your state has a person who coordi-

nates programs for bicyclists, you certainly should contact him or her for legal, safety, and other information.

Bicyclists also should determine whether a local bicycle ordinance has been adopted by the city or country where they live or will be riding. Ask for a copy, and read it.

Determining what state and local laws provide with respect to bicycle ownership or use is very important. As a bicyclist, you cannot comply with the law if you don't know what it requires. And if you violate a law, even one you didn't know existed, that violation can result in your conviction by a judge in a traffic court. Further, if an accident occurred, your violation can be used against you in civil litigation either to deny recovery of any of your losses from a motorist, or to reduce the amount you can recover. Always know what the law is, and always comply with the law because our traffic laws are designed to expedite the flow of traffic and increase the likelihood of an accident-free trip. Violating those laws often causes accidents and disrupts traffic.

The traffic laws in most states and cities are based on the *Uniform Vehicle Code* and *Model Traffic Ordinance*. These documents are revised and published by the National Committee on Uniform Traffic Laws and Ordinances, 1776 Massachusetts Ave., N.W., Washington, D.C. 20036. Provisions in these documents relating to bicycling were revised in 1975 and have been published

by the American Automobile Association in a pamphlet entitled *Model Bicycle Ordinance*. You can obtain a copy of this 13-page pamphlet from your local AAA.

Driver's License is Not Required

No state, county, or city requires you to have a driver's license to operate a bicycle on the highways. All states require drivers of "*motor* vehicles" to have a license, but a bicyclist is not operating a "*motor* vehicle." A few cities in the United States may have laws requiring bicyclists to be at least 12 years of age before riding on the part of the highway used by motor vehicles.

Registering Your Bicycle

In one recent study of 50 cities selected at random, 27 had ordinances requiring all bicycles to be registered. Another four had voluntary registration programs. A few states have adopted statewide bicycle-registration programs.

If you live in a state or city that registers bicycles, be thankful and eager to comply. Registration programs reduce bicycle theft and sharply increase the number of stolen bicycles that are returned to their owners.

As to bicycle registration, you should find out:

1. Whether your state, county, or city has a registration program.
2. Which state or local department registers bicycles.

Ed Kearney *cycles each day to his job as Executive Director of the National Committee on Uniform Traffic Laws and Ordinances, Washington, D.C. He continually studies the vehicle codes of every state, and has written chapters for driver education textbooks. He is a frequent contributor to bicycling publications and has written numerous articles on traffic laws, safe riding practices, commuting, and safe nighttime cycling.*

47

3. The amount of the registration fee.

4. How often the registration must be renewed.

5. What proof of ownership must be submitted to get the bicycle registered.

6. Whether there are any special equipment requirements (such as a bell or horn), or whether your bicycle must pass a safety check.

7. The type of plate or decal that serves as an indication that your bicycle is registered, and the proper place to display it on your bicycle.

8. What you should do upon selling or buying a registered bicycle.

RULES OF THE ROAD
General Rules and Why They Apply

Bicyclists generally must comply with the same rules of the road as the drivers of other kinds of vehicles. For instance, cyclists must:

Ride on the right side of the roadway.

Comply with all official traffic-control devices, such as signs, signals, and roadway markings.

Obey speed limits.

Stop at red lights. If it is legal in your state to turn right on red, and you do so, be sure to yield to pedestrians in crosswalks and drivers on the intersecting street.

Stop and yield the right-of-way at stop signs.

Slow and yield the right-of-way at yield signs.

Yield the right-of-way to oncoming traffic when making a left turn.

Yield the right-of-way to pedestrians in crosswalks.

Give a signal before turning or stopping.

State vehicle codes take different approaches to requiring bicyclists to comply with the same rules as other drivers. In some states, bicycles are defined as "vehicles" and most rules of the road apply to the driver of a "vehicle." For instance, read this rule of the road:

The *driver of a vehicle* intending to turn to the left within an intersection or into an alley, private road, or driveway shall yield the right-of-way to any vehicle approaching from the opposite direction which is within the intersection or so close thereto as to constitute an immediate hazard.

But, in other states, bicycles are not considered to be "vehicles." In these states, there should be a law which reads like this:

Every person riding a bicycle upon a roadway shall be granted all of the rights and shall be subject to all of the duties applicable to the driver of a vehicle, except as to special regulations in this article and except as to those provisions of this act which by their nature can have no application.

In other words, even though a person operating a bicycle is not operating a vehicle, he has the same rights and duties that vehicle operators do *if his "bicycle" fits the legal definition of "bicycle."* Since its revision in 1975, the *Uniform Vehicle Code* provides that bicycles are "vehicles." All states should adopt this revision because it simplifies the law and recognizes the bicycle as a significant means of transportation.

This chapter does not cover all the rules you as a driver must comply with because it is devoted more to special rules which have been adopted for cyclists. If you are interested in reading all the rules of the road, get a copy of your state vehicle code. All state departments of motor vehicles have a special pamphlet explaining the traffic laws for people preparing for the driver licensing examination. You may find this more helpful than reading your state traffic laws.

SPECIAL RULES FOR BICYCLISTS
Ride on Right Near Curb

Most state vehicle codes provide that a bicycle generally must be operated as close to the right curb or edge of the roadway as is practicable (possible, safe, and reasonable). Naturally, this rule does not apply when you are passing another vehicle, when you are preparing to make a left turn, nor when some other position is required because of the presence of official signs or roadway markings.

A few states have amended this law to

Photographs of New York's Short-lived Sixth Avenue Bike Lane by John Krausz

48

apply only when the bicyclist is moving more slowly than other traffic. Some states allow riding near the left curb on a one-way city street.

If your state does not have a special rule governing the proper position on the roadway for bicyclists, then you would be expected to comply with the same rules applicable to other drivers:

1. Remain on the right half of the roadway except when passing, driving around an obstruction, or driving on one-way roadways.

2. Use the right lane, or be near the right curb, when proceeding more slowly than the normal speed of traffic ("slower moving traffic, keep right" is the way this rule is often posted on signs).

Always ride a bicycle in the same direction as the rest of the traffic. Never ride a bicycle facing oncoming cars — not only is such riding against the law, recent studies indicate that such a position on the roadway causes accidents and is very dangerous.

Mandatory Use of Bike Path

Laws in most states require a bicyclist to use a bike path if one has been provided. The path must meet certain standards, however. It generally must be "usable" and "adjacent to the roadway." A few states have added other qualifications or have adopted special rules for use of "bike only" lanes. Because this law is opposed by organizations representing bicyclists, you should anticipate its repeal or amendment in your state.

Riding Two Abreast

In most states, it is lawful for two bicyclists to ride abreast of each other, but three may not do so. Some states require riding single file. Find out what your law provides and where it applies.

Riding on Sidewalks

As a general rule, it is lawful to ride a bicycle on a sidewalk as long as the bicyclist yields the right-of-way to pedestrians. A few states prohibit older bicyclists from using sidewalks, and many cities ban riding bicycles on sidewalks in the central business district.

Turns and Turn Signals

State vehicle codes require all drivers to signal their intention to turn or to move right or left on the roadway. As a general rule, this signal must be given continuously for at least 100 feet before the turn is made. The *Uniform Vehicle Code* was recently changed to provide that a bicyclist need not give the signal continuously if the signal is by hand and arm and if the hand is needed to control or operate the bicycle. Most state vehicle codes require use of the left arm to

give a hand and arm signal but a few allow a bicyclist to use his right arm to indicate a right turn.

As to the course for making a left turn, a bicyclist generally is required to follow the same course as other drivers: Move into the extreme left-hand lane available for traffic moving in your direction, turn to the left of the center of the intersection, and leave the intersection in the extreme left-hand lane available to traffic moving in your direction. A few states allow you to leave the intersection in any lane available to traffic moving in your direction.

Some states provide a special alternative course for bicyclists making a left turn: They may stay near the right curb, proceed through the intersection, and make the left turn at the far side of the intersection. After making the latter turn, a bicyclist must comply with signals, signs, or officers controlling traffic on the highway along which he intends to proceed. In European countries, this alternate course for a left turn is called a "big left turn."

Carrying Articles and Passengers

Many state vehicle codes and local ordinances prohibit carrying more passengers on a bicycle than it was designed for, or is equipped to carry. Before carrying a small child on a bicycle, make certain it is legal to do so in your state. If it is legal, be sure to comply with any special equipment regulations.

Laws also commonly require keeping at least one hand on the handlebars at all times, and prohibit carrying any item which prevents the use of both hands to control the bicycle.

Parking

A section was recently added to the *Uniform Vehicle Code* on bicycle parking. It reads as follows:

Bicycle parking

(a) A person may park a bicycle on a sidewalk unless prohibited or restricted by an official traffic control device.

(b) A bicycle parked on a sidewalk shall not impede the normal and reasonable movement of pedestrian or other traffic.

(c) A bicycle may be parked on the roadway at any angle to the curb or edge of the roadway at any location where parking is allowed.

(d) A bicycle may be parked on the roadway abreast of another bicycle or bicycles near the side of the roadway at any location where parking is allowed.

(e) A person shall not park a bicycle on a roadway in such a manner as to obstruct the movement of a legally parked motor vehicle.

(f) In all other respects, bicycles parked anywhere on a highway shall conform with the provisions of Article 10 regulating the parking of vehicles.

Some cities and a few states have similar laws.

Bicycle Racing

The laws of several states have been amended to allow bicycle racing events that have been approved by the appropriate state and local officials.

Bicycle Parking in Tokyo. Photograph by Alan Geiger 49

Parents Responsible for Children

The vehicle codes of most states make it unlawful for a parent knowingly to permit his or her child to violate any rules of the road or equipment requirement that applies to bicyclists.

MOTORISTS' DUTIES TOWARD CYCLISTS

Motorists are required by the laws of most states to recognize that bicyclists have the same rights as the driver of other vehicles. For instance, a previously quoted rule of the road requires a driver turning left to yield to any vehicle approaching from the opposite direction. In situations where a bicyclist is going straight through an intersection and a motorist turns left in front of the cyclist, the motorist would have to yield the right-of-way to the bicyclist.

Why is this true? Well, the law says that a person turning left must yield "to any *vehicle* approaching from the opposite direction." In some states, a bicycle is a "vehicle," so a motorist turning left would be required to yield for that reason. In most states where a bicycle is not a vehicle, there is a law granting a bicyclist the same rights as a person operating a vehicle. In these states, it is the latter law which would have the effect of requiring the turning motorist to yield to an oncoming bicyclist if he is operating a "bicycle."

But no bicyclist should ever assume a motorist has seen him and will in fact yield. And, remember, *no one ever has the right-of-way*. Our laws assign the duty to yield but do not grant any one the right-of-way.

Here are some more important general rules of the road governing a motorist's duties toward cyclists:

A driver who overtakes a bicyclist must pass at a safe distance to the left and not drive to the right until safely clear of the overtaken bicyclist.

A driver at a stop or yield sign must yield the right-of-way to a cyclist on the intersecting roadway.

The *Uniform Vehicle Code* requires all drivers to avoid colliding with any pedestrian "or any person propelling a human powered vehicle." Next to providing that a bicycle is a "vehicle," this was the most important revision adopted by the National Committee on Uniform Traffic Laws and Ordinances in 1975.

All drivers must proceed at a speed that is reasonable for existing conditions. They also may not exceed limits specified by law or by signs.

A person may not open a door on a vehicle unless it is safe to do so and will not interfere with moving traffic.

Motorists crossing a sidewalk must yield the right-of-way to bicycles on the sidewalk.

A motorist who turns right or left must make certain it is safe to turn, and must give a signal.

There is a chance that your state has not adopted all the above rules from the *Uniform Vehicle Code*. You may wish to contact bicycling organizations and legislators in your state about this. In a few states, there are laws which have been interpreted in such a way as to give bicyclists duties *but no rights*. That should be of great concern to all bicyclists.

Except for the rule about opening doors, bicyclists as well as motorists must comply with the above rules because they apply to the drivers of all vehicles.

EQUIPMENT REQUIREMENTS

Horns

Laws in about half the states require a bicycle to be equipped with a bell or horn. Having or using sirens or whistles is illegal.

Brakes

Most state vehicle codes require bicycles to have a braking system which will either cause the braked wheel to skid or bring the bicycle to a stop in 25 feet from a speed of 10 miles per hour on dry, level, clean pavement.

Equipment Required for Nighttime Riding

All 50 states require a bicycle used at night to have a lamp emitting a white light to the front. In most states, this lamp must be attached to the bicycle and it must be clearly visible for 500 feet. A few states require that the lamp be lighted only when the bicycle is in motion. California requires the light to be visible both to the front *and to the sides*.

Most states also require a red reflector facing to the rear. A few require a tail light and some require either a tail light or a reflector.

For additional nighttime equipment requirements, consult your state and local traffic laws. Some laws require that lights or reflectors be visible to the sides. A few require pedal reflectors. Find out what these requirements are and be sure to comply with them whenever you ride after dark.

Helmets

Though one jurisdiction (Puerto Rico) has had a law requiring bicyclists to wear a helmet, this requirement is believed to be unique.

ACCIDENTS

If a bicyclist is involved in an accident, the bicyclist must stop, identify himself, and render aid to any person injured in the accident. If death, injury, or substantial property damage resulted from the accident, the bicyclist also should notify the police immediately. In addition, the bicyclist may have to file a written accident report with the state department of motor vehicles within five to ten days after the accident.

None of these requirements are special to bicyclists. They apply to all drivers. Please note that you can "be involved" in an accident without having physical contact with a motor vehicle or pedestrian. For instance, if a motorist passes a bicyclist and collides with an oncoming car, the bicyclist is involved in that accident.

A bicyclist involved in an accident also should notify his homeowners' and his automobile insurance company of any accident resulting in death, injury, or substantial property damage. Failure to provide such notice may give an insurance company the right to refuse paying your claim.

LIABILITY AND INSURANCE

Injury to Another Person

If a bicyclist violates a law and causes an accident resulting in another person's suffering $10,000 in medical bills and lost wages, that bicyclist can be sued for the $10,000 and might be required by a court to pay that amount to the injured person. Naturally, $10,000 is just an example. The amount could be more or less. Though no state or city requires bicyclists to carry liability insurance, it is desirable that you do have liability insurance.

Most homeowners' or tenant's insurance provides liability protection for bicyclists. Check your policy and the amount of coverage. Coverage of $25,000 is typical and can be increased to $300,000 for a small additional annual premium. If you do not have such insurance, consult an insurance agent about this and other types of insurance that you may be eligible to purchase. Automobile insurance policies generally do not provide liability protection for bicyclists!

Injury to the Bicyclist

If a bicyclist is injured in a collision with a motor vehicle, the "medical payments" part of the bicyclist's own automobile insurance policy may cover some of his medical and hospital bills. If a bicyclist is injured by an uninsured motorist or by one that cannot be identified, the "uninsured motorist" part of the bicyclist's auto insurance policy may cover some of his losses. In states with "no-fault" insurance laws, the bicyclist's medical expenses, hospital bills, and some lost wages will be paid either by the cyclist's auto insurance policy or by the policy covering the car that struck him. In hit-and-run driving cases, there may be an "assigned claims plan" in these no-fault states. The bicyclist would be eligible for these forms of compensation even though he caused the accident.

CONCLUDING THOUGHTS

Though you should know and comply with the laws in your state and city, this alone may not be enough to assure your safety. True, knowing and observing the laws is basic to the safe use of a bicycle.

Over and beyond this, however, you should strive to develop common sense and a consistent willingness to yield to other road users whenever safety considerations so require. After all, your personal safety in bicycling is worth far more than "winning" an argument with a road user who violates a traffic law. Always drive defensively and never assume a motorist or a pedestrian has seen you.

If you do not agree with provisions you find in your state and local laws, you should, of course, request your state legislators and city council members to consider changing those provisions.

Laws can be changed, and often are, to improve safety, or in response to a sufficient demand from enough voters. Please remember that it is your responsibility to keep abreast of changes in laws relating to bicycling.

What to Do at the Scene of an Accident

Fred Time

Fred Time, an experienced bicycle commuter who has toured extensively (9100 miles in 1979 alone), is a firm believer in cyclists' rights ("Take a whole lane when you need it without worrying about inconveniencing someone"). He is also a prominent Texas lawyer and chairman of the legal section of the League of American Wheelmen. His advice:

"As a cyclist, the first rule to observe if stopped by a police officer for a traffic violation, such as running a red light (alleged), or speeding (a boast), or being involved in an accident (regardless of who's to blame), is *never* to show a driver's license. You are not required to have a driver's license to pedal a bike; if you show your driver's license and then lose the court case, it is possible that the violation will be reported to the State Highway Department, which could affect your insurance rate and possibly your driving record. I recently wrote a letter to a law enforcement agency in another state where the fellow did show his driver's license and the mishap was reported on his record. We got that expunged. We showed them it wasn't proper, because it had nothing to do with driving a motorized vehicle on a highway.

"Don't show your driver's license, but do show some other I.D. In a lot of states, if you don't identify yourself you go to jail. Cooperate with the police because you want a favorable report, you don't want to seem to be withholding information. Whether you're riding a bicycle or talking to someone in a restaurant, you don't want to seem antagonistic. It's no different from sitting in a car—you don't argue with a police officer.

"If you are hit by a car while cycling, or if you're involved in an accident that is not your fault, then call the police to the scene and have them make an accident report. They should procure the culprit's name, address, phone number, and driver's license number. Be sure your side is heard by the police. If a protagonist says something you disagree with, don't argue with him. Make a statement to the police, be as cool as you can be. He'll write his report the way he wants to. If the officer seems inclined to be prejudiced against cyclists and his report reflects inaccuracies, ask to see his superior for the purpose of filing a revised report. Actually, what a policeman writes in his report is important only to the insurance adjuster who sees it and usually takes it to be true. But once you show the adjuster that it's wrong, the police report's not that important. To protect yourself with the insurance company, get it revised.

"Make sure you always carry a pen or pencil and paper to record the culprit's license number in case of hit-and-run, then call the police. The odds are, the offender may be arrested for leaving the scene of an accident if you have that information about him.

"Be alert, although irate, and grab any witnesses who saw the accident. Get their names, addresses, and phone numbers. If the police come to the scene of the battle, have them talk to the witnesses so everything will be recorded on the accident report.

"Don't move your bicycle or allow the demon to move his vehicle until the police arrive. (Be judicial in your ability to maintain the status quo according to your assailant's size.) Don't move your bike for anybody's convenience until the police officer makes his diagram. If the officer tries to move it without doing that, ask him politely to note the bike's location on his accident report. Draw a diagram or sketch of the scene of the accident, showing such landmarks as stop signs, intersections, red lights, etc. Face off the steps from the curb to the place of impact, and from the place of impact to the now-stationary vehicle. If there's a witness around, see if he or she will agree to your drawing and get that person to initial it.

"Of course, if you're hurt, stay on the ground and ask for an ambulance; if you're not, you should get up and get witnesses' names. You shouldn't play a game. If you are injured, go to the hospital or to a doctor as soon as possible. It is my experience that soft tissue injuries such as whiplash, back sprains, etc., can appear days after the impact.

"You have now investigated the case, so call a local attorney. Hire him on a contingency fee basis (percentage of the damages awarded) and have him handle your case. In all likelihood, if you are not totally at fault, your attorney can settle the case for more money than you could, including his fee.

"Be sure to take your bike to your local dealer and get an estimate of repair or replacement, and notify your lawyer of that, as well as of the result of your visit to the doctor.

"If the settlement does not satisfy you, take your case to trial by jury and let your community decide the right of the cyclist to use the streets he's paying taxes on.

"If a dog bites you or unseats you, find out the name of the owner—that's whom you're going to sue. Of course, don't walk up to the dog that just bit you to look at his tag! But you might follow that dog home and find out where he goes. Call the police and have the dog pound pick up the dog; they'll find out who the owner is and then you can go after him after you've had a report made on the case.

"If you get hit by a car and the driver says he didn't see you, though you had the reflector that is all that's required by law, your defense is, 'I did everything that's necessary.'

"If someone riding at night takes more precautions, for instance, if the rider has a front and a rear light and other things to make him visible, he has a better chance of collecting. The same is true for wearing bright clothes during the day. If the defense is that the car operator still didn't see the rider, then he doesn't have the ability to see a cyclist; that's the driver's problem; he shouldn't have been on the road, and that fact should be brought out in court."

Good Roads

John Krausz

If the bicycle was to be a useful form of transportation it had to have access to the public roads. Although the need for good roads was evident everywhere, bicyclists had to continue using what roads there were, while hoping for better ones in the future. In 1881 the founders of the League of American Wheelmen (LAW) reported to the bicycle press that cyclists should reject the idea of using side paths and the temptation to use the sidewalks during the muddy time of spring, because once regulated off the roads, the bicycle could not easily reclaim its former privilege and use them when the weather got drier.

In 1890, cyclists could safely say that there wasn't a single road in the entire United States outside of the cities where one could bicycle five miles continuously in all kinds of weather without dismounting. Karl Kron, in his monumental *Ten Thousand Miles on a Bicycle*, published in 1887, reported that because of road conditions, sixty and a half miles was the longest he had ever ridden without dismounting, using his trusty Columbia "highwheeler" Number 234.

Just one year after the introduction of the safety bicycle in 1888, the LAW established a Committee for Improvement of Public Roads, which issued a booklet comparing the superior roads of Europe with the rutted

and muddy American ones. This booklet, *The Gospel of Good Roads,* was to help change the entire face of America, and with the League's magazine *Good Roads,* would sell over a million copies in the next three years.

GOOD ROAD SERMON

Do you know a Good Road Sermon when you hear it? If you do, here is one in a nutshell. On the poorest of earth roads, not muddy, but sandy, a horse can drag twice as much as he can carry on his back; on a fair road, three and a half times as much; on a good macadamized road, nine times as much; on a smooth plank road, twenty-five times as much; on a stone trackway, thirty-five times as much, and on metal rails, fifty-four times as much. Those who use roads can therefore make money by improving the roads rather than buying new horses every year.

Yes, and further, if you have sandy roads, you may possibly get one new settler per year; if you have fair roads, two; good smooth stone or shell, fifty or more! One little city in this state has recently completed miles of beautiful roads about the city, and the number of ten-thousand-dollar homes going up in that town this year is amazing. Good roads work all around, and for the benefit of all.

—*News,* St. Augustine, Fla. (1896)

The response to this form of persuasion was immediate. Countless newspapers reprinted *The Gospel of Good Roads*. In the future, many state legislators were to be controlled by the "bicycling lobby."

With the generous backing of Colonel Pope, the president of Columbia Bicycles, who later attempted to control the entire industry with the aid of John D. Rockefeller and A.H. Overman (afterward one of the largest car manufacturers), the LAW formed a very powerful political force, which was to influence local governments to pave the streets of the cities and force the state governments to pass legislation creating good roads. By 1891, in New Jersey, the idea of easements for roads was triumphant; if two-thirds of the landowners wanted a road, the state would pick up 90 percent of the costs. By 1892, more than $20,000,000 had been voted for this purpose.

By 1894 *Harper's Magazine* was to say that more than 90 percent of the expert road builders and fighters for better roads in the United States were to be found among the ranks of the LAW.

America had gone mad over the bicycle during the Gay Nineties, and in many ways it was the bicycle that made the Nineties gay. By 1897 the League had more than 100,000 members and had organized the more than 1,000,000 serious cyclists in the country into a powerful political force behind the *Good Roads Movement*. America was about to be paved and was about to stop paying what Colonel Pope termed its "billion dollar a year tribute to mud."

The cyclists had found powerful allies in both the military and the Department of Agriculture. Mile-a-minute Murphy became a national hero by riding behind a windscreen attached to a Long Island Railroad train. Barney Oldfield, who started his professional racing career as a bike racer, didn't exceed this speed till many years later as a race-car driver.

In this brief moment, the Golden Age of Cycling, the bicycle changed the world. It opened up the suburbs to the working class, making it independent of horses. It made the countryside available to the city dweller. It acted as a catalytic agent in the liberation of women, both in its effect on women's clothing, and in giving women for the first time a healthy form of exercise. It was both father and mother to the automobile and the airplane.

But it wasn't just in fighting for good roads that the League of American Wheelmen led the cyclists and affected the nation. Their maps were the first modern road maps (some state chapters printed weekly editions showing road conditions). They also issued stencil kits, which became the forerunner of modern traffic signs; fought for and obtained free baggage for bicycles on the trains and ferries; stopped restrictions on the use of bicycles on toll roads and bridges; and were instrumental in the establishment of rational traffic laws and proper signage.

The same spirit of adventure that put someone on a high wheeler put him behind the wheel of the early car. The car and the bicycle coexisted for many years on America's fine new roads. But by the mid-1960's, cars and the road-building boom had relegated the bicycle to a toy for children. Only about one in thirty American bicycles were made for adults, so it seemed natural to pass laws to protect the children. But by the year of the bike boom, 1973, the ratio had changed to fifty percent

"The farmer has always wanted good roads, but he knows that the farmer has always had to pay for them. Consequently he has generally looked upon any movement in this direction as a raid upon his pocket.

"It is no wonder that the farmer feared the cycler at first. The man on wheels was at first looked down upon as a dude in knee-breeches, out for an airing with his best girl, who demanded that others should, without cost to him, smooth the roads that he alone might have more pleasure. For years the farmer drove behind his horse with many a bumpety-bump, and the horse became stalled without ever swearing about it or writing a long protest to the county paper."*LAW Bulletin*,(1896).

Engravings from editors' archives

adult models. A society accustomed to protecting children was, by extension, treating adult riders the same way. Bicyclists' rights to use the streets had been seriously eroded. And because the bike was considered a child's plaything rather than a lawful vehicle, safety education usually consisted of "Watch out for the cars!"

The bicycle won the battle for good roads, but lost the war to the automobile. Many of the rights for cyclists that the League fought for and won must be fought for all over again. Thus, a century later, the LAW is once again emphasizing the rights of cyclists.

Before there were really any decent roads and before there were any traffic laws at all, these cyclists saw that for the bike to be a practical form of transport it would have to be treated like any other vehicle. Today that means using the good roads for serious cycling and using bikeways for light recreation.

Bikeways can be useful as a way for a child to get to school without having to interface with cars, a way for people to have fun, learn to ride a bike: All these are useful functions. But efforts to encourage the recreational cyclist should be funded by the recreational budget. The existence of bike paths should not then deny the more practical everyday cyclist safe and comfortable use of the roads.

Building a bike path is not sufficient to make it useful for transportation. It must have proper maintenance. One cannot now, any more than in the 1890's, ride "on the memory of a good road." This is another reason the LAW prefers widened roads for multiple vehicle use to bike paths that soon turn into grassy trails and ultimately benefit the pedestrian, the runner, and the dog walker. If bike paths facilitated someone's getting to work or to the store, serious cyclists would be for them, especially if they were maintained and traffic laws were enforced on them. Because that is usually not the case, and because more cycling accidents happen on bikeways than on regular roads, we must condemn them for serious transportation.

Ninety percent of all car trips are less than ten miles long. The person who, by using his bike for utility purposes, like commuting, cuts this wasteful car use, should have higher priority in national and local transportation planning. In some ways, changes have not been for the better: Ten years ago it was easier to take a bike on a bus, train, or plane. Those changes must be reversed.

The LAW is following its old technique in the new drive for good cycling roads: It is calling on engineers as well as enthusiasts to help plan for the mutual benefit of all road users.

Many cyclists are not ready to share the road safely and comfortably with motorists. The League knows the value of the applied experience and the accumulated knowledge of five generations of cyclists. Its Effective Cycling Course systematizes this into a coherent form, and a network of instructors has been established. Spin-off programs are making this knowledge more accessible. Entire cities and huge factories have formed programs of their own. Tens of thousands of people are learning on the road the principles the League was founded on: That the bicycle is a vehicle and should be operated in a lawful and predictable manner.

Recently, the LAW hired an experienced lifetime cyclist as a paid lobbyist who acts both as "our man in Washington" and also as an advisor to regional and

54

Volume XXIX.   Boston, January 13, 1899.   Number 2.

THE ROAD IS A CREATION OF MAN AND A TYPE OF CIVILIZED SOCIETY.

OFFICIAL ORGAN OF THE LEAGUE OF AMERICAN WHEELMEN

BULLETIN AND GOOD ROADS

Subscription, $1.00 per Year.   Special Club Rate to League Members Only, 25c.
Entered at Boston Post-office as Second-Class Matter.   **Price, 5 cents.**

PAID CIRCULATION, 73,070.

state committees on legal matters. The LAW, long known to many cyclists only for its annual fall Century runs, is now working toward building political clout and acting as an early warning system when cyclists' rights as users of the road are threatened.

If the League, still America's only national organization of cyclists, were to have just the numerical strength that it had at the turn of the century, when one in ten American cyclists belonged, its effect for gaining bike rights and good roads would be tremendous. It deserves the support of all cyclists, particularly America's more than 500,000 regular bike commuters.

L.A.W. MEANS GOOD ROADS

You Can't Get There From Here

Walter K. Ezell

Cyclists will smile grimly in remembering the old story of the New England farmer who was asked for directions. He scratched his head, made a couple of false starts at describing a route, and finally said, "You can't get there from here."

If we find this amusing it's because in the United States we know there are no destinations beyond our reach. The United States is crisscrossed by nearly two million miles of paved roads, connecting every burg with the largest metropolis.

And these are not just roads. They are what crusading wheelmen of eighty years ago referred to as "good roads." They are paved. A wagon or motor car or bicycle will not bog down in them. On almost all roads and on most bridges it is possible for cars going in opposite directions to pass each other at full clip. Once-forbidding bodies of water have been conquered with magnificent spans, making most ferries unnecessary. Sixteen of the twenty longest bridges in the world are in the United States.

And there is the wonderful interstate highway system, the backbone of American transportation, built over thirty-five years at a staggering cost. The design and construction of these roads far exceed anything our cycling ancestors dreamed of during the nineties – roads connecting all of the forty-eight contiguous states, with design speeds of 60 to 70 miles per hour, no intersections, separation of oncoming traffic, always at least one passing lane, 11- to 12-foot-wide lanes, usually

8-foot shoulders, grades seldom exceeding five percent, and limited access through acceleration and deceleration lanes.

So of course it's absurd to say, "You can't get there from here." Or is it?

The United States has the best network of roads in the world, and most of them are suitable for cycling by those who know how to cycle. But the good cycling roads are interrupted by bottlenecks–places where the roads are too narrow and the traffic too heavy for comfortable cycling. Although only the interstates and similar expressways were designed deliberately to exclude cyclists, few roads were designed with cyclists in mind. As Ralph Hirsch, the League of American Wheelmen's Legislative Director, notes, "Between 1956 and 1975, the peak period of highway building in this country, a total of $325 billion was spent on highways by federal, state and local governments, and this vast expenditure was made without considering the bicycle in the design of the system."

Imagine the chaos that motorists and

railroads would face if every bridge were suddenly washed away. Bridges illustrate the difference between a continuous transportation network and a network with gaps in it. One is a system; the other is a mockery. For cyclists, the "network" is a mockery. Safe, comfortable places to ride are interrupted by roads where it is dangerous or frightening or even illegal to ride. Closing these gaps will give cyclists a continous network to ride on, and make the bicycle part of a transportation system.

What's needed is a lot of road improvements and a few well-designed bikeways.

These improvements will cost many millions, even billions, over the coming decades, but they're a bargain when we realize that for perhaps ten or fifteen percent of the cost of rebuilding the road system, we can close the gaps; we can convert the road network into one that cyclists can share safely, comfortably, equally with motorists. Energy pressures convince me that these improvements are not only necessary but inevitable, and when coupled with education and enforcement, will

Walter Ezell *is the editor of* American Wheelmen, *the bulletin of the League of American Wheelmen. His job gives him the opportunity to cycle and to talk to cyclists all over this country.*

George Washington Bridge. Photograph by Karl W. Bruning

generate millions of new everyday utilitarian cyclists. The House Appropriations Committee reported in June 1979 that 62.4 percent of all automobile trips in the United States are five miles or less, and that if only one percent of these trips were to be made by bicycle, it would save approximately 131 million gallons of gasoline per year.

Until recently, highway engineers who designed for bicycles thought only in terms of bikeways–that is, separate paths, separate lanes, or green and white "Bike Route" signs on existing roads. Although it has not been shown that bikeways are effective means of reducing bicycle accidents or their severity, bikeways have nonetheless been promoted as a safety measure. But they have seldom been designed or advocated as a means of promoting cyclists' mobility. Cyclists want to travel at speeds possible on well-designed roads, and to travel without interruption to the same destinations motorists travel to. The fact is, if giving up a car for a bicycle cuts off some desired destinations, a motorist is unlikely to make the switch.

Highly mobile everyday cyclists are often cynics about the "safety" objectives of bikeway advocates. These cyclists know that many motorists are impatient with cyclists using "their" roads. They know that law-enforcement officers often prefer to treat cyclists as if they're not there, refusing to ticket cyclists who run traffic lights and ride against traffic, and failing to cite drivers when they do wrong and collide with cyclists. They suspect that bikeways are designed to get cyclists off the roads, out of motorists' way, out of officials' hair. Never mind that bikeways exacerbate conflicts with motorists by creating new intersections; never mind that skaters, joggers, dog walkers, and baby strollers are attracted to the bikeway, endangering themselves and the bicyclists, decreasing the cyclists' mobility, opening up new enforcement problems.

What confirms the cyclists' suspicions that they are being shunted aside for motorists' convenience rather than for cyclists' safety are laws in many jurisdictions requiring that cyclists use an available bikeway rather than an adjoining roadway. Even where such laws are not in effect, cyclists who use a road near a bikeway are harassed by motorists who think good money has been spent to get the cyclist out of the way.

Mandatory side path laws are discriminatory. When a special facility such as an expressway is built for motor vehicles, it is assumed that those who find the motor vehicle facility convenient and useful will use it. No one thinks it necessary to pass laws forcing motorists onto an expressway, and no one harasses motorists who use a parallel road. If a bicycle facility is well-designed, patrolled, and maintained, it will attract those who find it gives them adequate access, safety, and mobility. Those who don't find it so will use a convenient roadway.

The paternalistic regard for cyclists' "safety" at the expense of their mobility extends to rules in most states forbidding cyclists to use all interstates, even when there is no other reasonable access.

The interstate dilemma illustrates how cyclists have been designed out of the roadway system. Designers didn't deliberately exclude cyclists from certain destinations. They just neglected to consider that cyclists are ordinary people who want to go to the same places as motorists–to airports, across bays, beyond tunnels, to the other side of the railroad tracks. Engineers didn't deliberately design sewer grates to trap bike tires and kill or maim cyclists; they just didn't think about it one way or the other.

In an effort to keep noise, dirt, and high-speed traffic out of residential areas, planners have established a grid of commercial arterials separated by

exaggerated distances and filled in by residential cul-de-sacs that seldom go all the way through. If this system requires a motorist to travel a few extra miles, the loss in time and comfort is minimal, since the big roads allow for high speeds. But this same system forces the cyclist to pedal four miles to cover two, to share a heavily traveled road, and to breathe a car-polluted atmosphere. Often when he gets to a bridge, he is told to dismount and walk, or travel extra miles to another bridge where cyclists are allowed, or wait for unreliable public transportation that will, if the schedule permits, and if there is room, take him and his machine across. This is what I mean when I say cyclists have, through negligence, been designed out of the road system.

But the outlook has improved. Federal funds that might once have been spent only on bikeways can now go for roadway improvements, such as wide curb lanes, wider or smoother shoulders, and other appropriate physical measures to make bicycling safer and more attractive. These include providing bike parking facilities, fixing wrong-way sewer grates, and installing bike racks on buses. Also eligible are non-construction projects "which can reasonably be expected to enhance the safety and use of bicycles," such as training for improved law enforcement, mapping projects, and safety education.

Instead of special lanes that endanger cyclists and narrow the roadway for everyone else, cyclists are better served by continued maintenance and improvement of the existing road system. Left- and right-turn lanes, left-turn traffic signals, and wide outside lanes benefit motorists as well as cyclists by improving the traffic flow.

Cyclists may differ from motorists about where such improvements are most needed, so they should try to get represented on the Citizens Advisory Committees of the Regional Transportation Studies that exist for every metropolitan planning organization in the United States. Cyclists can help themselves by being visible and vocal. Then they can be designed into, rather than out of, the road system.

Build facilities, yes, but not to shunt bicycle riders aside in the name of safety. Give them access. Give them mobility. Make it possible for everyone to "get there from here." Then cyclists' numbers will increase and they will save the nation and themselves energy, money, and needless hassle.

The Bicycle Interfacing with Traffic

Alex Sorton

During the past decade, the United States has witnessed a tremendous increase in bicycling. The number of bicycle riders has doubled every ten years since 1940. The total number of bicycles in use is between 80 and 100 million, and over fifty percent of the new bicycles sold today are adult size.

Public officials are wrestling with difficult decisions about how the bicycle's potential as a form of transportation can best be realized. Citizen demands for action have made federal, state, and local officials increasingly aware of the need for bicycle-transportation planning. Competition is intense for very limited financial resources, and there is no assurance that extensive governmental investments can be justified by the projected number of people who will be encouraged to use bicycles for transportation.

As a result, many agencies are proceeding simultaneously with planning and design projects. Because of limited information about facility development and limited funding, shortcuts are taken and mistakes are sometimes made. There is little uniformity in procedures and design standards.

Many planners and engineers involved in planning, design, and operation of bicycle facilities are motor-vehicle oriented. Thus, many bikeway master plans and programs are developed that tend to separate the motor vehicles from the bicycles. This is done

Alex Sorton *is a transportation engineer at Northwestern University's Traffic Institute. He is an instructor for a series of workshops sponsored by the Federal Highway Administration entitled* Bicycle Considerations in Urban Areas. *These workshops have been greatly praised by previous participants, including professionals in planning, engineering, architecture, education, parks and recreation, and cycling enthusiasts.*

because these agencies feel this is the only safe place for a bicyclist to ride, or because they believe that this is where bicyclists want to ride.

It is simply not possible to create a comprehensive bikeway system to any significant extent in most of our urban areas. The difficulty of finding suitable locations for bikeways in cities has led them to be built where opportunities are available, rather than where the demand exists. Another problem is finding enough money to implement this type of plan on a large scale. Most bikeways of any length frequently intersect with existing streets, thus the potential for bicycle/motor vehicle conflict is not eliminated.

Many parallel separate bikeways do not serve the needs of the transportation bicyclist, are inadequately designed, and are poorly maintained. Local agencies become very frustrated when they find that some bicyclists avoid these separated bicycle facilities, preferring to ride in the streets.

Planners and engineers must realize that the bicyclist population is not homogeneous. In fact there are several distinct groups of bicyclists that have differing abilities, differing trip purposes, are capable of riding different distances, and so prefer different riding environments. Once these differences are recognized it becomes easier to plan and design facilities.

In general terms, there are three distinct types of bicycle riders: the child bicyclist, for whom the bicycle is the only form of personal transportation; the inexperienced bicyclist, whose age may range from sixteen to over seventy; and the experienced bicyclist, who is comfortable and willing to bicycle in a mixed traffic environment.

The first two categories form the largest part of the total bicycling popula-

tion. Most of their riding is done for recreation, and trips are around two miles long. They prefer to bicycle on roads with little traffic, which provides a more relaxing riding environment. These types of riders enjoy separated recreational bicycle paths because time and speed are a low priority. The emphasis is on having fun and riding in pleasing surroundings away from heavy motor traffic. These riders may subsequently think seriously about bicycling for other purposes, such as commuting.

Experienced bicyclists have confidence in their ability to ride in traffic. They use the bicycle as a vehicle and may be outspoken concerning the bicyclist's rights to the road. They may prefer to ride on arterial streets with more traffic rather than use side streets or alternate routes. At intersections, the arterial street has priority and often advantageous traffic signals, on side streets or on a separated bicycle facility, the bicyclist's speed is impaired every time a street has to be crossed. Arterial roads are usually the shortest and the best routes to the bicyclist's destination. Surface conditions are usually better in the curb lane of an arterial than on low volume streets because it has less debris, better maintenance, a smoother riding surface, and, sometimes, more width.

Transportation planners and engineers, as well as elected officials, tend to forget that traffic rules apply equally to bicyclists and motorists. It was determined during the earliest days of traffic regulation that the bicycle would be operated according to the long-established rules of the road. Vehicle codes in most states have applied to bicycles as they have to motor vehicles. The bicycle is regarded as a slow-moving vehicle subject to the rules for a vehicle of this class. These simple rules are generally known,

A mandatory bike path in the Southeast. The path is just left of the guardrail, covered with sand. The ocean can be seen at left through trees.

The guardrail was put up to discourage motorists from parking across the bike path. When the guardrail was put up, sand was washed from the shoulder onto the bike path, making it unusable. Still, bikes are not allowed on the street because of the existence of the path.

A mandatory bicycle path in the Northeast. Cars stopping across the bicycle path while in the intersection create problems for bicyclists.

A mandatory two-way bicycle path on a sidewalk in a southeastern state. Notice the poor sight distance at driveways and intersection, and the narrowness of the obstructed sidewalk. Also notice how wide the street curb lane is. It would be ideal for bicycle commuters, yet, because of the path, bicycles can't use the street.

A bicycle path in central United States. The black asphalt portion is the two-way bicycle path. It is about three to four miles long and was built for commuting bicyclists.

If the tree well does not get the bicyclist, the tree branches will. Beyond the trees are sign poles, telephone poles, street lights, and many undulating driveways.

The unfortunate thing is that the local community's bicycle club *endorsed* this bicycle path. The bicycle club officers were recreational bicyclists, not commuters. Moral – bicycle clubs may not provide the necessary answers; authorities should talk to cyclists who commute.

Photographs courtesy of Alex Sorton

although widely disregarded. The bicyclist is to move in the direction of traffic, keep to the right, observe traffic control devices, signal for turns, and provide illumination at night.

Some provisions of the vehicle code may present potential problems for bicyclists. One states that whenever bicycle facilities parallel the streets, the bicyclist must use the facilities, not the street. When bicycle facilities have been built adjacent to sidewalks in urban areas, or when signs indicate sidewalks for bicycle travel, some unsatisfactory situations result.

Since bicycle facilities tend to be used in both directions, bicycles may go unnoticed by motorists crossing these routes at intersections and driveways. In addition, vision is often impaired at intersections by parked cars, and at driveways by property fences and shrubbery. Motorists do not always look for bicyclists entering the crossing area, particularly when they are making turns. They tend to expect pedestrians, who move more slowly.

Sidewalks are designed for pedestrians. When bicycles, with their higher speeds, use them at the same time, they are not safe. Conflicts between bicyclists and pedestrians exiting from stores or stepping out from between parked cars are common because of their different speeds. So are collisions with fixed objects such as parking meters, utility poles, signposts, bus benches, trees, hydrants, or mailboxes.

Accidents have occurred because of these unsatisfactory conditions. Some have resulted in liability suits filed by the bicyclist involved in the accident against the governmental agencies that have built or designated these types of bicycle facilities.

When sidewalks or similar types of bicycle facilities are not made mandatory, the bicyclist has the option of choosing to ride in the street. Some of the accidents and lawsuits just mentioned may be avoided in that way.

Another problem may arise when a facility is designated only for bicycle travel. Such a designation implies that the facility is able to accommodate all different types of bicyclists. This is true of very few facilities. For example, a bicycle lane in the street may be easy for the experienced bicyclist to use, but may present potential problems for a child because of the hazards of motor vehicles turning at intersections. A sidewalk designated for bicycle travel may be convenient for children or adult learners, but the higher speed of the experienced bicyclist may create dangerous situations for himself and others.

Bicycle safety problems cannot be solved merely by creating bikeways. What can be done to reduce the potential hazards to bicyclists as bicyclists are integrated into the world of motor vehicles?

We have the answer for motor vehicles, but have not applied it to bicycles. Motoring problems have been reduced by what safety experts call the three E's: Education, Enforcement, and Engineering. The principles embodied in the three E's apply not only to motor vehicle operation, but also to bicycle riding.

Neither beginners nor veteran riders automatically ride bicycles correctly or consistently. Everyone must be properly instructed and reminded to obey the rules of the road. Continuous traffic safety education in the schools, in the media, and in the home is a must.

Most adult bicyclists are licensed drivers fully aware of the rules of the road. Educating them to operate their bicycles as they do their automobiles is important for all, whether they are experienced or casual recreational riders.

A large proportion of bicycle accidents cannot be avoided purely by engineering means. The accidents are often caused by careless riding habits or disregard for the rules of the road. Enforcement measures are needed in addition to education to improve the bicyclist's ability, road sense, and conformity to the rules of the road, as well as improving the motorist's attitude and awareness toward the bicycle rider. Education and enforcement programs may be more cost-effective than providing certain types of bicycle facilities.

Engineers and planners can implement the following suggestions to promote bicycling at all levels of competency and to encourage transportation related bicycle travel.

• Engineers could help provide adequate space for safe and convenient bicycle travel. The width of the outside traffic lane should be no less than fourteen feet for bicycles and motor vehicles to share. (Usually traffic lanes are twelve feet wide.) It becomes difficult to create a wide outside curb lane with a fixed curb-to-curb street width unless other lanes or medians are correspondingly narrowed or street parking is prohibited. Providing wide outside lanes is less confusing and sometimes more economical than building bicycle facilities behind the curb or designating sidewalks for bicycle travel, because no distinctive signs are required. Neither is it necessary to modify the rules of the road or contend with questions of liability.

The motorist in a wide outside lane is less likely to be forced into the adjacent lane because of obstructions along the roadside. The driver's view of oncoming traffic is not blocked by trees, parking meters, or light poles that line the street. About fifty to one hundred more motor vehicles per hour can be accommodated in a fourteen-foot lane as opposed to a twelve-foot lane; thus the primary benefit of a wide outside lane in terms of safety and capacity is enjoyed by the motor vehicles, and the secondary benefit goes to the cyclists.

• Paving shoulders in outlying urban areas and rural areas is another way of accommodating both bicycles and motor vehicles. Paved shoulders increase safety for the motorists, as has been borne out by studies in California and North Carolina. In California, the accident rate was reduced by 16, 35, and 29 percent respectively when two-, four-, and eight-foot paved shoulders were added to existing roads. In North Carolina, a significantly lower accident rate was associated with highway sections having three- to four-foot paved shoulders compared to identical highways having unpaved shoulders.

Planners should consider the importance of secure bicycle parking at common destinations. The lack of adequate bicycle parking is one of the biggest deterrents to the use of bicycles for commuting to work. The cost of providing secure bicycle storage is often considered prohibitively high by employers. The cost of bicycle storage facilities presently on the market ranges from $50 to more than $180 per bicycle. However, compare those figures to the cost of a motor vehicle parking space. In a parking lot, each space costs about $400 to $500; in open parking garages, $2,000 to $3,000 per space; underground garages, $4,000 to $5,000 per space, and underground garages with a landscaped park on top, $7,000 to $10,000 per space.

• A good riding environment in residential neighborhoods can be provided for the young or novice bicyclist by maintaining the streets and keeping large numbers of motorists from taking shortcuts through these areas. Grates that could be dangerous to the bicyclist should be replaced.

Traffic engineers could design bikeways that complement the existing road system yet are independent of it. If the bikeways were designed and maintained to be safe up to twenty miles an hour, bicyclists would be able to obey the rules of the road easily. Contrary to general public belief, bicyclists are no more capable of coping with substandard facilities than motorists. These bikeways could be built in parks, beside rivers, and along forest preserve property. Barriers and bottlenecks such as bridges, freeway crossings, and railroad tracks, should be avoided wherever possible.

It is hoped that planners, engineers, and public officials will look at more than engineering to encourage bicycle use as an alternative means of serious transportation in urban areas. Education and enforcement, as well as engineering, must be used in conjunction with each other in order to make bicycling safe.

Some Call It Paradise: Bicycling in Holland

Rob Van der Plas

Now I'm going to see what a bicycling paradise looks like, I thought as I left the arrivals hall of Amsterdam's Schiphol Airport. The airport itself looked like any other modern airport in the United States or Europe, and the same could be said of the road that connected it to the real world. The only bicycles in sight were our own. The freeway that led to Amsterdam and The Hague was much like any other freeway–familiar enough after ten years in California. Except, there it was–around the periphery of the freeway proper: a *fietspad,* the famous Dutch bike path, acclaimed and copied around the world as the solution to the bicyclist's problems.

It was 1974, the first time I had returned to my native Holland with a bike, after fifteen years in England and the United States. Back in California, bicycling had gone through the first great boom. Everybody had bought a bike and was just waiting for an opportunity to use it: The only thing missing was the bikeways. Now I was back in Holland and was going to see how effective those bikeways were, how safe and convenient they had made cycling, and how the United States ought to copy them.

What a disappointment: Not even these much-praised Dutch bikeways had succeeded in keeping the bicyclist on the road. Few if any visitors and workers at Schiphol Airport had traveled the eight miles from the capital city by bike. Elsewhere too, the car was almost as prominent as it was in the States. It soon became obvious that the bike, which I had used for all my transportation needs back in the fifties, had been relegated to a very distinct but minor role: short-distance transportation within the cities and in the country. For a trip longer than three miles the bike had become an anachronism of a few eccentrics and small numbers of those socially disadvantaged who could not afford to use the–admittedly excellent–public transportation system, or their own car. The bicycle had become, and still is today, little more than a "pedestrian accelerator."

To what extent the institution of the bike path had been responsible for this "pedestrianizing" of the

Rob Van der Plas *has been active as a bicycle advocate in several countries since 1960. He is the author of several bicycling books published in Holland, Germany, and Great Britain. He's a specialist in managing small oil refineries.*

The Press and Cultural Section of the Consulate General of the Netherlands

cyclist, I was to experience soon enough myself. In the fifties I had often traveled the eighteen miles between Baarn and Amersfoort–two medium-sized towns in the suburban zone east of Amsterdam–visiting relatives and friends. I'd made it a point to cover the distance as fast as I could–one hour and ten minutes, one hour, then finally fifty-five minutes–on a clunker 3-speed weighing forty pounds or more. This time I had my twenty-two pounds of double-butted alloy steel and precision aluminum to break all previous records–so I thought.

Not so. The still-scenic trip became a nightmare of stop-and-go cycling that was to take nearly two hours and prove more exhausting than the Mount Hamilton Hillclimb. Cycling in Holland is neither convenient nor safe, much less fast, at least when you use the bike paths. The motorist does fine in Holland: the arterials and freeways, the highways, and even most residential streets are among the best in Europe. Motorized traffic flows smoothly and swiftly, if not with quite the murderous speeds common in neighboring Germany. The bicycle traffic is given a different treatment entirely.

On almost all major roads the bicyclist is taken off the road and led over separate bike paths which are routed around the periphery of the road proper. At intersections the cyclist is not abandoned: He gets separate bicycle-traffic lights. That's when the frustration sets in: The only maneuver that doesn't require additional waiting is the right turn. Even in the case of straight-through cycling the cyclist's intersection clearing time is a multiple of the motorist's.

Imagine the intersection of two arterials with center dividers, protected by traffic lights. If the lights are synchronized with others in a system, the approaching motorist will usually arrive during the green phase—he can go straight or turn right (or sometimes left). The cyclist wanting to continue straight is first forced to wait until all right-turning motor traffic has cleared. Subsequently, cross traffic gets the green light: The cyclist must also wait for it to clear. Next is the cyclist's green phase: He can cross only to the center divide of the cross street. At this point the motor traffic in the same direction gets the green light. Depending on whether left turns are allowed, the cyclist may now have to wait another full cycle or may be able to complete his "crossing" (which was not meant to be a crossing at all but a straight through, remember?). The time delay is significant and the repeated acceleration required in the stop-and-go situation becomes exhausting. Eventually the cyclist, even the most sincere law-and-order advocate, gets impatient and starts trying to cheat the system. The situation then becomes dangerous as well.

Of course this is a grim picture. It shows the limitations of bike paths in urban and suburban transportation, but it is not necessarily true for rural cycling. Indeed, many thousands of miles of bike paths are quite good. Most freeways either have bike paths parallel to them on the same right-of-way, or

The Press and Cultural Section of the Consulate General of the Netherlands

The Press and Cultural Section of the Consulate General of the Netherlands

separate secondary roads, either exclusively for cyclists, or at least suitable and permitted for cycling. Where the bikeway joins the freeway, it often takes advantage of the same safe multi-level crossing facilities. Where it follows a nonfreeway highway, or is routed farther away, the crossings remain dangerous and time consuming, but the distances between crossings are usually so great that the net effect of the protection formed by the separate rights-of-way probably outweighs the inconvenience and danger of the crossing.

To me, the most unpleasant aspect of biking in Holland is that the cyclist is considered a second-class vehicle operator. Traditionally, the Dutch vehicle code has distinguished between *snelverkeer* (literally "fast traffic," i.e., motorized traffic) and *langzaamverkeer* ("slow" or nonmotorized traffic, primarily bicyclists). An elementary rule has always been that nonmotorized traffic must yield to motorized traffic (except that straight through traffic has preference over turning traffic). This may have been practical until the fifties, when a few cars competed with many bikes, because cars might never have had a chance to cross a dense stream of bicyclists otherwise; but today it makes little sense. The now relatively few cyclists have a hard enough time competing with the dense streams of motorists without such artificial and arbitrary discrimination.

The other major legal disadvantage is that it is compulsory for cyclists to use bike paths or bike lanes if they are provided. Also, there is an ever-increasing custom of banishing cyclists from major arteries by means of traffic signs (the dreaded bicycle sign in a red circle: Bicycles Prohibited). The winter of 1978-1979 clearly brought home the absurdity of this rule. As all Holland was covered weeks on end under a thick layer of snow, only the "real" roads were cleared—the bike paths were allowed to get ever slicker and more dangerous. One responsible official explained, "Since bicycling is too dangerous under these conditions, it should not be encouraged"!

Amsterdam, in front of the Reichsmuseum.

Opposition among cyclists against such public callousness has been increasing since 1975, when some cyclists who had been active in safety campaigns and environmental fights founded the ENWB, since then renamed ENFB, which stands for *Echte Nederlandse Fietsers Bond* or Real Dutch Bicyclists Association. It is quite separate from the Dutch equivalent of the AAA, the ANWB. The ANWB was founded as a bicyclists' association, but in recent years, though still bearing its old bicycling name, has concerned itself very little with the bicycle and its rider.

Another organization which is concerned with bicycling in Holland is the *"stichting: fiets!"* (the quotation marks and exclamation point are all part of the registered name). It is essentially financed and run by the bicycle trade and is closely linked to the motor lobby—it even uses the same mailing address. It will not surprise anybody to hear that the organization has found the answer to all the bicyclist's problems in bikeways. Its literature bristles with quotations from American bikeway literature. It is rather ironic that while bikeway advocates in the States point to Holland to justify their schemes, their Dutch counterparts point to the U.S.A.

All this need not be read as a discouragement to cycling in Holland: A lot of good cycling still can be done, and in some aspects that country shows some very positive developments. You can cross Holland on good scenic roads without being forced to take either a bike path or a serious detour. You can explore the cities (once you get used to avoiding the arterials) on streets which have been "humanized" in an often successful attempt to achieve something known as "traffic relief": city-sponsored programs considered exemplary by planners and environmentalists around the world. It is still a bicycle-oriented country.

Though bicycle use in Holland has decreased since the fifties, the bicycle is still a more common sight there than anywhere·else in the Western world. On Sundays especially, the bike parts the country lanes, and the purely recreational paths are alive with cyclists when most other Europeans take strolls or tour the countryside in their cars. Indeed, the recrea-

tional use of the bicycle has been greatly emphasized

since the early seventies and, it must be admitted, not without effect. Each of the provinces has prepared a bikeway plan, in the spirit of relegating the bicycle to a purely recreational function.

Some, such as the rural province of Drenthe, have succeeded in creating bikeways which have gone far beyond their original intention. These bikeway systems are really bicycle freeways: They have well-designed crossings with other roads, often form the most direct link between towns and villages, and are well surfaced. They are indeed used during the week for transportation purposes, because they do not delay the cyclist like conventional bikeways.

Other provinces, on the other hand, have come up with designs that neither encourage transportational use, nor have significant effects on the behavior of recreational cyclists. The Dutch will use their bikes—those same clunkers they use during the week, although you also see 10-speeds nowadays—for recreational purposes, whether they are offered bikeways or not.

In fact, most Dutch vacationers prefer to take their bikes with them at home and abroad. Like most European railway systems, Holland's *Nederlandse Spoorwegen* offers bike transportation. Unfortunately, the attempts to increase speed and frequency of the railway system have led to deterioration of this essential service. Taking the bike with you on the same train is rarely possible. Instead, the NS runs special bicycle trains during the summer months, taking the bikes but not the passengers. Though the railways are very proud of this service, my experience in 1978 was less than positive: The bikes took five days to arrive in Zutphen from Amersfoort—a distance of only thirty miles. No information about them could be obtained over the phone, so I had to make several trips to the station to inquire.

Definite praise, on the other hand, should go to this same NS organization for its bicycle storage and rental service at railway stations. Administered by the *Servex* office in Utrecht's NS headquarters, this system allows a visitor to almost any town in the Netherlands to rent a bike right at the railway station, while local citizens, whether they use the railway or not, can store their bikes in covered and

The Press and Cultural Section of the Consulate General of the Netherlands

guarded storage facilities. Because the railway station is invariably also the terminal for most local and cross-country bus services, all transportation is conveniently linked. It is this kind of setup that has made the bicycle attractive—much more so than the building of thousands of miles of bikeways ever will.

Perhaps the most important thing to be learned from Holland is the skill that can be achieved by ordinary cyclists. Because the bicycle was never a mere toy in an automobile-oriented world, the cyclists take themselves and traffic seriously. Kids and housewives, old folks and students, all ride like pros. Because parents are cyclists themselves, they teach their children how to ride safely. In part, this high level of skill derives from greater experience: Holland's population of 14 million owns 8.5 million bikes

which average 1,500-plus miles annually. But the school system does not ignore the bicycle: Traffic education is essentially bicycle education. A course given in the third and fourth grade teaches the student how to behave in traffic, not just how to keep out of the traffic, as happens only too often in the United States!

Of course, the utilitarian character of cycling in Holland has its effect on the equipment too. You'll see few light bikes. The Dutch clunker is many classes superior to the American clunker, or, for that matter, to the clunkers seen in many other countries. The quality of frame and moving parts is high, and the accessories are good and useful. Practically every bike has generator lighting. A large rectangular red unidirectional reflector helps out when the lights fail. The luggage rack on the Dutch bike is adequate to carry a crate of beer, a sack of cement, or your mother-in-law. The wheels are rather large, usually 28 inches (the small-wheeled folding bike, popular in many other European countries, never made it quite so big in Holland), with rather hefty tires an inch and a half wide, or more. Tires an inch and three-eighths wide give you a

Photographs courtesy of the Press and Cultural Section of the Consulate General of the Netherlands

Sportfiets—a sports bike. The brake is usually a coaster brake, even a 3-speed makes your bike a deluxe version. Fenders are a must, and excellent protection of the chain is provided by a fully enclosed chain guard.

The construction of facilities has unfortunately been almost entirely standardized on the basis of this kind of vehicle. Finding a rack to hold a 10-speed with narrow wheels is difficult; road surfaces that seem acceptable to a man with balloon tires will drive you bonkers in a hurry. On the other hand, inclines which can be easily handled with a 3-speed are barred to cyclists and considered too formidable. However, handling the facilities problem has in general been positive: Access is almost always guaranteed, the purely mechanical aspect of bikeway design is of a high standard (apart from the often rather uneven surfaces), sign posting is usually very good, and the design of bridges and tunnels, building entrances, and crossings is quite satisfactory. These details show how it should be done *if* it is to be done. My only complaint is that often it should not have been done, because there are better ways than routing the cycling traffic along the periphery of the "real" road. Though I'm convinced the bicycle is not about to die out in Holland, I do fear that the separation approach has reached the end of the road. To make bicycling more attractive and practical, the bicycle must be allowed to take advantage of the same plans and designs which have been provided—and only too often reserved—for the automobile, not only on quiet country lanes and residential streets for low speeds, but equally as much on the highways, the freeways, and the busy arterials—in short, where people need to travel.

Cycling in the Northwest

Paul Boyer

In Seattle and King County there are bicycles everywhere. They're not about to crowd the cars off the roads, but they are visible. There are people who commute to work, there are racers, and there are recreational riders who take advantage of any and all free time to get together with their friends for a ride. With such an obvious show of support for bicycling, the local politicians are an easier mark for bicyclists' requests than their state-level colleagues, whose constituents may only see a handful of cyclists each year.

The nature of those requests has changed during the past ten years. Then, bicyclists asked for bikeways so they could be separated from car travel. Now they spend their time working for facilities that would permit the bicycle to move safely alongside car traffic. The Burke-Gilman Trail, a Seattle and King County project, was a product of the earlier thinking. It was a bold stroke.

It utilized an unused railroad right-of-way that ran from the north shore of Lake Union near the heart of Seattle, along the campus of the University of Washington, past the city limits to the north end of Lake Washington—a distance of some twelve miles.

Much of the success of the Burke-Gilman Trail lies in the fact that it links the neighborhoods of Northeast Seattle with the University of Washington. As one might expect, the university is the greatest center of bicycle commuting in the state. The Trail is used constantly, carrying a steady stream of commuters during workdays and recreational traffic the rest of the time. It is used by bicyclists, joggers, roller skaters, pedestrians year-round. Real estate ads now tout proximity to the Burke-Gilman Trail the way they once boasted proximity to schools, churches, and shopping centers.

There are problems, though. At times the Trail is overused. The different kinds of traffic—commuting and recreational—don't always mix well. On a sunny Sunday afternoon it can be a harrowing experience to ride its length.

Attitudes have changed in ten years, however. At last, bicyclists seem ready to accept the fact that the automobile will not go away tomorrow. It is impossible to build a bike trail to every place any cyclist might want to go. So attention is beginning to turn to such irritating and dangerous obstacles to bicycle travel as railroad tracks that cross the streets at odd angles and bridge gratings that get slippery and unmanageable in the rain.

As the result of ten years of hard work by Northwest bicycle organizations, cyclists now find themselves in a position to influence public thinking.

Paul Boyer *regularly contributes both stories and photographs to Seattle's* The Bicycle Paper. *He has acted as president of the Cascade Bicycle Club, and runs the Wet Weather Company, which manufactures a complete line of bicycle clothing designed by his wife, Sally. The Boyers are also among the bicycle people featured in our tandem section.*

In Seattle, for example, the city engineering department has a bicycle coordinator who manages bicycle-related programs. The city council and the mayor have a bicycle advisory board. The King County planning division maintains close ties with an informal advisory group that consists mostly of bicyclists. While nobody has yet been elected to public office on a bicycle-oriented platform, at least bicyclists are in a position to make themselves heard.

The early years of the seventies were a whirlwind that picked up, sorted through, tossed around, and dropped again almost every element of American society. As thousands of people jumped on bicycles to show support for a new order, a significant handful, when the storm died down, was left to come to terms with the world of the bicycle. Those who stayed on their bikes were the movers of change. With each successive wave of environmental enthusiasm or gas shortage, they were joined by a few more who, like themselves, had discovered a true affinity with the bicycle. In short, they loved everything about the bicycle – its simple form, its silence, commuting to work, touring long distances, riding city streets on warm summer nights, screaming down from mountain passes into cool valleys.

What happened was, no doubt, a nationwide phenomenon. Reading the bicycle journals makes it clear that the situation has a broad base. But the Pacific Northwest, probably because it sits in relative isolation in the corner of the country and has, therefore, developed somewhat independently of outside forces, provides a kind of control group for measuring the degree of change.

It was very simple: The act of riding a bicycle became a form of social comment.

Those early years of the seventies set the tone for a powerful combination of political statement and good, clean fun. In Seattle, that combination gave rise to two institutions that are alive and well after ten years: the Cascade Bicycle Club and The Bicycle Paper. Both of these were established because people felt that riding a bicycle wasn't enough, that it was necessary to be politically active at the same time.

Since any bicycle club is essentially an organization of amateurs, the focus of activity changes with each change in administration. Cascade Bicycle Club is no exception. Some years, the work has been mainly political; others, it has been social and recreational. The political work is usually managed through the Bicycle Action Committee, one of the standing committees. This group has never moved mountains. But it has applied a sort of constant, steady pressure to assure that bicyclists' interests be considered when government organizations spend money.

The Bicycle Action Committee has met with success in its dealing on the local level – Seattle and King County. It has been markedly less successful in dealing with state organizations. Possibly that is because of the great amount of money required to lobby successfully on the state level. More likely, though, it is because bicycles are less visible statewide than they are locally. Politicians from the state's rural areas, where agriculture and logging interests dominate

public thinking, would be very forward looking indeed if they were to support bicycle causes. Usually they are not.

Like Cascade Bicycle Club, The Bicycle Paper came out of the early seventies idealism. Started by Chuck and Peggy Steward, it was originally called The Great Bicycle Conspiracy. The Stewards now smile at the thought of all the great dreams that were incorporated in that splashy beginning.

But The Bicycle Paper is still alive in 1980. It's not a newsletter and it's not one of those government-subsidized educational projects. It is a viable and functioning business, sustained through subscriptions and advertising. Its readers have learned about the progress of bicycle projects, such as the Burke-Gilman Trail. They have gotten information about touring in the Northwest. They have read about the work of the area's framebuilders (most of them started work in the early seventies, too). In 1977, they read about the USCF National Championships, which were held in Seattle. In 1975, they read about the opening of the Marymoor Velodrome. There have been meeting notices, race results, and calendars of events.

It would be wrong to create the impression that Seattle is the center of all the activity in the Northwest. A current list of Northwest bicycle clubs and organizations shows fifty-seven separate groups in Washington, Oregon, and Idaho. Work being done by Portland and Eugene activists rivals the work being done in Seattle.

Bicycling is a major activity in this corner of the United States. It is especially so in the urban areas where the numbers of cyclists are great enough to allow them to get together for races, rides, political activities.

If anything can be said to characterize the bicyclists and the bicycling organizations in the Northwest, perhaps it is that they provide a helping hand to people who need a gentle nudge, who need to be reminded that it's possible to get there on a bike if it's possible to get there at all. The political work that they do is strictly amateur; it gets done in fits and starts. The glue that holds everything together is the act itself, the process of pushing on the pedal and rolling forward.

There now seems to be widespread agreement that there's only one way to change society's mind about the relationship between the automobile and the bicycle: People have to ride their bicycles. Lobbying, dropping leaflets, and writing books are useless activities if the public never sees bicycles on the road. The whole process of making change happen begins when one person sees another person doing something he had thought was impossible.

Photograph by Paul Boyer

NORTHWEST RAIN

Once I was at a meeting where people were discussing bicycling facilities. On one side was a group of merchants who opposed spending money for bicycle transportation. On the other side were some bicycle commuters and planners. One of the merchants stood up and said that people can't ride bicycles in Seattle anyway because the weather is so bad. It was January, and I had ridden my bicycle to the meeting. There was light rain.

I've lived in places where weather stops bicyclists, places where snow and ice cover the streets from December through March, where the temperature stays below 0° F. for a month at a time. Seattle isn't like that. There's rain, no doubt about it. But it's usually gentle rain. No thunderstorms, no howling winds (well, maybe an occasional howling wind). It's usually just a cloud moving through. Quite often, cyclists get wet and cold, and sometimes they curse (or so I've heard) at the persistence of the rain. But they keep going, year-round, whenever they have the chance.

Under average conditions it's quite possible for a bicyclist to stay dry while riding. Nothing works better than a simple bicycle poncho used in combination with leg gaiters, and a bike cap to keep rain off your glasses.

Perhaps the clearest example of the way Northwesterners regard the rain happened in the summer of 1979. The occasion was the first running of the Seattle to Portland ride, a marathon event for competitive and touring cyclists. It rained hard all day long. The wind blew from the South—into the riders' faces—all day long.

There's very little chance of staying dry when weather gets that bad, and when a cyclist has to ride in the rain for 200 miles. Most people tried to keep warm and accepted being wet as a fact of life. There was no single remedy. Some riders smeared their legs and arms with olive oil; some wore Windbreakers and light wool leggings; some used wool exclusively and tried to keep bare skin to a minimum. Yet, whatever the method, people accepted the rain as a fact and did what they could to cope with it.

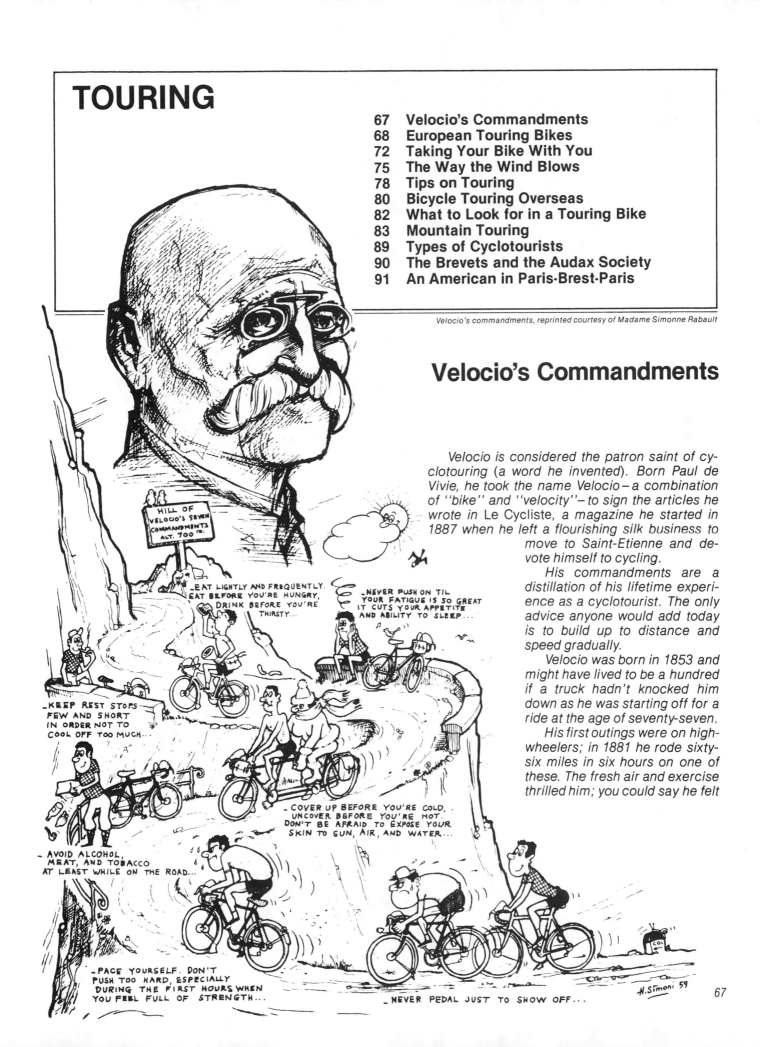

TOURING

Velocio's commandments, reprinted courtesy of Madame Simonne Rabault

Velocio's Commandments

Velocio is considered the patron saint of cyclotouring (a word he invented). Born Paul de Vivie, he took the name Velocio – a combination of ''bike'' and ''velocity'' – to sign the articles he wrote in Le Cycliste, a magazine he started in 1887 when he left a flourishing silk business to move to Saint-Etienne and devote himself to cycling.

His commandments are a distillation of his lifetime experience as a cyclotourist. The only advice anyone would add today is to build up to distance and speed gradually.

Velocio was born in 1853 and might have lived to be a hundred if a truck hadn't knocked him down as he was starting off for a ride at the age of seventy-seven.

His first outings were on highwheelers; in 1881 he rode sixty-six miles in six hours on one of these. The fresh air and exercise thrilled him; you could say he felt

67

what nowadays is called "a runner's high."

Velocio felt that vigorous riding sharpened your perceptions, made you feel refreshed and purified. Your blood circulated faster, your brain functioned better. At the age of fifty-nine he still rode 400 miles in forty-six hours.

Velocio maintained that every cyclist between twenty and sixty who was in good health could ride 130 miles a day with some climbing, providing he rode sensibly, ate properly, and had a bicycle with a long wheelbase, wide tires, and a wide range of gears. A racing bike might roll better at first, he admitted, but it would wear you out on a long ride.

Finding a comfortable touring bike was difficult. Saint-Etienne is in mountainous country, so one gear was not enough. Velocio helped develop the derailleur to solve the problem. Getting it accepted was another story, because using variable gears was considered a sign of weakness.

Velocio suggested a test that the Touring Club of France ran in 1902: Edouard Fischer, a champion racer, on a single-speed versus Marthe Hesse on a 3-speed. The course: 150 miles of mountainous country with a total climb of 12,000 feet. The woman won decisively.

Velocio's favorite wakeup ride was an eight-mile climb from the outskirts of Saint-Etienne to the top of the Col du Grand Bois. In 1922 his disciples invited all cyclists in the area to join the ride as a gesture of homage to their teacher. That was the first Velocio Day. Nowadays thousands gather once a year to make the climb, picnic at the top, and listen to speeches about this great and good man.

European Touring Bikes

Michel Delore

Translated from the French by Vera van der Reis Krausz

European cyclotouring bikes are very different from those used in North America. Of course, everything depends on what kind of tour is involved.

For half-day outings or purely athletic training some people use a racing bike.

For a one-day trip they use a bike with fenders and a handlebar bag supported so it doesn't touch the

Michel Delore *is a full-time cyclo-journalist, cycling specialist for* Le Monde, L'Equipe, Velo-Quebec, Velo, *and one of the mainstays of* Cyclo 2000, *the internationally famous cyclotouring magazine of his hometown, Lyon. Through Editions Amphora, you can get his* Cyclotouring (*health through cycling*), Ma Bicyclette (*technical initiation into maintenance and repair*), *and* Pratique de la bicyclette (*advice for the user and racer*). *He is also a contributor to Hachette's prestigious* Les Joies de la bicyclette.

Courtesy of the French Government Tourist Office

front brake cable or the wheel. (Routens' handy stem-attached gadget can take the place of this support on a racing bike.) In Europe you can find handlebar bags of all sizes, including tiny ones that are meant to only hold a light Windbreaker, a few tools, a little food. Even for a two or three hour trip, this means you don't have to stuff your pockets. It is getting harder and harder to find cycling jerseys with five pockets (two in front and three in back), and they rarely have buttonholes permitting them to be closed securely. Carrying a backpack is tiring after a half-hour or so and can cause the cyclist to lose his balance, particularly when turning.

For a trip of over two days most of our cyclotouring bikes have clinchers, racks for panniers both in the

Departure for Around-the-World Tour. Courtesy of Michel Delore

front and in the back, fenders, and generator lighting. According to the model (and the price!), they have five, eight, ten, or fifteen speeds.

We think European bikes are the best in the world because of the fantastic popularity of both bike racing and touring. Nineteen thousand races are organized each year in France alone, scarcely fewer in Italy. There are also races every Sunday and sometimes during the week in Belgium, Holland, Switzerland, Spain, Portugal, and West Germany. Television and radio stations (sometimes all channels at the same time!) transmit the larger races live. Newspapers publish whole pages on bike races, and there are magazines that specialize in the sport. French newsstands distribute 100,000 copies a month each of *Velo* and *Miroir du cyclisme*. The French Cycling Federation publishes a monthly with a circulation of 25,000. There are also two cyclotouring magazines that have a combined run of 70,000 copies, and a technical magazine that spreads the word to another 20,000 enthusiasts.

The organization of great cyclotouring tests that require perfect equipment are also stimulants for industry. In France we organize very difficult rides that have a rather extraordinary popular success. For example, Paris-Brest-Paris (1,200 kilometers to cover in under 90 hours) had more than 1,800 starters in 1979, and only twelve percent abandoned – proof of the high level of both material and physical preparation.

We also have innumerable medium-distance *brevets* to complete in a day, such as the Pyrenean Mountain Pass Randonnée (nearly 200 kilometers, and including the most famous climbs of the Tour de France) or the Randonneur of the Alps (260 kilometers and five climbs, including one of 2,700 meters, and a total of 4,600 meters of elevation). In 1979 this event attracted 5,000 starters, and another 5,000 were turned back. I must emphasize that these are not races; all the finishers, from the first to the last, receive the same medals.

Therefore the European public is very well informed and very demanding about the quality of equipment.

The Metals

For frames we recommend drawn steel tubing of high quality. You can choose between Reynolds (British), Supervitus and Vitus (French), Columbus (Italian), and Tange and Ishawata (Japanese). Get it at least 6/10 millimeters thick. If the weight of the rider is over 75 kilos (160 pounds), get 7/10 millimeter. In ordinary tubes the mechanical advantage is less and the weight more, so thickness is not a problem; those tubes are always from 10 to 12/10 in thickness.

Titanium has no utility in bicycling. It is very expensive because it is rare, and is heavier than Dural (light aluminum alloy), something many people don't realize. A titanium frame, just like a plastic one, lacks rigidity and cannot be recommended for traveling with luggage.

Steel cranksets with cotter pins are the most widely diffused in the world, so replacing parts is easy off the beaten track. But light aluminum alloy has numerous advantages for the real cyclotourist: It is more esthetic than steel, lighter, and doesn't rust. Besides the crankset, it is a good choice for brakes, seat post, rims, and hubs. But get a steel freewheel. A light alloy freewheel can only be recommended for time trials; the steel ball bearings wear it out very quickly (after 1,500 to 2,000 kilometers) and the inside is more apt to crumble; so keep to a steel freewheel.

Gearing

One can still see fifty-two teeth in the front and fourteen in the rear of an assembly-line bike, even in Europe. This is too big, except for playing at being a racer. Competition chainwheels like this must be forbidden in touring. For the front, choose a double chain ring (50 and 38, for example) or better yet, a triple (50 x 42 x 30). As for the freewheel, we recommend starting with fifteen or sixteen teeth and going at least as high as twenty-four. This gives a low gear of about 2.50 meters (32 inches) with both 650c and 700c wheels. This type of gearing means that the cyclotourist will never be at a loss on a climb. Remember that even in areas lacking high mountains one can run across a short but very steep hill. We think that for the "honor" of the cyclotourist concerned, as well as for the good reputation of the bicycle, it is preferable that the public see people riding rather than pushing bikes up hills as often as possible! So insure yourself against bad surprises by getting a triple put on. Racers don't like them because they displace the right leg by a half-centimeter since the axle of the crankset must be a half-centimeter longer than for a double. But in

France there are tens of thousands using this system with success and pleasure, without any mechanical problems or hindrance in pedaling motion. In 1966 the first two finishers of Paris-Brest-Paris used a triple; they did the 1,200 kilometers in 44 hours and 20 minutes. In 1971 De Muynck lowered this record with an 18-speed bike. Brest is in Britanny, where hills are numerous, steep, and long. Besides, at the end of hundreds of kilometers fatigue makes even short hills feel like mountains.

In the name of justice we should remember that it was the cyclotourists and not the racers who caused progress in bicycle technology. The cyclotourists used multispeed bikes as early as 1906. Paul de Vivie, nicknamed Velocio, who is considered the patron saint of cyclotouring, traveled with his friends on bikes with sixteen speeds! (A range of 2 to 10 meters – or 25 to 125 inches.) It took until 1937 for the derailleur to be accepted officially in the Tour de France, and the double chain ring didn't make its appearance until 1947. Racers mistrust innovations.

We prefer the triple plateau to the double because the double does not allow a large range of gearing, and forces you to use two or three very large, heavy, and ugly cogs. To avoid chain crossover you really only have eight usable speeds. With a triple you only have twelve, but with twelve speeds you have a real cadence regulator, which permits you to maintain your pedaling rhythm as the slope changes. Naturally, you must also get derailleurs that can handle large gear changes (a rear derailleur with a long arm like Huret's Duopar).

Fenders

We recommend full fenders. Using the horizontal position for reference, they should rise to the middle of the wheel and have an apron on the bottom to keep rain off the feet. Aluminum is infinitely preferable because it is stronger.

Spokes

On a normal wheel there are usually thirty-six. We recommend forty or up to forty-eight on the rear wheel to add security and minimize breakage. These spokes should also be thicker than usual.

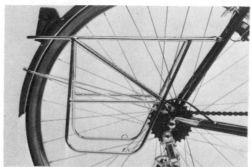

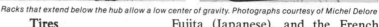

Racks that extend below the hub allow a low center of gravity. Photographs courtesy of Michel Delore

Tires

Use tires at least 28 mm wide; 35 mm are even better. The majority of bikes have 700c wheels, and tires 35 mm wide are sometimes hard to find because they are principally mounted on tandems, and tandems are still rare. 650c wheels allow use of tires from 35 to 40 millimeters wide. The bike frame should permit one to place these smaller wheels (if changing, check that the brakes still land on the rim). 35-40 mm tires are called "half-balloon."

Saddles

The plastic saddles on the majority of mass-produced bikes are completely unsuitable for a long outing. They are too hard, even if covered with foam. Of course, there is foam and foam! Plastic foam is no good whatever, but latex foam is very good, and European professional racers use it often – the Ideale 2002 saddle won the twenty-one-day Tour de France twice with Thevenet on it.

Even the best racing saddles are too narrow for cyclotourists. A racer's weight is mostly on the pedals and on the handlebar; besides, a racer spends a large part of a race standing on the pedals. This is not the case with tourists, or with urban cyclists who use their bikes to do errands and to go to work. On an upright utility bike almost all the weight of the body is on the saddle and the rear wheel. In cyclotouring, with the hands on the upper part of the handlebars, seventy-five percent of the body weight rests on the saddle; it should therefore be wider, shorter, and more comfortable than a racer's.

Leather, a living material that in time takes on the form of the posterior of its habitual user, is recommended. There are three world-famous brands: Brooks (English),

Fujita (Japanese), and the French Ideale, whose "90" and "92" have already been oiled and partially broken in by hand, eliminating hundreds of painful miles of breaking in on the road.

Lighting

A dynamo system is indispensable. Its main advantage is to have lighting always available. It does have three drawbacks; it slows you down a bit (one-sixteenth of a horsepower, according to a dynamo manufacturer), at high speed you risk the bulbs burning out, and at too low a speed (climbing at 7 km/h, for instance) the bulb lights neither the user nor the road brightly enough. So, while it's a very useful and inexpensive lighting system, it is not enough. In Europe we supplement it with battery-powered lights, a very bright torch-lamp in front – so strong that a car facing us has on occasion flashed its headlights, which meant the driver was blinded by our light – and in the back a battery lamp to guarantee being seen by drivers in all circumstances – including when not moving.

Flashlights can be easily removed from the bike to help with a nighttime repair or to light up a camping site. It is prudent to carry extra batteries, especially if you have to ride at night for a long time, or if you're riding in a region where there aren't many villages. Buy long-life batteries; they are more expensive but more dependable.

Carrying Baggage

Without a doubt the best solution is to carry bags laterally (panniers). We're always astonished that in many countries, particularly in North America, people attach bags to the top of the carrier, making the rear wheel even more weighted down. From the previous discussion of saddles, it is clear that this system is not rational on a bike.

Racks are an integral part of the frame design of a good cyclotouring bike. Mass-produced bikes are often only built for short outings and have no such provisions brazed on. Your safety on one of these is not guaranteed if you carry much over twelve kilos (twenty-four pounds) of baggage. Descents on a loaded bicycle are particularly dangerous. An American study of touring accidents found that over seventy-five percent of all fractured bones occurred on the downhills. Day tourers and riders covering the same route with sag wagons had far fewer accidents. Racing-type bicyles, which are not designed to carry weight other than the rider, may develop a sort of shimmy or machine clatter 'at the front. This can also happen on an improperly designed or poorly a-ligned machine. Fear can make this situation worse, causing the rider to grasp the handlebars too firmly. Shimmy can sometimes be stopped by placing the knee or hand against the top tube.

Use side racks for panniers; buy them ready-made if you can, have them made, or make them yourself. These racks are a kind of rectangular metallic grill. It is of prime importance that they be made of steel wire six to eight millimeters thick, and that they be screwed onto the eyelets of the fork-blades and the rear drop-outs, not the fenders. Their bottom should extend below the hub to assure maximum stability to the bicycle and to keep the saddlebags from getting caught in the spokes.

The center of gravity of the bags should be found in the plan of the fork (the smaller the trail of the fork and the steeper the steering angle, the higher and farther the load must be from the center of gravity of the bike and the rider). The tops of the bags should be no higher than two-thirds of the diameter of the wheel.

Saddlebags should be of coated nylon; it's waterproof and rotproof. Its only drawback is that it doesn't hold its shape when not loaded, a fairly minor disadvantage since saddlebags don't stay empty long. Nylon saddlebags seem more sturdily sewn than cotton ones.

Pack two-thirds of the baggage on the front wheel, or chance having the bike rear up like a motorcycle trial bike or a BMX! This is most likely to happen in a low-gear situation. The weight of a motorcycle rider with hands on the tops of the handlebars (also the cyclotourist's favorite position) is mainly on the rear wheel, so don't burden this heavily stressed wheel any more than you have to! The back wheel is also the driving wheel, so tires wear much faster than on the front wheel; don't aggravate this tire wear and spoke strain further.

Another point in favor of putting more weight on the front wheel: It's better to push than to pull. Don't confuse the size of saddlebags with their weight; you can have large bags in the rear but put light things in them; what's important is the weight distribution.

Steering is obviously more difficult with the bike loaded this way, but at the end of a few kilometers you get used to having more weight on the front than on the rear, and it doesn't stop you from taking a hand off the bar for a few seconds to signal a turn. A driving mirror helps make it unnecessary to turn your head, something that's always hard to do when a bike is heavily loaded. Before the big departure we suggest you take a few short trips to get used to handling the loaded bike, and to make final adjustments. After which we wish you Bon Voyage!

Courtesy of the French Government Tourist Office

Taking Your Bike With You

John Dowlin

If properly introduced, clean lightweight bicycles and clean modern transit, both public and private, can hit it off. To insure a full and attractive partnership, however, more research is needed on how to get bicycles and crowded trains, buses, and planes better equipped and designed for one another. What needs to be overcome is the contradiction between a loaded bicycle that is easily maneuvered and a heavy box plus baggage that isn't.

Clearly, innovations are needed at both ends: Public transit must be designed to accomodate passengers' *wheels* —bicycles *as well as* wheelchairs and baby strollers. Conversely, passengers' wheels must compact or collapse quickly and easily to occupy a minimum of space when catching a lift or when being stored at work or home.

Catching The Bus

The nice thing about buses is that they go virtually everywhere, serving the smallest towns and most rural areas.

The bicycle policy of most small rural bus companies is usually left to the driver's discretion. Often the driver is also the company president! Generally speaking, the smaller the bus line, the more helpful and obliging to individual passengers and their baggage. Bikes are accepted as baggage on almost all buses as long as the bus is not too crowded and there's space below. This is the policy of Transport of New Jersey, for example, which is currently the largest privately owned commuter bus company in the United States.

Among the major carriers, Greyhound will carry bicycles as checked baggage, provided they are carried in a "wood, leather, canvas, or substantial carrying case, which does not exceed 8 by 32 inches or 60 inches, and which is securely roped, strapped, tied, or otherwise fastened." Greyhound accepts a bi-

cycle as part of the regular baggage allowance of two checked pieces per person. To ship a bicycle as package express, it must be similarly enclosed so that the sum of the extreme measurements of length, width and height is 141 inches or less, with the longest measurement 60 inches or less.

Trailways and the Canadian Voyageur line policies are pretty much identical to Greyhound's, which makes the subject of a suitable bike bag an important one.

Bag It!

For both folders and regular-size bicycles a lightweight, preferably opaque bike bag is surprisingly useful, particularly if the contents can pass as something else, a French horn, for example. One should assume that there will always be a driver or a conductor or an assistant purser who is unaware of his company's policy. For this reason, and in the absence of an affirmative letter from the management, a bike bag that does not say BICYCLE is preferable. A number of excellent commercial bags are available in Japan and Europe, and

Drawings by Bob Thomas

at least one in the United States. These are expensive, but so is your time and peace of mind. Homemade bags of burlap or nylon are usually acceptable. If large enough, recycled mail or sail bags might also work. In the Netherlands, tulip bags are popular.

Cyclists who are traveling long distances or sending their bikes as express baggage will probably want to box their bikes for maximum security. Bicycle boxes, usually in two sizes, are available at most bike shops for no charge.

The long box, easier to pack but harder to carry, requires that the bike's front wheel and seat be removed, the handlebars turned (or removed, depending on the style), and the pedals reversed, i.e. removed and rescrewed so

that they're tucked in. The short box requires that both wheels be removed and placed on either side of the frame, along with the handlebars, seat, and pedals. Small loose parts and components should be taped to the frame or carried separately.

John Dowlin *is the founder of the Bicycle Network, an international news exchange pool, and editor of* Network News, *P.O. Box 8194, Philadelphia, PA 19101.*

Mail Your Bike

Probably the cheapest and simplest method of shipping a bicycle long distance is by United Parcel or Federal Express, if you don't mind dismantling your bike to fit into a carton measuring 108 inches combined length and girth, or 100 inches combined for Parcel Post.

The Airlines

A few years ago, the Boston Area Bicycle Coalition surveyed the major airlines and found that almost all of them carry bicycles as part of the regular baggage allowance, and many provide their own bags or cartons.

Like the bus lines, the airlines require that a bicycle be checked in a suitable package with the wheel(s) removed, the handlebars turned, and the pedals reversed. Occasionally they'll accept an unpackaged bicycle, contrary to policy. As a rule, it's a good idea to let the air out of your tires to prevent a blow-out at high altitudes.

While most airlines are accomodating, a number of domestic airlines now charge a bicycle fee, so it's worth calling in advance and patronizing the airline that tries hardest!

Small, lightweight folding bicycles, such as the Bickerton, the Micro, and the Pocket, can actually pass as carry-on luggage, provided they're tightly folded and bagged.

As for insurance, airlines usually treat bikes like baggage, and reward about $750 for loss or damage. Additional insurance can be purchased at the ticket counter if necessary.

Bicycles can also be shipped as air freight, although at prices much higher than via bus or train.

By Boat

Probably one of the nicest connections a bike traveler can make is by boat or ferry. The Vancouver Sea Bus on weekends and the Staten Island Ferry any time of day are two outstanding urban connections for touring as well as commuting cyclists. There are hundreds more, and cyclists can usually make the connections without much difficulty.

Prior to a long distance tour, it's a good idea to check out water crossings in advance, as well as the *rates for bicycles.* The latter should be investigated if only to insure that the boat does in fact carry bicycles, as most boats do, on the lower level(s) with vehicles, if not on the main deck. But there are always exceptions, so it pays to do some homework.

A number of directories are available, many of them at no charge, which list boat schedules and fares. Canada's "Ferries, Bridges, and Cruises," an excellent resource published by the Canadian Ministry of Industry, Trade and Commerce, is available at any Canadian

Waiting for the Ferry. Photograph by Bernard Thompson

government tourist office. Just give them a call and they'll send you a copy. The booklet lists by province the fares, schedules, operating season, capacity, and restrictions of every ferry, bridge, and cruise in Canada. The charge for bicycles on bridges operated by the Niagara Falls Bridge Commission, for example, was ten cents in 1980. Welcome information, not so much because of the fare, but because it alerts cyclists to an alternative should the local ferry have reversed its position on bicycles (which that ferry did!).

In the United States, travelers should contact individual state tourist offices; the most up-to-date information on water crossings is available state by state. Alaska and Washington are two states which publish separate guides to their boats and ferries. The United States Travel Service, it is hoped, will eventually

publish a national directory similar to Canada's. For cruises, the "Official Steamship Guide International" (published by Transportation Guides Inc. in Westport, Connecticut) is the most definitive source. This is a monthly publication used by travel agents and can be found in most libraries. Other sources, always dependable, are national cycling organizations such as Bikecentennial and American Youth Hostels. If they can't help you with a specific crossing, they'll put you in touch with local cycling clubs that can.

Of course the simplest method, tried and tested in dozens of countries, is to ask at local stores and gas stations in advance. A boat's schedule and fares are usually common knowledge within a fifty- or one-hundred-mile radius.

Getting a Lift

Hitchhiking with a bicycle is always possible and sometimes very necessary. One way to do it, if you need a ride in a hurry, is to hold up your front wheel. In Europe this is a familiar signal used by cyclists wanting a ride up a mountain, and it could catch on quickly in the United States, with a little roadside practice! A cyclist holding up a front wheel tells a motorist that there's a problem: a flat tire, a departing ferry, an approaching thunderstorm, road construction, mountains.... In most cases a motorist will stop, particularly truck drivers or cars with empty trunks or rear bike racks.

Another good way to catch a lift — with or without your bike — is through Travelmate, a national ride board that operates from Portland, Oregon. Utilizing a computer and a toll-free phone (800-547-0933), Travelmate puts regis-

Touring Mid-Wales. Photograph by Bernard Thompson

Bike tour leaves 30th Street Station, Philadelphia. Photograph by Gihon Jordan

tered riders and drivers together almost around the clock. Individual membership is $25 for six months ($40 per year) and entitles you to service, as either a rider or driver, between 7:00 A.M. and 7:00 P.M., six days a week. A registered driver about to travel cross-country, for example, will call in for a rider (and often will continue to call in after departing) in the interest of sharing the expense and driving. If there's room for a bicycle, no problem. Membership in Travelmate is a good back-up for bicycle tourists and is also useful for one or partway portions of a tour. Travelmate now has more than 100,000 members, including 2,000 private pilots.

Bikes On Cars

Probably the most common way of traveling with a bicycle in the United States or any other automotive society is by car, and the increasing number of rear bike racks on cars is evidence of this. Indeed, during the summer in popular resort areas, on Cape Cod for example, one gets the impression that one out of four cars is so equipped, and that in a few years, given the rising cost of gasoline and auto maintenance, perhaps all cars will carry bicycles much as sailboats carry dinghies. For commuters, "park and pedal" could become as familiar and convenient as "park and ride."

A roof rack, while not the most convenient, is definitely the safest for expensive bicycles, because the bike is less likely to be damaged in the event of a front or rear end collision. Almost all roof racks, whether commercial or the homemade two-by-four variety, attach to the roof gutters, some better and more safely than others. As Raymond Bridge puts it in *The Sierra Club Guide to Bike Touring,* "racks that depend solely on hooks that pull against the gutters are not safe, either for bikes or for other users of the highway. Each support for the rack should have a sturdy leg that rests in the gutter and holds up the rack, with a hook that screws in from the side to hold the leg firmly in place. All the hardware should be very sturdy; wind and inertia can exert fairly large forces on a rack full of bikes."

Rear bike racks, of which there are now about a dozen on the North American market, are in most cases preferable for the average bicycle, and they're certainly easier to use – less lifting. To secure a bike onto most rear racks, a few bungie cords are adequate plus locks, of course, where there's more than bumps and wind.

Train Your Bike

In the United States, "training" your bike isn't easy. Unlike Canadian and Mexican National Railways, Amtrak requires that all but folding bicycles be boxed and carried on only those trains that have baggage cars. Why the 1980 policy?

In the mid-1970's, Amtrak incurred as much as $17,000 in claims for damaged bicycles in a single year. Amtrak's management was confronted with the choice of discontinuing all provision for bicycles or instituting a policy that would be more practical from their standpoint. A consulting firm was hired and the box policy adopted, effective May 1, 1979. The new policy provides for transporting bicycles at no charge, but requires that bicycles be enclosed in an Amtrak or owner's bike box and checked as Amtrak baggage. Cyclists are required to dismantle and box their own bicycles, using their own tools and tape, with the weight of a boxed bicycle not to exceed 75 pounds. Boxes are theoretically available at most Amtrak stations. When they're not, and you haven't a box of your own, you're out of luck.

The obvious problems with Amtrak's box policy are the hassle and expense to cyclists, considering that any Amtrak passenger is allowed as much as 150 pounds of carry-on baggage at no charge. The snags, specifically, are the following:

• Temporary storage of boxes at Amtrak stations is not provided, nor is the box easily preserved and carried by bicycle for use on the return trip.

• The sale/no-rental policy promotes a nonreturnable box that often ends up as litter.

• The policy requires that boxed bicycles be checked, preventing cyclists from personally loading and storing their cycles in the available space at the end of most Amcoach cars.

• Checked baggage must wait for a baggage car, in short supply with Amtrak. As few as 282 baggage cars are in use – or disuse – on the entire Amtrak system.

Is there any hope for the "trained" bike? Yes. The League of American Wheelmen constantly reviews Amtrak policies and welcomes constructive suggestions from touring and commuting cyclists. Correspondence should be addressed to: LAW (Attention: Amtrak Project), P.O. Box 988, Baltimore, Maryland 21203, U.S.A.

Travelers in Canada and Mexico have it easier, because the bicycle policy for both VIA Rail (the National Canadian Railways) and the National Railways of Mexico is to carry bicycles on all trains with baggage cars at no extra charge. Once again, cyclists should check in advance on the availability of baggage cars.

Photograph by Bernard Thompson

The Way the Wind Blows (Especially in the USA)

Tom Cuthbertson

Wind, the invisible element, is disregarded by most travelers. But to the cyclist, wind is of the utmost importance. A stiff tail wind can increase speed by 50 percent. A strong head wind can reduce the cyclist to a blithering, dead-tired mess. When planning a bike trip of any distance, try to psych out the wind beforehand. This isn't easy. But you can at least learn what the prevailing winds are in a given area, and then learn some of the basic things about local thermal and terrain-controlled winds, so that you can make educated guesses as to which way the winds are

going to blow, before you get out and tangle with them.

First, remember the general rule that winds blow least early in the morning, and most in the early part of the afternoon. If you are making a loop ride, in other words, ride against the wind in the morning, and let the increasing prevailing wind blow you back toward home in the afternoon.

To learn what the prevailing winds are in your area for any given time of the year, look at the appropriate map of the United States on these pages, check the arrow next to the city nearest you for the prevailing wind direction,

then look at the little sunburst around the city to see how often the wind actually blows in the prevailing direction. The sunburst rays have nothing to do with the sun. The rays point out the wind directions. The number in the middle of the sunburst tells you what percentage of the time during the month there is no appreciable wind at all. The length of each little ray of the sunburst tells you how often the wind blows *from* the direction in which the ray points.

Some examples will make things clearer. Let's pretend you live in Brownsville, Texas, and you want to go on a ride in July. Turn to

Tom Cuthbertson *wrote this piece for* Bike Tripping, *one of the great presents Ten-Speed Press has given bicyclists. For their other gifts to cycling, see "Our Own Bookshelf."*

Maps by Rick Morrell

75

the July map of the United States and find Brownsville, the southernmost town in the country. Look at that prevailing wind arrow. You are obviously not going to want to ride twenty miles or so out of town to the northwest, then turn around and have to struggle against the wind all the way home. Brownsville doesn't lend itself to long rides to the east, because of the water there, but you might try riding down into Mexico a ways, then letting the wind blow you back up to town. If you live in Brownsville, you won't be able to count on having any completely calm days during July, because the little number in the middle of the sunburst shows that it is dead calm only two percent of the time. And that might well be at night. So for short, twenty-mile or less country escape trips around Brownsville, or towns like it with very lopsided sunbursts, leave early in the day and ride first *toward* the wind, in the directions that the long sunburst rays point. Then you can sail home with the wind.

If you are planning a long trip north from Brownsville in July, such as up to Corpus Christi or even up to Austin, you can tell that the wind will be behind you all the

way. The prevailing wind arrows for Austin, Galveston, and Corpus Christi all point to the north, and there are virtually no sunburst rays pointing to the north from any of these cities.

For a somewhat more difficult example, look at the wind map for April, and pretend you live in Boston. The prevailing wind is neither strong nor constant in its direction. For this sort of wind condition, it is best to limit country escape trips to short rides, early in the day, and to areas where there are alternate routes, so you can shorten any ride if it gets unpleasantly windy. One way to avoid most of the wind problems around places like Boston is to ride into the prevailing wind and uphill on your way out on any trip, then you can come back downhill without much trouble even if the wind does turn and blow against you. For longer trips, try to break them up into short, forty-mile segments or less, and ride in the morning. Also, try riding in small groups, so each of you can take a turn at the lead, while the others "sit in" right behind, taking advantage of the leader's draft.

There are some areas where the winds blow in opposing direc-

tions. Take Phoenix, for instance, on the July map. The prevailing wind is not only weak—it isn't the main wind. The most common winds, according to the sunburst rays, are the one that blows from the east (this wind happens to blow during the night and early morning), and the one that blows from the west in the afternoon, especially on those hot summer days. Now, there's no way you can tell *when* the winds blow from the different directions by looking at the wind maps, but in cases like Phoenix, the surrounding terrain gives you a tip-off. Phoenix is in a valley, surrounded by mountains. On warm days, the slopes of the mountains and steep upper valleys heat up first, before the valley floor. Air rises off the mountains, and by afternoon wind is being sucked up from the valley to fill the gap. Breezes like this, known as "valley breezes," are common in many hilly parts of the country on warm afternoons. At night, the mountains cool quickly, and the valleys stay warm, so air rises off the lower valleys, and cold mountain air rushes down the slopes to fill the gap. These "mountain breezes," or *katabatic*, or drainage breezes occur during the

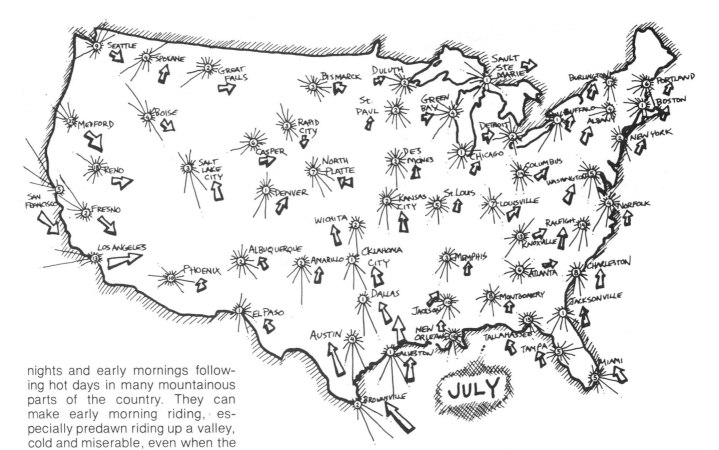

nights and early mornings following hot days in many mountainous parts of the country. They can make early morning riding, especially predawn riding up a valley, cold and miserable, even when the daytime temperatures in the same area are high. If you live in an area that has local wind conditions like those in Phoenix during the warmest parts of the year, you may want to ride from eight to twelve in the morning, instead of earlier.

Sometimes there might be a calm period just before sunset for riding. Otherwise, try to do your uphill riding in the afternoon, and your downhill trips during the early morning, in order to keep the wind at your back.

Another example of winds that blow diurnally in opposite directions can be found in coast towns. Turn to the wind map for January, and look at Los Angeles. There are winds blowing from the west and the east, according to the sunburst rays. The west winds blow in the afternoons, and the east winds blow in the night and early morning. These are the familiar land and sea breezes. During the day, the land heats up faster than the sea, air rises over the land, and the wind blows in from the sea to fill the gap. These onshore winds blow strongest between noon and three or so in the afternoon. The offshores blow as the land cools, between sunset and eight or nine in the evening. So if you want to avoid the breezes, ride in the morning, or just before sunset. Remember, too, that these coastal breezes can appear even when the prevailing winds indicated on the map are different. In Charleston, for instance, on the July wind map, the prevailing winds are from the south. But onshore and offshore breezes can be expected as well.

The fact is, the wind is the result of an infinitely complex interplay of different factors, only a few of which are described here.

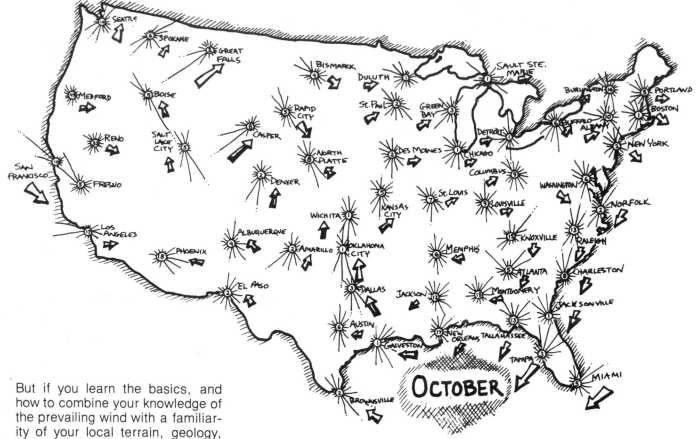

But if you learn the basics, and how to combine your knowledge of the prevailing wind with a familiarity of your local terrain, geology, and daily heat changes, you can make fairly educated guesses as to which direction the wind is going to arrive from, and plan your bike trips to keep it coming from behind you.

One other way of keeping one step in front of the wind is to phone ahead. If you are going to ride a long distance, or drive some distance out of a town and then do a lot of riding, call a friend who lives in the area, or call the local police or fire department, or Coast Guard if you're going to be near the coast.

Tips on Touring

Hartley Alley

Packing list. Make a list of everything you take on tour. After the tour is over place an X next to every item you did not need or use. This list then becomes the model for your pack list for subsequent tours.

Travel light. Get yourself a postal scale and weigh every item that you intend to take on tour. Record the individual weights on

---

Jean and Hartley Alley *have led tours, founded touring clubs and the famous Hilly Hundred Weekend, and cycled in North, Central, and South America and Europe. They shifted from careers in photojournalism to fill the need for quality touring equipment by designing and manufacturing it themselves. The tips printed here come from their bike catalog. For a copy write Touring Cyclist Shop, 2639 Spruce Street, Boulder, CO 80306.*

your packing list. This will help you to think light. If you eliminate ounces here and there, you'll soon get rid of pounds. After just one day of steep mountain roads in Guatemala I mailed home seven pounds of not needed items.

Secrets of packing bicycle bags. It's just common sense. Keep the heavy things low and toward the center of the bike. Us old wizards of touring have two other secrets–rubber bands and plastic bags. Roll each piece of clothing into a tight roll and secure with a rubber band to keep it compact. (Wrinkles will shake out of double-knit stuff.) The plastic bag serves several purposes. It is waterproof and dirtproof. Plastic bags are slippery –you can cram more things in. You can also label as to contents and thus not leave things behind.

Rain protection. Hard-driving rain will seep through zippers and seams on any make of bicycle touring bags. The answer is simple. Line each pocket and compartment with a good, thick plastic bag. This will not only keep your clothes from getting wet but will make it easier to slip things in and out of the compartment. You'll pack faster in the morning.

European bike shops. Contrary to what you'd expect, bike shops in Europe are apt to be very basic, quite often only equipped to handle repairs on 1-speed "transportation type" bikes. You'll find them friendly and helpful, but they just won't have the parts and tools. After many tours and mechanical failures, we've come to believe that you need to be independent–and prepared. Before you leave home you should have your bike completely overhauled. (To get tender loving care you should do the job yourself.) And you should have new tires, new tubes, new brake blocks, and all new cables. For spare parts and tools you should carry: two inner tubes, tire levers and a patch kit. Six spokes, spoke wrench and freewheel remover. Two brake blocks, one rear derailleur cable and one rear brake cable. Small screwdriver, chain tool, 6" crescent wrench, 4" crescent wrench, and the proper Allen wrenches. If your bunch rides together, one set of tools will do for a

Windy touring in the Flat Fenland, Lincolnshire, England. Bernard Thompson

whole gang. Of course, each cyclist should have a complete set of spare parts. Added note: Twice on tour I've broken a toeclip. You'll find it very hard to ride with a broken toeclip. This happened in rural Mexico. I now carry a spare.

Learn the language. Everybody's heard that touring abroad is more fun if you can speak the language. It's true. You don't need to be an expert. But at least get a phrase book before your trip and work on it. I find that the most important phrase to learn in any language is this: "What do you call this in your language?" For instance, in Germany you point at an article or act out a concept and then you ask, "*Wie nennen sie das auf Deutsch?*" You're asking, "What do you call this in German?" When you get the answer you can add that word to your growing vocabulary of German words that you need to carry on your everyday existence. It's fun. And you'll get a lot of special attention and help because you are showing that you have a respect for their language and culture.

Speaking English. You can expect that many big-city Europeans will speak some English. Small town and rural people will usually not speak English. On most bicycle tours you'll spend most of your time in the country and in small towns. It stands to reason that you should make an effort to

communicate in the local language. Get out the phrase book and give it a try. You'll get to meet more people that way.

Traveling by air. Some airlines insist that you put your bicycle in a box, in which case you have no choice. Other airlines will accept your bike as it is – just as it stands. After some twenty-five plane trips with a bike we believe that your bike is less apt to get damaged when it is not in a box. Not knowing what it contains, a baggage handler quite often will give rough treatment to a boxed bike. On the other hand he will be more apt to show respect for your shiny, clean bicycle if he can see it and roll it along. If you're worried about scratched paint, put some tape or padding on the most exposed spots.

Bicycle Clubs and Touring Groups

The best way to learn more about the fine points of cycling is by joining a club. You get the benefits of the combined knowledge of the members. We are members of the following clubs. We endorse, support, and participate in their activities.

The League of American Wheelmen

A well-organized national group, established 1880. Many benefits; monthly magazine, directory of members (25,000), patch, decals, group accident and life insurance, na-

tional and regional rallies. Write to LAW, P.O. Box 988, Baltimore, MD 21203.

International Bicycle Touring Society

Has ten or more tours per year in Europe and U.S. Sagwagon, good hotels, experienced leaders. Expensive touring but worth it. Directory of members (1,000), patch, schedules, and info sheets. Write to IBTS, 2115 Paseo Dorado, La Jolla, CA 92037.

Cyclists' Touring Club

England's national cycling club (29,000 members), established 1878. CTC provides touring info on British Isles and Europe, suggested tours, directory of accommodations (for bed and breakfast, hotels, hostels), ferry and train tips, repair shop list. An invaluable connection for Americans. Excellent bimonthly magazine. Write to CTC, 69 Meadrow, Godalming, Surrey, England G07 3HS.

Bicycle Touring Overseas

Clifford Graves, M.D.

Dr. Clifford Graves, a California surgeon, returned to cycling when his commanding officer decided the patriotic way to save gasoline was to come to the base hospital on a horse! Later in World War Two he escaped from a Nazi Panzer division on a lightweight bicycle he just happened to have packed in his ambulance. In the fall of 1964 he invited friends and fellow cyclists to join him on a tour of New England. Writers, artists, executives, and professional people came from all over the world. They had such a good time that before they disbanded they formed the International Bicycle Touring Society, which owes its continued success to the volunteer leaders who so carefully scout the rides, and, no doubt, to Dr. Graves' enthusiastic leadership.

Although my first bicycle tour overseas was hardly an unqualified success, it made a lasting impression on me and in a way opened a new life.

In the fall of 1942 I had been sent overseas with a medical unit, and we were quartered in Cowley Barracks near Oxford. Gas rationing had eliminated practically all motor traffic in England in those days. Watching hundreds, nay thousands of Oxford citizens on bicycles pass in review, I decided that this must be the way to travel. When I could stand it no longer, I went to Halford's on the High and bought a bicycle. Not a very good one. Good bicycles were no longer being made. But a bicycle nevertheless.

Old as it was, this bicycle gave me so much pleasure that I formed a bold plan. Oxford is 60 miles from London. I would ride my bicycle to London, stay overnight, and return the next day! Unfortunately, the late November rains fell without interruption for weeks on end. Finally, a few days before Christmas, the sky cleared and I was off. Never have I felt such anticipation. The challenge, the adventure, the freedom. Everything was new and unknown.

The start was auspicious. Favored with a strong tail wind, I kept the pedals spinning merrily. Progress was smooth, elegant, restful. Thatched cottages and vine-clad homes dotted my route. The fields spread a carpet of greenest green. Here and there a clump of beech trees beckoned me on. I was tasting a country that poets have praised for centuries.

At the Chiltern escarpment, I had a rude awakening. The road started to rise. The sun was blotted out. The fog rolled in. I felt a few drops of rain. Visibility was cut to a few hundred feet. The rain increased. Totally unprepared for this revolting development, I stopped and sought shelter under the canopy of a bus stop. How much farther to London? I studied the map. Holy smokes.

I wasn't even halfway. Maybe a bicycle wasn't so wonderful after all.

"Can I help you?" The voice came from a fellow cyclist who had joined me under the canopy. I told him of my plan to ride to London. He shook his head.

"London is a long way. Better have a cup of tea at my house. It's just around the corner."

I accepted eagerly because I knew that I would find no restaurants until I got to London. We turned into a side street, stopped at a neat house, and entered after parking our bikes. A fire was going in the fireplace, and we sat down. Presently, my new friend's wife came in. She brewed us a pot of tea, and we chatted. I was discovering the fellowship of the road.

The tea revived me. Refreshed, I said goodbye and faced the rain once more. It stayed with me the rest of the day. Slowed by wet roads, unfamiliar territory, and creeping fatigue, I limped down Oxford Street in London in almost total darkness. I did not have a map, but I had been told that all roads lead to Piccadilly Circus where the Piccadilly Hotel would surely have a room for me. I was aware of people around me, but I could not see them except through a veil. Blackout regulations had made a ghost city of London and moles of its citizens. Occasionally I could see the cat's eyes of a bus at arm's length. Completely unnerved, I relied more on my ears than on my eyes. At long last, I found myself on Piccadilly Circus and groped for the door of the hotel.

In contrast to the unreal blackness outside, the lobby was bright with light and alive with people. A long line had formed at the reception desk. I joined the line but became more and more apprehensive. These people were all terribly correct and important. By comparison, I was just a tramp. How was I to conduct myself? Before I could decide, I was shoved into the confrontation. Can I have a room here? The clerk gave me a disdainful look. Do you have a reservation, sir? Well, no. Sorry, no room. Next!

Slowly I walked out. Leaning against the massive walls of this imposing hostelry on which I had pinned all my hopes, I tried to figure out what next. Cabs whizzed by. Buses loomed up. People brushed past. They talked and laughed just like people do everywhere, but they were separated from me by a heavy curtain. Apparently, everybody knew where he was going. I was the only one lost. What was I doing here anyway? The rain came down harder than ever. An air raid alarm sounded in the distance. People started running. Then all motion stopped. I was trapped. Not only trapped but abandoned, forsaken, betrayed. Sweat poured down my brow.

"Can I help you?" An air raid warden!

I explained my problem.

"Ah — . You should go to the American officers' club on Jermyn Street. Here, I'll show you how to get there."

Rescued at last.

I tell this little story because it illustrates the fortunes of the bicycle traveler so perfectly. First, the lure of the open road. Excitement, high spirits, a spurt of energy. Then the sobering reality. Rain, fatigue, cold, shivers, hunger, tension, weariness, imminent defeat. You go limp. Eventually, the reprieve. How marvelous. And how mindless to forego all this fun for the sake of a car. A car has its place: to go somewhere quickly and effortlessly. But as an instrument of travel? Sterile.

So what advice do I have for the person who wants to use his bicycle for travel in distant lands? It seems to me that he needs advice on where to go, what to take, and how to find his way.

Where to go? A bicyclist needs highly specific conditions: quiet roads, attractive towns, a varying landscape. These can be found in limitless quantity in the countries of Europe, particularly northern Europe. I would put France first, then England, the Low Countries, Germany, Switzerland and Austria. The Alps are gorgeous but only for the experienced. The same can be said for the Norwegian fjord country. Personally, I avoid Italy. Even in the most remote areas, drivers start blowing their horns at you a mile away. Spain in the summer is hot in the interior and mobbed on the coast. As for eastern Europe, it peters out long before you reach the Bosphorus.

I want to stress that the highways of Europe are just as noisy, smelly, and debilitating as ours. Heavy traffic eats you up. If I have one bit of advice for the bicyclist, it is this: Stay on the little roads.

What to take? Your own bicycle. Rental bikes are not satisfactory. If you must rent, at least take your comfortable old saddle with you. Clothes? Cycling is best done in shorts and a jersey, which can be of cotton, wool, or a material like banlon. For cold weather, add a nylon, unlined Windbreaker. For wet weather, add a cape. Shoes should have hard rubber soles for non-slip contact with the pedals. Tennis shoes are not suitable because the soles are too soft. It is now possible, using drip-dry materials, to be neat with one shirt, one dress, one pair of shoes, one coat, one pair of slacks, etc.

How to pack? Here is my system. First, I write out what I think I am going to take. Then I spread all the articles on the

Map Reading on tour in Yorkshire, England. Bernard Thompson

table in front of me, and I weigh everything. Down to the last ounce. When I get to 15 pounds, I stop. The rest is ballast. I now put every article in its own plastic bag and secure the bag with a rubber band.

How to find your way? Before you can make an intelligent choice, you need to know the basics of European geography. First, get a general idea of a country and learn the names of the regions. Then, get a detailed map of the area you plan to tour. A detail map is a map on a scale of about 1 to 200,000. You buy them in a local bookstore. In England, ask for the Bartholomew series, half inch to the mile. In France and the Low Countries, ask for the Michelin maps, scale 1 to 200,000. In Germany, ask for the SHELL Generalkarte, scale 1 to 200,000. Many people think that Europe is full of bicycle paths. It is not. The only country that has such paths is Holland, and you never find them unless you use the special maps, scale 1 to 100,000, issued by the Dutch Touring Club, 5 Museumplein, Amsterdam. Without maps like these you will never find the little roads you are looking for.

For the first-timer who is not sure of himself and wants to take it easy, I suggest a tour of the Cotswolds in England or the chateau country in France. The chateau country can be combined with Brittany. A second suggestion is the area just south of the Austrian Alps, from the Lake of Constance to Salzburg. You will be traveling in southern Bavaria. Avoid the direct route through the valley of the Inn. It is too crowded.

For the person with some experience, I suggest the Lake district or the Yorkshire Dales in England. In France, the Juras and the Vosges. In Germany, the Black Forest. In Luxemburg, the Ardennes. These are all hilly. Remember that you will be riding a loaded bicycle.

For the tiger, I recommend the Pyrenees, the Norwegian fjords, and of course the Alps.

Whereas a conventional tourist spends most of his time in the capitals, a cycle tourist spends most of his time in the country. Still, you want to see a little of the glamour too. For sightseeing, make up a list of places and go there by train. You can park your bicycle at the station.

Where to stay? Hotels are plentiful, but expensive. ''Pensions'' cost less, and are equivalent to our tourist homes. Or you can stay at a youth hostel and sleep in the dormitory (but not in Germany and Switzerland if you are over 25). And for nothing at all, you can pitch a tent. However, there are some drawbacks to a tent. First, you need extra equipment, which is heavy. Second, you spend much time shopping, cooking, cleaning, and packing. Third, rain. Most cyclists would rather spend a little extra money for a roof over their head.

Inn in Slaidburn, Lancashire, England. Bernard Thompson

HARK TO BOUNTY

How to meet other cyclists? The best place is at the rallies. These are put on by the national organizations, to which you should write for details. In England, the York rally is organized by the Cyclists Touring Club, 69 Meadrow, Godalming, Surrey. The date varies. Lately, it has been the last weekend in June. The York rally is mostly a spectator event. In France, the national rally is organized by the Federation Française de Cyclotourisme, 8 rue Jean-Marie-Jego, Paris 75013. Date and place vary. It is a riding rally, as opposed to a spectator rally. Another interesting event that attracts thousands is Velocio Day in St. Etienne. Write to the Chambre Syndicale du Cycle, 7 Karl Marx Boulevard, St. Etienne for the date. Finally, there is the international rally of the Alliance Internationale de Tourisme, or AIT. For information, write to the chairman, Leslie Warner, CTC, 69 Meadrow, Godalming, Surrey, England. The address of the AIT is 9 rue Pierre Fatio, Geneva, Switzerland.

How to get your bicycle on the plane? For years, this was no problem. You just handed over your bike at the check-in counter. But lately, the airlines have been getting skittish, and they have a point. A bicycle is an awkward package. Today, I use a plastic bag that encases the entire machine and keeps it from scratching other baggage. No dismantling. The advantage of a bag is that the baggage handler can see what he is dealing with.

The other method is the carton. A carton has several disadvantages. First, it requires that you dismantle the bike. Second, it is an encumbrance when you get to your destination. Third, the carton gets thrown around because nobody knows what's in it. Even after many flights, I am still a little uneasy about my bicycle in the hold. Damage can happen, but fortunately it is rare. Don't lose your temper at the check-in counter. And don't call up beforehand. You always find yourself talking to an underling who gets rattled.

In summary, a bicycle tour overseas is a great adventure. But it is even greater if you do your homework first. Get thoroughly acquainted with your bike. Take it on a shake-down cruise. Tame your saddle. Use low gears. Take only what you need. Study the map. Read a book. Get primed. You will have the time of your life.

What to Look for in a Touring Bike

Clifford Graves, M.D.

Comfort is the first consideration, not speed. To begin with, the frame should have a long wheelbase and more rake in the fork to absorb road shock. Unfortunately, racers have determined what the modern American 10-speed would look like, and they need a more upright frame for quick maneuvering at speed. Since they were often the only cyclists willing to pay for quality, their requirements have been met.

The new high-pressure clincher tires, while suitable for short trips on good roads, will shake you to bits on the rougher scenic roads that are universal once you leave the highways of Europe and the rest of the world—including America. You need a tire with about seventy pounds of pressure, not ninety. Even

Photograph courtesy of Dr. Graves.

if I wanted to use high-pressure tires, I wouldn't get wheels with rims that restricted me to them. I'd want to be able to put on a heavier tire. Tubulars are completely unsuitable, since they are almost impossible to find away from the big cities.

The new thick handlebar covers are a big help in preventing pain in your hands and shoulders and pay for themselves in no time, because they eliminate the need for special bike gloves that are so expensive and so easy to lose.

Besides being designed to absorb road shock, a touring bike should have fenders, carriers, and lights. Brackets for these should be brazed on at the time of manufacture. Only too often accidents occur because fittings are put on as an afterthought. Someone may be perfectly competent to build a bike from scratch and not have the expertise to braze on fittings. That is because fittings are very

For light but bulky packing. Courtesy of Michel Delore

thick, and the tubing is very thin, so getting the temperatures just right and not weakening the frame is a real problem. The solution may be to have the bike store import a touring bike for you. They are standard equipment in France.

You should have the advice of an experienced bicycle tourist in helping you set up the bike to fit. Many people have the seat too high or too low. Then they try to copy the racer's aerodynamic position, with the stem two inches lower than the seat. I have my stem as high as my seat.

French Touring Bike. Courtesy of Michel Delore

This permits me to see the road without straining my neck. I use randonneur handlebars, which have a little rise so that I can use a handlebar bag and still have room to move my hands.

Handlebar bags should rest on the front carrier and have solid support so they don't flop around. The higher they are, the more they interfere with steering. A third of the total baggage should be carried up front; the rest divided among the rear panniers. The load must be carefully distributed for safe riding.

All this weight means you need wide-range gearing; a fully loaded touring bike is a completely different animal from an unloaded one.

Bike riding in any new situation calls for great alertness—animals may stray across your path, or traffic may go in the opposite direction, as in England. You have to be careful not to go into automatic, and keep telling youself, "Stay on the left, stay on the left," when you enter an intersection. New Zealand also has British-style traffic and very few cars. I highly recommend New Zealand for its scenic beauty, but it's a long way to go for a bike ride.

—Clifford Graves, M.D.

Mountain Touring

John Haigh

Just as being able to make a left turn is the mark of an accomplished urban cyclist, a safe mountain descent remains the test of a competent cyclotourist, for it is while descending a mountain that most serious touring accidents occur. John Haigh's experience climbing passes both in Europe and on our Bikecentennial trail qualifies him to give advice on how to enjoy both climbing and descending mountains. John has toured the Alps and the Rockies and is one of the stalwarts who does hill-climb racing every fall. He is secretary of OCD, the Ordre des Cols Durs (League of Hard Climbs), and was kind enough to share his insights and photographs with us to initiate us into what is perhaps the most challenging form of touring.

Many of us think that cycle touring is at its best in places with long climbs to high summits. Here we find scenery that towers over human efforts and makes the road look trivial. There is the challenge of climbs and the exhilaration of fast descents. Tremendous contrasts are encountered when riding from valleys in summer heat up to heights in arctic conditions and back again in a few hours. The most dramatic of my own experiences of this was in the Oregon Cascades where forty minutes of fast descent raised the temperature by 50°F, taking us from snowy wastes to semidesert.

This was on the transcontinental "Bikecentennial" ride, which provided the first experience of cycling among high mountains for several thousand Americans. Usually with little or no difficulty they reached their highest summit at over 11,000 feet above sea level, emphasizing on a grand scale that hills and mountains are not a barrier to cycling, but instead are a source of enjoyment. Admittedly, in Colorado, the grades were quite easy, as they were rarely steeper than 5 percent; but, curiously enough, other major mountain ranges also have many roads with well-engineered climbs. For instance, the European Alpine climbs are rarely steeper than 6 to 8 percent (except in Austria where it can be up to 20 percent). It is often the more minor mountains that have the really difficult ascents, such as the English Lake District where anything between 20 and 33 percent is common.

The perfectly smooth roads of the Bikecentennial route in Colorado are not always equaled elsewhere. In Norway and South America the more remote areas have gravel or hard-packed earth roads.

Here, slower climbing and shorter mileages are inevitable, but have their advantages, leaving more time to enjoy the scenery. Indeed, harder areas usually have the increased natural beauty that comes with wild conditions. Thus we can argue either that the riding provides few problems or that the harder

Photograph by John Haigh

stretches have the most enjoyable views and the quietest roads. However, both ways it is wise to plan ahead so that you cover the areas as easily and safely as possible, whatever conditions Nature throws at you.

PLANNING

Apart from being advisable, much of the planning for a tour should be pure enjoyment as you anticipate the sights from the maps you have bought. Get the best maps you can, ideally with heights of summits and valleys marked. Scales of two to three miles to the inch are ideal, as they give all the details required without needing too many sheets. Good maps give a clear idea of the effort needed, where food and accommodations are available, and the quality of the road surfaces. Even more detailed maps are needed if you use tracks and paths, in which case you would have to plan almost as for a walking tour.

The most important rule of planning is to stay within your known capabilities, assuming that we are talking about a holiday rather than an endurance test! More ambitious rides can always be done once you find that easier plans are achieved with time to spare. Mountain cycling benefits more from experience than most other branches of the sport. For instance, the mighty storm clouds or fresh snow that so enchance your holiday memories and photographs are also enemies to be treated with respect. Perhaps

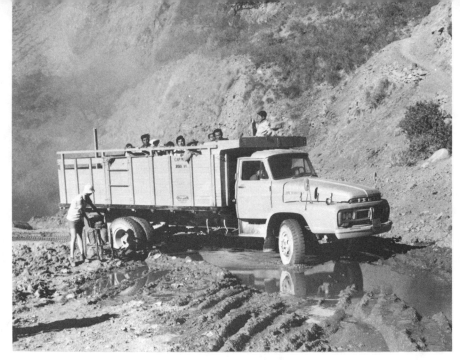

Touring Bolivia with Lightweight Tricycles. Photograph by Martin Purser

you will be remote from help, so take enough supplies to be able to meet likely problems such as bad weather, lack of food for sale along sparsely populated roads, and the breakdowns that can occur on even the best-maintained machines. We should emphasize the most common problems only, as you can usually get help from passing vehicles in an emergency. Emergencies should be very rare if you have prepared properly. There is no sense in taking too much luggage because it causes more problems than it solves.

Assuming, as we should, that you already have some experience of cycle touring in easier conditions, aim to cover only about half to two thirds of your usual daily mileage. Also pay attention to the

height gained on climbs that you see on the map. Three thousand feet gained in a day is enough climbing for the inexperienced or even the moderately fit cyclist, while ten thousand feet will be a hard challenge for anyone.

SOME SUGGESTED PLANS

In the United States you cannot do better than to follow part or all (2,000 miles) of the western half of the Bikecentennial route over the Cascade and Rocky mountains. The climbs are mostly well graded and run through much superb scenery. The Bikecentennial Organization (P.O. Box 8308, Missoula, Montana 59807) supplies detailed books and maps that tell you all you are likely to want to know.

A good place to start in Europe is in the Alps among the French, people who know about and respect cycling. A good cross section of the area can be seen going south from Aix-les-Bains (rail connection from Paris) to Nice. Michelin maps at about three miles to the inch cover the route. Some suggested stops: Grenoble, Briancon, Izoard, Cayolle, Col St. Raphael. There are plenty of small hotels and campsites all along the route, particularly where place names are underlined in red on the recommended maps. Obviously the ride can be done in reverse, but for the beginner the climbs are better split up by stopping places for food and accommodations in the southward direction. As these details are

On the Bikecentennial route. In the snow at 10,000 feet. Wyoming. John Haigh

given in metric units, it is easy to work with the figures available and adapt them to your capabilities. Thus you can expect to cover as many kilometers (km) in the mountains as you would miles in flat country.

The route includes 7,700 meters of climbing on gradients mostly easier than 9 percent and is about right for a week on a first mountain tour. Other scenic areas for tours include the (Italian) Dolomites, (French and Spanish) Pyrenees, and the (French) Massif Central, on the European mainland; the Scottish Highlands, Wales, and the northern Pennines in Britain; and the Sierras in California for an earlier or later season tour in the United States. Note that many mountain areas are only open for a few months each summer. For instance, early June to late September are the limits for the French alpine route suggested earlier.

THE MACHINE

For a mountainous tour you need a machine with the right components and one that has been proved to be reliable with a good day's ride. Everything should be in a comfortable position and the various mechanisms well adjusted. Otherwise the first steep hill that you find will cause you to wrap the chain firmly around the rear hub, or provide other problems that could have been detected, and put right, before the tour.

We will start, as most tours do, with the climbing, and here your choice of gears will go a long way toward deciding how much you enjoy the tour. It is easy enough to spend three-quarters of the riding time on climbs. In most conditions a very strong rider should have gears down to about 40 inches, and the less fit down toward 30. Below that, nature has provided a 24-inch (your own two feet!) ratio for the steepest or loosest-surfaced roads. Two possible combinations are suggested below.

Gear Ratios in Inches for 27-inch Wheels

STRONG RIDERS

CHAIN	COGS				
RING	14	17	20	24	28
52	100	83	70	59	(48)
40	(77)	63	54	45	38

AVERAGE OR TANDEM RIDERS

CHAIN	COGS				
RING	14	17	21	25	30
46	93	76	61	52	(41)
36	(69)	57	46	39	32

Each of these combinations allows two choices while riding most ratios; either move the front changer to get a large reduction of gearing, or move the rear changer to get a finer adjustment. Gear ratios shown in parentheses may be usable, but do not work efficiently because the chain crosses at a severe angle. The suggested gearing combinations require a large capacity rear mechanism to accommodate the different lengths of chain on the various ratios. Most manufacturers produce such a mechanism but they are rarely fitted to new machines.

Now that our gears have got us to the summit it is time to consider braking equipment needed for safe descents, particularly for use in bad weather and on tandems, both cases where safety margins are much reduced. First of all each wheel needs a separate brake for use together in emergencies to minimize the chances of skidding. There is a wide choice of brakes for rims and hubs. Taking rim brakes first, it is unlikely that you will be able to stop on a steep descent in the rain with a combination of hard-rubber brake blocks and chrome-plated rims! Use soft rubber blocks and aluminium alloy rims. At a higher price than average ones, but well justified for a heavily laden machine, it is also possible to get chrome-leather brake blocks that work nearly as well in rain as in dry conditions.

Well-designed brakes of side-pull, center-pull, or brazed-on designs are all adequate, with the best performance coming from the last because they are the most rigid. Before starting a mountainous tour, new brake blocks, brake shoes, and cables should be fitted.

The author pushes his tandem up a hill. Photo by Christine Haigh.

13,500 feet up on the Bikecentennial trail in Mount Evans, Colorado. John Haigh

Hard going in the English Lake District. Photograph by John Haigh

Tandems generate so much heat at the brakes that a third and even fourth mechanism of disc or drum type can usefully be fitted. These are fully enclosed and therefore work well in rain. They can also be run hotter than rims because there is no adjacent tire to burst. However, their main advantage is to spread the heating problems on long descents.

Tires, especially rear ones, wear much more quickly in mountainous country than on the flat. Thus a new pair should be fitted before you start and then exchanged, back for front, before there is serious wear in the back tire. It is important to use an adequate front tire as punctures can be dangerous on a fast descent. They cause loss of steering control as well as braking ability, and therefore a spare tire should be carried on long tours. Many tires only last about a thousand miles on a tandem rear wheel or 1,500 on a single machine, so plan accordingly.

Sufficient tools and spare parts are needed for mending punctures, shortening a chain, removing wheels, and repairing broken spokes. For the latter you should have a spoke wrench and a freewheel remover for use in a vice (available at most garages). Other tools are less necessary and probably not worth the additional weight unless you are one of a group. Then you can share heavier tools and spare parts such as spare freewheels and axles. Obviously, the more remote the area you visit, the more spares and equipment you need.

LUGGAGE

After over gearing, luggage is the second factor most likely to deter a rider from making a second tour in the mountains. Please don't take the kitchen sink, or even the metal bucket once seen by the author! Unless you are camping, fifteen pounds in a saddlebag or small pair of rear panniers is more than enough for a month's tour. Only then will you climb and descend happily unaware of your luggage. Even camping, which the author does not favor in mountainous areas because of the extra bulk and weight, should not increase the basic load beyond twenty-five pounds, and will need at least a five percent reduction in the gear ratios suggested here, to keep your working rate equivalent to the lighter loading plan.

Weight should be fixed firmly to the machine, never – repeat never – on yourself. This keeps climbing

smoother and easier and allows the use of the efficient riding methods we'll recommend later. Having the weight as low as possible improves control while riding fast descents. Keep the weight down in both senses of the word to enjoy your tour.

FOOD, DRINK AND SALT

Energy needs for cycling increase dramatically with long or frequent climbs. Indeed, cycling in the mountains is the ideal excuse for gluttony, as it is difficult to eat too much. To eat little and often is ideal during the ride. After a few days, evening meals tend to get bigger; there are plenty of true stories of tourists eating a meal in one restaurant and then going next door to another and starting again.

Always carry some food with you so that you can eat before hunger becomes a serious problem. Running out of energy on a long climb is extremely unpleasant, particularly as it makes progress to the next food supply very slow. It is also remarkable how quickly this phenomenon, known as "bonk" in Britain, disappears as soon as you eat – certainly much quicker than you absorb sugar into the bloodstream. However, although the trouble is partly in the mind, it is always a huge physical barrier. Put more positively, a steady supply of food and drink during a ride makes the range of a fit rider almost limitless.

Thirst is another danger; you can lose a lot of moisture in a day's ride, and water needs to be replaced as you go, otherwise you will drink uncomfortably large

Along the Bikecentennial Route in Colorado. Photo by John Haigh

amounts in the evening. It is a good plan to carry two water bottles on your machine in hot weather. If you need to use purifying tablets, one bottle can be treated (this takes about half an hour) while you drink from the other. Salt, while obviously very necessary, can be absorbed quite adequately in moderate amounts with meals. Extra tablets should rarely be necessary, and in fact they are best avoided because they dry you out.

RIDING

A good rule for a long climb, whether on tour or in competition, is to start at a pace that feels easy. Thus you keep tiredness for the end of the day, if at all. Riding uphill should not require a lot of force on your knees or the pedals. A comfortable gear ratio is 10 to 15 inches lower than for the same gradient met on a shorter climb. It is efficient to ride mainly on the saddle, holding the tops of dropped handlebars and pedaling fairly quickly, say 70 to 80 revolutions per minute. Use only short spells of standing on the pedals (holding the bars near the brake levers) for a relaxing change of position or for *short* steeper sections such as hairpin bends. Even the latter can often be ridden more easily on quiet roads by swinging out wide. Riding off the saddle, especially into a wind or on a well-loaded machine, is a waste of energy. If you feel the need to be off the saddle for long periods, you are using too high a gear. Ultimately, if you have no lower gear left, as on a very steep or loose-surfaced road, then walking is perfectly reasonable, and is an excellent idea early in the day, particularly. Anyway, you are supposed to be on holiday!

A steady effort with few stops is preferable to a series of punishing bursts and the rests which are then required. A slower, steadier climb keeps you comfortably warm. Surprisingly little clothing is needed for climbing, even when snow is lying in banks on both sides of the road.

Sooner or later even the longest climb comes to an end and the summit provides a good opportunity to eat and drink. (Put warm clothing on first, though.) By eating at the top you avoid having to climb

New Stony Farm. Exmoor, England. Courtesy of Rough Stuff Fellowship

with a full stomach, and anyway the view should be worth stopping to see. Many major road passes have a cafe on top, although you should have taken the precaution of bringing some food with you.

Descents can be very cold because of the high speeds and the absence of work. Thus a windproof jacket, which can also serve as your rainwear, long trousers, gloves, and hat may be needed. Take particular care to protect knees and chest against the cold. Turning the pedals occasionally will help keep the knees warm and you might follow the habit of cyclists in the Tour de France who put newspapers or polyethylene bags down the fronts of their jerseys.

The brakes provide the opposite problem by getting very hot. All the energy you have gained earlier in the work against gravity has to be lost as heat by the brakes or, if you go fast enough, by wind resistance.

Alison Purser, president of the Women's Tricycle Association, on a 12,800 pass in Bolivia. Martin Purser.

A long and steadily graded descent on a single machine can usually be achieved without the rims overheating but, with a tandem, or more generally on very steep drops, some pauses are needed to let the brakes cool. If, as suggested for a tandem, you have fitted three or four brakes, you can alternate between them to spread the heating effects.

The first rule in getting down safely is not to go beyond what you can do confidently. As a general guide to speed, you should be able to stop comfortably short of visible obstructions with only one brake. Bear in mind some of the unexpected hazards commonly met on descents, such as piles of gravel at bends, holes in the road, unlit and badly surfaced sections in tunnels, and animals. When descending fast you should move well out from the side of the road, particularly in crosswinds. Quite often it is possible to overtake motor vehicles, but make sure you have plenty of speed and braking power to spare when you do this. There are few sensations more exhilarating than a fast descent on a well-engineered road. Even though quite cautious, the author has averaged 37 mph for seven miles on one Alpine pass.

A fast descent has the advantage of providing strong air currents, which cool the brakes as well as providing wind resistance. The latter applies particularly if you

Snow sheds in the Austrian Lake District. John Haigh

sit well up. Descending slowly makes the brakes much hotter. Stop occasionally and check the rims or hub brakes and, if too hot to touch, let them cool before continuing. These delays are almost inevitable with a tandem on long descents, but such pauses are not necessarily wasted time, because it would be a pity to rush through the scenery you came to see.

Long and sharp bends are a common feature on mountain passes. Most of the braking should be done before entering the curve. As you lean over, raise the pedal facing the inside of the curve to

avoid scraping it on the road. Greater care is needed in bad weather because it is then much easier to skid, and rim brakes become less effective when wet. Keep squeezing the brake levers to clear water off the rims during the flatter sections so that you are sure that they will work when needed. In dry conditions avoid harsh braking, because this seriously shortens the lives of tires and spokes. Smooth and gentle braking on both wheels is the ideal method.

THE CLIMBERS

A group of really "converted" riders has formed the Ordre des Cols Durs, originally a French organization, which now has an English-speaking branch. The basic activity of the club is the compiling of annual claims which add up the summit heights achieved. There are several ranks of membership according to the rider's total claim, starting at 50,000 meters for an ordinary member and culminating with a "venerable" at one million. The club also has a magazine, occasional weekends, and an information service that currently deals mainly with European climbs. Further details are available from the author at 39 Delahays Road, Hale, Altrincham, Cheshire, England, who would particularly like to hear from riders interested in founding a United States branch.

The enthusiasm of members is obvious from details received with the claims. For instance, multiple claims for individual mountain roads have been made for hill-climb races (warming up and then racing) and, on one occasion, by a member who left his pajamas at a hotel and went back up a whole pass to collect them! Meanwhile other members have accumulated huge claims by tremendous feats of endurance, such as covering the thirteen major climbs of the English Lake District in one day. Another rider did a detour off a 400-mile tourist trial just to include a nearby climb. Obviously there are many levels of interest less ambitious than these, but they are all witness to the lure of mountain scenery and the personal sense of achievement in completing long climbs.

Beside Lake Thon. Photograph by John Haigh

Types of Cyclotourists

Jacques Faizant

Translated from the French by Vera van der Reis Krausz

A *cyclotourist* cycles leisurely. He visits museums, churches, castles, and so on. He is also often a photographer, and stops every two miles to get a snapshot, which considerably bothers any randonneur who happens to be with him.

A *randonneur* cycles for the sake of cycling. Being on a bike is the main part of his fun. Of course, he looks at the scenery, and appreciates the sights, but he doesn't stop every now and then to pick flowers or look at a little birdie.

A *cyclosportif* is a guy who, deep in the bottom of his heart, regrets not having become a racer when he was still young enough. Accordingly, he dresses himself in a racer's outfit (even if his belly is a little bulging), uses a racing bike with tubulars instead of clinchers, and pedals at full speed as long as he can. (And some of them can go far and fast!)

The cyclosportif despises the cyclotourist,

Stopping for Postcards in Yorkshire, England. Photo by Bernard Thompson

Jacques Faizant *is almost as well-known in France for his love of cyclotouring as for his political cartoons. His books have won several prizes for humor, and we know of no funnier or more insightful works about bicycling than his* Albina *series, published by Calmann-Levy in Paris.*

Touring on the Isle of Jura, off the West Coast of Scotland. Bernard Thompson

whom he mockingly calls "contemplatif." In turn, the cyclotourist despises the cyclosportif, whom he calls "couraillon," which is a very disreputable word for racer.

The quarrel between these two philosophies has been going on for a long time in our little world, as long as the quarrel about the use of 650 or 700c wheels, the use of clinchers or tubulars, and the easiest side to climb to the top of Mount Ventoux.

The randonneur is the sensible fellow in the middle. He seldom stops, seldom races, but nevertheless, can do both when he feels like it.

Actually the word "randonneur" is used for both cyclotourists and randonneurs. There are so many jokes about people loitering in the fields with their bikes at their sides, that cyclotourists prefer to call themselves randonneurs to keep their morale high.

Human nature, you know!

The cyclotourist uses a rather heavy bike with 650c tires, the randonneur uses a "randonneuse" which is a lightweight bike with 700c tires (clinchers) and fenders. The cyclosportif uses a racing bike with tubulars and no fenders. When it rains he is covered with mud from head to toe, but he loves it.

89

The Brevets and the Audax Society

Jacques Seray

Translated from the French by Vera van der Reis Krausz

The normal way to start bicycling (the term cyclotouring indicates a higher level) is simple and spontaneous: you take your two-wheeler, choose a road, and set off. Some time later you ride with a friend, then with a group – and you're on your way to perfecting your technique. In every country where the bike has its place, that's the order in which things happen.

Countries differ from each other, however, in the maximum distance or speed one can imagine achieving. By this, we mean the intensity of physical challenges. Of course, competitive racing is an option everywhere. If you're young, and have cycling talent, you can devote yourself to confrontations that give rise to a debauchery of effort; with success comes status and classification. But wearing a number, even if you're strong and swift, may not thrill you. The ambience of competition, with its permanent rivalries and the necessity of training during the week, is not to everyone's taste.

Not all countries have alternative systems that encourage development of physical capacities to a high level. Here in France we have found a formula that permits everyone to devote oneself to an elaborate form of cycling that is, nevertheless, not competitive. These are the *brevets*.

The idea goes back to 1890 and the first federation that ruled cycling in France, the UVF. As soon as the bicycle had begun to have a following, it launched its *brevets* of fifty and one hundred kilometers. At that time, when people first learned the use of the bicycle, the idea of the *brevet* as a proof of having pedaled a great distance was completely natural. This idea has survived to our time, with some improvements and a great many participants from every social and professional group.

Two types of brevets now exist in France, the *randonneurs,* where you

Jacques Seray, *the secretary of the Audax Association, explains some of the variations in cyclotouring in France. He often contributes both photographs and articles to the society's journal.*

choose your own speed, and the *audax,* where you ride in a group at a set pace. The classic distances are 200, 300, 400, 600, 1,000, and 1,200 kilometers, each distance to be finished in under a certain number of hours.

The distances are progressive and placed at a fixed date on the calendar. The first outings of 200 kilometers usually happen at the end of the winter. People aren't in shape yet and, after all, participants range from nineteen to seventy years in age. We even have a few eighty-year-olds.

The 200-kilometer outing gives beginners a chance to find out whether they can cover this minimal distance. A month later we offer 300 kilometers, and some cross this new frontier with apprehension. A little later in the season are 400-kilometer tours with fewer participants. Some years there are 500-kilometer challenges, and occasionally the great *brevets* of 1,000 and 1,200 kilometers, such as Paris-Brest-Paris.

The originality of the Audax brevet is that it is done in a group at a uniform speed. What is this speed?

Modern roads and materials permit quite a number of cyclists to keep going at 22.5 kilometers an hour. 20 kilometers is too slow, except in mountainous country, and 25 is wearing. The natural physiological speed seems to be 22.5, and that's how it was chosen.

The principle of a fixed median speed may seem a bit odd. Racers never know at what speed they are going to cover their ground. How do the Audax groups do it? The road captains' job is to regulate the speed. Habit is such that they often arrive on time without having to look at a watch. If there is a secret at all, it's in the choice of gear. It mustn't be too high; 42 x 18 is the standard Audax set-up, but knowing how to spin is an art, so most cyclotourists use 45 x 18 or its equivalent.

The wisdom of the Audax formula is to offer frequent stops to permit eating and recuperation. According to the distance of the *brevet,* these occur every thirty to seventy kilometers and last from fifteen to thirty minutes. There-

fore, those who were delayed by a flat or other mechanical problems have a chance to rejoin the group. Besides that, an hour and a half is set aside for a group meal at noon. On a 500-kilometer ride there are two meals, and many more at greater distances. An Audax group pedals, stops, eats, and pedals again. It can continue doing this for hour after hour and day after day.

What kind of ground does the peloton cover? 200 kilometers in 12 hours (14 permitted); 300 kilometers in 16 hours (20 permitted); 400 kilometers in 22 hours (27 permitted); 600 kilometers in 36 hours (40 permitted). Greater distances than that are done in stages that permit sleep.

Each participant is given a road map. The stops are also control points where cards are stamped to record ground covered.

What kinds of bikes do these *cyclos*

Monument to Henri Desgrange, founder of the Tour de France and the French Audax brevets. Audax Society.

use? In theory, touring machines adapted for probable road conditions, all kinds of weather, and nighttime as well as daytime riding. You see mudguards (duraluminum is preferred because it is more rigid), permanent dynamo lighting and lamp brackets at the front and the rear. There's no rule about all this though, so you often see cyclos with racing bikes to which plastic mudguards have been added. Some even ride without this protection, which, if it rains, doesn't please the other members of the pack too much. Audax president Guy Bossiere suggested recently that "those who don't have mudguards are requested to go sprinkle each other at the rear of the pack."

Good humor is more important than constraining rules. Only the traffic code is kept faithfully, though it is often difficult to keep right to let cars pass.

The idea of the brevet formula and the term *audax* (Latin for "audacious") both go back to an Italian railway engineer and passionate cyclist, Vito Pardo. In 1898 he and eleven companions set themselves the challenge of riding from Rome to Naples — 230 kilometers — "between the rising and the setting of the sun." Nine completed this first brevet.

Later that year he founded the Italian Audax Society, with the eagle as its symbol. In 1902 the "March of the Giants" took place. Fifty-five Audax members did 540 kilometers in 36 hours, proving that nonracers also have a lot of endurance.

One man in France noticed all this activity: Georges Lefevre. He not only managed to convince Henri Desgrange to organize the first Tour de France in 1903, but also talked him into establishing audax brevets a year later. The whole Audax movement would have disappeared if the idea hadn't traveled from Italy to France, because during the war of 1914, all the Italian Audax members belonged to a national corps of volunteer cyclists — and were almost all killed.

Today there are Audax members all over Europe, and the formula has been expanded to include walking, swimming, and rowing. If the idea appeals to you, write to Jacques Seray, residence Les Cedres, 40 rue Jean-Rey, 78220 Viroflay, France.

An American in Paris-Brest-Paris

Stephen Bauman

Steve Bauman tells how it was. Steve is one of the hard riders of the New York Cycle Club, staunch supporter of the LAW, leader of many American Youth Hostel rides, and someone well able to appreciate the organizational demands of Paris-Brest-Paris, as he is one of the organizers of the Five-Boro Bike Tour in New York City:

"Last year we had 8,000 entrants. This year we had 10,000. We have certain logistical problems the French don't have. American motorists are a lot less patient and understanding than the French if the traffic is tied up by bike riders. Fortunately, the police love the riders. All the city departments cooperate with us. The municipal authority helps plan the route. Even the Marine and Aviation Department is involved because we use the Staten Island Ferry. The most the ferry fleet can move in an hour is about 3,000 bicyclists. No one wants to wait much more than three hours to get back to Manhattan, and that limits the ride in its present form to 10,000 people."

We had the opportunity to be actors in one of the greatest plays or spectacles ever produced, the Paris-Brest-Paris race, and that in itself is a thrill. I just wish the ride weren't so difficult, so that everyone could have that opportunity.

There were 1,800 participants from nine countries. There were very few accidents, and only 16 percent failed to complete, so it was the cream of the crop in terms of the cyclists. The oldest person who completed the entire race was seventy-three. The youngest riders were eighteen; you're not allowed to be under eighteen.

Four of us went over about a week ahead of time to get our bodies acclimated to the water and climate of France, and also to get the road sense. There are subtle differences. For example, the placement of traffic lights. You can see only one light at an intersection; if you go beyond it you won't know when it's going to turn green. Arrows for directions go according to town rather than route number. The first fifty miles we had to cover had many turns, so we wanted to practice that part so as not to get lost.

We were in an area where there was a lot of training. It's close to Paris and there's a forest to ride through, so it's a nice biking area, with lots of individual towns. We often saw schoolboys cycling in a tight formation with the coach behind them—they learn to ride in a pack at an early age. Cycling is much more of a group activity in France than the individual thing it is in the United States—and the French are good.

It was cold on race day at the 4 A.M. start. The event was to be televised and the cameras were already there. My friend Max and I decided to get

Steve Bauman. *Photograph by John Krausz*

warmed up by the lights the crew had ready. As we were talking and waiting for the ride to start, the French announcer spotted us and we were on TV! He asked if we were really Americans, and if we spoke any French. We said we spoke a little, and suggested he keep the questions simple and speak slowly. He asked whether there were many bicyclists in the United States, whether Paris-Brest-Paris was well known, how many Americans had come over for the event, and how long we expected to take to finish. We told them we would be very happy to finish within the 90 hours!

IPD, a bike company with an unusual sort of transmission, sent their racing team over from the United States. Only amateurs are allowed in PBP. The IPD bikes made a sensation with a 68-tooth chain ring that absolutely shocked the French, they couldn't understand it. One of the IPD team finished second, which is a fantastic finish, so the Americans looked very good. Even our hackers finished.

Someone told me my picture was in the Brest paper, and showed it to me. It turned out to be Dick Seebode, a friend of mine from Ohio. We had Bell helmets on, so after the TV show anyone with a Bell helmet on was instantly identified as an American. The Europeans didn't wear helmets.

All the cyclists wore bike jerseys, the Welshmen had *Pays de Galles* on theirs. Because the national sport in France is cycling, bikers always wear racing clothes; so if you're on the road a motorist will give you plenty of room, because if he were to hurt you he might have hurt a national hero.

Starting was quite an experience. The 90-hour group had 1,100 people, and it rode in a tight pack for the first hundred miles. It is unusual for me to ride in a tight pack with people I don't know. In the United States you can't trust people's bike-handling skill, and if someone makes a mistake in a pack there's a big pileup. It was amazing to see so many, so well disciplined. They kept a tight pack without changing the distance between riders both going uphill and going downhill. Teams knew the speed of the slowest person so they didn't spread out and drop someone unintentionally.

The thing that was frightening to all the Americans was that tight pack going down a hill at 30 mph. People who normally think nothing of going down hills at 40 mph chickened out. One of the Americans later said, "Usually nobody beats me going down a hill, and here these guys are whizzing by me in tight formation!"

I couldn't get used to it. When I go down a hill I like to see the road, because I know there's going to be a pothole. That's from my experience in America.

The peloton broke up at the first control. After that it was catch-as-catch-can. I worked with several Frenchmen, but it was hard to hook up, and I was a little leery. I didn't know their hand signals, so I was afraid I'd cause an accident if I rode too close. If I needed a windscreen I'd catch onto the back of a pack; if more people caught on, I'd drop off the rear. I had to pay for that by taking more wind than I ordinarily would have. I wasn't in danger of not finishing, but it took longer than I had anticipated. After the second day I knew I had enough time.

The road surfaces were bluestone, a slow surface, but free of ruts and glass. It was terrible for the people using clincher tires because the tread caught on stone projections and gradually tore the rubber from the cord. Practically all of them wore out the rubber on their tires. PBP was a good test of equipment...it took a pounding!

No one had anticipated that the wind direction would change, so we had a head wind both ways; I timed it almost perfectly...I had 600 miles of head wind, mostly the first day and the third day...the third day was a killer.

The scenery was very nice. It's practically all farm

Photograph by Laurama Pixton

country. We went through a lot of forests as well. There are hills, but the climbing was a lot easier than what I'd been doing when I was training in Vermont. Climbing Roc Trevezel was one of the few times I was able to zoom past the Frenchmen. Incidentally, their technique in climbing hills is a lot different from ours. They don't use low gears to spin up. They use middle gears and stand up on the pedals and rock back and forth.

I never felt lonely; the Frenchmen, once they found out I spoke some French, were eager to find out why the devil I was there, how I found out about it, whether we had to do the qualifying rides, what it's like in the United States...so I made some friends.

Now I can see why athletes take all the pain and suffering. It's a big lift, being cheered by the people

as you go by, and waving back to the kids. There was one town where there was a fourteen-year-old boy who got his grandfather to bring him down just to see the riders, and he lived about twenty miles away. There must have been thousands cheering us on our way.

There were arrows on the ground, but arrows are hard to see at night even with a full moon. By the way, it's standard practice if you're going to organize a ride that is going to involve night riding, and you have a choice of dates, that you do it when you have a full moon. The moon gave us a lot of light, but many times we still weren't able to see the arrows. And in some towns we passed they turned off the streetlights after ten o'clock at night. Therefore some of the local residents—even some of the little children—were out there with flashlights to guide us. Everyone pitched in to help us out. They really got into the spirit of the thing.

They did a bang-up job in terms of the organization. I did not think they would be able to pull this thing off with so many people. I met Robert Lepertel, the organizer, before the ride. During the ride I saw him several times—he was haggard. He rode it in a car, but that put him out of communication. Charlie Price, the organizer of the TOSRV ride does it on a bike, but he's accompanied by a ham operator on another bike, so he's in instant communication and knows what's going on. Communication is the reason I don't ride the Five-Boro Tour on a bike...I'm in the lead police car, with radio. But they are more used to big tours in France. The cyclotourists have brevets for shorter distances—200 km, 400 km, 600 km, and 1,000 km; some of these will attract 4,000 people.

About the organization. First of all, the French Army put the arrows on the road. Then, we had a police escort for the first hundred miles. Now remember, they had three different starts, so they had three different police escorts...and I understand that in the racer's start, they made a wrong turn, and had to turn the peloton around! And that was at 4 P.M. during the Paris evening rush hour!

There were fourteen announced control points, plus three unannounced secret ones. You couldn't do any monkey business. Apparently there was a temptation, so not only was the route card turned in, but notes were taken at the individual towns so they could be checked against each other. That way they could tell that a person did not have anyone else take his place.

About one in three people had support vehicles. If they caught the support vehicle giving support further than three kilometers from the control town, the person involved was fined five hours . . . and if caught a second time, out of the race. They were not as successful guarding against that as they wanted to be, and there was some talk that for 1983 they will not allow support vehicles at all.

There were restaurants all along the way which were primed for us, and special restaurants at each of the controls. Most stores are usually closed from 12 to 2 P.M. though, and that sometimes posed a problem. People carried emergency rations and stocked up at grocery stores if there was a crowd at the restaurants.

Sleeping accomodations varied from checkpoint to checkpoint. The first night I got into town about midnight. Along with beds, there was food available. The second night I stayed in a college dormitory.

Brittany Encourages Paris-Brest-Paris riders. The Audax Society

I spent four days in Paris. Biking there is almost the same as in New York, but without the potholes or glass. You do have cobblestones. I stayed away from the Champs Elysees and biked in the outskirts of the city. Cabs don't threaten you, so it's much nicer there. Motorists have grown up with bicyclists. They took bicycling as a sport in high school, so they know what you're going through, and from what I could gather, the training they get in high school is pretty good. The caliber of their hackers is far better than what we have here. Here it's an individual thing, whereas there it's a team sport, so they're a lot less selfish both as riders and as motorists.

Jimmy Rex can now add Paris-Brest-Paris to all those ride patches. John Krausz

Courtesy of the Audax Society

They had run out of beds, but they had mattresses on the floor. The third day was the most interesting. It was probably the city hall and they had a combination gymnasium-auditorium. In one corner they had set up a cafeteria, in another corner space for the bicycles, and in the third corner they had heaped a big pile of straw, on which about seventy-five people were sleeping. They also had people who would wake you up at the time you requested. A keeper would ask what time you wanted to wake up, write it on a big piece of paper, and tell you to place it near you before you dozed off.

94

OFF – ROAD AND WINTER CYCLING

Rough Stuff

John Krausz

"Rough stuff" can range from a bicycle-assisted tramp through the woods to a combination of backpacking and cyclocross. The uncharitable describe it as "taking one's bike for a walk." Devotees take along what a hiker or backpacker takes plus a large-scale map and a compass. The compass is necessary to make a match between what you see on the map and what you see on the ground. It will also come in handy if you want to take a practice jaunt into the woods and return to the place you entered. Taking a bearing when you leave the road will save you from hunting for your gear, car, or friend on the way back.

In England there's an organization called The Rough-Stuff Fellowship, which has about a thousand members and publishes a lively bimonthly journal comparing routes and ordeals. It keeps a library of rough-stuff tracks/trails/paths/routes both for Great Britain and for the Continent.

One aim is to never see a car, and that's why "the rough stuff begins where the road ends." Routes vary from country roads to the open countryside, and include canal towpaths, fire roads, railroad tracks, and animal paths, so it can be seen why tubulars and other lightweight equipment are considered useless for this kind of riding. As it is considered illegal to ride a footpath in England, Rough-Stuffers who do so mentally work out arguments while they're riding, in case they meet the landowner. "No Cyclists" often means the local kids, not Rough-Stuffers, but in any event the worst that can happen is you have to turn back.

One of the joys is going into the countryside, riding some of the way, pushing and carrying the bike, finding a trail and being able to ride it to some delightful spot far from everything and "brewing up a cuppa tea." The bad

news is that sometimes the water you have used is the drainage from a garbage fill.

Since a ride may entail a push up a mountain so as to avoid a motoring road, it is hard to calculate how long a trip will take, what with having to ford streams, unload

Hard going at Croig, North Mull, Scotland. Bernard Thompson

A rest in the Olchon Valley. Maurice and Marion Teal, Rough-Stuff Fellowship

Glen Forsa, Isle of Mull, Scotland. Bernard Thompson

everything on the bike to get over a high fence, and dodge boulders. You might go no faster than a mile an hour in some places. So it can be a matter of fine calculation whether you can get from A to B before nightfall, "for who wants to be stranded on the side of a mountain or in the center of a large expanse of open moorland after dark?" as Archibald Woodward, editor of the *Rough-Stuff Journal*, noted.

Standard equipment is a touring bike equipped with a 3-speed internal gear and a chainwheel of about forty teeth (although there are low-gear advocates who use chainwheels that go as small as twenty-four, they have their critics who say that while that's fine in the rough, it's very, very slow in terms of getting anywhere to do some real riding). Any bicycle is deemed suitable except small wheelers and real lightweights; 10-speeds are fine. Most bikes have back racks and fenders (mudguards). The usual luggage is a large seat bag and/or a handlebar bag. Rubber pedals are used because good, stout walking shoes are far more important than toeclips. But for those unwilling to consider using rubber pedals and giving up toeclips, flat-bottom running shoes might be an alternative; these shoes are coming into use by mountain climbers for light climbing. A change of socks might not be a bad idea, and a pair of jeans might be appropriate even for the I-don't-go-anywhere-on-a-bike-without-riding-shorts person: A short trip through the bushes might save you several hundred yards of impassable ground.

Rough stuff combines the mobility of cyclotouring (in that you can get from here to there rapidly) with the special independence of the backpacker, and has the added advantage of not making you carry anything on your back. Along most trails and even in trailless country, the wheels of the bike rolling your load allows you to go faster than the unassisted walker, and easily makes up for any inconvenience caused by carrying your bike over an obstacle or through a streambed. Besides, the obstacles are all part of the game. A bike is a cyclist's best friend, and you wouldn't leave your best friend at home!

The Rough-Stuff Fellowship goes on group "rides." Many trails that would be unpassable alone become possible if there are two or more to manhandle the bikes through the really tough parts. Also, although you are certainly in no danger from cars, this kind of riding has its own dangers: Every year solitary mountain climbers and wild walkers are maimed and killed. This kind of riding becomes a test of your bike-handling skill because

of the instant retribution that the material world can take upon you because of a mistake in logic or a moment's inattention. Even the smoothest meadow may contain a rock. Of course, the slow speed is a safety feature: Hitting a rock at five miles an hour will damage you less than hitting the same rock at fifteen.

It's always a good idea to check out local conditions, so you'll know when to watch out for hunters, and where you're liable to run across drunken potshotters. And at a time when some trails are even marked "No Runners," cyclists should be mindful of the damage they might do to the ecology of certain delicate places.

There has been some spasmodic interest in trail biking in the United States, but this is not quite the same touring. Rough-Stuffers taking along their sleeping bags, a ground sheet (useful in case of rain) and as much as five days' food, prove the independence of the bicycle-sustained tourist. Once they leave the road they find many pleasant rides that the more road-dependent would never discover.

From *The Rough-Stuff Journal*:

"Ten members had a very muddy wallow along the riverside and then had to ride home through pouring rain."

"The magic of seeing a field of wildflowers."

". . . being completely alone and in nature only three or four miles from a large town."

". . . squelching up to the low pass."

". . . the track that climbs west out of the village and in wet weather doubles as a watercourse."

". . . slogging into a gale."

"My father lived here fifty years and he's *never* seen anyone come over there with bikes."

"In answer to our query as to whether we could get through on the road ahead, he was evasive, so from past experience we decided our best course was to continue, after thanking him for his no-doubt good intention. It is funny how some people are keen to encourage one to take the line of least resistance. They simply don't understand the art of 'cycling to see' and 'rough stuffing.' "

If you'd like to join, write the Rough-Stuff Fellowship, 1, The Close, Paignton, Devon, TQ4 6JQ, England.

Cyclocross

Laurence Malone

In Europe, cyclocross is a popular professional sport and wintertime conditioner for road racers. Thirty to fifty mud-drenched riders engage in mad steeplechase dashes, riding or carrying the bike over cobbles, through forests, down embankments, and across fields to the finish line--all this before large crowds and with able-bodied pit crews.

Cyclocross is off-road bicycle travel, a sometimes laughable, sometimes heroic combination of riding and carrying the bicycle, of pedaling and hoofing it. Cyclocross is more than specialized technique and equipment; it's an attitude, an approach, an assertion of greater mobility and versatility. It can be a bicycle excursion out in the wilds, away from pavement, traffic lights, and impatient motorists. Or it can be a necessary daily function in circumstances dictated by extreme weather or ground conditions.

Everyone can and should become a more proficient bike handler. It's a survival issue. Just as America, in self defense, has developed driver education, so Swiss schools conduct bicyclists' training classes. Few people realize that it is possible, for example, to mount and dismount from a bicycle at fifteen miles per hour. Or to jump curbs and storm grates. Or literally to ride down a flight of stairs. Unwieldy and cumbersome beasts to carry they are often thought to be, yet bicycles have a balance point and a handhold that allow for almost effortless transport back up the stairs, onto boxcars, across streams, and up ravines.

Laurence Malone has won the American Cyclocross Championship five consecutive times, and has twice represented the United States in the Tour of Costa Rica, a nine-day stage race. He has written for many bicycle publications and considers his BA in history from the University of California a useful tool in his work as a bicycle advocate.

The good cyclocrosser assumes any place is accessible. There is the story of one West Coast fellow who strung rope around his wheels for traction, then rode up through the slush of a mountain road carrying skis that he then mounted for the snowy downhill run on the other side, bicycle slung over his shoulder! Generally speaking, cyclocoss requires a healthy mixture of skill and humility–the humility that precedes caution, the caution that precedes a willingness to walk the bicycle. Good nerves help at the racing level, but important for any practitioner are fundamental techniques such as mounting, dismounting, and carrying the bicycle.

It is a singular joy to explore old abandoned roads or well-traveled cow paths by bicycle. With the harrowing sounds and pressures of onrushing motorists left far behind, the cyclist has enough time and space to dally and weave, to indulge any escapist impulse. Cyclocross technique not only facilitates wilderness travel, but endows one with the necessary tools to cope with such urban hazards as potholes, soft shoulders, storm grates, and high-lipped driveways. It's an important developmental stage of the complete cyclist.

Not surprisingly, most youngsters, ready to explore and take risks, are very proficient cyclocrossers. This is reflected in the fast-growing sport of bicycle motocross, where riders jump, drift, and slalom their stingray-style machines over short, tricky courses. But the skills are too often lost or forgotten, except for the few who "graduate" into motorcycle racing. Most trade in that two-wheeled mobility and expertise for a driver's license, in observance of the American coming of age ritual.

Cyclocross, like skiing, involves a certain physical flair, a balance and

Paul Boyer for Velo-News and Bicycling.
Laurence Malone *winning his fifth National Championship.*

feel for the peculiar motion, a sense of confidence. Over rough terrain, the rider must read the ground well ahead to minimize surprises and reduce the need for constant split-second responses and decisions. The rider should be in tune with his or her own physical capabilities, as well as the features and handling characteristics of the machine.

What kind of bicycle is best suited for cyclocross? I started cyclocrossing on an old, straight-gauge Italian 10-speed costing a hundred dollars, but my basic skills were developed during a rural childhood, riding a simple 1-

speed on dirt trails and roads. Both these bikes were a far cry from the typical European cyclocross racing machine. Racing demands optimum form and function.

With the classic 'cross bike, clearance and flexibility count. The bottom bracket might be one-half to one inch higher than the normal road bike, critical on rough, undulating terrain. Extra clearance between frame and wheels allows for mud build-up, increased fork rake adds flexibility and a softer ride. Fingertip shifters give better control in rough conditions than the usual down tube affairs.

The seat is farther back, to place more weight over the rear wheel and thereby increase traction. A shorter stem makes this possible. Cantilever center-pull brakes, mounted on bosses brazed to the forks and seat stays, provide tremendous braking power and are not so readily clogged with mud as normal caliper brakes. Sew-up cyclocross tires are a happy compromise of durability, lightness, and traction; the rear features a knobby, "sculpted" tread, the front a wide-profile one. Each weighs between four and five hundred grams.

Such technological wonders are by no means imperative to enjoying cyclocross. Any bicycle will do—only a few modifications are necessary to provide greater safety, speed, and comfort. The 20-inch stingray models have evolved to a sophisticated level of engineering—we now have superlight motocross bikes capable of handling most any terrain. Their range, however, is limited, and most adults do not fit comfortably on a 20-inch wheel bicycle. For simplicity's sake, we will discuss later the various forms and modifications possible to the basic 10-speed design.

Every cyclist encounters moments requiring split-second decisions and responses. Though the hazard or condition generally determines the nature of the response, its effectiveness is ultimately dependent on the level of rapport between rider and machine. Few exercises place as high a demand on this rapport as cyclocross. Whether done for racing or simply for recreation, cyclocross involves torquing and braking dexterity of the first order, severe changes in bodyweight distribution, sudden mounts and dismounts, manual portage, and a degree of functional acrobatics. All these skills are quite applicable to the less extreme

Rick Ives makes clear why cyclocross riders are called "mudmen." By Bernard Thompson

though far more critical realm of the motorway.

Some of these "tricks" can be described, but there is no substitute for experience. Experience and ability are directly related to the level of risk or challenge taken—one learns faster tackling a twenty-five-degree grassy embankment on a bicycle than on a ten-degree slope. Dirt roads are good confidence builders; they enable you to develop a "feel" for the nuances of both machine and terrain, sensations not possible in the asphalt domain of the automobile.

Tackling a grassy ravine or a snowy embankment requires a mixture of nerves, balance, and knowledge of the bicycle's handling peculiarities. When going uphill, the major consideration is maintaining weight over the rear wheel—where the power is applied. This underlines the importance of the short stem and the seat slid well back on the post.

Downhills are trickier. One should be keenly aware of the different effects of the front and rear brakes. On any descent, application of the front brake shifts most of the rider's weight to the front end of the bicycle. The front brake is the main stopping brake; it should be applied judiciously to avoid any sudden over-the-handlebar acrobatics. The rear brake provides the finesse. European cyclocross pros lock the rear brake and fishtail down the steep, muddy slopes. Mud and snow exaggerate the rider's weight distribution; sometimes it's better to sit well back on the saddle and let the front wheel "feel" its way. Even with so mundane a nuisance as a pothole or sunken

manhole cover, weight should be taken off the front wheel. Tricky lateral movements in exaggerated conditions can only be learned through experience.

Many riders do not trust the brake levers to be reliable handholds. In fact, this position affords ample control of the bicycle, both laterally and fore-aft. The overhand grip of the brake levers allows the wrist action necessary for jumping curbs, potholes, small dogs, and branches. Young bicycle motocross experts can jump curbs head-on without benefit of toeclips—it's all in the wrists. Ten-speed riders, with their weight distributed a bit more horizontally, need toeclips and a secure grip on the brake levers for any Evel Knievelesque feats.

Jumping obstacles demands timing, strength, and a sense of weight distribution. Tighten your toe straps, then place pedals at three and nine o'clock as you approach the obstacle. With hands in the classic brake lever position, rest about seventy percent of body weight on the leveled pedals. You are now in a semi-crouch position, ready for take-off. As you jump, remember to lift the handlebars with the wrists, maintaining the bicycle in a fairly level position. This type of riding is dangerous enough to warrant practicing on grass, and jumping collapsible items.

Suppose you want to carry your bicycle up a flight of stairs or a slippery embankment. Your tool box or bag of groceries is in the other hand. Where to hold the bike? One very simple and effective way (assuming you are right-handed) is an overhand grip on the down tube about three to six inches up from the bottom bracket. In this position the top tube is on your shoulder, the seat tube rests against the forearm near the elbow. You are holding the bicycle at a critical balance point, and holding it away from your body—your legs don't knock against the pedals as they do with an over-the-bike grip of the seat tube. The front wheel rests a bit lower than the heavier rear end of the machine. A free left hand can reach over and steady the handlebars.

Cyclocross racing often requires you to run with the bike. When shouldering the bike, the hand slips under the down tube and back around to the left side of the bike to grab the butt end of the left handlebar. This allows superior control of the bike; some weight rests on top of the wrist at the down tube, some at the contact point of shoulder and top tube. People sometimes place foam pads to cushion the shoulder, but in time it gets used to the idea anyway. The advantage of this carrying style is vertical and horizontal control of the bike with only one hand, leaving the other hand free to reach for twigs, banisters, or rear jersey pockets.

Proper dismounting is a key element to cyclocross. Such a technique can instantly transform a rider into a pedestrian, a useful trick at crosswalks or in the event, heaven forbid, of brake failure. Assume a left-sided dismount. With the bike still moving, toe straps nice and loose, pull the right foot from the pedal, and bring it around to the left side of the bike. Instead of swinging the right foot behind the left foot, bring it between the still-stationary left foot and the bicycle itself. You are now poised to

step lightly forward with the right foot, simultaneously kicking out and backward with the left foot, which forces you into an automatic run. With cycling cleats, particular care must be taken to slightly disengage the cleat and loosen the toe straps of the left foot, assuring its departure from the pedal.

In racing, where everything depends on the smooth transition of mounting and dismounting, the rider will approach the obstacle, swing right foot between left pedal and bicycle as described above, and simultaneously reach for the down tube from the left side of the bike with the right hand. This prepares the rider to shoulder the bike immediately after "kicking out" from the pedals.

Mounting a bicycle on the run presents an even greater challenge than the dismount technique. The idea is to jump directly onto the seat, rodeo style. Both hands should be firmly gripping the handlebars, preferably at the tops or on the brake levers. There is no need for exaggerated elevation; jump not too much higher than the seat itself, to minimize the impact. The impact can

Cyclocross Mount

be lessened by transferring most of the body weight to the handlebars. Both legs should be poised and bent at the knee, ready to slap the feet into the toeclips. The leap must be forward as well as sideways, to keep up with the

Junior cyclocross. Photograph by Bernard Thompson

Cyclocross Dismount

moving bicycle and to maintain momentum.

Cyclocross races are, in some sense, mad spectacles. Imagine forty or fifty contestants, all vying to be first through that initial funneled-down section of the course, through which only one rider at a time can pass. The thundering herd thins out rapidly, the stronger riders moving to the front, for there can be no drafting or "wheelsucking" in the lower speeds of the quagmire. The footsteps and breathing get heavier as the crowd presses closer to catch the fatigue and exhaustion behind the film of mud covering the rider's face. The once pristine machines are logged and caked with goo, pieces of ice and reeds cling to the frame and wheels. Meanwhile, the pit crews ready the spare bikes. The rider storms into the pit area, expertly dismounts, tosses the mud-laden bike aside, picks up the spare, jumps on and is off, while the pit crew gets busy with sponge and bucket for the next time around.

In cyclocross racing the line between heroics and buffoonery is a fine one. The racer constantly assesses the relative advantages of riding or running through a tricky or dangerous section. Crashing generally has mild consequences; landing in soft mud is more comic than anything else–a small price for riding "close to the edge." The spectators tend to congregate at the more challenging sections, sometimes only a few feet away from the action, in an intimate proximity to the contestants unknown in motor sports.

Yet to call it only sport is demeaning. As people seek increasingly creative and self-reliant means of transportation, this hybrid of foot and bicycle travel will take on new dimension and importance. As perceptions of the bicycle shift from that of toy to tool (and they will), two-wheeled expertise cannot remain confined to sport alone. What is regarded as "recreation," "sport," or "leisure" today will be the challenge of mobility tomorrow.

Junior cyclocross. Photograph by Bernard Thompson

John Atkins, 13 times British champion.
Bernard Thompson

Want to Try Cyclocross?

Cyclocrossing is hard on bikes. Choose an older, more expendable model, as rigorous cyclocrossing has its risks. Maneuverability suggests a frame about an inch smaller than usual. The seat post is usually lowered a half inch or so for a lower center of gravity and increased stability in mud or snow. A higher bottom bracket means better ground clearance; eleven inches from ground to center of bottom bracket is adequate.

Strong spokes help ensure wheel longevity. In the absence of the more expensive sealed-bearing hubs, lower quality hubs bring less grief when wintertime moisture and grit take their toll. Sew-up rims are remarkably strong, but how long they last is again a function of prudence. Make sure the tires are well glued to the rim--this is especially critical in the rough.

Special cyclocross tires, both the sculpted and nonsculpted kind, may well be the best tire investment where sew-ups are concerned. The extra weight is but a small concession to the effectiveness and durability. When riding in mud, snow, or ice, lower tire pressure to 45 to 60 psi (depending on the rider's weight). This increases traction and stability, though care must be observed when approaching driveway lips, railroad tracks, and other objects that might dent the rim.

A wide-range cluster (14 to 28 teeth minimum) should be adequate for any off-road use. A racer considers 28 teeth enough—any lower makes running with the bike a preferred option. Normal 52-42 front sprocket combinations are okay though some riders prefer close-range gearings of 45-36 or 46-42 for finer selection. Even simpler and appropriate for wilderness travel is a single front sprocket with a chain guard. Some have fashioned homemade guards out of old 54-tooth chainwheels with the teeth ground away. Triple chainwheel bolts are needed for setups like this. Chain guards serve to keep the chain on and protect the chainwheel from logs and brambles. Derailleurs are a matter of personal preference; a rear chain guard gives some protection against possible entanglement of spokes, grass, and derailleur.

Another possibility is a sew-up rim built to a 3-speed internal hub, a 36 to 40-tooth front track chainwheel and a 3-speed chain, providing quick, thumb-activated gearing range. Five- or 10-speed arrangements still give the most range and selection, both for on- and off-road travel.

Longer cranks, whether cottered or cotterless, provide more leverage, but reduce ground clearance. A personal matter.

Bar and stem should be of high quality, as cyclocross at times requires strenuous wrestling with the bicycle.

Exotic looking and functional, cantilever center-pull brakes give a cyclocross bike its distinctive appearance. The bosses don't flex and the brakes themselves are quite inexpensive and lightweight. Side-pull and center-pull calipers of nominal good quality both work adequately except in heavy mud conditions. In either case, high quality brake pads are a sound investment.

Wide touring pedals provide better grip and foot contact than racing pedals. And both sides of such pedals are usable.

Toeclips and straps present one of bicycling's major mythologies. ''What happens when you fall?'' is a favorite question of those who suspiciously eye rat traps for the first time. One might retort mischievously, ''What happens anyway?'' But the fact is, toeclips increase stability and facilitate bike handling, especially on rough terrain and bumpy roads. Toeclips enable the rider to jump and lift the bike over potholes and logs, they provide extra footing and control on rough, steep descents,

Number 1 is Norbert Dedeckere of Belgium, former World Champion. Bernard Thompson

and added leverage on slippery hills, where smooth 360-degree pedal pressure is particularly important. They make the rider, in the Zen parlance, one with the bike.

Most European racers ''double'' their toeclips. This is done by filing out the rivets holding the toe strap loop, punching out the remains of the rivet, and then re-riveting two toeclips and the loop. Double toeclips act as leaf springs; they resist abuse and seldom break.

Where the mixed and integrated blessings of running/riding/walking are concerned, stiff-soled cycling shoes are impracticable. Shoe companies are waking up to the need for a shoe suitable for both walking and riding, but ingenuity and improvisation can serve in the meantime. Hard-soled soc-

cer shoes with the front cleats ground down for easy pedal insertion provide excellent support and are inexpensive. Tennis shoes are nice for running, but lack stiffness and protection at the contact point with the pedal. European racers employ custom-made shoes with a flexible, ripple-tread toe section and a steel plate/cleat into which two cramp-on-like spikes are threaded, depending upon the severity of conditions. The steel plate in this arrangement acts as buffer between foot and pedal. An extra-long shoelace fits around the ankle to ensure the shoes are not lost in the bog while running!

Saddle choice is another personal decision. The seat post, however, should be high quality, to withstand the effects of rodeo-like leaps onto the bike.

Klunkers

Darryl Skrabak

When the modern bike boom began, one of the first desires of new bicyclists was for roads without cars, or bikeways. These were in great demand until a few were built, and it was discovered that bikeways were not without problems. Many were poorly designed and unsafe. Most went unmaintained.

Bike paths also proved costly. Often they were insinuated into odd places, where builders could afford to put them, rather than where bicyclists might need them.

Out in Marin County, California, are bikers who don't dream about roads without cars; they ride on them.

These riders have discovered an entire system of auto-free roads virtually in their own backyard. And in taking to them, they are pioneering a new kind of bicycling, one just starting to spread to other sections of the country.

What the Mariners are doing is riding without pavement. Thereby they buck a trend, one as old as bicycling. Back in the days of the first bike booms, in the late 1880's, bicyclists so despaired of the rough, dusty –or muddy, depending on the season – wagon tracks they had to contend with, that they founded the Good Roads Movement. The object was to pave roads to make them rideable.

Bicyclists had gotten the Movement going pretty well by the advent of motorcars. Motorists didn't like wagon tracks either. They took over the Movement and the roads, too, and went on to great things, like interstate highways.

The long eclipse of bicycling did nothing to diminish preference for pavement. Just the opposite. When bikes re-emerged in the modern boom, they emerged onto dramatically better road surfaces. So improved had paving techniques become that bicycle builders were able to alter frame design. Preferred frames became stiffer, more "responsive." Everyday 10-speeds have more upright geometry than 1950's racing bikes. This accommodation is not without penalty, however. On harsh surfaces, the ride is jolting.

Thus when Marin bikers began to take to the roads of yesteryear, they not only bucked the trend toward pavement, they went against the evolutionary trend in quality bikes. This was particularly so because of the manner in which Mariners went off-roading.

The initial venture beyond pavement probably hadn't much to do with a desire to leave cars behind. More likely

Darryl Skrabak *has been covering the klunker phenomenon from its early days as "repack." He combines journalism with teaching bike repair clinics. He also wrote "A Case for Hands-On Experience."*

Modern Mountain Bike. "Repack" T-shirt refers to the good old days when coaster brakes often had to be repacked at the end of a run. Drawing by Barbara Remington

it was born of the cops having chased a dirt-digging motorbike rider off the fire roads once too often. Or maybe it was a spinoff from kids' BMX bikes. For whatever reason, some unknown instigator had himself and an old-style American bike driven up the flanks of Mt. Tamalpais. This pinnacle dominates southern Marin vistas. It overlooks a quantity of territory remarkable for its wildness on the edge of urbanization. For much of the area the only incursions of civilization are fire roads. It was on these dusty, precipitous tracks that Marin off-road biking began.

Taking to a steep Marin fire road on a bicycle is like boarding a bobsled at the St. Moritz course in Switzerland. Speed is determined by the ability to hang on, stay on the course, and stay off the brake.

This thrill-seeking approach to bicycling was possible since motor vehicles are prohibited from fire roads. No need to worry about oncoming traffic. Only about dodging the rocks and gullies and not overshooting the next corner.

It is this emphasis on fast downhill riding that distinguishes Marin off-road biking and has led to development of an especially hardy sort of bicycle known as a klunker. The bikes that came to be favored might have been quite different if the preferred fire roads had been

Photograph by Waldo Bascom

relatively level routes through the woods. Ordinary 10-speeds are not so out of place on roads like that.

On the flanks of Mt. Tam, the roads are not like that. They are steep. Too steep to ride up, it was thought. So Marin fire-road riders emulated alpine skiers. Skiers ride lifts. Station wagons and pickups became the downhill bikers' lifts. One enterprising trucker even went into the lift business, charging a buck a ride. Business was brisk until authorities got word of it. Seems you can't hire out for public transport without proper certification.

Barreling down rutted fire roads proved tremendously abusive of equipment. It is one thing to hop a front wheel over a rock at five miles an hour. It is another to crash over it at twenty-five. This brutal treatment destroys ordinary bikes like clay targets at a shooting gallery. Everything breaks, from rims to stems to frames.

Fortunately for those engaged in early downhilling, a certain ethic was attached to acquisition of equipment. It was considered bad form among adherents to pay more than five dollars for a mount. These were picked up at local thrift shops, which were overstocked with old-style fat-tired American bikes. Once the sole offerings on the American market, they had been rendered despised relics by the 10-speed trend. Disparaged as klunkers, they gave their name to the new sport.

With long wheelbase, heavy, fat tires, and motorcycle-like seating position, klunkers were better fire-road bikes than anything else available. And they were so cheap it didn't matter much when one broke. Just throw it in a dumpster and buy another at the nearest thrift store.

Such were the carefree attitudes of early klunking. Since those time – less than ten years ago – klunkers have evolved into something more than castoffs.

What has evolved are machines that will go like hell downhill and not break, and that can be nimbly ridden uphill as well. Klunker bikes, in fact, can be ridden just about anyplace, depending on the strength and skill of the rider. And when an unrideable obstacle is encoun-

tered – wall, chasm, whatever – just carry the bike past and continue. (Try that with your XT500.)

These light, tough bikes have expanded the scope of Marin off-road biking. Although high-speed downhill runs remain a central activity, klunking has grown beyond the pull of gravity. A lift up the mountain is no longer necessary. One can ride into the back country on roads and trails that wind for miles. These venues are utterly devoid of motors. They comprise a biking resource previously overlooked.

Similar unpaved tracks exist in nearly every part of the country. The West is covered with fire roads and unmapped logging roads. So are the forests of the North and South. Even the populated East is not without nearly unused unpaved back lanes. A Boston motorcycle-magazine publisher once described how riders in that metropolitan area seeking new terrain turned to court-house records. They located historic but long-disused roads, which they proceeded to open.

To give biking beyond pavement a try, almost any bike will do. An ordinary 10-speed is reasonably adaptable. It helps if the machine has low gearing, an aid when forcing through soft surfaces. It helps, too, if the bike is not shod with the skinny high-pressure tires now in vogue for road use.

But for Marin-style off-roading, more specialized equipment is in order. Most Marin riders start out with a heavy-duty American bike, a balloon-tire bomber, as writer Tom Cuthbertson describes the type. Of mass-produced bikes, Schwinn frames are strongest; the best-handling of the Schwinns is the Excelsior model. Manufactured in the late thirties and early forties, these are now rare.

Shod with the most formidable knobby tires one can buy (26 x 2.125-inch size), the Schwinn makes a fair downhill bike. But it's heavy, about fifty pounds. That and its single gear make it hard to push along flats, much less up hills.

To make the bike more versatile, a series of modifications is undertaken.

Derailleur gearing is the usual first step. Adding it means adding several other things, too, such as a new rear hub. And hand brakes. The original coaster brake won't work with a freewheel.

What sort of brakes? Calipers offer the simplest and least expensive option. Special large caliper units are available to fit the large tire and rim. Some custom-bike buyers specify cantilevers. But most Marin riders prefer hub-mounted drum brakes. These are less affected by dirt and water and not at all affected by a rim knocked out of true or bent. The latter condition is not unusual.

If you opt for hub brakes, you must have wheels built around them, so it's timely to consider rims. Good steel rims are strong but heavy. Marin riders report excellent results with aluminum rims which are very expensive and still somewhat scarce. Fourteen-gauge DT spokes are preferred. Weight savings with aluminum rims: about two pounds per wheel.

The favored brake levers – mounted on motocross-style handlebars – are Magura-style motocross models. To these are fitted large-diameter motorcycle cables, large-diameter motocross grips, and derailleur shift lever(s). Highly favored are Sun Tour "thumb shifters."

These are stock catalog items, not to be confused with end shifters.

A stock 10-speed stem will break in a fall; it is replaced with a heavy-duty BMX type.

Back to gearing. With the stock crank, choose a freewheel carrying the largest sprocket to be had (34 tooth). This provides five speeds. For ten speeds fit a two-sprocket Ashtabula (inexpensive but heavy) or alloy cotterless. Extra-long BMX or TA cranks (185 mm) are favored by some riders.

A useful final option: quick-release seat-post clamp. It allows lowering seat for better control on downhills, raising it for better pedaling efficiency on other terrain.

Frames: There are several special frames now available for off-road specials. Marin-developed frames are usually distinguished by larger-diameter tubing, larger than the one-inch standard for most American frames. The special frames are lighter, stronger, better handling.

Final note: No piece on klunking would be complete without a mention of klunking's premier event – the annual Repack race, so named because a single pass down the course will burn the lubricant right out of a coaster brake. One is then obliged to repack the brake with grease. The course drops some 1,300 feet over a 2.2 mile length.

BMX in a Nutshell

John Krausz

This is the way a fourteen-year-old high school science student explained it:

Traction is where it's at; you keep traction by moving your body weight around on the seat and using the handlebars, or by shifting your weight on the pedals. It's just like regular bike riding, but you can't use toe-clips in BMX, so you do more with your weight on the pedals; and you want to stay more upright than on a 10-speed so you can use the wide tires to get traction.

You're also more over the back wheel on a BMX than on a regular bike, and the frames are quite whippy because the seat tube is only about twelve inches high. The seats are smooth to make it easy to slide back – almost exactly like plastic racing seats. But on a lot of moves you just lean back and pull on the handlebars a little.

It's hard to get hurt in BMX racing because you have so much protective equipment – gloves, helmets, face masks, and pads all over the place. It can get pretty hot, but races don't last long. The biggest track I've heard of is only three-quarters of a mile long. With all that protective stuff on you're not afraid to make a dangerous move in a race that you might think twice about if you were just fooling around, and seeing

Photograph by BMX Plus! magazine.

will probably take over; it's easier to change the gears on them than on hub brakes. Of course the bikes would be more useful for just riding around if they had brakes front and back.

Front brakes aren't too popular. You don't want brakes to stop with, you just want to control the bike. The chrome-moly forks are tremendously strong but

some jumps will get you seven to eight feet off the ground, so you don't want to weaken them by drilling a hole for a front brake. I also think people are afraid that little kids won't be able to handle them and will go flying off the bike.

When you cross a railroad track or an expansion joint of a bridge you want to keep your bike upright

someone else do something makes you sure it's possible, so you'll try it too.

If your handlebars aren't in a straight line with the bike you're not going as fast as you can, so to get top speed you stay upright and crank hard. When you take a turn the weight is on the outside pedal, with just enough weight forward to keep the front end down. You want to go as fast as you can, because the faster you go the more stable the bike is; what would throw you at fifteen miles per hour, you plane over at thirty . . . you sail over the ruts instead of into them, so you have to take the downhills as fast as you can.

In a skid you bring your back wheel around so you stay straight—it causes lots of dust and roostertails and that's neat. It can also cause a lot of wipeouts if you don't weight the outside pedal or pull enough.

In a way it's like biking on ice-covered roads, you only use your brake in the straight or in setting up for a move—it all takes practice. But it's better to go off the course than to always brake; after a while you'll learn the right moves and may not have to brake. But the courses are getting more difficult so rim brakes

105

Harry Larry kicked back and flew free. BMX Plus! *magazine.*

Photograph by BMX Plus! *magazine*

and cross straight-on, so the front wheel won't be deflected. You ease up on the handlebar or maybe even pull it toward you, then slip back on the seat so the front wheel can come over . . . then you rock forward so the back wheel can come over. Starting a jump involves moves like that. You've got to worry about your line, but it's traction that lets you hold your line.

If you can't set up at a right angle to the obstacle what you do is wait for the last instant and then bring the front wheel around to as near a right angle as possible – the back wheel will follow if you use a little body English. You can do that in traffic, too – when you're in with a lot of cars you often don't have enough room to steer around a pothole or something like that.

In making any jumps – and BMX racing is all turns and sprints and jumps – you want your feet at 3 and 9 o'clock for clearance; it also minimizes the shock of landing and you can start to rev as soon as you hit. And it's easier to pull and twist so you can deflect the back end and change direction.

The front tires are bigger than the back to get better "gription" and to absorb the shock of landing.

It's important to get a good start at the beginning of a race to build up speed. If you can get away clean you get to choose your line and not have to eat someone else's dust or take the muddy patches, so first off

is usually first over. The right gearing is important, and we use two-sided hubs and chainwheels that are easy to change. You usually start at 40 x 16 or 40 x 18 – it depends on the track and track conditions – because you want to be able to rev.

Riding BMX is finding out what a bike can really do. It's made me a much better bike rider. Most people riding around on bikes don't know nothing. Something happens and they don't do anything about it or else do exactly the wrong thing – like pulling away if they get leaned against instead of knowing to lean back, or pulling away if they tick a back wheel instead of turning into it for a second – the same way you maximize a right-hand turn by momentarily turning to the left to switch your balance. Freezing is the worst thing you can do – do *anything* rather than freeze.

There are a lot of things you can do on a bike that most people never try – setting up for a jump teaches you to take an obstacle head-on and to pull; that keeps you on the bike and back over the rear wheel so you don't go flying. And getting used to controlling a skid means you don't have to wipe out if you hit a patch of ice in the winter. If you do lose your back wheel stay with the bike and you won't roll. As long as you're on the bike you can do something. In most cases if you do go down it's better to stay with the bike anyway. Of course you bail out if you're heading for a truck or a cliff or something.

Winter Cycling in Finland

Alan Robson

Alan Robson with Lentava Possu "The Flying Pig"

Last winter ("The worst since the Winter War in 1939-40," they said), I, along with a few thousand other idiots, continued to use bicycles. My personal record was -22° C. If bicycles can be used in Finland in winter, they can be used practically anywhere.

The first principle of winter cycling is to forget any ideas about competition, faster or better or whatever. All you're trying to do is keep moving and stay alive. Never do anything suddenly—accelerating, braking or turning. Smoothness is the key to it all.

In the case of braking, the best advice is, don't. If something is coming at you, steer, don't brake. Even if you don't fall off from slamming on the brakes, you may skid from safety to danger. If you see that there

Alan Robson *is an architect and permanent resident of Finland. Major portions of this article previously appeared in* Freewheeling, *the Scottish monthly.*

isn't space for both of you on the road (unless you're on a good surface like hard-packed snow), steer for the ditch and get ready to roll. On most roads there is plenty of space, so don't panic. If you do brake, the safest way is to pull the front brake slightly sooner than the back. I keep my front brake more tightly adjusted so I get this result when I pull both levers simultaneously. To slow down, use feather braking—small, light pulls on the lever, letting go as soon as you feel any tendency for the wheel to lock.

Beware of rim brakes. Ice can form on the rim, and when you pull the brake nothing happens. So you pull harder in desperation, the heat soon melts the ice layer, the block suddenly bites hard, the wheel locks, and the next thing you know the bike is on top of you. Unlike a soft snow skid, this is so fast you don't know it's happening until you're in a heap.

If you think the rims may ice up or get wet, pull the brakes very gently to dry them out, then check the response.

On a steep downward hill you have two alternatives: to let go and ride it out if you're sure you can handle it, corners and all, or to use both brakes very smoothly to make a very slow descent. Never, never, use a brake halfway down a steep hill on ice. If in any doubt, get off and walk.

Cornering is the next most dangerous operation. First, make sure everybody knows that you intend to turn, by giving a clear signal. Then make sure your speed is appropriate, by braking or accelerating before you start turning. When you turn make sure that you lean while the bike stays as nearly vertical as possible. This is in direct contradiction to the normal "natural" method in which the rider stays upright while the bike leans. That will work, though badly, on a dry surface, but on ice the bike will merely slide from under you.

Using gears is a matter of common sense. On a steep hill wheel spin can be reduced by using a very low gear and pedaling rapidly and smoothly. Use of a high gear in a car will reduce the chance of skidding but I haven't noticed a similar effect on a bicycle.

Normal danger spots are obvious, such as bus stops where spinning wheels change the surface to a highly polished, wave-shaped, oiled glass. Avoid them if at all possible, otherwise get up just enough speed to coast over. Don't pedal, don't brake, don't turn.

Then there is the deep slush which gets left at road junctions. This is tricky, as the correct response depends on the depth of the slush and if it's frozen hard or not. If in doubt, get off and push. If you're sure it's not too hard or deep, build up as much speed as possible and smash through, holding the handlebars very firmly. Near pedestrian crossings, remember that your braking distance is enormous, and that nobody can jump out of your way on a frozen road. Snow piled at the side of the road can hide you and obscure your vision.

Winter road surfaces are quite different from summer ones. Hard-packed snow with sand on top is about as fast a surface as asphalt. Slush of the wet variety is heavy but not too dangerous, and everything happens slowly on it. Frozen hard slush is another story, and is usually a get-off-and-push surface, as a bicycle just doesn't have the weight needed to crush it enough to move forward. Cobbles are pure murder except with dry, very cold snow. If they get slightly wet and freeze, it's next to impossible to stay upright, and under the same heading, watch out for ice-covered manhole covers. The worst surface bar none is black ice covered lightly with powdery snow. No matter how good your tires, the snow just fills up the treads and lubricates the ice (as if it needed it). Leave it well alone unless absolutely unavoidable, in which case, glide over it. We have special delights here that you don't find everywhere, namely tram tracks at road junctions which get covered with slippery slush.

And if, in spite of everything, you do skid? Well, skidding isn't the end of the world. In winter you will skid at some time on every trip and you have to learn how to maintain control. Don't panic, don't pedal, don't brake, *steer.* If your back wheel skids, turn the front wheel in the direction you want to go; if your front wheel skids, hold the front wheel straight. Don't jerk anything. It's different from a car, in that cars don't usually fall over when they skid.

I've a strong feeling that there is such a thing as a psychologically produced skid. You're on a bad surface and you feel a perfectly normal movement in the bike which, because you're expecting to skid, you interpret as a skid, and promptly skid the bike.

Perhaps the most important thing to add is that you need to know when not to ride. For instance, yesterday was very warm and a lot of snow melted then froze hard at night, after which it snowed. I tried to cycle to work this morning and after some horrible moments came back and went by bus. I could have risked it, but with the bike sometimes less than a yard from very heavy traffic it would have taken only one bad skid.

Secondly I recommend an open, so-called "lady's" frame, because there will be times when you are going to have to get off fast, and you don't want a crossbar trapping you in front of that sliding truck. (The principle is to save yourself, not the bike.)

I have used a 10-speed tourer in -22° C, and it worked, but it was hell. A hard-packed snow surface will shake a lightweight frame to pieces.

Now in this country many people normally cycle all year round, mainly on a weird assortment of what looks at first sight like scrap iron. Men as well as women prefer open frames because then you can fasten enormous cardboard boxes to the equally immense rear carriers and still mount the bike. The wheels have broad tires, 1 5/8-inch being standard, fine for the kind of dirt roads which abound here, even within the Helsinki city boundaries.

Still, on a daily round trip often approaching 50 kilometers something more flexible than a single speed *traktorcykel* as the Swedish Sport mob disdainfully calls the standard machine, would be an advantage. So, Lentava Possu, the "Flying Pig," came into my possession when, before last winter, I found that 27-inch stud tires were not made to fit my 10-speed tourer. I could have changed the wheels, but for a long time I'd wanted a *traktorcykel*, one with an open, curved frame, slow, steady, and beautiful. Its low gearing of 44.22 began at times to annoy, and I decided to convert the Flying Pig into a Super Traktor. I changed the rear wheel to a 5-speed with a 28-24-20-17-14 block, put a caliper brake and a worn-out Simplex changer on it to see what happened. The changer worked reasonably well at first but more or less collapsed a week later.

Wheels and spokes need to be massive. Partly for strength, partly for comfort (bouncy tires on rough ice), but mainly because you need the extra gripping surface that broad tires give. I use 26 x 1-5/8-inch. I have ridden on a machine with 1¼-inch racing tires on frozen snow and slush but I wouldn't recommend it. The Finnish Army uses 2-inch tires for boondock bouncing but the loss of efficiency on a good surface is high. I use stud tires made by Oy Nokia Ab and they are excellent. Other tires can be used, but preferably knobbies only. If you have a tourer, Trellegorg Ab in Sweden make very good high-pressure grip tires. They give, considering the small contact area, quite as good a grip as the stud tires on everything except hard ice. Unfortunately, so far Nokia only makes the stud tires in 26 x 1½-inch and 28 x 1½-inch sizes. The principle is that the heavier the tread the better, i.e. worn tires are out. Remember to check tire pressure every day before leaving. Empty tires are lethal.

It helps to lower the saddle slightly during the winter so that you can get your foot quickly to the ground during a skid without leaning the bike too much. Handlebars should not, *repeat one thousand times,* be the drop type. The reason is that to control a skid you need a handlebar that will give very firm leverage, and drops are too narrow. For deep snow you need very firm steady leverage also. I use motocross grips so that my heavily gloved hand won't slip easily. They must have a good surface, and be thick enough for heavy gloves to grip round.

Perhaps the most important item is brakes. On ice I've used almost every type known to man, and prefer a mixed system. I use an Oglaend "Giant" drum brake on the front wheel. This is the most important brake in bad conditions and a drum brake will operate quite as well in wet slush as in dry weather. Blowing wet snow *can* slightly affect it but very little. Also a drum brake is less liable than a rim brake to grip violently and throw you. However, I have used center-pull rim brakes, front and back, and provided you've *very* careful how you use them, they're okay even at -22° C. The standard coaster brake is what most people use here. It's normally a good, gentle brake, dependable in all conditions, but you can apply it very fast, and in a moment of panic you can skid the bike very easily. Hand levers slow down your reaction a little. Brake blocks should be adjusted so that they don't bite very hard.

Gears aren't essential but I've found that in very deep snow a low ratio will keep you ploughing on where otherwise you'd flounder. Gear changers seem to be relatively unaffected by extreme cold. Remember to keep the changer clean if you use a bike in salted slush, or it will vanish before your very eyes.

Remember too to lubricate the bike well before winter with water-free Vaseline in all bearings. However, even that will freeze below -15° C and you'll be running on dry bearings. You'll feel the difference and usually hear it clearly, so be gentle to your bike at these times.

Lighting is important, both to see where you're going on dark country roads, and, more importantly, to make sure others can see you. Battery lamps are fine but heavy and get used up fast in winter. Surprisingly, dynamos work perfectly well in everything except deep, wet snow. Even then there are big differences between makes, and some will operate under almost any conditions. Remember that in very bad weather your speed will be low and your need to be seen correspondingly high, so think well before fitting a larger pulley to a dynamo in winter. Despite adverse comments from people who ought to know better, reflectors do help in the dark. Especially recommended are the type that fold on a fluorescent stick. They give drivers something to aim at that isn't rigidly fixed to the bike. Indeed, the Finnish police are so impressed by them that they want to make them compulsory.

Reflectors in the spokes help drivers coming from a side road to see you, but they have to be kept clean. From my own experience, hanging reflectors round yourself and bike like a Christmas tree noticeably increases the amount of road space you're given. Drivers are generally trying to give you space, but they have to be able to see you clearly. I also use reflective tape sewn round the wrists of my jacket so that hand signals can be seen better. You can sew reflective patches on your gloves too.

Clothing should be brightly colored or covered with reflectors so that you are seen, and preferably well padded and strong so that when you fall off damage is minimized. Clothing must be warm and loose enough to let you move. Your face will be colder than anywhere else, but using a scarf over your nose and mouth can be uncomfortable. If it's very, very cold and windy then I wrap a scarf across my nose in addition to wearing a Chinese dog-fur hat with the ear flaps firmly down.

Baggage and freight must be securely attached to a rigid carrier. Keep the center of gravity low and as well centered as possible. Carriers and baskets hung on the handlebars can help to induce front wheel skids. Wobbly rear carriers can help to induce rear wheel skids. It doesn't pay to carry heavy loads on the back carrier. When you're on a slippery surface, you can feel it sliding. Carry heavy things on your back.

Mirrors are a vexed subject, but anyone attempting a left turn on a main street among the kind of aggressive idiocy that characterizes Finnish driving better have one even in summer. In winter, on a narrow road, it gives you some warning of what the car following you is going to do. To my mind they are useful at all times, and essential in winter. Apart from seeing behind you, a mirror is useful for checking your face from time to time for frostbite.

The Monk's Road in Mid-Wales. Garet Cox, The Rough-Stuff Fellowship

Rollers, the All-Weather Bike Route

John Pixton

Serious cyclists in northern latitudes run, swim, play tennis, ski, skate, maybe shovel snow and chop wood to stay in shape during the winter. Most of them probably find these activities less fun and less effective as conditioners than bicycling. The sovereign quality of bicycling is its steady, rhythmic character, perfectly contrived to elevate the heart rate to whatever level you require, and sustain it there for as long as you like. Only running approaches cycling in this quality of steadiness, and it is much harder on the leg joints. Anyone with garden-variety aches and pains in the legs or back is likely to find that cycling will ease them, maybe eliminate them.

If you want to enjoy this salubrious exercise when snow, salt, and cold make the road inhospitable, get some rollers, the all-weather bike route. Learning to ride them is not difficult. Set them up near a wall or heavy table and get someone to steady you while you get comfortable on the seat and pedals. Start pedaling while your helper holds the bike under the seat, *not* by the handlebars or stem. The helper should hold you as lightly as possible. You quickly discover that if you are smooth, keep the bike vertical, and maintain a certain minimum rpm, the bike will just about steer itself. High-pressure tires and round wheels help.

In roller workouts you will get thoroughly warmed up – perhaps get hotter and perspire more than you ever have before. (I cover my stem and the floor with a piece of towel.) I think this is salutary provided you work up to it gradually and do not exceed pulse rate limits for your age and experience. (Rule of thumb: 220 minus age equals maximum pulse rate; workouts should take you to 75 percent of maximum for at least twenty minutes.) I find I tolerate heat very well; maybe 1,500 miles per year on the rollers has something to do with it.

John Pixton uses rollers as part of the college course in cycling described earlier. He is also chairman of the Bicycling Federation of Pennsylvania, which promotes safe cycling and represents bike interests. He regularly wins USCF-sponsored races (Veteran Class).

Rollers can help you develop dynamic skills that will make you a more competent and secure rider generally, and a safer rider in traffic. Practice these drills: Ride tops, drops, and brakes with one hand while signaling or shifting with the other; sit up, coasting, put your left hand on your left knee and look over your shoulder; go as slowly as you can without falling, then as fast as you can without bouncing; wipe front and rear tires (with gloves, on the road, to clear glass fragments).

Rollers are useful in fitting and adjusting your bike before you go on the road. Proper adjustment of stem extension and height, as well as of seat height, angle, and fore and aft position, takes more care than most people give it. Trial and adjustment on the rollers is easy. A good set of rollers will also tell you if your frame, especially the fork, is out of alignment, and if your wheels or tires are out of round.

If you are serious about conditioning, get a speedometer-odometer and a stopwatch. The rolling resistance of rollers, unlike that of stationary bicycles, is not controllable, and rollers are lighter than the flywheels found on the former. So generally you are pedaling faster, more continuously, and against lower resistance than on a stationary bicycle. Your bike also fits you better. Most stationary bicycles have shallow seat tube angles and high handlebars.

Set time and distance objectives and keep a log or diary in which you record these objectives and your pulse rate at the end of the workout. One of my standard routines is to warm up, usually in a 78- to 88-inch gear, for about ten minutes, zero the stopwatch, and do a thirty-minute time trial, usually in a 102-inch gear. I have calibrated my speedometer, but that is not necessary; all you need is one that is consistent so that comparisons of your performance will indicate your progress. A variation is to do intervals, thirty to sixty seconds at maximum rpm, followed by a similar period at some slower pace. They are tough, and one session a week is plenty unless you

John Pixton at left. Photograph by Pat Little

are racing. I have found the rollers helpful in cultivating the mental-physical discipline needed in time trials, but also useful in hill climbing and touring when the wind is against you or the day longer than you figured. Decide what your workout program is going to be in advance, and stick to the time or distance objective even if you fall behind the pace you had hoped to maintain.

With all these advantages, why shovel snow or chop wood in the winter? Keep rolling on the bike!

CYCLE SPORT

British Bicycle Polo

Tony Knight

Bicycle polo was first played in 1891. The sport started when Richard Mecredi, an Irish racing cyclist, decided he was no longer able to continue competing, and not being capable of accepting a premature retirement, he invented Bicycle Polo as a means of keeping fit and of keeping his cycling blood flowing. The first game was played at the Scalp, just outside Dublin.

The game grew in popularity and spread to England in the early 1900's. One of the highlights was the Olympic games at Shepherd's Bush, London, in 1908, when an experienced Irish team beat England on their home ground. Then came the First World War which dealt a body blow to bicycle polo in terms of players, and interest slowly waned.

In 1930 a gentleman by the name of Cyril Scott found himself in much the same position as the game's founder and reinvented the game, not having heard of the earlier version. The Bicycle Polo Association of Great Britain was formed that year when the constitution was drawn up at a

meeting at Cyril's house, so 1980 sees its fiftieth anniversary.

The game spread quickly and several bicycle polo clubs, often affiliated to cycling clubs, were formed. Competitions and leagues were also formed including the English Cup, which is still regarded as the major domestic competition.

A bicycle polo team consists of six players, male or female, five of whom (including the goalkeeper) may be on the field at any one time. The sixth

person may be used as a substitute at the beginning of a period, or at any other time at the discretion of the referee. The game is divided into six fifteen-minute periods called chukkas. Pitch (field) dimensions are similar to those of soccer, but the goalposts are set four yards apart with a crossbar nine feet up.

The game is started by a sprint. One player from each team lines up his front wheel on the goal line on the left-hand side of his goalposts. At a

State-of-the-Art British Bicycle Polo Bike

Tony Knight *is a competitor and secretary of the Bicycle Polo Association of Great Britain. He can be reached at 72 Upton Road, Haylands, Ryde, Isle of Wight, PO 33 3HX, England.*

Bicycle Polo in England. Photograph by Bernard Thompson

of the fast pace of the sport.

The bicycle, which may be bought either new or built up at relatively low cost from spare parts, must conform to safety regulations laid down by the association. For instance, handlebars are kept quite short, and brakes and metal pedals are forbidden because of the danger of cuts. The main conversion from a standard bike is the fixed wheel. I started my polo career on such a crude conversion. In fact, my first ever experience of polo was on a grocery delivery bike, complete with basket! The gearing is on the low side–this helps to get maximum acceleration and speed over minimum distance, which of course makes the game faster and more exciting. The wheels are usually twenty-six inches in diameter and one and three-eighths inches across the rim. A normal tire is used in front, but a special spud tire is used in the rear.

The mallet must be held in the right hand and can be either thirty-two or thirty-four inches long, with a head of either four or seven inches. Wrist straps are not allowed, and metal must not be incorporated into the head, although this does not apply to the shaft.

The ball has a diameter of three and a quarter inches and is usually made of bamboo. In recent years, limited success has been experienced with a plastic version that tends to last several games, as opposed to the bamboo counterpart which usually needs replacing every fifteen minutes.

signal from the referee each races toward the center spot to gain possession of the ball. The best way to "trap" the ball is to use the wheels but it can be stopped by any part of the body to bring it under control. The ball may be struck in any direction but not while the player is dismounted (one foot on the ground is deemed dismounted). You may not catch and throw the ball but it is permissible to use the hand to stop or knock it; you may kick it as well, but only when it is airborne. Although play can be robust it is not dangerous. It is very rare for a player to receive an injury worse than a minor bruise or two, yet players are allowed to shoulder charge, tackle, crook a mallet, or "ride off" an opponent challenging for the ball.

Once a player graduates from the initial stage he begins to learn the finer points: stroke-play, bike handling, and team tactics. It is a delight to watch two top teams in action –the high-speed interpassing and clever "practiced" attacks with the resultant abundance of shots. The referee (who, incidentally, is on foot) is usually assisted by two goal judges and two linesmen–necessary because

American Bicycle Polo

Walter K. Ezell

Walter Ezell reports on all phases of the cycling scene for the LAW Bulletin, *of which he is editor. He also contributed the plea for cyclists' right to the road, "You Can't Get There from Here."*

"Bicycle polo fills a gap in cycling," says Richard Grubb of the United States Bicycle Polo Association. "You don't have to be in super shape to enjoy it, so it fills the gap between touring and racing, a sport you can do on a bicycle that you don't have to spend ten hours a day practicing.

"There are plenty of cyclists who will go out and play softball on the weekends and later ride their bike. Bicycle polo enables them to 'play softball' and ride their bikes at the same time."

With four teams and a twelve-game season, Charlotte, North Carolina, probably has the most bicycle polo activity in the United States. There are also teams in Chicago, Wisconsin, California, and possibly Colorado. There is also some interest in starting teams in Oklahoma and Minnesota, according to Grubb.

In 1897 in Milton, Massachusetts, a bicycle polo club was formed, but with the decline in popularity of the bicycle in the early twentieth century, the sport lost ground in the United States. It has experienced several faddish revivals since, but has never gained a strong footing.

Bicycle polo has been described as the "poor man's polo," though the bicycle polo enthusiast can spend five hundred dollars on equipment if he wants to do it the deluxe way. The sport greatly resembles horse polo, and some people play both sports. But just as field hockey and ice hockey have developed some basic differences, so have bicycle and horse polo.

The field is one third the size of the horse polo field, with maximum dimensions of 140 by 60 yards, the same as a football field. There is a goal at each end of the field, marked by posts twelve feet apart. A point is scored when a player knocks the ball between the goalposts of the opposing team.

Because of the reduced size of the field the player may only hit the ball three times in a row, while the horse polo player is allowed an unlimited number of hits. As a result, team play is important, with passing patterns to move the ball down the field.

American Bicycle Polo.   John H. Bowers, Jr. Charlotte Bicycle Polo League

Bicycle polo is also much less of a contact sport than horse polo, with "riding off" forbidden. Riding off allows an equestrian player to bump into an opponent, preventing him from lining up the shot correctly. But since bicycles don't have the resiliency of horses, contact is more hazardous and is not allowed.

Polo ponies are trained to follow the ball. "When horse polo players play bicycle polo," says Grubb, "it takes a while for them to get used to the fact that their 'horse' doesn't just take off after the ball."

Who plays bicycle polo? John Bowers, chairman of the Charlotte Bicycle Polo League, says that no more than twenty-five percent are avid bicycle riders. "Bicycle riders are about the last people to take it seriously, because almost all other phases of bicycle sport are actually solitary. Even though bike racing has teams, their tactics are not equal to the kind of teamwork required to win a polo match.

"Very few sports lend themselves to family activity the way this one does. Most are involved with matching people of the same ages, but that just hasn't proved to be necessary with bicycle polo. It is good for all ages, from about twelve up.

"The younger one starts to learn this game the better. With handlebar modifications, the small scrambler or motocross-type bike that most kids ride would be ideal for the young player," Bowers said.

In the Northeast United States, where bicycle polo enjoyed passing popularity a few years ago, the sport drew almost all its players from the ranks of horse polo players.

But the Charlotte players learned the sport the hard way. John Bowers became interested in the game after reading about it in the League of American Wheelmen magazine in 1974. He and others studied the rules, went to a horse polo match in South Carolina, and learned by doing.

Their first encounter with other players was at a tournament last year in Chicago—which they won. "We learned a lot," says Bowers. "Having now had the experience of playing against Bill Matheson's team of horse polo players on bikes, I feel that our emphasis on the bicycle equipment was somewhat misplaced. The name of the game is stick skill and play anticipation. The bicycle itself can definitely help or hurt one's game, but can never compensate for lack of skill and knowledge of play."

Bowers says September through November is a good time for the season, because other bicycling activities are tapering off. "It is a good cold-weather sport. You generate a certain amount of heat."

Grubb advised starting out with inexpensive bicycles. "Get a twenty-six-inch wheel coaster brake bike with a drop frame, straighten the front forks, and substitute a twenty-four-inch front wheel. Slice the handlebars down. Remember, the less bike the better. Inevitably you are going to fall, and you don't want protruding parts or a high top tube to hurt you or another player.

The mallets and balls and often the helmets used in horse polo are also used in bicycle polo, and it is therefore not too difficult to get these items.

But the polo helmets are expensive—retailing at fifty to seventy dollars. Bicycle helmets are not adequate as they lack crucial face protection. The teams in Charlotte and Chicago use construction helmets with clear Lexan face protectors added.

Grubb used to build polo bikes of his own design one at a time, till his physician told him the fumes from brazing were causing lung problems. Bowers bought about a dozen of the frames from Grubb, and still owns nine. He rents them to players on a per-game basis to cover maintenance costs.

Because of the short forks which fit the twenty-inch wheels, the steering tube is unusually long. Compared to a motocross bike the Grubb polo bikes have a shorter wheelbase and a longer trail—two and a half inches.

The bikes are light—twenty or twenty-one pounds. And strong? Grubb claims one "took the door off a taxi and only bent one of the front forks." (The rider suffered a broken collar bone and the woman in the taxi became hysterical.)

Some of the Chicago players including Grubb use a fixed gear—like track bikes use. Others use a coaster brake or disc brake, sometimes in combination with a front caliper brake.

Professionally Bowers is an industrial designer. He likes the polo bike design so much he has no other kind of frame. He has set up one of his frames as a touring bike with a six-speed freewheel. He is working on designing a bag that will hold the bike so he can carry it on an airliner like a garment bag.

He has used the bike on sixty and one-hundred mile tours, and likes the quick steering. He finds it fits nicely with the front wheel removed in the back seat of a VW Rabbit.

But like Grubb, Bowers suggests that newcomers to bicycle polo put together bicycles from readily available parts.

Grubb Polo Bike

Artistic Cycling and Cycleball

John Krausz

Artistic cycling looks like cycling in a dream. The rider does a series of seemingly impossible things: riding backward from a wheelie, standing still, pirouetting, then, turning to face the front of the bike, he sits on the handlebar and does a headstand on the seat—all the time riding in neat circles and figure eights in an area not much bigger than the shooting circle of a basketball court.

It seems akin to some fantastic circus trick, something only an acrobat with steel nerves is capable of doing, yet in western and central Europe there are tens of thousands of people who participate in this strange sport, *Hallenradsport*, or indoor cycling, of which trick riding is only a part. Similar machines with different handlebars are used in a game called cycleball, played as doubles on a court about the size of a tennis court. It is similar to soccer, except the ball is hit with the front or rear wheel. Ten goals in a fourteen-minute game is not unusual, giving you some idea of the speed of play. There are national, regional, European and world championship matches, since it is played all over Europe, plus in the USSR, in Japan, Hong Kong, and Canada.

Indoor cycling has existed for a hundred years and is a major sport in West Germany, where there are about 6,000 competitors, roughly twice as many peo-

Cycleball in Play.

ple as in bike racing, and there is much TV coverage. That's not surprising, because it is breathtaking to watch. With the aid of specially designed gym equipment, competitors on specially designed bikes practice the more than 700 moves that have been graded into a scoring system similar to the ones used in figure skating, gymnastics, or diving. It's worth only two points to ride the bike backward and jump from sitting on the handlebar to sitting on the front tube, but you can earn 5.8 points for doing a figure eight while you're in a handstand on the handlebars. Competitors work out six-minute routines and compete singly or in pairs on the bike. Movement 365b involves doing a wheelie with someone standing on your shoulders while you're sitting on the handlebars. A forward figure eight is worth 6.8 points, a backward circle is worth 7.2. Artistic cycling is also practiced in groups of fours and sixes, in which complex Busby Berkeley routines are performed. Franz Kratochvil amassed 327.60 points in his six minutes to win the 1979 world championship.

The machine, a fixed wheel, is built with large clearances to permit it to be ridden in tandem during some of the more extreme exercises. It is geared one to one, meaning that one turn of the cranks equals one turn of the wheel. Alloy 26-inch wheels with 1 1/8-inch tubular tires are used. The fork is absolutely straight so the front wheel can be spun—many of the figures involve complete rotation of the front wheel. A

Bicycle used for Artistic Cycling

Cycleball Bicycle

An Artistic Cycling Sequence

special saddle post permits the seat to be far back so the center of gravity is way over the back wheel, making raising the front wheel, "risers" (or wheelies), easy. The saddle is wide enough to stand on, with half-moon scales like a snakeskin that catch your clothing if you start to slide off the back. There are dorns (axle extenders) that make it possible to walk all around the machine while it's going! Because soft gymnastic-type slippers are worn, the pedals are rubber. The handlebar is upside-down, dropped-type, steel, and made in one piece with the stem – the whole must be strong enough to support two riders! Adult bikes are 52 and 55 cm, and there are 46 and 40 cm ones with 24- and 20-inch wheels, respectively, for children.

Special training equipment includes a low vaulting stand with a handlebar on top of it, a front-wheel trolley that keeps the bike upright while practicing various stands, and a carousel about five feet in diameter for practicing wheeling and other moves alone or in a group. Teeterboards are used to learn balance on, and weight lifting is practiced to develop the upper arms. There is even a rigid bike to leap about on.

A scarcity of equipment seems to be slowing the growth of the sport. Breuer's bikes, which are the artistic cycling equivalent of Hetchins, Cinellis, and Singers, are no longer made. All artistic cycling bikes must be as carefully crafted as any custom bike and have one feature that all bikes could benefit from: Because a lot of tension is put on the seat clamp by the various changes of position, these bikes use a bolt in the seat tube to both register and lock the seat post and keep it from turning. This can be used to lock an index point on the seat post so that the bike can be shared by many people. Because the seat post is locked in two positions, overtightening of the seat-clamp bolt (a common occurrence on even the best bicycles) is avoided.

The photographs in this article were contributed by Hans Born, who also sent us the yearbook of the International Commission on Indoor Cycling, from which we reprinted the championship routine at right. Mr. Born is secretary of the commission, which is a member of both the Union Cycliste Internationale and the Federation Internationale Amateur de Cyclisme. For more information on Artistic Cycling or Cycleball, write Hans Born, Gaustrasse 77, D-6520 Worms, West Germany.

Courtesy of Hans Born, International Commission on Indoor Cycling

Champion artistic cyclist Kurt Hunsanger recently represented West Germany against Czechoslovakia at Nachod. In his last competition he set a world record with a score of 324.05 points. Jaroslav Stepan, the methodical coach of artistic cycling in Czechoslovakia, has noted Hunsanger's routine in detail.

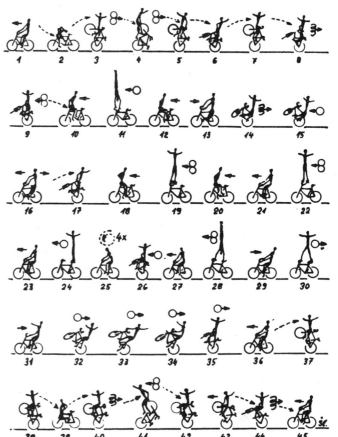

Cycle Speedway

Rod Witham

The sport was spawned on the bomb sites of the East End of London in the gray, postwar days when motorized speedway was at its height and every youngster attempted to copy his leather-clad hero by skidding sister's bike on the wastelands so thoughtfully provided by the Luftwaffe. The ensuing thirty years have seen the sport make giant strides in establishing itself as a vigourous, independent, cycle sport – progress that was rapidly accelerated in 1971 when the Cycle Speedway Council came into being. It has close to a hundred clubs in active membership. Some two thousand competitors race every weekend (and mid-week in minor local leagues) from April to October in team and individual competitions at seventy-five tracks organized into six leagues throughout Wales, England, and Scotland.

Since Cycle Speedway has its roots in motorized speedway, naturally it still retains a degree of similarity. Races – or, to use the correct phraseology, heats – take place in a counterclockwise direction on an oval, shale-surfaced track. Four riders battle for four laps earning points for positions gained – four to the winner, three to the second, two to the third, and one to the fourth. When a rider is excluded or fails to finish through mechanical or other mishap, he doesn't score.

Varying from 90 to 110 meters, raceways are situated in public parks, sports complexes, and recreation centers. Despite the present economic climate, racing facilities have multiplied as local authorities became aware that capital investment costs are low in comparison with benefits for participant and spectator alike.

Spectators are vital to the sport. They are pampered and kept informed. Track and club management place great emphasis on providing printed programs, seating, car parking, and refreshment facilities. They are kept informed throughout the race with public-address announcements and race commentary. And it pays handsome dividends as the spiraling crowd statistics readily reflect.

State-of-the-Art Cycle Speedway Bike. Photograph by Roger Nicholson

Individual events are the icing on the cake and while the rules stipulate that riders cannot receive cash payments, generous sponsorships ensure that competitors receive very worthwhile prizes. All the top clubs promote these "Grand Prix"-style events and the galaxy of star riders visiting from many parts of the country usually guarantees big crowds and excellent publicity for Cycle Speedway.

Photograph by Roger Nicholson

Rod Witham *is press and publicity officer of The Cycle Speedway Council, 14 Joy Avenue, Newton Flotman, Norwich, Norfolk, NR15 IRD, England.*

Photographs by Roger Nicholson

What does it take to be good at Cycle Speedway? Bike handling, technical ability, and physical fitness all play an important part in the makeup of a top rider. As these only come from experience it's not surprising that many of the people on the National Grand Prix circuit are in their late twenties or early thirties. Some stay at the top even longer, like Derek Garnett, a living legend in the sport, four-time British champion, forty-two years old and still going strong. However, there's plenty of racing to be had for the younger riders. Most leagues and clubs promote schoolboy (under sixteen), junior (under eighteen), and youth (under twenty-one) events. And of course there's always advice and encouragement from the older riders, such as help in polishing techniques, advice on equipment, suggestions on what national events should be entered, and often donations of equipment.

The Cycle Speedway bike is a very special machine. It's built round a distinctive frameset, is compact, responsive, and lacking in all accessories — including brakes! Cornering techniques require the

117

frame to be small (usually twenty-one inches) in comparision with rider height, while straight forks and ultrashort wheelbases aid stability in cornering. A wide choice of brand-name, "off-the-peg" frames are readily available, although the connoisseur often has a machine built to his individual specifications.

The saddle is positioned low enough so that feet touch the ground on both sides when seated. Handlebar fashions have changed over the years and gone are the old "cowhorns" that were popular in the 1950's and 1960's. They are set as low as possible into the stem, to get the best leverage for the start.

Pedals must be rubber; the narrow type used on children's and ladies' 3-speeds is ideal because these pedals don't clip the track when you pedal out of a corner during a race.

Cranks are of cotterless alloy, usually 180mm, to gain the maximum leverage from the starts. So the bottom bracket has to be set especially high – twelve-inch clearance is not uncommon.

If you think you can spin a low gear, just watch a Cycle Speedway star ply his trade! A 46-inch gearing gives explosive starts as riders jump into the first corner and sprint up the straights. Most common transmission is a 32-tooth chain ring/18-tooth freewheel combination.

Wheels are 26 x 1 3/8 inch – the only size able to accommodate the exclusive Cycle Speedway "Gripster" tires available only from Sweden or Taiwan. Thirty-six spoke alloy rims, large flange hubs, and 14-gauge double-butted spokes complete the wheel.

The ingenuity of manufacturers never ceases! One British company has recently introduced offset bottom bracket spindles that enable riders to pick their pedals up quicker from the gate. Tailor-made to suit left- or right-foot pushers, one degree offset is equivalent to one-eighth-inch misalignment!

The Council rules state that hands and limbs must be adequately protected, so a long-sleeved shirt or track suit is essential. Black track-suit bottoms or jeans are most commonly used and tucked into a pair of heavy-duty football socks, so there is nothing loose to catch on the chain. Gloves must be worn and should cover the fingers and palms completely. Sturdy shoes should have protective uppers.

"Widespread media coverage and substantial backing from sponsors have helped to rid Cycle Speedway once and for all of the ' skid kid ' tag picked up on the postwar bomb sites when the sport first evolved," states the 1980 *International Cycling Guide*.

With motorcycle speedway again emerging in the United States, I see no reason, given the necessary encouragement from trade and commercial interests, Cycle Speedway shouldn't blossom in America. It's not far removed from BMX, and what a huge success story that has been! Who knows – perhaps United States versus Great Britain tests are not all that far away!

If you would like to know more about Cycle Speedway, please do not hesitate to contact: Rod Witham, Press and Publicity Officer, The Cycle Speedway Council, 14 Joy Avenue, Newton Flotman, Norwich, Norfolk, NR15 1RD, England.

Photograph by Roger Nicholson

Photograph by Roger Nicholson

Photograph by Roger Nicholson

SPECIAL BIKES, SPECIAL SKILLS

How to Ride a High-Wheeler

The Timsley Brothers

An ounce of knowledge is worth a ton of theory, and there is no royal road to bicycle riding any more than there is to the attainment of any other desirable object. Cases are on record of persons learning the art in an incredibly short space of time, and we were informed the other day of an instance of a rider who purchased a machine at a large provincial factory, and after being shown simply how to mount, actually rode away on it, without any previous practice. Such instances are, however, extremely rare, and must not be allowed to mislead. Patient persevering practice is required to become a proficient and elegant bicyclist.

In the choice of a bicycle it is undoubtedly the truest economy to purchase only the best quality, and that from a well-known manufacturer, whose reputation is the buyer's best safeguard for the superiority of the machine he sells.

For if it be considered that a bicycle, which must bear the wear and tear of all kinds of roads, and carry a weight of ten to fourteen stone at a rate of twelve to fifteen miles an hour, for days together if necessary, weighs only forty-five pounds, it will be at once conceded that not only must it be made of the very best materials that money can buy, but that its con-

The Timsley Brothers originally published this in Bicycling *in 1879. The small-wheeled machine referred to is the front-wheel driven "bone-shaker."*

struction demands also the finest mechanical skill and ability that can be bestowed upon it.

Second-rate material, and second-rate labor, are not only absolutely unreliable, but perilous to life and limb. This warning cannot be too strenuously enforced.

It is well for the beginner not to be too ambitious about the size of the driving wheel; confidence is more certainly acquirable on a small wheel, although that is pretty certain to be soon discarded for the largest possible radius the rider's length of leg can compass, for the sake of the speed thereby to be obtained without any greater labor.

Where practicable, it is very advisable to learn on a small wooden machine, and we say *experto crede*, this will not be injured in appearance by the few harmless falls that the tyro generally has to take in the beginning, with the best grace he may. Decidedly the better way in the first instance is to obtain the assistance of a friend, and this there can be little difficulty in doing. The knack of *balancing* is really all there is to be actually learned, the rest comes by practice, and that gives the confidence that enables riders to do the great things in the way of speed and distance that the equestrian may sigh for in vain.

On a gentle slope and on a machine with a small wheel, you may then, alone if necessary, take your seat and proceed, grasping the handle, not too tightly but *never leaning on it*, and if your machine

FRIENDLY HELP

be low enough for your feet to just touch the ground, so much the better. If you find the balance difficult to acquire on starting, and that the machine has an inclination to fall, a mere touch with the toe, on the ground, on whichever side the machine is falling, will right you again. The pedals must not be used in the first essays, the impetus given by the incline being sufficient to move the machine with quite enough velocity for you to learn to balance and steer. When you have mastered this, you have learned all that a bicyclist needs by way of precept. The next thing is to accustom the feet and legs to the motion of the pedals, in order to do which, it is necessary to place the feet lightly on them, allowing the motion of the machine to carry them round.

Do not attempt to exert any pressure on the pedals until you become thoroughly accustomed to their motion. As

119

your feet are now employed and cannot touch the ground to restore equilibrium, if you experience a tendency to fall, bear in mind, *to turn the wheel gently and without the slightest jerk in the direction the bicycle is falling.* This is the whole secret of success in bicycle riding, and cannot be too attentively observed. To a finished rider this motion is an instinct, but, until you arrive at this stage of perfection, it will need to be carefully remembered and practiced. If you turn the wheel in the opposite direction you will assuredly fall.

A FRIENDLY WALL

After a little experience in riding, so that you have become somewhat accustomed to the balance and the pedals, you may endeavor to mount. This, it is advisable, should be first attempted from some support, such as a wall or post, and not by the step. You will by this means gradually acquire the confidence necessary to mount and also dismount by means of the step in the proper manner. To mount by a wall you place the machine in a nearly upright position against it, placing the pedal that is away from the wall, just past the top of the throw. This is to ensure your getting a good start with your outside foot. Mount your machine and take hold of the outside handle, but with the other hand steady yourself against the wall, gently bringing the machine into a perpendicular position. As soon as it has attained this, push your outside pedal downward; this will give you the requisite start and enable you to bring your other foot into use. This way of mounting will answer your purpose until you have arrived at some proficiency as a rider; you may then endeavor to do so in the ordinary way, by means of

MOUNTING

120

the step. To do this, take the machine by both handles, place the left toe upon the step, and, taking two or three short hops to get a little "way" on the machine, raise yourself on the step and drop into the saddle. In learning, it is always best to do this on a gentle descent; it is also desirable, in order to avoid a fall, to keep the wheel turned about two inches out of the perpendicular and toward you, so that, in the event of your not succeeding in reaching the saddle at the first attempt, you will drop on the side you started from.

It is quite impossible to state arbitrarily how long this state of pupilage will last. No two riders, on comparing notes, ever find their experiences coincident. We can only counsel patience and resolution, and give the assurance that bicycling is not so difficult after all, and that success is within easy reach of all who persevere; a few hours being generally enough to learn each successive stage on the way to complete mastery over the machine. Frequent practice (but not by exhaustive spells of work) is of the greatest importance; and a sure aid to the maintenance of self-possession is to bear continually in mind the few precepts we venture to give.

DISMOUNTING   FALLING

The acquisition of a graceful and easy seat, and the economy of your motive power are the next two things to be striven for. Avoid stiffness, whether in the joints of the legs and arms, or in the pose of the body, and do not attempt to sit rigidly upright with military exactness. The act of dismounting being exactly the converse of mounting, it is scarcely necessary to say more than that the left toe should be accustomed to seek the step and find it with ease, whereupon the rider can drop lightly on the ground on his right foot, not relinquishing his hold of the machine handle until he is safe on terra firma. Experienced riders generally acquire the habit of descending without using the step, and leave the machine from the treadle direct, or by throwing the left leg over the handle. A tyro should never attempt this.

The use of the leg rest permits the rider, on descending hills, to rest from the labor of working the treadles, and

THE LEG-REST—DOWNHILL

merely steer his course with the handle.

Acrobatic performances, such as riding sidesaddle and standing on the seat like a circus rider, are occasionally to be seen. The learner should never attempt anything of the sort until his mastery over the machine is quite perfect, even then he will do well to avoid these displays, and give his attention to the increase of his speed of traveling.

For racing, the best dress is that usually worn by runners, consisting of a thin jersey, with knickerbockers, or trousers cut to the knee, made of silk, or some such light material.

The tourist has to take into consideration what is most useful and comfortable for a long ride, as well as what is least likely to hamper his movements. For a long journey, riders will find knickerbockers more comfortable than trousers and gaiters. A flannel shirt and a short yachting coat will complete the costume (serge is the best wearing material), though a mackintosh strapped to the machine is indispensable. A light gun or fishing rod can be tied along the spring, as well as a bag containing sponge, brushes, etc. Thus equipped, a rider may travel for days among the Highlands of Scotland, or through the wildest parts of Ireland.

PRACTICE MAKES PERFECT

How to Ride a Unicycle

John Jenack

Many people think that riding a unicycle is a practice limited to a few very coordinated and slightly eccentric circus performers. To these people, unicycling is closely akin to roller skating on ice during an earthquake: in other words, impossible. Actually, the balance used in riding a unicycle is most similar to the balance used in walking, and anyone capable of walking is capable of riding – in a very short time!

The best wheel size for a beginner is 20-inch, with the tire slightly under-inflated to increase its surface friction. This makes turning sluggish, and helps to prevent the unexpected spins so common to beginning unicyclists.

Adjusting the seat is very important (see "The Saddle"), for if the seat is set right it will save your legs from unnecessary strain and allow you to practice twice as long. The front of the saddle should be slightly higher than the rear, and allow you to slip onto it

John Jenack *is one of America's most skilled unicyclists and is an instructor of circus arts in the New York State school system. For more information, write The Unicycling Society of America, P.O. Box 40534, Redford, MI, 48240.*

easily but still hold the unicycle snugly to you when you mount. When seated on the unicycle with one or the other of the pedals in the "down" position, your leg should just be able to straighten out completely, without really stretching.

When learning to ride it is best to work with two volunteers – helpers or "spotters" – one on each side. If you're unable to find two willing volunteers, one person and a wall or fence will suffice. If all your friends are wary and no one will volunteer, it is possible to learn with just a wall or fence, but much of the difficulty encountered in the early stages of learning can be eliminated by using one or two helpers.

To mount, put the saddle comfortably but securely into your crotch area. The pedals should be in a near-horizontal position, with the rear pedal just slightly lower than the front one. With a helper on each side of you, put your foot on the rear pedal and, resting your body weight on the saddle, ease yourself forward and upward and draw the pedals backward for one half revolution of the wheel until you are balanced over the unicycle. Your helpers should be holding your hands out at arm's length on each side

of you, and the palms of their hands should be facing upward. (Aside from being the most comfortable hand-holding position, the "helper's palm up" is not as tiring and allows the rider to push rather than pull to maintain balance.) When you feel yourself balanced over the wheel, stand up immediately.

Because this is your first attempt at mounting, a certain amount of shakiness is inevitable. Some people, finding they gave too much push, pass right over the wheel and off the front of the unicycle. In just a minute or two this problem should disappear, though, and won't be a problem after that. You should now be standing up on the unicycle, looking forward, with both legs completely straightened. Posture plays a key role in riding the unicycle, and sitting up straight and looking forward rather than down will make everything much easier. By standing up immediately you will force your posture to improve, and you'll also force the pedals of the unicycle into the "safety" position.

When you stand up with both legs completely straightened, the pedals ro-

Fairchild Republic Co., Farmingdale, L.I., N.Y. Lunch hour unicyclists. Bill Jenack, founder of the Unicycling Society, is at far right.

Start of a "slow" race at an annual Unicycling Society meet. Photo courtesy of The Unicycling Society of America, Inc. Newsletter

tate to a horizontal position. In this position it's possible to apply forward or backward force to maintain your balance. This is called the "safety" position. (When one or the other of the pedals is held in a "down" position, the rider has no control of the cycle and will usually be forced to dismount.) Finding yourself in the "safety" position, you can now lower your weight onto the saddle. If at any time you feel yourself losing your balance, stand up immediately and start again.

While you are mastering this basic mount, it's a good time to learn how to dismount as well. To dismount, move the pedals into a near-horizontal position, with the rear pedal slightly lower than the front one. With your weight resting on the seat and the rear pedal, take your foot off the front pedal and slowly step backward. (You may wish to put one hand on the saddle to keep it from falling, but to begin with, this isn't necessary.) While dismounting may seem like a difficult feat at first, you are actually barely six inches off the floor and the step is a small one. A few tries will diminish any fears you have of doing it. And once you have learned how to mount and dismount, you're ready to learn how to ride.

When you first begin to ride the unicycle, your helpers can make all the difference in the world. Make sure that they stay at your sides at all times, for if one leads or falls behind, it will hinder the balance you're trying to develop. Also, make sure that they keep your arms extended outward. With your arms fully extended you have a natural balance pole, similar in its effect to those used by tightrope walkers; use it and it will considerably help you in balancing. Make sure that your helpers are not pulling you to the side, for that can prevent any balance from developing. Have one helper keep an eye on your posture, and if necessary, have him tell you to "look up" or "sit up straight" every thirty seconds. With your concentration on a number of things at once, this nagging will be a useful reminder.

Ready to ride? Good. First, mount the unicycle and move the pedals into the safety position. Try to get comfortable, and make sure to let your weight rest on the seat. Taking the weight off your legs and relaxing is half the battle, so if you concentrate on this from the first you'll find it much easier. Get used to the feeling of your feet on the pedals, and try to find the position that makes you feel most secure. It is rare that your feet will

ever slip off the pedals, but the psychological advantage of feeling that your feet are firmly positioned is helpful.

Next, try to move the unicycle just a few inches forward and a few inches back. As you are doing this try to concentrate on keeping the seat (and your body!) over the wheel, and try to move smoothly, rather than jerking as you start and stop. When you first try this you'll have a tendency to pedal much more than is necessary; instead of covering a few inches you'll probably be covering a few feet. Try, though, to develop the control necessary to move the unicycle just a few inches at a time.

After you feel comfortable with this small back-and-forth movement, it's time to make a half revolution of the wheel. To do this, you'll start from the basic safety position, sitting up straight with your forces "trimmed out." (This means that you should be depending on your helpers equally, not favoring one or the other side, and not leaning forward or backward.) When you are ready to go, you should be relaxed and your weight should be on the seat, not on the pedals. To begin, back up three or four inches and immediately pedal forward for one half revolution of the wheel. As soon as you have completed pedaling, stand up immediately to re-establish your control and return the pedals to the safety position. The reason for backing up initially is to establish a forward lean necessary for you to be able to ride forward. If you were to begin pedaling forward from a complete rest, the unicycle would fall in front of you just as your body would be falling behind the unicycle. Like balancing a broomstick on your finger, it is necessary to back up before making a forward movement.

Once you have re-established your balance in the safety position, you are ready to sit back down and try it again. Remember that your posture is tremendously important, so check to see that you are sitting up straight and looking forward before each attempt. Eventually you should be able to make a half a revolution each time without having to stand up, finding the safety position by feel. When you can do this confidently, you're ready for a full revolution.

The most important thing to remember in making a full revolution of the pedals is do it smoothly. Just as you did with the half revolution, back up and immediately pedal forward one full revolution. You may find yourself hesitating at the halfway point, but keep on pedaling! Once you have made a full revolution stand up immediately to catch your balance. As you are already familiar with the feel of this, you'll probably pick it up very quickly. Don't pedal beyond one revolution yet, because your control won't be that good and you'll have difficulty stopping. Take it one step at a time, and by the time you feel confident doing a single revolution you'll be able to start putting them together.

When you do start pedaling for more than one revolution, set a goal each time and stick to it. If you plan to pedal for three, then pedal for three and stop. This will make it much easier for your helpers to help you, and will prevent a lot of unnecessary falls. By the time you can make five or six full revolutions without stopping or losing your balance, you'll be able to get rid of one of your helpers.

Sitting on the unicycle with the pedals in the safety position, extend one of your arms fully to the side and let go of that helper. Keep that arm extended, and don't be afraid to use it for balance. Repeat the steps for half and full revolutions of pedaling, and when you've mastered them try several revolutions without stopping. At this point you're just about ready to start riding by yourself.

John Jenack, *the author, riding a Big Wheel converted from a wagon wheel. Photograph by John Krausz*

When you really feel good riding with just one helper, and don't have to stop any more for support or to catch your balance, it's time for you to start soloing. As you ride along with your one helper, try clapping your hands. You may think that this should be very easy, but don't underestimate the power of panic. Many people discover that they're fine riding along with someone, but as soon as they let go, they freeze up and panic, forgetting everything they have learned. Take it easy, take it slow, and relax. Don't attempt a thunderous ovation when you should just be clapping your hands once. As you develop your proficiency you can increase the number of claps each time and eventually let go of your helper for complete revolutions at a time. Just don't rush it. When you feel that you no longer need your helper except to get on the unicycle, it's time for you to learn a solo mount.

The solo mount is virtually identical to the mount you learned to do with your helpers, but instead of stopping in the safety position after you have drawn the unicycle under you by backpedaling, you continue to backpedal just a little bit more – establishing your forward lean. Once you are leaning forward you have no choice but to pedal forward to catch your balance, and if you can do this, you're riding.

Once you are able to mount and ride in a straight line, it's only a matter of practice to develop your turning skills. To turn, it is necessary to develop a lean in the direction you wish to turn. Once that lean is established you can then turn into it, usually accelerating just slightly to catch your balance. If you

attempt to turn without establishing a lean in a certain direction, you'll find that your center of gravity is no longer over the unicycle and you'll be forced to dismount. This shouldn't really be a problem though, for turning on the unicycle rapidly becomes an intuitive process – almost like a reflex.

An important skill to master once you have learned the basics on the unicycle is rocking in place, or idling. Essentially, rocking in place is a forward and backward movement of the wheel that allows the unicyclist to maintain his balance without traveling. Rocking is accomplished by pedaling forward and backward one half revolution of the wheel – from one safety position to the next, and back again. The easiest way to learn how to rock is to hold on to a wall or fence with one hand, begin rocking back and forth, and gradually let up the pressure on that hand. Soon you'll hardly need the wall at all, and then you'll be rocking by yourself.

The real key to learning to do anything on the unicycle is practice. If you practice systematically, a high level of skill can be developed in a very short time. All of the unicycle skill mentioned to this point can be learned in three or four days, provided you follow the methods described closely and devote a couple of hours to practice each day. Advanced skills will certainly take a bit more time, but not half as long as most people might think. Some advanced skills are: jump mount, riding backward, riding with one foot, and shuffling (walking on the wheel in place of pedaling).

The unicycle is considered by many to be a recent and highly specialized addition to the world of cycling. In fact, it can be traced back to the early 1880's, making its first appearance during the era of the high wheelers. Many cyclists of that era have laid claim to the "invention" of the unicycle, each believing himself to be the first ever to ride on one wheel. Sebastian Merrill Neuhausen, an inventor, cyclist, and business associate of the Wright brothers, claimed to have ridden on the front wheel of an Ordinary, holding the rear wheel off the ground. George Hendee, a well-known trick cyclist of the time, went one step further and completely removed the rear wheel. Ahrens, a California cycle inventor, built a unicycle that was displayed for many years as the "world's first." And Lou Lacher, a New York cycling performer of the 1890's, claimed not only to have been the first unicyclist, but also to have been the first to ride one on a tightwire! These claims were all very original, but also very dated, because Leonardo da Vinci had made drawings of a "monocycle" as early as the mid-fifteenth century.

As for being "invented," most researchers agree that the unicycle was not invented, but rather discovered – by many people at the same time. Cyclists riding their high wheelers found that as they braked, the rear wheel of the bicycle often came off the ground, leaving them riding on just the large front wheel. From there it was a small step to removing the rear wheel completely, and discovering the unicycle.

In the few years following its discovery, unicycling became highly developed as a sport, and unicycles often appeared at the bicycle competitions of the day. In 1888, the bulletin of the League of American Wheelmen carried a listing of unicycle speed records set at Lake View Park in Peoria, Illinois. Similar records were being set throughout the country. Far from being just a curiosity to bicyclists, unicycling was a challenge and a welcome diversion from the often grueling bicycle competitions. The unicycle was "in vogue," and would remain so for the next dozen years.

Around the turn of the century, as high wheelers began to disappear in favor of safety bicycles, the unicycle became less and less common. Rarely was one seen outside of a circus tent or vaudeville show.

The saddle design of a unicycle is particularly important, for a comfortable and properly adjusted saddle can make all the difference in learning to ride. Most of the commercially available unicycle saddles have very narrow center portions that widen at each end – an esthetically pleasing design that is unfortunately neither practical nor comfortable. As this type of saddle falls and hits the ground it tends to widen at the ends, restricting leg movement and making pedaling extremely uncomfortable. The metal seat frame also tends to buckle and kink, tearing through the seat cover and gouging the rider's legs. The narrow center portion of the saddle results in the seat belt protruding on one side, digging into the rider's thigh, and creating a lopsided effect.

These problems can be overcome, though, by customizing your own unicycle saddle. A few simple modifications will greatly improve the comfort of the saddle, and this should improve your riding. First off, once the seat is properly adjusted, the protruding seat bolt can be hacksawed off at the nut, filed down smooth, and capped. This will save the rider's thighs. Then the seat itself can be redesigned like this:

First, hammer the ends of the saddle outward, as the arrows show.

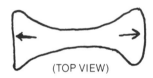
(TOP VIEW)

Then lay the saddle on its side and hammer the wider ends in, making it long and slender (See arrows.)

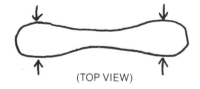
(TOP VIEW)

The shape of the saddle should have been altered as follows:

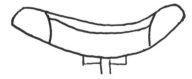
Side view before hammering

(Custom saddle design by William Jenack – Founder, Unicycling Society of America, Inc.)

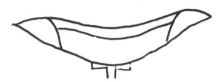
Side view after hammering

Next, a padding layer of foam rubber is added. The foam rubber is then taped to the saddle with one-inch masking tape – but not too tightly as the cushioning effect will then be lost.

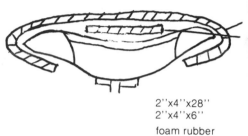
2''x4''x28''
2''x4''x6''
foam rubber

1'' wide masking tape

Finally, a seat cover made of some durable material should be added. Many unicyclists use a pair of athletic tube socks – slipping one over each end of the seat, overlapping them (as shown in the diagram) and overhand stitching them together. In addition to the socks, an additional seat cover can be made for protection or just for show. Denim blue jean material is ideal for this, but any strong material can be used. Elastic slip covers – coordinated to costume color, etc. – are also easy to make and will considerably extend the lifetime of the saddle.

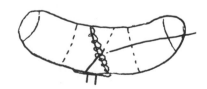
Tube socks sewn together with an overhand stitch

Hurray for Fixed Wheels

John Krausz

Riding a fixed wheel is completely different from riding a bike that free wheels, but knowing how to ride "fixed" is perhaps the only shortcut there is to learning to be a good bike rider.

Grace, balance, economy of movement, conservation of momentum, "setting up for a sprint," rushing a medium-sized hill, alertness to changing road and traffic conditions, even and continous pedaling are all things that a good bike rider does, and are all sort of thrown in "free" as one learns to ride a fixed wheel.

Once you know how, there is little left to learn about bike riding besides shifting gears and learning how to do without the control that a fixed-wheel bicycle gives you.

A fixed wheel bicycle is simplicity itself. Pedaled forward, it goes forward, restrained, it slows. If you pedaled backward it would go backward. This direct drive allows you to use "negative work." When you walk down a flight of stairs you use negative work-- you are still going forward, but most of the energy you are using is in restraining yourself. Backward pressure on the pedal slows, then stops, the bike. Why this is difficult to understand seems strange to anyone who knows how to do it.

If you rode a tricycle as a child or one of those little brakeless sidewalk bicycles they sell to unknowing parents, you know how to make many of the moves necessary to ride a fixed wheel. A front wheel driven tricycle *is* a fixed wheel.

Up until 1897 almost every bike was a fixed wheel.

Highly skilled people can learn to ride in a few minutes. A sixty-five-year-old dancer learned immediately (she had never ridden a bike so she didn't know that you were "supposed" to be able to coast.) So did a mountain-climbing instructor. He was able to go faster than I could, as he was stronger and better coordinated. People whose cycling has been restricted to Exercycles learn equally rapidly. So for riders of ordinary bicycles, the problem is not learning to pedal all the time, but learning not to coast.

Because, of course, you can't coast with a fixed gear. You can "empty pedal," which means keeping up with the pedals but producing no pressure. This is called "fanning" by the racers who do it when their downhill speed exceeds their gear. Others apply slightly negative pressure, so that their speed doesn't exceed their ability to spin.

Some physiologists think that we can do more negative than positive work, which gives credence to the fixed wheelers' idea that it is possible to stop a fixed-wheel bike faster than a bike with brakes.

Fixed wheelers are a very clannish lot, happy to meet each other or expound on their favorite subject. They often demonstrate, and will sometimes even admit, a feeling of moral and technical. superiority over other cyclists. That's because they share certain secrets: the added safety in traffic because of their greater ability to change speed, their much greater degree of control in the rain because they are not dependent on a brake, the bike's mechanical simplicity and greater efficiency, (at least five to eight percent more than a 10-speed), and most of all, the delight of being really with the bike. They know that riding a fixed is more fun, and they know that it has made them better bike riders, and they are very amused by all the people who call themselves bike riders but are afraid to learn!

Technique, of course, differs from bicycling with a freewheel. Hills have to be rushed, and special care must be taken when riding with people on road bikes, particularly where drafting is concerned, because of the difference in stopping ability of the two bikes. A skilled fixed wheeler can sometimes stop faster than a road bike, and tends to ride much more evenly except on hills.

A fixed wheel can be used on almost any bicycle. The picture shows a fixed wheel on a 20-inch Peugeot folder. Photograph by John Krausz

125

Not that fixed wheeling is without its special dangers. A fixed wheel is so unforgiving that if your pedal rhythm is poor you wonder how anyone ever gets used to it. Miss just one part of a pedal stroke and the pedals remind you, forcibly. Make a more serious error in judgment and the bike rejects you—it may even eject you!

There is no way you can fake riding a fixed wheel. There are lots of ways of faking on a bike that coasts. But if you don't hurt yourself or scare yourself silly the first time out on a fixed, and have enough self-discipline to learn the inevitable lessons that it has to teach you, riding fixed makes you a better bike rider. Any unevenness is immediately signaled to the rider by the drive train. On a free-wheel bicycle there is no way of knowing whether you are completely in gear during an entire rotation of the pedals, or if what you are doing is high speed "twiddling"—catching up with yourself as the bike slows. On a fixed it becomes very clear that you steer with your body and the handlebars become something to pull against. The laws of physics are non-negotiable and this is never more clear to a bike rider than when riding a fixed.

People ask how you climb a hill on a fixed wheel. This is not a problem unless it is geared too high. You roll up a hill the way you roll·up a carpet. Hill-climbing competitions are usually on fixed wheels. Going up is not the problem, though sometimes the competitors carry their bikes on the way down.

The first time that you ride down a very long hill on a fixed wheel is really exciting and you can learn a new definition of fear.

Practice in a parking lot, or at least in an area where there is little traffic, to gain some experience before you try the road or a downhill of any size.

Riding fixed wheel is getting back to basics. It's so much fun that it's hard to get back on a bike that free wheels. No matter how good you get, every ride leaves you with the feeling that you've learned something.

It's perfect for urban transportation, winter cycling, and riding with someone who's much slower than you are.

Besides involving more muscles in the legs by back-pedaling to restrain the bike on downhills and to slow and stop, fixed wheeling involves using the arms and the back muscles to a much greater extent than regular bike riding. That allows you to warm up much faster on cold winter days. And your legs don't cool on downhills. It's an old truism in bicycling that "you're not a complete bike rider until you've done at least one winter on a fixed."

With its greater efficiency and mechanical simplicity, the fixed-wheeled bicycle is the basis of many special forms of cycling: track racing, hill climbing as a competitive sport, bicycle polo, trick and artistic cycling.

Bicycle racers use it as a spring training machine to get the winter out of their legs and ensure good pedal action. Traditionally, it was used on rollers as well. It is the "hack" everyday bike for many long-time bicycle riders.

On the road fixed wheels are usually ridden with a front brake. They are always used with toeclips.

Classic gears are 63 inches with high-pressure tires, and 72 with tubulars. Almost everyone gears down a bit in the winter, so that the rider warms up faster because he's spinning more. One fixed wheeler I know cut his gear back from 72 to 68 on his seventy-second birthday!

The term "fixed wheeling" is British and is used to describe this type of gearing when used to ride on the road. A fixed wheel can be any type of bike that is used to do fixed wheeling. A track bike is, of course, a fixed wheel, but specially built for racing on a track.

A track bike is a pure racing machine. Take all the junk and cables off a modern road bike and it would look like a track bike. Built for stiffness, with severe angles, it has rear-facing horizontal dropouts so that chain tension can be adjusted by pulling the back wheel backward. The fork may or may not be drilled to accept a front brake. Although designed for the track, track bikes equipped with a front brake are sometimes used in time trialing, hill climbs, and club races. And it wasn't until the early 1950's that road bikes could consistently beat track bikes on certain race courses.

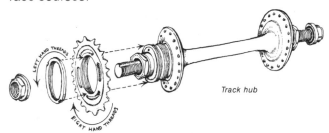

Track hub

A fixed wheel doesn't have to be a track bike. Any bike can be converted into a fixed by using a track hub, which has a locking ring that screws in the opposite direction from the cog to prevent it from unscrewing when pressure is put on in stopping or slowing down. But even a track hub can be improvised on a steel hub by having the sprocket welded on. There are enough problems learning to ride a fixed without the cog coming loose.

A track wheel isn't dished, it doesn't have to be. But you may have trouble getting a good chain line if you're converting a road bike to fixed. On a 10-speed choose the front ring that gives you the best line, making use of whatever adjustment of the front spindle is possible. (Track spindles are shorter than 5- or 10-speed spindles.) A 5-speed will probably give a better chain line than a 10-speed. You may also not be able to use the rear sprocket you want to because front-facing dropouts leave little room for adjustment. If you get serious and can't afford another bike, the thing to do is have track ends put on your frame.

Regular track sprockets are 1/8-inch wide (same as on a 3-speed); they are available in half-inch pitch in 13 to mid-20 tooth size, and in derailleur width (sometimes used in pursuit racing because the thinner chain is thought to be smoother), and in one-inch pitch for people who want to use the older block or roller chain . . . the skipped tooth means that 7-tooth gives the equivalent gearing of 14, 10 the equivalent of 20, etc.

Fixed wheels are more fun when they have light wheels and tubulars, but the thin one-inch clinchers will serve. Heavier clinchers can be used, but it's hard to bring the wheel around for either jumping or stopping, so that the trade-off between heavier wheels and safety must be considered.

If you buy a new track bike that is not street approved, there are certain additions you'll want to make. A front brake, first of all; then a pump clip and a spare-tire carrier (though a used toe strap will do for that). If the fork is not drilled out for a brake, don't let someone attack it with a quarter-inch drill unless you trust them! You may also want to change the chainwheel, which is usually a 50 or a 52. A 48 or 46 will give you a larger choice of gears when combined with 13 to 18-tooth sprockets. Larger sprockets are hard to find and often of inferior quality. If the bike comes with Campagnolo cranks and hubs, get a Campy crank wrench; it's strong, inexpensive, and efficient. (It's sometimes called a peanut-butter wrench because it's also useful for spreading peanut butter.) If the cranks aren't Campy, find out if Campy crank bolts will fit, as they are the strongest.

When sold for street use, most new fixed-wheel bikes at least have bridges with holes for brakes, and often come with road bars, chainguards and front and back brakes in order to meet Consumer Product Safety Commission rules.

The Tandem Story

Malcolm Boyd

Tandem bicycles, or "twicers," have a certain mystique about them that sets them apart from other bicycles. Dazzling speed, exotic prices, mechanical orneriness, and scarcity combine to lend them a uniqueness. But are tandems really so different? The answer is an unqualified yes. In almost any aspect – handling technique, equipment, mechanical tricks, versatility – twicers differ from solo bicycles. Let's look at what makes them different.

First and foremost, the riding relationship is expanded to include three—pilot, stoker, and machine. All must function in a synergistic relationship if a happy cycling experience is to be had. The classic twicer joke that the pilot accidentally leaves the stoker behind doesn't happen to those who are attuned to the beast. This may seem trivial, but thirty miles out on a ride, it's clear to a tandemist that tandeming is cycling's teamwork sport.

A favorite myth among the uninitiated is that two big lugs can jump on a twicer and blow the pack away. While they are somewhat faster, consider this case in point.

I ride tandem with my wife, and I also occasionally ride with a Category One racer. While my wife is in no way as strong as an experienced racer, she drives the machine around a timed course every bit as fast. Why? Personal communication.

Some of the simplest aspects of cycling must be rethought to accomodate a tandem. How one starts a tandem from a stop is dependent on whether cranks are in phase or 90 degrees out of phase. In the former case two feet are on the ground, whereas out-of-phase machines generally keep the stoker fully clipped in, which increases the acceleration from full stops. This has nothing to do with stopping, but rather with hill-climbing, where out-of-phase cranks are often preferred for smoother power application.

A survey revealed that sixty-nine percent of all tandemists ride cranks in phase, and one suspects this is so because

Tandems on a tour. Photograph by Janet Carothers

Malcolm Boyd *is the founder of the Tandem Club of America and a 25,000 mile tandemist with his wife Judy.*

the bikes come that way from the manufacturer. Those who ride in phase may never have tried the alternative.

While making a decision about crank-phase angle should be easy, this offers a perfect example of how tandems differ from solo bicycles. The problem encompasses technique as well as mechanical know-how, has no set, pat answer, and widespread disagreement exists among tandemists. The search for solutions to this basic problem—power transmission within the man-machine triad—leads tandemists toward invention and improvisation. Nowhere else in cycling is so much experimentation and modification seen, and this is one of the things that makes tandems so exciting.

What are some of the things a person thinking about tandeming should consider? First, because riding a tandem requires two people, the machine doesn't get on the road quite as often as a solo. Second, the return on investment in dollars per ride is less—because it gets out less often, and also because tandems cost more initially.

Tandeming requires a good, steady relationship—such as marriage—that won't easily break up. Tandeming can take a toll on a team, especially toward the crest of long hills. Tandemists are not especially combative, but spending two hours on the side of a mountain with someone feeling peaked early on can try one's temper. "If your marriage can stand a tandem, it can stand anything," notes one knowledgeable, if cynical, observer.

When buying a tandem, consider how much and what type of use the tandem will have. For virtually any type of solo, there is a tandem counterpart: for racing, day touring, camping, or just riding to the beach. For beginning tandemists, the choice is between a $200 bomber and a minimum of $500 for a light touring machine. Most people considering more than around-the-block activity choose the more expensive machine, which can be readily modified for camping or racing by adding or changing gears. While not ideally specialized for any one function, the light touring machine can perform adequately in several. Unadulterated tandem enthusiasts buy several tandems for different uses.

When riding, a tandem team is exposed to an amazing barrage of questions from nontandem cyclists. "How do you tighten the transfer chain?" one will ask. With an eccentric bottom-bracket casing. "But why do stokers' crank rates appear higher than pilots' in out-of-phase machines?" Optical illusion. "My, what a lot of teeth you have on that chainring!" It's a 56. And finally, "Jeez, your cute little stoker doesn't seem to be working at all!" In a flash, the stoker is out of the saddle, the chain is on the 56 and the questioner is left far behind. Ah, tandeming—it's a different trip.

Problems with riding twicers uphill has given the breed a bad name in bicycling circles. The truth is that good hill-climbing ability is a matter of technique. A strong team on the flats will pull each other apart on the grades if it doesn't learn to work together. Unfortunately, most tandemists believe the problem can't be overcome, so they stay away from mountainous terrain. Thus, with little or no practice climbing hills, tandem teams tend to be slow, and a self-fulfilling prophecy is generated.

The essence of efficient technique is a smooth application of power. Because of any tandem's increased weight, any decrease in speed or inertia demands a greater power application to reaccelerate. Either out- or in-phase machines must concentrate on "thinking round" and pedaling fully and smoothly through the cycle. The bike must be held upright with little side-to-side fluctuation or rocking, which requires a good deal of concentration on the part of driver and stoker to keep their combined body weight in line with the forward vector. Stokers can normally drive a tandem considerable distances sideways by weight shifting. On a hill, bad technique can force the driver to constantly be correcting the steering, which requires a good portion of his or her strength.

If maximum speed uphill is required, both riders can stand out of the saddle. This is particularly easy on a stiff frame, which does not twist, then spring back under stress. It is also easier if the pedals are out of phase, since power is applied at all times. In-phase uphill standing drives the bike side to side in a swaying motion, particularly if the gear is too high or the hill too steep. This can happen even on the

---

Come Ride With Me

Michael Roeder

What follows are a few things we've learned in the past couple of years about a peculiar disease—tandemitis.

Mike hates to chase the tandems that his friends ride to work each day. Tandem owners don't like to let friends ride their bikes. A person who lets Mike borrow his custom George Stratton for the summer is a great guy! Laurie is very impressed by the tandem, as are some other women who have since faded from the picture. Laurie likes riding to the beach on the tandem. Laurie doesn't like

Mike and Laurie Roeder *first delighted the readers of the bulletin of the Tandem Club of America with this article.*

riding up the mountains in a slither of sweat on a 95-degree day. Neither does Mike, but they do it anyway.

Mike discovers that heavy guys with muscles are not necessarily better tandem partners than light girls with enthusiasm. He also discovers that the Stratton tourer will not keep up with a Pogliagli tandem. Ridding the bike of steel rims, hub brake, pannier racks, lights, generator, fenders, horn, and water bottles drops it from 56 to 42 pounds. It goes faster, rides harder, and bends the axles on his single-bike racing wheels. Eventually, even great guys want their tandems back.

Honeymoons are a great excuse for a tandem tour. Tandem tours are a great reason to buy a tandem. Tandems are not so easy to get on a week's notice. They cost lots of money. An unexpected inheritance is best spent on a Paramount. Stone Cyclery in Alameda, California has six in stock—what color would

we like? Black is beautiful.

Tandems are fun to put together. Tandems are lousy to get fine tuned. Cables break—where do you get a tandem fingertip shifter rear cable? Cinelli seats look great and sit terribly. Weinmann rims flex. Mike's legs hit the rear bars; Laurie's nose hits Mike's rear.

After ten days of development time, the honeymoon begins. Contrary to popular opinion among cyclists, there are other things to do on a honeymoon besides ride a bike, so we borrow the seat off the Stratton to assure a good time will be had by all.

Next, we learn that bicycling does not necessarily ruin one's sex life, but 6,000-foot elevations, tandems, and a 40-inch low gear do not mix. Walking a tandem uphill is not fun. TA chainwheel bolts loosen up, fall out, and are not available in hardware stores. Long fender screws, jillions of washers, and a couple of nuts are an acceptable substitute for a while.

flats if the team isn't aware of transverse body-weight movement.

A particularly helpful uphill technique is alternate standing out of saddle. Either pilot or stoker can individually stand on alternate short hills in a series of rolls, or he or she can alternate standing on a long hill. If you're being overtaken on a hill, a particularly devastating technique is to have your female teammate stand to match the speed of the passing bike. Having given the potential passer about ten seconds to assess the situation, the driver can then also jump out of the saddle and deliver the bad news, leaving the challenger in the dust.

When riding tandems in mountains, particular care should be taken to smooth the grade. Ride as far as you can to the left of the lane on right-hand uphill corners, and keep to the right on left-hand corners. Obviously, traffic takes precedence, but on an empty mountain climb, this minimizes the grade. If the road curves sharply, this reduces the number of gear shifts required. This is especially important on a tandem, since gear shifting often takes a little longer. Also, a tandem's great weight requires more frequent shifts on a grade, much as a truck's does.

Thus far, all the emphasis has been on uphill speed. Mention should be made of getting back down. This is no trivial matter on a tandem, where speeds on a long downhill can exceed 60 miles per hour. Riding a twisting mountain road and trailing behind cars, it is quite possible to blow out tires if a few precautions are not followed.

Applying your brakes should be avoided, if possible. While not braking will lead to descending at high speeds, it is safer in the long run. Much has been made in tandem circles of drag brakes, such as disc or drums, yet these only marginally reduce speed at the cost of overheating and fading the brake so it can't be used later if it's really needed to stop. A better technique is for the stoker to use his or her chest as an air brake by sitting up with hands on the top of the bars. This is especially useful in steep, straight descents, where perfect balance isn't needed.

Descending at a high speed allows the tandem to fully enter the stream of traffic. Solos are at a distinct disadvantage here, because their slower speed invites cars to pass, often where they shouldn't. The faster tandem can take a full lane, leaving room for errors in gauging a corner's speed or difficulties caused by wind gusts, and preventing being squeezed by passing cars. When room is available, passing slower cars is preferable to braking and staying behind. Continual braking behind a car will not only fade the brakes, but possibly overheat the rim and cause a tube blowout. Also, because of their more powerful brakes, most cars stop faster than most tandems.

When descending curving, steep roads, both pilot and stoker should ride the drops to gain maximum control. The tandem should be set up on a proper line through the corner, and brakes should be applied firmly to slow the machine before entering the curve. Once in the corner it is equally important to stay off the brakes because it upsets the balance of the machine in the corner and could lead to loss of control.

If the corner is being negotiated at too high a speed, the proper way to exit is to lean more, not to brake. Racers have proven that virtually no one has sufficient machismo to lean a bike over so far that it washes out on dry pavement. Some particularly rabid stokers are finely attuned to this, and can be relied upon to "lay it over" by shifting their weight at the critical moment. A fully loaded touring machine can be tremendously exciting to descend upon, because of its stable frame geometry and lowered center of gravity.

Although seldom used in this fashion, twicers make an interesting vehicle for long-distance touring and cycle camping. Thorough experience with a machine is desirable, because handling and performance of a tandem loaded with gear are different from the response of a light touring tandem.

Because a low center of gravity markedly assists downhill performance, panniers are a must. The tandem tourist will quickly find space in those panniers at a premium, because two people's gear must be accomodated; thus, front panniers abound. The price paid in stiffened steering and increased air resistance is noticeable, and one should consider choosing a bike with an increased fork rake for stability if

---

A small handlebar bag will not carry two warm-up suits. You need two water bottles, not one. Don't carry a new tandem with leather seats on the roof when a thunderstorm breaks. A Paramount tandem can be crammed into a Volvo 122 sedan in less than five minutes when a thunderstorm breaks.

When we get home, we find out other bits of fascinating information. Changing a Paramount to crossover drive and fifteen speeds can be elusive and expensive. It can be done for $70 if you're in the right place at the right time with green stuff to wave.

Regina freewheels on tandems never come off. Exception – a Regina freewheel body that has been stripped of its slots, cogs, pawls, and balls can be removed with a 16-inch pipe wrench. Suntour Winner steel freewheels work great. Weinmann rims keep flexing, spokes begin to break, and break and break.

A famous tandem shop takes 83 days to reply to a letter about better wheels, and their prices are high. Ray Blum in L.A. builds great wheels, in one week, for $110. They are guaranteed and have lasted more than 2,500 miles without truing. Phil Wood hubs are neat.

Tires and tubes and Super Champion rims don't get along. The tires will not seat on the rims. Mike tosses a wheel across the garage and it still retains its trueness! Schwinn LeTours will take 150 psi before seating evenly on the rim.

Most rear racks do not fit on a 19-inch rear. Karrimor can be persuaded onto the seat bolt with a few sheet metal tabs. Long tent poles fit well beneath the boob tube, slung by two toeclip straps. B-72 saddles are very comfortable on the rear but seat wires will break when clamped on a Campy seat post. Anybody need a leather seat? Laurie and Avocet's new ladies' touring seat get along very well.

Mathauser pads are phenomenal in the rain. Of course, it helps if the pads are sanded with sandpaper after a thousand miles. Suntour Cyclone long front derailleurs twist on the seat tube under the pressure of a five-hour Century. Some riders actually carry and loan out 4mm Allen wrenches to tandems with twisted derailleurs. Paramounts eat headsets regularly. Your local bike builder-brazer can fit other ones for about $15 and a few minutes to put in spacers. Black is not only beautiful, it is easy to match braze-burned paint!

Laurie and Mike ride home, downhill, with the wind, on a beautiful day. Black Beauty has done her best and all is well. In the mailbox are a new bike magazine, a catalog ordered months ago and forgotten, and the Tandem Club of America bulletin. New products! Lighter! Stronger! Faster! Better looking! And all this for only $$$! Mike heads for the bathroom with all the information. Laurie hides the checkbooks, Master Charge, wallets, coins. . . .

many touring miles are anticipated. A partial fairing may provide some compensation for the increased drag. While most distance tourists recognize the journey as the goal, and rate speed second, a fairing used to decrease the work load rather than increase speed can make the trip more enjoyable.

Other accomodations to tandem touring extend to the equipment carried. Although light weight is always important, size is equally noteworthy. The largest panniers available are necessary and are usually supplemented with auxiliary bags on the top of the racks. Don't overlook the possibilities of mid-frame bags, either. A tandem's large frame can accomodate a surprisingly large amount of extra gear when it is mounted this way. If you are at all handy, some very nice custom bags can be made to house awkward objects such as tent poles, a handbag or a camera.

Changes in the transmission and brake systems are helpful in outfitting a light touring tandem for carrying heavy loads. Gearing on these tandems routinely drops into the high 20's to assist teams in mountainous terrain. Similarly, when touring, increased drag and long distances conspire to promote coasting downhill, so a top gear of 100 is all that is required. Additionally, unless the touring tandem's road weight is less than 350 pounds, a hub brake for quicker stops is mandatory.

Tandem road racing is non-existent as a recognized or organized sport in the United States. So few tandems travel the roads that the sport is kept from progressing.

Since a tandem team generates about 150 percent of the power of a solo, you can often enjoy training rides with racers. First you have to get solo riders willing to have you ride with them. Many have the idea that a tandem is slow and hard to maneuver simply because it is big. The quickest way to dispel this idea is to ride at the head of a pace line for twenty-five miles. This permits you to mix with the faster riders at the front. It just isn't in the interest of a tandem to get stuck in the back of the pack. A tandem's high inertia makes for great work accelerating and decelerating, and being at the back of any pack makes this necessary. More than three singles out in front is unnecessarily tiring to a trailing tandem, as the peloton will accordion.

A tandem must be inserted smoothly into the pace line, but this is usually easy, because soloists are understandably nervous about being run over by a twicer—besides being eager to take advantage of the huge draft provided the person immediately behind a tandem. This wind screen is why tandems were traditionally used as a training aid for racers.

Riding tandem invariably attracts solo riders, the worst of which become inveterate tandem vultures. They are a distinct danger, since many are riding at unusually high speed, above their true physical and bike-handling capacity.

Naturally, the best way to ride is with another tandem. If you can ride side by side while warming up, you can catch up on local bike gossip twice as fast. Both tandems will go more or less at the same speed and accelerate at the same time. With a little care to switch pace smoothly, two twicers can drop all followers without undue strain.

Sooner or later, any discussion of tandem bicycles centers on mechanical aspects. To avoid the subject is a little like trying to write history without characterizing individuals. Tandems are very much individuals, each with its own personality and aptitudes.

Tandem frames differ from solo frames; weight doesn't really matter, but stiffness does. Since full tandems average three hundred and fifty pounds and are eight feet long overall, a frame capable of being stomped up a hill is necessary.

Low-carbon steel, such as 531, Columbus, Isawata, or 4130 should always be used. Oversized tubing in bottom, down, and steer tubes as well as massive forks and stays are commonly used to anchor the front bottom bracket. Tandem frame styles enjoy much greater freedom than do solos', with double diamond, twin 5/8-inch lateral pencil stays, double-twin lateral stays, single 1-inch middle stays, bobtails and mixtes seen in all permutations. Fork rakes range from 3 to 1½ inches, seat-mast angles from 75 to 65 degrees, and chain stays from 15 to 18 inches—all greater than on solos.

Buy steep, short-wheelbase bikes from a racing builder and relaxed, hands-off cruisers from a tourist shop. Try to buy small—big tandems are awkward and loose jointed.

Most tandem frames are built with sloping top tubes to accomodate different sized riders. However, if the frame is built with lugs and standard-size tubes, its top tube will be either horizontal or offset parallel, because of the array of lugs needed if the top tubes are sloped. Some fine tandems are also composites with upper joints lugged and bottom ones lugless to avoid casting specialty lugs and bottom brackets.

Component choice is contingent on anticipated use. In all cases, buy the best you can afford. Cheap equipment that's

Tandem People by Ruth Rapp from *The Bicycle Paper*

"Aw, look at that! That's a little kid!"
"Someone else noticed us, Mom."

The secret is out!—the reason so many of Ruth Rapp's Bicycle People are tandemists! Who but another tandemist could keep up with them long enough for an interview!

Besides writing for Seattle's The Bicycle Paper, holding workshops on safe riding, and being active in bicycle politics for ten years, Ruth rides a specially adapted 10-speed tandem with her five-year-old son. Before her "retirement" from teaching junior high school, she commuted by bike to school, including through eight months of pregnancy.

The Bicycle Paper is this country's best regional newspaper, covering every aspect of Seattle's lively bicycle scene. For a sample copy, write The Bicycle Paper, P.O. Box 842, Seattle, WA 98111.

Way back in the mid-sixties, when most of America thought of bicycles as kids' toys, two lone figures biked between home and the University of Washington Seattle campus. For Sally and Paul Boyer, bicycles were their only means of transportation during college.

After graduation they sold their bicycles because they were on their way to North Dakota where winters seemed too harsh for bicycle travel. But they ended up buying 1-speeds and pedaling everywhere, even through the snow.

When they decided to go to Italy, they sold the 1-speeds, and rented bicycles. At a flea market in Holland they found bicycles for $15, rode all over Holland for a month, and sold them for $10 on a boat going down the Rhine!

Once back in Seattle, they bought 10-speeds two days after unpacking and have ridden everywhere since. During the winter, their bicycles see about 100 miles a week, and in the summer, many more. They ride for both exercise and recreation, and enjoy both city and country travel. But they don't ride as a twosome any longer. Their children now ride with them.

marginal on a solo is intolerable on a tandem. Break the habit of buying cheap parts so it won't come to haunt you when you break down miles from home. In the long run, it's a whole lot cheaper to buy parts once.

On the other hand, an all-Campy tandem isn't good for much except impressing friends. With a few notable exceptions, Campagnolo goods are designed primarily for racing, and their sidepulls really should be limited to lighter, slower solos and their bottom brackets to bikes with 120-milimeter rear axles, rare for a twicer. Consider the special features tandems need, and select a particular component from a suitable manufacturer rather than buying a whole component line.

Tandem cranksets are still being developed and refined. The original "safety"-framed derailleur tandem cranks used the rear inside chainwheel of a rudimentary 10-speed to transfer the power from the front crankset to the rear, resulting in a 5-speed. The Schwinn Paramount used this development for years, using a 15-speed crankset to yield a 10-speed tandem. This was a workable proposition, but perhaps the limited gear range (40 to 100 inches) first won the tandem's unjust reputation as a flatland machine.

Recent widespread use of the crossover drive, with transfer chainwheels on the left-hand side, freed up the inner rear chainwheel, and developments in front and rear derailleur capacity and extended freewheel range have made the 15-speed tandem the benchmark. Tandem gearing currently extends to 18, 24, and 28 speeds with the addition of up to four drive chain rings and seven freewheel cogs. Gear range runs from 26x36 to 64x12.

The standard for tandem cranksets is the TA cotterless triple-crossover set. The reason is its great setup flexibility and 26-to-64-tooth chainring capacity. Some Campagnolo and Campy-copy sets are seen, but they are limited by their sole 36-tooth inner chain ring. A few tandem Stronglight 49D cranksets still exist, with chainrings interchangeable with TA's. You'll see cottered cranksets on a few less expensive tandems, but when their cotter pins start breaking and bending, they'll cause you more trouble than the savings justify.

The transmission also includes two hanger assemblies, two chains, and the freewheel. It pays to spend money here. The strongest riders face a continual stream of loosened bearings, stretched chains, broken pawls, and twisted hanger axles. Many tandemists swear by Phil Wood hangers because they offer good adjustability from side to side for proper chain line, and because when they break they are guaranteed. Because of the high wear problems, most chains and freewheel cogs are often replaced. Proper preventive maintenance helps both inside and outside the freewheel body.

With the recent surge in cycle touring and camping, some very wide-range derailleurs have appeared on the market. Here's the place to save money, because all of them perform more or less equally. The Suntour Duopar, Rally, Cyclone, and old VGT series (listed in decreasing price) all perform rather well. A recent trend has been toward bar-end controls, which allow both hands to remain on the bars at all times — helpful with a squirmish stoker. A tandem has miles of cable, and the price paid in sluggish control caused by added cable length is hardly noticeable.

The weakest part of the whole tandem is the wheels. The rear wheel supports up to 300 pounds, and tandem wheels are notorious for self destructing in short order. Yet sheer weight is not the sole factor in failure; equally important is crank phase, terrain, and how the team rides.

Some teams seem to never break or even untrue their wheels. Typically, they are sane, sedate, cautious, and pothole-wary people who venture out on Sunday afternoon flat thirty-milers.

By contrast are the pair of young, meat-eating club racers who are less concerned with wheel failure than with dropping that pesky solo they picked up sixty miles back. A quick sprint at the crest of a hill combined with jamming the brakes to get through a curve may drop the follower, but snap, crackle, and pop!

About $110 later, they have a new wheel even they can't break.

I've heard of 15,000 miles being bagged on 48-spoked, 5-cross, Superchampion clincher-rimmed Phil-Wood-hub wheels shod with either Schwinn Letours or Super Record tires, with only the tires going.

If the wheels are of marginal durability, with spokes breaking at a nominal rate of one per hundred miles, the alternative is to tie and solder the wheels. This supports the spokes so well that next-to-worthless wheels can be used.

Another fine trick is to put Loctite, Tubasti, or a slight crimp in the nipple to prevent the nipple from unscrewing during rim compression. Wheels with loose spokes are much more susceptible to breakage than when spokes are tight.

Special arrangements have been made to accommodate two little Boyers. Pia has been riding since she was five months old, starting out in a backpack, graduating to a seat on the rear of the bicycle, and she's now doing post-grad work as stoker on a tandem. Isabella has been riding since she was one month old, starting in a soft pack and graduating to a seat where she is now. She soon will be stoker on a second tandem.

On any weekend of the year the Boyers can be seen somewhere, pedaling merrily along. They're a good example that as families grow bigger bicycling becomes even more fun.

Sally and Paul Boyer. Photograph by Ruth Rapp

Happily, this all relates to rear-wheel problems. The only exception is if the driver sprints too suddenly or applies a front hub brake too forcefully, which can break front spokes.

The choice of the rear-wheel hub is important for several reasons. First, tandems bend axles. After seeing bent axles on all but Maxicar drum-brake hubs and Phil Wood hubs, I can only recommend these. Some dealers carry heat-treated axles for other makes. Avoid rear quick releases on tandems if possible. If tightened sufficiently to guarantee they won't slip, they may fracture or the threads may strip.

Many tandemists choose to put a rear-hub brake as a third brake on their machines. This baffles me because the rear wheel is already badly stressed, and braking the hub stresses the spokes. A front brake has better stopping potential, and the cable run is shorter to a front brake.

Some people have a mistaken idea that the front wheel could lock with a drum or disc, although I've never seen the brake that could do it. Maxicar, Exceltoo, Atom, Bridgestone, and Phil Wood all make hub brakes. The latter is overpriced and overrated, in my opinion.

The other choices for brakes are simple. Rim brakes should be Mafac tandem cantilevers, preferably with a set of the new, harder pads, such as Mathauser. The long-arm cantilevers are much more powerful than short-armed models, such as Mafac's cyclecross or Shimano's touring models. Sidepulls and centerpulls do not compete in price or braking ability. Many good tandem frames lack conventional brake mounts entirely.

A team's success, at any speed, depends not only on mechanical reliability and maintenance programs; it relies also on the ability of the team to work with each other and with the tandem. This aspect, familiar to any experienced

TANDEM PEOPLE by Ruth Rapp from *The Bicycle Paper*

Lisa Loran and Frank Weldon. Photograph by Ruth Rapp

According to Frank Weldon of Tacoma, Washington, the prettiest bicycle route anywhere begins in Tacoma, crosses Puget Sound over the Narrows Bridge, passes through Port Orchard, follows the Hood Canal, runs through Olympia, and back home to Tacoma. Frank and his tandem partner, Lisa Loran, make the 120-mile trip in a day.

For anyone interested, Frank and Lisa can enthusiastically recommend where to find the best cinnamon rolls or the best brunch stop along the route.

Frank describes himself as "strictly a flower sniffer." He's never in such a hurry that he can't stop to enjoy the scenery. His goal is bicycling, not trying to get somewhere at a certain time.

Just coincidentally, Frank's bicycle career began at the same time as the 1972 gas ordeal. He started bicycling as a "health thing." He needed an exercise program "as everybody does." He started bicycling at 240 pounds with diabetes – the diabetes is gone and so are the excess pounds!

Frank had developed diabetes in 1968, and for four years he took thirty units of insulin each day to keep the condition under control. With bicycling and a special diet for diabetes, Frank lost seventy pounds, and could stop taking insulin. He now holds his own at 180 pounds.

When he moved to Tacoma, he found that commuting to work by bicycle took less time than commuting by car and then exercising after work, and bicycling was more interesting than any other type of exercise. He used to have a problem deciding whether to take his 18-foot boat or his bicycle out – and every time, the boat lost! Now he just wonders when he'll be off his bicycle long enough to get around to selling the boat!

A few years ago Frank was part owner of a tandem, but conflicts arose about where and when to ride, so he bought his own tandem and started riding with Lisa. With Frank as captain and Lisa as stoker, they've covered a lot of ground. Last year they spent their vacation bicycling from Tacoma to San Francisco with seven other bicyclists. They are planning to do the Northern Parks Tour that Bikecentennial has laid out.

When Frank is not riding, what does he do? Fixes bicycles! "Bicycling takes up almost all of my time." Since he started bicycling, he hasn't felt the need or desire for any other hobby.

Lisa likes bicycling because "I can eat! I can eat pancakes and not feel guilty." She also enjoys being outside and getting a suntan – although a funny one.

Both Frank and Lisa have been active in organized bicycling. Frank is a past president and Lisa is current president of the Tacoma Wheelmen. Frank has an unfulfilled goal – to form a federation of clubs so bicyclists can be more effective in speaking to local governments. "Bicyclists could speak as one voice and be more effective." He thinks it will happen, and would like to see it under the League of American Wheelmen sponsorship.

In the year and a half they have been tandem partners, Frank and Lisa have worked up to 150-mile days, which they ride often. Lisa would like to see more people bicycling. "A lot of people don't know what they're missing."

tandemist, was made more poignant in a recent article by a medical doctor recommending solo bicyclists use a tandem to help "cheat" the wind and distance when riding a double century. Not a bad idea—after 2000 miles of training.

When we first bought a tandem, I was depressed by how slow we were on it. True, we were faster over short distances than on our solos, but the machine just wasn't moving. A year passed before we saw significant change. As we learned each other's reactions and the tandem's capabilities, our speed, acceleration and handling abilities improved markedly. Our initial chatter to synchronize our moves fell off dramatically, replaced by an occasional quiet cheer when we "nicked" together particularly well. Non-verbal communication, transmitted through the frame and pedals, blossomed.

If both bodies are attuned to it, it's amazing what you can tell another person through a tandem.

Photograph by Janet Carothers

TANDEM PEOPLE by Ruth Rapp from *The Bicycle Paper*

Lynda and Dan King. Photograph by Ruth Rapp

Only the birds are awake to watch Dan and Lynda King bicycle around their neighborhood at 5:30 in the morning three or four days a week. They put in five or so miles in the early hours just for exercise.

After trying commuting from Kenmore to the University of Washington in Seattle a couple times, they decided that fighting traffic during rush hour on Lake City Way was not worth the energy. So now they do most of their bicycling on weekend tours. They bicycle year-round, but most of the 1,500 miles they travel each year is in the summer.

The Kings started bicycling in a rather roundabout way. In a V.A. hospital in Maryland, in 1969, recovering from an injury suffered in Viet Nam which left him blind, Dan heard someone suggest that tandem bicycling might be exciting. With an $85 1-speed Huffy tandem, Dan

and Lynda entered the world of tandem riding. Well, sort of. The bicycle didn't fit, was heavy, and they didn't know what to do or where to ride with it.

In 1972, they bought a 10-speed tandem, but it wasn't until two and a half years ago that they started riding frequently. Now they have plans for a bicycle trip in Hawaii or Europe somewhere.

Their favorite riding is in the rural areas of Washington on long weekend trips away from noise and cars. Usually they ride alone. But two years ago they took their first organized group ride.

They slipped in gravel and crashed and for three weeks, Dan complained of a sore arm. Finally, a checkup by a doctor revealed a fracture that had already healed. Group rides haven't been as appealing to them since then as they might have been!

To make their bicycle trips more enjoyable, Dan and Lynda will soon have a specially made Jack Taylor tandem to ride. Because of the difference in their sizes, their new tandem will be a conversation piece—an 18-inch front, 23-inch rear frame! With it, they plan to take many extended tours, and continue their weekday exercise rides with the birds. The Kings are an example of how a little imagination and dedication can make life enjoyable on a bicycle.

Photograph by Janet Carothers

The Tricyclists

Dennis Donovan

Beards are no longer *de rigeur* for trikers, but they do fit an image of offbeat casualness that the tricycle fraternity has built up over a number of years in order to combat the general public's opinion that tricycles are ridden by geriatrics, invalids, or people simply unable to balance on two wheels.

Though there are tricyclists who fall into these three categories, the majority of trike riders ride on three wheels just for the hell of it, and these very tough *hombres* are usually very competent on two wheels as well.

Eric Tremaine at six feet four inches is a giant in a world where trikers tend to be around five feet eight, and it was in 1972 that his great strength propelled him to a British record of 457.89 miles for a 24-hour time trial. Why does he ride a trike?

"Why does anyone ride a trike? Logically, they shouldn't. The trike is heavier, more awkward to ride, and takes up more room on the road. It's awkward to park, too. I guess it's because of the challenge. It's something different from conventional cycling."

Why use three wheels when two wheels are doing very nicely, thank you? Why trikes anyway? The explanation is that the tricycle is a living ancestor of the many dinosaurs that sprang up around the turn of the century when man the inventor looked for alternatives to the bicycle. It was found necessary to provide a more stable form of riding for the idle rich who at times had difficulty standing on their own two feet, let alone trying to balance on a bicycle.

From this notion grew tricycles with two front wheels and one rear one; four-wheeled vehicles; triplets, quads, quintets, sextuplets, and other abortions from the tandem distaff side; tandem tricycles—there are still a few of them around today, and being raced—side-by-side sociable machines for Mr. and Mrs. and many others that are now found in museums and private collections. Of all these, only the trike has survived in quantity, exerting a fascination to its riders that is hard to define to the layman, and a challenge to anyone who has ever tried to steer one of these broad-gauge machines—not many people can steer one at the first attempt.

This was brought home quite visibly some twenty years ago when many of the top European riders came to Britain for the Isle of Man Cycling Week, and to ride the big professional race on the famous motorbike racing circuit. World champion Andre Darrigade, five-time Tour de France winner Jacques Anquetil, the Irishman Seamus Elliott, and the late-lamented Britisher Tom Simpson, all had a go on a trike. Simpson found he could, but then he had the advantage of having seen one before. His fellow professionals hadn't and found they couldn't.

It was explained to Tom and the others that the best method of countering the trike's tendency to steer into the left-hand curb—remember the British still drive on the left!—was to cross the hands when hold-

Eric Tremaine. Photograph courtesy of Harold Harvey

Dennis Donovan *is a reporter. His wit and keen observation are enjoyed regularly by readers of the British weekly,* Cycling. *We thank Rex Coley, dean of cycling journalists, for recommending Dennis to us. Dennis also contributed "Hill-Climb Racing—Cycling's Toughest Event."*

A Winter run during the thirties. Courtesy of the Tricycle Association

ing the handlebars, and then steer. Most of the professionals either fell off at the first attempt, kept turning full circle, or launched themselves into space as a wheel lifted off the ground.

The reason was quite a simple one why they—the world's best cyclists—couldn't ride this strange machine. It was simply because they were expert cyclists, and over a period of time would react instinctively to a bike's steering peculiarities. A complete beginner to any form of nonmotorized transport would have simply pointed the front wheel in the right direction and ridden off into the sunset.

The average trike nowadays is twenty-eight inches wide across its back, though elderly trikes would probably be around thirty-two inches across the beam, the same measurement that a tandem trike has to be, otherwise it would tip over when the driver and his stoker lean when cornering.

The machine is driven by the left wheel on an axle (average length 15½ inches) which is split in two. The long part of the axle drives the left wheel and at the other end engages the chainwheel, bottom bracket, etc. The right part of the axle is simply a stub on which the right wheel is fastened by a split nut and bolt. A brazed-on boss takes the derailleur gears.

The Tricycle Association, which celebrated its fiftieth anniversary in 1978, helped to frame one of the British laws when it insisted that trikes should be equipped with two front brakes, usually a conventional caliper brake and a cantilever brake, or a rear hub brake that binds into the axle.

Tubing used for a trike is of a bigger gauge than for a bike, because of the stresses encountered when cornering. Forks too have to be stronger because they tend to bend with the effort. The head angles are shallower to prevent speed wobble, but the seat angles are more upright.

Gearing is usually lower than for a two-wheeled machine—116 to 118 inches, but even that theory is being made a mockery of now as bikers take to the three-wheeled beast and ignore all the conventions. Lower gears are needed for climbing and a certain amount of wheel spin can be met with if conditions are wet and greasy. A good bottom gear is needed on hills because of the dragging effect.

Though trikes are slower uphill than bikes, they are often faster downhill—providing there are no difficult bends to contend with.

Cornering is the main obstacle to a biker on a trike for the first time, but the golden rule is when cornering left, lean left. That way the center of gravity is kept, otherwise the off-side wheel simply lifts off the ground and you become the next rider to be propelled into space.

Triking has its advantages in bad winter weather. You have three wheels on the ground at the same time, and you are therefore more stable. Indeed many cyclists in Britain switch over to three wheels when there is ice and snow about, and while their contemporaries visit hospitals for broken limbs, they stay mobile and accident free.

Finally, there is one more advantage to those who like to say they have ridden every inch of the way. On a trike you never need to put your feet to the ground, not even for traffic lights!

Lightweight Tricycles

Martin Purser

Formed in 1928 at the instigation of Alec Glass, the Tricycle Association is totally different from any other cycling organization in character. Every member is a keen and experienced cyclist, which results in the association having a stability and atmosphere that is quite unique. The association organizes racing, social, and touring activities throughout Great Britain, which is divided into geographical regions. The membership usually numbers about four hundred and forms another community within the cycling world. A typical regional program would include time-trial events and club runs. All members receive the *Gazette* quarterly and so keep informed on national and regional activities, and have an opportunity to exchange views.

Racing is mainly confined to time trials at 10, 25, 50, 100 miles and 12 and 24 hours. There are a few *kermesses* (around the house races) organized around the country, the most famous and popular ones being held on the Isle of Man during Cycling Week. These races are exceptionally exciting. The corners, and difficult ascents and descents make the courses very interesting to ride: The spectators are enthralled. Our late president Ed Green used to ride every year. He competed last year at the age of seventy-one. He was a wonderful character – cheerful, bluff and tough, and a tricyclist through and through. He always used to win the first lap at the island races – sort of a tradition! He would also always be first man off during a time trial so that if a course official was missing he could take his place so as not to spoil the others' race.

Stan Spelling was another incredible character. Any man who can have both legs, arms, pelvis, back, spine, and skull broken in a car/cycle colli-

Cornering on a tricycle. Courtesy of the Tricycle Association

---

Martin Purser *is the treasurer of the Tricycle Association of Great Britain. He uses a tricycle for both touring and racing, and is an expert tandem tricyclist.*

136

Grass-track racing at the York Rally. Bernard Thompson

sion on a San Francisco, California, freeway in 1958, become registered as disabled, and then ten years later come back and break several national trike records and a tandem trike record at the age of fifty has just got to be a character. Sadly, he was killed during the Mersey 24-hour time trial in 1972 when his idle wheel came off his trike and he went under a car.

Alf Layzell, the legendary "mile eater," accumulated more than 472,000 miles on a tricycle (and a further 150,000 on a bicycle) since about 1935.

Touring events in this country are mainly the continental style "brevet" or "randonnée" events. These are long-distance reliability trials to be completed at the rider's own pace, but within a set time limit. These include Brevet Cymni and Chester-Windsor-Chester. Barry Parslow is a well-known tricycle rider who competes in these events. He had ridden Paris-Brest-Paris on his trike.

During a protracted tricycle tour in South America in 1973-74 my wife Alison and I used our one-wheel drive machines. These we loaded up with cycle camping equipment and souvenirs. The wheel slip experienced on unmade surfaces made progress very exasperating at times. Uneven surfaces cause the axle to bounce, both vertically and horizontally, and apart from slow progress, one is apt to fall

off! Tire wear is an additional disadvantage.

The men and women who ride with clubs, either racing or touring, favor a lightweight tricycle frame. The equipment used on the basic frame is a matter of personal preference; but generally speaking, clinchers for touring and tubulars for racing. Ten speeds and five speeds are popular driving through the left-hand wheel. It would be a comparatively easy engineering task to produce an axle driving through the right-hand wheel. But as there is no point or demand for right-hand drive tricycles in Britain (and I think we're about the only country in the world to manufacture sports tricyles) none are produced.

There are a small number of tandem racing tricycles. The axle width is usually thirty-two inches and these are accepted in tandem bicycle time trials. These machines are said to be easier to ride than solo tricycles, although the steering is heavier. Both solo and tandem tricycles are about ten percent slower than their two-wheeled counterparts. This is accounted for by the greater wind resistance, slightly increased road drag from the third wheel, the greater weight, and possibly the handling characteristics on corners and hills. This last depends on the expertise of the rider, for tricycling *fast* is a real

art and skill as well as a test of physical ability.

The machine is steered round corners as it cannot be leaned over. The center of gravity of the rider and machine must be adjusted to counteract centrifugal force by the rider moving his body weight over and into the corner. At low speeds this can be achieved by merely bending the body at the waist. At high speeds a great deal of nerve and acrobatic skill are required by the rider to get out of the saddle and move the body weight right out from the machine center line and into the corner. Cornering quickly is an art: Some riders are very spectacular and may, in certain situations, be faster than their two-wheeled colleagues. (Consider a tandem tricycle circumnavigating a traffic island at full speed!)

A cambered road presents the tricyclist with an almost constant problem. If there is little traffic about, one can hog the center of the road to keep one's axle level. If one is forced to ride on the camber, one has to adopt a position suggesting one is riding round a continuous corner! If the camber is constant, this position, if it is not too exaggerated, will soon grow on one! If camber is steep and constantly changing in degree, one is tried to the limit in one's proficiency in trike handling. It is usually camber that throws the novice, for the

Tricycling in South America. Photo by Martin Purser

deliver the drive through both rear wheels. A solid axle connecting both wheels would not work effectively, and so to facilitate this type of drive through the axles, a number of differential designs have been developed for tricycles. The most well-known are the Starley, patented by James Starley in 1877 and first used on the Salvo tricycle; the Abingdon, patented by Starley in 1892 and used extensively through to the 1940's; and more recently, the Higgins. I know of no tricycle differentials in production today, although many riders favor them in spite of the disadvantage of additional revolving weight.

The advantages are that there is less chance of wheel slip, there is constant gearing while cornering, the ride is generally "smoother," and braking becomes possible through both rear wheels.

The Road Traffic Laws allow tricyclists to have two independent brakes operating on the front wheel if there is a freewheel on the machine. (Bicycles must have an independently operated brake on each wheel.) The most usual arrangement is a brazed-on cantilever brake with another center-pull brake on a short metal extension brazed to the fork crown. (A side-pull brake may be substituted for the centerpull.) Drum brakes may be on any wheel, and are substituted for one of the rim brakes obligatory on the front wheel if there are no brakes on the rear wheels. A drum or disc brake on a differential is quite effective, either may also be mounted on the gear boss on a one-wheel drive axle. Note that the arrangement must be incorporated in the design of the axle and cannot be added on as an afterthought, or as

natural tendency of the front wheel is to steer downward toward the curb, road edge, drainage ditch, etc., and consequently a fall.

As the tricyle is basically heavier than a bicycle it requires more effort to propel it up gradients. Providing the road is tolerably smooth and firm it is mainly a matter of choosing an appropriate gear and pedaling up. If one wishes to get up out of the saddle and "honk" (stand on the pedals), this is quite possible, but as one cannot sway the machine slightly from side to side, as with a bicycle, the body must be moved up and down vertically, if you see what I mean. (Consider riding out of the saddle up a steep hill with bad camber and surface!) If too low a gear is selected on very steep climbs there is a tendency for the front wheel, being

"light" on the road, to lose its adhesion, and the drive wheel to force the machine to turn to the right. Of course, this turning force is always present while the machine is being pedaled, but it only becomes obvious on steep climbs.

On wet, loose, or uneven surfaces there is a tendency for the drive wheel to lose adhesion and slip or spin. This is a trait the rider learns to live with and there is not much one can do about it apart from replace worn-out tires! Seriously, one can shift one's weight over onto the drive side to try and obtain more adhesion. Obviously, if an exaggerated position must be adopted to keep the wheel down, then the rider will become uncomfortable and so the effort put into pedaling decreases. It would follow that it would be a good idea to

Martin and Alison Purser in Argentina.
Photo by David Sarsby

Stan Spelling in Royal Navy 30 mile Time Trial in 1972. Courtesy Tricycle Association

Down-hill cornering. Courtesy Tricycle Association

an extra brake. Under normal circumstances the twin front brakes are quite adequate. However, long, sinuous mountain descents will cause the rim to cook up unless care is taken. Drum brakes are not very popular, as they are not usually very efficient, they are cumbersome, and, of course, they are distinctly heavier to the weight-conscious racing man.

A purpose-built trike is lighter and more rigid than a conversion of a 10-speed bike. A conversion tricycle always has a extra pair of seat stays.

One can convert an ordinary tandem frame to a tandem tricycle by merely fixing on a conversion set – these axles are thirty-two inches wide and of a heavier construction than the solo versions. Conversions of tandems suffer the same problems that solos do. Of course, you can always change your mind with a "con" set and revert to two wheels.

A fairly shallow fork rake and head tube ensures that the machine follows a straight line and does not wander too much on unpredictable road surfaces.

The stoker of a tandem tricycle rides the machine as if it were a solo tricycle and all that entails – leaning out on corners, etc. On our machine, the gears are in the hands of the stoker but that is peculiar to us – the gear levers can be wherever you wish.

ADVICE TO NOVICE

It is usual for a cyclist's tricycle frame to be about one inch smaller than his bicycle frame. This is to

make cornering easier – one can hook one's knee over the top tube to lean out further. One does not lean a tri-

cycle round a corner, and it is surprising how difficult it is for a bicycle rider to learn how to *steer* the machine. The reflex action is to lean on a corner. As one cannot take such liberties with a trike, one falls off or crashes into the curb!

Some riders recommend that a novice trike rider find a quiet backyard to practice the art in, and for the rider to cross his hands, i.e. left hand to right brake hood, and right hand to left brake hood (only in the backyard *not* on the road!). This is to make the rider concentrate on steering. I think the best way to learn is to find a quiet road and get on and learn through experience.

Of course a trike has tremendous advantages over a bicycle in icy conditions, but there is a tendency for them to crab sideways a bit. In deep snow I think the bicycle regains the advantage as one only has one track to carve, one third of the tricycle's laborious path. On ice – whoopee!

Photograph by Bernard Thompson

Ed Green

ED GREEN:

"There is a fascination about riding a trike that you can't get on a bicycle. You're more stable, particularly on greasy or icy roads, and feel safer in traffic – the average driver gives you far more room than you need.

"Top-notch racers won't give the time and energy to mastering the intricacies of the trike because they seek competition and international recognition. They pack up work all summer to compete. Bicycle racing has got to such a peak they won't even speak to one another when they're racing, while in the tricycle world they'll say to me,

'Permission to pass, Mr. President.'

"I'd like to think my last years were spent riding, and I shall ride again in the Isle of Man next year if I'm well enough."

Harold Catling: re Ed Green:

"It is in the nature of the Yorkshireman to combine a quite remarkable singleness of purpose with a degree of determination to reach his chosen goal, which a lesser man might unkindly regard as fanaticism. In this, Ed was the archetypal Yorkshireman, doggedly prepared to move mountains rather than be beaten where anything in which he sincerely believed was concerned – and he most sincerely believed in cycling as a philosophy of life, and in tricycling as being the highest embodiment of that philosophy.

"Although no stylist, he had strength and an aggressive spirit that I could not match, but above all he was a master of time-trial tactics. However complex the course he knew instinctively how best to ride it, and however varied the field he knew to a hair's breadth just what his handicap was worth . . . he is probably still chuckling to himself over an incident in a '12' in the early forties. By resting by the roadside and letting me get ahead of him, he was able to take a diversion, avoiding a particularly hard leg of the course and leaving me with a false sense of security, and thereby contrived to take First Handicap from me by one furlong.

"The end came dramatically at about mid-distance in a tricycle '50' and I suspect that, at the moment of death, he felt a great regret that the timekeeper would have to record DNF (did not finish) against his name."

Ed Green about to cross the finish line. Courtesy of the Tricycle Association

Tricycling in Century Village

Anita Linda Furst

Photographs for this article by Anita Linda Furst

Six mornings a week, the members of the Century Village Tricycle Club in West Palm Beach, Florida, form an elephant train of a line, sometimes as many as forty trikers long. Pedaling at a steady pace, safety flags periscoping up behind each trike, the riders move along the side of the roadway, wary of the cars and trucks that pass them at 45 miles an hour. What is responsible for this phenomenon?

Our older population is increasing in number. Wishing to take advantage of the years that remain for them, people are retiring early. The last ten years have seen a massive migration of people out of urban centers into retirement communities in Florida, California, and Arizona. They move to an environment where the weather, the social activities, and the relaxed atmosphere have a dramatic effect on their habits and lifestyle.

For some, there are disadvantages. Removed from the convenience of urban transportation systems, people who never learned to drive begin to experience transportation problems. So do those who had to stop driving because of failing health. All of them need to shop, to visit their physician, to do their laundry. Available transportation facilities are often inadequate.

By relocating, many have left behind friends and family. Illness and death bring further losses. Retirement stops the socialization that business contacts provide. Half the women over sixty-five are widows. They in particular, need to overcome their loneliness, social isolation, and physical dependence on neighbors and friends.

Many symptoms and complaints associated with old age are really the result of muscular and cardiovascular disuse. Research has shown that though aging cannot be stopped, it can be slowed. Exercise increases blood flow to organs and muscles and oxygen to the brain. It slows the loss of muscle tissue and the conversion of lean body mass into fat. It reduces tension. People who exercise have less arthritic changes than sedentary people of the same age. They look better and feel better.

Anita Linda Furst is a West Palm Beach based writer and videographer who is active in projects involving senior citizens.

Three major problems encountered by older people – the need for mobility and independence, a means of safe exercise, and a pleasant way to meet friends – are solved by riding a tricycle.

In the 1950's the trike was only used for industrial purposes in America. The gleaming white refrigerator that was pedaled through the streets of New York by the Good Humor Ice Cream vendor

was the most visible use of the trike concept.

Al Cook, Jr., of Alco Cycle Products, manufactures the Villager Tryke in Largo, Florida. He remembers people who had trouble riding a standard two-wheeler going to his father for help.

"My dad wanted to see if he could develop an alternative vehicle. He remembered the Good Humor trike, and using that as a starting point, he began experimenting in our garage. Regular training wheels are not stable enough for adults, so he designed large, fifty-pound wheels that were stable but which were too heavy for people with physical disabilities to pedal. He created a conversion unit which would be adaptable to any two-wheel bike."

When people began to retire to Florida, they saw these trikes and wanted them for mobility, for exercise, and for the camaraderie that triking creates. The triking boom began.

Alco started manufacturing sturdy, stable tricycles for recreational use. A rear-end double axle adds strength and easy chain adjustment and alignment. Accessories include 3-speed gearing, child carriers, rear baskets, and even surried canopies!

The Century Village Trikers praise these trikes: Most of the 125 members of the club had never ridden a bike – how did these 75-year-olds feel when they mounted a trike for the first time?

Selma Koenig explains, "I felt great, like a child. I was able to do things on my own. I didn't have to wait to have someone take me somewhere by car. Riding gave me a feeling of being free. It's the greatest thing that could have happened!"

She added, "The club is the pivotal point in my life. I have made friends with other members. We socialize. I use my trike to shop and to do my laundry. I even go out and ride in addition to the rides I take with the club."

Riding helps alleviate loneliness. Ruth Crandall confides, "When my husband died, I felt that my life had ended. I had already belonged to the club, but after his death I went out riding every single day. Riding gave me a lift. It helped me forget about my problems. It brought me into contact with other people."

The club has spawned five marriages. Sophie Adler Blum married another member of the club five years ago. She says, "I have been riding for eight years now and I had never ridden a bike before that. Now, I have biked over 13,000 miles. When I first got on the trike I felt young and spirited and very, very happy, and I've been on it every day since. We didn't have a car, so the trike gave me freedom. My basket has a covering that closes up for when I do my marketing. The first trip I took with the trike was at a place that had a hill and it was quite a thrill going down that hill. I was a little frightened, but I enjoyed it. It was exciting."

One of the fifteen male members, Reuben Sussman, rides with the club for the exercise: "I like riding with the group because it's safer to ride that way. The

longer the ride, the better I like it."

Another male member, Murray Pikoff, says, "I have enjoyed my seven years with the trike club. I have the distinction of making 10,000 miles which shows on my badge. The trike adds years to your life because it keeps you healthy and it keeps you happy."

Not everyone who belongs to the Trike Club rides a trike. Jean Zohn, the president, and Albert Stillman, the club leader, ride two-wheelers. Jean Zohn says, "Albert is responsible for the safety of the group. He rides at the head of the procession and when he leads us we feel safe and secure."

Albert received instructions from the Florida Highway Patrol on how to lead the group and how to take it through intersections. Florida is still being developed and there aren't many bike paths. Often the only thoroughfares into certain parts of town do not even have sidewalks. It is within this environment that the trikers must travel. They are subject to the buzz of fast-moving vehicles, the fume of exhausts, and the fuming of automobile drivers, some of whom yell at the trikers. Ironically, studies have shown that these oldsters who bike fifty to sixty miles a week, exercise more than the automobile drivers who throw out their epithets about old age.

Stillman is not overly concerned. "The attitude by some toward us is bad, and sometimes I don't blame them because the traffic can be heavy, but we have no alternative. Most of the club members do not want to restrict their riding to the village because the circular bike path is only two miles around. They like to ride outside. Some people feel that it is dangerous for us to be out riding on the road. But in the eight years that I have been leading the club, we have never had a single mishap. There have been injuries within the village but none where a club member was involved. Club members have to obey orders, they have to give hand signals, ride in single file of about one and a half tricycles apart to allow room for emergency braking, and never pass each other. We always observe bike safety. We take one rest stop for five or ten minutes on the way to our destination. When we

are finished, the mileage coordinator marks down the mileage for each club member."

Club members do not actively encourage other people to join. When someone wants to join, they ride with the group for two or three weeks until Stillman sees that they will obey the safety rules.

Because they are so dependent upon their trikes, the trikers are concerned about trike quality. Jim Ribar has sold a thousand trikes in the last ten years, five hundred of them to people in Century Village. He recommends the Alco Villager because it has only one wearing feature, the tire. The repair rate with less expensive trikes is higher. As a result, most of the trikers in the Village have Alco trikes.

Ribar is also concerned with bike safety; "I feel a moral obligation to explain to them how to ride the trike. Some of them are advanced in years and may never have ridden a bike of any kind before. I tell them that they may feel a little awkward at first and that they should take their time getting used to the trike, that they shouldn't let their enthusiasm interfere with sound judgment."

The difference between riding a trike and riding a two-wheeler is that the trike requires no balancing. When you are on a trike it is as though you are sitting in a car, steering it. People who have ridden two-wheelers have to unlearn the need to balance. It takes them longer to get used to riding a trike than it does a person who has never ridden a bike before. The seat is farther back than on a standard bicycle, so that the triker is pedaling into the pedals, pushing them forward rather than pushing downward as one does with a two-wheeler.

Because Century Village was far from a bicycle repair shop, Ribar at one time had a repair van that would come into the village three times a week to maintain the trikes. There is a high rate of flat tires because most of the riding outside of the village is done on the side of the road with the debris; also tread loss occurs from high mileage and deterioration of the rubber because of Florida's heat. If the maintenance was quite simple, like a patch or a tire change, it was done while

the triker waited. For more substantial repairs, the trike was taken back to the shop and loaners were made available. If someone was interested in buying a new trike, one would be left for a week's trial. The van was indispensable. But in the past few years, a number of bike shops have opened that are easily accessible to the trikers.

Women seem to prefer their trikes in bright colors – blue, yellow, white, and orange – while the men prefer a darker one, mocha, or blue. Most riders choose a wide western saddle. These are cushioned still further by homemade knitted covers and fluffy toilet seat covers that are unashamedly tied to the saddle. Although gas and electric motors can be added to a tricycle, most riders prefer pedal power.

Cook and Ribar agree that proper maintenance will increase the life of the trike. Cook recommends biweekly maintenance: checking tires for air pressure (between forty and forty-five pounds), cleaning and waxing painted parts, spraying chrome with protective coating and spray, lubricating the brake-handle pivot bolt, top caliper-brake bolt; inside pedal bearing, chain, and free-wheel face.

No longer considered just a "granny bike," the trike has proven itself to be a sensible and efficient way for people of all ages to solve transportation problems, as well as providing the physical and emotional uplifting that is important for the life satisfaction of older people.

The Trike — Hand-Powered Mobility

The Trike is a hand-powered machine especially designed for the active handicapped population. It vastly outperforms a wheelchair. You can average eight to twelve miles per hour over trips of five to fifteen miles, and top speed in a sprint is about eighteen miles an hour.

Because many paraplegics can get around with crutches, the Trike is perfect for them: They can ride it to their destination, and then get up and walk inside, locking the Trike as others would a bike.

The 27-inch width allows it to go through most doorways and into elevators, the 54-inch wheelbase gives it stability and maneuverability. Built of 4130 (chrome-moly), it weighs 50 pounds. The parts list will sound familiar to any cyclist: TA cranks, Phil Wood hubs, Campy derailleur, and Shimano disc brake. A roller clutch-and-cam follower work the brake when the cranks are backpedaled. The Trike has fifteen speeds, although on this model only five can be used at a time. There are three chainwheels (27-40-52), but the chain has to be moved manually from one to another, the derailleur works the 14-34 freewheel. Driving the 20-inch front wheel, that gives gearing from 16 to 74 inches.

The current model is available from Dan Gould, a custom builder in Missoula, Montana.

Using that model, two Trike owners averaged thirteen miles an hour in a one-hour race in the 1978 Human Powered Speed Championships. In 1979 Bill Warner took time out from his studies at MIT to enter and reached a top speed of 17.86. Handicapped as a result of a car accident, Bill found the Trike a liberation; he did six hundred miles during a New England winter; does twice as much the rest of the year. He takes it up and down a five-inch curb

Bill Warner on his Trike by James B. Kesseli

without difficulty, and likes riding it at night. Bill says Trike riders in good shape can keep pace with regular cyclists in leisurely touring, and can leave a casual cyclist on a 3-speed clunker in the dust.

Bill has used his engineering know-how to design an improved and less expensive Trike: It has a vastly simplified frame, easier seat adjustment, and two derailleurs which can produce twenty-five usable gear combinations. A continuing effort is being made to find an established firm to produce the Trike in quantity.

Anyone interested in hand-powered cycles – building, designing, or using them – should get in touch with Bill Warner, c/o Hand-Powered Cyclists of America, 228 Winchester Street, Brookline, Massachusetts 02146.

BICYCLE RACING

How to Watch a Bicycle Race

Robert A. Potts, Jr.

Scene one: Fred and Joe and I are on a footbridge over the Long Island Expressway, the busiest road in New York. We are covering the seventy-five-mile Apple Lap bike race for NBC News. The sports department isn't interested at all, but the hard news people have been attracted to the event because they are interested in anything that could empty that road even for five minutes. An empty L.I.E. could only mean a major calamity or a major celebrity, so a few of the local residents have come out to find out why everything is so quiet. Is it the President, the Pope, Yasir Arafat? Have the Arabs cut off all our fuel? We tell them that it's just a bike race and that everything will be back to smelly, noisy, normal in five minutes. As we speak, the first police escort goes by, and over the rise comes the whizzing herd of America's best bike racers, about 150 of them. They are a compact group, splashed with color. They wear shirts like jockeys' colors. The bikes are bright enamel and polished metal. In the quiet you can hear the hiss and hum of the machinery. That they are not out of breath is evident, because some of the riders yap at each other. At the rear, two or three riders are having trouble keeping up after thirty-five hard miles. Was that it? the local people want to know. Who was leading? We were too busy making our shot to notice much. We explain that they had just seen part of a seventy-five-mile race on streets and freeways that started in

Staten Island and would end on Fifth Avenue and that some of America's top riders were in there somewhere. The locals shrug and go back to the Sunday papers and football, a sport that does not run away from the fans.

We began our day at the starting line, Fred sitting in the hatchback to catch the first turn of the pedals. Then we followed the race for a few miles just ahead of it. We knew more about the race than most of the bystanders along the way, but we didn't know much because it's almost impossible to watch a bike race unless you're in it. Or unless you own a helicopter.

Here's another scene: All-star night on the board track of the Velodrome d'Hiver, the main indoor arena in Paris. At the middle of the straightaway closest to me, trainers hold Jacques Anquetil upright, his feet strapped to pedals, ready. On the opposite straightaway his seconds hold Fausto Coppi, whom some would say is the best racing cyclist in the history of the sport. A lot of the guys who hold up Paris bars think their boy Anquetil is better. We are about to see a test. Gunshot, off they go. The point is to catch the rider ahead of you. These men are both very strong and smooth, they know how to pace themselves. They're doing it for money, but they know that this is a test of nations—France versus Italy—and men, two of the best, each trying to gain on the other. On the first few laps, they're even. You can tell as they cross the median line on opposite sides of the oval. Neither gains or loses an inch, they cross the line in almost perfect synch. Drops of sweat glint and splash on the boards. Anquetil has a few inches, Coppi takes them back and gains a few. There is a constant hubbub

Photo: Alfred Letourneur, "The Red Devil," Madison Square Garden, by Fred Hamel

Robert A. Potts Jr. *has allowed daily journalism to distract him from a two-hundred-mile-a-week riding schedule.*

Memorial Day Race, Somerville, New Jersey, One of America's Classics. Photograph by Fred Hamel

from that crowd, its collective voice seems controlled by the rise and fall of the battle. Now Fausto Coppi turns calm and supple. He turns up the heat and gains steadily on the Frenchman. The hubbub becomes a rhythmic chant: "COP-PI, COP-PI, COP-PI. . .," Anquetil can feel the surge behind him and he weakens. Coppi takes it. The Parisian crowd would have loved an Anquetil win, but they love Fausto Coppi too, because although he is the best, he doesn't put on airs. He rolls up to Anquetil and puts an arm around him as they coast into the pits.

That was the main event. There were also sprints: all-out two-man races to the finish – still, silent jockeying and then a blast of speed – Arie Van Vliet the great Dutch sprinter cleaned up, almost mangling his bicycle into knots of tubing and wire as he applied his huge strength to showing the upstarts who was still the boss of the track. There was racing paced by motorcycles, bikes dancing along behind at fifty miles an hour. Bike racing for the masses. And they paid to watch.

Who would blame Americans for not watching a bike race on the road even for free? The bike racers do. Everyone knows about Shorter and Rodgers. Your third-grade teacher runs the marathon in less than four hours. They put marathons on television and the runners sign their books in the shopping center. Runners get on the talk shows. But who has ever heard of George Mount, Tom Officer, and the Stetina brothers? No one outside the bike game knows who they are, but they all put out as much as any marathon runner. How about a hundred miles up- and downhill, into the wind and with it, in less than four hours – better than twenty-five miles in the hour? That's what George Mount and those other guys can do. Don't say you know all about it. One day on a clear bit of road (flat), try and get your Sears 10-speed up to twenty-five, even for a minute.

It does not put runners down to say that all they have to do is stay in shape and run. That's hard enough. The bike racer has to push the pedals around until it hurts and, on top of that, he must play a game if he's to score. The game makes bike racing more fun than running.

The bike-racing game is all in the physics. The bicycle-equipped human being is *the most efficient* device for turning energy into motion, more efficient than a 747 or a dolphin or a diesel locomotive. That explains why Aunt Maude on a bicycle can go faster than Frank Shorter, who must expend most of his energy heaving his own weight into the air at every step. The bicycle carries all of Aunt Maude's weight on ball bearings, however she must push her way through the air and at her usual speeds that's fairly easy. At fifteen miles an hour or less the air is a gentle fluid. It gets thicker as you go faster. At twenty miles an hour it has become sea water. At thirty it feels like a wall.

The racing cyclist soon learns, if no one tells him, that the solution to the air-resistance problem is to ride behind something, most often another racing cyclist. The sheltering principle works so well that riders have pedaled more or less standard bicycles to well over a hundred miles an hour behind race cars with windbreak shields attached to the back. The hero of the film "Breaking Away" follows a magnificent Kenworth truck to sixty per and a man named Murphy rode to sixty-plus behind a Long Island Railroad train several decades ago. Tucked well inside a group of riders, it can feel positively restful; you might even see a rider coasting along behind hard-pedaling competitors.

The trouble is that *all* riders are aware of these physical facts of life at high speed on a bicycle. Naturally they all try, therefore, to make certain someone else is out front to buck the air, not to mention a head wind that makes a hard job harder. There is an unwritten rule that everyone in a race is expected to do some of the hard work up front some of the time. If that rule did not apply, riders would jockey for rear positions and the race would come to a stop, which has happened. There is almost certain to be a certain amount of crabbing about how little work certain riders are doing, often justified.

Not all riders have the same skills and strengths in this group that has settled down to a race. Some are capable of very rapid acceleration: sprinters. They may not be as strong as some others, but they are quick. Their strategy will be to do as little hard windbreaking work as possible to save strength for that last sprint, where they'll show their stuff. The stronger pluggers are not going to peaceably tow the sprinters to the finish line; they will force the pace to wear the sprinters down, or they will try to get out ahead of the main pack of riders – that's what "breaking away" means. Only an uncommon rider can manage to break away alone and that is where teams come into the picture.

At the very start of the Apple Lap race, three riders broke away right at the start. We had to get the speed of our car up in order to stay ahead of them; we were expecting a slow start, lots of jockeying. Just holding position ahead of the three so that Fred could tape them, our speedometer climbed up over thirty-five. These three brave souls were members of a team, a loose grouping, often sponsored by a bike shop or maker of bicycle parts, which pay some of the costs of racing. (At this writing a competitive road bike is up to $1,200.) The team's aim is to place at least one member as highly as possible. If one member has a really good chance of winning, the others will subordinate their efforts to his win. In the break we were watching, the three were fairly even; they were going to share the work of building a lead on the pack. If they were successful in staying away, it would be each man for himself at the finish line, but if they were indeed successful, they would be dividing up the first three places, and the pack would be arguing about fourth and so on down. Team members may be assigned to slow the pack down—sitting out front and cutting the speed of the pack, while other team members take off. If another team makes a break, members of opposing teams are supposed to leap out of the pack and sit right on those departing wheels, doing no wind-breaking work, forcing the breakaway artists to tow them along. This often has a discouraging effect, and the break melts back into the pack.

In the Apple Lap, the breakaway group weakened. The pack was moving very fast on flat roads, and they soon swallowed up the breakaway. George Mount won that race. He made his own break closer to the finish line and easily won a long sprint.

The drafting principle works best at high speeds. There does come a time in most races when everyone must slow down: the first big hill. What does the supple sprinter do now? He hangs on for dear life. What does the brute do? He presses his advantage of strength for all he's worth, pulling relentlessly away from the weaker rides. In the Tour de France, the month-long international professional race, it is the mountains that decide the outcome. Climbs of twenty miles, grades that cars have to creep up in first gear, dirt surfaces, snow, wind. That is where the great champions like Fausto Coppi and Jacques Anquetil have done their breaking away, sometimes with help, if any of their teammates can stay with them, but often alone. There are some crazies among the pros who can and do count on dropping down the other side of the mountain at fifty miles an hour and more, and sometimes they make it if they don't hit a sheep in the fog, or skid off down a cliff.

The mountain-climbing brute would be at a disadvantage in another kind of race that is probably not as common as it should be in this country: the criterium. Such races are run on a closed loop of road or the streets of a town. The course may be only a mile or two. It is a race that is more likely to reward the audience who can watch riders' progress as the laps go by. Criteriums generally include sprints every four or five laps, with special prizes for the winners. Our sprint artist is happiest here, whizzing along at high speeds, dodging in and out of shelter showing his elbows to those powerhouse locomotive types who wish they were back in the mountains. One such race in Somerville, New Jersey, has been a season opener in the East for decades and one result is that many people in Somerville are up on bike racing whether they ride themselves or not.

The high-speed, closed circuit might draw better audiences, but the unwatchable point-to-point road race has the fascination for bike riders that the marathon has for runners. If television covered the big road races, there would be more fans for that sort of madness, but television won't cover them because there aren't enough fans to make a profitable audience. So it goes, around and around.

Running gets the attention it does because so many people run. Lots of people ride bicycles too, but they go so slowly, they have no sense of the racer's high-speed world. Runners are benign and sportsmanlike. The masters welcome beginners, or at least they don't sneer at them. Any runner can take satisfaction home from a race he has no hope of winning simply by finishing or beating a previous time. Bike racing is not that gentle. If you can't stay with the leaders, you don't count. Stragglers are likely to find the timers have packed up and gone by the time they get to the finish line. Within that whizzing pack on the road there is constant jostling, lots of competitive tension. They won't go out of their way to hurt you, but they won't make a beginner feel good either. They snap at each other, complain about each other's tactics and there is no sport that has developed more excuses: "I had a soft tire;" "I put on the wrong sprockets for the course" (pretty dumb, if true, which it never is); "I haven't trained for weeks;" "I've been sick;" "I am sick." Most of them will say anything to diminish the winner's glory and explain their own failure. The winner, of course, wears a smug smile, but even he has complaints about teammates who didn't

Waiting for the Start. Photograph by Karl W. Bruning

work hard enough, officials who weren't paying attention, and he will have a faultless excuse from the above list to explain why he didn't break the course record.

They are a crabby lot, but in their defense it should be said that racing cyclists are under a lot more pressure than, say, runners. Running may be more punishing, but pushing pedals is not easy, and many cyclists do ride themselves into exhaustion. Even when they're tired they've got to keep that game in their heads. They ride at great physical risk from traffic, potholes, and dogs. That drafting technique requires that your front wheel practically touch the back wheel of the rider in front of you. If he wobbles or hits his brakes hard, down you go, and if you do down in a pack, others go down with you. Coming off onto concrete at twenty-seven miles an hour can break bones, and it always rips skin off leaving pain that lasts for weeks.

The risk, the strain, the physical and mental skills of the riders, the excitement of the speed, the flash and blaze of color – these are all characteristics of good sport, however hard it may be to watch. If the pack flashes whirring and yapping past you one day, give them an encouraging yell, no matter how general. They won't look up, they're too busy, but they'll be glad you noticed.

Advice to Beginning Racers

Bjarne Rostaing & John Allis

Going fast is only part of being a good racer – many of the skills needed have survival value for any cyclist. Bjarne Rostaing, U. S. Editor for the annual International Cycling Guide, *has covered European and American bicycle racing for Velo-News, Olympian, Cycling, and other publications. John Allis, now an executive at TI-Raleigh (USA), was US National Road Champion, a three-time Olympian, and also raced successfully in Europe.*

Poor conditioning, lack of technique, confusion, and fear are problems for most beginning racers, and usually only the first is dealt with seriously. Training rides are often thought of only in terms of physical fitness. But pure "fitness rides" of either LSD (Long Slow Distance) or Interval type can be dull, and will not teach you techniques you need to know. You will lack confidence if you do not know how to respond to problems and remain upright, and that lack will affect your riding style and your results. The pack-shy rider is a danger to himself and others.

Staying upright in a near-crash situation is not just a matter of balance. Close-quarters bike handling is an art; A peloton is a large group of competitors, many of whom want to be in the same place at the same time, with resultant jockeying and jostling. Contact is inevitable, and you must get used to it. This is done much more safely in training: Ride with another rider and get used to knuckles and shoulders touching. Practice steering (slightly) into each other and riding close for periods of time. When you are used to this, find a grassy area and practice touching your front wheel to the side of the other rider's rear wheel. By bouncing your wheel against his rather than leaning away, you can stay upright when wheels accidentally overlap. Many amateurs crash in this very common situation. (Wear a long-sleeved shirt and long pants when trying this; you'll go down, and the clothes will help prevent road rash.)

With this practice, you will be a more confident and therefore a safer rider. Learn to sense the flow of the peloton. While glory is one of several possibilities for the experienced rider, it can be a blinding obsession for the strong, inexperienced one. Being aware of nothing but your own excitement, you ride without response to the traffic flow established by experienced riders, ignoring physical and verbal suggestions. This brings the spirit of free enterprise directly into conflict with the laws of physics, which dictate whether you maintain balance and adhesion.

Although it is possible to spill anywhere, corners are the most likely place to go down, because riders have different ideas about which cornering line to follow. Cornering in a pack is a compromise between the best line and what is forced on you by those around you. The following rules apply, modified as circumstances demand:

1. The best line is from the outside of the turn to the inside. Really talented bike handlers can pass inside less agile riders, but this is not for everyone. Cornering too tightly raises the possibility of being forced into the curb by the outside rider. Keep your inside shoulder as low as possible; cocking your knee out does not help.

2. Avoid altering your line substantially once you are in the corner; the shift of weight and wheel movement reduce adhesion. It may be better to make temporary, controlled contact with another rider.

3. Avoid entering a corner too fast. This can lead to overshooting, or the cardinal sin of braking in the corner.

4. Don't try to pedal all the way through sharp corners unless your bike has a high bottom bracket and/or short crank arms. Instead, drop the outside pedal to the bottom of its stroke and put

Photograph by Bernard Thompson

your weight on it. Contorted positions don't help; a low center of gravity and smoothness do.

5. Avoid following too closely (in corners or anywhere). Overlapped wheels are very dangerous. Even if you have mastered the technique of regaining balance by controlled tire-touching, you lose speed and get in the way of some other rider—who may panic and bring you down.

Obviously you want to know the course — especially with criteriums, where bike handling can be a decisive advantage. After taking a corner three times, you'll know something about it. Watch the best riders. Watch the bad ones too; even a halfway serious competitor has a ''book'' on his competition. Avoid known crashers, and sudden ''switchers.'' Don't be trapped behind one without room to maneuver. The best riders are observant and rarely crash. Low-category amateurs often display road rash as if it were a badge of honor, like duelling scars.

While a certain amount of contact will always exist, it will be more under control at the front of the field. This is where the action is. Not only are the successful moves made from here, but those at the front avoid what is sometimes called the ''rubber band'' effect. The peloton alternately strings out and bunches up during the course of a race. This means that those toward the back have to constantly slow down and speed up. Hills and turns accentuate this. And the rider in the rear has little idea of what is going on at the front. Staying with the first twenty while doing a reasonable amount of work is a fine art.

Moving to the front can be done in different ways. Some have to go to the outside and move up alongside the pack. Others can create openings and move up through a field without creating problems. This is dependent not only on skill and reaction time, but on peripheral vision. At close quarters, you need to see not only the wheel in front, but all the bikes around you.

Another thing you need to know is whose wheels to follow and whose to avoid; the biggest name is not necessarily the best wheel, and trying to move up behind a really slick sprinter is like trying to thread a very small needle. (They see openings as they start to happen, and fill them just as fast.) Generally the good wheel to follow belongs to a biggish, smooth rider — experienced, reliable, efficient; but of course others will want the same spot, which introduces the question of just how aggressive you can afford to be in fighting for position.

The answer is a matter of how good a bike handler you are, and how important the situation is tactically. If you always yield, it will become a habit. If you force the situation crudely or at the wrong time, you are dangerous; expect out-of-control aggression to lead to spills. (Spills make you lose time on the bike, form, and confidence. Crashing is bad news.)

What should you do if someone goes down in front of you? Don't jam brakes. Whichever way he is falling, try to go the other way, and if you brake, do so just enough to avoid contact. If someone is right under your wheels all you can do is ride and hope . . . it is frequently possible to cycle across impressive piles of arms, legs, wheels, and tubing, if you remember to lift your front wheel. Sounds sadistic, but it's usually better

for those below than having you and your bike fall on them, bringing down yet others.

In road racing, bike handling is important but can be compensated for by strength in the hills, determination, endurance. The road rider can be conservative, but for the criterium rider, handling skill is essential; a great many escapes will occur after corners, when the pack is elongated. The best place to refine handling skills is the track; there everything is fast and close. Awareness is heightened, aggression is everywhere, and the atmosphere is supercharged.

No matter how the chipping, bluffing, hooking, and crowding make you feel, ride the mass-start track events, and do it before you get a lot of bad habits. The track riders will let you know what's happening real quick — they're not bashful.

This is where you move away from the fantasy world of the rider who trains alone without ever really learning to race, and move toward a real perception of what is going on around you even at maxed-out tempos. Because confidence is basic to quick decisions, the track can reduce fear, the greatest enemy of performance. You will feel loose and easy on the road after going through some madisons and points races.

As for wheels and tires, it is no accident that a 3-cross wheel with a 260-gram cotton mixed-tread is found on more racing wheels than any other. On United States roads this is the best all-purpose, all-weather, good-durability compromise. While matte and linear-tread tires may be marginally faster, they are more unpredictable in the wet, particularly when worn. Traditionally,

Photograph by John Krausz

"reds" are unreliable in the rain, and all silks tend to deteriorate when wet. Vary tire pressure to change handling characteristics. A good racing tire should tolerate as much as 110 to 120 pounds of pressure; with a light rider it may be advisable. But 90 to 95 pounds is better in slippery conditions.

TRAINING

The purpose is to interface your particular body with a bicycle to go as fast as possible for a given distance. This means, first of all, fitting the bicycle to yourself correctly. Because of almost infinite variations in the human body, theories will always fall short of expert advice from an experienced director.

No matter what your event, you are pedaling, and this is often ignored. It is applied strength that counts, and efficient use of energy. Weights, exercise machines, and exercise will not teach you to pedal; you have to learn how, and it should become so automatic that when fatigue hits, you don't forget how to do it.

Pedalers are broadly divided into smoothies who spin, and punchers who tend to stamp down and pull up sharply. (Then there are those bike-benders who slog along in too-big gears getting nowhere.) It pays to be smooth for several reasons: Bad, hard pedaling for long periods can strain muscles and ligaments and damage knees. Bad pedaling is inefficient and wastes strength. Whatever the terrain, whatever the gear, pedal smoothly. This allows you to relax, and blood to flow more freely through the muscles with many benefits. Tight, awkward pedaling interferes with this. Often it is connected with nervousness and confusion.

There are a number of approaches to pedaling, which apply to both flat and climbing situations. You can twiddle a small gear, pedal a medium gear, or move back on the saddle and smoothly work a bigger gear. Or you can get out of the saddle, which is commonly done in attacking, when closing gaps, or on climbs. (On climbs, the out-of-saddle position is usually combined with a more upright position, the hands on top of the brake levers.) But no matter how you go at it, the art of the bicycle comes down to making perfect little circles with your feet. If you're not doing this, you're wasting energy; and in a four-hour road race, this matters. The rider

Photograph by John Krausz

who makes it a habit to concentrate on this skill is the one who can keep going when his legs are shattered and unresponsive.

Technically, the problem is to spread the energy of pushing down and pulling up over a longer arc. If the pedal stroke is divided into four quadrants, in only one of these do most untrained riders push down with effective force. This can be doubled — most of the downstroke can effectively transmit energy. The shorter pulling up motion can be also extended, so that all of the stroke is useful. Eventually the whole process can become smooth and natural, but it is not at all easy, which is why it is often ignored.

While rollers do not develop strength, they can teach you to transmit your strength to the pedals smoothly. Riding fixed gear can and does build strength in addition, and the backpedaling develops muscles that tend to atrophy when riding only a derailleur bicycle. But whenever you are pedaling, the idea is to apply force perpendicular to the crank arm all the way around the pedal stroke. In doing so, you would use only the muscles required for that part of the pedal stroke, while relaxing the other muscles.

A low aerodynamic position is also very important, because at racing speeds most of your work goes into overcoming wind resistance. Pictures of professional racers show a marked difference in position from those of most amateurs — even the six-foot-tall Merckx disappears into the peloton. This position should become habit, not

just be adopted for races, because it involves the back muscles in pedaling, and these need exercise if demands are going to be made on them. Breathing will be different as a result, you must adapt to this.

Methods of training vary quite widely among amateurs, much less among professionals who race so often that training as such is limited to preseason miles.

Ideally, you want to avoid going into anaerobic effort — you want to raise that threshold. It is a tricky process. You are trying to build yourself up without running yourself down. With serious training this is a fine line; peak form is just this side of losing form and the training process does not work without adequate rest, a balanced diet, and a disciplined approach. Despite the carbohydrate-loading craze, professionals eat a basic balanced diet and get plenty of fats — which pound-for-pound are much more efficient, though the ability to use them varies from person to person.

Training begins during the off-season. General fitness allows you to enter on-bike training from a certain plateau of overall strength. Skating, running, cross-country skiing, and circuit training all develop aerobic capacity, while basketball, soccer, hockey, and calisthenics keep you nimble. Strength can be developed from chopping wood—or light varied work with weights and exercise machines. Caution should be used with the former, and supervision with the latter.

There is a definite distinction between general strength and the ability to go fast on a bicycle. A look at the bodies of the better professional road men is revealing: They do not have big arms, or even extremely big legs; they have bodies specifically adapted to going fast and long on a bicycle, because this is what it takes to win. Track riders are often of a different type – there are more big men, since distances are short, strength and speed are the main issues.

Broadly speaking, there are two current schools of training. The Long Slow Distance (LSD) method traditional to Western Europe, and the "Interval" approach, popular in Eastern Europe. Both have produced good international riders. More important, both Eastern and Western European riders race very frequently. After early-season conditioning miles, racing is the best training. It not only gives mileage, but fast tempos and intervals as you attack and counterattack. Beyond this, it sharpens your bike handling and your sense of what is likely to succeed and what is wasted effort –tactics, in other words.

But before racing begins, conditioning miles are needed. In late winter many will do this on a track bike or road bike converted to fixed gear, with about a 63 to 72 inch gear depending on terrain and rider. This arrangement limbers the muscles and helps develop a quick, smooth, supple pedaling motion. The fixed gear forces you to pedal well and constantly, and it handles more precisely, especially in slippery road conditions.

Photograph by Paul Boyer

Photograph by Paul Boyer

For the beginning senior rider something like 80 to 120 miles the first week and about 25 to 30 miles more each subsequent week is reasonable. Some calisthenics and stretches followed by a roller session on bad-weather days is a good idea too; anything to build overall fitness and strength. For the inexperienced, rest days are a good idea. Enthusiasm can lead to early peaking, followed by a let down. The art of training is to be super fit at the right time.

After a month or more on the fixed gear (upwards of 600 miles) the road bike can come out, but with fairly heavy wheels and tires. The new, light, high-pressure clinchers are very good for this time of year, both tough and cheap. Mileage should continue to build gradually and level off at somewhere between 250 and 300 per week, for most riders.

With 1,000 miles in the legs you can think about limited speed work without fear of muscle strain. Training should resemble racing closely and be a mix of long slow distance and intervals or pace-line. Always warm up on the bike for twenty to twenty-five minutes before such an effort. Intervals stress the system, on the theory that stress will make it develop. They can also stress muscles and joints, sometimes too much, particularly if the body has not warmed up. (LSD theorizes that the body is best developed by exercising below the anaerobic threshold.) But theories are of limited use; no one training schedule can fit all riders

preparing for a given event. You must work from information fed back by your body and overall state (pulse, weight, sleep). Thirty-second intervals are vastly different from "pursuit type" intervals of two to five minutes. The former will develop your jump, the latter your ability to escape and stay off the front. Don't overdo intervals, or do them every day. Many riders do not feel the effect immediately; the basic, safe pattern is to go hard one day, easy the next. When racing begins, the day before a race should be easy. How easy is hard to say; some riders take a day off prior to racing, but most do better to put in about an hour of low-gear spinning. Gearing is important too; big-gear intervals can damage riders whose gift is for smooth pedaling in low gears.

Equally important is training your mind. A bike race is a series of episodes alternating stress and relative relaxation. What distinguishes winners is consistency, and what makes for consistency is a certain attitude toward pain and discouragement. Even very good riders have periods during a race when everything seems to fall apart. But things often come back together unexpectedly when you are at the point of giving up. This is not to say that the symptoms of fatigue should be ignored, but that various types and levels of fatigue must be distinguished. The rider who manages to push himself through these thresholds will often defeat a faster rider who is up and down emotionally, looking for sympathy, or for an excuse to abandon.

151

It is a tough sport, and toughening yourself is something that should not be avoided. Toughness can be developed from method and discipline in training. A no-nonsense frame of mind helps you concentrate on what you are doing. A regular schedule in training, eating, and sleeping helps maintain a calmness that is definitely needed in a race; calmness goes with concentration. Control over the situation leads to confidence both on and off the bike. This can affect a coach's decision when teams are being picked.

Coaches also much prefer the rider who shows maturity by being able to take care of his needs efficiently. Food, clothing, equipment, transportation, and adequate rest are the obvious essentials. "Neither a borrower nor a lender be" is more or less impossible, but it's not a bad way to think about things if you are not with a team. Self-sufficiency requires organization, but it generates respect. Other riders are more likely to be cooperative about giving you a ride to a race (or working with you in a race) if

that respect has been established. There are plenty of strong, fast riders nobody wants to know because of their whining, demanding behavior and endless distracting requests.

To be very specific, you need not only to own at least two pair of pants and jerseys, you need to wash them on a regular basis, and have a set dry and ready on race day. Your bike must be maintained regularly, not the night before a race, and you must know how you are getting to a race well beforehand. Have food and drink ready to take along so you don't have to stop on the way.

What is often ignored here is that failure in any of these areas makes you anxious and gets in the way of good rest. Nervous and anxious is exactly what you don't want to be. In stage six-day racing, preparation becomes particularly important, because you will have to take care of obligations just when you would like to avoid them. If you have no pattern – no habit of taking care of yourself effectively – you are subject to the bonk (no food), dehydration

(no liquids), breakdowns (bad maintenance), and saddle boils (dirty shorts). Any of these can put you out of competition, if you managed to get to the race in the first place. Cycling, particularly road racing, is not so much a matter of pure "talent" – speed and coordination – as it is of putting together a lot of seemingly secondary and uninteresting skills and habits.

EQUIPMENT — PRINCIPLES

Despite a continuing obsession with trick equipment and light, drilled-out components, reliability is crucial. Good wheels in particular are important, preferably having more than one set. You really need a separate set of training wheels with heavier rims and tires. The basic parameters are: training tires, 290 to 400 grams, racing tires, 230-260.

Frame weight is not very important (rolling or rotating weight in the wheel and crankset is more important, but still

152

George Mount gets a good push-off after a puncture. Bernard Thompson

not critical). What you want is a frame that fits and is "true"; if it doesn't fit, you will feel uncomfortable and be unable to use your strength efficiently, and if it isn't built true you may get a flutter at certain speeds that is unnerving and hard to stop. Most racing frames are made of double-butted tubings, of which Reynolds and Columbus are the best known. But the quality of the construction is more important; too-cold or too-hot brazing can both lead to failure.

The same principles apply to all components: reliability, repair-ability, and reasonable price. For the cost of a few titanium components you can start thinking about an extra set of wheels, and any racer will tell you that this is where it's at. A few ounces here and there mean nothing, if there is a loss in reliability. In time trialing and track pursuit, this is less true, but what you want first of all is a bike that works.

And that you can repair. This is something you must face. Unless you have a truly breathtaking potential, no one is going to true your wheels, patch your tires, tighten your bottom bracket and headset.

There is no avoiding these chores until you are at least a National Class rider, which takes a few years for just about everyone. You won't get there if your bike doesn't work. You will also become unpopular if you constantly seek help. Other riders have their own maintenance to think about; they may show you once, but after that they're helping the competition.

What Makes a Winner

Paul Harris, M.D.

Dr. Harris is a lifetime cyclist who has been racing ever since he got his first good bike. He is also the parent of a state champion, and club doctor. Therefore he has been able to judge what makes a champion both as a participant and as an interested observer. His medical background makes him a bit cynical about the efficacies of most fads. He is medical editor of this book, and wrote the article, "Children and Bicycles." He trains every day and participates in club races on weekends.

Great athletes and winners are frequently unaware of what really makes them win, or they attribute their success to various rituals, beliefs, or personal superstitions. Their admiring press or competitive colleagues are only too happy to look for some factor – equipment, diet, training routine, etc. that accounts for consistently great performance, but which may or may not, in fact, be related.

I know of riders who rest before a race, and others who ride the day before, riders who fast, and riders who eat heartily, riders who eat only health foods, and others who

down Cokes. Each seems to feel that his special regime is responsible for a great performance.

In fact, the reasons that a particular individual is successful in an extremely demanding and competitive sport such as cycling are very complex and not well understood. But they are surely not due to any specific fad or diet, equipment, ritual, routine, or superstition.

The great and successful bike-racing athlete must possess several assets and cultivate them in order to win. The single most important factor in winning is psychological. You must want to win very badly, know you can do it, and be able to work hard and endure great pain to accomplish this goal. A cyclist must have unbelievable determination and willpower that allows him to continue under extreme conditions of fatigue and even boredom. To be psyched up for an event also means that the event is suited to the individual's temperament, as the differences between track sprinting and stage racing are remarkable. A time trialist who has inner consistency and endurance does not need the same

kind of stimulation to proceed as does the road sprinter, who depends upon competitors to urge him on as well as team spirit and individual courage.

Basic health and coordination and a good build are all needed to start with, but no particular advantage is gained or lost by adhering to any special diet—vegetarian, natural, or meat, perhaps with the exception of carbohydrate loading prior to long distance events.

It is a well-known observation that the winners of most events are not the most exhausted—it is the runners-up or losers who have worked the hardest just to keep up with the pace set by the leaders. This is because winning riders are in top form—physically and psychologically – and have both the experience and the confidence gained from frequent hard training and competition to achieve a certain standard of performance. Age can be a factor, but racers may begin success in senior events by seventeen or eighteen and can remain competitive into the forties – remarkable for a sport requiring such devotion. Riders usually peak 153 at between twenty-one and thirty, or even later.

Specific goals in winning races revolve around motivation and training for the event with general long distance conditioning, endurance training, and intervals to build speed. Sufficient sleep and abstinence from intoxicants, tobacco, and other drugs are needed for optimal performance, and coaching, which is tactical, practical, and psychologically oriented, must be effective.

I have never known the best or most expensive equipment to be the determining factor in winning — you still have to pedal it to win — but functional, aesthetically pleasing, light, strong, mechanically-sound stuff helps, or is a bare minimum. Getting good advice, coaching, and team and family support for the bike racer's activity is probably one of the most essential needs, because to really do well

takes full-time effort — the amateur, leisure-time racer is at a disadvantage here.

Another critical factor in maximizing one's performance in racing to win is the delicate balance between overtraining and undertraining. This depends a great deal on the individual and the events being prepared for. Most active racers in full season need little additional training if they are racing three or four times a week. What they do need is to assure themselves of adequate rest, fluids, calories, and relaxation. The Europeans believe very strongly in massage, which is not well practiced here. I suppose that it does help, mostly to relax physically and emotionally.

When all is said about factors that make a winner, it must be realized that not all men and women are created physically equal. What we must strive for is to create the

conditions that allow each of us to perform to the best of our ability and to select events that will bring out the best of our natural talents. However, because there will only be one champion, the others who participate will also need to enjoy what they are doing and will need to receive some compensation, or the event will be meaningless for all. A good race should bring out the best in all the competitors and enable those special talents or qualities that individuals have mastered to flourish.

In the final analysis, the polemic between environment versus genetic factors that go into making us all what we are is being played out on the track and road in competitive cycling as it is in life in general. Probably it takes a good dose of each factor, and a fair amount of good fortune as well, to be truly successful and consistent.

Time Trialing

Vera van der Reis Krausz

"Cycling is sustained in all its phases by a fierce independent spirit of loyalty, dedication, and sacrifice insulating functional, touring, and competitive cycling against the indifferent media, lack of public support, and legislative restriction . . . the suppression of open-road racing probably symbolizes more an expression of conservative opinion against the sport than any danger to the dog-cart owner.

"This ban stimulated the remarkable network of events, always unpublicized prior to the start, of unpaced time-trialing and road records, with its almost underground movement in common dress of black alpaca jacket and tights . . . the present acceptance . . . the enthusiastic flamboyancy of multicolored advertising sweaters sweeping in group formation has not obliterated the most genuine amateur of all, the British time-trial rider.

"There are more than 800 clubs in the United Kingdom, many with riders and races unnoted, but every weekend they meet and sweat and suffer in lonely individual battles against time and distance."

Sir Hubert "Oppy" Opperman, Australian diplomat and holder of many long-distance cycling records, thus recently glorified the sport in Melbourne's *National Cycling*.

Time trialing is sometimes called the British obsession. There is no doubt it is that country's most popular form of amateur racing for both men and women, one that many people enter as teenagers, and keep up all their lives. A reading of the bulletin of any of the many clubs in England shows that some rivalries have gone on for over fifty years.

In 1888 British authorities banned mass-start road

Time trial photographs by Bernard Thompson

races and transferred most events to the many tracks that dotted England. For those who refused to give up road racing, they established the Road Records Association to keep track of long-distance record events. The first to be recognized are still among the most important—50 miles, 100 miles, 24 hours, and Lands End to John O'Groats—the 850-mile run from one end of the island to the other. Even then separate records were kept for bicycles, tricycles, tandems, and tandem tricycles.

F. T. Bidlake, who in 1895 set tricycle records for 50 miles, 100 miles, 12 hours, and 24 hours, that same year added a competitive aspect to record racing by helping run the first real time trial—a fifty-miler (twenty-five miles out and twenty-five miles back) on the Great North Road out of London. The same rules apply today: Racers are to cover the same course on the same day, each starting alone, separated by a time interval of at least a minute. People try to catch their "minute man," but most are well satisfied if they can establish or equal a personal best time for a course.

The form's continued success is no doubt helped by being open to everyone, having a full-season program, and culminating with the competition for the BBAR—the British Best All Rounder—run by *Cycling* magazine, where each season winners' speed is averaged on three events. For men that is 50 miles, 100 miles, and 12 hours; for women, 25, 50, and 100 miles. In both cases the average is over 25 miles an hour!

Since 1938 the Road Time Trials Council (RTTC) has supervised races, which are open to every cycling club in England and Wales. There are separate classifications for boys, girls, juniors, men, women, and veterans, as well as a handicap system. The RTTC must approve the watches and timekeepers, as well as distances and times. National championships are held in different places; they start in June with the 25-mile championship and do not end until October.

While time-trialing does eliminate the dangers of mass-start racing, it can present the cyclist with other interesting obstacles, as can be seen from Bernard Thompson's accompanying photographs.

Only since World War Two were time trials part of major stage races, but now winners of the Tour de France are often great time trialers as well. Only the team time trial is a World Championship event, but there are famous continental time trials such as the Grand Prix des Nations, a hilly course outside Paris when Anquetil won it nine times between 1953 and 1966, and the Grand Prix de Lugano, where 50,000 spectators saw Eddy Merckx set the record at 26.65 miles per hour.

The time trial is favored by many clubs in the United States, both as an individual and a team event. The United States Cycling Federation ratifies all records, and verifies times and distances. National championships include twenty-five-mile competitions for men, women, veterans, and juniors.

Since events may be won or lost by fractions of a second, time trials have been a spur to equipment development. Until 1976 major emphasis was on lightness—titanium, ultralight often lugless frames, and drilled-out parts. The last few years the emphasis has shifted to aerodynamics, with Hinault's time trial bike for the 1979 Tour de France featuring hidden brake cables, a totally new handlebar assembly, and wheels with oval spokes and recessed valves. Riding at constant speed without drafting makes rolling weight particularly important. Michel Delore, in *Cyclo 2000* notes that air resistance on traditional wheels absorbs twenty percent of the power of the racer, versus two percent for the rest of the bike.

Use radial front wheels, and back wheels with compensated spoking, eight on the left and sixteen on the right. Tires must hold as much air as possible; 125 pounds is not unusual, so silk or silk-polyester tubulars at the lightest weight possible for the road surface are used. Most courses are flat, which encourages high gearing and only one chainring in the front, or else fixed gears for the smoother pedaling and weight saving. Nylon or silk jerseys without pockets are worn. Holding as aerodynamic a position as possible means the bike must fit just right, so many time trialers use micro-adjusting seatposts and adjustable stems, plus, of course, a watch mounted on the handlebars.

The Tour Transforms a Small French Town

Samuel Abt

The window of a beauty parlor in Fleurance, a sleepy town in southwestern France, was drawn over in lipstick with a map of the country. Only two places were identified: Fleurance, where the Tour de France bicycle endurance race began in 1977 and again in 1979, and Paris, where it ends each year.

Not often are these two municipalities paired, but for a few days before the start of the race, the map was valid. The Tour de France does that for a small town, gives it a touch of importance, an international dateline, a place on European television.

Suddenly the world has heard of Fleurance or Luchon or Saint-Brieuc or any of the other obscure corners where the racers stop for the night.

It is in the small towns that the riders are most fussed over. Shops, even banks, close because the residents are thronging the arrival and departure areas to look closely at the bicycles and to stare at the racers.

The welcome in the evening can sometimes be brisk. The riders sprint past the finish, push through the crowds, and vanish in their team cars. The best a fan can do is perhaps touch a bicycle as it is wheeled away, or watch as the day's winner receives the inevitable kiss and flowers wrapped in cellophane.

But each morning, in the half hour before the departure for another stage in the month-long race, riders and public meet.

Old men turn up in full racing regalia to glide on their bicycles among the riders, mimicking youth's pursuit. The police are notably lenient about letting young children wander around asking for autographs. The riders hide their tension by chatting with their fans.

Then whistles blow and the riders gather at the starting line. The real start usually takes place outside town, on an otherwise-empty road, but the Tour de France likes to pretend, just one more time each day, that the town it is visiting is really the focus of the race.

The signal is given and the riders move out. Down the street they go, around a corner and then they are

Tour de France photographs by Barbara Bell

gone. For a few minutes, the town seems empty, but down the road lie other towns waiting for a few hours of recognition.

They will be thronged also, even though their citizens can see the race better, and certainly more comfortably, at home on television. Every finish is shown live each afternoon, with filmed highlights shown later each evening. There is also live radio coverage every day. Both television and radio coverage reach throughout Europe, but it is in France that the saturation point is attained.

Newspapers throughout the country are full of articles about the Tour de France before, during, and long after the race. Photographs of spectacular finishes are often on page 1, and commentaries and lists of standings and points fill inside pages.

Samuel Abt *is a journalist for the Paris-based* International Herald Tribune *and often reports from everybody's dream job for* The New York Times.

In short, the Tour de France is the center of French life in July. Why this is so has been the subject of learned discussions for years, but the best explanation may be, as it has often been remarked, that the French love sports, especially when they are being played by somebody else. They also love a spectacle, a winner, and a free outing — all of which the barnstorming Tour de France provides.

This excitement is obvious to the racers, who like to see the huge crowds that pour out to watch the passing parade. While the Tour moves through about 2,000 miles of France, it is watched by nearly a third of the population. The official figure is that fifteen million people will line the sides of the road, which is closed to all other traffic for ninety minutes before and ten minutes after the passage of the race.

On the flat, a spectator can expect to see a few minutes' worth of the race, preceded and followed by advertising trucks, official cars, squads of motorcycle policemen, and reporters and photographers using all known modes of conveyance except bicycles. The official party of the Tour exceeds 2,000 people, only 150 of them racers.

In the mountains, as the pack strings out for the slow climbs, the view of the race lasts longer. Families bring picnic lunches and make a day of it in vast numbers. More than 150,000 people showed up in 1979 for the mountain finish at Alpe d'Huez and traffic down from the peak was still bottlenecked at 4 o'clock the next morning.

Except for the seats in a short stretch of grandstand at each finish, the entertainment is free. The money that fuels the Tour comes from team entrance fees, from purses put up by towns and cities eager to have the race stop there, and from patrons. These include the companies that join the blaring publicity caravan: makers of ice cream, vacation cottages, insecticides, tires, clothes, and bicycles.

There are other Tours, of course, notably in Spain and Italy. Britain has an equivalent race and so do Belgium, Switzerland, West Germany, the Netherlands, and Luxembourg. In Eastern Europe, the Peace Race passes through Czechoslovakia, Poland, and East Germany. Bicycling fans follow the races in all these countries, but only the Tour de France has managed to involve the general populace.

It is not simply a race, the French say, but a gift, like spring.

157

The Tour de France

Nicolas Freeling

The Tour de France is a phenomenon: No other sporting event is in the least like it. It might at first be thought to resemble some ferocious car rally, trans-Andean in character, for the champion riders do have much in common with a Fangio or a Stewart: men of speed, extracting the maximum advantage from physical and mental strength and skill upon roads chosen for their difficulty. But the comparison breaks down at once, for the Tour rider has no mechanical aids beyond the simple system of levers and pulleys — which even I can understand — of a bicycle: This is stick and strong. He has no motor, helmet, armor, or safety belt. He is virtually naked – the modern gladiator. The combat is of man against man, man against mountain, and, above all, man against himself.

The temperature can be anything from freezing to the high 90's Fahrenheit, neither in the least infrequent. For the one or the other, a folded newspaper upon your chest under the shirt, and a cabbage leaf over your neck are diversely recommended.

There have been Tours when it never stopped raining. You may meet the Pyrenean thunderstorm, another impressive phenomenon.

A Tour's length (averaged out over the years) is around 2,400 miles – a single day's stage around 120 miles – covered at an average speed of about 21 mph. The best average speed over an entire Tour was made by France's Jacques Anquetil in 1962, at 37.3 kmh.

The numbers engaged are about 144, say 12 teams of 12 riders each. These teams have been, in the past, national or regional, but nowadays bear the names of their commercial sponsors. Of this number of riders, nearly half fail to finish the course.

Officially, the prize to the winner is around $75,000: In practice it is far more (his contracts and "appearance money" for the following season will be three times that, and publicity payments as much again). A host of other prizes in proportion can be won, by the stage winners, the best climbers, the fastest sprinters – there is even a prize for the unluckiest rider. In general, the rewards for the star riders are comparable to those for top professional footballers.

Nicolas Freeling, *creator of Inspector Van der Valk and thus of some of the best-loved and best-written mystery stories ever, uses his skill to explain the mysteries and triumphs of the Tour de France.*

Explanations, however brief, do not cover the complexity of this gigantic circus; for the Tour is a show as well as a race.

But the first phenomenon to look at, in order to understand the rest, must be *L'Equipe*, the Parisian daily paper devoted to sport (and nothing else), within whose bureau the Tour is organized. Here in the Faubourg Montmartre, between bourgeois boulevards and raucous street markets, are some of the best sports journalists in Europe, and in the unpretentious offices a handful of extremely able men spend the entire year in the staggeringly complex organization of the Tour. Fifteen hundred persons continuously on the move for 22 days.

Like running the Principality of Monaco, in the sense that at the top is a prince: This prince is Jacques Goddet. He would be a remarkable man in any company. Princely the beautiful manners, the

Bernard Hinault at start of the 1979 Tour which he won. Barbara Bell

A Peugeot rider during the 1979 Tour. Photograph courtesy of the Liaison Agency

power and authority, the responsibility, the devotion. And princely in the Machiavellian sense the eye, the force and judgment. A universal man. Even over a lunch table he is the Tour de France.

Words come drilling round the oyster shells like machine-gun fire. ''The rider suffers acutely in his body – tendons, muscles, nerves. It is natural that he should suffer also deeply in his morale.''

Every sport produces exceptional champions: the bicycle more perhaps than others because of its exceptional nature, allying the demands made upon the climber, the downhill skier, the long-distance runner, the boxer. Jacques Goddet needs to be an exceptional man: His life is spent among more such.

The supreme champions have been Jacques Anquetil and Belgium's Eddy Merckx, who have each won five times (and each four in a row). Follow the Frenchman Bobet and the Belgian Thys, with three wins each. The most spectacular and brilliant rider ever seen was perhaps the Italian Fausto Coppi, who won twice, in 1949 and 1952.

Anquetil, the supreme stylist, once said of a great rider that he looked like a postman on a bike. What then can one say of Merckx of the awkward bobbing head, the cramped heaving back and grimacing face?

That it has no importance. Monsieur can do anything: climb against anyone, sprint against anyone — and when the entire Tour, himself included, is falling over with exhaustion, he will move off irresistibly in a lone run to the finish.

For the press, perhaps, he is ''Eddy''. But to the riders, and the followers, he is always Monsieur Merckx. The boss. It might sometimes be sarcastic — ''Mossieu'' — or half in mockery, but there will always be respect. Not to speak of fear. Even Jacques Goddet gives him his title.

The best, the *campionissimi*, have more than physical force and concentration. Merckx has an exceptional lucidity, and the moral power of a superior general.

In a famous hour he was left beaten. Smashed even, swept away by a superb Spanish climber, Luis Ocana, on an Alpine pass. No one forgets Merckx agonizing, the face distorted, struggling in to Orcieres-Merlette speechless and half blind, ten minutes late.

He led the race, next day, through the entire stage, not looking round, as though they were all beneath contempt. Ocana stuck to his heels, but the superiority was gone, and two days later, on a water-sloshed road under Wagnerian thunder in the Pyrenees, Monsieur M took his Tour back.

Anquetil was thin and quiet. Blond hair, a hollow face; the boy from Normandy. Cold – and the hotter the weather the more he liked it, and the hotter the rivalry too. He also looked a killer, and was. He fed you through the mincer; he had a gait superior to others and held it till you fell down.

Alone against the clock, in his balanced, elegant style, he was incomparable, seeming neither to suffer nor sweat. He won, and the others wobbling in rather later took their hats off, once they could breathe.

Of course he suffered: He was often close to disaster, but his moral force was such that one did not believe in it. He was not the best of climbers, but the most gifted Spaniards, astounding in tranquil ease, turned on the high mountain to glance nervously behind them. Maitre Jacques was there, the crocodile ready to devour.

Eddy Merckx, five-time winner, flashes a rare smile as he receives a piece of the ribbon opening the 1977 Tour in Fleurance. To his right is Bernard Thevenet, who won his second Tour that year. Barbara Bell.

Anquetil never sprinted. Despite rules, and severe sanctions, you are bumped, held by the shirt, knocked sprawling at sixty kilometers an hour. It is for the tough, brawling middleweights, generally Belgian sons of big shoulders and thick thighs.

I have a memory too of a "Giro," a tour of Italy, of the riders climbing a long, straight, killing slope. The fanatic supporters, the dread *tifosi*, were flagrantly pushing the Italian bikes, catapulting the rider upward. Not, of course, Anquetil, the cold, the French, the detested. Insults for him, and spittle. Expressionless, he climbed his line without yielding, without varying: Roman. He won, to be sure, but I have never admired him more.

Of all the moments in the legend, most would choose, perhaps, his electric ride against the clock in 1964, on his fifth and finest winning Tour: the twenty-seven kilometers through the Valley de Chevreuse on the way home to Paris that wrote "paid" against the name of Raymond Poulidor. The margin at the end, after a Tour lasting 127 hours and 9 minutes, was 55 seconds.

All the Tour countries have their exceptional names: Switzerland a Kubler and a Hugo Koblet; Italy a Bartali and the legendary Coppi; Spain the imperial Federico Bahamontes. Perhaps it is fair that France should be richest in characters, but since the Tour's most famous day of all back in the heroic time before 1914—when Chistophe the Gaulois stopped on the slopes of the Tourmalet, to mend the broken front fork

of his bicycle himself, at the village forge of Sainte-Marie-de-Campan—there has never been a rider, neither Anquetil nor Louison Bobet himself, like Raymond Poulidor.

He is the rarest bird of all, the champion loved as much as he is respected.

Nobody ever had more ill luck: Raymond has been knocked over by everything imaginable, right down to a motorcycle cop, and covered in blood more often than you or I have had hot cups of tea. He shrugs it off. Splendid looks, an enchanting slow smile, a voice like a soft song, exquisite manners. A man humble, gentle, generous, good. And has never won a Tour. . .

Won everything else; since 1970 he has taken Paris-Nice away from Monsieur Merckx twice in a row. On a fine day in the high Pyrenees, he rode away alone from all those fleas that tease, and left a leaden, anguished Merckx two minutes off. But it was too late: Poupou had had a mysterious bad hour on the Galibier a week earlier. It has always been too late.

He has invariably been beaten by first Anquetil and then Merckx, and many would say he was better than either. In the high hills nobody has excelled him, and only the aerial Bahamontes has been his peer. And of course he is very rich, very successful, very happy. He has just never won, that's all.

Other aspects there are of glory. The sprinters for example, and surely first Andre Darrigade, who got his nose in front 24 times to forge a stage win in the last 200 meters. The Spanish climbers, who really do float like the butterfly and sting like the bee. And, for many besides me, the common soldiers, who leave the peloton in a solitary effort and manage sometimes to maintain it till the end of the stage. Of all things in the Tour this is the hardest and best. The Tour is generous: The second- or even third-rate rider can have his hour. As the Spaniards remark, it is absurd to call so-and-so brave. He was brave on such a day.

One can see this. A famished Spanish lynx, an Ocana or a Fuente, alone in the mountain. Or after the dreariest of flat stages in the rain a combat of brave bulls, Belgian sprinters responding to the scrap of rag called the "red flame" which marks one kilometer to the finish. No horse could do it: It is sly, brutal, reckless, ugly: It is man.

Photograph by Barbara Bell

Mercifully, it is impossible to corrupt a Tour. Nobody could bribe 140 riders for three weeks. But there has been collusion, sometimes, between teams, and attempts to intimidate riders who showed up too often, for some tastes, at the front of sprints.

Teams are built where possible around a star. The best teams will also have specialists in sprinting, in climbing, in the tactical battling — and in the plain day-by-day graft. They are managed, as a rule, by ex-champions, who accompany the race in their cars, close enough to encourage and advise, and yell too in fury. A rider has at least two bicycles, often three or four. Stars have special featherweights, hand built of titanium, for time trials.

They push off, each morning, in a massed group (unless it is against the clock). They loiter at first, taking time to warm up, at a tourist's 20 to the hour, laughing and chatting. Staying alert though, for the first of the day's breakaways — a series of feints as a rule, to confuse, to provoke, and to fatigue the adversary. Farther on, a jockeying for good placing at the "hot points." This continual testing tells the shrewd who is looking strong and hungry, and who is showing signs of ambition. . . .

There is no stop for lunch, but a kind of truce while the picnic bags are handed out on the run. The wise drink little ("dryest is fastest") but all must eat. Neglect your food—cold meat, salad, fresh and dried fruit—and you risk collapse; you are burning energy at the highest metabolic rate.

The tension builds up in the early afternoon, roughly two thirds of the way through a stage. The serious break of the day is due, which may snap the peloton into fragments. The star, and his designated watchdogs, must be alert. To stay always at the front sounds the easiest way of doing this, and such indeed is the simple and effective tactical formula of a Merckx. In practice it is very difficult. To reply to every

Photograph by Barbara Bell

challenge takes a huge toll, and the greatest riders have their days of loitering at the back of the peloton, getting a tow — and suddenly trapped, and in trouble. A group is watching for signs of fatigue or wandering attention, fatally easy in the heat and dust, in the monotonous turn of the pedals; or in a gusting head wind, or driving rain. . . .

Or a puncture. Racing tires are thin and fragile: It will take twenty seconds for the mechanic's car to pull alongside, ten more to change the wheel. That is enough and more, on a twisting winding road, for get-

At the start. Photograph by Barbara Bell

ting left behind, and the pursuit may be bitter, sapping the reserves. One can never know, in the changing kaleidoscope of a Tour stage, when a break will come.

To guard against apathy and to continue to establish the time classification, especially in a Tour's early stages and on flat terrain, the first half-dozen in stage and "hot-point" sprints are rewarded with a few seconds of bonus, and time trials add a few more: There are plenty of ways of picking up odd seconds. But the classic manner, the only real way of telling the men from the boys, is the forthright road break. Hugo Koblet on his first Tour in 1951 had a final win of twenty-two minutes. He won five stages, including two against the clock. But his moral win was made on the road in 135 kilometers alone between Brive and Agen. He took "only" two and a half minutes from his closest pursuers, but he had run the entire peloton into the ground.

You choose your terrain with care. A sharp slope may add lead to the usually fleet; a narrow lane with room for only two abreast may favor the adroit. Or a bad road surface – rarer too, nowadays. Put your head down and Do Not Look Round. Most breaks are in twos or threes. Much depends upon your reputation and your time position. If you are small fry, the peloton may not deploy its entire strength to chase you. And if you are big, they may not have the force to try.

Half a dozen may favor your enterprise, relaying you at intervals. And twice as many might be sitting on your back wheel, waiting if need be to swamp you at the finish. You may well have nothing to show, in the end, for all your effort. Nowadays it is only in the mountains that even a flyer can count with any certainty on putting real time and distance between himself and the infantry.

Mountain stage – a day with four or even five hill passes, including at least one of "first category" and maximum difficulty. Each Tour contains several, but always the top "classics": The Galibier in the Alps, over 8,000 feet high and a perfect terror; worse still, it is generally linked with the Col du Telegraphe, itself over 5,000 feet. The Tourmalet in the Pyrenees, over 7,500 feet high; appalling, especially in hot weather; generally grouped with the Col de l'Aubisque, which is over 4,500 feet. On either or both of these, the crack

The Col du Tourmalet. Courtesy of the French Government Tourist Office

rider may have a huge win. It can and does happen that he is brilliant on the one and has a horrible collapse on the other.

The crack climber is light and small, and generally Spanish. He stands on his pedals *en danseuse*, on his points as it might be called, bicycle loose and flexible below him. He seems to use no effort. But the power climbers, Merckx or Anquetil, stay in their saddles, change grip on the handlebar, lift the head to get more oxygen; veins stand out; the strain is gigantic.

A pure climber, not complete in other talents, has only once won a Tour. Bahamontes of course, the Eagle of Toledo, in 1959, leaving Anquetil five minutes away. As a rule they are not strong enough against the clock.

The Tour can indeed be dangerous, but there are surprisingly few bad accidents. The Dutchman Van Est wrote a page in Tour history (and earned his name of Iron Willem) by once accomplishing a horrific tumble into a ravine; was picked up unscathed, to general disbelief. Ocana, Zoetemelk, and the inevitable Merckx had a vile crash at high speed, aquaplaning down a storm-drenched pass. The one was taken to

In the mountains. Courtesy of the French Government Tourist Office

hospital. The others went on to be second, and first, in Paris. . . . The smashes and collapses are the business of the celebrated Doctor Dumas, who can tell you at a glance the incipient bronchial pneumonia, or the penalty for too much mayonnaise last night.

Most accidents are caused by careless spectators. Since the downhill runners reach 100 kilometers an hour the record is good, better by far than rugby, or skiing. Sprints cause cuts and bruises, plenty of broken collarbones, the odd leg. The rider's most vulnerable point is at all times the articulation of the knee.

The whole tempestuous caravan does not reach Paris without drama. In 1950 both Italian teams walked out after words, and more than words, had flown; the eternal Franco–Belgian rivalry has made broken faces. Monsieur Goddet, the tiger hunter, has quelled the oafish and the ruffianly, the vengeful and embittered, by the force of his character. Nowadays it is Felix Levitan who controls the race from the command car, through a complex system of hand signals and shortwave radio. But the master is present. He makes the decisions; the responsibility is his. When politics threatened the Tour with cars bombed and a menace of violence toward the Spaniards, it was Goddet who paid no attention. He is the direct descendant of Henri Desgranges, who created the Tour. When a black day comes, and the master is no longer there, we will have a remembrance stage, as now on the Galibier we have the "Souvenir Henri Desgranges," and on the Mont Ventoux for poor Tommy Simpson. I do not know what form the day will take. But quite certainly there is a corner of heaven too where it is July, and a cloudless sparkle on the snow of the Pyrenees, and the smell of hot asphalt. And eighty boys climbing the Aubisque, with the Tourmalet, the big bad wolf, towering up behind.

Photograph by Barbara Bell

Many riders have glorious days, and a few have years. But there are all the others, who never for more than a few minutes unite mind to wrist to ankle and leave the peloton behind. So few will remember how good, that day, that boy was. Happy is he who paddles in to the Parc des Princes after 2,500 miles, unnoticed but for the official clock. Forty-third; sixty-third. No flowers or cameras or splashy kisses from beauty queens, or even a banner to hold advertising

Photograph by Barbara Bell

somebody's yogurt. A nod, maybe, from his manager. The boy stayed behind, it might be, on that tough stretch from Luchon to Pau, when his leader had a spill into the ditch; nursed him back, relaying nearly all the way, in a hundred kilometers of pursuit to a peloton that was fairly flying. A good boy. So a few good contracts from now till the end of the season. It's a fair living. And it's a life.

If you wish to catch a glimpse of a Tour, and nothing is easier, avoid the flat country where it screams past and you see nothing but the ten-foot-high models of somebody's chocolate biscuit in the publicity caravan. Try to post yourself, rather, near the top of the Tourmalet. Be prepared for it being either extremely hot or vilely cold. Either way have plenty of hot tea. There will be a colorful chatterbox, folklore crowd that writes slogans on the road. Scream with the others. It is forbidden to catapult the riders. And even if it is nearly a hundred degrees, do not throw water over them.

You will see a very splendid sight, as great a feat of courage as exists on earth.

If you prefer comfort, roughly the last thirty kilometers of every stage – and of course, the arrivals are televised daily.

And now thanks – to all the riders who ever finished, or did not finish, a Tour.

Photograph by Barbara Bell

Spring, 1975. Strasbourg – 17 times a stage halt for the Tour de France.

Hill Climbing – Cycling's Toughest Event

Dennis Donovan

For a few brief, mad, and hectic weeks, as the British time-trialing and road-racing season comes to a close, the hill-climbing season occurs. This annual tilt against gravity starts around the end of September and finishes with the national championship toward the end of October on a hill selected during the short season; the governing body—the Road Time Trials Council (RTTC)—moving the venue to a different part of the country each year. During this period the climbers can be expected to race up anything from a 400-yard hill in 75 or 80 seconds to a 3-mile mountain pass at 12 miles an hour.

It's a kind of symbolic—Don Quixote-like—gesture of defiance for many racers before winter sets the countryside into an icy grip; and on country lanes carpeted with russet-brown leaves, these heroes gasp the thin air into tortured lungs before returning to their snug homes to enjoy the social life that has been denied them since early February.

Out of all the forms of bike racing that every bike rider tries at least once in his lifetime, hill climbing is the hardest—even harder than riding a kilometer time trial on the track — for the effects of sprinting up a gradient as steep as twenty-five percent can be extremely vicious, leaving the rider completely speechless for several minutes and feeling the effects sometimes for two or three days.

British geography determines the use of hills during this short season, with the hills in the north of the country generally rated harder and longer than their southern counterparts, and as a result it's the northern guys who tend to dominate every year, especially those from Lancashire and Yorkshire, where climbing hills is an everyday fact of life for a bike rider.

Inevitably there are specialists at hill climbing, people who go against nature by hibernating all summer, emerging as the leaves begin to fall, only to disappear until the next hill-climbing season comes around. During this brief period they will race up to a dozen times, sometimes achieving two or three climbs in one weekend, and then that's it for another year.

The rules of this exacting form of racing are simple: Each rider starts at a minute interval from the next man in a prearranged starting order, and the fastest man up the hill is the winner. No part of the course may be covered on foot, which means no walking, no running, or pushing, or assistance of any kind. Once dismounted, the rider is automatically disqualified from starting again.

Unlike other time trials, there is no push start, and a steward will simply hold the rider upright by grasping

British National championship at Winnats Hill. Bernard Thompson

Dennis Donovan *regularly reports on all aspects of racing for the British weekly,* Cycling. *He also contributed the "Triking" story to this book.*

Photograph by Bernard Thompson

by today's climbers, the traditional fixed wheel is still used by many because it transmits effort instantly, and provides the rider with good control and rhythm, two basic requirements in any form of racing. Gearing for the shorter climbs is usually between 48x24 (54 inches) to 46x20 (62.1 inches), and on medium-length hills where gradients can vary, the gear is needed to be high enough to be pushed on the flatter sections, but not so high as to cause the effects of "dead-centering" occurring on the agony sections. Something between 47x21 (60.4 inches) to 48x19 (68.2 inches) is usually chosen. Long, steady hills can be climbed on gears between 44x18 (66 inches) to 44x16 (74.2 inches), providing there are no freak gradients en route to the summit.

In the 1979 British championship, the winner – Jeff Williams from Manchester – used rings of 42 and 53 for the 3-mile climb of Haytor in the National Park of

his frame by its head and by its rear fork ends. Once the timekeeper has intoned the familiar "five-four-three-two-one" of the final five seconds of countdown, the steward will simply let go of the bike on the command "go" and man launches himself into space.

Usually the starting effort is an out-of-the-saddle one. The nature of the hill will determine whether you will dance on the pedals all the way to the top, or whether you will be able to sit down for an armchair ride. Most of the top guys will sit down on the easy sections, pedaling their way out of trouble, then get out of the saddle on the harder parts, gripping either their brake hoods or the bottom of the bars, transferring their weight most heavily over the pedals to give more downward thrust and produce a stamping motion. It's also customary to adopt a more upright position than normal to allow for better lung expansion and better breathing. Deep breathing before the start to build up some air into the lungs is also practiced.

The choice of hill used will determine the type of gearing required. For the short, sharp hills that are common in southern events, most will turn out on track bikes and fixed wheels, whereas in the north, summer road bikes and derailleur gears can be used to better effect on the longer climbs.

A track machine, which under the rules of racing must have a front brake and lock ring to keep the fixed cog fixed in place, provides a very light and responsive machine for the shorter hill, and with twenty-eight-spoked wheels shod with tubular tires as light as the road surface will allow, a strong track sprinter will be favored to win.

On the shorter hills, some riders fit double toe straps to their toeclips, one at the base of the clip, the other in the usual place, because the strain of liftoff can cause feet to come out of the clips – with disastrous effects – well-fitted, strong, steel toeclips are a must. Straps, clips, pedals, and shoe plates should all be inspected well before the day of the race, for failure of any of these four can mean a ruined ride. In this type of effort the pedal must be dragged around as well as pushed down, so a spell of pedal maintenance is considered a good idea.

Though derailleur gears are used more and more

Photograph by Bernard Thompson

Dartmoor in picturesque Devon in the southwest corner of England. He started on 42x16, then shifted to the 15 sprocket for the flatter middle section, changed to his outside ring of 53 with a 16 sprocket for a downhill section, then it was back on to the 42 and his biggest sprocket, an 18, for the last lunge to the finish. The deposed champion, Gareth Armitage, from the same area as Williams, used a wide-ratio block (14 to 18) and similar chainrings. Very few used fixed wheel on this hill, and handlebar control gear changers were also a rarity, most using down-tube shifters instead.

Preparation is all important for this specialized event, and that starts with breakfast. As most hill climbs are held mid-morning to midday, it's fatal to climb on a full stomach, so you'll find riders breakfasting at least two hours beforehand. As there is no time to eat or drink on the way up, and nervous tension will have been doing strange things to the stomach, it's essential to eat something substantial to combat tension and hunger knock which can leave a racer feeling legless. Perhaps not surprisingly, very few can eat for some time after a race, nausea being a frequent reason. They can drink plenty, but eat, no. Those that have eaten too near to the climb will be self-evident at the finish, usually being violently ill. They stop and are caught by helpers who help them off their bikes and lay them to rest on blankets until the world stops spinning and starts to slow down. Laid out like wounded soldiers, they stare blankly into space for a while, then gradually come to and then the story of the race begins for anyone who cares to listen.

Warming-up is essential because of the explosive nature of the event, to ensure that muscles don't suffer damage from the suddenness of the starting effort. It doesn't necessarily have to be done on a hill. As hill climbs are generally conducted in cold weather, riders wear track suits with plenty of protection for the knees, which not only take enormous strain from the "off," and on every inch of the climb, but will also take unkindly to any chill winds that are blowing. Extra clothes are needed at the finish where the air may be colder; it's easy to contract a chill as the sweat dries on the body.

Climbers, except for the sprinter types on shorter hills, are usually about five feet eight inches or five feet nine inches tall, wiry, and weigh around 112 to 128 pounds, deriving their strength from arms, back muscles, and thighs. Stringy muscles rather than the bulging calf variety seem to be the norm. There are exceptions of course, but generally tall men or heavy ones have enough to do on the flat without dragging their bulk up hills. Off the bike, hill climbers are kind to children and animals, and pay their mortgages regularly – yet can produce enough venom, fury, and energy during four to ten minutes duration, to make the vertical seem horizontal. Nerves and temperament, naturally, will be more evident in this type of racing, with all the usual psyching moves known universally to sportsmen, used to maximum effort.

Added Advice from a Competitor

John Haigh

Hill climbing is the part of cycling where wind resistance has least effect. Hill climbs have more in common with running races of similar durations. The same talents are helpful on mountainous courses. The major battles in the ultimate of cycle races, the Tour de France, are usually won in the Alps.

Machines and Equipment

The most common machine has a light but rigid frame with a short wheelbase. A single fixed wheel is ideal for short climbs, as the rider then has nothing else to do but get

Photograph by Bernard Thompson

John Haigh loves everything about mountains – even racing up them: For advice on enjoying them in a more leisurely way, read his "Mountain Touring."

Photograph by John Haigh

Reinforced handlebars. Bernard Thompson

on with the racing. Mechanically, it is also the most efficient transmission method. Chains waste energy at the angles used for low gears and there is always the danger of a missed connection, which brings the rider to an embarrassing halt. However, multiple gearing has obvious advantages when the gradient varies. To avoid problems, it is wise to use the limiting screws on the rear mechanism, to restrict the choice to two or three cogs. Thus a positive change can be guaranteed by going against either of the stops. A front mechanism tends to be less reliable, especially under pressure. Satisfactory gear changes must be proved possible before the race starts. A former champion lost out badly in a recent national event when he brought his chain off. This

in an event that can be decided by fifths of a second.

It can pay to know the course. The author once won two successive events on the same course by changing down to a bottom gear of 40 inches on a finishing slope of 25 percent. This had almost stopped most of his rivals, who were using fixed ratios 20 inches higher.

The law requires one brake for a fixed wheel and two for gears. These are also very sensible for getting down safely to the start! To be equipped with light wheels and tires may seem obvious but there are factors other than weight. The events are often held on roads covered with wet leaves, so use a well-patterned tire. The rear wheel should be tightly constructed with strong spokes to resist the particularly large forces applied on low gears. Otherwise a broken spoke will make the wheel rub against the brakes or frame, and waste a lot of energy.

Riding Techniques

A good warm-up is essential. Ten to fifteen miles riding on gently graded roads before the event is ideal, even if you have to change wheels for the race itself. Then the hill should be ridden once at just a little below maximum effort for the legs and lungs. (Tour de France riders have been observed to ride a whole forty-five-minute climb of a time-trial stage before the race itself.) This practice ride is also a

useful rehearsal for planning gear changes or for checking that you have the right ratio on a fixed wheel. (Weather conditions can change your plans from hour to hour.) Ride the last few yards to the start with the right gear for setting off to ensure that there is no slip. You will be supported at the start, but not pushed forward. Several novices have fallen off in surprise, so be warned.

Always start slightly below the maximum effort you can manage. Fatigue catches up quickly enough anyway, and two or three seconds gained by going flat-out near the start are likely to cost much more time later on. You should be able to judge your capabilities from training sessions, even on different courses. Indeed, one successful British hill climber of recent years, Joe Waugh, claims to do nearly all his training on the flat.

The first half minute or so of the event will usually be a settling-in period, while you establish a steady rhythm that can be maintained without slowing down right through to the finish.

Photograph by John Haigh

For longer races, at points you have chosen earlier, change gears while on the saddle, slightly reducing the pressure on the pedals. When changing down for a steeper section it is important to make the shift while your pedaling speed is still high enough for a smooth change. Indeed, a winning ride requires a good pedaling speed throughout, certainly never much slower than sixty revolutions per minute.

Then, on approaching the end, and regardless of distance, it should be possible to go flat-out for the last minute. This way you use up every bit of available energy. In well-organized events there will be helpers to hold you up once you have crossed the finishing line, so you can then concentrate on recovery. Otherwise be careful to unstrap your feet before you try to get off!

Photograph by Bernard Thompson

The Track

Bjarne Rostaing

Bjarne Rostaing, keen observer and veteran reporter of racing, is currently American editor for the annual International Cycling Guide, *and collaborated with John Allis on "Advice to Beginning Racers."*

The common denominator of all track racing is speed. Like any arena sport, it evokes and recycles energy from the crowd, which can see every move, if it knows how to look. In the mass-start events, clearance between riders is infinitesimal, much closer than on the road. Contact is the rule rather than the exception. Speeds approach forty miles an hour at times; it is hairy and high-strung, and the rider who anticipates rather than simply reacting has the advantage; there is little time to think. Even solo events against the clock can be intense.

Unlike road racing, amateur and professional track are very different sports. The so-called Olympic events (match

sprint, kilometer, individual, and team pursuit) dominate amateur track, particularly in the Eastern European countries, while madison and points races are oddly slighted. Oddly, because the madison is the heart of the six-day (which in turn is the heart of pro track racing, except in Japan).

The tracks themselves reflect this. To be in the Montreal Velodrome is to immediately sense a kind of Olympian architectural boldness and grandeur. The track is long (333 meters), majestic, beautifully finished and maintained. But Montreal is somehow more like Trexlertown (an outdoor composition track) than the indoor Ghent track, a small (200-meter), fast, funky place with the smell of pro competition about it. Lapping the field in Montreal or on any "Olympic-design" track is quite a number; so difficult that without the existence of combines among the teams it would happen rarely. But these long

tracks yield fast pursuit and kilo times because of the gradual turns. The design of any given track is as crucial as the difference between baseball fields.

Generally, the real bike rider (the one the other riders respect) likes a shortish, indoor, wood track with steep banking. A skillful rider can play the angles on such a track and do consistently better against stronger, clumsier opponents. Balance becomes a greater factor, the experience of rider and spectator rises in sophistication accordingly. Owing to some as yet undefined laws of cycling physics and crowd dynamics, more electricity is generated by tracks about two thirds the Olympic length.

MATCH SPRINT

Most electric and perhaps most tactically sophisticated of all cycling events is the match sprint, with its long professional and Olympic tradition. It brings two riders head to head, alone on the track. (Early seedings will have three-ups, but this causes as many tactical problems as it solves logistically.) The only slow thing about match sprinting is the tedious elimination system, which is complicated by the *repechage,* through which defeated riders get another chance to reenter competition. Because of this elimination system, one basic element of strategic preparation is that the rider must be physically and psychologically ready to face as many as five heats in a day's racing, which accounts for the unexpectedly long training distances ridden by some top sprinters.

Nominal distance of the match sprint is 1,000 meters, but after the gentle, low-speed hand-held start, the most usual thing is a slow-to-medium speed circling, with both riders watching each other very carefully. Quick-jump specialists often prefer the rear position, while those with more windup than jump will often accept the front. As the circling proceeds, both may prefer the rear position, which can lead to their coming to a dead stop on the banking. This trackstand is almost impossible to do in the turns. Additionally there is the question of who is blocking whom when it occurs, whether the front wheel is pointed down (good) or up (bad), and finally, the position of the pedals, which should be such that the rider can bite into the fat part of the stroke. Split-second advantages being crucial in this event, these fine points can be the difference between winning and losing.

Also crucial are complete confidence about one's relation to the bike in any and all circumstances, and a knowledge of the track itself. Different tracks make certain moves advantageous. There is a stupefying variety of track configurations, from 175-meter whizzers to enormous 400-meter absurdities where the banking fails to counteract centrifugal force. Steepness of the banking also directly affects the speed by which a diving attack can be made from a high position. This dive to the blue sprinter's line is a very basic tactic, executed preferably at a moment when the lead rider has lost sight of the follower — who then assumes the lead, but under very favorable circumstances, with surprise, good momentum, and usually a gap that denies the other rider his slipstream. The best sprinters seem to sense moments of lapsed concentration and follow body language very easily.

Major action generally is delayed until the turn before last, where a sudden

dive can be sustained to the line by many riders. What tends not to happen is for both riders to go side by side for any longer than the last fifty meters. Generally there is a leader and a follower, and the situation is dictated by the leader. If he commits himself soon to the sprint line (which offers the minimum distance around the track) he is obliged to stay there, and the follower cannot chop down into this ''lane''; but if he has not made this commitment, a skillful competitor can ride his opponent all over the track. According to the rules, he can do this only so long as the bikes are overlapped, with the follower on top.

That is one basic situation. Another is for the leader, inside the sprint line on the final turn, to allow his opponent to come almost alongside, thus depriving him of the draft or slipstream (''starv-

ing'' him used to be the term). Because the rider on the outside travels a longer distance, this technique can effectively tease and tire him, especially on shorter tracks where the sharper curve enlarges the outside rider's line proportionately more.

But this side by side position, common in the last fifty to one hundred meters, can be dangerous when employed with certain riders: John Nicholson, former professional world champion, was notorious in these wars, suddenly becoming all elbows, teeth, snarls, and hooks.

When the sprint pits riders of roughly equal ability against each other, the combination of physical and psychological competition creates abrupt, subtle, and exciting variations that are a connoisseur's delight. Decisive moves are

Madison Square Garden. Photograph by Fred Hamel

Jockeying for position. Photograph by Paul Boyer

fleeting and elusive; much like the multiple body, head, and eye fakes that enable a basketball player to be going up to the basket while the man guarding him is on the way down.

KILO

The kilometer is ridden against the clock, rather than another rider, and it is a one-shot; there are no qualifications, no heats, and no need for repeated efforts. Recuperation, agility, bike handling are not issues — only the ability to peak mentally and physically for a single, perfect effort of a little over a minute. Yet the event is so demanding that, like marathoners, kilo specialists may do only half a dozen all-out efforts in a season.

No athlete could be more alone than the kilo rider. During his minute-plus he is in virtually full sprint for almost twice as long as the human biological machinery allows this anaerobic effort to be sustained. The last third of a kilo is a matter of rapidly increasing physical agony as lactic acid and other wastes clog the muscles, including the heart. At some point between the start of the last turn and the finish, the rider almost invariably hits what is known as "the wall" – an occurrence clearly visible to observers. Sometimes the rider comes apart completely in the last fifty meters of a perfect effort as the oxygen debt overwhelms him. And before this stage, any distraction, anything that takes him from concentration on perfect execution, can undo a season's effort.

Typically, a good kilo is followed by severe, generalized abdominal and lower body pain, often accompanied by dizziness, faintness, cramps, inability to walk, vomiting, or some combination thereof. Pierre Trentin's Mexico City world record is generally regarded as the perfect kilo; it resulted in oxygen debt so massive that Trentin lost consciousness for several minutes afterward.

The kilometer (a World's and Olympic

event) draws from roughly the same talent pool as the match sprint – big, anaerobic fast-twitch, muscle-types abound. But psychologically and physiologically it is totally different.

PURSUIT

As in the kilometer, qualifications are against the clock, but the ensuing heats are run rider versus rider, with opponents starting on opposite sides of the track, in plain view of each other. Eliminations proceed pretty much as with the match sprint, but without the complications of the *repechage*. Qualification time is extremely important, because heats are run fastest versus slowest, next fastest versus next slowest, etc. A fast qualifying time allows an easy first round — which allows recuperation. Unlike the kilometer, the pursuit offers plenty of opportunity for tactical sophistication, particularly in terms of going very fast only when it is necessary, not when you happen to feel like it. In the Montreal Olympics, Russian Vladimir Osokin recorded the fastest time of the games — and left without a medal. This came about because the exuberant and well-peaked Osokin let loose with a scorching run in an early heat. He simply did not recover from this gratuitous effort. Holland's Herman Ponsteen qualified decently, won his heats in a series of unspectacular times, gradually improving over the heats as required. None of his times approached Osokin's, but he took the Silver from the Russian because he was strong when he had to be.

Serious pursuiters operate on schedules, particularly in the qualifications, and it is essential, as in the kilo, for the rider to have the gift of smooth, metronomic effort. But some riders come to life when faced with another rider.

The team pursuit, an important amateur men's event, is generally similar to the individual, with teams of four starting on opposite sides of the track. Three must finish, and time is taken on the

third rider to cross the finish line. During the event, riders take turns at the front. A pursuit team goes very fast, and as riders shift off the pull and up the banking, it is essential that they do so smoothly, and fall into the end position accurately. Otherwise they can either touch wheels with the third rider (usually crashing), or find themselves chasing the train. This switching of the lead is an art some riders never quite learn. A single, clumsy, inexperienced, or tired rider can break the flow or cause a crash. But out of the need for smooth, harmonious, relaxed effort, seemingly limited riders sometimes appear in the team pursuit as key members. Interpersonal chemistry, technique, and attitude must adjust to the whole – if the whole of a pursuit team is not more than the sum of its parts, something is definitely wrong. This is even more true here than in the team time trial, a road event, also with teams of four riders who alternate work.

POINTS RACE

Exciting, dangerous, much like a miniature mass-start road race, this is generally a ten to twenty kilometer affair. It brings together road and pursuit types (who endeavor to break away) and sprint-kilo types who sit on them with determination until the bell sounds for a points lap.

As with the pursuit, practical evidence indicates that the advantages of racing against the best road competition in fast, flat events may outweigh a more special-

Changing off in a team time trial. Photograph by Paul Boyer

ized strategy in preparing for the event, and there is no question that it comes closer to the demands of the madison than any other.

THE MADISON AND THE SIX-DAY

Originated in the United States, named after Madison Square Garden, but long ago taken over by Europeans, the madison is the test. Riders who cannot handle its demands have no professional future on the track, and like the team pursuit, it sometimes brings out the best in riders who do not shine elsewhere.

The madison (and a six-day is essentially a series of madisons) is a mass-start event, a combination of distance and points races, in which the final advantage is to gain a lap. Because it is raced by teams of two riders who alternate at will, there are constant high-speed exchanges going on, and the tempo can be phenomenal. But a pro madison is invariably orderly no matter how frenzied the pace, with the pack clearly separate from those circling above (or below, depending on the banking) waiting to take their turn. An amateur madison often has riders all over the track, making it difficult for observers to keep track of things. To master this event and its techniques will give a rider a certain respect in France, Belgium, Holland, and especially Germany, a very track-oriented cycling power. Thus Roger Young is overshadowed in the United States each year by some new face, while in Europe he is

Photograph by Paul Boyer

Pijnen gives Harts a hand sling. Photo courtesy of T.I. Raleigh (USA) Inc.

one of the few Americans not subject to the usual criticisms.

The madison is first of all a test of bike handling in a pack. The track is crowded, exchanges are constant, riders are weaving in and out, and attacking is very frequent, stimulated by periodic points laps. As the jams boil up, position becomes important, and because a hand sling (favored in better competition) is both faster and more erratic than a seat (pants) sling, the threat of spills is very real. It was this mixture of speed, danger, and surprises that filled Madison Square Garden with celebrities to watch the pre-World War II six-days. Experienced riders transform this dangerous dance into the ultimate sports experience. It is heady, grueling, and capable of driving crowds into sustained delirium, particularly on the small, steep European tracks that evolved in connection with the sixes, where everything is more easily seen.

Teams generally tend to combine the talents of a sprint-kilo-type rider (expected to take sprint points) and a

pursuiter type, who is expected to do more than his share of work when the team is going for a lap or chasing. Although lapping the field is the main goal, it is not uncommon for several teams to finish a madison (or a six-day) tied in laps covered. The decision then rests on how a team has fared in the points competition. Thus a team tied with several others at, say, two laps behind the winners, could place as badly as fourth or fifth on the basis of points.

Preparation for the madison and six-day do not require as much specialization as other track events, but mastery of skills is essential, as is basic tactical intuition. Good nerves help, too, and endurance is very important: The six-day is the stage race of track cycling. Consequently, many road riders can and do make the conversion, but only if the basic skills and speed are there. Patrick Sercu and Eddy Merckx were a very great team, but, on the other hand, Tour de France winners have been known to disgrace themselves on the boards.

171

Keirin – Parimutuel Bicycle Racing in Japan

Vera van der Reis Krausz

In Japan more people attend bike races than horse races, and there are four times as many professional cyclists as in Europe. From April 1978 to March 1979, 36,000 races were held, at which 37,593,800 spectators bet five and a half billion dollars. Nakano, World Professional track champion, earned $383,200 in 1979, making him Japan's highest paid athlete. Racers' average earnings were $37,200, with 711 earning over $46,000. And all that from prize money–they receive no salaries or contracts.

Japanese Keirin races seem to resemble horse races more than bike races. Racers are put in starting blocks, eight-or-nine-up, and bettors can bet win, place, show, or first and second in any order. Bookies aren't legal, but touting, tip sheets, and small bets are.

There are usually ten races a day, from 1000 to 4000 meters. Pack racing is common, but there are some handicap and some tandem races for variety. One racer in a special shirt acts as rabbit to keep the pace fast, but no bets are placed on him because he is not expected to finish. Racers must wear hard helmets, and all equipment must be manufactured in Japan.

Most of the fifty open-air velodromes are 400 meters long; nine are 500, seven are 333.3. They are more gently banked than most Western tracks, with surfaces of asphalt or cement. The majority of them are owned by municipalities, who have to follow strict rules to get the license to sponsor twelve meets, or Keirins, a year, each to last no more than six days.

All of this was spelled out in 1948, part of the government's farsighted way of rebuilding the country after the Second World War. While seventy five percent of the money is paid back in bets, fifteen percent goes to public welfare–schools, roads, medical research, facilities for the old or handicapped, disaster relief–and building sports centers and lodges near the tracks.

The remaining ten percent goes back to bicycling–some to the municipalities and local clubs for building and main-

The start of a Keirin race. Photographs by Alan Geiger

taining tracks and for organizing races; some to the bicycle industry for research, development, and to help small manufacturers; the rest to the Professional Cycle Racing Association that administers, organizes, and develops the sport, while barred from running the races.

The PCRA trains, registers, and licenses referees and racers. Rigorous examinations of physical and mental aptitude help select 110 out of the thousand or so yearly candidates to its Keirin School. There apprentices spend ten months learning how to be Keirin racers in near wilderness among 15% incline hills to train on, with two full size tracks, a weight-training room that accomodates 110 people, another with 110 rollers, plus a sophisticated sports performance laboratory manned by a permanent staff.

Each day half of the students do road work, while the rest have a two-part track session. Warmup: Groups of twelve led by motorcycles or tandems circle the

track at thirty miles an hour. Those who drop out receive an extra dose of roller work later.

Then the famous starting blocks are put on the track, and races are run with all the trappings of Keirin, including an appreciative audience of those waiting to race or having just finished. Teachers are also watching and noting times and performances, using the camera in the middle of the track to supplement subjective judgment. Each race is videotaped and will be part of the next morning's theory lesson.

And so it goes, five days a week. Lest students get stale, there are cultural lectures, music, golf, and karate. Cycleball is used as a means of relaxation and to develop speed and bike handling skills in an informal setting. Skills that will be called on when the apprentice is licensed as a full-fledged Keirin racer.

TRAINING AND FITNESS

Bicycling and Your Heart —
An Interview with Dr. Samuel M. Fox III, Cardiologist

Dr. Fox regularly cycles the seven miles and four hills to his job as director of the Cardiology Exercise Program at Georgetown University Hospital in Washington, D.C. He is past president of the American College of Cardiology, and past chairman of the American Heart Association Committee on Exercise. He was kind enough to take time out from his busy schedule of teaching and lecturing to answer all the questions we had always wanted to ask a cardiologist.

Would you care to comment on exercise in general and cycling in particular?

Ralph Paffenbarger's data on Harvard alumni showed that the greatest reduction in incidence of coronary disease is found in those who expend 2,000 kilocalories or more a week in extra energy expenditure from exercise. That's biking sixty miles a week, or the equivalent of jogging or running twenty miles a week. Paffenbarger also demonstrated a gradual but very meaningful associated reduction of coronary events when expending from five hundred to a thousand kilocalories, so that the amount of exercise does not have to be excessive to give good results.

The unfortunate thing we have to recognize is that the people who are the most active usually are the most slender and the better conditioned. They have the natural constitution and energy level that makes physical activity attractive for them. The factor of self-selection is very important, but the effects are beneficial even at the top of the age scale, when people are in their 60's and 70's.

The atherosclerotic process starts back in your subteens; the milkshake, hamburger, or pizza snack that we all enjoy, two eggs for breakfast and so forth, that's all "bad news," and the best recommendation seems to be to get away from it. You can certainly improve your risk status, but we don't know for sure whether the improvement in risk factors is accompanied by a real lessening of mortality. There has been a turndown in coronary mortality that started in 1968, but we don't know exactly why: better control of blood pressure, diet, exercise, less smoking in the middle-aged group, as well as earlier detection and weight loss could all contribute.

At a conference in late 1979 on the reduction in cardiovascular disease mortality, none of us could say with confidence that an increase in physical activity had actually contributed to the decline in mortality, because the number of people who have been exercising sufficiently over a long period of time might not be large enough to make a significant difference.

How much exercise is good?

Paul Dudley White said, "That which increases the heart rate (he didn't quantify it particularly), increases the rate of breathing, produces a perspiration and a pleasant sense of fatigue." I think this is very appropriate. If you wake up in the morning and you can hardly get out of bed, you overdid it; if when you wake up you can say, "I feel sort of shaken out, I've got some stiff muscles, I really worked yesterday, but I slept it off well," that's good.

Enough intensity to develop perspiration is considered of importance. It usually takes six to ten minutes to generate a sweat except in very hot weather. Keep it up for five or ten minutes.

Conceptually, it should be better to have high-intensity exercise with a high internal heat load. You "overload" the system and it adapts more rapidly day by day.

Alternating hard and easy days is important from the standpoint of muscles and joints, to avoid the "overuse syndrome," but it is not so important for the heart.

As we get older we become more vulnerable to the stress of sudden exercise of high intensity, so warm up and slow down gradually. Exercise per unit time on the stationary bike is often better for you than out on the road. And in the winter you won't have the chilling effect of getting started which is more than a little bit uncomfortable; even in the fifties you are usually dressed for the last six miles and are pretty cool the first three or four.

Too much exercise can lead to insomnia. Grinding away on a stationary bicycle during the eleven o'clock news will wake some people up when otherwise they'd be slowly cooling down. So it would be better to exercise during the six o'clock news, especially since exercising before dinner acts as an appetite inhibiter, which helps with efforts at weight reduction.

It's important to remember to replace fluid when you sit down for that meal, though. You have to be careful with the increased exercise to keep your hydration up. Eat foods that contain fiber, such as bran, celery, fruits with skins, or prunes. These are necessary to absorb fluid and provide bulk in the bowels so you don't get constipated.

Once you're fit you go through the oscillations of what we call the "hunting" frequency; you work a little harder and say, "Well, I didn't get any particularly great extra reward from that time and effort, so I'll try a little less." Then if you start to find you're not sleeping so well, or getting winded when you're playing tennis, you move up the intensity of effort again. Of course if you're interested in going to the Olympics you keep training harder and harder.

Basically, being fit should help you to have restful nights, enjoy the physical exercise you do, and help you "hassle" with the stressful world.

I find it very difficult to get my pulse rate up to the recommended rate on my stationary bicycle.

You can get training effects at a slightly lower heart rate on a bicycle; you usually have a lower heart rate

---

Biking and Cholesterol Marianne H. Durgin

A surprisingly small amount of bicycle riding may help you prevent heart disease. As little as three and a half miles a day (or five miles daily Monday through Friday) cannot only get you to work and back, but are as good for you as jogging.

The Framingham Heart Study in Massachusetts has been conducting vast statistical studies over the past thirty years trying to learn why so many people have coronary heart disease. They have isolated the risk factors most of us are now familiar with: too little exercise, too much weight, smoking, and cholesterol.

The deposits of cholesterol particles can start forming surprisingly early in life. If the cholesterol blocking the arteries is not removed it becomes hardened by calcium deposits later in life (arteriosclerosis) and cannot be absorbed by HDL cholesterol.

Cholesterol is made up of different types of particles. Four of these are called lipoprotein particles. The three lightest in weight are the ones that collect on artery walls, making it hard for the blood to circulate properly, and eventually cause the coronary disease called atherosclerosis. But the fourth lipoprotein, HDL (high density lipoprotein), helps clear off arterial walls and makes coronary disease less likely to happen. That's because it can absorb some of the

Marianne Durgin *has been following the Framingham study from nearby Wellesley College, where she was first a student and is now a librarian.*

other lipoproteins as it courses through the arteries, and can carry them through the bloodstream to the liver. There, they pass off through the bile ducts as excess waste and reusable bile salts.

The higher the HDL cholesterol content in the total cholesterol, the better for the flow of blood to the heart and brain. And the HDL cholesterol content can be increased by exercise.

The study has shown that men with an average risk of coronary heart disease have 350 mg. per 100 ml. total cholesterol. When that number is divided by the average HDL cholesterol (70 mg. per 100 ml.), the ratio is 5. This is what is meant by "TOTAL/HDL cholesterol ratio." Women have a lower average ratio of 4.4. When the HDL cholesterol is increased, through the exercise of bicycling, for example, the TOTAL/HDL cholesterol ratio is lowered, and so is the danger of coronary heart disease. Eating foods low in cholesterol and exercising lower the ratio even more. A strict vegetarian who also exercises may have a TOTAL/HDL cholesterol ratio as low as 2.8. A person who is overweight, sedentary, and/or smokes may have a ratio as high as 9.6 (two times as great a danger of having coronary heart disease) or even as high as 23.4 (three times as great a danger).

Tests have been carried out on cross-country skiers, marathon runners, joggers, and swimmers. Bicyclists were tested for the first time in 1979. The Charles River Wheelmen had planned long (forty-four mile) and short (twenty-two mile) bicycle trips for July 1. It rained, so only sixteen people completed the bicycle trips and returned to the Framingham Heart Study to have blood samples taken.

Dr. William Castelli, director of the study, said that the marathon runners tested had an average ratio of 3.4, and that he expected the Charles River Wheelmen to also have low TOTAL/HDL cholesterol ratios. He was right. The men had an average of 3.9 and the women an even 3.

Of the Charles River Wheelmen participating on July 1, six were women and ten were men. The women usually averaged about twenty-five miles of bicycling a week; the men, three times that much. The women's average age was 40.5 years, while half the men were over fifty. And half of the cyclists jogged, played tennis, or participated in other sports.

Dr. Castelli noted that twenty-five miles of cycling a week was enough to produce the women's low ratio. That's the equivalent of bike-commuting to a job two and a half miles away, running errands, or any combination of daily and weekend riding. Frequent moderate exercise to maintain a constant flow of HDL cholesterol through the bloodstream is better than a lot of exercising done only once a week, and cycling's gentle treatment of joints makes it an ideal choice.

and higher blood pressure on a bicycle than you do running. And the bicycle is so much kinder than jogging . . . even with today's very much improved running shoes, there's still a good chance of ripping things up a bit, and there's a certain amount of unavoidable overuse syndrome in running for many people.

In the early 1960's, Dr. Bill Haskell and I looked at the literature on heart rates of people relative to their age. There seemed to be a variability in the maximum heart rate, and we wanted to find a simple way to state it. We reviewed ten studies, put the data on a graph, and then drew a line through the data points that went from a little over age twenty to over sixty-four. What we found was that the maximum heart rate likely for any age can be described pretty well by taking the formulation "210 minus one half the age." This gives the highest estimate. On the low side there's a reasonable fit with "220 minus the age," and it's this last phrase which has been used to describe the expected maximum heart rate.

If you're coasting down a hill are you getting any training effect?

Hilly courses give you the same effect as the Swedish "fartlek" – intermittent high-intensity training or interval training, if you will. Although you coast down the other side of the hill, you will get more effective training than if you were on a flat course. On level ground you have to pedal three or perhaps four times as far on a bicycle than you have to go running to acquire the same benefits (assuming it's the modern lightweight 10-speed derailleur type bike weighing thirty pounds or less). If you're talking about 40 miles of running a week you may need to ride 120 to 160 miles per week on a bike to get the same cardiovascular training effect, but it also depends on the amount of either hilliness or else speed. On a stationary bicycle you could impose the same resistance that you have on the road, which is something you can learn to approximate, so you could have to ride thirty to forty miles on your stationary bicycle to get the same effect as your ten-mile-a-week running minimum. By increasing the resistance, you can get the same effect in fewer miles, which is usually desirable.

When people commute on a heavier bike are they getting a better workout?

If you ride on a heavier bike you're getting a better workout, of course; it's in direct proportion to the power requirement. The more work you do per unit time the more total work in the sense of pounds moved through feet, or kilogram meters, or whatever way you measure the work performed.

Does training increase your ability to deal with the heat?

Biking helps increase your ability to deal with both heat and cold. A particularly relevant comment to make now, when we attempt to reduce power requirements by putting the air conditioner on less in the summer and pushing the thermostat down in the winter, is that people will tolerate extremes of heat and cold better at any given body weight if they have good regular physical exercise. The exercise helps them adapt. We don't tend to think about physical benefits in terms of saving energy, but it's an opportunity too good to miss.

Some good studies on temperature adaptation have been done by groups at the Pierce Foundation at Yale and in the mountains in Norway. The latter compared the temperature adaptation response of young troops with middle-aged people. Everyone's adaptation increased according to the amount of exercise they had had before the temperature test. There's no doubt you get better adaptation when you have been exercising regularly.

It is a help from the standpoint of heat dissipation if you are slim, you have less fat. The obese person who has more body mass has more difficulty in dissipating heat. In cold weather your adaptation is better also, so the benefit is mostly from the vascular distribution and return.

As you get older should you be more careful in the heat?

As a person gets older, two things happen: one, the arteries and arterioles dilate less and the arterial circulation opens up less during exercise in hot weather. As a result, they're less apt to move blood out to the periphery to permit heat loss. Two, the heart is less capable and the vessels are less prompt in responding with appropriate constrictions. An older person is often more vulnerable to high heat challenges. Lightheadedness after a heavy meal or exercise may suggest that one of these processes is at work.

Older people must be more careful in the heat; there's a hazard to the cardiovascular system from not enough blood being available to the heart upon a sudden movement. The alarm reaction this causes will produce adrenalin and bring things back into line, but it also leads to irregularities of the electrical stimulus that could be hazardous.

After any exercise, wind down slowly. Always taper off, particularly if it's hot. You can eliminate the feeling of lightheadedness just by shifting your weight back and forth, walking around a bit or pedaling down a hill after pedaling up it: These are other ways to slow down gradually. The very fact that you feel faint if you stop suddenly is proof of the increased circulation, of the fact that the legs are like a second heart.

So cycling must be good for circulation problems like edema?

Asa Kilbom of Stockholm made a study that is certainly a justification for biking as a way of keeping down ugly ankle swelling, as well as enhancing the circulation. She observed some salesgirls and measured the volume of the lower leg early in the day and again at four o'clock in the afternoon. When they had 15 minutes of stationary bicycle work at some resistance, both morning and afternoon they had less swelling of the legs at the end of the day. In other words, there was improved venous drainage and better lymphatic drainage achieved by the exercise, which supports the concept that there'll be reduction in the tendency for thrombophlebitis (clots in the veins).

I understand cycling is good for blood pressure also.

Blood pressure is better regulated if a patient combines drugs with exercise. It also helps both the diabetic and the hypertensive whose excess tension is under moderate control. If you exercise hypertensive patients over a period of three or more weeks they will usually need less medication to keep their pressure down. My personal recommendation for the hypertensive patient is to get out and get exercise producing a sweat every day. Keep it up thereafter for at least ten minutes. Exercise helps dilate vessels and block the increased vasoconstriction that leads to the increased resistance that is the basic problem. In the hypertensive person, the resistance through the blood vessels is elevated, and there's constriction of the muscles in the linings of the very small arteries, which decreases the diameter of the cross-section and requires a higher pressure to maintain the same flow through a segment than where the artery is wider. One of the benefits of exercise is that it breaks down that hypertonic or increased tone as it dilates the vessels of the skin and the vessels to and in the muscles. Local tissue chemical responses do this, it is not something that is centrally mediated.

Can you get fit with just cycling?

It's good to vary the kind of exercise you do. I commute by bicycle. The fourteen miles to and from work are very pleasant in spite of the fact that I have to "play dodge" with some cars. Some of them are driven by rude and reckless people who seem mad at the world and take it out on bicyclists. Still, I look forward to it as a stimulating introduction to getting started in the morning, and as a break after the hospital day before I get back to writing or reading in the evening.

Cycling uses a wider range of muscular contractions than running, through a longer length change in the hamstrings and quadriceps in the legs. You have more use of the back, abdominal, trunk, shoulder, and arm muscles in biking than in running, and yet both have to be considered very restricted, repetitive, tightly routinized maneuvers. As such, there is some real advantage in getting into something that moves you around a great deal more. I like tennis, and mostly play on weekends; it's worthwhile for me for bending down, reaching up, twisting, a lot of movements I think I'd like to preserve that I do not get with cycling or running. Aerobic dancing and swimming would also be good. If you wish to go skiing, the value of your bicycling will be apparent; many other people will get tired because their legs just haven't been conditioned. Biking is excellent training for either downhill or cross-country skiing.

What advice would you have for beginners?

What we are all interested in knowing is whether a person can get started with a pleasant bicycle routine without a formal exercise clearance test. I hope we don't have to recommend that every forty-year-old individual who is going back to bicycling, or is going to take it up for the first time, needs an exercise test. Experience suggests that a return to bike riding can be done at acceptably low hazard.

If one can get started with a pleasant bicycle routine, and avoid tackling steep hills, or trying to go too fast, or trying to keep up with people with much more experience, there is little reason to require an exercise tolerance test. Just don't be tempted into overdoing. Any sense of physical incapacity should prompt a consultation with your physician.

Duration itself is rarely dangerous; you may end up being "pooped," and you'll have sore muscles and maybe sore joints if you try too long a duration initially, but you probably will not expose yourself to cardiovascular hazards unless you're tempted into overdoing the intensity.

Not only that, but exercise tests can produce false-positive results, creating the impression that there is cardiovascular trouble where there isn't. Some people have isolated T-wave inversions that make interpretation somewhat difficult, but they are not an indicator of latent or incipient disease. Then again, tall people are more inclined to have these abnormalities. Dr. Sheehan, our happy running "guru," used to say, "Don't go to a cardiologist if you're a runner, he'll just get perplexed by things he may not be familiar with as being part of the running scene." I think that's less true now for all athletically involved people, as cardiologists are learning what things are part of the training adaptation seen in athletes.

It's almost predictable; if you follow the program three or four times a week for half an hour after a warm-up, followed by a cooling down of activity, and if you get your pulse above seventy-five percent of age-predicted maximum, chances are good of your having enhanced physical performance which you can readily appreciate. Then continuing the routine becomes automatic.

Are there conditions during which people shouldn't exercise?

• Immediately after a heart attack or any other acute process, cardiovascular or otherwise.
• Myocarditis: inflammation of the heart muscle itself.
• Hepatitis or mononucleosis; usually temporary conditions, we used to think people had to be put to bed, now we know they can mosey around the house.
• Active phlebitis (clots in the veins), either superficial or deep; you have the danger of chunks getting into the lungs and causing pulmonary embolism.

One must be very careful not to overdo it if one has:

• Active tuberculosis.
• Severe allergic tendencies, such as asthma. One should exercise within the limits that can be tolerated but one has to be careful not to overexert or go out in adverse environments, such as extreme cold or smog-filled areas.
• Arthritis, because it can become aggravated; yet when rheumatoid arthritis is not severe you get beneficial responses from exercise. It can increase your mobility and make you feel better.

- Gastrointestinal problems: colitis, Crohn's disease, ileitis, and such can flare up with heavy exercise.
- Badly controlled diabetes: hypoglycemia can occur if the patient doesn't remember to take sugar to balance out caloric expenditure.
- Ill-controlled blood pressure. Immediately after exercise there is lowered blood pressure. Sometimes it goes too low when the person is also taking medication.
- Severe irregularities of heart rhythm. Bicycling might be ill advised, though walking may be all right, since the patient can sit down or lie down.

Consult your physician for guidelines on all of these.

What are signs of overdoing, and how should you react to them?

Dizziness or heavy pounding or irregularities in the chest are indications. Discomfort more than just the discomfort of having to move air more rapidly than you are accustomed to doing; though severe breath-lessness would be an adverse sign. Any constricting heaviness in the chest, any tightness in the chest, shoulders, down the arms, up in the neck, jaw, teeth, back of the neck. A gut ache or stitch in the side is seldom a sign of real hazard, but any discomfort that cannot easily be explained on the basis of muscular effort or pulling on the handlebars should prompt a medical review. (Pulling on the handlebars can squeeze the stomach, and compression of the abdominal contents can cause some acid to regurgitate into the esophagus and cause it to go into spasm; this is not abnormal.)

In conclusion, any discomfort not easily explained as a result of the exercise challenge should be discussed with your physician. If you experience this type of discomfort while exercising, ease off, but not abruptly; possibly walk the rest of the hill, or walk very quietly on the horizontal, or even lie down. An adequate recommendation is hard to make; the individual must have the perception and maturity to respond to the symptoms in an intelligent manner.

Interview with Frank Westell, Cycling Coach

Frank Westell is at present chairman of both the British Cycling Coaching Scheme and the Fellowship of Sport Masseurs and Therapists. He is a regular contributor to Cycling, the British weekly, and has shown great kindness to the American team both in England and at the Montreal Olympics. His training program should be of interest to any serious cyclist, whether tourist or racer. We were fortunate enough to interview him on the occasion of his last visit to the States, where he was exploring the possibility of setting up a school for soigneurs.

Do you believe in interval training, circuit training, and rollers?

Yes, they all have their specific place in the racer's time schedule. The rollers are more for limbering up. After you've been out in a hard race of a Sunday, you can get on the rollers and work the stiffness out of your legs.

Would that be good for tourists, too?

Yes. You're riding without resistance, you can just roll the legs around and get them supple. The blood circulates and the pains and aches are worked out.

Are there different kinds of riders?

Some people have a natural ability to pedal and others have a natural strength. It's a matter for the coach to guide a particular rider into his niche. There's no point in trying to get someone who's a very strong rider into very low gears, or vice versa. Every individual is different and has his particular assets. . . Strength, stamina, speed, and skill make up a racer.

I am a coach and soigneur, which has some advantages as you can help the rider over the final stages before an important competition and help bring him to his peak.

How important is peaking?

Peaking is the name of the game. At the beginning of the year we sit down and look at the calendar. We designate the peak time. Then we have training races with the idea of getting to peak form at a particular period of time. At those times top racers are under a lot of psychological pressure; you have to watch that they don't go over the top.

Too many people worry about peaking too early and then they never peak. It's easier to get out of a tailspin than to get fit . . . you can always rest a little.

What are signs of someone getting stale?

Performance levels below par, legs aching more than usual, not sleeping too well, possible loss of weight.

The times go off?

Performances definitely go off. Many people experiencing this slump fall into the trap of doing more work. That's when the coach should say, ''Enough is enough, rest now and get away from the bike.''

I see you have to be a psychologist. How big a team can you work with?

Eight or ten. Well, it depends on the level. On a 177

grass-roots level you can work with a lot more. But if you've got national or international champions, you can really only bring your mind to bear on one or two. The higher up the ladder of success, the greater the concentration and the psychological pressures. Every race is a grand prix.

Is there a team doctor also?

In most cases I'm the team doctor unless there is an emergency. Cycling is a sport where there aren't too many complications. There are very few fatal or serious accidents. You know, it looks like a spectacular crash, but once the blood is out of the way and you get down to it, it's not too bad in most cases. It is important to only work to the level of one's medical training – if in doubt, send the rider to the hospital.

What do you do if there's a fall?

First you have to see that there is no further damage done to the rider, so you get out in the road to protect them from cars and bikes. Usually the rider moves out of the way and you know he's all right.

If you fall on the road, is there any self-help that is important?

You're talking about an abrasion, aren't you? All you need to do is just clean it off. Put a Telfa pad on and keep it on.

Should the rider warm up?

I believe in warming up on the bike. If it's an important race, I usually also recommend a short, brisk massage for about ten mintues. Too much massage can lose you the race.

I presume that would be with a qualified masseur?

Definitely. You've got to have some training and know what you're doing. There are people all over the world who like the idea of being a soigneur. That's not enough. You need to know about anatomy and physiology. And the higher on the team you work, the more you need to know. You need a lot of experience before you get to world championships. I can teach someone to massage correctly in a week, but this does not make them an experienced soigneur.

How much massage can you do for yourself?

Quite a bit, because you're on the performing end and the receiving end, so if it doesn't feel right, you know you're not doing it right. It should never hurt . . . only perhaps when using friction. Stroking and kneading are best to do yourself, percussion not so much.

Frank Westell's Training Program

Speed has often been termed "applied strength," but it is in the tough races where strength really counts. When every nerve, every muscle, every sinew is strained to the limit, it is the rider with the depth of strength and stamina who wins.

I cannot overemphasize the need for personal supervision, because no two riders are alike. What is good for one could be useless for another. The real worth of any training program is for you to start thinking along the right lines.

Strengthening: Cycling will build up your legs. But what about your arms, shoulders, and abdomen? Setting up a daily exercise routine auxiliary to your cycling program will build up muscular power throughout the body. Think of your exercise routine as a diet. If you do not have a balanced physical program, you will not reach the limits of your physical potential. Start a program gently, and as you improve, progressively increase the amount of repetitions of each exercise.

Stretching: To improve muscular efficiency, you must have fully stretched muscles. Stretching exercises should be done every day of the year. They only take a few minutes and will help prevent muscle strains and sprains. They can be done any time – first thing in the morning, during the day, or before you go to bed at night – whenever it is most convenient.

Running: Another good general fitness exercise is running. Some people say that running is no good for bike riding, but generally speaking, any form of physical exercise is good for bike riding. The object is to develop a high level of physical fitness. Running in the off season is excellent. Start with a run of about five minutes and gradually build up to forty-five. The pace should be steady and the effort progressive, as with everything.

Using the home exercises as a foundation, join a class for circuit and/or weight training.

Circuit training aims at the development of all-round fitness.

Weight training aims at the development of strength.

Circuit training, developed at Leeds University by Morgan and Adamson in 1956, was quickly adopted by all sports as a good method of training. It is self-regulated; excellent for developing the cardiovascular system to a good fitness standard and to the stamina essential for bike riding.

Circuit training is a series of exercises performed against the clock. For example, a series may consist of ten pushups, ten situps, ten rope climbs, ten chinnings on the bar, and so forth. The first time you complete the series it takes five minutes. Then you immediately start another circuit and try to do it in less time. The next session you try to beat your best time. All you need is a set of cards for the exercises and they can be done anywhere. Over a period of time, you get faster; it's partly anaerobic training.

Weights: Weights are used to develop strength for all sports. They are the safest way to achieve strength because they consist of a controlled, progressive overload series. However, like anything that can help you in a short period of time, it can also harm you in a short period of time. Therefore, it is essential to do weight training with a qualified coach. If you have never learned the right way to do weight training, I strongly advise you to contact an expert. Unless the exercises are done correctly and the weights treated with respect, you can do more harm than good.

Training Progression: Training progresses from steady miles to speedwork, then to interval training to develop the cardiac muscles. As soon as possible move to the bike; you become a bike rider by riding a bike.

Your first training runs should be long steady miles to get your muscles used to prolonged activity. A small group of

Always massage toward the heart; the whole of the muscle must be massaged; and for the best result you should be warm and relaxed during the whole process. Use a good quality massage medium, such as Johnson's baby oil; if you prefer cream the choice is very wide.

There are four basic massage movements, and they are performed in the following sequence:

Stroking helps relaxation and aids circulation.

The hands should be shaped to the contours of the areas that are being treated and should travel the full length of the muscle, stroking toward the heart and the lymph glands. As you will be mainly concerned with your aching legs, the lymph glands referred to are those situated behind the knees and in the groin.

Kneading tones up the muscles and induces the flow of blood and lymph. The movement is a rhythmical, kneading, rolling, and squeezing of the muscles. Care must be taken not to nip. Again, you work toward the heart in a smooth manner.

Percussion stimulates the muscles; it will suffice to explain the movements easiest to master:

Cupping is performed by cupping your hands; flexible, light, sharp blows are made with alternate hands in quick succession. This should not be done over a

English racing cyclists train in the early season. Bernard Thompson

about six is ideal for this, riding in twos in a medium gear for about thirty-five to forty miles.

Over the next few weeks the mileage should be gradually increased to sixty or sixty-five. This is sometimes termed "getting the rough off," but if you have been working properly in the gym and doing home exercises, you should not have any "rough" to get off; the riding will condition your muscles, giving them tone.

Use Variety to Get Form and Avoid Staleness: All successful training methods have one factor in common – hard work. I have always been in favor of varying training to include as wide a variety of workouts as possible, such as interval, speed, group, and *fartlek*. This will not only give you good form, but will help you to fight off staleness brought about by the same old routine.

The amount of training depends so much on your physical ability, time available, and ambitions that it is impossible to set down a rigid plan. But in order to help you build your own program, I have made out a schedule as an example of how to balance your training.

Sample training schedule, assuming a Sunday race:

Monday and Saturday, steady ride (done at between 18 and 20 mph), possibly with a short fast period of Saturday, once in shape. Tuesdays, Wednesdays, and Thursdays, alternate speed, interval, kermess, and group riding. Friday, at first rest or do a steady ride, fartlek training once well in shape.

Train at racing speed and cut down the distance: Conditioning your body to

the speed and method of racing can be done most effectively by training at racing speeds. Of course, one can always go faster and longer in a race because of the environmental stimuli. The logical conclusion is that in order to train at racing speed one must cut down on the distance.

Interval training is a system of one fast period followed by a slower, or interval, period to permit recovery. To start with, the interval period can be two or three times longer than the fast period, then as you improve, cut down the interval time. The speed of your fast period should always be that of your projected racing speed. It should be treated as a time trial, going at racing speed, each time trying to smash your personal best time. Pick several courses of a fairly flat nature and set times for each. The schedule should be set before you start and kept to with no cheating.

Kermess training develops bike handling, speed, strength, and stamina and can be fitted into your schedule at any time. It is best done with a group of about eight riders of similar ability, around a small circuit for a specific number of laps or period of time. If this is done at racing speed, sprinting out of corners, and for predetermined primes, you will notice a great improvement within a few weeks.

Group training: The operant word is *training*. It is not meant as a night off or as a ride to hide among others' wheels and sprint for the town sign at the finish. It is meant as a training session to develop bunch-riding techniques such as

trading off, echelon riding, and the various skills that add together to make a complete road racer.

Fartlek training: This is a Swedish word that freely translated means speed play. It can be useful in overcoming boredom or it can be made a regular part of your training session to prevent staleness.

Fartlek training is usually started once a decent standard of form has been developed. Its aim is to encourage riders to engage in a free, untimed variation in pace. It is not done at racing speed, but at a comfortable speed, with a small group of riders in a relaxed frame of mind, playing at racing with spontaneous sprints and periods of effort. If you're at your peak and you still have a couple of weeks to an important race, you can switch to fartlek training, enjoy what you're doing, and sprint to have a bit of competition.

The importance of sleep: No matter how well you eat or how hard you train, it will all be of little use unless you get enough sleep. Sleep is necessary for your system to relax, your tissues to repair, and for your general well-being. Though your own personal requirements remain fairly constant, there is considerable variation between the needs of individuals. For one rider six hours of sleep is sufficient, but for another eight hours is not enough.

Look upon sleep as part of your preparation and go to bed at a regular time to insure that you get enough. A succession of late nights will soon result in a definite lack of punch.

bony prominence. The other movement is simply shaking the muscle and vibrating it with the fingertips.

Friction is performed with fingertips and thumb, moving the skin in spiral movements over the Achilles tendon, ankles, and knees to loosen adhesions.

Finish. Always finish as you start, with smooth, stroking movements.

Would you recommend massage for cycletourists?

They would get more enjoyment out of cycling if they did stretching or massage or both. Some tourists do a lot of strenuous work muscle-wise, but they don't look after themselves. Most of them are riding one day after the other, not giving their muscles a chance to recover. Their muscles get harder and harder and they tend to think this proves they're tough. But their muscles would recover far more efficiently if they would work them out.

Are they asking for tears?

Yes. If you have a tight, hard muscle and then go for a long hard ride, especially in cold weather, you stand the chance of tearing ligaments. Whenever it's cold, warm up your knees with massage and possibly stretching. I always recommend putting some warm embrocation on knees on the borderline days when people wear shorts.

What about after a ride?

After a long ride it's good to have a short, light ride to work it out, if not a massage. Better cool off by riding. If you stop suddenly, you're asking for cramps and aches. You should limber down, warm down. It pushes out the lactic acid of effort and consequently you recover far more easily. Sprinting to your door and getting off still shaking and getting right into a bath is abusing your system.

What about a cramp?

Now that's a different matter. Then I put the muscles in a position of stretch; I find the belly of the muscle and press down with my thumb with something like five or six pounds of pressure. What happens in a cramp is that the fibers go into each other and most of them have gone into the belly of the muscle where the denser fibers are. If you put pressure there you get a chemical reaction within the muscle and it releases. It's like acupressure technique, but instead of looking for the meridian, you're looking for the belly of the muscle. It's far easier. In the thigh the main muscle that goes is the middle one, so just press it in its middle. In any case, if you press the wrong spot you won't do any harm. You can find the spot to press in your foot also, but a little differently.

Should you wash down after a hard ride?

If the body's not clean, you're asking for trouble. All sorts of bacteria set up. Sweat is fine when it's fresh and soap and water are fine to wash if off. If you can't get a shower, soak a towel in warm water for a brisk rubdown; then dry off; or carry cologne and have a quick antiseptic rubdown that leaves you feeling fresh. This is for after a massage, too.

What about shorts?

Buy the best shorts you can afford—they may not be the most expensive. Wash them carefully in soap,

Photograph by Paul Boyer for The Bicycle Paper

not detergent. Rinse the soap out well, dry away from heat. Dress with an antiseptic preparation such as Jecovital; failing that, lanolin. Check chamois to make sure the seams are bedded down and the leather is not torn. Change them every day. Not many people do that, but that's ideal. Most bike riders need three pairs.

Keep the perineum clean with white soap, splash with cold water, dry, dab carefully with alcohol assuming no chafing or open wounds.

Any underwear with the shorts?

If a six-day rider were to wear underpants, he'd have no skin left. As it is he ends up very sore. The harder you're riding, the less you want on the chamois.

Should you ride with a boil?

If you look after yourself in training, you usually don't get a boil. You *can* get a blood cyst—a blood vessel breaks, and the blood encapsulates. Then you must go to a doctor and get it lanced. This must not be handled by a soigneur. Avoid boils as much as possible by keeping yourself as clean as possible. If you still get one, set about getting medical treatment.

What about foot care?

The feet are important because that's where you transfer your energy. See a chiropodist if you have any problems. Dry and powder between toes. Foot cream helps relax the feet; a menthol-base cream has a cooling effect.

Always use clean socks and never wear them more than once between washes. Make sure shoes fit well and have a thick reinforced sole. Don't walk around in bare feet after taking racing shoes off. Put on sandals or slippers, anything. Certainly don't walk on a cold surface. There's also the chance of grit or glass cuts.

Some people give themselves ingrown toenails by the way they cut their nails. Some don't even cut them, just let them grow and grow, and then the nails turn in, and they wonder why they have pain. It's worth having a look at your feet—you tend to ignore them.

Should you use cleats?

A number of people get knee trouble messing around with them. Also inexperienced trainers and coaches give them knee trouble with the cleats in the wrong position or having a bent pedal. But knee trouble is more likely caused by going out again before the muscles are recovered.

What preparation do you recommend for a new season?

Dental and medical checkup. Make sure your tetanus shots are up to date and you know your blood group.

Make use of any coaching schemes in your area; write to the governing body and they will tell you the nearest one. Go and see a coach with your training diary for a personal schedule. The time to make yourself known to a coach is during the off-season, because he will probably have more time to talk about training and get to know you.

If you're lucky enough to have a training bike, it should have a good overhaul before winter use. When it's cold it's no joke for you or your training companions to carry out roadside repairs that could have been avoided. The bike should have mudguards, good brakes and tires, bearing in mind weather and road conditions.

Your racing frame should be checked for dents or cracks, and if necessary, put in for repair early.

Check and clean all equipment and make a list of items to be renewed.

Tubulars should be checked and repaired when necessary, and a list made of new requirements for the coming season, to be purchased as soon as cash permits.

It is always advisable to buy tubulars in advance and store them in a cool place inflated with just a puff of air. Do not forget to remove the plastic wrapping.

Do you suggest protection from rain and cold?

Especially early in the season it is far better to be too warm than too cold. You'll survive being too warm, you may not survive being too cold. You've got to keep your upper body warm, and if it's cold, dress accordingly; that means covering up the legs, either wearing tights or track bottoms. Put plastic, foil, or newspaper between jerseys to retain body heat and keep out the wind; avoid chest infection. If you get one, stop riding and go to the doctor.

Wear warm clothing, wool preferably; tops long enough to cover the lower back when on the drops; training trousers with a loose waistband to be held up by suspenders; if very cold, long johns.

Wear wool socks and shoes large enough for slight toe movement (not perforated!), gloves, warm but not tight, and to top it all off, a woolen hat will keep your

British pros in a criterium race on a wet and dirty day. Bernard Thompson

head warm but not sweaty.

Warm embrocation on the small of your back and down the spine will not only give you a pleasant warm feeling, but lessen the chances of backache.

The legs should also be massaged with embrocation, and if very cold Capsicum or Musculor No. 3 applied to knees and Achilles tendon.

What's cold?

That's individual. I trained a guy some years ago who didn't feel the cold. He never wanted to wear more than one jersey. I used to say, "For goodness sake, put another jersey on." But he put it to me one day, "Don't you think with so much at stake I would put extra clothes on if I felt cold?"

And never once during his cycling years did he 181

ever get a strain due to being improperly dressed.

Is he an exception?

Oh yes. That's one end of the scale, there are others that feel the cold as soon as there's a breath of wind. Somewhere between the two is everyone else.

Do you ever recommend salt tablets?

Never. Well, very rarely. The summer of 1976 when there was a real heat wave in England was probably the only time I ever gave salt. In certain parts of the country, say in Florida, one needs to look to the electrolyte levels. Salt on its own I feel is ineffective; people tend to take too much of it anyway.

Do you recommend Dynamo or Gatorade?

They're different. Dynamo is basically a glucose solution with some electrolytes, whereas Gatorade is an electrolyte preparation with some glucose in it. Anyway, you take either of them little and often. If you glug it down all at once, you're going to get glucose imbalance because of the overworking of the insulin. You start getting problems riding after that.

Compare them with tea and honey.

Everyone has their own particular way of refreshing themselves. But when it comes down to it, if you need instant energy, glucose syrup is the best way of replacing it because it's easily assimilated.

Do you recommend eating while riding?

I recommend that one eat little and often. I've never recommended having items like Dynamo to the exclusion of eating during a race. In a long stage race a piece of food like a roll or milk will take up some of the acids in your stomach. There are so many things to consider about eating. And again, there are individual likes and dislikes. I took one rider to the Peace Race who could have nothing but bananas; they had to import some for him.

Do you advocate carbohydrate loading?

It's a dangerous toy to play with. I recommend it only when I can monitor it, as you can retain too much body fluid and be more sluggish. I tend to do a more moderate version without the midweek draining. It's something that should only be done under a qualified coach.

What do you recommend be eaten the day before a race?

Eat well, but don't stuff yourself, with plenty of carbohydrates, such as potatoes and cereal, which will be converted to glycogen and stored in the liver ready for competition.

How long before a race should you eat?

No nearer than three hours. Actually, you're getting your energy needs from the meal you ate the night before. Rest has not burned off a lot of that. The day before a big race I suggest a light ride to keep your suppleness up. Eat your carbohydrate food, go to bed, wake up and have what you like, but not too near the competition.

What kind of diet do you recommend?

Balanced and of good quality. Mealtimes regular, not just chocolate and cola drinks, a fair mixture of meat, fish, dairy, fresh fruit and vegetables to give adequate vitamins and minerals.

A lot of young riders are vegetarians and others have fad training regimes.

That's not necessarily bad. If you're going to be a vegetarian or a vegan, you tend to understand a lot of what your body is doing. You're actually more likely to take care of yourself. I do suggest you take vitamin B12 as a safeguard, though you only need it in microscopic doses, assuming your stomach is working effectively.

What about protecting young riders from quacks and drug pushers?

It's not much of a problem with me. I know it sounds a bit big-headed, but I've got a reasonable enough reputation that they sort of take my word for the fact that you can get better performances by scientific training and vitamin preparation than by taking dope. There is always the danger that somebody will get in the hands of people who are less informed who might recommend a dope point of view. This is a thing I fear very much in America.

Besides, ultimately you can't get away with it. What's the point of winning races and getting to international standards only to find out you can't take the drug you've been taking en route. All you do is lose confidence. That has happened to some racers; they fall apart in the big-time when the psychological crutch they've been walking on is taken away from them.

It's very important that doctors keep abreast of the regulations and testing facilities. In Europe doctors are very interested in cycling and want to get the trade of the bike riders and so are quite ready to help them. But all it takes is the wrong cold medicine and you're disqualified from a race.

One of the drawbacks to sending untrained soigneurs and coaches to world championships and Olympics and other important events is that unless someone is fully conversant with the properties of the medicines that they're prescribing, they stand a chance of getting someone in trouble.

I'm very much interested in the American scene and would hate to see it go backward because of the wrong sort of backup. I would like someone to run a course on coaching and being a soigneur so the riders can have the backup they deserve.

How did you get into this?

I was a rider myself. First category. I rode in Europe; mostly road, some track. I became a trained physiotherapist and while I was still racing was asked to become a professional team manager. I was team manager for the Mackeson team for twelve years, and during that time acted as manager-soigneur. The soigneur aspects I mainly learned in the field, the patching-up and what have you. I was involved long before the Italian training book was written in 1972. A group of us formed the Sports-Masseurs-Therapists Guild. There are only two in Europe, the one that started in Italy and the Dutch school for sports masseurs.

What kinds of events have you covered?

Pretty well everything. Long distance record events, most of the major tours, right down to the kilometer. Lands-end to John O'Groats.

Advice from a Sports Physiologist

Edmund R. Burke, Ph.D.

Ed Burke, a former racer, turned his interest in cycling into his major field of study, and is using his Ph.D. in exercise physiology at the Cardiovascular Division of the Department of Internal Medicine at the University of Iowa Hospitals. He is chairman of the Medical Committee of the USCF and consultant to the Olympic cycling team. He has a regular column (and also answers cyclists' questions) in Velo-News, a monthly journal on bicycle racing. "If you need help, go to an athlete doctor" was reprinted from Inside the Cyclist by permission of Velo-News, Box 1257, Brattleboro, Vt. 05301.

If home remedies can't cope with your injury, you should seek medical help. But where can you go to find the best treatment for an injury resulting from cycling?

There are good reasons why you should seek out a physician who is familiar with sports medicine and the treatment of sports injuries. You may not find one knowledgeable about cycling, but a sports physician understands the physical, psychological and emotional differences between athletes and sedentary individuals.

Many physicians are not familiar with the laboratory test results that an athlete in training will produce. For example, a trained cyclist's blood test may show red cell values which are low for an average individual. Anemia may be the diagnosis. It is now known, however, that athletes actually have an *increased* blood volume from training; the cyclist may even have a higher number of red blood cells than a sedentary individual. But the increased blood volume lowered the concentration of cells, making the rider appear somewhat anemic.

Many physicians are not aware that injuries to athletes such as cyclists often require non-standard treatments. Furthermore, some treatments that produce good results with nonathletes may have an adverse effect on cyclists. The use of corti-sone to help ease tendon inflammation is common. But cortisone reduces the blood supply to the tendons, and if an athlete were to work the muscle tendon maximally there is a greater possibility of tearing it.

I recommend that you search for a physician who is also an athlete. He or she may have had problems similar to yours. Call the local high school or college trainer and ask for names of physicians experienced in treating athletic injuries. There is also the possibility of the trainer offering to help you. Contact the nearest medical school; it will have contacts with physicians who work with athletes.

If all else fails, call the local chapter of the American Medical Association for information. If the local chapter is not listed, contact the main office at 535 N. Dearborn St., Chicago, IL 60610.

If your injury involves bone or muscle, contact a sports orthopedist. To find those closest to you, contact the American Orthopaedic Society of Sports Medicine, 430 N. Michigan Ave., Chicago, IL 60611.

Chronic problems associated with the legs and feet should be examined by a sports podiatrist. If you cannot find one, contact the sources of information listed above. Ask for those who are members of the American Academy of Podiatric Sports Medicine.

Though the number of doctors and related personnel in sports medicine is small, the specialty is growing and the future looks very bright for the athlete. I also see benefits for the physicians who work with athletes. A better knowledge of rehabilitative principles and methods will help doctors return any patient to health more quickly, and close contacts with school-age athletes will keep them "in tune" with the younger generation.

If a physician is interested in working with cycling, a local coach or club will likely greet the idea with enthusiasm. Any medical person can gain important experience this way. Much information about treatment of sports injuries is becoming available in seminars across the country and in books and magazines, e.g., *The Physician and Sports Medicine*.

If a physician is thinking of getting involved in sports medicine for the financial rewards, he can forget it. Office and emergency visits are covered by health insurance, but travel, advice about health care, extra time spent with local athletes, and other time-consuming items are not. Sports medicine means being involved, having interest, and giving time and effort. The specialty is open to those aggressive enough to undertake its challenge.

EASY WAYS TO MONITOR YOUR FORM

A steadily descending waking heart rate is a good indication that cardiovascular training is effective. This rate is used as a baseline by many coaches to measure the effectiveness of the training program. Traditionally, swimming trainers compare it to the heart rate after a fifteen-minute workout. Cycling coaches often ask riders to take two readings, as the difference between the lying-down rate and the standing-up rate can be used as a measure of stress.

Each morning before getting out of bed count your pulse for fifteen seconds; wait one minute, then stand up and count it again for fifteen seconds. Do this daily and record the difference between the rates. If there is a sudden rise in the difference between the two rates, it is a sign your body has not recovered from yesterday's training.

Recording your morning weight will give you an indication if you are eating enough or are dehydrated from the previous day's exercise. In hot weather don't allow your body to get into a state of chronic dehydration. Thirst is not always a good indicator of the need for fluids. You should make an effort in hot weather to drink plenty of fluids while riding, between meals, and in the evening.

If you haven't recovered, training should either be suspended for that day or done less strenuously. This daily monitoring will give you a general guideline for judging fitness and will enable you to better evalute the effects of cycling and other stresses encountered each day.

A Bicycle Autobiography, or How I Came to Be A Cycling Doctor

Jean-Pierre de Mondenard, M.D.

Translated from the French by Vera van der Reis Krausz

Dr. Jean-Pierre de Mondenard, doctor at the French National Institute of Sports, Associate in Functional Reeducation at Mondor Hospital in Paris, Member of the French-Language Association for the Study of Diabetes and Metabolic Illnesses, has been kind enough to let us reprint some of the articles that make Cadu-cycle (*the magazine of the Friends of Cycling in the Health Professions*) *such interesting reading. Dr. de Mondenard's book,* La consultation medicale du cycliste, *Amphora, 1979, consists of full answers to letters cyclists have sent him about common accidents; cures, prevention.*

Dr. de Mondenard *testing Poulidor's lung capacity.* Photographs courtesy of Jean-Pierre de Mondenard.

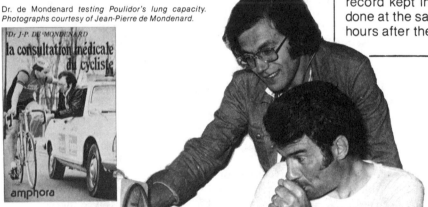

I was born March 18, 1943 at Nimes in the south of France. I lived in Marrakech, Morocco until 1957, then moved to Toulouse where I stayed until 1973, and have lived in Paris since.

During my studies I played rugby, which is normal for a young man living in Toulouse. When I started medical school, I couldn't reconcile rugby with my studies, so I turned to bicycling.

The bike offers the advantage of being practiced without a partner and at any moment of the day. As soon as I had a free moment, since I lived in the suburbs of Toulouse it was easy to do an hour or more of biking. This was very important for my equilibrium.

I was always interested in cycling. At thirteen I was already buying sports and cycling magazines.

I bought my first racing bike in 1965 and was quickly confronted with the incompetence of certain bike sellers. I was neither a doctor nor knowledgeable yet and went to buy it with unsuspecting

self-confident naivete. No problem with the frame: They'd given me a 60 cm, which was right for my one meter ninety. But the width of the handlebars would have barely been enough for a boy of fourteen, and the toeclips were two sizes too small, as was the jersey the owner threw in.

Then I moved, and cycling luck was with me because my new home was opposite a bike store. Very rapidly I became a faithful customer of this velocist who taught me all the basics needed so that my setup would fit my morphology.

From that moment on, my love of cycling grew and grew. I participated regularly in the training outings of the club directed by the bike store owner, who was the father of two sons who raced. Even during the week I went training with them. From that time on I did between 5,000 and 10,000 kilometers a year. I was soon asked by the directors of the club to help them organize the medical supervision of the cyclists, which

CYCLISTS CONTROL YOUR OWN PHYSICAL CONDITION

Periodic checking of physical condition helps the success of any training program. It is regrettable that the amateur cyclist doesn't know any objective way of verifying that his physical condition is getting better thanks to his training; he generally knows the way his bike works better than the way his body works.

To overcome this lack we present three very simple ways to permit a racer to check his progress. These checks should be made once a month, and the record kept in a training log. They should always be done at the same time of day, preferably at least three hours after the last meal. On waking is best.

was considered insufficient at the level of the associations and even at the level of the official regional committees. So I had the luck of being designated assistant to the doctor of the Tour de L'Avenir (the Amateur Tour de France) in 1972, 1973, and 1974. From 1973 until February 1979 I was doctor at the National Institute of Sports.

During all this time, I accompanied, as a doctor, the most important professional races (Tour de France, Paris-Roubaix, Bordeaux-Paris, Paris-Tours, the Grand Prix of Nations, etc.) and amateur races (Tour de L'Avenir, Route de France, etc.)

If I followed the racers, that didn't mean I abandoned my bicycle, and during the month of August, after the Tour de France, I tried to make up for lost time with an orgy of cycling outings, each year in a different region.

During the 1973 Tour, I handled the racers in the Gitane team, led by Joop Zoetemelk. There was a rest day at Divonne-les-Bains. The racers, in order not to have stiff legs the next day at the start, did about fifty kilometers during their rest day. I accompanied them on my bike to try out Le Saleve, a first category climb and the main difficulty of the next day's stage.

The Saleve is very hard, with a slope that approaches thirteen percent for eight kilometers. The inside of the turns are impracticable because they are too steep

184

Pulse Rate

There are as many pulsations as there are beats of the heart. In a healthy adult pulse rate is 60 to 80 a minute; in a trained athlete, 40 to 60; it is more rapid evening than morning. Physical effort, meals, fear, and other emotions speed it up. During illness the pulse generally accelerates.

Significance. The resting pulse can be considered a sign of general endurance; the lower it is, the better the endurance (44 for Eddy Merckx). Even more remarkable is its stability—a speeding up of six to eight pulsations a minute (all other things being equal) indicates excess fatigue or the beginning of over-training or illness.

Usefulness. The lowering of the pulse during the season is a good sign of cardiac adaptation to effort and a confirmation of the adaptation of the cyclist to the training he's undergoing.

Technique. The pulse can be taken on the radial artery of the wrist that runs below the thumb. Don't use the other thumb, but the index and second finger instead. Count the pulsations for fifteen seconds and multiply by four.

Body Weight

Cyclists and coaches know that this is an important element in the preservation of training. Each athlete, strangely enough, has a training weight and a competitive weight; there is no general rule, but each athlete should know what they are.

In youths checking weight helps evaluate growth; in adults it can indicate the elimination of excess fat, the growth of muscle, or the level of form due to training.

Technique. Make sure the scale is accurate; always use the same one; weigh after urinating; and never after exertion.

Ruffier's Test

This test measures heart resistance. All exercise makes the heart work, which is translated into a speeding up of the pulse. If the heart is strong, this acceleration will be small and of short duration; if the heart is not adapted to effort, the change will be great and persistent. The sooner the heart comes back to its original resting rate, the stronger and more resistant it is.

Technique. Sit for two minutes, then count the pulse for fifteen seconds; multiply the result by four to get the first number, P1.

Stand and do thirty knee bends in forty-five seconds to the rhythm of a metronome (the heels stay on the ground). As soon as you've finished, count your pulse for fifteen seconds, multiply by four; this is P2.

Sit and rest for exactly one minute. Take the pulse for fifteen seconds, multiply by four; that's P3.

(17 percent). From the first turns, after about twenty kilometers on the flat, the majority of the racers decided to do the rest of the climb in the car that followed us. I remained the only one with Zoetemelk. My gearing was 42x26 and I was in agony. Zoetemelk, on a 42x23, rolled along telling me the story of his life, expecting answers that never came because I was completely incapable of speaking during this climb. That day I finally realized that there really were phenomenons in cycling.

I went back and climbed the Saleve in 1979. It hadn't gotten any easier.

In 1974 I submitted my thesis at the Faculty of Medicine in Toulouse on "Medical Activities at the Heart of Competitive Cycling." This work summed up my medico-cycling activities during 1972, 1973, and 1974.

During this time I was able to study the very numerous aspects of medical activity before and during the large competitions and to observe the very singular conditions of this type of medical practice.

Competitive cycling is an exceptionally painful and dangerous sport. The mileage of the races, racing in stages, the high average speeds realized, and the weather conditions that are often extreme necessitate an exceptional level of training, staying power, and health.

Desire for money and advancement exists not only among the professionals but also among the amateurs of whom a large number hope to quickly turn professional. It is easy to understand why all, or almost all bike racers have looked to doping as a way to better their results and to fulfill an abnormally heavy program of competition. European bike racers are generally of modest origins. Their level of education is not very high and their credulity is great. It thus seems important to give them a sound education in medical hygiene.

The role of the doctor should be to protect these athletes from themselves and from procedures that might very gravely compromise their health.

In my thesis I tried to cover the major aspects of medical activity: prevention of doping and controls, medical supervision of training and competition, emergency medicine and first aid care during competition, and giving medical information to racers and trainers.

It seems to me that the doctor who's working in the midst of competitive cycling has to assume functions in all four of these areas at the same time. The doctor whose job is controlling drugs is considered a policeman and not accepted well. But doctors who supervise the training or help cure illness are much in demand; in fact, they're asked to do more than any doctor can; so it's important competent education be available in the athletic milieu. In this way the racer will no longer disassociate himself from the activities of the doctor, who can become a counselor, nay, a friend, even if he has to monitor the antidoping controls.

I have been working since 1974 to make medical information available to racers and trainers. To that end I have medical columns in various popular cycling magazines like *Cyclisme*, *La cycle*, *La France cycliste*, and *Caducycle*, which I've been editing since 1973 and in which I present basic articles on medical problems tied to the practice of cycling.

I have a sports medicine practice in the east of Paris where two thirds of my patients are cyclists who come sometimes from great distances to consult me. I am also attached to two Paris hospitals where I examine athletes: Henri Mondor and Herold.

I believe that to do a good job of practicing sports medicine one has to be athletic oneself. Often the pathology is related to the technology of the sport. Cyclists who come to consult me about problems related to bike usage come with their bicycle, otherwise it's not possible for me to take care of them properly.

Since 1976 my cycling passion has been concentrated on climbing mountains. To date, October 1979, I count 178 passes, 109 different ones, including all those that make the more difficult Tour de France stages.

Add P1, P2, and P3 together, subtract 200, and divide by 10. The lower the number, the better the heart. 0 is exceptional; 1 to 5 is good, 6 to 10 can be improved, 11 to 15 is weak, 16 to 20 is dangerously weak.

While this test is not perfect, it can help you check if your training is helping your conditioning. The test is of no value checked against anyone else's, and in particular should not be compared with that of athletes in other specialties because the amount of effort required to do knee bends depends on how much knee bends resemble moves in a particular sport. It is not a perfect test for cycling because there is no warmup, as there always is in cycling, and that lack can cause some good athletes to have bad indexes. However, done once a month under identical conditions, it should at the end of a year give another indication as to when form was achieved.

Precautions. Wear no tight clothes that restrict abdominal breathing. Breathe out while bending, breathe in while standing. Stand up completely each time. The bends must be total, with the thighs touching the heels, the trunk remaining straight.

Diet for Cyclists, Whether Racers or Not Jean-Pierre de Mondenard, M.D.

Law of Three Hours. The last meal should be eaten at least three hours, and even four for some people, prior to an intense effort. After eating, the blood is concentrated in the digestive apparatus to the detriment of the muscles and brain. If exercise causes the blood to speed to the muscles and brain, you risk having cramps, nausea, breathlessness, and an accelerated cardiac rhythm.

What should be eaten at the last meal before competition? Generally racers have changed from steaks and heavy stews to lighter, easier-to-digest meals. However, eating is a personal matter. One racer was observed to down a dozen eggs, a large steak, and four beers before a race. It was Van Looy, who later won the race. On the other hand, I know a judo champion who could manage nothing but liquids during the whole day of his Olympic competition.

During effort. Eat regularly, in small quantities. Eat easily digestible food like dried fruit and drink glycogen-enriched water. If exercise is intense, the body calls on glucides or carbohydrates to supply the oxygen necessary to the muscles. The body holds about 400 grams of glucides in reserve (50 in the liver and 350 in the muscles and extracellular fluid). It uses three grams a minute during effort, so two hours is the maximum supply stored. A concentration of sugar between fifty and a hundred grams a liter permits the stomach to empty rapidly and to maintain blood sugar at a sufficiently high level during an intense and prolonged effort. But don't drink too much at once; this can raise the sugar level to such a point that it precipitates insulin secretion that wipes out all the added glucose and can bring on "the knocks" (hypoglycemia). Potassium should not be added because very little is lost in sweat, and a balanced diet is enough to make up for loss in anyone with normal kidney function.

Drink enough. Exercise causes dehydration. We know many cyclists think our advice is hard to follow, but remember that Olympic-level long-distance skiers drink a half a water bottle every twenty minutes, so it's not impossible.

After effort. Eat as much sugar as is necessary to replace what's been lost. And of course, drink enough water.

Vitamins. The word fascinates the athlete as it has a magical aura. Their real effect on cellular metabolism turns him away from dangerous doping substances but still permits him to keep his morale high, an important factor in performance.

Morehouse's research proves, however, that adding vitamins to a balanced diet in no way betters the aptitude for work, neither in a brief intense effort, nor in one of long duration. Only in the case of a deficiency does vitamin therapy have any benefits. The conclusion must be that it is up to the doctor to decide if supplementary vitamins are needed. Deficiencies can be brought on by the use of antibiotics (a loss of B vitamins), aspirin, whose prolonged use lowers the concentration of vitamin C, and oral contraceptives, which also favor the degradation of vitamins C, B12, and B6.

The recommended diet for athletes, high in cereals and fruit, has the added advantage of supplying large amounts of vitamins B and C to replace those lost through heavy training and a diet rich in refined sugar.

Preserving vitamins in food. After forty-eight hours green vegetables lose ninety percent of their vitamin C. Keep vegetables out of light, do not peel, chop, or grate them too long before eating. Don't soak vegetables; wash them in running water. Cook fruits whole, skin on. Cover cooking food so that vitamins don't evaporate with the water. Use vinegar and lemon as much as possible; vitamins keep better in an acid environment. Don't overcook.

Fighting obesity. Weight can't just be sweated off. Overheating the body simply causes dehydration, and any weight lost is replaced as soon as you've replaced the water. To really lose weight, you have to exercise at fifty percent of your maximum capacity, that's when fats start to be broken down.

Proteins and meat. Many athletes eat too much meat because they think it helps form muscle. Actually, protein is not used any faster during physical effort than at rest. If more than twenty percent of the calories consumed are proteins, the excess is merely destroyed. While, of course, protein is important during growth, for adults too much meat adds uric acid, which can cause muscle and tendon problems, in addition to providing too much fat to the diet.

Carbohydrate Loading *A special use of diet for racers.*

Jean-Pierre de Mondenard, M.D.

For healthy people carbohydrate loading is a way of bettering competitive performance in events over ninety minutes long. The only dangers seem to be certain digestive disturbances such as more gas, which can be cured by stopping the diet or by using intestinal absorbents. Anxious types are more likely to suffer from aftereffects.

Assuming a Sunday race, carbohydrate loading involves using up one's store of glycogen on Monday by making an effort at eighty percent of capacity for two hours, using the same muscles as in competition. This is followed by a diet rich in proteins and fats (ninety percent), with a very important ten percent carbohydrates to help assimilate the fats. If there is no sugar at all, there will be thirst, difficulty training, excess uric acid, and excess cholesterol.

Friday the diet shifts to ninety percent carbohydrates, which is maintained until the day of the race. The most common error is to overeat at this stage, but it is not the quantity of nourishment that's important, but the percentage of carbohydrate. Each gram of glycogen should fix three grams of water, so it is necessary to drink much more than usual during the carbo-loading stage. This will result in a weight gain of from two to three kilos, but this disappears rapidly during the first part of the competition. In races under conditions of extreme heat, it can be an important advantage to have a supplementary reserve of liquid if it is difficult to drink while racing.

This diet is only possible for a few races and certainly is not meant to be followed all year long. Always try it out in a race of secondary importance to see if there are any problems that should be corrected before you use it when it counts.

It is not a miracle cure. Nothing can ever replace training to heighten aerobic endurance, however, it demonstrates that there are natural methods to improve performance.

Carbohydrate loading is not a form of doping. Doping has three criteria: artificial stimulation, danger, and giving an unfair edge in performance. Carbohydrate loading is not stimulating, since it only betters performance after ninety minutes; it is not artificial, as eating is normal, it is not dangerous, the only problems being easily solved digestive ones, and it gives no more unfair advantage than having a good coach would over having a poor one.

A Myth to Dispel — Driest is Fastest ### Jean-Pierre de Mondenard, M.D.

Dr. de Mondenard *getting ready for a race. The ACCS on the jersey stands for Friends of Cycling in the Health Professions. Courtesy of Dr. de Mondenard.*

Cells get the energy they need and get rid of wastes by the intermediary of liquids. All cells contain and are surrounded by water. When the athlete gets dehydrated, the liquids in which the cells bathe diminish. Muscle cells in particular cannot work well until proper liquid level is reestablished.

Exercise dehydrates the body. Oxygen consumption at rest is about 0.2 liters per minute. During exercise it climbs to 2.5 to 3.5 liters per minute in an untrained person, and 5 to 6 liters in a trained athlete. In two hours this translates into 700 kilocalories for untrained athletes and 1,400 kilocalories for trained athletes. The body is only capable of transforming twenty to twenty-five percent of this huge amount of energy into work; the rest is heat. Muscle temperature goes from 36°C at rest to 40°C at submaximal effort. The heat liberated in the muscles is carried by the warmed blood to all the rest of the body. Muscle temperature climbs rapidly during the first minutes and stabilizes about a half-hour later. Rectal temperature climbs less quickly and takes about forty-five minutes to stabilize. After this equilibration the temperature climbs no further even if the effort is prolonged. On the other hand, if the intensity increases, the temperature rises again, but also stabilizes at a constant level forty to fifty minutes later.

Body temperature climbs proportionately to the intensity of effort. A well-trained person's temperature rises less than in an untrained individual. However, they would have the same temperature for the same relative effort. Trained or untrained, everyone using fifty percent of his maximal oxygen consumption has a body temperature of 38°C.

The amount of heat that can be stored by the body is very small. The excess heat must be eliminated or the body temperature would rise 1.5 degrees per hour at rest, and 10 to 15 degrees during every thirty minutes of intense effort. Fortunately the body has a perfect means of eliminating heat that can be compared to the water reservoir of a car; however, as the water evaporates, we do not have a closed system.

The quantity of heat removed by radiation and conduction depends on the difference between the temperature of the skin and the air. When the ambient temperature is 20°C, 100 to 200 kilocalories an hour are eliminated by radiation and conduction. The rest must be eliminated by perspiration. The evaporation of a liter of water requires 580 kilocalories, so to eliminate 1,000 kilocalories an hour, you have to sweat 1.5 to 2 liters an hour. These theoretic estimations agree with measurements taken during cycling, and cross-country and long distance skiing races.

When the ambient temperature is lower, the evaporation of sweat is less important and can drop to half a liter an hour.

Effort also vastly increases the amount of water lost through breathing: 400 milliliters in 24 hours at rest, 200 milliliters in one hour during effort.

Origin of Eliminated Liquids

Experiments have shown that liquids come from different tissues when the body is active than when at rest. At rest, with high ambient temperature, the liquids come mostly from the blood; this is proven by loss of blood volume. Measurements taken during exercise show an astonishingly constant volume of blood in spite of heavy loss of liquid; physiological functions require this constancy. These lost liquids must come from the cells, probably the muscle cells.

How is This Water Loss Compensated for by the Muscle Cells?

The combustion of fat and carbohydrates frees carbon dioxide and water. The "water of combustion" liberated is about 150 milliliters an hour. About three grams of water are also freed from each gram of glycogen used. Thus during effort the body can lose about 800 grams of water an hour without disturbing the hydric balance of the muscle cells. But this released water is insufficient for an intense physical effort when the ambient temperature is high.

Water loss of four percent of body weight diminishes the capacity to sustain intense physical effort by forty percent when the temperature is 18°C and by sixty percent if the temperature is 41°C. A loss of ten percent of body weight can be fatal.

How much water must be replenished during muscular effort depends not only on air temperature, but also on whether it is cloudy or sunny. One loses almost 0.7 of a liter more water an hour on a sunny day than on a cloudy day.

Since one must drink 1.3 liters every hour to replace water lost working hard at 20°C, it's obvious that one should respect the rule, little and often. In 1971, H. Staff and S. Nilsson showed that 225 milliliters of liquid have to be ingested every fifteen minutes during muscular effort of long duration.

A feeling of thirst only appears when perspiration loss is over a half liter an hour, too late to reestablish fluid balance. So it is fundamental during physical effort to drink without being thirsty, that is to say, to drink systematically before feeling the need for it.

What Should You Drink?

Pure water will be eliminated through the skin immediately, so you must drink water with carbohydrates in it; the best proportion is 2.5 grams of glucose per liter when it is hot. When it is cold, drink small quantities of heavily sweetened water (150 to 400 grams per liter). In cold weather the slow emptying of the stomach assures a regular transport of glucides to the liver and the muscles in activity.

The speed with which the stomach is emptied depends on the osmolarity of the liquid. Both sugar and potassium slow the absorption of liquid from the stomach. Small quantities of salt, however, speed it up. Cool water is absorbed faster; about 15°C is ideal. Five to six hundred milliliters of water can be tolerated without slowing down absorption, and absorption does not depend on intensity of effort below seventy percent of maximum.

Should salt be added? Normally this is unnecessary because the percentage of salt in sweat is only 0.2 to 0.3 percent, while that in the blood is 0.9 percent. When we perspire we lose more water than salt, so the concentration of salt in the body goes up. However, after five hours of riding, it is advisable to add a little salt to the water or to take a salt tablet. Salt should also be added after the race (as well as sugar) to help speed recuperation.

Until 1972 giving racers drinks during the stages of the Tour de France was forbidden. The organizers then accepted the recommendations of doctors about the usefulness of fluid and electrolyte replacement during effort, and racers may now receive drinks practically throughout each stage.

During certain stages of the Tour de France, run in great heat and with steep climbs, it was not uncommon to see racers consume enormous quantities of liquids—up to 8 liters at a time. Such a practice is not good for the digestive tract. If you drink before you feel thirsty, you can prevent dehydration without harming your form and recuperation this way.

Photograph by Bernard Thompson

188

Muscle Energetics

Edward Bottone, Ph.D.

Ed Bottone's article draws on his expert knowledge of two areas – microbiology and racing. He is both director of the Department of Microbiology of The Mount Sinai Hospital in New York City, and president of the Century Road Club Association, America's oldest racing club. Dr. Bottone competes regularly in club and open races, and won the Excellence in Teaching Award at the Mount Sinai School of Medicine where he is an associate professor. He is the author and editor of numerous books and articles on microbiology.

Cycling, although basically an individual activity, is a total sport that challenges both body and mind and unifies these two forces.

The renaissance of cycling shows a high degree of sophistication among its more serious practitioners. A growing number of cyclists have gone beyond the purely mechanical aspects and now concern themselves with the physiology of cycling. Present-day cyclists are attuned to concepts of aerobic and anaerobic energy metabolism as it relates to cycling. It is not uncommon on a "training ride" to hear such terms as "oxygen debt," "lactic acid build-up," "ATP," or "glucose metabolism" being bandied about. Augmenting such interest are numerous articles and books about sports medicine that use cycling as a physiologic model.[1]

Current interest in cycling is focused on acquiring a sense of fitness or shape. Shape is the body's ability to transfer atmospheric oxygen to working muscle cells, enhancing aerobic metabolism.

Metabolism is the sum total of the various reactions occurring in a cell. While no common food

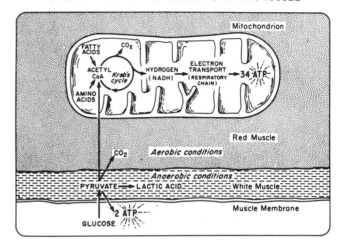

FLOW SHEET OF
ENERGY-YIELDING METABOLIC ACTIVITY IN MUSCLE

Mitochondrion

FATTY ACIDS → CO_2

ACETYL CoA — *Kreb's cycle*

AMINO ACIDS

HYDROGEN (NADH) → ELECTRON TRANSPORT (RESPIRATORY CHAIN) → 34 ATP

CO_2

Aerobic conditions

Red Muscle

Anaerobic conditions

PYRUVATE → LACTIC ACID

White Muscle

Muscle Membrane

2 ATP

GLUCOSE

source could possibly contain the multiplicity of different molecules found in a given cell, a single carbon substrate such as glucose can serve for the synthesis of numerous organic molecules. Upon entry into the cell, this carbohydrate can be chemically transformed into various structural components. This process is the focal point for muscular activity.

Striated muscle may be distinguished on the basis of color intensity into thinner, dark colored fibers (red) and thicker, pale fibers (white).[2] The color intensity of muscle is directly related to its myoglobin content, which in turn indicates its function and biochemical activity.

Red muscle fibers contract slowly, contain a greater degree of myoglobin, have decreased

Ed Bottone. *Photographs by Karl W. Bruning*

amounts of high energy phosphate containing compounds, and have a rich blood supply, suggesting greater oxygenation for the aerobic metabolic processes. To accommodate oxidative metabolism resulting in greater energy as adenosine triphosphate (ATP), numerous mitochondria (the "power plants" of cells) speckle the muscle fibers.[4] White fibers, in contrast, contract rapidly, have a somewhat poorer blood supply, are rich in glycogen, high-energy phosphate compounds such as creatine phosphate (CP), and in the extra-mitochondrial enzymes essential for the anaerobic glycolysis leading to lactic acid formation. The interrelationship between structure and function is beautifully shown in skeletal muscle: The red fibers are adapted to the aerobic metabolism of fatty acids and metabolites of glycolysis through the respiratory Krebs cycle, while the white fibers are concerned with the anaerobic cleavage of glycogen to pyruvate.

In order for chemical energy to be transformed into work (muscular contraction), a series of cellular reactions must occur converting carbohydrates such as glucose into more usable forms of energy.

Before talking about pulmonary and muscle physiology as they relate to cycling, it is important to discuss what is meant by "getting in shape." Each year as the new cycling season looms on the horizon, the ritual of "getting in shape" commences anew with a flurry of activity. Great care is devoted to preparing the bicycle for the strenuous task ahead. Gear ratios are lowered to ease the forthcoming miles after a winter's hiatus. Training schedules are planned with meticulous care as to distance, terrain, and speed. The mind and body are galvanized into action in an effort to achieve "shape."

"Shape" has different meanings for different individuals and is influenced by sex, age, vocation, and extraneous interests. In cycling, "shape" is excellence of metabolic exchange coupled with a sense of well-being. The juxtaposition of mind and body may be achieved in cycling or other endurance sports by achieving endurance fitness, defined by R.J. Shepard[7] as "maintaining the various processes involved in metabolic exchange as close to the resting state as is mutually possible during performance of a fully learned task for moderate time (from one to sixty minutes) with a capacity to reach a higher steady state of working than the unfit and to restore promptly after exercise all equilibriums which are disturbed."

The marvel of "shape" as it relates to cycling is inherent in its beneficial effect on one's outlook. The cyclist who has acquired this state of being is also in possession of a mental status that accepts challenge as a daily endeavor. Think of the highly positive frame of mind one must have to cycle across the United States, to embark upon a bike ride to a friend's house some distance away, or to compete in a rigorous bicycle race. When out of shape, the thought alone of such undertakings is met with a multitude of excuses as to why not to do it!

It cannot be the task of this brief article to examine all the metabolic processes that take place in pulmonary and muscle cells. It is hoped that enough interest will have been generated so that the reader may pursue greater detail concerning those systems (cardiovascular, genito-urinary, gastrointestinal) and their functioning during exercise. In this regard, the text edited by W.R. Johnson and E.R. Buskirk[3] may prove beneficial.

According to A.W. Hubbard[2] "the apparent multiplicity of responses in living organisms can be reduced ultimately to two basic forms: movement and secretion." Physical activity such as cycling requires energy for its performance. The energy must be mobilized from the oxidation of carbohydrates and fats. In turn, such energy expenditure is directly related to oxygen consumption and its availability to the muscle cells, which will markedly influence their mode of metabolism i.e., aerobic versus anaerobic. The interrelationship between the oxygen intake demanded by the physical activity and the oxygen requirement to sustain a maximal effort is crucial to the mode of muscle metabolism. As the oxygen requirement increases, a point will be reached wherein the cardiovascular respiratory system can no longer deliver the required amount of oxygen to the muscle cells to sustain the maximal effort. As the maximal oxygen requirement exceeds the intake rate, metabolism in the muscle takes place by the less energy efficient anaerobic pathway (glycolysis), with glycogen serving as the primary foodstuff. The net result of sustaining this maximal effort under conditions of oxygen debt is the accumulation of lactic acid and other products of metabolism (metabolites) in the muscle cells resulting in the all too familiar pain.

"Shape" is the conditioning of the cardiovascular-pulmonary system to increase its efficiency in the delivery of oxygen to muscle tissue in order to sustain the highly productive aerobic metabolism. All cellular activity, especially muscular activity, is energy dependent relying primarily upon the oxidation of essential carbohydrates and lipids and the "excretion" of metabolic end products, such as lactic acid, which may accumulate in varying amounts depending on the availability of oxygen. The energy necessary for muscle contraction, however, is drawn from the high-energy phosphate compounds, which are generated as a result of glycolysis (anaerobic) and respiratory (aerobic) metabolic activity. Thus, energy is stored in the muscle in the form of glycogen and high-energy phosphate containing compounds and can be called upon for muscular work in the absence of active metabolism. In the absence of active metabolism, however, the amount of physical work is strictly limited lest active metabolism ensues to restore energy stores to the muscle.

"Shape" is directly related to the ability of the body to transfer atmospheric oxygen to sites of marked biochemical activity in various body tissues. During periods of moderate activity, oxygen intake exceeds oxygen requirements and has been calculated to be three to five liters per minute under standard conditions.[7] At the inception of high-intensity activity such as in sprinting or "breaking away," the energy demands depending on "shape" may not be adequately met by aerobic metabolism (oxidation) in the muscles. Part of the work force must be supplied anaerobically, as an oxygen deficit develops that is proportional to the intensity of the physical demand. Upon completion of the driving activity, during the recovery phase, there is an excess oxygen intake in comparison to the resting value prior to the activity. Thus as the cyclist enters the high-intensity period he incurs a sort of "oxygen debt" that may be as high as twenty liters,[3] and which must be repaid upon cessation of activity. When considering the three phases, rest (pacing), high-intensity activity (sprinting), and recovery, the excess amount of oxygen taken in during recovery equals the oxygen debt incurred during the high-intensity stage. In a sense, the "oxygen debt" is the amount of oxygen necessary for the aerobic (oxidative) resynthesis of the high-energy phosphates and the restoration of the oxygen reserves in the muscle in the form of myoglobin (oxygen carrying protein in muscle).

The biochemical events at the initiation of exercise may be reconstructed as follows: (a) utilization of the small amount of oxygen stored in muscle as myoglobin for aerobic metabolism (oxidation) with no increase in lactic acid production, but generation of high-energy phosphate compounds (ATP, PEP); (b) as the physical stress is prolonged, the oxygen stored as myoglobin is depleted and the oxygen intake is not equivalent to the oxygen demand and delivery (oxygen deficit). Anaerobic metabolism ensues, resulting in the accumulation of lactic acid. There is some overlapping of energy sources, for as oxygen is being depleted some of the energy requirements may also be met through the exhaustion of the readily available high-energy phosphates. In the absence of oxygen they are replenished more slowly via the glycolytic anaerobic process and ultimately more efficiently during the recovery phase in which oxygen excess prevails, thereby favoring oxidative phosphorylation. The lactic acid that accumulates during strenous activity is transferred from the skeletal muscle cells to the blood for further metabolism in the liver and other tissues (heart, kidney, resting skeletal muscle) where it is dehydrogenated back to pyruvate which is further degraded to CO_2 and H_2O.[3] In contrast to muscle, in the liver lactate is resynthesized into glucose and glycogen (gluconeogenesis). From this site, glucose can be released into the blood and serve as a substrate either for energy production of for the synthesis of glycogen.

It is to be appreciated that under prolonged stress, muscle fatigue, as evidenced by a diminution of muscle contraction, may be directly attributable to depletion of high-energy phosphate compounds. An energy supply from the breakdown of glycogen to lactate (2 ATP's liberated) is not sufficient to sustain high-level muscular contraction. The more primitive anaerobic glycolytic pathway is simply not sufficient to supply the energy needs during prolonged high-intensity periods. Additionally, as lactic acid accumulates, the pH of the cell is lowered below 6.4, causing an inhibition of glycolysis. If the oxygen debt is not met promptly, the accumulation of unoxidized metabolites, especially lactic acid, lead to the well-known muscle discomfort (pain) and excessive breathing. It can readily be seen why pacing oneself during a cycling event is critical to keeping the level of unoxidized lactic acid to a minimum and delaying the oxygen debt until the all-out final sprint.

The degree of tolerance of the oxygen debt as overt pain will vary with each individual's threshold and state of physical conditioning. The better trained the individual, the greater the efficiency of cardiopulmonary function. In trained individuals there is the availability of a larger blood supply and a decrease in muscle mass in which unoxidized metabolites can accumulate.[3]

Prolonged exercise may result in depletion of glucose stores (hypoglycemia), and ingestion of glucose enhances endurance. In this regard, the capacity for prolonged vigorous exercise is greater for individuals maintained on high-carbohydrate diets. Thus the concept of "carbohydrate loading" may be related to increasing the glycogen content in muscle, thereby increasing endurance.

The beneficial effect of carbohydrate loading is directly related to the total duration and quality of exercise. Thus in terms of cycling if one is stressed, as during "jamming," then glycogen is rapidly converted to glucose, which is actively metabolized either aerobically or anaerobically depending on "shape." If the metabolic pathway shifts to anaerobiosis because of ensuing oxygen debt, then lactic acid levels will become elevated. To simultaneously enjoy the beneficial aspects of carbohydrate loading and keep lactic acid levels at minimum during maximum exercise, a warm-up prior to maximal effort is beneficial.

The inherent value of a warm-up prior to engaging in strenuous activity could be related to gradual elevation or priming of cardiovascular and pulmonary function prior to stress. Such preliminary activity would result in an accelerated adaptation of metabolic activity in the muscle cell by virtue of improved blood flow and hence oxygen transport. The net result would be a diminution in lactic acid buildup as aerobic metabolism would be favored, thereby preventing a pH drop in the cell which could result in, as noted earlier, decreased performance capacity of the muscle cell.

References:

1. Conrad, C.C. How Different Sports Rate in Promoting Physical Fitness. President's Council on Physical Fitness and Sports, U.S. Dept. of Health, Education and Welfare, Public Health Service, 1978.

2. Hubbard, A.W. "Homokinetics: Muscular Function in Human Movement," eds. Johnson, W.R., and E.R. Buskirk. Science and Medicine of Exercise and Sport, 2nd ed., New York: Harper and Row, 1974.

3. Johnson, W.R., and E.R. Buskirk, eds. Science and Medicine of Exercise and Sport, 2nd ed., New York: Harper and Row, 1974.

4. Keul, J., E. Doll, and D. Keppler. "Energy Metabolism of Human Muscle," Medicine and Sport, 7:19-51, New York: 1972.

5. Lehninger, A.L. Biochemistry. New York: Worth Publishers, Inc., 1971.

6. Lehninger, A.L. Bioenergetics. 2nd ed., New York: W.A. Benjamin, 1971.

7. Shephard, R.J. Endurance Fitness. University of Toronto Press, 1969.

8. Watson, J.D. Molecular Biology of The Gene, 2nd ed., New York: W.A. Benjamin, 1970.

CALORIES AND POWER

Calories and Power

David Gordon Wilson

David Gordon Wilson is professor of mechanical engineering at the Massachusetts Institute of Technology. In 1967 he sponsored a prize design competition for improvements in human-powered land transport. There were seventy-three entrants from six countries. He later coauthored Bicycling Science *with Frank Rowland Whitt, one of the competition's entrants. David Wilson is an enthusiastic designer and rider of recumbent bicycles (his designs are being manufactured by FOMAC, Inc., of Wilmington, MA.). He believes he has bicycled between a quarter and a third of a million miles, in Europe, Africa, and America.*

This section gives some guidelines on the energy and calories expended by average people in different circumstances on different types of bicycles. The range is wide. Fig. 1 shows that a rider on a "racing" bicycle going quite slowly could cover a mile with the expenditure of only four calories, while someone on a heavier "roadster" bike going against a twenty-mile-per-hour head wind would use up more than sixty calories.

There are many reasons why the calories expended could be even more than is shown on fig. 1, and a few reasons why they could be less. So that we may be a little more rigorous, we need to be more precise about what we mean by the terms we are using.

Definitions

A calorie is a measure of energy. In physics, a calorie is the heat or work energy required to raise one kilogram of water one degree centigrade. In nutrition, unfortunately, a "calorie" means one thousand of the physics' calories, or one kilocalorie. From here on, I will use the nutrition calorie in the text, but for precision will use the abbreviation "kcal" in the graphs.

These calories of energy, which may be stored in your food or in the body fat you want to burn off, may all be transformed into heat, or some may be converted into work. Work is defined in thermodynamics as the energy necessary to lift a weight –which then gives the weight potential energy– and work may also appear as kinetic energy. The new S.I. units of energy are joules. A kcal is 4,186.8 joules.

Power is the rate of change of energy, measured in watts or horsepower. A watt is a joule per second. A horsepower is 746 watts.

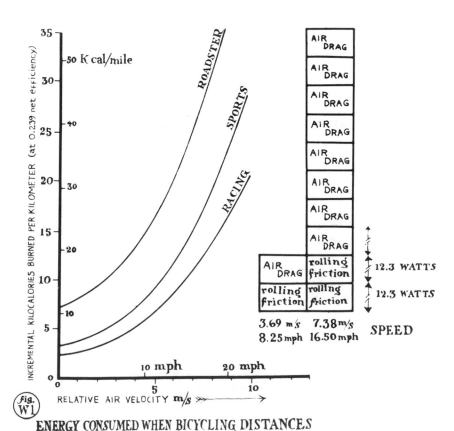

ENERGY CONSUMED WHEN BICYCLING DISTANCES
assuming equal "incremental" (net) metabolic efficiencies.

A human being is like a fuel cell, taking in chemical energy in food or fat and putting out work energy. The efficiency is defined as the amount of work energy divided by the chemical or food energy. Now a human being obviously needs some food energy just to live and keep warm, even if no work or other activity is undertaken. We then define the "net" metabolic efficiency as the ratio of work output to the *incremental* food-energy intake over that necessary to support life. Values between twenty and thirty percent have been measured for trained athletes. We have used a reasonable mean number for fit people of 0.2388, or 23.88 percent, because when multiplied by 4,186.8 it gives 1,000, for the calculation of fig. 1. For this value of net efficiency, an expenditure of one calorie produces one kilojoule of work. We shall comment later on the effects of differing efficiencies.

Bicycle Specifications

We made calculations for three types of bicycles and their riders. One was for a "roadster," which is more popularly referred to as a "3-speed bicycle." The important characteristic is that the rider sits more or less upright, presenting more area to the wind in a rather "high-drag" shape, i.e. flat-on to the wind. Although this type was known a decade or so ago as the "English lightweight," it is light only in comparison with the old domestic, heavy-duty single-speed "clunker" bikes, which have almost disappeared from the catalogs. The second bike we calculated we called a "sports," known generally as a "10-speed." It has dropped handlebars so that the rider, when using the lower handgrips, not only presents a smaller frontal area than when on a roadster, but does so with a more streamlined, i.e. lower-drag, shape. The sports bike is lighter than the roadster, and in particular it has lighter, smaller-section wheels with higher pressure, though still wired-on (clincher) tires. We assumed that the rider plus clothing would generally weigh less than would the typical rider plus clothing on a roadster.

The third bicycle we took was a true racing model, considerably lighter still than the sports, with very lightweight tubular tires. The rider would adopt an even more "tucked-down" position than for the sports bike.

The assumptions coming from these considerations are summarized in the tables below.

For the rider on a typical sports bicycle, the power going to air drag equals that overcoming rolling friction (12.3 watts) at 8.25 mph (3.69 m/s). At twice this speed, the rolling-friction power doubles to equal the total power previously expended. But the power required to overcome air drag is eight times as much, and the total power is, then, five times the total power at the lower speed (123 watts, or about one-sixth of a horsepower). The bar chart shows how the power losses at the two speeds compare.

Power Curves

The power requirements for moving the three types of bicycles and their riders at various speeds are shown on figs. 2 and 3. The air-drag power is for sea level, moderate-temperature (15°C.) conditions. The rolling-resistance power is for riding on a smooth, level road. The power to ride up a gentle hill of 2.5-percent slope is also shown on fig. 2.

It can be seen that for the slow-speed commuting or shopping bicyclist who travels at around 10 mph, the rolling and air-drag powers are similar (assuming no wind). Hills and head winds are very important to these riders.

For the higher-speed riders, air drag becomes dominant. One-hour races are usually won at over 25 mph, at which speed the power going to conquer air

David Gordon Wilson *on a recumbent of his own design.*
MIT photo by Calvin Campbell

resistance may be five times or more that being lost in rolling resistance. At these speeds it may even be easier riding up a hill with the wind behind one than down the hill with the wind in one's face.

The rolling and air-drag powers have

| | Bicycle Type | | |
	Roadster RR	Sports SS	Racing RG
Frontal area, sq. m.	0.5	0.4	0.33
Drag coefficient	1.2	1.0	0.9
Bicycle mass, kg	15	10	6
Rider & clothing mass, kg	80	75	75
Total mass, kg	95	85	81
Rolling-resistance coeff.	0.008	0.004	0.003

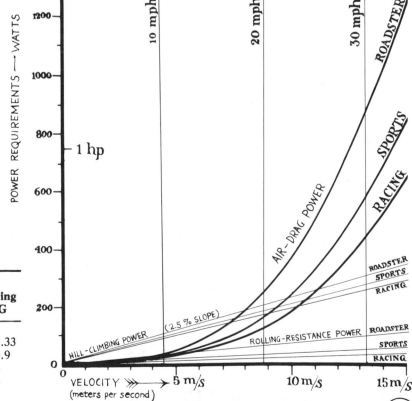

POWER REQUIREMENTS FOR BICYCLES (fig. W2)

been added in fig. 3 for only the lower end of the speed range. These curves can be accurate only, of course, for still-air conditions. Plotted this way, these curves show just how great the penalty of riding a roadster is versus a sports or racing bike. At ten miles an hour, about twice as much power is required for the roadster as for a sports bicycle. Another way of looking at the difference is to take a figure of one-tenth of a horse-power, about 75 watts, as the output which most fit adults feel that they could keep up for hours. At this power level, the rider of the roadster would be going at about 10 mph, and the racer about 15 mph.

The best guide to calories expended is still, however, fig. 1, because here the true relative air velocity can be entered, so accounting for head and tail winds, and the results will be the sum of the expenditures over rolling resistance and air drag. The effects of hill climbing can also be added: 0.932 calories per meter climbed for the roadster rider, and 0.834 and 0.795 for the sports and racing riders.

If you and your bicycle together weigh more than or less than the amounts taken as typical in the table, you should multiply the rolling losses and the hill-climbing expenditures by the ratio of your combined weight (mass) to that in the table. (A kilogram is about 2.2 pounds.) It is less easy to judge the effects of different frontal areas, drag coefficients, and rolling-resistance coefficients. But if you ride with under-inflated tires, or travel on sandy, slushy, or cobbled roads, you can be sure that your rolling losses will be much higher than the values calculated here for smooth surfaces and well-inflated tires.

Metabolic Efficiency

These charts are based on a uniform net metabolic efficiency of 0.2388, a figure chosen purely for convenience. If you are in the peak of condition and training, your efficiency might be 28 or 30 percent. If, on the other hand, you are in poor condition and out of training, your efficiency might be down at the 10-percent level, and you will burn correspondingly more energy per mile. (I confess that I have not been able to find reliable figures for nonathletic bicyclists.)

Your efficiency will also be low, however fit and well-trained you are, if you use an inappropriate gear ratio or foot motion. For instance, imagine trying to pedal a bicycle at 25 mph in a very low bottom gear. You would not be able to feel any pedal reaction at all, and your efficiency would be zero or negative. The same goes for trying to ride up the Mt. Washington toll road in a high top gear, except that here you would experience plenty of pedal reaction but no forward movement, and again your efficiency would be zero or negative (if you were rolling back). Human beings seem to be tolerant to a rather wide range of gear ratios, so that there isn't one definite optimum for any set of conditions, but there is a certain range of ratios within which one's efficiency will be at, or very close to, maximum.

Your efficiency will also be lower if you decide to give one leg a rest and to pedal with the other alone. People have often wondered if the converse was true –that one's efficiency would increase if one involved as many muscles as possible. At least within limits, it appears that this is so. People can develop 10 to 20 percent more power if they hand crank in addition to pedaling, and it is a fair assumption that when they produce equal power by the two methods, their efficiency will be higher when they are using more muscles. There have been many designs and patents of hand-and-foot-cranked, single-rider bicycles, but none has been wholly successful. But we can infer that using toe straps and training oneself to pull on the pedals as well as push, and using other muscles to push the pedals over "top dead-center," will increase one's efficiency.

Bicyclists' Miles per Gallon

All this information has important implications for the energy crisis. We can see from fig. 1 that a racing bicyclist at 20 mph can travel more than 240 miles per gallon–of homogenized grade-A milk.

Bicyclists could help to solve our energy crisis and our milk surpluses simultaneously.

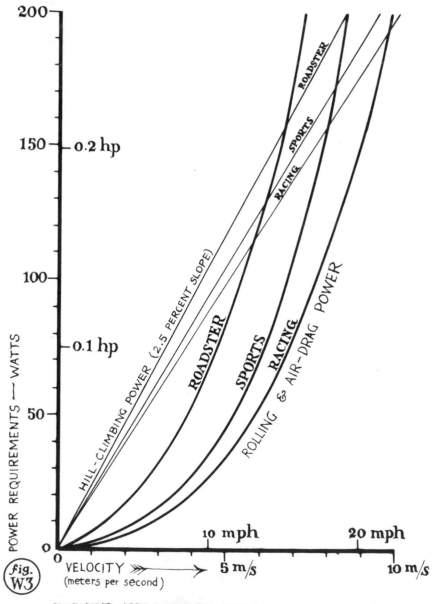

POWER REQUIREMENTS FOR BICYCLES

ORTHOPEDICS

Cycling Injury

Wayne B. Leadbetter, M.D. &
Myles J. Schneider, D.P.M.

Since the bicycle acts as an exoskeleton and relieves your body of carrying much of its weight, it permits you to exercise with a minimum of jarring to joints and muscles. That's why it is often prescribed for runners who can't run, walkers who can't walk, and even people with advanced arthritis. It will help keep you fit by retarding the advance of osteoporosis, and by keeping all those veins and arteries cholesterol-free to an advanced age.

Yet to take advantage of this most human machine, certain rules of biodynamics must be followed. There is nothing sadder than a biker watching the world roll by because his knee or his foot hurts. And in this world of running doctors, how hard it is to find someone who knows enough to tell you when it's safe to get back on the bike.

So we knew we needed orthopedic advice. But who to go to? And how many people had been shuttled from foot specialist to knee specialist and back again, without anyone being able to come up with a cure?

Then we learned that cyclists in the Washington, D.C. area were blessed with an orthopedist who routinely worked with a podiatrist. We jumped at the chance of having them contribute advice on how to avoid injury and what to do if it happened.

What they did surpassed our expectations. Drawing on their own experience plus what was published in France, England, and America, they produced the most authoritative and complete statement in English to date. Don't just take our word for it: We had it reviewed by our medical consultant, who is both a physician and an accomplished racer; he was thrilled. It describes the mechanisms of injury, tells you when you can treat yourself, and gives you enough information to meet your doctor more than halfway.

Since not everyone is lucky enough to be treated by Dr. Wayne B. Leadbetter and Dr. Myles T. Schneider, they suggest that you take this section to your doctor if you don't think he understands the dynamics of cycling. Good advice, like the rest of this chapter!

Writing this chapter was a challenge to us. We think cyclists, like all athletes, have a responsibility to know the basic principles of their sport and to prepare themselves properly to avoid needless injury. Prevention is a lot more effective than cure. So we tried to identify just what does happen in cycling, and then put into perspective some of the rare effects without making you neurotic. Our offices are already filled with worried well people.

So, we don't want to scare people. Cycling is very safe if done properly, but there are some dangers everyone should know about. Compartmentalization of the lower leg muscles is extremely rare, and you shouldn't think you have it because you ache a bit. But someone who is in very poor shape and goes way beyond his physiological conditioning limits—like riding a hundred miles when they're really only capable of twenty—might get it, and it's a disaster! It could happen on the second or third day of a tour. Whenever it happens, it means a trip to a hospital emergency room and should be recognized as such.

Cycling is good for you, and we don't want this chapter to be an excuse for you not to go out and do it. Conditioning is uncomfortable; we call it Grade I pain, to help you realize you're not falling apart just because you're a little sore. There are a lot of complaints in cycling, but not very many injuries; and even most injuries are self-limiting and not serious. Anything that doesn't go away soon can usually be cured by an adjustment of riding equipment or technique.

Cycling can be beneficial to the hip; in fact, it's used as rehabilitation after hip joint replacement surgery, as well as in helping older people regain mobility. Even walking has greater impact than cycling. So, doctor, if you want your patient to avoid impact and torque (like in golf), cycling is a very good compromise that lets him maintain a healthful heart.

There *are* a lot of creaky knees out there. Lots of cyclists sound as if they have chondromalacia, but they don't show any of the pain patterns. Oh, a knee might hurt after fifty miles, but it doesn't really bother them the rest of the time. And that can be a problem when a non-sports-medicine doctor looks at a cyclist's knee. He'll feel that knee, and look at it, and listen to it, and say, "That's awful! You'd better stop cycling! You've got crepitations, you're going to have arthritis and have to have your knee replaced!" Yet this noise is endemic to a lot of touring cyclists, and we don't know what its significance is, but it doesn't seem to do them any harm.

Of course, if a knee or a tendon swells, that can be serious.

What we're trying to stop is the person who gets a very expensive bike, has a very rough idea of how to put the cleats on, goes out and rides a hundred miles without any idea of what they're supposed to be doing, and then has to go to the doctor because everything hurts. If they're in an organized club, they're going to be talking with people who will set them straight, but it's amazing some of the problems that are born of ignorance.

Who is at greatest risk?

The beginner is likely to experience pain that is considered part of the conditioning process. Muscle soreness, mild aching of the thighs and kneecap area, occasional soreness in the feet and ankles, as well as the all-too-frequent saddle soreness are part of the beginner's experience.

Eventually the cyclist graduates to regular rider status and may be commuting to work on his cycle and certainly is engaging in regular rides on weekends. The knees become the trouble spot in this group, and complaints centering on the hands begin to appear.

The tourist will engage in rides of many hundreds of miles. He experiences a high percentage of knee complaints as well as hand and back symptoms. He is especially vulnerable to overuse conditions and to injury of the knee and patello-femoral joint because of the frequent hill climbing that touring implies.

The racer, by sprinting, exposes himself to muscle tears and strains, as well as the danger of collisions and falls. Because of hard training and the high forces generated in racing, these injuries can be difficult to treat.

As a general rule, the cyclist in transition from level to level is at greatest risk. Sudden changes in training routine including frequency, distance, and intensity of riding all contribute to injury. Any change in the cycle or the equipment, especially the cleat alignment of the serious cyclist, has importance when a new pain or problem arises. Riders with poor muscle conditioning, poor flexibility, and structural weakness of the foot and lower extremity are all at risk.

The middle-aged rider, thirty-five to fifty-five years old, is the most likely to overindulge in riding after a period of inactivity and to experience an overuse injury.

Riders who are relatively free from pain include children, those who ride frequently enough to remain in condition, the strong and flexible rider, and the rider who performs other athletic activities that promote the proper balance of flexibility and strength.

Why does injury occur?

There are six basic causes for all sports injury: impact, overuse, muscle imbalance, inflexibility, dynamic overload, and structural weakness. An understanding of these mechanisms is the first step in recognizing why pain is experienced and in identifying measures necessary to avoid its occurrence.

Impact

It is easy to understand the role of impact in falls or collisions; less obvious but equally important is impact or contact occurring at all times at three points: the foot with the pedal, the buttocks or ischia with the saddle, and the hands with the handlebar. Pain at any of these sites requires attention as to riding technique, the fit of the cycle, and the nature of the cyclist's equipment. Properly chosen and correctly fitted footwear, saddles, and riding gloves, as well as handlebar covers, decrease the risk of impact injury.

The most life-threatening form of impact injury in cycling is head injury. Vigilant, competent cycling; with proper braking technique and the use of a hardshell helmet lined with noncompressible foam offers the highest degree of protection.

Overuse

Overuse injuries are caused by mistakes in training or riding technique. They occur gradually, accompanied by warning signs of soreness and pain, and therefore are often predictable and preventable. Most of your body's responses to cycling are beneficial, such as improved cardiovascular function, more efficient oxygen utilization, excess calorie consumption, improved muscle tone, increased physical endurance, and a sense of well-being.

But riding too fast, too long, or too often does not allow the body to keep up. When body stress is excessive, strengthening and improved function cannot occur. You get out of equilibrium; we call this "breaking down." Breaking down is heralded by feelings of fatigue and pain. So listening to your body is important.

Overstressing is another way a rider can get hurt. You might ride at an easy pace during the week and then go out on the weekend for a very fast or very hilly or very long ride when you're not really trained for it yet. In this case, you would be undertrained and overstressing yourself. You have to build up: Get in some harder or faster or longer workouts during the week, so that you stress your body gradually.

How to tell when you're overtrained. This syndrome has many of the characteristics of a depression. You feel any combination of these: fatigue, soreness, a heavy feeling in legs, frequent colds or other infections, a loss of interest in cycling or in work. There may be constipation or diarrhea, menstrual problems, loss of weight and appetite, a rise in resting pulse rate. A series of minor injuries, aches, or pains make you seem to go from one injury to another.

Since muscle recovery often takes twenty-four to forty-eight hours with any type of athletic activity, cyclists as well as runners should alternate hard and easy days, with a day of recovery between hard workouts. If you feel fatigued on an easy day, chances are you're overtraining.

Overtraining is not only related to distance and time spent on the bike. Changes in diet, especially eating less, lack of sleep, emotional stress, overwork at job or at home all have a place. Remember: Overtraining is the most common cause of pain and injury, and is directly related to errors in cycling technique and frequency: I DID IT! (Injury = Daily, Intense, Distance = Improper Training).

Muscle Imbalance and Inflexibility

These two are grouped together because they are two sides of the same coin. Cycling tends to over-strengthen the extensor muscles of the hip and of the knee, the flexors of the toe and ankle. This results in shortening of resting length and increased resting tension. It is the direct result of muscle use and is sports specific: For example, while the cyclist has generally stronger quadriceps and weaker hamstrings, the runner has just the reverse. Injury may result when weaker muscles are stressed to exhaustion or strong tight muscles tear. Painful spasm or cramping is another stress response of muscle, which represents a titanic contracture promoted by metabolic imbalance in the tissues caused by excessive exercise and loss of electrolytes. This problem is helped by improved conditioning.

Muscles are made to move joints and allow motion and purposeful activity. When they shorten, joints are directly affected; ligaments and periarticular capsules contract, further aggravating inflexibility. Engaging in activities that require a full range of motion of the joint or produce stretching beyond the limit of a contracture will cause discomfort or pain.

Because the effects of muscle shortening are unavoidable, it is normal for the cyclist to feel stiff after a period of inactivity. It's also the reason warmup is so important in all sports. The cyclist should warm up for at least five to ten minutes by riding at a gentle and comfortable pace. This will allow increased blood flow to leg muscles and their relaxation to proper resting length. At the end of a ride it is equally important to cool down by riding at a slower pace to avoid muscle spasm and tightening.

Although cyclists as a group tend to be more flexible than runners, a maintenance program of stretching and strengthening may help you ride better. To do your best riding, you need a flexible spine, knee, foot, and ankle; strong arms, shoulders, abdomen, hip extensors, knee flexors, and foot and ankle extensors.

Stretching should be done before and after riding.

Each stretch should be done slowly with no bouncing or jerky motion. There should be no pain or burning. The beginning stretch lasts for twenty to thirty seconds; gently relax into the position and remember to breathe deeply; during this time the stretch reflexes will relax and the muscles will become more pliable. Next, gently try to further reach in the direction of the stretch for another thirty seconds or more. Strain—a tearing of the muscle fibers—is to be avoided. It is important to understand that a slow gentle approach to stretching reduces the action of the "stretch reflex," which is a tendency for muscles to shorten in response to the stretch lengthening; it is a protective reflex to prevent tearing of the muscle from over-extension, and most active during an unexpected exaggerated motion, such as bouncing. When brought into play, it prevents you from obtaining a maximum stretch and thus maximum flexibility.

The tighter you are, the more you need a stretching program. Set your own goals—people vary a lot in how flexible they are. Many people have one side tighter than the other; always stretch that side first. If you're right-handed and right-legged, that's usually the tighter side, and needs stretching the most.

Strengthening is an important part of cycling conditioning. Body motion results from the coordinated contraction of muscles and/or groups of muscles that flex and extend joints. The contracting muscle that initiates the desired movement is called the agonist. All agonist muscle functions are balanced by counter-acting muscles, the antagonist. Smooth, efficient motion is achieved by the balance of these two functional groups; antagonist muscles control the speed, range, and force of the agonist muscles. An example would be the controlled stretching or relaxation of the hamstrings (knee flexors) as the quadriceps (knee extensors) drive the pedal downward. If the hamstring is too tight (inflexible), or if it stretches too easily (weakness), a tear or a pull will result.

Any sport will produce muscle imbalances. In cycling, the predominant downward thrusting movement leads to dominance of muscles that extend or straighten the hip, the knee, and the ankle joints in either leg. Proper pedaling technique, with spinning and pulling up on the backstroke, decreases this dominance.

Improved muscle strength allows for increased endurance, proper muscle balance, and better riding performance with less soreness, fatigue, and injury.

Dynamic Overload

Dynamic overload describes the muscle strains or tears that can result from suddenly accelerating in a race. The sudden violent contracture of the muscles caused by the tremendous intrinsic structural force that's applied at such a time can tear quadriceps, hamstring, or calf. It's rare in the tourist or noncompetitive cyclist, but it can happen with too high gears, especially in hill-climbing. Flexibility helps prevent it—another good argument for the stretching exercises.

Structural Weaknesses

A lot of people go to the doctor unnecessarily to find out whether they are knock-kneed or their feet are flat. This section is going to tell you how you can find these things out for yourself. No one is perfectly symmetrical, and if you're not having any pain or problem, you do not need any treatment for these conditions. I knew a marathoner who ran heel-to-toe with one foot, and toe-to-heel with the other, but he had no pain. If I'd tried to treat him, I'd have ruined him.

Anatomical variations can be subtle and may be the cause of a painful complaint, so you should become familiar with your own body characteristics if you're having cycling pain that can't be explained by lack of conditioning. There are various foot, leg, and structural weaknesses that can be recognized either by looking in a mirror or by having someone else look at you.

First, stand in front of a mirror, facing forward. Notice whether your feet turn in or out, that is, do you toe in or out? If you place your legs together, is there a space between your knees? You're bow-legged. If your knees touch firmly and there's a space between your ankles, you're knock-kneed. Notice whether you have high arches (cavus foot) or low arches (flat or planus foot); do your ankles roll inward?

When one hip and knee are lower than the other, the two feet will not look the same. A low arch on one foot and a normal or high arch on the other implies a leg-length discrepancy.

A significant number of people involved in athletics have a leg-length discrepancy where one leg is actually shorter or functions shorter than the other. A difference of a half-inch or less usually causes no problems in a person not involved in athletic activities. However, a difference as small as a quarter-inch can sometimes lead to problems in an active person. Anyone with a leg-length differential greater than a half-inch must compensate for it when involved in cycling. On the other hand, if the cyclist has a limb-length discrepancy a half-inch or less and has no other problems, then the situation is best left alone. Problems that are usually associated with limb-length difference are knee, hip, or low-back pain.

A curvature of the spine will also cause the legs to look unequal. With shoulders level, is one arm longer than the other? Is one kneecap or hipbone higher than the other? These might be clues to curvature of the spine, leg-length difference, or angular deformity, which might affect alignment of the knee, foot, and ankle. Next, turn to the side; is your pelvis tilted forward into a swayback; is your back rounded or hunched? These might increase stress of riding on your spine. Lastly, turn your back to the mirror and study the way your Achilles tendon is inserted into the back of the heel. Is it inserted straight or does it bow in or curve out? Excess in either direction may make your heel hurt.

Structural weaknesses can be significant in transmitting force from the leg to the pedal. The extended leg, like the standing leg, does best with no excess deviation, medial or lateral, to the line of force or weight transmission. Whether treatment is needed depends on the symptoms of the rider and the amount of stress to which his body is exposed. Small leg-length discrepancies or flat feet or knock-knees may only become a problem at the touring level of participation. Until then, it would be wrong to treat them.

When injuries occur only on one side of the body, think of limb-length problems.

If you have a leg-length problem, how do you measure how great a differential you have? If pants are altered, must one leg be made shorter than the other? If not, lie on your back on a flat surface and have the protruding portion of the hipbones marked with an X. Use a tape measure to measure the distance from the right hipbone to the inside of the right anklebone and vice versa for the left limb. Then measure the distance from the navel to the inside of the right ankle and the navel to the inside of the left ankle. Repeat the same measures standing up. Obviously there should be no difference between the two limbs.

If the measurements are different on lying and standing because one foot has a lower arch and the other has a normal or higher arch, then this is probably a functional limb-length discrepancy and the correction should be made by utilizing an arch support in the shorter limb or the limb with the flatter foot.

A similar discrepancy in both sitting and standing measurements suggests a structural difference in the limbs, and that correction should be made by using a sole raise. You or a shoemaker should glue an extra sole to the bottom of your cycling shoe. If a lot of walking is done in your cycling shoes, you may want to carry an extra shoe or build up both the heel and the sole.

Since more time is spent in your everyday shoes than in your cycling shoes, all shoes must be corrected. In walking shoes, correction should be made in the heel.

To make a heel raise, take some felt a quarter inch thick, cut it the shape of your heel, thin (skive) it down so that the front end is thinner than the back, and place it in the heel of the shoe with the shorter limb. More than one heel raise may be needed. Double check by putting the heel raises in your shoes and measure that the limb-length discrepancy has been corrected.

Common Cycling Faults Leading to Injury

These fall into two categories: static—caused by improper equipment or cycle fit; and dynamic—caused by improper riding technique.

Cycle Fit

A properly fitted bike is designed to establish and maintain a series of bio-mechanical relationships:

1. The foot and knee circle in a plane parallel to the bike frame.
2. The knee is directly above the pedal axis at the midpoint of the power stroke.
3. The leg is extended, but the knee is not locked at the bottom of the stroke. The hips remain parallel to the ground.

Failure to maintain these relationships, either because of improperly fitted equipment or skeletal problems can lead to pain and/or loss of efficiency. Improper frame sizing, seat height, foot pedal alignment, and handlebar adjustment can all contribute to injury.

Bicycle frames should be proportional to the rider. The rider should be able to straddle the top tube and raise the bike a half inch without making contact with the crotch. One method to measure height is to measure crotch-to-floor with feet slightly spread apart, and use two thirds of this measurement as the frame size. The importance of a proper size frame cannot be overemphasized. Straddle injuries to the perineum while coming off the seat or slipping off the pedals, as well as during mounting and dismounting, are painful results of a too-large frame; more subtle are the problems of improper arm positioning with extension of the elbows, too forward a lean, or excess curvature of the back to reach the handlebar. Knee injury results from overextension on too large a frame and excessive flexion on too small a frame.

Unfortunately, small frames are not always available, and every size isn't available in every make. You should aim to fit the bike to your measurements, not yourself to a bike you happen to want. Be careful! A patient came to us with hamstring strain and bursitis of the ischia. Her use of a new larger frame for a distance ride had resulted in overstretching her hamstrings and hip extensors.

Seat adjustment includes four variables: height, tilt angle, front-to-back position, and intra-seat tension. Differences as small as a quarter inch may matter a great deal in all of these. Begin by sitting on the bicycle wearing shoes you plan to cycle in. Place your heel on the pedal, with the pedal at the bottom of the stroke. The ankle should be at a neutral position, with the sole of the foot parallel to the floor. Assume a normal riding position, hips square and comfortable and arms on the handlebar with elbow slightly bent. The leg should be almost fully extended with the pedal at the bottom position, but the knee should not be locked.

Improper seat height influences all parts of the body. Too high a seat results in overextension of the knee, which causes the patella to be pulled out of the femoral groove of the femur. This loss of channeling plus the angular pull of the muscles on the kneecap, combined with any angular deformity such as knock-knee, will definitely result in pain. In addition, increased flexion-extension of the ankle will be required, placing additional stresses on it. Placing the seat too low causes excessive flexion of the leg, which places excessive pressure on the sides of the knee, and can lead to softening of the cartilage, progress to fracturing of the kneecap, and end in degenerative arthritis.

Correct front-to-back adjustment is just as important in avoiding injury. The center of the pedal should be almost directly under the knee at its most forward position. In no case should the knee be farther forward than that, though tourists could have it be as much as two fingers farther back. One way to measure this is to place the crankshaft horizontal to the floor, with the ball of the foot on the pedal; drop a plumb line (piece of string with weight) from the front of the kneecap—it should pass through the axis of the pedal spindle. Forward of this point increases knee flexion and so the force on the patello-femoral joint; backward placement allows greater extension thrust with increased muscle stress.

Because the seat-tube is at an angle, raising the seat automatically moves it backward, while lowering it moves it forward.

Seat tilt angle can also be regulated, using a ruler as a guide. The seat should usually be absolutely level, but some men prefer a very slight upward tilt, most women level or very slightly downward. Improper tilt can result in painful impingement on the pubic bone or on the genitalia. It can lead to urethritis, scrotal contusion, prostatitis, and penile numbness. Excessive downward tilt also adds pressure to the hands, while excessive upward tilt causes a sliding backward on the seat, producing friction that can result in saddle boils.

Saddle shape should support the ischia and pelvic bones without causing impact injury. Intra-saddle tension can control this to some degree; also, in time, a good saddle molds itself to the rider's shape. If body weight is light, this may not happen, and the saddle must be broken in artificially.

During the power phase of a spin cycle, the forces on the weight-bearing leg may exceed four to six times body weight. This weight is transmitted by the lever of the foot to the spindle and pedal. A rigid lever helps distribute this force over the entire foot. For this reason, cycling shoes are inflexible and often reinforced with a steel or synthetic shank in the sole. We strongly recommend their use. For a more thorough discussion, read the last part of the *Sites of Injury* section.

The most efficient foot-pedal contact requires the ball of the foot to be placed over the axis of the spindle. Slight variations (within a millimeter or two) are not critical in terms of injury. Toeclips or cleats hold the foot in this position without strain, but care must be taken that they not place an artificial constraint to side-to-side placement of the foot.

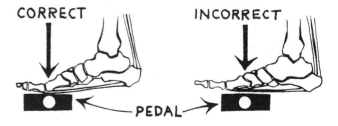

CORRECT   INCORRECT

←PEDAL→

In our experience, if an individual rider has a natural out-toed gait on standing, then to impose an unnatural in-toed position (as is often recommended) has been associated with a marked increase in painful syndromes, especially at the knee.

Check standing alignment of the foot as follows: Walk or run in place for a minute or two; stop in a relaxed position with the legs slightly apart. Notice whether the foot faces straight forward or toes in or out. Permit the toeclip or cleat to hold each foot in its individual natural position. Many ride without cleats until a wear pattern is established on the riding shoe and use this as a guide for alignment. When pain occurs, no rule is invariable, and *slight* adjustments in alignment may be helpful and should be tried. Proper alignment cannot be determined by sitting in a chair and noticing which way your feet point; a reading of the section on knee injury will make this clear.

Upper Body Placement

Once the seat is at the correct height, the stem must be adjusted to assure that the top of the body can reach the handlebars (and the brakes!) comfortably. This usually means no more than a forty-five degree forward lean. This is no problem on a 3-speed. On 10-speeds, it may be. Stems can be raised and lowered and come in different lengths. Racers generally have the stem as much as two inches below the level of the seat because this cuts wind resistance. It also places a strain on the neck, back, and arms if you have to raise your head to look forward. Most racers are young and supple and strong; they pull on the handlebars and develop the strength to maintain this position. Back flexibility often decreases with age, so most older riders should have the stem level with the seat. Women, whose upper-body strength is usually less than men's and who also want to avoid pressure on the front of the genitalia, may have the stem as much as two inches higher. However, make sure this leaves an inch and a half of stem inside the headset.

Handlebars must be wide enough to permit easy breathing, but not so wide that the arms splay out; for men this means bars the width of the shoulders; women's bars should be relative to chest width.

Dropped handlebars are recommended because they permit a variety of hand placements and body positions, depending on whether the hands are on the tops of the bars, on the brake-handle levers, on the drops, or in some in-between position. This variation in hand placement and body positioning gives relief and comfort during a long ride.

In the "rest positions," the hands are placed centrally on the top or to the sides of the bar, the trunk and spine flexed no more than forty-five degrees forward from the hip. Position two, common both during touring and racing, has the hands on the brake levers. This decreases wind resistance and thus energy consumption and stress on the legs. However, because it increases body flexion, it requires more flexibility in the neck and may be uncomfortable for riders with conditions of the spine that prevent easy forward flexion or neck extension. Such riders must totally avoid the third basic position, with the hands in the drops, even though it offers the least wind resistance. In hill climbing, a pull back on the handlebar adds efficiency; this can be accomplished from position two either seated or standing on the pedals out of the seat.

Riding Technique

Commonly the beginning cyclist will err in favor of too high a gear ratio with a slow spin. This not only prolongs the period of stress upon the lower extremity during each individual spin, but also vastly increases the torque upon the hip, knee, and ankle. This tendency is parallel to the tendency of the beginning runner to overstride and to push off too vigorously. This error in technique will result in increased overuse injuries in the lower extremities, muscle soreness, and knee pain. The experienced cyclist rarely spins at a rate below seventy-five or above one hundred revolutions per minute and will favor a lower gear selection under average riding conditions. The cure for

high gear injury is low gear selection and less ankling.

When traversing rough terrain, the experienced rider learns to cushion the shock by holding the handlebars firmly but not tightly, and by posting off the saddle very much as in riding a horse. This way the muscles of his legs act as springs to absorb the jarring impact, and this helps avoid impact injuries to the seat, the palms of the hands, and the feet, as well as reducing shock to the spine and knees.

A rider may have an asymmetrical riding habit due to leggedness, which often follows handedness. This can result in stressing one side of the body over the other. Some doctors advocate strengthening the weaker leg, while others feel that the problem cannot be corrected and should not be interfered with. Eventually the dominant leg tires because it is working the hardest, and the nondominant leg then picks up the workload. Therefore the actual significance to the cyclist is questionable. We have not seen leggedness cause a significant problem in the cyclist.

If you are not a conditioned athlete, never ride or work yourself excessively more than three days of the week and never two days in a row. This has been mentioned in the section on overuse, but bears repeating here.

If Pain Occurs

This section will help to guide you in both self-diagnosis and treatment. Combined with the section on specific sites of pain, it will help you decide whether to continue cycling activity, and clarify when medical advice could be useful.

The first step in evaluating pain is to attempt to classify its severity and character. There are four grades of athletic pain, each characterized by a specific pain pattern and by a general treatment guide.

Classifying Pain

Grade I Pain. There is no limitation of motion—therefore no great change in routine is required other than a more thorough warmup, with stretching and strengthening exercises. If there is a low-grade pain at the start that decreases as the ride progresses, work past the pain in a low gear before undertaking heavy speed or hill work. This kind of pain is the common experience of the beginner and the person starting to cycle after a layoff; it is relieved by a gradual increase in speed and distance, and an every-other-day cycling program.

Grade II Pain. There is little effect on riding form. Eliminate the activity that causes pain to increase, such as races, hard hill work, or very long rides. If pain is constant or increases as the ride goes on, check clothes, shoes, and bike for fit and alignment. This kind of pain requires reducing intensity, frequency, and duration, as permanent injury could result if the cause of the pain is not discovered and eliminated.

Grade II Pain. There is mild pain on an easy ride, and severe pain on a hard ride, with disturbance of riding form. Start slowly and cautiously; when pain builds to a form-disturbing level, gear down or do stretching exercises. Limited rest is indicated—from seven to ten days. This type of pain implies the beginning of structural breakdown, so a thorough checking for causes in the "Common Sites Of Injury" section of this chapter is indicated.

Grade IV Pain. It is impossible to ride without great pain. The body is undergoing a significant breakdown problem. Examples are a severe patello-femoral or chondromalacia pain of the knee, or a fulminant Achilles tendonitis. Rest must be part of the formula for recovery; extended rest, from three to six weeks. Often an aerobic alternative, such as swimming or walking, can be done to allow cardiovascular benefits to be maintained while the cyclist recovers from his injury. According to Dr. Kenneth Cooper, a quarter mile of swimming or two-and-a-half miles of walking are the equivalent of cycling for five miles.

Joint Problems

There are also five criterions for a "sound joint": (1) Full motion, (2) no instability, (3) no swelling, (4) no warmth, and (5) no persistent pain. If any of them are not met, medical attention should be sought.

Conditions that respond rapidly to rest or changes in riding pattern suggest overuse as the underlying cause. (This should alert the rider to analyze his riding habits.) Pain that is not affected by rest and is present with other activities is more serious and may imply an anatomic lesion or some other problem unrelated to cycling and coincidental to or aggravated by cycling stress. Such complaints deserve medical attention when they are not responding to the measures described in this chapter.

Inflammatory Syndromes

For all inflammatory syndromes (bursitis, tendonitis, strain) local ice applied for fifteen to thirty minutes immediately after riding is helpful. Always warm a chronic condition *before* riding (i.e., liniments, stretch, massage). Buffered aspirin (two tablets) a half-hour before riding may reduce pain or swelling; however, the authors do not recommend more than four adult aspirin a day for longer than three days, due to the high risk of gastrointestinal bleeding. If these measures fail to help, seek professional evaluation.

Muscle Cramps

Muscle cramps are spasms that occur in the calf, thigh, or foot and are fairly common among athletes in general. Cyclists are certainly prone to this problem. The most common treatment for a cramp entails applying pressure to the involved muscle and slowly trying to take it through a normal range of motion. For a calf cramp: Sit down and grab the calf with one hand while pulling the top of the foot toward your face with the other. Hold this position until the cramp is released. Buffered aspirin as recommended for inflammatory syndromes and a gentle massage once or twice a day after the cramp has occurred are indicated. If a cramp occurs while on a ride or a tour and you want to continue riding that day, it would be a good idea to wrap the involved area with an Ace bandage. If the cramps tend to be repetitive or chronic, the problem may be due to a structural weakness as described earlier in this chapter. If you feel it is possible that your arches are flattening out too much or your ankles are rolling in too much, an arch support may be helpful.

Do not overlook metabolic imbalance as a cause. In hot weather, or whenever sweating a great deal, water and increased dietary salt and potassium are needed. Racers traditionally stock up on bananas, oranges, and pretzels. Salt tablets are not recommended as they provide too much replacement or are not assimilated by the body at all.

Sites of Injury and Their Treatment
(Neck, Shoulder, Hand, Back, Hips, Knee, Lower Leg, Foot)

Neck

Neck discomforts are not uncommon in both the beginning cyclist and in the middle-aged or older cyclist. In the beginning cyclist, wearing head protection that may weigh one to two pounds is an added aggravation to the postural stress to the cervical spine of riding a 10-speed. The normal cervical spine has a gentle lordosis, which is acquired during infant years when the head is first held upright while crawling. The structures that are important in supporting the weight of the head are the paracervical muscles and the powerful posterior interspinous ligaments. Both of these structures can suffer from overuse during the conditioning phase of cycling, but this neck pain will lessen with increased cycling. A more upright position makes it easier for the rider to control the weight of the head. If riding continues to aggravate the neck, it must be stopped to allow healing, and when riding is resumed, be resumed gradually enough to permit conditioning to take place without undue stress. In the middle-aged and older cyclist, a different type of neck pain sometimes appears – a dull aching between the shoulder blades and over the top of the shoulders, accompanied by tingling or numbness into the fingers and occasional weakness in the upper extremities. This pain is aggravated by neck motion and may be preceded by a whiplash-type injury in an auto accident. X-rays will show the onset of cervical degenerative arthritis involving the small joints in the cervical spine or the degeneration of the small masses of soft tissue that cushion the vertebrae of the spine known as the cervical discs. This results in pain on hyperextension of the neck and holding it in the riding position. Paravertebral muscle spasm will often result in response to the pain, causing further problems. If there is nerve root compression, there may be intractable pain in the arms plus a numbness in the hands, and even an inability to hold the handlebar well. Cervical arthritis requires medical attention for control. It is commonly advocated for such conditions to use an anti-inflammatory such as aspirin or some of the stronger medications such as Butazolidin or Indomethacin to control the arthritic symptoms. Physical therapy that includes cervical traction may also be useful. Helmet mirrors to reduce the need to turn the head while riding are of great help. A brace or soft collar can be used when not riding. It has not been shown, on the other hand, that life-long riding produced cervical arthritis.

Shoulder, arms, and elbow

The shoulders are most vulnerable in those sports that require circumduction and rotatory motions such as the throwing sports. Cycling requires a fairly stationary posture to the shoulder and therefore complaints are fewer. Previously existing conditions such as bursitis, arthritis, or tendonitis of the shoulder may be aggravated by the fixed posture of the rider, although minor adjustments usually bring relief. Occasionally the

Treatment Chart

TISSUE	INJURY	DESCRIPTION	FIRST AID	LATER TREATMENT	TIME OUT
Skin	Abrasion	Surface scratch without penetration of all layers; often dirty and contaminated.	Clean: soap and water. Apply an antiseptic and sterile dressing.	Observe for infection.	1-10 days
Skin	Blister	Superficial layers separated by fluid.	Cool compress, sterile drainage, compressive dressing.	Remove cause, lubricate with Vaseline.	1-7 days
Skin	Callus, Corn	Skin thickened from friction or pressure.	Trim excess skin, pad around lesions to relieve pressure.	Keep pressure off with pads, arch supports, and/or avoiding certain types of shoes.	1-2 days
Skin	Laceration or Puncture	Laceration is a separation by sharp instrument. Puncture is penetrating-object wound.	Clean, control bleeding with ice and compression.	Possible PC to suture edges. Watch for infection.	1-3 weeks
Soft Tissue	Contusion	Bruising of underlying tissue often with infiltration of blood.	Cold, compression, immobilize for 24-48 hours.	Protect from further injury. Local heat, immobilization, rest. Evaluate extent. Possible PC.	1-4 weeks
Soft Tissue	Hematoma	Pooled blood in a restricted area.	Cold, compression, immobilize for 24-48 hours. Possible PC.	Protect against further bleeding. Evacuate blood. Heat, rest, protect until healed. Possible PC.	1-6 weeks
Tendon	Strain	From minor irritation to actual tear or rupture.	Rest, ice, compression, elevation. Often PC.	Evaluate extent. Heat, rest; protect from movements that irritate. Often PC, possible immobilization.	4-6 weeks
Tendon	Tendonitis	Inflamed tendon sheath or tissue around it.	Rest, ice, possibly immobilize for 24-48 hours.	Heat; prevent irritation. Possible PC.	2-6 weeks
Ligaments	Sprain	From a stretch to partial tear, to complete tear.	Rest, ice, compression, elevate, immobilize for 24-48 hours.	Heat; protect from further injury. Possible PC and immobilization.	2-6 weeks
Muscle	Cramp	Sudden involuntary contraction from diminished blood supply and/or fluid imbalance.	Local pressure, guidance through a normal range of motion; then gentle massage.	Depends on cause. A blow: protect from further injury. Overuse: prevent, maintain good muscle balance and flexibility. Fluid imbalance: banana, orange, dietary salt.	Brief
Muscle	Pull or Strain	From stretch to partial tear to complete tear.	Rest, ice, compression; elevate, immobilize for 24-48 hours.	Heat; protect from further injury. Possible PC and immobilization.	2-4 weeks
Nerve	Neuritis	Injury from trauma or impingement of adjacent bones or tissues.	Heat, rest. Relieve impingement if possible. Trauma: protect.	Prolonged relief of impingement; protect from further injury. Possible PC if no relief after several days.	2-3 weeks
Soft Tissue: Bursa	Bursitis	Inflamed fluid-filled sac.	Protect from trauma, compression bandage.	Eliminate irritating factors. Possible PC.	2-6 weeks
Joint	Dislocation	Displacement of bones in a joint.	Rest, ice, immobilize. PC help.	Immobilize to prevent further injury; tape, elastic support; PC.	2-6 weeks
Cartilage	Chondromalacia	Thinning and softening, often under kneecap.	Rest, ice, restrict movement.	Eliminate or compensate for cause of stress. Often PC needed.	2-8 weeks
Bone	Periostitis	Inflamed bone covering.	Rest, ice, compression, immobilization.	Eliminate or compensate for cause of stress. Often PC needed.	1-2 weeks
Bone	Stress Fracture	Cracks from overuse, jarring.	Rest, ice, compression, support. PC.	Minimize movement. PC advised.	2-6 weeks
Bone	Complete Fracture	Complete break.	PC diagnosis, proper alignment, immobilization.	Immobilization. PC guidance, checking.	4 weeks- 6 months

202   PC = Professional Care

narrowness of a handlebar will create a hunched posture and lead to discomfort. The upper arm and elbow are vulnerable to impact if handlebar and seat alignment do not allow flexion of the arms to accept the shock from the ground. Strength conditioning will help. If pain persists despite adjustment in position, medical attention is required for further evaluation.

Hand

Hand numbness is a well-recognized complaint of the high-mileage cyclist. It may involve only the little finger and the ring finger or the whole hand. It is caused by the pressure of the hand against the handlebar and is an impact injury, a peripheral neuropathy involving a motor branch of the ulnar nerve as it passes from the wrist into the hand. Damage to this sensory and motor nerve results in both numbness and loss of the ability to bring the little finger close to the ring finger. Proper prevention is the most important recommendation; cycling gloves with adequate padding of the palm as well as handlebar padding prevent the pressure on the nerve from occurring. The median nerve is another major nerve to the hand that can be

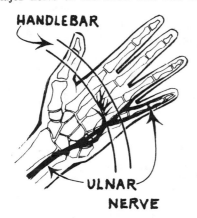

involved by a similar mechanism. Prevention is also the best treatment for this problem. Once weakness in the little finger or in the ability to pinch has developed, it may not improve. The second riding position, with the hand on the brake handles, may contribute to the development of this condition, especially on rough roads, due to the direct contact of the outer border of the palm with the handlebar. Frequent changing of grip position is very important on long rides.

Lower back

Despite an occasional backache occurring after a long ride, many cyclists find relief and relaxation of tension-aggravated back ailments because of the reversal of the lordosis and the flexed posture required during cycling. Sports activities that cause serious back injury encourage forced hyperextension (such as gymnastics) or hyperflexion with impact (such as

football). Nevertheless, leaning far forward over the handlebars for a long time will reverse the normal lordosis and place a burden on the supporting muscles of the lower lumbar vertebrae. This can result in muscle spasm or a dull aching back pain, usually without any radiation into the legs. It can be cured by stretching before the ride, adjustment in posture during it, and local heat and rest after it.

More serious backache implies either the aggravation of a pre-existing condition, such as degenerative arthritis or a disc injury. Disc injury with nerve root compression invariably will be signaled by pain that extends well below the knee, often to the calf or foot. This may be accompanied by numbness or a feeling of weakness in the involved extremity, although it can be as subtle as a dull aching pain in the buttock or hip. It is not responsive to rest or simple measures, will produce a marked limp in many cases, and be so painful that medical attention will be sought. The axial compression to the vertebral spine while riding, although it is not as jarring as may be experienced in jogging or running, can be significant over rough terrain and may aggravate such a condition. Conditioning of the back is the best method of treatment and includes gradual abdominal strengthening exercises, working toward bent knee situps to give front support to the vertebral column and a stretching program to alleviate the muscle spasm of the ilio-lumbar muscles. Although braces or corsets can be prescribed, it is the authors' experience that they are rarely needed for the average cyclist.

Normally, the skin over the hip joint and buttock will move up and down nearly two inches as the cyclist shifts body weight to the power leg.

A seat set too high or low will exaggerate this excursion leading to pronounced side bending at the lumbosacral junction, as well as shearing stress at the sacroiliac joints. This excessive rocking motion will also lead to saddle irritation.

Buttocks and hips

The buttocks, and specifically the ischial portion of the pelvic ring, provide the main support of body weight on the saddle. All riders experience some saddle discomfort. This is especially true of the tourist or beginning rider who assumes a more upright posture than the racer. The female pelvis can be 1-1/8 inches wider than the male's and will require a more contoured support to the saddle for optimum comfort. Impact on the ischia may result in ischial bursitis, which is an inflammation of the small anatomic fluid-filled sacs that are natural cushions over these bony prominences, and the complication of calcific bursitis can also occur. In most riders, seat impact does not lead to such advanced conditions,

and once the beginning period of "saddle soreness" abates and the saddle is broken in, problems become infrequent. During touring distances, saddle boils, which are true cutaneous boils resulting from friction and irritation of glands in the skin with subsequent infection, can result or be aggravated by poor saddle fit and impact on the skin, as well as friction. This can be prevented by the use of pants with a chamois lining, perhaps lubricated with an antibiotic or Vaseline-type ointment to assure a gentle surface of contact between the skin and the supporting saddle. If severe inflammation occurs (ischial bursitis), pain can be palpated on the hard bone at the base of the buttock and sitting will be most uncomfortable. Anti-inflammatory medications, warm soaks, and an occasional cortisone injection may be helpful in controlling this condition. Prevention and lasting improvement is made by improved conditioning and a proper seat adjustment.

Crotch

Crotch numbness has been recorded in touring cyclists. This may involve both the scrotum and the penis and seems to be aggravated by hill climbing and by placing pressure on cutaneous nerves to the genital area. A case of ischemic neuropathy of the penis has been reported in the male rider.

Hip

The hip can be vulnerable to overuse specifically with regard to the greater trochanter and the hipbone and the iliotibial band which runs to below the knee. The iliotibial band is a broad fascial structure, which originates from the iliac crest on the outer side of the pelvis and is an extension of the tendons of the tensor fascialata outside of the legs, and the gluteus maximus muscle of the buttocks. The band runs as a distinct structure along the side of the leg, and inserts on the side of the tibia below the knee. It acts as a tension band and provides a counter-pull to the weight of the body when the rider shifts weight onto the

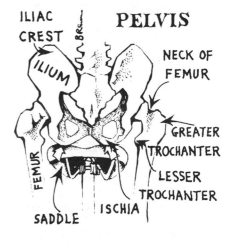

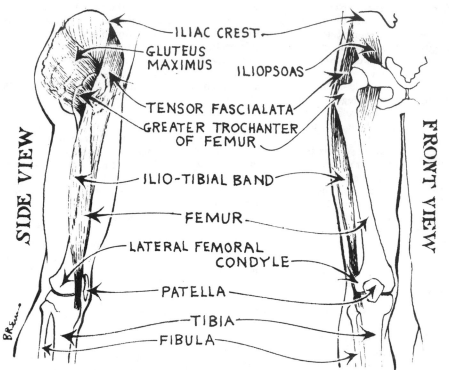

SIDE VIEW

- ILIAC CREST
- GLUTEUS MAXIMUS
- ILIOPSOAS
- TENSOR FASCIALATA
- GREATER TROCHANTER OF FEMUR
- ILIO-TIBIAL BAND
- FEMUR
- LATERAL FEMORAL CONDYLE
- PATELLA
- TIBIA
- FIBULA

FRONT VIEW

BREnn

ments that cross and support the knee, it has two cushions of cartilage known as menisci, or semi-lunar cartilages because of their half moon shape, which act as shock absorbers and stabilizers between the femoral and tibial articular surfaces.

However, the site of concern and interest to the cyclist is not this femoral-tibial articulation, but rather the unique and highly stressed patello-femoral articulation, which works in cooperation with the quadriceps muscle and the infra-patella tendon to power extension of the knee itself. The kneecap is a bone located in the substance of the quadriceps tendon, which serves the mechanical purpose of augmenting by fifty percent the power of the quadriceps muscle. It accomplishes this by displacing forward the fulcrum of action of the quadriceps tendon. The patella itself is keel shaped with two main faces or facets, the medial and lateral facet, in addition to smaller facets that come into contact with the femoral articular surface during

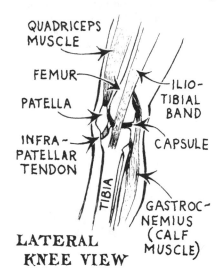

- QUADRICEPS MUSCLE
- FEMUR
- PATELLA
- INFRA-PATELLAR TENDON
- ILIO-TIBIAL BAND
- CAPSULE
- TIBIA
- GASTROC-NEMIUS (CALF MUSCLE)

LATERAL KNEE VIEW

power pedal at mid-spin. It passes over a prominence of the femur, or thighbone, known as the greater trochanter. The greater trochanter can be palpated at the prominent bony bulge at the level of the groin on the outer side of the hip. Pain may occur in the form of point tenderness over this bony prominence and may represent either an inflammation of the lubricating tissue sac (bursa), which protects this bony prominence from the abrasion of the iliotibial band, or may result from a frictional irritation of the iliotibial band itself as it passes forward and backward over the trochanter during the raising and lowering of the hip in cycling. Occasionally this will produce a "snapping hip" syndrome, which will be recognized by a clicking sensation as the hip is carried through the pedal cycle. Greater trochanteric bursitis is an explosive painful condition, which not only inhibits cycling, but which also inhibits walking. A pronounced limp as well as severe pain will demand medical attention. Treatment involves potent anti-inflammatory medications and in the authors' experience, it is very effectively treated by local cortisone injection. Ilio-tibial band tendonitis is helped by a stretching program as well as by icing the local area immediately after cycling, then using local heat, and when all else fails, an extended period of rest, which may be longer than four to six weeks. This is an overuse condition that is brought on by overtraining or overriding and is relieved best by corrections in the level of riding.

It is a striking characteristic of the cyclist that hip flexibility is well preserved. Cyclists can often externally rotate or toe out almost ninety degrees at the hip. This is allowed primarily by the periarticular ligaments and capsule being stretched as well as, in the authors' opinion, the iliopsoas muscles. The iliopsoas is the most powerful hip flexor and also a strong external rotator of the leg. Its use in cycling is difficult to assess as it lies deep in the root of the leg and pelvis. In running sports the iliopsoas becomes overstrengthened and shortens, placing increased lordotic stress on the lumbar spine as well as limiting internal rotation of the leg. In theory the cyclist produces the same stress response to a lesser degree and may develop backache due to tightness or spasm of the psoas after a hard ride. In stretching, the iliopsoas should not be overlooked.

Knee

The knee is by far the most common site of complaints and worries for the cyclist. It is the largest joint in the human body and truly a strange and perilous structure; strange because of the complexity of its anatomy, and perilous because of the high incidence of injury or pain in almost all leg-dependent sports, much of which appears very puzzling to both the injured athlete and his physician.

The knee is often described as a modified hinge joint, which slides or glides while it flexes and extends around a moving instant center of rotation in the thighbone. It is formed by the junction of four bones, the thighbone, or femur, the kneecap, or patella, and the two bones of the lower leg, the larger tibia, and the smaller side bone, or fibula. In addition to the multitude of muscles and liga-

the course of knee flexion and extension. The compressive force upon the patello-femoral articulation is increased as the knee flexes and decreased as the knee extends. During knee extension, no contact between the patella and femur takes place and the patella rides above the groove in the femur. As knee flexion progresses, an increasing band of surface contact involving the medial and lateral facets of the patella distributes the pressure across the patello-femoral joint. Patello-femoral contact begins at ten to twenty degrees of flexion and increases in area to ninety degrees of flexion and then begins to decrease in area. It is important to note that the range of motion of the knee during cycling, which averages from twenty to 110 degrees of flexion, places the patella in constant contact with the femur and under constant pressure, often at high load. As the knee bends, this pressure becomes six times greater than at knee extension.

Another important feature of knee function is the "law of valgus." It has been noted by several investigators that there is a definite "Q" or quadriceps angle that normally does not exceed fifteen degrees formed by the quadriceps and the infrapatellar tendon. This is a result of normal leg alignment and is a characteristic most highly developed in animals that walk on their hind legs. It allows for the line of support to more closely approach the center of gravity of the body when weight is shifted onto the extended leg. In cycling, this occurs when the power leg extends and the pedal is at its lowest point. This characteristic of normal leg alignment produces a resultant outward pull on the patella, which can exceed tolerable limits if there is distortion in the shape of the patella, the shape of the femur, or a pronounced knock-knee deformity. Such findings combined with the force overload experienced in cycling can produce a variety of patello-femoral injuries.

The balance between the quadriceps and hamstring pull across the knee is important, although not as critical in the cyclist as it is in the running athlete. Hamstring pulls do not occur as frequently because full knee extension does not occur and full stretching of the hamstrings is avoided, unless the cyclist rises out of the saddle and stands on the pedals, as in hill climbing. Nevertheless, tightness in the hamstrings will create a counter force that the quadriceps must overcome during the power phase of the pedal stroke, and this will add to the work of the quadriceps with increased fatigue as well as force on the patello-femoral joint.

The dramatic knee injury of the field athlete with ligament damage or cartilage tears is not often experienced by the cyclist except as a result of a fall. The mechanisms of injury in the cyclist knee involves combinations of overuse, structural weakness, and muscle imbalances, which primarily affect the patello-femoral joint.

The diagnosis "cyclist's knee" is in reality a variety of pain syndromes, some difficult to evaluate even with professional help and many of which produce overlapping qualities of pain. A knee pain common to the beginner is insertional strain of the quadriceps on the patella as well as infrapatellar tendon strain. This is heralded by a dull aching located vaguely over the front of the knee, often with palpable tenderness at the upper outer border of the patella; it is readily relieved by rest and aggravated by excessive riding. This is a microtrauma of conditioning that the body seems capable of recovering from without totally stopping riding, and often represents a Grade I pain syndrome. It is *not* accompanied by knee swelling, is

likely to be bilateral, will last only a few days after riding, but will be aggravated by bending the knee while sitting or stair climbing. This type of knee condition can be self-treated and recognized by the grading of the pain, as well as the lack of swelling and the rapid recovery, with progressive decrease in its incidence as conditioning improves. An every-other-day riding program is recommended for treatment of this syndrome.

Infrapatellar tendonitis is a more pronounced overload or overuse syndrome of the tough tendon that connects the kneecap to the tibia. There will be tenderness over this structure or at the lower pole of the patella. It is a condition related to "jumpers knee" in basketball and will respond to a combination of rest, oral anti-inflammatory medication, local ice after exercise, and an attempt to spin smoothly rather than push high gears. Braces are now available that spare stress across the infrapatellar tendon and decrease the stress on this structure. These can be provided by an orthopedist.

A related condition that results from overstress of the quadriceps mechanism is retropatellar tendon bursitis, which produces a pain described as "below the kneecap." This bursa lies behind the patellar tendon insertion on the tibia and normally protects the tendon from abrasion against the tibial plateau as the knee goes into flexion. It is difficult to palpate the area of tenderness deep to the tendon, but high torque stress on the knee, such as hill climbing, will definitely produce pronounced pain at this site. This is a condition that may be isolated in the dominant leg. Although it is often said that the infrapatellar tendon will not rupture, persistent or increasing grades of pain in this structure are worrisome to the authors, as one such rupture in an otherwise "healthy athlete" has recently been treated.

A common, but until only recently unrecognized, syndrome producing patello-femoral pain is the excessive lateral pressure syndrome (ELPS). This condition is produced by a variety of circumstances, especially distortion in the natural shape of the patella or excessive knock-knee or foot pronation and increased Q-angle in the quadriceps alignment. This results in excessive side force on the side of the patella and leads to a spectrum of changes that includes softening of the cartilage surface, progresses to fracturing of the margin of the patella, and can end in degenerative arthritis. It is characterized by pain during flexion of the knee that is most prominent over the outer aspect of the patella and may be accompanied by some swelling. The diagnosis depends primarily on identifying the structural characteristics of the rider and on obtaining an X-ray that shows the profile or shape of the

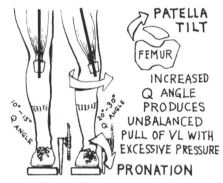

patella in the femoral groove. This view is known as a sunrise, or profile, view of the patella and should be obtained if there is concern regarding the patello-femoral articulation. Often this view will show a tilt of the patella, implying a maldistribution of force. While this is a condition that is brought on by a variety of physical activities, ELPS is being increasingly seen in the knee-flexion sport of cycling.

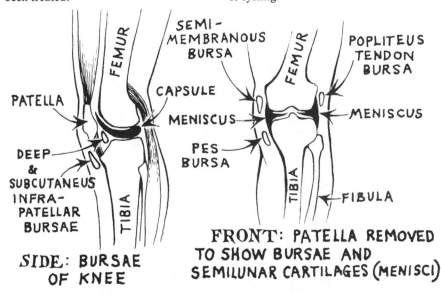

SIDE: BURSAE OF KNEE

FRONT: PATELLA REMOVED TO SHOW BURSAE AND SEMILUNAR CARTILAGES (MENISCI)

Early treatment involves the reduction of stress in the knee by analyzing and changing the static forces across it. Lowering the seat has the effect of increasing patello-femoral force and aggravating this condition. Raising the seat should improve it for most people. Exercises to strengthen the quadriceps, especially the medial or inner portion of its fibers, are one of the mainstays of rehabilitation. It should be emphasized that at no time should bent-knee exercises be prescribed for patello-femoral pain. Isometric exercises in no greater than twenty to thirty degrees of flexion accompanied by straight-leg raises and quad-set exercises are of use. It should be pointed out that although commonly the quadriceps are well conditioned in the cycling athlete, the medial portion of the quadriceps, which is responsible for the last twenty degrees of extension, is not called on to function during the average spin cycle, as the knee never passes the minus twenty degree extension point. For this reason, the vastus medialist oblique may not have a balanced function on the patellar tracking and excursion in the otherwise conditioned leg. Professional help is needed in evaluating serious malalignment of the quadriceps mechanism. Quadriceps angles greater than fifteen

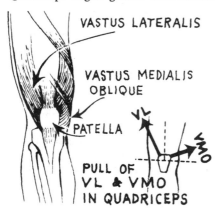

VASTUS LATERALIS

VASTUS MEDIALIS OBLIQUE

PATELLA

PULL OF VL & VMO IN QUADRICEPS

degrees are often refractory to an exercise program. Anti-inflammatory medication may help in controlling the symptoms, but treatment must affect the malalignment of the quadriceps pull. In some situations, surgical treatment is justified and is performed to realign the infrapatellar tendon, thereby decreasing the quadriceps angle; however, too great a realignment can produce worse problems for the rider! Often all that is required is to surgically release the tight ligamentous attachments of the patella on the outer aspect of the kneecap in order to rebalance the forces of pull. This is the simplest surgical treatment and the least likely to have an adverse affect. Nonoperative treatment can include a slip-on knee brace to control the tracking of the patella in the femoral groove during its upward and downward excursion, thereby avoiding the tilting or

tendency to shift out of the groove (called subluxation), which leads to the excessive pressure.

Chondromalacia patella (Chondro = cartilage, malacia = softening) is a much-feared condition that fortunately is rare in cycling. Normal cartilage on the surface of the kneecap, when exposed to excessive pressure as in the ELP syndrome or when injured by a fall onto the front of the knee, will undergo necrosis or cell death, and when exposed to imbalances of pressure or force, will follow a progressive course of softening and eventual degeneration that leads to loss of the normal cartilage surface and eventually the exposure of the bone itself.

When softening of joint cartilage becomes symptomatic, the knee will often make noises that sound like walking on snow. This crunching noise is known as crepitation. It often can be felt rather than heard. Crepitation is a curious finding, which does not always correlate with incapacitating pain or even restriction of cycling performance. It is the authors' impression from treating a great number of cyclists that the majority of distance riders will eventually develop such noises in the knees. Why some of these riders will develop pain and others will remain asymptomatic is not entirely understood.

True chondromalacia patella is a serious condition and one of the few conditions that can end a cyclist's career. The diagnosis of chondromalacia can be inferred by a patella X-ray if advanced. In the early stages, the only accurate assessment is provided by the arthroscope. The arthroscope is an endoscopic tool used by the orthopedic surgeon to look inside the knee without actually making an incision. A small puncture wound made either under local anesthesia or in an operating room setting allows inspection of the patello-femoral surface under direct vision.

The presence of crepitation alone should not be a prohibition to cycling, but may be a warning to analyze the static alignment and dynamic factors of the rider and bike to uncover any circumstances promoting knee wear. A definite source of imposed knee stress can be the improper positon of the foot on the pedal due to toeclip or cleat malalignment. Many times chondromalacia patella is improved by changing the cleat alignment or toeclip angle. Other mechanical causes could be a bent pedal axle or crank, an asymmetrical seat, leg-length imbalance, or even worn shoes.

This emphasizes an additional characteristic of knee joint function known as the screw-home mechanism. The screw-home mechanism refers to the external rotation of the tibia in relation to the femur during the terminal degrees of extension of the knee. This is a stabilizing quality of the knee in extension and

must be provided for when considering foot pedal alignment. With the knee bent in a sitting position, there is a rotational freedom of the tibia, which can be demonstrated by the ease with which the foot can be rotated externally or internally. This freedom of rotation does not exist and becomes progressively controlled as the knee approaches full extension. For this reason, the authors disagree with sitting and noting foot angle to determine cleat placement, and would emphasize the hazard to the patella of imposing a restriction on the screw-home mechanism by forced intoeing of the cleat.

If crepitation of the knee is accompanied by increasing grades of pain and is associated with the symptoms of an unsound joint, then a careful analysis of all knee stress factors must be systematically carried out. Treatment initially includes an anti-inflammatory medication often as potent as Butazolidin or Indomethacin, accompanied by quadriceps conditioning, which is always carried out in a relatively straight-leg position and with an isokinetic or isometric conditioning program. Intra-articular injections of cortisone are highly controversial and in the authors' opinion contraindicated in the young athlete as will be discussed further. The most rewarding treatment for chondromalacia patella will seek to uncover the reason for the force imbalance or mechanical injury to the patello-femoral joint and thereby treat the cause and not the symptom of the condition.

Recently, developments with the arthroscope have allowed patella shaving of the degenerated cartilage surface with some success, although the results in high-stress activity such as cycling are not fully known at this time. The early results in a variety of knee-bending activities are encouraging, although this treatment is no justification for overlooking an obvious malalignment or overstress cause for the condition.

Chronic synovitis of the knee joint is characterized by prominent swelling, warmth, and diffuse pain. The synovium is the lining of the knee joint and the inflammation of this lining results in the production of a vast variety of inflammatory substances and chemicals known as lysomes, which basically pollute the internal environment of the knee joint. Synovitis and its production of harmful inflammatory by-products seems to be promoted by the breakdown products of cartilage wear and chondromalacia. Swelling and warmth are signs of an unsound joint and are never to be regarded lightly. The most common cause of mild synovitis in the cyclist is chondromalacia patella.

When synovitis involves both knees, it is either related to overstress or can in rare instances, especially in the middle aged, be the harbinger of a systemic arthritis such as gout. Systemic arthritis is best evaluated by laboratory tests and an analysis of the fluid acquired by aspiration to search for the crystals of gout.

If swelling occurs in only one knee, after checking for mechanical causes, the cyclist should suspect an injury that can occur on an isolated basis. A torn meniscus, a loose "joint mouse" or fragment of free cartilage, or some other unique tumor or lesion should be considered in the diagnosis. If the cyclist is unable to squat comfortably and bring the knee into flexion past ninety degrees without pain, and there is instability or inability to move the joint to a full range of motion, meniscal injury is highly likely and an arthrogram is indicated. In an arthrogram dye is placed in the knee joint by a radiologist, and the outline of the meniscus with its tear can be seen. An arthroscope is also an acceptable way to make this type of diagnosis. Most loose body fragments can be seen on a regular X-ray of the knee although some are more elusive and require an arthrogram and an arthroscope.

Pain can be localized to the sides of the knee. On the inside of the knee is a bursa known as the pes anserinus bursa, so named for the tendons that pass across this area and form a shape not unlike the web-foot of the goose (pes = foot, anserinus = goose). Palpation will reveal point tenderness that is aggravated by bent-knee exercise and riding, and is often responsive to anti-inflammatory medication or local cortisone injection.

Outside knee pain in the authors' experience is most commonly due to iliotibial band tendonitis caused by frictional irritation as this structure passes across the outer aspect of the femoral condyle. It is responsive to a stretching program, anti-inflammatory medications, rest, and occasional injection. Neither the pes anserinus bursitis or the iliotibial band tendonitis are serious or very frequent causes of pain in the cyclist.

It should be emphasized that the cyclist rarely experiences a torn cartilage due to cycling activity alone. However, many cyclists are also engaged in other athletic activity and may sustain a meniscal injury, which is then exposed by the stress of cycling. These are almost always only in one knee, which is a helpful differential.

Fat pad syndrome refers to a painful syndrome that has been denied by some but is felt to exist in some form, especially in women. The infrapatellar fat pad may be traumatized by a direct blow or impinged between the femoral condyles and tibial plateau during extension of the knee. Palpation of this structure will reveal tenderness. Its treatment is the same as for the other inflammatory conditions that affect the knee such as sy-

novitis, which it is often associated with.

Ligamentous instability of the knee is not caused by cycling. However cyclists with previous ligament injury in other contact sports may experience pain and swelling of the knee during cycling due to derangement of the normal mechanics of the knee with excessive pressure distribution, especially on the patello-femoral joint. Nevertheless, cycling is a more satisfactory exercise for such a knee than the more stressful impact of running. Bracing of the knee can be successful in controlling the symptoms; an operation to stabilize the ligaments will also create a better cycling knee.

Finally, we are left with a condition commonly known as wobbly knee – a darting of the knee either toward or away from the top tube during the pedal revolution. This should not be treated in a cyclist with no other symptoms. The exact mechanics and significance of these peculiar knee motions has not been fully explained. Occasionally, an analysis of the structural characteristics of the rider will reveal excessive ankle pronation, which can be treated according to the recommendations in the section on foot injury.

Thigh

Most of the power that propels a cyclist comes from his leg and thigh muscles. Therefore overuse injuries can occur to these muscles, too. These injuries are usually muscle strains with an actual mini-tear or micro-tear at the muscle tendon connection or the muscle bone junction. As they are gradual in onset, strains may not even show up in the form of pain or swelling until a day or two after the injury actually was sustained. The more serious complete tear of the thigh muscle is very rare in the touring cyclist, but can occur in the racer. It would be accompanied by severe discomfort, swelling, and black-and-blue discoloration, and requires immediate medical attention.

Most muscle strains take between three and six weeks to heal. Depending on the severity, two to seven days of absolute rest from cycling and other athletic activities are needed to control the acute stage of the injury. Place an ice pack on the injured area for the first twenty-four to forty-eight hours. The ice applications will be for periods of thirty minutes with a rest period of at least thirty minutes between renewed applications. Compression by wrapping an Ace bandage around the thigh and anchoring it around the waist is helpful. Elevation of the involved extremity above the level of the heart is also wise for the first twenty-four to forty-eight hours.

Cycling can be resumed when there is little or no pain on walking.

If after forty-eight hours pain is still pronounced, it is not just a simple strain

and you must consider taking several more days off. At this time switch from using regular ice pack applications and elevation to using ice therapy and exercises to help speed up recovery. Ice the injured area for six to ten minutes or until it is numb. Then move the muscles until pain or burning is felt. Even if no pain or burning sensation occurs, stop the exercises after five minutes. Repeat the icing. This entire process is repeated a second time, so that the sequence is ice, exercise, ice, exercise, ice. If the thigh-muscle pull is in the back of the thigh, for example, stretch the hamstring muscle group.

With a problem in the front of the thigh, like a quadriceps injury, lay down on your stomach and for the right quadricep grab the right foot and pull it back as far as possible, trying to touch the buttocks with the bottom of the foot. Hold this for fifteen to thirty seconds and do it two to four times. If there is severe pain or burning, you are stretching too far.

When pain on walking is minimal or nonexistent, then try cycling again. Before cycling, apply a heat-inducing ointment such as Ben-Gay and cover the thigh with an Ace bandage for compression. Warm up gradually and also do a good stretch routine before and after riding. At first avoid all hill climbing, sprinting, and very long distances. If there is any discomfort at all from the ride, ice down for fifteen to thirty minutes afterward. Gradually return to normal cycling distances or routine, using lack of pain as a guide.

If after several weeks of self-treatment and rest, pain is still present, or there is severe swelling or discoloration in the thigh after several days, then visit a sports doctor.

An important complication of muscle tears or injury is myositis ossificans. Damaged muscle may develop deposits of bone. These bony masses are sources of chronic pain and inflammation and can be a serious problem in the hamstrings or quadriceps. Incomplete rest and repetitive reinjury by too early a return to cycling increase the risk of myositis ossificans. While the bone deposits can disappear spontaneously or be surgically excised, the result is not always satisfactory. Prevention by taking muscle tears seriously is the best course. Warmth, swelling, or pain lasting more than two or three weeks may imply the beginning of myositis ossificans.

Lower leg and foot

A serious threat to the unconditioned or overtraining cyclist is a *compartment syndrome*. This is a direct result of overuse of lower leg muscles. The four compartments of the lower leg have only small openings for tendons, nerves, and blood vessels. Strenuous exercise can cause swelling that compresses and obstructs the veins. This is a medical emergency because the circulation of the lower leg is severely compromised and permanent disability and loss of limb can occur. Excruciating pain, swelling, hot red skin, and numbness or partial paralysis of toes, foot, or ankle develop rapidly a few hours after a ride. Never regard these symptoms lightly. Any rider complaining of them should receive immediate hospital evaluation because surgical intervention is required. Treatment is usually surgical release (fasciotomy) of the tight compartment, with complete cure seen a few hours afterward.

The most common injury in the front of the lower leg that occurs to cyclists is *tibial tendonitis.* Anterior tibial tendonitis is characterized by minor tears of the tendon or the muscle as it attaches to the fibula bone in the lower leg and is associated with pain in the front and outside of the lower leg. Posterior tibial tendonitis may be either a minor tear in the muscle complex on the inside of the lower leg or an overstress associated with excessive rolling-in (pronation) in the flat-foot. This will be associated with pain along the inside of the anklebone and even into the inside portion or the inner border of the foot. These conditions can occasionally be overcome without discontinuing cycling, but are typical overuse conditions demanding seven to ten days of rest if persistent.

Initial treatment is twenty-four to forty-eight hours without cycling to control the acute stage, followed by the treatment described for thigh muscles. Daily massage of the involved area is also indicated. Baby oil or lotion will reduce friction and allow proper massage. Use pain as a guide to intensity of pressure. If the area is very tender, ice it down for ten minutes to numb it before massaging.

When you can walk without discomfort, the initial stage is under control and cycling can be resumed. Make certain that cleats or toeclips are placed in the proper position, as improper alignment can lead to *shin splints,* especially on the inside or behind the ankles. In most cases, feet should be lined up straight ahead or in an in-toed position in order to relieve stress in shin splints that occur on the inside of the leg. The opposite would be true for pain or tendonitis along the front or outside of the leg. If your foot flattens out significantly or rolls in at the ankles (pronation), then an arch support inside your cycling shoes would definitely be beneficial. This is especially true for tendonitis on the inner side of the leg or foot. For tendonitis along the outside of the leg or the front of the leg, cycling shoes should be used to relieve stress in the ball of the foot.

Icing after riding is helpful.

Daily massages of the involved leg should be continued in the evenings or before retiring as long as there is discomfort. As with all injuries, a good pre-cycling stretch routine is strongly suggested as well as one following your ride.

The stairs stretch is another exercise that can be helpful here. Stand on your toes at the step of a staircase, holding onto a wall or bannister for support. Lower the heels two times for thirty seconds each time, with each leg.

Lower leg tendonitis problems such as these are often due to a lower leg muscle imbalance; the calf muscles are over-utilized and overpower the muscles in the front of the leg. So, in addition to the stretching exercises described above, exercises to strengthen the front leg muscles – the anterior and posterior tibial muscles and tendons – should be done three times a week. They can be done at any time during the day, not necessarily in conjunction with cycling.

Occasionally, there is some pain at the *peroneal tendons* along the outside of the foot and ankle. This is not very common, but can occur in track riders or anyone who often uses tight toe straps. This puts pressure on the peroneal tendons where they insert into the base of the fifth metatarsal bone. Loosening the toe straps usually solves the problem.

For any of the tendon inflammations just described, professional care, if needed, would usually involve the use of oral anti-inflammatory medications, injections of corticosteroids, and the use of certain physiotherapy modalities. Casting or supportive immobilization of the involved lower leg is very rarely indicated.

Achilles tendonitis is the major ankle injury common to cyclists. It is an irritation and inflammation of the tendon that inserts into the heel bone. It often occurs in middle-aged riders, and is due to overuse – excessive ankling, excessive duration, or using excessive force in hill climbing. Insufficient warmup in colder weather can also be a factor. Swelling is prominent along the course of the tendon, with severe pain on ankle motion.

Rest, ice, and immobilization with a plaster splint for five to seven days, accompanied by strong anti-inflammatory medication (like Butazolidin) are all often needed. Achilles tendonitis is serious; it is disabling, painful, and can be a prelude to rupture. No cycling should be attempted for seven to ten days following lessening of the swelling. If cycling is accompanied by a recurrence of symptoms, double the amount of time taken off before attempting to cycle again.

Ice therapy and passive exercising to stretch out the Achilles tendon should be instituted after the first two days. Ice the Achilles tendon down for five to ten minutes or until numbness occurs. The exercise to do is:

Sit on the floor and extend the legs straight out in front of you; bend the foot toward the head as far as you can. Hold it there for ten seconds; relax. Repeat five to ten times. The same exercise should be repeated pulling against a rope, a towel, or a tie for better leverage.

This injury is often painful even when walking. High-heeled shoes take pressure off the Achilles. A man should try boots, like cowboy boots. If this is not possible, take a quarter-inch piece of felt and cut it to the shape of your heel. Carve it down so that the front end is thinner than the back and put it in the shoe. This has to be done to both shoes to avoid any difference in leg length.

Be wary of returning to cycling without proper healing. The relief of pain does not mean healing has occurred, but merely that the threshold of discomfort is no longer exceeded. In chronic overuse injury such as tendonitis, when injury occurs over several weeks, the body often requires several weeks to repair. Use the pain guide to help assess progress.

Heating the chronic Achilles tendonitis before cycling is often helpful and can be done with a heat-inducing ointment such as Ben-Gay; wear soft socks over it to keep the heat in.

A limp or pain and swelling when walking should be evaluated by a doctor.

Professional treatment will usually involve the use of anti-inflammatory drugs and occasionally immobilization with special strapping, prolonged rest, or rarely, casting. Corticosteroid injections should not be given because they have been shown to weaken the Achilles tendon, which can lead to further damage or rupture when beginning to cycle. Fortunately, rupture is rare, as will be explained shortly.

Remember that excessive ankling or using too much power on the ankles when climbing hills can definitely irritate this problem; therefore, pushing high gears, sprinting, racing, hilly and long-distance rides are definitely contraindicated until the problem is under control. Relief can be obtained and no harm done, except loss of efficiency, by riding with the instep or even the heel on the pedal. You will have to lower the seat a bit to make this possible.

It is interesting to note that normal range of motion at the ankle joint is twenty degrees dorsiflexion (moving the foot and the toes toward the head) and fifty degrees plantarflexion (moving the toes toward the ground). The cyclist's ankle normally ranges from zero to fifteen degrees plantarflexion and he rarely dorsiflexes. So Achilles tendon ruptures or serious Achilles tendon injuries are infrequent in cyclists because the ankle motion does not overstretch the tendon under normal riding conditions. This physiologic protection cannot be relied upon in every case; and rupture requires surgery or prolonged casting (six months).

Calf strain is a partial tear to the posterior muscle group in the lower leg. This is the gastrocnemius, which is used greatly in cycling. Strain is usually characterized by gradual localized pain in the back of the calf, which is sometimes accompanied by black-and-blue discoloration. Initial treatment is basically the same as for Achilles tendonitis. In addition, an Ace bandage is useful for compression and should be wrapped first around the foot for stability, and then wrapped around the leg in an upward direction to support the calf muscle belly all the way up to just below the knee. Ice therapy is also useful. If you have discomfort in walking, then an Ace bandage should be worn whether cycling or not, and the use of a heel raise as described under Achilles tendonitis is also useful here.

Cycling activities can be started once there is no discomfort walking with an Ace bandage and heel raise. For the first week or two, the heel raise and Ace bandage should be used as a precaution. Before cycling, if there is any discomfort, a heat-inducing ointment should be applied to the back of the calf under the Ace bandage. Again good warmup, cycling, plus pre-cycling stretching and post-cycling stretching including wall pushes should all be done. The chronic calf strain problem in a cyclist can also be due to a muscle imbalance; strengthening exercises correct this problem. It is advisable not to go barefooted and not to wear negative-heeled shoes (e.g. Earth Shoes) for everyday use until the problem is completely under control.

Pronation: An abnormal lowering of the arch and an excessive rolling inward of the ankle. This is often a mechanical weakness built into one's foot and leg structure. People with a Morton's foot are particularly prone to it. A Morton's foot can often be recognized by a second toe that is significantly longer than the first one.

Pronation has been linked to various overuse injuries in cyclists and can lead to problems with the knee, lower-leg tendonitis, Achilles tendonitis, in addition to intrinsic foot pain.

A simple solution is a Spenco inlay. It can be purchased in a sporting goods store or cycling shop and is a friction-resistant inlay that is fit to your shoe size. Place the Spenco inlay against your foot with the bottom facing the floor, then take an eighth inch to a quarter inch of felt, fill in the arch area, and extend it all the way up to the big toe. This inlay can then be moved from shoe to shoe but should especially be used when cycling. Cyclists sometimes prefer putting a wedge on the pedal itself, between the pedal and the bottom of the shoe. If you continue to have problems despite your homemade compensation, then visit a sports podiatrist to be fitted for a spe-cially-made arch support called an orthotic. This often allows the feet and legs to act more efficiently, cuts down on injury, and increases your performance levels.

Numbness: Foot numbness is a common problem in cyclists. It is caused by irritation to the small nerves that become pinched between two adjacent metatarsal bones. Symptoms range from numbness and pain to burning or tingling in the front of the foot or into adjacent toes. It is called Morton's neuroma (not to be confused with Morton's foot).

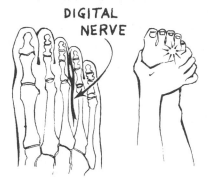

DIGITAL NERVE

Initial treatment is to massage the feet, moving the toes in an up-and-down direction. A heating pad wrapped around the foot for about twenty minutes two or three times a day is also helpful.

The cause is too much pressure on the forefoot. Stiff-soled cycling shoes help distribute this pressure over the whole foot and so are recommended as a preventive measure for this condition, but they must fit well. If the toe box in the cycling shoes is narrow, as is often the case, then take a sock, fill it with sand, and stuff it in the front of the shoe. Take a towel, wet it with hot water, wrap it around the front of the shoe, and let the shoe sit for a day or two, rewetting the towel with hot water as often as possible. This will often increase the toe box area in the front of the shoe. In addition, make sure not to lace the shoe too tightly, and if using toe straps, make sure they are not too tight. Finally, pulling upward on the upstroke tends to take pressure off the foot.

If after following these recommendations, the numbness persists, then a visit to a sports doctor is indicated. The use of corticosteroid injections, orthotic foot-brace devices, and surgical intervention may be necessary in order to alleviate the problem permanently.

Bunions: Bunions are inflammations that can occur just behind the big toe joint on the inside of the foot or behind the little toe on the outside of the foot. This condition results from abnormal bony alignment with friction between the enlarged bone underneath the skin and the shoe wear enclosing the foot, leading to soft tissue irritation with redness, swelling, local heat, and pain.

Initially, apply ice to the painful bunion area for five to ten minutes following the ride. Next, remove the pressure by using a commercially available bunion pad. Try making your own pad by taking some moleskin or an eighth-inch adhesive felt or foam and cutting a hole in the middle to surround the bump. Place some Vaseline in the hole created and cover this with some gauze and tape it down. Take a quarter to an eighth inch of polyurethane foam or some moleskin, put it between the first and second toes for a big-toe bunion, or between the fourth and fifth toes for a little-toe bunion.

Check shoe fit. Cycling shoes are of value because they are rigid so they do not allow excessive mobility in the joints of the foot. In addition they usually are made of softer leather-type material, which will conform more easily to the abnormally-shaped bunion. Toeclip or cleat position can be changed so that the front of the foot and bunion are located slightly (perhaps a quarter-inch) more forward than would normally be the case, thereby alleviating pressure.

Refractory conditions may require corticosteroid injections or anti-inflammatory medications, which are useful for the acute phase. It is often necessary to have surgical correction of the existing problem, and this is the treatment of choice and advised. The use of specially made orthotics to control abnormal pronation, which often leads to bunions, can also be helpful in alleviating the problem.

Toe Jamming: Toe jamming is associated with black-and-blue, thickened, and often painful toenails. This often occurs when shoes are the improper length or there is not enough room in the toe box area. Cycling without socks results in excessive sweating, causing abnormal friction and pressure on the toenails. Occasionally, this injury results from uncut toenails jamming against the end of the shoe. Abnormally shaped toes may require surgical intervention.

It is helpful to relieve pressure by draining the blood from underneath the nail as soon as possible. Ice the toe for five or ten minutes to make it numb, and then sterilize an instrument (a paper clip that has been straightened works well) by heating the tip in the flame of a match for a minute or so. Put the hot sterile point of the clip onto the top of the nail plate and push downward to create a hole. Do this two or three times and then press down and drain the blood from under the nail. Then clean the area with soap and water and apply an antiseptic spray or cream, cover with a Band-Aid. If any buildup of fluid occurs under the nail, soak the toe in Epsom salts two or three times a day for about two days.

Check for the proper fit of the cycling shoes, make sure the toe box has enough room, and make sure there is no seam or part of the shoe that is irritating that particular part of the toe. There should be a thumb's width between the end of your longest toe and the end of your shoe. Also make sure that you cut your nails straight across and don't let them get too long.

Excessive Perspiration and Athlete's Foot: Excessive perspiration can lead to athlete's foot – an actual fungal infection of the skin. The best way to deal with this problem is to scrub the feet thoroughly with soap and water and pat dry. Then soak the feet in a mild household detergent for five to ten minutes, using two tablespoons of the detergent to a gallon or gallon and a half of water. Put a medicated powder such as Tinaction Powder between the toes or on the feet before bed and in the mornings. Air out shoes for twelve to twenty-four hours before using again and spray the shoes themselves with Desenex Spray. Johnson's Odoreaters are often useful in eliminating some of the odors from the feet. For everyday, wear well-ventilated shoes or sandals. For cycling use cycling shoes that are made of perforated leather, which has a good breathing capability.

Corns and Calluses: Corns and calluses are thickened skin that occur on pressure areas of the foot. Thickened skin areas on the tops of toes are known as hard corns, between two toes, as soft corns. Calluses are thickened areas of skin that occur on the bottom of the feet and differ from corns only in that the pressure area is much larger. The best way to treat these conditions is to peel off some of the thickened skin and then pad around it to remove the pressure.

Wash the feet with soap and water and pat dry, then soak in an Epsom salts solution for about ten minutes in order to soften up the hard skin areas. (One or two tablespoons of Epsom salts in a gallon of warm water.) Rub some mineral oil onto the involved areas before trying to remove the thickened layers of skin. Then take a callous file or pumice stone (found at drug stores) and file back and forth to get as much skin off as possible. To pad around corns, take moleskin, make a hole in it, and leave about an eighth-inch diameter of the moleskin to go around the corn to relieve the pressure. Place it on the involved toe, put some Vaseline in it and put some Band-Aids over it or tape it down. For alleviating pressure for soft corns between toes, file it down as described above, then place Vaseline with lambswool between the toes. Do not use cotton in here because this will absorb moisture and make the problem worse.

For calluses on the bottom of the foot, take an eighth inch to quarter inch foam or felt and cut a hole in the middle of it and leave about an eighth to quarter inch of padding in the diameter around the opening. Place some Vaseline or ointment around the opening and cover it

with gauze and tape it down. It is a good idea to use a Spenco inlay. Cycle shoes will help reduce the pressure on the foot. Try to adjust your cleats or toeclips so that the front of the foot is slightly more forward than normal (an eighth to a quarter inch is usually sufficient), taking pressure off of the callus or corn.

Ingrown Toenails: Ingrown toenails occur when there is excessive pressure on the toes, especially the big toe, and the toenail actually cuts through the surrounding skin. Many cyclists have learned this can often be painful, with infection and a pussy exudate. Home care or self-help is geared toward removing the offending portion of the nail. Wash the foot with soap and water and pat dry. Soak the foot in a solution of Epsom salts for approximately ten to fifteen minutes, then try to remove the offending portion of the nail with a nail cutter, cutting it at an angle. Once the part of the nail that is causing the pressure is removed, soak the foot in a solution of Epsom salts two or three times a day for two to three days. Infected ingrown nails are a serious threat to the cyclist with diabetes or poor circulation and should be immediately seen by a physician or podiatrist.

To avoid this problem, make sure shoe size is correct, that the toe box of the cycling shoes has enough room so that toes can wiggle, that socks are not too tight, and always cut toenails straight across.

Blisters: Blisters are an accumulation of fluid due to friction between skin layers. They are often very painful, sensitive to pressure, and can become infected. Treatment is aimed at reducing the pressure by draining the blister. After washing the foot in soap and water, ice is applied to the area for five to ten minutes to make it as numb as possible. Then take a pin that has been sterilized by placing it to the tip of a flame for a minute or so and puncture the blister several times. Squeeze the blister gently from the sides so that the fluid is released. Apply an antiseptic cream and a piece of gauze and a compression bandage, putting some pressure on it, then taping it down. Soak the foot in a solution of Epsom salts once or twice a day for a couple of days after this. The blister itself may continue to fill up with fluid for several days and so this process may have to be repeated.

Cycling can still be comfortable by applying the following treatment. For a blister on the bottom of the foot, take an eighth- or quarter-inch foam or felt and cut a hole in it to alleviate pressure around the blister. Make sure there is about an eighth- or quarter-inch diameter in the surrounding portion of the pad. Apply an antiseptic cream and two-by-two inch gauze and tape it down. For a blister on the toes, follow the same

method, using moleskin instead of felt.

Never remove the roof of the blister until it is almost healed. To prevent blisters, stretch the part of the shoe that is rubbing, and do not use socks that are dirty or wrinkled. For blisters on the bottom of the foot, Spenco inlays are useful, as they resist friction. Another prevention method is to apply Vaseline liberally to areas that are blistering.

Objection is sometimes raised to the recommendation of piercing the blister with a pin because of possible infection. In the authors' experience, as well as that of physicians responsible for US Army infantry, infections are rare and readily treated by soaks if they occur. The advantage of early return to, or continued cycling seems to far outweigh such rare occurrences.

Metatarsal Head Pain: Cycling utilizes the ball of the foot for contact on the pedal. This can often lead to undue stress on the heads of the metatarsal bones, which are the long bones of the foot that start just behind the toes. This may result in callus buildup. Pads or inlays usually curtail pain. All previous recommendations on forefoot ailments may apply to "metatarsalgia" – rigid-soled shoes to spread the pressure, proper fit, and placing the forefoot a little forward of the pedal spindle.

For persistent problems, orthotics or a shoe change may be needed.

Cycling Shoes

The use of cycling shoes as opposed to regular canvas shoes, tennis shoes, sneakers, or running shoes is strongly recommended. As mentioned in the section on cycle fit, each time you push down on the pedal you're transferring force four to six times your body weight from your lower back and hip to where the foot comes in contact with the pedal. In most cases, the ball of the foot receives the full amount of this force.

In an extreme racing shoe, the sole is molded with the heel elevated, so that downward pressure can be transmitted by the whole foot. A cycling shoe is made with a hard leather, wood, or plastic sole and a steel shank between the inner and outer shoes to distribute force over a large area. Wearing a stiff-soled shoe automatically cuts down on foot pain. The rigid cycling shoe also lessens foot-joint movement, so there is less chance of irritation to the foot from blisters or bursitis caused by faulty foot structure (e.g. bunions and hammer toes).

Cycling shoes are wedge-shaped and laced to the toe in order to restrain the top of the foot and keep the toes from being forced against the end of the shoe, which would otherwise happen from the force of pedaling. If your toes start to hurt after a long ride, tighten the laces again.

Cycling shoes are not made for walking: Many have no heels because racers want as little "revolving weight" as possible, and cleats get worn very quickly if they are walked on. Racers usually have fold-up slippers or sneakers to change into after the race.

Tourists (or their shoemakers) often add a thin, nonslip rubber sole and a small heel to a cycling shoe–though some enjoy the new stiff-soled cycling sneakers. A bowling shoe with an extra sole glued on can serve the same purpose.

If cycling shoes look too bizarre for your taste, or you can't get any that fit, stiff-soled leather shoes can be reinforced with an extra sole.

Seat height is critical in avoiding knee pain, and it depends in part on the thickness of the sole. If you start wearing thicker-soled shoes, be sure to raise your seat; if soles become worn, lower it. On a long ride a quarter-inch difference in seat height can cause knee problems.

When purchasing cycle shoes, make sure to get a proper fit. Whatever is worn when cycling should also be worn when purchasing new shoes. If you wear two pairs of socks, then make sure you have them on at the time. Any pads or arch supports should be present when fitting the shoes. Cycling shoes should fit rather snugly, but make sure there is about a thumb's width between the end of the shoe and the end of the longest toe. Note: It is important to be aware of the fact that many people have the second toe and some people the third toe as their longest toe. In addition, there should be an extra pinch of leather available across the upper portion of the shoe.

Men often complain that cycling shoes are too narrow in the forefoot or the toe box area. If this is the case and you have already purchased the cycling shoe best for you for other reasons, then you can increase the toe box area as mentioned under "Numbness."

Women have problems because there are no special cycling shoes for them and shoes are often too wide or too large. There are several ways to decrease the size of a cycling shoe. By using a Spenco inlay, approximately one letter size in width can be eliminated; they come in shoe sizes and are often available in sporting good stores. Secondly, placing an eighth to a quarter inch of adhesive foam or felt on the underside of the tongue of the cycling shoe gives a snugger fit around the forefoot area and helps keep the heel down better. Thirdly, placing moleskin on either side of the heel can help narrow the heel area; an eighth-inch foam can be used here if more filler is needed. Finally, polyurethane foam between a quarter inch and an inch and a quarter thick can be stuffed into the forefoot part of the cycle shoe to decrease the toe box size.

If you do finally find a cycling shoe that you like, make sure that you order one or two extra pairs right away. It can take quite a long time to get a specially ordered shoe in.

Toeclips keep the foot on the proper part of the pedal. They give extra support especially useful climbing hills or accelerating, and lead to better stability in foot position on the pedal. They have the advantage of being less constraining on the foot and transmitting less stress to the knee than cleats do. Properly placed cleats have an even greater stabilizing action on the foot. This allows for more efficient cycling, as it cuts down on slippage. Slippage wastes energy and can lead to fatigue and sloppy form, and subsequently overuse injury.

After purchasing shoes, plan to ride without cleats for a hundred miles or so, so that the pedal will make an impression on the bottom of the shoe. The cleat should be placed somewhere in back of this line, or alternately, tape should be wound around the front of the toeclip to act as a stop so that when the cleat is set, there'll be a little clearance between the end of the shoe and the toeclip. Perhaps a better method of setting cleats is to have a friend scribe a line after checking out the location of the ball of the foot on the pedal. Although fore and aft position is important for maximizing leverage, from an orthopedic standpoint, the foot angle is what is important (toe-in, front, or toe-out) and should be the same as in walking. Remember–having the foot pointing straight ahead, or held to a slightly in-toed position according to some "rule," is not necessarily correct. Some people are much better off with their foot turned outward. A good way to determine cleat angle is to walk barefoot for five or ten steps. Stop with your feet apart a few inches and note their position. That should be your cleat angle.

For more detailed information on foot care, read Dr. Myles Schneider's How to Doctor Your Feet Without the Doctor, *Running Times Publications, Woodbridge, VA., 1980.*

What to do when an injury occurs

Proper evaluation and treatment of any injury must begin with accurate diagnosis. If you sustain a painful injury, the first step to take is to consult the section on specific sites of injury to identify what problem you have acquired. Be sure to analyze your pain characteristic to judge how serious the injury has become. By judging the grade of pain you can decide with some accuracy whether riding should be discontinued. Notice that it is not an arbitrary medical statement but rather the quality of your own body's symptoms that will dictate whether abstinence from riding will be required as part of the healing process.

The ability to heal is dependent on various factors: age, inheritance, nutrition, the severity of the injury, and rest. No oral medication can speed healing. Oral medications treat the symptoms of breakdown, which are pain, local swelling, and tenderness. Their use is justified to improve comfort and to ease recovery, but should not be an excuse to overstress or overuse the injured part.

The most commonly prescribed medication for athletic injury is aspirin. Its advantages are that it's available, cheap, and relatively safe (safer than many other medications). It should not be used for extended periods of time, however, for two reasons: Although aspirin is the drug of choice for musculo-skeletal inflammation, much of what aspirin does is symptomatic treatment. If you suppress, say, your sore-knee symptom, you're not treating the cause. If you have to keep taking it, you obviously haven't solved your problem, but only the symptom of it. Two, it is dangerous to your health taken cumulatively for a long period of time because of the high rate of gastrointestinal irritation and bleeding, and because there's a tendency to take too much at one time—ten to twelve pills a day. You can get toxic—actually poison yourself—with aspirin.

The use of cortisone in athletic injury remains controversial and misunderstood. It has been the experience of sports physicians and podiatrists that local cortisone injection for such conditions as bursitis and tendonitis has been highly effective in large numbers of patients. How this effectiveness is achieved is not clear. Experimental evidence would suggest that there is some detriment to the healing process at the site of injury over the initial two weeks after injection, followed by a reparative phase that requires a total of six weeks to fully mature. Three local effects of cortisone that should be emphasized as potential risks before its use is accepted: (1) subcutaneous atrophy, (2) depigmentation at the site of injection, and (3) collagen or tendon damage. Subcutaneous atrophy refers to the loss of fat in the subcutaneous tissues, which results in dimpling of the skin and sometimes results in a hypersensitive thinning of the skin at the site of the injection. This is rare if one or two injections are given, but is a real risk if more than three or four are given in any one anatomic site. The loss of skin coloration is an effect on melanin-containing cells of the dermis and may be permanent in the black or dark skinned person but can also occur in the Caucasian. Tendon damage is the most often quoted reason for not using cortisone as a local treatment. This can occur at the Achilles tendon, at the infrapatellar tendon, and at the biceps tendon (which is not a common injury complaint of the cyclist). As can best be understood, local cortisone activity seems to set the stage for the body's repair efforts. Therefore a mandatory period of rest must be given to the injured part before cycling can be resumed if the curative effect of cortisone is to occur. A current guideline suggests using no more than three to four injections in any one anatomic site, to be spaced over a period of several weeks. If after this treatment no response has occurred, it can be safely assumed that some other form of treatment or possibly a surgical solution will have to be considered.

Regarding the other factors that affect the ability to heal, it is recognized that the younger athlete heals more quickly, that there are persons who are naturally quick healers, and that *rest* is a common denominator to almost *all* successful treatment programs involving Grade III or IV pain syndromes.

Local treatment of acute injury traditionally includes the use of ice. Often, there is confusion as to whether ice or heat should be applied to the injured part. In the acute or early phases of pain ice is always helpful. This is especially true after activity. The purpose of ice is to reduce blood flow to the injured part and thus hopefully decrease the development of either bleeding or soft-tissue swelling. After the first twenty-four to forty-eight hours, warming the injured part aids in promoting local blood flow, which increases the rate of removal of breakdown products and seems to promote the cellular healing forces of the body. This is empirical; but there seems to be absolute agreement that acute injury should not be warmed or swelling and pain will increase.

Professional help should be sought when either the guidelines of this chapter do not alleviate the problem or they point out danger signs of more serious injury. In seeking the attention of a physician or podiatrist, you may be fortunate in having access to a sports clinic or you may be relying on your family physician to guide you in treatment. It is safe to assume that the majority of physicians are not avid cyclists and may have far less experience with cycling than you. This is not to say that they will not be interested in your condition or wish to help. Often, if you can provide some insight into cycling, the medical professional can provide some insight into the medical nature of your problem. It may be helpful to bring this book and refer to the section you feel pertains to your injury, so that

cyclist and physician together can come to a reasonable conclusion as to treatment. Remember also that cyclists are people first and cyclists second. As such, the cyclist can develop any condition, complaint, or health problem that the average noncyclist would be exposed to. Any symptom or complaint that does not appear to have any similarity to the discussion in this chapter should signal the possibility of a coincidental condition.

Special Considerations

The Child Cyclist. It is important to recognize that the child is not a little adult, but has several unique characteristics, one of which is the fact that both the ends of his bones (epiphyses) and the sites of his tendon insertions (apophyses) are growing. The child athlete is particularly vulnerable to apophysitis (inflammation of tendon insertions) typified by Osgood Schlatter's condition of the knee at the site of the infrapatellar tendon insertion on the tibia.

Osgood Schlatter's condition is best understood as a stress-induced fracture accompanied by inflammation of the ununited apophysis, aggravated by knee-flexion activities such as cycling or kicking. It often appears in the twelve- to fourteen-year-old population, especially in boys who go through a pronounced growth spurt at this age, thereby placing an additional stress and stretch on the infrapatellar tendon. It is treated best by rest, splinting of the knee to reduce the bending forces, and oral medication—although strong anti-inflammatory medications such as Butazolidin are contraindicated below the age of fourteen. While some specialists advocate injection of the inflammatory site, the authors do not, because the risk of rupture—though low—is present, and other treatment seems to correct this condition quite well. A cardinal sign of its presence is a swelling of the tibial apophysis with a large bump or prominence at the site of the patella tendon insertion that is exquisitely tender to palpation. This is often a bilateral condition.

Another apophyseal injury seen in the child cyclist is Sever's disease of the heel, or calcaneal apophysitis, again due to stress on the Achilles tendon at the apophysis at the calcaneus (heelbone). Its treatment is similar to that for the knee.

Children rarely complain of persistent back pain. A painful lower back in the child cyclist should point to an underlying cause. This may be an anatomic lesion, such as a stress-induced fracture of the vertebrae or an excessive curvature. A child with back pain of longer than a few weeks should be evaluated by an orthopedic surgeon.

Conditions of the hip, which are often of concern in children, are not known to be caused or promoted by cycling activity. Slipped capital femoral epiphysis and Legg-Perthes disease of the femoral head are two conditions characterized by injury to the growth center of the femoral head, which seem to be related to collision trauma, jumping-type sports, and other factors not fully understood.

It should be remembered that cycling is not known to produce limp and any limp that develops in a child cyclist should be regarded as a sign for thorough orthopedic evaluation. If a hip problem were to develop in a child, bicycling may become difficult or painful and will reveal the coincident condition.

In the knee, in addition to Osgood-Schlatter's condition, the child cyclist may experience osteochondritis dissecans. This represents a local death of bone and cartilage with the resulting formation of a loose fragment that may separate from the articular surface and drop into the knee joint. This will produce symptoms of an unsound joint, and is to be suspected if a child has a recurrent swollen knee. But remember that juvenile rheumatoid arthritis, infections, and some blood-cell diseases may also cause knee swelling, so swelling of the knee is never to be ignored.

Since one of the unique qualities of the child is the presence of growth centers in the bones, concern has always been that cycling activity could do harm and affect growth. At the present time there is no evidence that such injury occurs as a result of reasonable cycling activity. However, the encouragement of children to pursue high levels of touring or competition certainly has been associated with the apophyseal injuries previously described. Perhaps even more important are the strong psychological and sociological pressures that result from early forced participation and specialization in sports. Intensive training schedules, especially an emphasis on anaerobic training, should be discouraged in children, based on present psychological and physiological information. Current research does support the positive aspects of aerobic conditioning in children, but we would recommend that cycling distance and gear size be carefully controlled in order to avoid overstressing the skeletal and cardiovascular systems of the growing child.

The Geriatric Cyclist. The advantages of cycling to the older athlete include aerobic conditioning for cardiovascular health maintenance, the promotion of flexibility, and the prolongation of a younger functional capacity to recover from physiologic stress.

Although impact is present in cycling, its effects are almost entirely preventable by the previously described adjustments in equipment. Cycling provides the older athlete with a vigorous aerobic sport without the inherent joint trauma seen in running. Aging is characterized by a progressive decrease in flexibility that is counteracted by cycling's promotion of flexibility in the lower extremities. Cycling has long been prescribed for the rehabilitation of hip disease in the geriatric patient.

The geriatric rider is exposed to certain aggravations of pre-existing disease that the younger rider does not experience. Degenerative cervical arthritis or lumbar spine inflexibility due to the processes of aging will make it more difficult to ride without some modification in bicycle adjustment. This is also true for deformities associated with previous trauma or fracture, or congenital skeletal anomalies. It may be necessary to go to a custom builder. A loss in balance may suggest the use of a tricycle.

The presence of joint replacement common in our society is not a contraindication to cycling activity providing the role of impact is minimized. The beneficial effects of range of motion of the knee and hip far outweigh any criticism of such activity.

The Overweight Cyclist. Cycling offers the obese patient one of his few opportunities to participate in a stimulating cardiovascular exercise without the worry of intolerable punishment to the weight-bearing joints of the leg. The energy consumption and calories consumption in cycling, although it does not have the efficiency of the running sports, is still sufficient to benefit most obese riders.

The overweight rider is particularly vulnerable to saddle impact and may have to make modifications such as getting a sling seat.

Preventing Injury

The following recommendations are an overview of this entire chapter with some additional comments:
• Prevention of injury starts with proper bike fit. This takes into consideration frame size, seat adjustments, shoe and cleat position, and finally handlebar position.
• Proper shoe wear. It is our recommendation that firm-soled cycling shoes should be used for cycling.
• Proper riding position and form. It is important to develop a comfortable and relaxed form of cycling. You should be very comfortable with your arms and legs extended—the arms slightly bent at the elbow—the legs slightly bent at the knee. While it is important to develop a relaxed position on the bike, it is not advisable to daydream, and one should be alert at all times to the variety of obstacles to be dealt with.
• Proper maintenance. Correct alignment and roadworthiness are essential to avoiding accident. Any fall requires thorough checking for alignment, particularly of handlebars, cranks, and pedals.
• Pre- and post-cycling stretching and strengthening routines.
• Warm into the ride.
• Follow accepted training principles: Alternate hard and easy days, don't overuse or overstress the body, and very gradually increase distances and speeds.
• Don't ignore pain. Respect any achiness or fatigue or soreness that cannot be explained by conditioning.
• Read the weather article in the opening section of the book and follow its guidelines. In particular, drink plenty of fluids before, during, and after long rides to avoid hyperthermia and heatstroke. Water is the best fluid replacement; salt tablets are dangerous and unnecessary.

Being dehydrated or losing excessive body heat will mean that you will fatigue more easily and so increase your chance of injury.

During cold weather, it is important to stretch more and to warm up properly to avoid injury to tendons, muscles, and joints. The worst danger is hypothermia, when body temperature drops abnormally due to exposure to cold. Signs of this include: mental confusion, slurred speech, extreme fatigue, coordination problems. These can be followed by unconsciousness and even death.
• Previous injuries. An example is the knee, which is so commonly injured during youth. If you had an injury to a specific area, it is very possible that you will have problems with that area if you overdo it on the bicycle. Consider it a warning if a chronic area of injury starts to be achy or painful—it may be a sign that you are overtraining.
• Recovery from recent injury. Many of us try to do

too much too soon. For every day of training or cycling you lose, you are actually losing three days of conditioning, so if you are out for a week, it is actually the equivalent of almost three weeks of conditioning loss. Therefore you must gradually work up to past levels of speed and duration.

Accidents

Cycling is not an intrinsically safe sport. In 1971, the estimated annual rate of injury approached one million cyclists, including 120 thousand fractures and sixty thousand concussions. An on-the-road injury most often involves falls or collision of a rider with another cyclist or auto vehicle . A recent study of 684 accidents at the University of California over a six year period revealed that a collison of two bicycles was the most frequent type of accident, 26%. Collision of a bicycle with various other objects occurred in 17.6% of the accidents, while a car was involved in 10%. Abrasions and lacerations occurred in 76% of the accidents, sprains and other soft tissue injuries in 11%, fractures in 5%, and loss of consciousness in 2%. Less than 1% of the injured riders required hospitalization. These statistics imply that the cyclist who is "going on the road" should be prepared to meet a variety of first-aid situations.

It is the responsibility of the leader of cycling groups to prepare for common emergencies. The first requirement is that someone be trained in simple first-aid. Training in cardiopulmonary resuscitation should be acquired by every citizen, certainly by every touring cyclist. A first-aid kit should be carried. It need not be expensive, and will prove its worth countless times during a tour.

Head injury accompanied by any period of dizziness, headache, incoordination, convulsions, loss of consciousness, or vomiting demands immediate medical evaluation. The cyclist should be kept lying down and transported by station wagon or emergency vehicle. The concern in head injury is expanding intracranial bleeding, and minutes to only a few hours are available before collapse may occur.

The most common fracture in cycling is injury to the clavicle (collar bone) or to the point of the shoulder at the site of the acromioclavicular joint. Injury to this joint is commonly called a separation. These injuries occur when the cyclist falls onto the point of the shoulder while holding onto the handlebars of his cycle. After such an injury, the cyclist holds his arm to the side and supports it with the opposite hand. There is tenderness and pain at the site of trauma. The arm should be immobilized, splinted, and supported by a triangle bandage. The cyclist should be transported to the emergency room for X-ray. Occasionally, dislocation of the shoulder will occur and on-the-road treatment also demands support of the joint until emergency treatment can be obtained. Relocation of a dislocated joint should not be attempted without previous X-ray and medical evaluation.

A fall onto the outstretched hand may injure its small bones, particularly the carpal navicular bone. Pain at the base of the thumb and at the first web space of the hand, accompanied by inability to grip and local swelling, demands an X-ray of this area. This seemingly minor injury can require extensive casting and is notorious for failing to heal, resulting in prolonged hand disability. Injuries to the hand should be evaluated by X-ray as early as possible. Fractures of the wrist are also common and are usually obvious because the forearm looks deformed.

Open fractures – in which the bone pierces the skin and is exposed – are emergencies due to the risk of infection. Immediately splint with any available device, put on a sterile gauze dressing to prevent further contamination, and transfer to a hospital emergency room.

Injury to the spine is rare. No cyclist should be moved if there is concern for a possible fracture of the neck or back.

Minor sprains are incomplete tears of the ligaments that hold joints together, major sprains are complete severe tears. A fracture of a bone is a break and is best understood as a soft tissue injury accompanied by a break in the bone. Using the ankle as an example, it cannot be determined by the outward appearance of a swollen and acutely painful ankle, whether a break or a sprain or both has occurred. An X-ray and careful physical evaluation are required. If any bruising or swelling can be seen, X-rays are warranted. Always apply ice (or at least cold water) to acute injury until medical care can be obtained.

Abrasions are easily treated by cleansing and applying a sterile dressing with an antibiotic ointment. Deep wounds or wounds accompanied by heavy bleeding require direct pressure to control bleeding, a sterile dressing to protect against contamination, and referral to a physician. If a tourniquet is required to control massive hemorrhage, remember that once it is applied, only a few hours exist before permanent damage to the part is caused by the loss of circulation. Gently release the tourniquet for a few seconds every half-hour to hour to allow a flow of blood to the limb.

Cycling after surgery or injury

Cycling is an excellent exercise alternative after surgery of the hip or knee. It helps rehabilitate the patient who requires hip replacement or repair of a hip fracture by re-establishing the range of motion of the hip; the forces across the hip are not detrimental in most cases.

Selective analysis of quadriceps rehabilitation with enzymatic studies has also substantiated that cycling permits rapid rehabilitation of the quadriceps muscle after knee surgery. Removal of a knee cartilage and ligamentous repairs are often rehabilitated by cycling when motion will allow. Often an athlete will have instability in the knee joint after severe ligamentous injury; though running and sports requiring changes of direction are not always tolerated, cycling is often an excellent aerobic alternative for this group of people.

Cycling, however, does stress an injured part. The presence of swelling in the knee joint or ankle is not to be regarded lightly and is not to be "pedaled out." Swelling implies intra-articular injury which has not completely healed. Medical guidance should be obtained before cycling is resumed.

The grading classification of pain is a useful guideline for return to cycling activity.

...So You've Had an Accident

Diane Shafer, M.D.

Diane Shafer is an orthopedic surgeon and has been a bike rider for twenty-five years. She says that her bike saved her sanity in medical school, and that she didn't drive a car until she became an M.D. She has made house calls, gone to graduation, and gone to church on her bike.

She has been attending physician in emergency rooms in four different areas of Pennsylvania, and has conducted a survey of bicycle accidents treated at those facilities. The type and severity of accident differed with location.

In Philadelphia the biker was rarely at fault, but had been forced into the sidewalk or otherwise squeezed by traffic.

Erie's accidents were rare but usually extremely serious, as they happened in conditions of ice and fog when visibility was minimal.

Titusville accidents were caused by gravel and twisting roads, as well as hitting wild animals.

In a low-income section of Harrisburg, 80% of the accidents involved thirteen- to seventeen-year olds who had darted into traffic or knocked down pedestrians.

PUMP SPLINT. INNER TUBE.

MAGAZINE SECURED WITH HANDLEBAR TAPE OR INNER TUBE.

Before you examine your bicycle assess your own injuries and plan treatment that will get you home or to a health care facility. As soon as possible place ice on the injured part, elevate it, and rest it.

For minor injuries such as bruises and road rash, be sure to remove the sticks and stones. Clean the wound with soap and water and put a sterile dressing on it once you get home. A brush sometimes helps remove road grit that can cause an infection.

If you injure a joint such as an elbow or a shoulder, do not try to "work it out." Instead, apply a sling to protect and rest the injured joint. Use a scarf, shirt, or jacket folded to the correct shape. A spare tube doubled or tied to proper length also works well, as does a Windbreaker with the sleeve pinned to the pocket for support.

Splints can be improvised from pumps. If you sustain a forearm or wrist injury, place the pump on the palm side and secure with inner tube, handlebar tape, or whatever you have. If you have a magazine along, place the arm in it for support. If a hand is injured, splint it with an orange and an Ace bandage, or ball up your shirt, place it in your palm, and cover it with a sock. If a knee, ankle, or foot is injured be sure to protect it and *don't put your weight on it*. A pillow taped around an ankle, foot, or knee makes a comfortable splint.

INNER TUBE AS A SLING

HAND SPLINTED WITH ORANGE. WRAP WITH ACE BANDAGE.

In helping accident victims, remember your ABC's—maintain Airway, Breathing, Circulation (i.e. a pulse). If they are unconscious and something is broken, splint them where they are lying. Treat the head, neck, and shoulder region as a unit. If you suspect any injury to the head or spinal column, do not move the person. If the person is lying in a dangerous place and must be moved to safety, place a board under the head-neck-shoulder area *in position found*. But better yet, block traffic until help arrives.

If you think that a large bone of the leg is broken, splint it to the other leg with inner tube or tape.

Backaches

Glenn Goldfinger, R.P.T.

Fear was man's main form of transportation in caveman days, as Mel Brooks noted when speaking as the "Two Thousand Year Old Man."

The evolution of man was structured on a high-activity level. Early man did not have to plan his daily exercise routine; physical exertion was inherent in his life and survival. Our bodies were designed for activities consisting of hard, fast, and prolonged work. Exercise, in almost any form, is a positive input to our bodies.

Although today's fight for survival does not include running away from wild animals, the world we live in appears to be one of ever-increasing tension, crisis, and conflict. Urban man, however, has been moving farther away from physical exertion, and more toward a life with minimal levels of physical activity.

Sources of tension and conflict are one's family, job, environment, and societal pressures. The coupling of ever-increasing tensions and diminishing physical exercise produce abnormal levels of muscular tension in the body, which, when combined with slight physical activity, yield strains, sprains, and a condition called tension myositis.

It is impossible to number the various treatment techniques currently used in modern medicine to treat these pathologies. However, examining *all* the reasons one has pain, not just examining the pain, is the key to a successful treatment program.

The interesting and most important fact about tension myositis is that the causative agent is usually very ordinary: A sneeze, cough, reach, or move that is well within one's normal movement repertoire suddenly brings on pain. Physical therapists who specialize in musculo-skeletal disorders can relieve this pain, but a long-term aerobic exercise program should also be initiated to reduce the tension levels in the body.

Because tension myositis usually strikes the neck, shoulder, and low-back regions, care must be taken to select the best form of aerobic exercise.

Bicycle riding, specifically stationary bicycle riding, is probably the safest, most consistent, nonweather-dependent, and cheapest form of intense aerobic exercise existing today.

Glenn Goldfinger *is project coordinator of the New York Regional Spinal Cord Injury System at the New York University Medical Center Institute of Rehabilitation Medicine in New York City.*

Inherent in running, jogging, and jump-roping, are severe jarring and pounding forces placed on the legs, hips, and vertebral column, including the low-back, high-back, and neck regions. Witness the multitude of severe ankle, foot, knee, hip, and back problems that often plague weekend and long-distance runners. Cross-country skiing is fine, but, like swimming, is weather dependent for most people.

The stationary bicycle, whether at home or in a health club, is accessible 365 days a year. The body will not be jarred while riding it, and one can breathe relatively clean indoor air as opposed to exhaust fumes from the street. One can even enjoy the pleasures of stereo or television while pedaling.

Regular bicycles cannot offer the constant, objectively measured inputs that stationary bicycles give. They can also produce a jarring ride, if ridden on poor roadbeds, and should not be used when the rider has pain. Until large metropolitan areas create bicycle lanes with good surfaces, indoor stationary bicycling remains the most perfect means of developing an aerobic-conditioning exercise program.

Minimal equipment on a stationary bicycle should include a variable-resistance control to allow the body gradual training, and a speedometer to exactly measure one's speed or pace. The stationary bicycle should be adjustable to fit the body properly, and can even include a timer to help measure workout times. Look for easily adjustable seat and handlebar locks, especially if more than one person will be riding the bicycle. The seat should be comfortable, and the handlebars able to meet your height requirements. A weighted wheel and sturdy construction will yield a comfortable, smooth, and vibration-free ride.

The Schwinn and the Tunturi bicycle companies both have fine examples of stationary exercise bicycles. The Dynavit incorporates a computer and a pulse-monitor to automatically adjust the exercise resistance appropriate to your conditioning.

A good guide for aerobic conditioning is the paperback book entitled *The Aerobic Way*, by Dr. Kenneth Cooper.

Check with your family physician before starting any exercise program, and if you are over thirty, have a stress EKG done at a testing center that uses stationary bicycles. Names of facilities are available from a local chapter of the American Heart Association.

WOMEN AND CYCLING

American women have brought home most of the medals in international cycling competition, and cycling may be the first sport in which a well-trained woman will be able to beat the best man because of her greater potential for endurance strength. Races so far haven't been long enough, and at short distances women are about seven percent weaker than men of the same age and level of fitness.

Good technique can go a long way toward making up for strength. That means spinning rather than pushing pedals, pulling on the handlebars when going uphill, anticipating when you should change gears to keep your cadence constant, making sure your seat is high enough to give your legs proper extension, and hardly ever coasting – saving the high gears for pedaling downhill.

If you want to use the bike for fitness as well as fun, a week is long enough to get out of training. To do long weekend rides you really should run, skate, dance, or bike for a half-hour at least two other times a week. Cardiovascular training should be combined with strengthening exercises for the upper body and the abdomen. The only woman racer we spoke to who doesn't train with weights is Beryl Burton – and she works on a farm! There are books on weight training for women that describe how to firm just about every muscle without making you look muscular. (By the way, bent-knee lifts feel just like climbing a hill.)

Once you can ride decent distances, you should know your bike well enough to avoid its breaking down on the road, and to repair it if it does. Skill in handling tools comes from practice, and what better place to practice than on your own bike. Search out a hands-on class; every cyclist owes it to himself or herself to understand how a bike works. There's nothing very mysterious about it; there are women bicycle mechanics all over the country, many teaching classes in bike repair and maintenance. The basic minimum is knowing how to change a flat and how to adjust derailleur and brake cables.

Since bike riders are often helpful types, it's easy for a woman to get spoiled and never even have to pump up her own tires. Of course, if you take care of the shopping, cooking, and cleaning, there's no reason you should do the mechanical maintenance of the bike as well. That's not liberation, that's exploitation.

So is carrying the kid on a 3-speed while a male companion whizzes along on a 10-speed. A 3-speed is very good for what traffic planners call the average bike ride – two miles each way. It can't be beat for the run to the store, going somewhere with a child, avoiding inefficient mass transit. And their design suits the average woman's shorter arms, lack of upper-body strength, and wider bottom. But the upright position and heavier wheels slow you down, make staying on a bike any length of time unpleasant, and make keeping up with someone on a lightweight 10-speed an impossibility.

When women want the better quality equipment you need for touring, racing, and the long-distance recreational riding that is so exhilarating and so good for you their way is barred. Quality small frames are hard to find, as are bike stores willing to make the changes necessary to suit women's proportions. (Right now, the nearer you are in size to a fourteen-year-old boy, the easier it is to find cycling gear that fits.) But sale of women's seats and the new thick handlebar padding are signs that manufacturers are beginning to pay attention. When women in the Seattle area got together and formed the Northwest Women's Cycling Coalition, four stores in the area started catering to women.

Finding a bike that fits, riding in traffic without fear, climbing hills without getting out of breath or hurting your knees, keeping a bike in working order: These are problems all cyclists have. When we first started to write this section, we found ourselves recapitulating the whole book.

On our own we could find no studies on women and cycling, so we got in touch with Dorothy Harris, director of the Center for Women and Sports at Pennsylvania State University, the first research organization in the country devoted entirely to the scientific study of the woman athlete. Very little research had been done about cycling, but quite a bit about women athletes in general. We thought Dr. Harris had done a brilliant job of explaining the important points in her columns in Womensports, and were fortunate enough to receive her permission to reprint them.

While studying women and sports, the name Mona

Shangold came up whenever there were discussions of a gynecological nature. A marathon runner whose favorite patients are athletes, Dr. Shangold agreed to answer our questions and to study the relationship between cycling and gynecology and obstetrics.

We also called Nina Kuscsik because she is active in the women's sports movement – and we remembered that she had, as Nina Marmorina, been New York State cycling champion before she won the women's division of the Boston Marathon. Nina uses her track bike as part of her running training program to develop balanced muscles – good hamstrings from running, and good quadriceps from cycling. She also thinks going down hills fast on a track bike is good for leg speed work.

Nina said that before research would happen, the knowledge of the riders had to be tapped, and that a more open discussion by women cyclists would produce more and better research by doctors and physiologists. We should speak to women cyclists who had longevity in their careers, and ask them what attitudes they had found in the medical profession in pursuit of their own health, and what they had found out for themselves.

Nina suggested we get in touch with Jeanne Omelenchuk, who started cycling competition at seventeen, was national champion in 1952 and 1955, and is still winning veterans' championships thirty years later. Jeanne is living proof that Mona Shangold knows what she's talking about. She says, "While pregnant with our daughter I rode twenty-five to thirty miles daily until two weeks before she was born and never had an ill moment." Jeanne says, "If normal health is present, women should engage in some form of vigorous sport. Whether competition is essential is debatable, but a regular form of exercise is so beneficial to both psychological well-being as well as physiological. Cycling is ideal, since it can be combined with your normal day's routine, going shopping, visiting, daily errands, etc. Cycling this way we can pile up miles without seeming to.

"Ordinary housewives in Europe get more exer-

The Uniped Theory

George Gipe

People are always talking about the change in women's lives the bicycle caused. We've never heard it put quite the way George Gipe did in The Great American Sports Book, *Doubleday, 1978. If you missed it, the book takes cycling quite seriously, which sets it apart from the run-of-the-mill general sports book.*

The bicycle . . . involved the average woman in sports for the first time. "It is safe to say," wrote an official of the United States Census Bureau in 1900, "that few articles ever used by man created so great a revolution as the bicycle." The gentleman was absolutely right, for the bicycle not only put a small army of vibrant young women on the road with their male counterparts, it also changed the very nature of American womanhood as well as the style of clothing she wore and the way she acted toward men.

Before the 1880's when "wheeling" became popular, the American woman was a uniped. No profes-

sor of comparative anatomy would have admitted this in print, but it was nevertheless a fact of life in the United States as well as most other Western nations. Man at this time flaunted his two-leggedness by wearing tight trousers, crossing his legs, and walking with long strides. When he mounted a horse, he casually threw one leg across the animal's back and rode astride his mount.

In contrast, the normal woman was forced to sit bolt upright in her floor-length skirt with her feet together. When she walked, her gait was mincing, rather like that of a trained seal, and when she rode a horse, it was sidesaddle, in a manner that not only diminished her security but also practically wore holes in the poor creature's back. In this way, people of good breeding preserved the myth that woman was a one-legged animal, which solved many problems of a carnal nature.

Accepting this myth was a relatively simple matter – until the bicycle came along. Then a startling fact emerged. It was not – and still is not – possible for a person to ride a bicycle comfortably with one leg. To properly manipulate the pedals the rider must have two separate limbs. Even worse, the limbs must work

cise on bikes than what some of our athletes get here in the United States. They go up and down hills and ride from store to store on bikes instead of jumping into the auto and turning the ignition key.

"After winning the National Veteran Women's title these last two years, I'm especially aware of the wealth of talent in women thirty-five and over who never competed while younger."

While many sophisticated runners like Nina use bicycles for speedwork and as a way to maintain cardiovascular fitness while recovering from an injury, speed skaters traditionally cycle in the summer. It is no surprise to anyone in either sport that Beth and Eric Heiden, Sheila and Roger Young, and Jeanne Omelenchuk are at the same time speed-skating and cycling stars. What is surprising to anyone who doesn't know Jeanne is that at forty-nine she still competes in both sports, and was a member of three Olympic skating teams—in 1960, 1968, and 1972.

Photograph courtesy of Jeanne Omelenchuk

in such a manner as to emphasize the contours of the upper thigh and hemispheric undulations of the buttocks.

This was more than the dedicated moralists could stand. At first, bans were tried. In Flushing, New York, a school board resolved that it was immoral for any young lady to ride a bicycle and further noted that if the lady happened to be a teacher, "the practice had a tendency to create immorality among the children of both sexes." Alarmed at the report, Justice of the Peace William Sutton proposed a resolution that banned women teachers from riding their vehicles to and from the schoolroom. Such tactics, of course, served only to make the bicycle more attractive to all women.

Thus thwarted, the opponents of bicycle riding for ladies dreamed up a variety of outfits for the women to wear as a means of disguising the fact that they had two legs instead of one. Baggy Zouave trousers or ingeniously designed split skirts became the order of the day. In February of 1895, the battle was still being fought when Mrs. Frank Sittig announced an exhibition of her new duplex bicycle skirt. On the day of the show, models Eva A. McKean, "the talented

young elocutionist," and Vietta Huyler, "the well-known amateur actress," pedaled decorously around a rink in Brooklyn, each wearing a combination skirt-trouser set later adjudged by *The New York Times* to be "an ideal suit for cycling, to which even the most prudish could not object."

Some persons, naturally, would settle for no compromise. In Delaware County, New York, a farmer put up a sign reading, "Any idiot of the new women species found riding or walking on these premises will be arrested." When asked to elaborate on what he meant by "new women species," the farmer defined her as "one of these fools in bloomer costume on a wheel." Even someone as worldly as actress Sarah Bernhardt objected to the bicycle on the grounds that "It brings young people together in conditions unfavorable to strict surveillance."

By the turn of the century, however, the bicycle had done its work. Women were two-legged creatures who were more than ever interested in all sports. Observing this new breed of woman, her grandmother, who grew up before the Civil War, could hardly be blamed if she experienced and expressed a sense of outrage liberally tinged with envy.

Women and Exercise

Dorothy Harris, Ph.D.

The importance of regular, vigorous physical exercise for women has not received the same attention that it has for men, yet the benefits are just as important for them, perhaps even more so in some respects.

By now, almost everyone knows about the value of exercise in maintaining cardiovascular efficiency, but less publicized research indicates that exercise is also essential for keeping one's bones intact into old age.

Bones

Without the push and pull of muscle on bone that comes from physical activity, limbs develop lighter, more porous bones that can be dangerously brittle. Bones need muscle stimulation to develop to their sturdiest potential. Limbs that have been confined in casts or otherwise immobilized tend to become lighter in weight because of mineral loss. It seems that the prime bone mineral, calcium, is not metabolized effectively without muscle activity. Scientists have also noted a significant weakening of the bones in astronauts after only one week in simulated space or zero gravity.

As the above examples indicate, bone growth is stimulated by muscle growth. The amount of muscle determines the degree of force that is exerted on bones to which it is attached, thereby influencing the degree of bone mass. In short, bones adapt to stresses and strains placed upon them.

Osteoporosis is a bone condition that is practically an inevitable accompaniment to old age in both sexes. It is characterized by a loss of calcium that results in a decrease of bone matrix formation and in the formation of abnormal spaces in bones. It is far more prevalent among women, and results in their greater vulnerability to bone fractures in old age. But it is also common among women as early as their immediate postmenopausal years. The onset of osteoporosis among women at this age has been related to the decrease in levels of estrogen, since estrogen stimulates bone maintenance.

Mindful of the female's greater tendency toward osteoporosis, three important points regarding bone development and maintenance should be emphasized. (1) As a safeguard against early onset of osteoporosis, young girls should participate in vigorous activity during their growing years to generate maximal bone strength and density. (2) Since activity stimulates bone maintenance, the way to stave off the threat of osteoporosis in later years is to continue a physically active life-style. (3) Each person's diet should include sufficient levels of calcium in order to maintain proper calcium concentration in the body. When calcium intake is low, the calcium stored in bones and teeth is released to meet the body's needs. A high calcium concentration in extracellular fluids stimulates release of calcitonin, which inhibits release of calcium from bone, the effect is that calcitonin lowers extracellular fluid calcium. Older people often develop an intolerance to milk products and their diet should be supplemented with dolomite, which gives the proper amount of magnesium to help with calcium . . . vitamin D is also needed for proper calcium assimilation.

Obesity

Lack of physical activity cannot only weaken your bones, but also be a more significant factor in becoming overweight than overeating. In one recent study of 350 obese subjects, the onset of obesity was related to inactivity in nearly 70 percent of the cases; in only 3.2 percent of the cases was increased food intake related to weight gain.

Another misconception about the relationship between exercise and fat loss is the idea that appetite increases with exercise. Dr. Jean Mayer, an internationally recognized nutrition and weight specialist, demonstrated in a classic Harvard study in the fifties that a decrease in appetite occurs with moderate physical activity, that is, up to one hour of daily exercise. The increase in metabolic rate – the rate at which energy is used – that occurs during exercise is the main cause of weight loss. And several studies indicate that the metabolic rate remains high even hours after one has finished exercising. One University of Southern California study reported that four hours after strenuous activity, the resting metabolic rate was 7.5 to 28 percent higher than at the same time of day when the subject did not exercise. Another study suggested that six hours after exercise, you are still burning more calories than you would be if you had not exercised.

Another misconception that has been widely exploited commercially is the concept of "spot reduction." Women are frequently told to use localized exercises to reduce fat deposits in specific "problem areas," but they are not informed that females are generally fatter than males. This additional fatty tissue is stored in sex-specific areas which include the hips, thighs, buttocks, and upper arms. The best evidence available suggests that exercise causes fat to be reduced from the areas of greatest concentration, regardless of how the exercise is performed, or what the exercise is.

To be effective in reducing body fat, activity must be vigorous and sustained. Exercise must gradually progress from a low to a higher level of intensity. Warming up is also important to minimize muscle soreness and prevent injury to bone and connective tissues. The intensity of the activity is critical, and a good indicator of it is heart rate. For a healthy young adult, a pulse rate below 120 beats per minute suggests light intensity; 120 to 150 beats, moderate intensity; and above 150, heavy intensity. (You can

Dr. Harris *is recognized nationally and internationally as one of the most knowledgeable individuals in the area of women and sport, and has spoken and published widely on the topic. She has devoted the last twenty years to sorting facts from myths and misconceptions about the physiological, psychological, and sociological responses of the physically active female. She is director of The Center for Women and Sport at The Pennsylvania State University.*

check that by stopping exercising and taking your pulse for ten seconds and multiplying by six.) If you want to lose weight, the intensity should be as high as one can maintain for approximately thirty minutes, the suggested duration for optimum results. As you continue on an exercise program, you will note that as a result of improved physical condition you will have to increase the intensity to elevate your heart rate. Research studies show that participation three or four times a week is sufficient.

Don't be discouraged if you don't lose pounds during the initial stages of your exercise program. For the first month or so, muscle gains may equal the fat reduction, and the scale will not indicate net weight loss. But the fit of your clothes will.

How much one weighs does not tell the whole story of body fat; one can be of normal weight and still be "over fat," or one can be overweight but still lean. Women, in general, have more body fat than men at birth, during childhood, and as adults. The proportion of fat to lean body mass in females increases with puberty, while in males, it decreases with adolescence.

An increasing number of studies that compare sedentary, moderately active, and highly trained females are beginning to provide exercise physiologists with a much better understanding of the influence of exercise on body composition. Changes in body composition associated with regular vigorous exercise include a slight overall decrease in body weight, a moderate decrease in body fat, and a moderate increase in muscle weight. One recent five-month study of 14-year-old girls reported an average gain of 6.9 pounds in lean body weight, but a 7.2 pound loss in body fat. There is no evidence to suggest that men respond to vigorous exercise any differently.

Advantages of Fat?

Because of the higher proportion of fat, women are much more buoyant in water. Additional subcutaneous fat (fat layers deposited under the skin) also provides greater insulation from the cold, which partially accounts for the fact that women hold many of the open-water swimming records. Both van Aaken, a German physiologist, and Dr. Joan Ullyot, a physiologist and marathon runner, theorize that women may be better suited to long-distance running than men because of their ability to utilize stored fat for fuel.

But in an article entitled "Hitting the Gender Wall" which appeared in *The Runner* in October 1979, David L. Costill, exercise physiologist at Ball State University, stated that "those who suggest that women metabolize fat more efficiently may have gotten their theory backward. You have more fat because you cannot burn it; if you are converting fat efficiently you will not have an excess of fat. In fact, women may be at a disadvantage in fat metabolism because their fat cells release it more grudgingly – estrogen, the female hormone, is known to block fat oxidation." Costill came to this conclusion based on research comparing males and females who had comparable maximal oxygen uptake or the ability to deliver oxygen to the working muscle. They found that when males and females work at the same relative percentage of their maximal capacity, they will burn the same amounts of fats and carbohydrates.

Costill and his colleagues also did muscle biopsies to see if there were any differences between the muscles of males and females with regard to the capacity to burn fat. They discovered that males have an advantage in burning fat by as much as twenty percent when compared to females. It appears that when the ability to deliver oxygen to the working muscles is controlled, males may have yet another advantage in energy production. There exists the possibility that the ability to utilize fats for energy can be increased in the female through training, thus among females who are genetically endowed with high-oxygen capacity and train to maximize that ability, the difference might be less than Costill measured.

Sweat or Heat Stress

Studies of physical activity in heat show that men sweat more and sooner than women in response to an increase in their body temperature. Because sweat is the most obvious weapon against the

Courtesy of the Danish National Tourist Office

heat, and because women sweat less, it has been assumed that the female body is more vulnerable to heat stress. This may not be the case. In fact, differences in a woman's physiology may be providing her with other ways of cooling off, so that she doesn't need to rely upon sweating as much as a man.

On the average, women have a greater number of active sweat glands than men; however, a woman's internal body temperature must rise two or three degrees higher than a man's before sweating begins. What determines the amount of activation of the female's sweat glands is the amount of use.

In laboratory experiments conducted in hot environments, women have been able to accomplish the same workloads with less water loss than men. Observing that women sweat less than men under similar conditions, C.H. Wyndham and his colleagues at the Human Sciences Lab in Johannesburg, South Africa, suggested that "the male . . . is a prolific, wasteful sweater, whereas the female adjusts her sweat rate better to the required heat loss." K.P. Weinman and associates at the Department of Physiology and Biophysics at the University of Illinois, found that women seem to have not only lower total body-sweat rates than men but also lower heart rates when exposed to the same heat stress. Other investigators, including Dr. Christine Wells of Arizona State University, also have suggested that women regulate their body temperature more efficiently than men do.

The estrogen level in females tends to provide women with greater vascularization (the process of conveying blood through the body). This allows more blood to get to the surface of her body for cooling. Greater vascularization may compensate for her generally smaller body surface and for her additional subcutaneous fat. This may explain why her body temperature is two to three degrees higher than the male's before sweating begins. Because more blood is brought to the female's skin surface for cooling, she does not have to start sweating as soon, nor does she have to sweat as much.

Furthermore, because she has a greater number of active sweat glands than the male, sweat is distributed more uniformly over her body surface to produce maximum cooling by evaporation. This increased efficiency may compensate for her lesser body surface. In other words, although the male sweats sooner, the female may sweat better.

For both men and women, however, the ability to combat heat stress may be a matter of nurture as well as nature. People who live in the tropics have more sweat glands than people living in cooler climates. It also appears that people who lived in the tropics during their childhood are better at adapting to heat as adults. Repeated exposure to heat stress will result in lower core and skin temperatures, accompanied by a decrease in heart rate and an increase in the toleration time of the heat stress. And studies have shown that physically fit men adjusted to hot environments much more easily than their untrained, unfit counterparts. Therefore, young girls should be encouraged to exercise in hot weather, not dissuaded from it. For maximal acclimatization to heat stress, women should develop their ability to dissipate heat early in their development and maintain a good level of physical fitness throughout life.

Anemic?

Iron is one ingredient in a complex biochemical chain that is necessary for carrying oxygen through the body. Specifically, iron is an essential component of hemoglobin, the compound that carries most of the oxygen from the lungs to the muscles. The whole issue of iron deficiency is particularly important to the female athlete because physical performance depends to a large degree on the ability to take in and use oxygen.

On the average, the adult male has approximately one million more red blood cells than a child or an adult female. This would seem to suggest that it is not women who change with the onset of puberty, but that something happens to the male during puberty, raising his red blood count and increasing his ability to store and produce iron. An investigation of androgens (male hormones) and their effect on red blood cell production conducted by David Lamb at the University of Toledo provides some insight. When testosterone (the most potent androgen) was injected into castrated male animals, there was an approximate twenty percent increase in their red blood cell counts.

There seems to be agreement among investigators that the bone marrow, which manufactures blood, actually becomes redder under the influence of regular exercise. This would seem to indicate an increased blood-forming activity. This may dilute the number of red-blood cells in a sample, and give the appearance of anemia. Two effects of very strenuous exercise – the compression of capillaries by muscular contractions and the increased velocity of blood flow – may, however, increase the destruction of red blood cells.

Foods with high iron content should be included in the female diet on a regular basis. Studies show that iron from animal tissue is absorbed by the body better than iron from vegetable sources. Liver of all kinds is tops on the list; oysters are next. Vegetarians must pay close attention to getting sufficient amounts of iron. Good sources are prunes, dates, kidney beans, and baked beans. For a female competitive athlete, adequate sources of iron in the diet are essential.

Obstetric & Gynecological Concerns of Cyclists

Mona Shangold, M.D.

Dr. Shangold *is assistant professor of Obstetrics and Gynecology at Cornell University Medical College. She practices obstetrics, gynecology, and reproductive endocrinology at New York Hospital/The Cornell Medical Center. She is a marathon runner and occasional cyclist and would cycle more if time permitted.*

Little attention has been directed toward the gynecological problems of cyclists, and little has been written about this subject. Areas of concern fall into two general groups: those that are common to athletes of other sports, and those that are unique to cyclists. Some of the reproductive concerns of all athletes involve the effect of training on the menstrual cycle; others involve the effect of the menstrual cycle on training; some involve the effect of training on pregnancy, and others the effect of pregnancy on training. The interdependence of these acts and consequences makes the overall picture complex and dynamic.

Healthy women should be encouraged

to practice regular physical exercise throughout life. In most cases, reproduction should not interfere with such activity. Cycling offers many options and benefits to serious athletes and to occasional practitioners of the sport. Women using common sense should be able to enjoy this sport throughout life.

Recently it has been observed that many athletes have menstrual irregularity; some report total cessation of menstruation. Cause and effect are extremely difficult to determine because of the complexity of the dynamics involved in training. Some investigators have found a higher incidence of menstrual irregularity among athletes than among nonathletes. Most of these reports did not describe the pretraining menstrual patterns of the athletes. Certainly, if a woman had irregular periods prior to athletic training, the training cannot be considered the cause of the menstrual irregularity.

In the course of training, a typical athlete is likely to be subjected to many factors: The immediate effect of the exercise itself, the long-term physical stress of training, the emotional stress of training or competing, weight loss, low weight, and low body fat. It is extremely difficult to separate all these variables in studying any one person. Any of these variables, alone or in combination, could lead to menstrual irregularity.

Perhaps even more important than any of the above is the emotional stress involved in coordinating a strenuous athletic training program with professional, domestic, and social responsibilities. It is very common for women to experience temporary menstrual irregularity in association with personal environmental stresses – e.g., changing jobs, losing a loved friend or relative, taking college examinations, moving to a new home, getting married or divorced, or vacationing in Europe. This phenomenon is neither uncommon nor abnormal. The brain is truly an endocrine gland, and it secretes hormones (chemicals produced in one part of the body and carried to another part of the body, where they produce their effects) in response to external stimuli, such as stress. The same stressful stimulus may be perceived differently by different individuals. Even if perceived similarly, the hormonal response may differ among individuals. Thus, two women undergoing the same physical or emotional stress can be expected to produce different amounts of many hormones, all of which will affect other organs, which

may also demonstrate a hormonal response. This phenomenon is the body's normal response, for both men and women.

When menstrual irregularity develops it is not necessarily dangerous. Any woman with irregular periods should consult a gynecologist specializing in endocrinology in order to determine if the problem is serious and/or in need of treatment. This advice is valid for both athletes and nonathletes. Interruption of training is not necessary in order to undergo evaluation and probably is not indicated to effect treatment.

A menstrual interval (defined as the number of days from the beginning of one period to the beginning of the next period) of between twenty-five and

Courtesy of the Danish National Tourist Office

thirty-two days probably reflects normal function; a menstrual interval between twenty and sixty days probably warrants no attention in the absence of infertility. An infertile couple should consult a specialist. A woman should consult her gynecologist if her menstrual interval is less than twenty days or more than sixty days, if she bleeds between periods, or if she has a breast discharge. Attention is also warranted if menstrual irregularity develops in association with increased training.

There is no evidence that any exercise-related menstrual problems are irreversible. The cardiovascular, psychological, and other benefits of physical exercise far outweigh any potential reproductive hazards, such as might be represented by menstrual irregularity.

Some investigators have reported puberty at later ages among athletes than among nonathletes. This phenomenon

may involve the same overlapping stresses described previously in reference to adult women. Delay of puberty is not harmful, except for social and emotional reasons. A girl showing no signs of puberty (appearance of breast tissue or axillary or pubic hair) by age fourteen deserves evaluation; a sixteen-year-old girl who has never menstruated deserves evaluation. Training need not be interrupted for either evaluation or treatment.

Dysmenorrhea (menstrual pain) has received much attention during past and recent years. While the causes may be complex, they are probably related to prostaglandin release. The pain and gastrointestinal symptoms are often effectively relieved by administration of prostaglandin inhibitors. Many athletes have reported relief of menstrual pain with exercise. While a number of explanations can be suggested for this, the truth remains unknown. Among the most plausible theories are improved pelvic circulation, increased metabolism of pain-inducing substances, and/or increased production of pain-alleviating substances. Clearly more research is needed.

Athletic women generally seem to be less incapacitated by menstrual or other pain than more sedentary women. Perhaps the self-discipline they have developed during training enables them to tolerate more pain, or perhaps the increased feeling of well-being brought about by exercise and the distraction of other activities diminishes their awareness of it; in any case, exercise may have both immediate and long-term benefits on many types of pain. Its role in dysmenorrhea is particularly striking.

A few investigators have studied athletic performance in different phases of the menstrual cycle. They found decreased athletic performance during menstruation, and even worse athletic performance during the few days immediately preceding menstruation. The best athletic performance was found immediately after menstruation. Hormonal manipulation for a single important event, like a World Championship, should not be undertaken prior to it for the first time, but rather this should be attempted on a trial basis several months in advance, in order to determine what side effects, if any, may be anticipated. A competitive cyclist should discuss this issue with a gynecologic endocrinologist specializing in the care of athletes.

The menstrual cycle can also be 223

manipulated by ingesting birth control pills to delay the onset of bleeding. However, this tactic might have a deleterious effect on performance. All birth control pills contain estrogen and progesterone. Side effects of estrogen include nausea and vomiting, fluid retention, headaches, breast tenderness, and carbohydrate intolerance. Progesterone may cause acne, weight gain, increased appetite, and depression. Ingestion of various combinations of these compounds may produce any combination of these undesirable effects. This, the entire picture of the premenstrual tension syndrome, including anxiety and moodiness, may appear in a woman taking oral contraceptive agents to delay bleeding. These unpleasant experiences might impair performance more than either bleeding or the hormonal events accompanying menstruation.

There is, of course, no reason to avoid athletic participation during menstruation. Most athletes find tampons more comfortable and aesthetic than sanitary napkins; both are medically acceptable during exercise. Many women have heavier menstrual flow during exercise and may need to change these at more frequent intervals, or wear additional absorptive protection.

Finding comfortable, stationary underwear is difficult for many cyclists. Many active women have solved this problem with bikini-style panties of a stretchable fabric. Although some women can recall being advised to wear cotton-crotch panties to avoid vaginal infections, there is no evidence to suggest that wearing nylon-crotch underwear causes or increases the incidence of vaginal infections. (Women gynecologists wear whatever they find most comfortable; in many cases this seems to be nylon stretch.) Chamois-lined shorts offer the cyclist another comfortable option.

While many cyclists report low back pain or discomfort, this problem seems to be annoying, but not serious in most cases. Alterations in handlebar or seat height or body posture may alleviate the discomfort; exercises to strengthen the muscles of the lower back and hips may also be beneficial. The wider bone structure of the female pelvis and the physiological tendency of the female to deposit fat tissue encourage use of the wider saddles made for women. Cycling itself tends to correct the problem of fat deposition as it firms the hips by developing muscle and reducing fat.

Pregnancy increases the work load imposed on any woman's body, athlete or nonathlete. This added work load exists both at rest and during exercise. In addition to supplying the caloric needs of the growing fetus, a pregnant woman works harder by carrying more weight. It has been shown that physically fit subjects can perform a standardized work load with less of a decrease in blood pH than physically unfit subjects. Thus, a woman entering pregnancy in a state of physical fitness can be expected to be better able to handle the added work load of pregnancy, labor, and delivery than a less fit woman.

It has been shown that more blood flows to skin and muscles and less flows to the liver and kidneys during exercise, in the presence or absence of pregnancy. It is not known how strenuously a pregnant woman can exercise before the blood supply to the uterus becomes compromised. (It is the blood supply to the uterus that nourishes the developing baby.) Animal studies have shown some harmful effects associated with prolonged and repetitive exercise, although considerable exercise in some species can be tolerated without harmful effect. Whether these data can be extrapolated to humans is not known. The risk of potential harm to a human is too great to justify such danger, since the entire lifetime of the affected individual is at stake. Therefore, it is probably reasonable for any pregnant woman to avoid exercising excessively or exhaustively in order to avoid potential risk to the fetus.

The caloric expenditure of strenuous physical exercise might benefit pregnant women with hearty appetites, but others might find it excessive. A pregnant woman should gain approximately twenty-five pounds during the course of her pregnancy. Weight loss or weight constancy is not advisable during pregnancy because inadequate nourishment is afforded the developing and growing baby. Weight gain in excess of twenty-five pounds does not provide any additional benefit and adds undesirable fat to the mother. Thus, it is important for all pregnant women to find the unique balance between food intake and physical exercise that permits optimal and gradual weight gain throughout pregnancy.

The fetus is very well-protected during early pregnancy by the bones and muscles of the mother's pelvis, and during later pregnancy by a generous cushion of amniotic fluid. The movements involved in strenuous cycling probably affect it negligibly, if at all. Many women find it physically uncomfortable to continue training after the fifth or sixth month because of the size of the pregnant uterus, but many have continued strenuous activity throughout pregnancy and have had no adverse effects. Cycling seems to produce less jarring movements than many other sports and, thus, may be better suited to continuation throughout pregnancy.

There is certainly no evidence to suggest that athletes have any more complications during pregnancy than the general population. Many obstetricians find that their athletic patients have less backache and fatigue. Some have even suggested that they have shorter labors and better endurance of pain during labor and delivery. While some have reported a lower incidence of Caesarean sections among athletes, such statistics were compiled prior to the modern age of obstetrics and its accompanying fetal monitoring techniques and updated indications for Caesarean section.

While cold weather should present no problem for the pregnant cyclist, heat and humidity might lead to greater discomfort and more postural hypotension. In addition, maternal hyperthermia during the first trimester has been associated with increased birth defects, and should therefore be avoided. High altitude cycling might be more difficult because of increased oxygen needs. While cycling on hills might seem to be harder work than in the nonpregnant state, this represents no greater danger. As long as the pregnant athlete listens to her body signals and trains at a comfortable pace, no deleterious effects should be expected.

Photograph by Bernard Thompson

After an uncomplicated pregnancy and vaginal delivery, a cyclist can resume training as soon as she can do so without experiencing pain. If she has had an episiotomy, she may find more prolonged pain than other athletes, since her activity involves direct pressure on her surgical scar. Absence of pain is a reasonably good indicator that healing is adequate, whether following vaginal delivery, Caesarean section delivery, or any other surgical procedure.

Any pregnant woman should consult her obstetrician before undertaking or continuing an exercise program. Pain, bleeding, or rupture of membranes warrants prompt evaluation by an obstetrician; training should cease until the problem is evaluated and should not be resumed until it has been determined that it can be resumed without risk.

The main guides to activity during pregnancy are the prepregnancy fitness and activity of any pregnant woman. Most women can safely continue any activity at the same level of exertion, although extremely active or inactive women might consider slightly modified guidelines. World-class athletes might be best advised to reduce intense train-ing slightly because of both the potential adverse affect of exhaustion on uterine blood flow and also the high caloric cost of strenuous exercise in a woman who should be gaining weight. (It must be emphasized that these are only potential, and as yet unproven, dangers.) Extremely sedentary women might be advised to increase activity slightly and gradually; however, pregnancy is not a good time to initiate a strenuous training program.

In a normal, uncomplicated pregnancy, cycling can provide excellent cardiovascular and psychological benefits throughout the entire pregnancy for both competitive athletes and less skilled participants. Stretching and strengthening exercises are recommended for all cyclists and may be even more beneficial during pregnancy.

If a healthy woman is dissatisfied with the antiexercise advice she receives from her obstetrician or gynecologist, she is always entitled to seek another opinion. She should recognize, however, that a second opinion is not necessarily better than the first, even though the two may differ. There may not be a "right answer" to every ques-tion. Physicians are human and make judgments based on reading, personal communication, and experience. The conservatism and/or athletic discouragement advocated by many obstetricians and gynecologists may reflect their own instincts and habits more than factual information.

Any cyclist seeking a physician interested in the care of athletes should consult local clubs (for runners or cyclists) or the specific specialty department (i.e., orthopedics, cardiology, obstetrics and gynecology) of the nearest medical school or major hospital; those with sports clinics are often especially helpful. Every athlete has the right to select a physician to whom he or she can relate.

It is worth repeating for emphasis that healthy women should be encouraged to practice regular physical exercise throughout life. Reproduction should not interfere with such activity in most cases. Cycling offers many options and benefits to both more serious and less serious athletes. Healthy women using sound judgment and common sense can expect to enjoy this sport throughout life.

Racing During the 1950's —
An Interview with Nancy Neiman Baranet

National Champion in the fifties, Nancy Neiman Baranet is still much involved with cycling. She is secretary of the United States Cycling Federation, and rides about sixteen miles a day before work. Our interview was done at the 1979 Nationals in Northbrook, Illinois – at the top of the officials stand. Nancy had just been typing up the sheets for the final events.

In 1952 I began my great joy by hosteling. Took a trip out East, went to Martha's Vineyard, Cape Cod, down into Rhode Island. When I came back, the group I was with formed a cycling club, and that's how I got into the sport. That was American Youth Hostels; way back in the fifties they had racing groups. They had a group in Detroit, the area I was from; later we broke off and formed our own club, the Spartan Cycling Club, named after the Spartans of Michigan. We weren't related to the college, it was the spirit of the thing.

We would go where they were building the expressways. At that time there was no traffic on the roads, and we could hold sprinting situations. You learned tactical maneuvers, how to use your strength best. Some girls could go from 230 yards at 18 miles an hour, some could only go from 210 yards to the finish line.

There were only two tracks in this country; one was in Wisconsin, the other way out in California. National Championship events were the same for men and women; there was no road race for women at that time. You had three events on the track, a half mile, a mile, and a two mile. They were much like today's scratch races in the Intermediate and Junior Divisions. There weren't National Track, Road and Pursuit Champions; just National Champions.

I was Champion for four years, and then I rode in Europe in 1955 and tied the existing world's record for 200 meters flying start. Since then it's been broken a number of times, but at that time, with our not having a track in Michigan, it was pretty sensational.

I liked racing in Europe tremendously. I loved France; it was super, the food, that's all I can remember! In France there were only two or three tracks, in the northern part around Paris; down south we did road racing, and that was my first road racing experience.

There were teams from a lot of countries. There was a sort of junior women's Tour de France, the first one ever. It lasted eight days. The first day when we started climbing into the mountains, all the trackies were at the end of the field. We'd all have to drop off, then we'd ride together in a group. But as time went on we got stronger, and we started to do a lot better than the roadie girls, because most of us could sprint, which the roadies couldn't. So it worked out really swell. I ended up fourteenth overall. When I went up to the podium in France, they said, "Numero 14, Nancy Neiman, des Etats-Unis." I went up and said, "My name's Nancy Neiman, champignon des Etats-Unis." I'd said, "American mushroom"!

I was working. I had aspirations in art, but at that time, it wasn't that long ago, you grew up to be either a housewife, nurse, or teacher, and I wasn't interested in any of those, so I took Business Education in school and some art courses afterward. I got a job as a secretary, which paid my way. I packed my money away and once I was in the sport, all I did was work and race. And that's what it takes to be a champion. You have to put all of yourself into it, there's no time for anything else.

Being a champion is a combination of a lot of things. Physically I'm not the world's strongest person, or perhaps the best built, but my vital capacity is good; I came from a good middle-class family that could afford to take care of my needs as I grew up. I have always been very strong willed; there were a lot of girls who were basically stronger than I was, but they didn't have—I don't like to use the words—the killer instinct; knowing exactly when to make your move. It's not smartness, it's not endurance, it's an instinct. Many times I've seen girls hesitate who could have beaten me.

We were very lucky because we had a team physician, Nick Gimbel (part of the New York Gimbel family) who rode a bicycle and took a very strong interest in our team. We also had a nutritionist who was years ahead of her field. Dr. Gimbel didn't travel with us, but he raced himself and went to races, and when we had problems (you know how female problems occur with women) he would consult with us. If you didn't have a period for four or five weeks after stenuous activity, you felt safe knowing it was a normal reaction to stress. I rode a twelve-hour once and I didn't have a period for about nine weeks; two hundred miles on a bike in twelve hours is an awful lot, and I'd never do it again.

Title Nine was the greatest thing to help women in general. It opened up opportunities for young girls to get into things they never had before. I'm not a Women's Libber, believe me, I'm not, but I believe in equal opportunity, and it has given us that. We also have equal funding for programs now.

When I was racing there was nothing for anybody, so we were equal. When I went overseas, it was with my money. The men were treated the same way. Once we got some international funding, though, it all went to the men, and the women were still forced to pay their own way. Finally, when Audrey McElmury won the World Championship Gold Medal in 1969, she went over on her own money, but they paid the ticket afterward. Even after that women had to pay their own way. We always got, "Well, there are only a few women in the sport."

I said, "Gentlemen, quantity is not quality, and it is the women who are bringing home the World Championship medals."

There's much less disparity now; it is equal on the Federation level. But private sponsors still don't put up as much for women as they do for men.

Sunday racing in a park in Paris, 1870. Editors' archives.

Advice from the World's Greatest Woman Cyclist

Beryl Burton, O.B.E.

Beryl Burton started winning the Women's BBAR (Best British All-Rounder) in 1958, and hasn't missed a year for 22 years. Besides winning over eighty titles at home, she's won seven World Championships. In 1967 she beat the men's 12-hour figure with 277.25 miles and became the idol of every woman cyclist.

We had always wanted to ask her what advice she would give to other cyclists. This book gave us the opportunity to send her a long list of questions – all of which she was kind enough to answer.

To go fast on a bike doesn't mean you have to be exceptionally strong. You can be very strong, but unless you have speed power, which only comes from riding your bike, you won't get that extra bit out of yourself when racing. Plenty of basic touring miles (done with high pressure tires and saddlebag) with my club, Morley Cycling Club, built my muscles up for the speed I needed when I began to race years later. When I first started racing, it was once every three weeks. The other weekends we would do a hundred mile touring ride with the club on a Sunday. I have tried the short, fast, interval training, which has been successful for some people, but it wasn't for me. Each Spring, I find I have to get about three thousand miles in my legs before I can produce any speed, those miles being done at about eighty-percent power.

If you are riding with a group of people that you know, people you have ridden with on several occasions, you get to know each person's style of riding. You will know how much you can let Joe ride to the left before using your brakes, or how fast you can follow Bob before slowing down, etc. If I am with a group of strangers, I always try to ride on the outside, as riding on the inside tends to get you boxed in. If someone in front of you falls off, you have no escape on the inside, but if you're riding on the outside you can go to the right (in England), assuming, of course, you don't hear a car coming. The main thing is to keep your eyes – not on the person immediately in front of you – but on the one two ahead; then if you suddenly see them swerve or move to one side, you will know straightaway that the person in front of you will do the same. Then you will be prepared to move whichever way you have to. Always make sure your brakes are working perfectly.

Don't try to go crossways on gravel too sharp. Riding in sleet or snow, go the speed at which you feel safe. Some people will go faster than others. Don't put your brakes on too hard (always use two brakes, same pressure on each) or you are bound to end up on the ground. Sometimes you are on the ground before you have even touched your brakes. That's what we call black ice on the roads!

If you have any advance warning that you're going to fall, try and relax. I am sure you will do more damage if you stiffen up. I have watched quite a few spills on the track and road, and the ones who seem to come away with the least injuries are the ones who roll when they fall, rather than going down with a thud. Sometimes I am afraid we haven't much choice, as it is over in a flash.

For many years I went uphill seated in the saddle. I dared not get out of the saddle, as I was never sure if I had worn a hole in my trousers. That was before all the fancy materials and cycle clothing had come out. Now I find if I am alone, I quite often get out of the saddle, but if I'm with other people I tend to sit down and really push with my legs, gripping the saddle with my bottom, and pulling hard on the handlebars.

I use my brakes going downhill as little as possible, so I go down quite fast. I tend to use the brakes more if with a group. The main thing is to lean your bike. If your bike is the right size, it is amazing how you can throw it about, or put it where you want it. One thing I have noticed with a lot of young riders, especially females, is that they tend to use only one brake. Often they can reach only one brake, because the bike is too big. They are reaching too far forward. Perhaps they don't realize they are only getting fifty percent braking power, not to mention ruining their headset.

I don't seem to have any problem breaking in a saddle. I ride a plastic saddle, covered with a thin layer of foam rubber with leather on the top to keep me from sliding about. People have asked my advice on saddles. With the females, I usually find the boyfriend or husband has adjusted the saddle height, and quite often the saddle is too high. This means the woman is pressing down on the delicate part of herself all the time, as her legs are stretching; or often the saddle is pointing uphill, and once again she is putting weight on the same spot. It is difficult to get a saddle perfectly level. I have mine slightly downhill, if it won't go level. Sometimes the saddle is okay and the problem is that the person is wearing nylon panties. This is okay if they have a cotton gussett. Some girls wear panties under racing shorts, which isn't very comfortable and is defeating the object of the chamois leather in the shorts. Chamois has to be washed fairly often, or it gets as hard as old bricks. When I wash my shorts, I always do so by hand, with a soap powder, *not detergent*, give them a good spin, and hang them outdoors to dry. When they are dry I rub the chamois together with my hands, and I find it comes lovely and soft. If it stays a bit hard, I usually put on a spot or two of olive oil.

When I am training I always wear a wool undershirt, a thick one. I perspire a lot, and wool is absorbent. It also retains heat longer than cotton or acrylic. I wear a pair of track training trousers, sometimes wool, sometimes acrylic, or a mixture of both. I always wear suspenders on my trousers. I can't stand tight elastic around my waist, as it restricts my breathing. When you are trying hard, your stomach muscles are going in and out. In the summertime I wear a long-sleeved jersey. Over it I wear a racing jersey with pockets in the back, into which I put a thin wool vest in case I have to stop at all. I find the extra length of the

Beryl winning the national championship in 1976. In winning the 1980 BBAR with an average speed of 25.733 miles an hour, she did the 25 mile in 54 minutes 54 seconds, the 50 mile in 1 hour 55 minutes and 38 seconds, the 100 mile in 4 hours, 10 minutes and 42 seconds. All three time trials were during the last week in August.

Photograph courtesy of Beryl Burton.

racing jerseys covers my back and waist well. I use old racing jerseys to work in, as I work on a farm and do a lot of bending.

In wintertime I have a cotton jacket with a zip-up front, as the wind just blows through any wool jerseys I put on. But a lot of the lads simply wear about four sweaters. The wind doesn't seem to worry them. I wear a woolly hat, which keeps a lot of the heat in your body, and a pair of soft, wool mittens, because I find having my fingers all together rather than separated keeps them warmer longer. Soft wool is good, as I can never get to my handkerchief quickly enough when my nose wants wiping.

If you are out all day in the Winter, it is nearly impossible not to get cold feet, as your feet are just flying in cold air with no real body weight on them. Some people get off and walk with their bikes in order to warm their feet. I can't do that because I'm usually so covered with sweat I would get cold before my feet got warm. Even if it's freezing, I sweat. In winter I

Until she restricted herself to time-trialing, this was one of the best-known views in women's cycle racing in England – the rear view of Beryl Burton! Photo and caption by Tim. Hughes.

wear a pair of fur-lined cycle boots, with a pair of soft plastic overshoes, which come mid-calf. They have a cut-out underneath for a cleat. Some have zips up the back, others Velcro, to give a snug fit, so they don't catch on the crank as you pedal. I do like to wear wool socks, or socks with a good percentage of wool. Acrylic is not very warm.

The only time I don't use mudguards is when I am racing. I just don't like getting my bottom, feet, the bottom bracket, and the rest of the bearings on my bike, wet. Occasionally I even race with mudguards on, usually at the beginning of the racing season when it is very cold.

Equipment is important, but I think it should be graded to your standard of riding. Perhaps I am a bit old-fashioned, but I always feel sorry when I see someone fourteen or fifteen years of age racing with equipment as good as mine. I feel that if they are to improve, they can only do it from themselves. They can't put a lighter tire on, or wheels, or change some of their steel equipment for alloy. Even now I keep certain wheels and tires especially for championship events. If I race without my pump or spare tire, I really mean business, and I am trying for a new record. I keep one bike just for racing on. I get such a thrill when I get on it. I know I am going to go faster, because it is my *racing* bike!

It is not just having the best equipment, but keeping it in one hundred percent working order that is important. Have the bearings cleaned out and greased, everything adjusted properly. I have seen people ride their racing bikes around all year, for racing and training, without mudguards even in the rain, and they never look at the bearings all year. What they must be like I dread to think!

I feel that if a woman races, her equipment should be as good as a man's. If only the man is racing, that doesn't mean that the woman's bike has to be just any old thing. It should be mechanically sound and reasonably light in weight. She doesn't necessarily

have to go to the expense of tubulars, but a good pair of alloy high pressures would help.

I feel I am as strong as a male rider. I ride in the same races. My bike is as good as theirs. But I have seen quite a few top male riders in my time, and the female, be it girl friend or wife, has her bike in a shocking condition. My husband on several occasions has had to adjust brakes or gears, and even stick tires on some of the bikes before the girls could race. One way of getting at the husband/boyfriend is to say one evening, "Sorry the dinner isn't cooked, darling, but I am busy trying to do my bike," or, "Sorry I can't go to the movies, I have my bike to fix." I am sure that will do the trick.

Everyone needs someone to give them confidence and help. It doesn't matter how far you have climbed up the ladder. Nowadays there are coaches. When I started racing it was either the boyfriend or a club member or a friend who helped you. In my case it was the boyfriend, later to be my husband. I have found that the higher up the ladder you climb, the more you need to lean on these people. In fact you get to the point where you have to keep being told that you can do that ride, that you are the best, that you will do a good ride today, or that you look good in training. It is only someone who really understands you that can do it. It's the way they say it; the tone of their voice as they shout to you when you are racing. They can read how you feel by just looking at you, so they adjust their shouting voice accordingly. It is something that you both have and understand, and no one else can take that person's place.

I find most doctors don't understand sports people. We are lucky in Yorkshire, we have a very good sports clinic, which is fourteen miles from my home. If I have any injuries I go there. They are very good.

I don't really know what caused my knee trouble, unless it was overuse. I was doing a lot of training six weeks before the big race, a twenty-four-hour time trial. Three days a week I was doing eighty miles a 229 day. The other two days, a hundred and forty miles a day, plus my housework, shopping, cooking, baking, gardening, etc. (I had been given six weeks leave from work to train for the race.) Some of the Sundays I was racing twenty-five-mile or fifty-mile time trials, then going riding after the race for the rest of the day. I suppose our bodies are like motorcars. Something gives way under pressure. With me it was my knees. I was terribly disappointed because I had to stop in the race. I was leading the field, faster than all the male riders, and I was still bubbling over with energy. I stopped at 17 hours; I had done 370 miles. I am pleased to say I haven't had much trouble with my knees since, just the odd occasion, and when it occurs, I don't do any training for about three days.

I have had massage for the last ten years, and to be quite honest, I can't say it makes me go faster on the bike, but I definitely feel more relaxed after a massage. I just go once a week, usually two days before I race. I don't use linament, just on the odd occasion. If it is very wet, I put a bit of Vaseline on my knees, as it keeps out the rain. That's what my masseur tells me.

If I have a cold, I find the best thing to do is put on a couple of wool undershirts and a sweater, put a jacket on top, get on my bike and try to go fast. Straight away I will be able to breathe through my nose. But if you have a fever, don't go out. Wrap up in warm clothes and go to bed with a drink of hot milk with a bit of ginger in it. It will make you sweat out the cold.

About "women's" problems, up to the age of thirty I didn't have any bother. I have even set up a new record when I had my period. After the age of thirty I find the day before my period is due, I can go like a rocket on the bike. Nothing is too much trouble. I sprint uphill, do anything. Distance is no effort. I feel I can go on all day thumping the pedals around, but I

Beryl and Charlie Burton returning from a race. Photographs courtesy of Beryl Burton.

sure pay for it the next day. I don't suffer with cramps but I feel very lethargic. I think it is a waste of time training, but I still go out. I feel as though someone has switched me off. I creep along at about fifteen miles per hour. I have raced and done some good times in time trials, but when I am racing, I feel as though that extra little zip isn't there. That feeling lasts for about two days. The funny thing is that during the winter my period falls twenty-eight, thirty, thirty-two, and even thirty-four days sometimes, but as soon as I start racing it falls smack bang on the Saturday and Sunday every time. I don't know if it is brought on by thinking about racing! Several times I have ridden World Championships when I had my period. I have both won and lost the Gold Medal. I think to myself, "Well, maybe the other girl is the same way."

About my famous twelve-hour ride. Over here in England we have what we call a "British Best All-Rounder Competition" for men and women in time trial races. The men's is taken on distances of fifty miles, a hundred miles and a time of twelve hours. An average speed of three distances is worked out. The women's is over distances of twenty-five, fifty, and a hundred miles, and an average miles per hour is worked out, so that the twelve-hour race I was in didn't count for anything other than personal satisfaction. I had raced in two twelve-hour races before. I did 237 miles in one, and 251 in the other. In the second one I had a spill and damaged my left shoulder, so I had to eat and drink with only my right hand,

Photographs courtesy of Beryl Burton

which was awkward. During both of these races I couldn't eat much. I couldn't get the hang of eating and breathing at the same time.

So for this third twelve-hour race, I made up my mind. It didn't matter how many miles I did. I was going to eat the pile of food I had put in the back of the car! Well, I ate everything. My husband was driving along, and our friend, Eddie, was busy cooking small pieces of filet steak on a Primus stove in the front of the car. I had sausage, soup, rice pudding with tinned fruit in it, tomatoes, malt bread with sultanas in the middle, just small pieces you can push to the side of your mouth and still breathe easily, Milky Way bars, licorice allsorts, tea, coffee, black currant juice, orange juice, fresh peach, melon, I never stopped eating. I think I had something about every twenty minutes, in small quantities. If I felt a bit sleepy, I got a bottle of water and poured it over my head. You have to be careful it doesn't go in your eyes.

Well, riding in the same race was a friend of mine, Mike McNamara. Big Mac we call him. Big Mac was trying to win the Men's British Best All-Rounder Competition, and had to do about 270 miles in this race. I remember watching him set off in the race and saying to my husband, "What a burden to have on your shoulders, knowing you have to do more than 270 miles to win the competition."

I set off in the race, nothing in particular on my mind, other than enjoying all the food in the car. I think I had done over 200 miles before I realized how well I was doing; after 210 miles everyone rides around what we call a finishing circuit. It is usually about fif-

Millie Robinson at left, near the end of a great career.
Beryl Burton at the right, near the beginning of hers.

Ready for the Word "Go"

teen miles around, and you ride round until you have finished your twelve hours. There are timekeepers every two miles. Well, I had started to go around the circuit when I saw this rider in front, and I was getting closer to him. I suddenly realized, as I was nearly up to him, that it was Big Mac. I was so taken by surprise, I put my hand in my back pocket and pulled out a licorice, and said, "Licorice allsort, Mac?" "Ta, love," he said, and I went by him and on my way. I finished at the timekeeper when my time was up, and not long after along came Big Mac to finish at the same timekeeper. We had both set new British Competition records, but mine was about half a mile longer than the men's. I did 277.37. I had stopped a couple of minutes before my time was up, because if I had gone to the next timekeeper, I would have been over the twelve hours. An average is taken between the last two timekeepers.

I remember lying in the back of the car afterward and saying that my stomach felt like a dustbin. I felt as though I could have done with about a dozen packets of stomach tablets.

I don't think the fact that I had gone faster than the men really hit me until the next day. Ever since then, men to me are just other competitors to beat. I don't mind admitting, when I see some of the men warming up before the race, and I look at their physique, I think, "Am I supposed to beat that hunk of muscle?" But I put it at the back of my mind straightaway.

I have won fourteen world championship medals, seven Gold (five pursuit, two road race). I'm not sure how the others are split up, four Silver and three Bronze, I think.

Photographs courtesy of Beryl Burton

Choosing Components

Donald Taylor

Donald Taylor's articles in Freewheeling *were so clear that they were responsible for our expanding the equipment section far beyond our original intent. Free-wheeling is a lively new magazine that reports on the development and use of the bicycle throughout the world. Its editors aim to encourage all forms of cycling, with particular emphasis on the bicycle as a means of transport.*

This article is intended as a guide to the informed choosing of components when specifying a bike or deciding between manufacturers' alternative specifications. It is best read in conjunction with a comprehensive component catalogue. Here we are considering lightweight touring and recreation machines, not heavy-duty roadsters or specialized racing machines.

There are four factors influencing the choice of a component: suitability for purpose, reliability and service life, cost, and effect on the rider's energy expenditure.

Of course, the choice must necessarily be a compromise between the four. The energy expenditure factor refers to the effect of weight, friction, and lack of rigidity in components. If a component's weight is pared too far, it is liable to flex under pedaling stresses, and energy is wasted bending the metal to and fro. Be wary of drilled-out components whose weight is reduced by a tiny amount but whose strength and rigidity are severely reduced. Titanium components are not recommended, because of their high cost in relation to weight saved, and their relatively short service life because of fatigue cracking. Remember that it is not the weight of the bike which is significant, but the total weight of bike and rider.

Wheels

Tire weight and tire pressure have a great effect on performance. The less rubber in the tire and the higher its pressure, the less energy is consumed by the flexing of the rubber as the tire rolls in contact with the road. The working pressure of a tire is governed by its width–a narrow tire requires more pressure over its smaller contact area to give the desired degree of support for its loading. Light tires, however, have a shorter life and are more prone to punctures and cuts. The fastest tire is the tubular (sew-up) at 200 to 400 grams, but this construction, where the outer casing is stitched round the inner tube, makes puncture repair extremely difficult and is not recommended. The amount of time spent repairing punctures is far greater than the time saved by riding on a more energy-efficient tire. Tubulars are often said to possess "feel" and "responsiveness"; these vague terms merely refer to the perceived increase in speed and acceleration when such a very light tire is fitted. High pressure clincher tires of equivalent weight "feel" the same. They are to be preferred to tubulars and are available in a wide range of weights–280 grams with tube (Michelin Elan TS) to 700 grams. Fatter tires are slightly more comfortable on bumpy surfaces. Forget about tread pattern–matt, file, ribbed, mixed–it is not important.

Alloy is the better rim material, as it gives thirty percent wet-weather braking distance improvement over steel. The alloy rim is also lighter (400 to 500 grams) compared to steel (800 grams) and is rustless. Smooth-surfaced sides as opposed to dimpled or ribbed, give better braking; claims to the contrary are not well substantiated. Two basic designs of alloy rim section are available–solid U-section and hollow-box section (e.g. Super Champion). The hollow type is light, strong, and builds to a very true wheel. Rims and tires are coded "27x1¼" or 700c–referring to the diameter, the 27 being about 7 millimeters larger than the 700. You must stick to one or the other. The larger 27 has marginally better rolling resistance, but 700c is becoming the standard size.

Spokes are double butted (D.B.) or plain gauge. Double butting is the thickening of either end of the spoke where stresses are greatest, giving a lighter construction. Spoke thickness is described by gauge numbers (the smaller, the thicker); 14 g. plain or 14-16 g. D.B., where 16 refers to the thin central section, 14 to the thickened ends. Light riders can use the thinner 15-17 or 15 g. Unfortunately, most of the brands of D.B. spokes are made of a material which, though strong, is relatively brittle, and spoke breakages can be expected. Chrome plating of spokes is expensive and mainly for appearance.

Hubs attract a degree of interest and financial outlay quite disproportionate to their importance. Here, price relates to the degree of hand polishing rather than quality. Expensive hubs do have better quality precision bearings, which last longer, but the additional life is not in proportion to the additional cost. Theory holds that high flange makes a more rigid wheel, low flange a more comfortable one; in practice this is difficult to perceive. Low-flange rear hubs have less problems with the rear derailleur fouling the spokes. If strength were the only consideration, you could forget quick-release hubs, they only make wheels easier to steal, and the hollow axle is weaker than the solid spindle. The sealed-bearing type of hub needs less maintenance but has very slightly more friction and there can be problems with the nonadjustable bearings when these do eventually wear.

Saddle

The choice of saddle is an important one—an uncomfortable saddle wrecks cycling enjoyment. Leather is uncomfortable at first, but "breaks in" to the rider's anatomy, and in the end is held to be slightly superior in comfort to the molded plastic variety. The plastic and leather-covered plastic types, however, are very much lighter and cheaper. It is worth experimenting with different saddles, including the "anatomic" designs, which have hollows positioned to correspond with human pressure points. In any case, do not buy cheap leather saddles as these develop uncomfortable ridges. A variety of "microadjusting" seat posts are available, highly polished and highly priced, offering some convenience. If available in the correct size, the traditional detachable post and clamp are fine.

Crankset

Alloy cotterless or steel cottered are the choices. The alloy set is 500 grams or so lighter than the steel (double chain ring). The accepted superiority of alloy cranks may be exaggerated because steel cranks consume less energy in flexing and air resistance. However, because of the almost universal preference for alloy cotterless, good-quality, precision-steel sets are not widely available. Most of the steel sets are poorly made; cranks are twisted and chain rings are buckled or out-of-round. The most expensive alloy sets have machined (rather than pressed) chain rings, which wear longer. All the well-known makes of alloy cranksets are good quality.

"Swaged" cranksets refer to a method of attaching the crank to the spider, where the two parts are force-fitted together in a manner akin to riveting. The joint can eventually work loose. The expensive sets have the crank and spider forged as one piece, a superior design. Spiders are 3-arm, 5-arm, or small diameter 5-pin. The 5-arm would be expected to be more rigid than the 3-arm. In either case thick, chunky spider arms are desirable to minimize the energy losses in flexing. The 5-pin (TA, Stronglight 49D) allows very small rings to be fitted; however, small rings instead of large cogs are not the best practice because of the very high pedaling force transmitted in the chain. The high chain force results in rapid wear and increased friction in the transmission, broken teeth, bent rings, and even shattered freewheels.

Transmission

European brands have a good reputation for reliability, adequate performance, and availability of spares, but the Japanese manufacturers have introduced a host of novel features in changers and freewheels, some of which have proved highly successful.

Freewheels

The Sun Tour "Ultra" has close spaced cogs and a cone adjustment for bearing wear, and is highly recommended. The close cog spacing allows the use of a less-dished (i.e. stronger) rear wheel; a narrow chain with flushed rivets is required with this freewheel. Standard freewheels are more difficult to adjust for bearing wear. Seven-speed blocks sound good, but problems can arise with dishing, insufficient fork end width, and excessive chain misalignment. Forget Dural freewheels, these are for racing only.

The Shimano free hub has the freewheel mechanism incorporated into the hub, giving a very light and neat arrangement. In this design, the hub bearings are spaced farther apart than on conventional hubs, which reduces the tendency for the axle to develop a bend. However the cogs used are thinner than standard, i.e. have less contact area with the chain, which would be expected to lead to reduced wear life.

Zig-zag cog teeth, where the teeth are bent alternately in the manner of a saw blade, and chamfered teeth tops, are both claimed to give smoother gear changing, especially on the very large cogs.

Generally, the more expensive freewheels have better quality bearings and more accurately cut, harder, longer lasting teeth.

Chains

There are no great design differences between the makes except for the Shimano Uniglide with bulged plates and the Sedisport with floating bushes, both claiming smoother gear changing.

Changers

Rear changers are rated according to their capacity to absorb chain slack, i.e. the range of the gear, and by their largest cog size. To find the range of a given transmission setup, add the freewheel tooth difference to the chainwheel difference—e.g. on 52-42 by 14-28 the range is 14 plus 10 equals 24 teeth.

This represents a chain slack needing to be absorbed equivalent to the length of chain which would wrap around twenty-four teeth. Choose a changer with no greater capacity than you actually need, because the long cage on wide ratio gears incurs less positive changing.

Avoid cheap steel or plastic gears, these wear quickly. Up to the mid-price range, money buys longer lasting pivot surfaces—sloppy worn pivots means poor shifting. The most expensive changers offer super-lightness.

The Sun Tour Slant Pantograph rear derailleur is an excellent design, having the mechanism angled to follow the contour of the different-sized cogs on the block. The idea is to keep the distance between the jockey pulley and the cog to a minimum, to reduce the lag between operation of the gear and the actual sideways chain jump. The design makes for crisp shifting. Shimano tackles this by having an additional tension spring between the mechanism and the fork end, as well as the tension on the jockey cage. The extra available movement allows the gear to "float" closer to the cogs. Most other makes of rear changer are standard parallelogram design.

Front changers follow a fairly standard pattern.

Shift Levers

Levers can be down-tube, handlebar end, or stem mounted—a matter of personal preference. Tall riders might find the bar end or stem controls more convenient than the long stretch to the down tube. It is sometimes claimed that the shorter cable of the down tube control results in a more positive gear change, but in practice this is not noticeable.

The argument against stem levers as being dangerous is somewhat superfluous, since in the event of a fall the stem itself would in any case cause injury. "Click stop" and "ratchet mechanism" levers use notches instead of a friction clamp to hold the lever in place against the pressure of the return spring—some people find these an aid to smooth shifting.

Brakes

Sidepull, centerpull, or cantilever are the choices. Cantilevers have the most powerful leverage but require special brazed-on pivots. Side-pull brakes have the least leverage but are the simplest in construction and fitting, and have a hard "feel," i.e., it is easy to judge exactly how much brake pressure is being applied to the wheel for a certain hand pressure on the brake lever. Centerpulls have more leverage but the "feel" is spongy because of the flex in the arms and cable hangers. The main difference between the makes of lever is in the shape of the hood in relation to hand comfort when riding "on the hoods." If, for instance, you like thick chunky levers, choose Universal.

Rubber lever hoods are recommended, the so-called "safety" add-on levers are not; these can actually be dangerous. Some riders descending a steep hill using these levers have discovered that the hands cannot apply enough braking pressure as the bike gathers speed; moving over to the more efficient normal levers incurs a sudden complete loss of braking—temporary, but liable to induce panic. Also that top position on the straight part of the handlebars is not the best for steering control on descents.

Very expensive brakes are no better in function than moderately priced ones—you are paying for fancy presentation boxes and meticulous hand polishing.

Pedals

Avoid the cheapest steel non-quill pedals; the joints between the component parts—plates, barrel and supports—come apart after a short period of use. Also, the cage tends to "lozenge," i.e., the rectangle distorts to a parallelogram shape. Cheap quills are not so bad, the quill helping to keep the assembly together. In the mid-price range are all-steel, steel barrel/alloy cage, and alloy barrel/steel cage. In all these designs the riveted joints eventually loosen. Best choice is the all-alloy pedal with an integrally formed barrel and supporting arms; these do not come apart and are the lightest. Although alloy cage plates do wear down where the shoe contacts, the bearings will in any case wear out by the time the plates are excessively worn. Heavy riders who break spindles should try K.K.T. pedals, which have very thick spindles. Pedals for use with alloy cranks need a longer threaded section on the spindle; do not use short thread pedals on alloy cranks—the crank will break. For shoe sizes above 8 or so, the wider type of pedal will be more comfortable.

Handlebars and Stem

Steel bars and stem are intended for track racing use; alloy is nearly always used on lightweights (note that steel bars will not fit alloy stems and vice versa). Make sure that bars and stem are of the same country of manufacture, since dimensions can differ sufficiently to prevent the bars fitting the stem.

Two methods of attachment for the stem to steering tube are used—cone expander and wedge expander. Both are okay, though sometimes the wedge type creaks a bit. Some trial and error is needed to find the most comfortable forward stem extension. Get handlebars with a bulged center section several inches long; bars with a bulge only the width of the stem clip eventually distort, preventing proper tightening of the clip.

Handlebars are made in different widths to suit chest width—the idea is that the arm should not angle in from the shoulder and restrict breathing. If in doubt, err toward wider bars.

Accessories

The remaining bike accessories can be selected by personal taste. Alloy mudguards tend to develop rattles; plastic ones crack more easily. Battery lamps are expensive to run; generators create a significant drag. Canvas saddlebags and panniers are heavy but very durable; nylon ones are light but tear easily. Alloy toeclips weigh less than steel but are much less durable. Frame-fit pumps and cageless bottles constitute very elegant and light designs and are worth considering.

Frames

Donald Taylor

Triangulation

Why are frames built in a standard "diamond" arrangement?

Ideally, a structure should consist of triangles to best sustain loads. Triangles are very resistant to deformation (Fig. 1), whereas the structure in Fig. 2 distorts or collapses very easily.

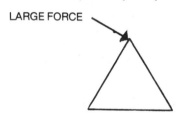

LARGE FORCE

Fig. 1. Triangle very resistant to deformation.

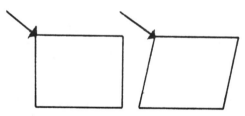

Fig. 2. Rectangle distorts or collapses (known as "lozenging" under a relatively small load.

Figs. 3 and 4 show examples of strong, triangulated construction.

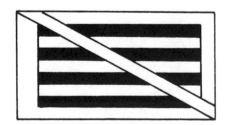

Fig. 3. Farm gate

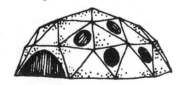

236   Fig. 4. Geodesic dome

Tension and compression

A structural member is strongest when forces are taken in at the ends rather than the middle (Fig. 5).

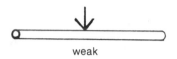

weak

Fig. 5

strong

For example, an empty beer can will easily stand a person's weight end on, but not sideways.

Tubular construction

For the same weight of material, a tube is far more resistant to bending than a solid rod (Fig. 6).

0.9	1.0	0.44
Rigidity = 10	Fig. 6	Rigidity = 1
Weight = 1		Weight = 1

An example of this is the stiffness of a drinking straw until it is collapsed (the same components but a different structure). Our basic frame is made of tubes arranged in triangles with the forces at the apexes.

Fig. 7

The two triangles taken together form the "diamond." The front fork isn't of course triangulated, but this is in fact an advantage, providing some suspension.

The traditional ladies' frame is inherently weak; the "mixte" design is to be preferred (Fig. 8).

Traditional ladies'

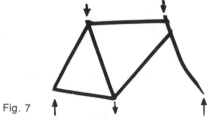

Fig. 8   "Mixte"

What do you pay for in a good frame?

A good quality, hand-built frame costs three to ten times as much as a cheap one. What's the difference? The expensive frame is lighter (about 5 lbs. compared with about 8 lbs.), stronger, more effective in converting energy to motion, and can be specified to suit an individual's requirements.

Tubing

Reynolds "531" Double Butted is the world famous name in tubing. The steel used is formulated for maximum strength and minimum weight. "Double Butted" refers to the thickened (butted) ends of the tube, where more strength is required than in the middle (Fig. 9).

butt   butt

Fig. 9. Double butting

Double butting itself saves about ½ lb. on a frame, the good quality steel a further 1 lb. Other well-known makes of tubing are Columbus (Italy), SuperVitus

(France), and Tange (Japan). Some frames are only 531 double-butted on the two main tubes, where the possible benefit is greatest. (The seat tube is always single butted, and the fork blade is tapered.)

531 front forks also give improved ride characteristics. A recent development, Reynolds 753, is even lighter (1 lb. less), and yet is stronger. This tubing is only supplied to certain builders who have the required skill for the very precise construction necessary with this thin material.

Good frames have ''mitered'' tubing, that is to say the tubes are shaped to joint to themselves as well as to the lug (Fig. 10). The down tube is the most highly stressed tube in the bike, and is made of heavier gauge, 28 mm diameter tube. The top tube is 25 mm, seat tube 28 mm, and head tube 32 mm.

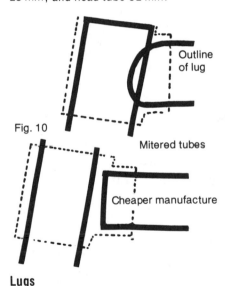

Fig. 10

Outline of lug

Mitered tubes

Cheaper manufacture

Lugs

Most frames are of lugged construction nowadays. Quality lugs have an irregularly shaped edge, to spread the stress over a large area of tube (Fig. 11).

Fig. 11

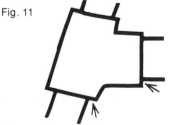

Plain Lugs stress concentration at abrupt changes in cross section, liable to break.

Irregular lug

A large part of the cost of a quality frame is due to the laborious process of filing the lugs to save weight and further reduce the abruptness of the cross-sectional area change at the lug edge (Fig. 12).

Fig. 12. FILED LUGS give almost completely smooth transition from tube to lug.

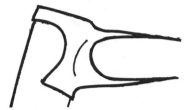

Some lugs have cut-outs as well as irregular edges. This is principally to assist the builder in judging whether the brazing material has penetrated to every part of the lug to make a strong joint.

Construction methods

A top builder possesses a high degree of skill. During building, it is necessary to ensure that no part of the metal is allowed to overheat beyond the critical temperature at which the steel's crystalline structure alters, thus seriously weakening the frame. Reynolds 753 has a low critical temperature, and for this reason silver solder (itself expensive) is used instead of brass.

Joining Process	Joining Material	Temp.
(soft) Soldering	lead	
(hard) Silver Soldering	silver	low
Brazing	brass	
Welding	steel	high

Accuracy

Quality frames are built in a precise manner and are in proper alignment without requiring ''cold setting.'' Cold setting is literally bending the frame to get the correct alignment after the brazed frame has cooled down and any untoward thermal distortion has appeared. The head and seat tube would be accurately reamed to accept the headset and seat pillar, and the bottom-bracket threads would be properly cut.

RIGID, RESILIENT, AND RESPONSIVE

In discussions of the qualities of bike frames, the terms rigid, resilient, and responsive appear frequently. But rigid (stiff) is apparently opposite in meaning to resilient (flexible) and responsive

doesn't seem to mean much at all. So what's afoot?

Among other functions, the frame must enable the rider to transfer as much pedaling energy as possible to the rear wheel, and must help smooth out road shocks in the manner of a suspension. The first function requires that the frame does not ''whip,'' a lateral movement of the bottom bracket under the alternate left-right pedal thrusting (Fig. 13).

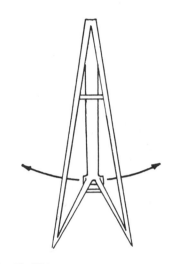

Fig. 13. Whip

The greater the whip, the more energy is absorbed in flexing the metal. Whip can be minimized by suitable design, material, and tube sizing. A frame with low whip is a rigid frame.

The second function requires a certain amount of flex in the vertical direction (Fig. 14). Most of this flex is made available by the curve in the front forks, and also by the relatively small gauge and diameter of the forks and rear stays. A frame designed to provide suitable suspension is said to be resilient.

A ''responsive'' frame responds to a rider's sudden increased pedaling thrust by going faster, not by flexing laterally, and responds to road irregularities by flexing vertically, and not jarring the rider.

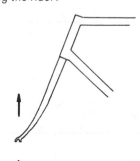

Fig. 14. Suspension

Fork ends

There is a choice of four types of fork ends. The track ends (Fig. 15) are used on fixed-gear machines and on old roadster models.

Fig. 15. Track

The forward dropout is fitted as standard to most machines. The wheel can be easily removed forward without entangling the gear mechanism, if fitted. When single-speed or hub gears are used the wheel position can be varied to adjust the chain tension. Sometimes it is claimed that the alternative wheelbase possible with this type of end (short and rigid wheelbase for efficiency or long and comfortable wheelbase for touring) is an advantage, but the effect is small and is difficult or impossible to detect. Adjustable stops can be fitted to allow rapid repositioning of the wheel.

Fig. 16. Forward dropout

Fig. 17. Vertical dropout

The vertical dropout can only be conveniently used with derailleurs, as there is no facility for chain-length adjustment. The fork end is of sound design, as the axle load is taken against solid metal rather than via the clamping forces of the axle nuts or quick-release skewer in the forward dropout. The vertical is the strongest and lightest of the road ends.

Fig. 18. Short forward dropout

The Campagnolo short forward, a compromise between the vertical and forward, has a slot 12 mm shorter than the forward.

Fig. 19. Claw

The three road ends are shown with integral gear ''hangers,'' which are bosses threaded to accept all derailleur makes without the need for a separate ''claw'' (Fig. 19), thus saving material. Cheaper bikes have plain fork ends; the integral hanger type is recommended.

Fig. 20. Front fork end

Front ends are a standard design (Fig. 20). Fork ends with threaded mudguard eyes are strongly recommended, except for purely racing machines.

Fork ends are described as ''forged'' (or ''drop forged'') or ''pressed.'' Ends manufactured by forging are stronger and have accurately machined surfaces to bear against the locknuts.

Seat stay attachment

The method of attaching the seat stays to the seat lug generates a particularly large number of vacuous claims and controversy. There are four main designs (Fig. 21). The choice is one of fashion, as no one has succeeded in establishing the mechanical superiority of any one.

Fig. 21.

Wrapover

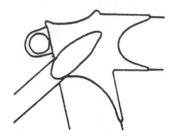

Semi-wrapover

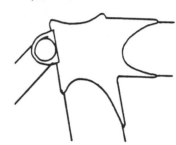

Fastback

Shot-in

Fork crowns

Three types available (Fig. 22). The sloping version is 100 g or so heavier than the flat, but is preferred by some for its elegance. The flat crown has the highest lateral strength (resists bending forces induced by sprinting). The semisloping represents the compromise between the two.

Fig. 22.

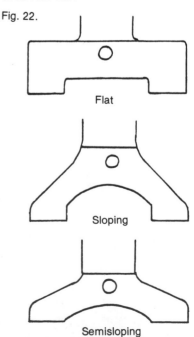

Flat

Sloping

Semisloping

Specifying the Dimensions of a Frame

The easy and foolproof way to specify a made-to-measure frame is to tell the builder your height, arm length, and inside leg measurement, exactly what equipment you are going to fit to the frame, and exactly what you are going to use the bike for. Using the enormous practical fund of knowledge accumulated over the last hundred years, they will build a frame to suit your purpose. All you need to decide on is braze-on fittings, color, and any fancy lugwork or paintwork desired.

Although it is possible to build a frame to suit your own exact specifications, a good framebuilder will generally have a better idea of the most suitable dimensions for your purpose. Most builders can recount tales of woe about people who specified strange angles or tube lengths and who ended up with most unsatisfactory frames.

In general, track racing frames are steep and utility frames are shallow, with touring frames in between these two extremes. This aspect of the frame is described in terms of the head and seat angles (Fig. 23). Typically, current frames have the seat and head angles equal — known as "parallel" design. This is simply coincidence and has no significance.

A 1-degree change in angle represents a forward or backward movement of about 1 cm.

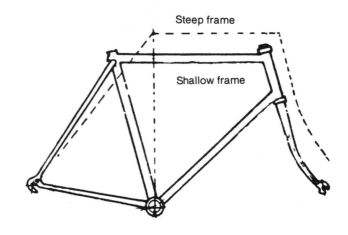

Fig. 23

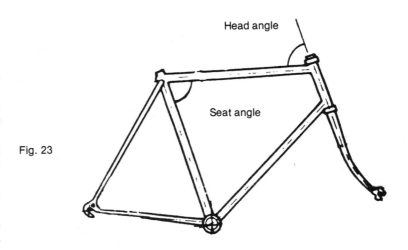

Brazed-on fittings

Fig. 24 shows a variety of brazed-on fittings. Clips are heavier and less neat than brazed fittings, and also damage the paint work. On the other hand, they allow components to be changed. For example, cantilever brake bosses will foul center-mounted side-pull or center-pull brakes, so you have to make up your mind which type you are going to stick with. The argument whether brazed-on fittings weaken the frame by local overheating has droned on for a century, but numerous tests have failed to detect any such weakening where the brazing is done by a skilled builder. Brazed fittings are not recommended for the special purpose, very thin "SL"-type tubing.

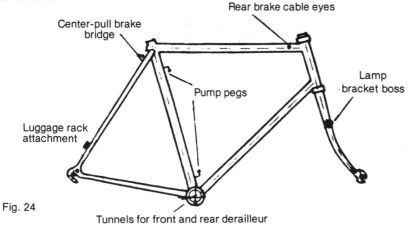

Fig. 24

Frame Angle — 70-71 deg.
Use—Utility
Characteristics — Long · wheelbase absorbs bumps. Whippy frame. Rider position upright and behind the bottom bracket. Comfortable. Stable steering.

Frame Angle — 72-73 deg.
Use — Touring on good roads

Frame Angle — 73-74 deg.
Use — Road racing

Frame Angle — 75-76 deg.
Use — Track racing
Characteristics—Short wheelbase, can only be used on very smooth surfaces without extreme jarring. Position of rider is pitched forward. Jittery steering. Maneuvers quickly. Low energy losses in frame.

Wheels and Wheel Building

Donald Taylor

The advent of the tension-spoked wheel was a spectacular technological leap. Solid wheels bear the weight of a vehicle downward to the ground via material in compression (Fig. 1).

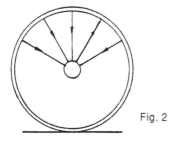

Fig. 1

In a tension-spoked wheel, the load is suspended from the top of a stiff rim via material in tension (Fig. 2). This method of construction is inherently much lighter than the solid-compression type.

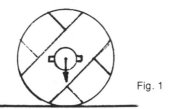

Fig. 2

A striking example of the two types of structure is shown in Fig. 3. The road and railway bridges over the River Forth sustain similar loads, but the suspension road bridge uses much less material than the girder-built railway bridge.

240   Fig. 3

Intricate Spoke Patterns

A bicycle wheel has an apparently complicated ''lattice work'' of spokes, crisscrossing in all directions (Fig. 4) in a pattern which seems an unfathomable mystery to the novice. All will become clear as we build up this spoke pattern from the basic spoked wheel.

Fig. 4

Radial Spoking

The simplest wheel is radially spoked. Fig. 5 shows the 12 spokes on one side of a 24-spoked wheel.

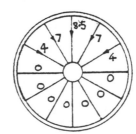

Fig. 5

The approximate tension generated in each spoke by an axle load of 50 kg is shown (in kg). On the other side of the wheel, the spokes are placed half way between the first set of spokes (dotted lines in Fig. 6). When the wheel is built,

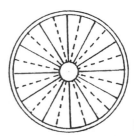

Fig. 6

the pre-tensioning (typically about 20 kg) in each spoke is adjusted so that the rim is central (Fig. 7) and concentric (Fig. 8) with the hub. The radial wheel is strong, stiff, and light, and is excellent for the purpose of supporting the axle weight (i.e., for a front wheel). But, to transmit pedaling torque (i.e., twisting effect) from the hub to the rim, a different pattern is needed.

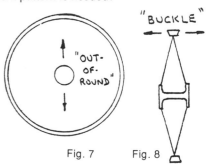

Fig. 7   Fig. 8

Tangent Spoking

If a torque is applied to the hub on a radial wheel, the wheel distorts to the pattern shown in Fig. 9 — viz., the tangent spoked wheel, where the forces are once more being transmitted along the length of the spoke.

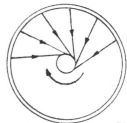

Fig. 9

A wire spoke cannot sustain a sideways force; this situation results when a radial wheel is subjected to torque. But a wheel built with the spoking in Fig. 9 will not hold its pattern when the driving torque is relaxed. As the hub with the overlong spokes would slop around, additional balancing spokes are added in the opposite direction, giving the characteristic pattern shown in Fig. 10.

Fig. 10

This figure shows one side of a 24-spoke wheel. On the more usual 36-spoke wheel, the pattern is more intricate, but the principle is the same. As well as having torque capacity, the tangent spoked wheel can also support axle load (Fig. 11), in a similar manner to radial wheels, so this design can be used for both front and rear wheels.

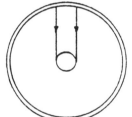

Fig. 11

2-, 3-, and 4-Cross Wheels

As well as pure radial and pure tangent patterns, a spoke may take a half-way position (Fig. 12), representing a compromise design between radial and tangent wheels.

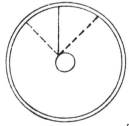

Fig. 12

Adding a few more spokes to the wheel (Fig. 13), we find that the spoke "crosses" the paths of three other spokes — a 3-cross wheel. If a spoke is angled closer to the tangent, it must cross more spokes.

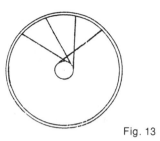

Fig. 13

Tangential spoking is represented by 4-cross, and radial spoking by 0-cross. Fig. 14 shows a 1-cross, while Fig. 10 is a 2-cross.

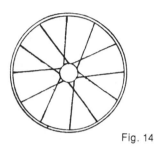

Fig. 14

Another property of tangent spoking is the suspension effect, as shown in an exaggerated fashion in Fig. 15. The scissors action of the spokes allows the axle to move slightly in relation to the rim, affording some cushioning against bumps. Which pattern is best?

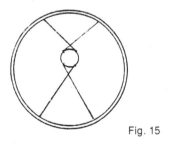

Fig. 15

The most suitable pattern depends on the use required:

RADIAL

0-cross
Stiff wheel, bumpy ride
Short (light) spokes
Spokes highly stressed

TANGENTIAL

4-cross
Suspension effect
Can transmit torque
Spokes not highly stressed

Commonly, spoke patterns are 3- or 4-cross on the rear, 2- or 3-cross on the front. "Tying and soldering" refers to the knotting of copper wire around each pair of spokes where they cross each other. This prevents scissoring movements of the spokes under very heavy pedaling forces, and this technique is often used on track racing machines.

Inside and Outside Spokes

Looking at the spokes entering the hub, half must be "inside" and half "outside," to allow them to cross each others' paths. The weakest part of the spoke is the bend at the head, and the bend itself is weakest when the spoke is on the inside. Fig. 16 shows how the tension is trying to open the bend of an inside spoke. Spokes eventually crack from fatigue at the inside of the bend. Metal fatigue arises from fluctuating stresses as the wheel rotates; each spoke in turn is subjected to an 8.5 kg force at the top of the wheel.

To make the best use of the spokes' strength, the pattern is arranged so that outside spokes take the driving torque on a rear wheel. On a radial wheel, all the spokes can be outside ones. (In Fig. 9 the spokes shown would be outside.)

OUTSIDE   INSIDE

Fig. 16

Initial Spoke Tension

If a wheel is built with the spokes at a low tension, the spokes can easily absorb the additional axle and pedaling loads without reaching their breaking point, but the wheel will be sloppy, i.e., it will distort, and thus waste the riders' energy. Such sloppiness is most noticeable when "honking" (climbing a hill out of the saddle). If the brake blocks are adjusted fairly close to the rim, the rim can be heard to scrape against alternate blocks at each pedal thrust. On the other hand, a tight wheel is energy efficient, but the spokes will break more often. Part of the knack of wheel building is to judge an appropriate compromise tension, by listening to the "ping" of each spoke as it is plucked.

Braking Forces on the Spokes

Braking generates large radial stresses in the spokes. In the particular case of a hub brake, very large tangential forces must also be transmitted from the hub to the rim. In Fig. 17, to achieve an effective braking force of 50 kg at the circumference, the transmitted force of 300 kg is shared by half of the spokes, 8.3 kg on each spoke for a 36-spoked wheel. It is these large forces that necessitate the heavy construction of wheels fitted with hub or disc brakes. Rim brakes, however, generate their braking effort near the circumference where it is required, and the number of crosses does not affect their operation.

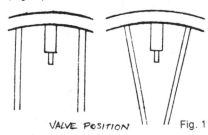

Fig. 17

WHEELBUILDING: How To Do It

Building a wheel is a fairly tricky task, but certainly a satisfying one. Until you have done it several times, expect to spend a few hours on building a wheel. Having purchased rim, hub spokes, nipples, and nipple key (your dealer will provide the correct length spokes for your rim/hub combination), your first step is lacing the wheel, i.e., loosely assembling the components before truing. The method described here is not the speediest, but it is designed to be least confusing for the beginner. The instructions refer to a 3-cross wheel, 36 spokes.

Lacing

Look at the valve position on a wheel — the valve lies in a rectangular spoke space rather than a triangular space (Fig. 1).

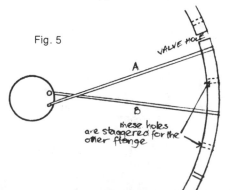

VALVE POSITION Fig. 1

This convention is not for structural reasons, but is to allow room for the pump connection.

Now look at the spoke holes in the rim — they are slightly staggered (Fig. 2).

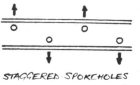

STAGGERED SPOKEHOLES
Fig. 2

Left-staggered holes are for spokes to the left hub flange, right staggered to the right flange. We will lace one side of 18 spokes, temporarily ignoring the 18 holes staggered in the opposite direction.

Insert three inside spokes into one flange (Fig. 3).

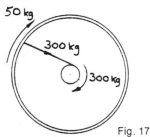

Fig. 3

Inside spokes occupy every second hub hole, the remaining holes are for outside spokes. If the hub holes are countersunk, arrange the spokes so that the heads sit in the countersinks. Now insert one outside spoke and fan out the four spokes so that the outside spoke crosses the three inside spokes (Fig. 4). Thus the basic three-cross pattern is arrived at.

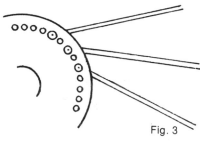

BASIC 3-CROSS PATTERN Fig. 4

Grip spokes A and B and align them adjacent to the valve hole (Fig. 5), forgetting the other two for a moment. Screw on the nipples.

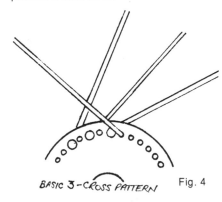

Fig. 5

When these two spokes are correctly located, all the others will fall into place. Attach the other two inside spokes as in Fig. 6.

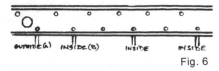

OUTSIDE(A) INSIDE(B) INSIDE INSIDE
Fig. 6

Following the pattern, insert the remaining 6 insides, then the remaining 8 outsides. Check that the sequence at both rim and hub is inside-outside-inside-outside. There is an opposite-staggered hole between each pair of spokes at the rim. Each spoke crosses three others.

Turn the wheel over and establish the "square valve space." Some trial and error is needed here. To check the four key spokes, look at the lean of the outside spoke (Fig. 7).

leans to left ("going left")

SPOKE LEAN Fig. 7

Turn the wheel over and look at the completed side. The outside spokes should again lean in the same direction. But, if you look at both sides from the same viewpoint, the outsides appear to lean oppositely (Fig. 8). It doesn't matter whether the lean is either left or

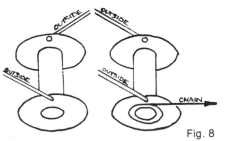

OUTSIDE OUTSIDE
OUTSIDE OUTSIDE
CHAIN
Fig. 8

right. The diagrams here have been drawn to show left leaning. The above applies to front wheels. For rear wheels, the free wheel outsides must go left so that the driving torque is taken by the stronger outside spokes. It is our recommendation, although some debate exists, that the nearside outsides be made right leaning.

So the rear hub looks like this.

When lacing the second side, the spokes have to be bent slightly to maneuver them past the first 18 already in position. When all are in, check the sequences again.

Renewing a rim on an existing wheel

Replacing a damaged rim is relatively straightforward if the spokes are undamaged. There is no need to dismantle the wheel; slacken the nipples, hold the new rim alongside the old, and transfer each spoke and nipple in turn.

Truing

To true the wheel, the tension in each spoke is adjusted by tightening or loosening the nipple, according to the principle shown in Fig. 10.

In addition to the truth of the rim, we are also aiming for equal spoke tension (so that the load is spread over all the available spokes) and a rim position central to the locknuts (which in a front

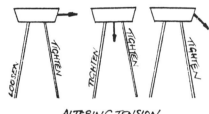

ALTERING TENSION TO CHANGE RIM POSITION — Fig. 9

wheel is the same as central to the flanges) (Fig. 11).

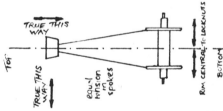

OBJECTIVES IN TRUING — Fig. 10

To start with, the wheel can be put in approximately the correct shape by screwing each nipple on the same number of turns. As a yardstick, tighten each nipple until, say, the spoke end is flush with the nipple top, or until the threaded portion has just disappeared into the nipple end. This trick won't work with old spokes which at some occasion have been filed and are not all the same length.

For a wheel jig, use the forks of an upturned bike or mount a pair of front forks in a vice. Rear spindles are thicker and rear locknut spacing is wider than front spindles, so a second set of forks with filed and spread tips is necessary for rear wheel truing.

Before starting truing, make sure that the cones are properly adjusted — any wobble will interfere with your judgment of rim corrections needed. Use the brake blocks as sideways truth indicators (upturned bike), or your thumb (vice) — loosen the brake adjustment

first to give clearance. At the high spots where the rim scrapes the block, tighten and loosen the appropriate spokes (Fig. 12).

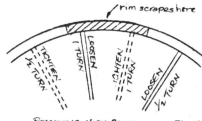

REMOVING HIGH SPOTS — Fig. 11

As the wheel improves, tighten the brake adjustment to bring the blocks closer to the rim. When the sideways high spots have been reduced to 3 mm either side, apply the same method to the roundways highspots. Hold a wrench across the blades as an indicator, or use your thumb. At first, you'll find that half of the wheel is a highspot (Fig. 13) — here you tighten 18 nipples and loosen the other 18.

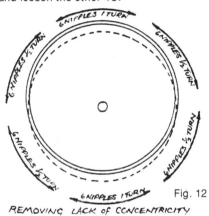

REMOVING LACK OF CONCENTRICITY — Fig. 12

By the time the rim is concentric to 3 mm, the sideways truth will have been thrown out, so this will have to be readjusted. Then recheck the roundways truth — and so on — making ever finer adjustments until both sideways and roundways high spots are less than 1 mm (on good quality alloy rims with pinned joints) or 2 mm (on steel and cheaper alloy rims with welded joints).

Now reverse the wheel in the forks and check for centrality between locknuts. Tighten or loosen all 18 nipples by the same amount on one side to move the rim over. Half-turn tightening or loosening will move the rim about 1 mm. Half-turn tightening AND loosening will move it about 4 mm.

Test for equal tension by pinging each spoke. The higher the tone, the tighter the spoke. Take extra tension off each tight spoke and load it on to the adjacent spokes without altering the overall pull on that section of the rim

(Fig. 14). With good quality rims and hubs, it's possible to get the tensions within half a semitone. Repeat the sideways, roundways, and centrality checks until everything is right. The "art" of wheel-building lies in adjusting to all four criteria at once – this takes practice.

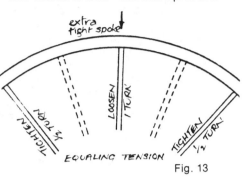

EQUALING TENSION — Fig. 13

Spoke tension

Ping the spokes on a fairly new bike to get an idea of the correct tension.

Tension too tight:
If great strength is needed to turn a nipple it is too tight. (Ignore creaking sounds when tightening; this is normal.) Spokes will break more often on a wheel that is too tight.

Tension too loose:
Wheel is floppy and the spokes will come loose in use. Under heavy pedaling, the rim will be heard to scrape the brake blocks as it distorts. Under normal pedaling, the spokes will rattle.

Dishing rear wheels

On derailleur wheels, the rim is central to the locknuts, but not to the flanges. On the tighter, freewheel side, use spokes 2mm shorter than on the other side. A separate tension equalization is needed for each side.

Filing spoke ends

If the spoke protrudes above the nipple inside the rim, file it flush, so that the inner tube will not be punctured.

Bedding down

When the wheel is first ridden, a chorus of tinkling will be heard for the first few seconds, as the spokes, rim, hub, and nipples bed down into each other. After several miles running, re-true the wheel. The bedding down can be accelerated by pressing hard down on the wheel against the floor on each part of the rim in turn, before fitting. The same tinkling will be heard.

Another meaning of lacing

Lacing means assembling the spokes in a wheel ready for truing. But the word is also used to refer to the interweaving of spokes as shown in Fig. 1.

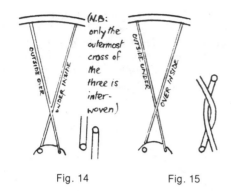

(N.B: only the outermost cross of the three is interwoven)

OUTSIDE OVER
UNDER INSIDE

OUTSIDE UNDER
OVER INSIDE

Fig. 14   Fig. 15

Some maintain that lacing gives a tighter wheel (spokes are less able to move because they are pressed against each other). Others claim a more flexible wheel (the spokes follow a curved instead of straight path and the available curvature can be converted to a slight movement). Also claimed for lacing is the fact that a broken-headed spoke cannot flop outside the wheel and become entangled with the frame or gear, with possible dire results. Perhaps the widespread use of laced wheels is because automatic wheel building machines, on which the majority of wheels are built nowadays, cannot operate any other way.

So, until the superiority of either design is established, beginners should stick to unlaced wheels.

Improving a 3-Speed

John Krausz

Many long-time riders' favorite bike is the 3-speed Clubman. Such bikes, unfortunately, are no longer distributed. Alloy 27-inch wheels, dropped handlebars, racing seat, metal rat-trap pedals with toeclips, and fenders were standard equipment, along with a wide-range 3-speed hub.

You can convert your favorite old 3-speed to a bike like this in stages. The simplest and cheapest thing to do is to change to metal pedals and use toeclips. (One of the many bicycling items made but not widely distributed are toeclips designed to fit on rubber pedals.)

Toeclips, besides giving you more power and keeping your foot in the proper pedaling position, allow you to relax and spin better because you no longer have to fight one leg against the other in an effort to keep your feet on the pedals. It is important they be the proper size.

If you're nervous about trying toeclips, you can either start with one, or get the short, strapless kind designed for urban riding. The toe straps needn't be tightened, and even experienced riders usually leave one very loose in stop-and-go traffic. A few trials in an empty parking lot should give you enough confidence to try the street, and a few hours' practice should perfect the ability to pick up the second pedal while riding.

Straight handlebars are a compromise between standard 3-speed handlebars and racing bars. Get some that fit the stem on your bike and use the brake handles you already have. The straighter bar will place more weight on the front wheel and allow you to pull on a hill; it will help cut wind resistance. With straight bars you can still use a 3-speed seat; dropped handlebars will probably require a racing seat.

If the main reason you don't use your 3-speed is that the lowest gear isn't low enough, have the 18-tooth rear sprocket (standard equipment) replaced with a larger one with more teeth. Sprockets are made with up to twenty-two teeth. An increase of three teeth will equal about a half-step in gear. You'll need a few more links of chain.

Get a new chain and remember to oil it regularly. If the rear hub and the chain are oiled regularly, this will probably equal a full step in gearing over a neglected bicycle.

If you still have a chain guard, leave it on or put it back on, because with a freshly oiled chain it does what it's meant to—it keeps the oil off your pants. Unless you have one that totally encloses the chain, don't trust it to keep your pants out of the chain.

The biggest change you can make in the performance of a 3-speed is to replace the 26 x 1-3/8 inch steel wheels

Drawing by Barbara Remington

244

with alloy ones for high-pressure tires; at that point it performs as well as a 10-speed with steel wheels. The reason alloy wheels are better is three-fold; they brake much better under wet conditions, they cut two pounds of rotating weight off the bike, and they offer a much wider choice of tires (some allow the use of tire pressures of up to ninety-five pounds). Better tires and higher pressure cut rolling resistance. The difference in performance is as great as the difference between shuffling and skipping. Higher pressure means you bounce over minor road irregularities, rather than sink wormlike into them. The lazier angles of the 3-speed absorb a lot of the road shock. As you'll need a high-pressure pump, the Zefal hp has a crack valve lever and is very good.

It has been suggested that standard 27 x 1¼ inch wheels will fit the average 3-speed frame, but this raises the bottom bracket, and may make other changes in the handling characteristics of the bike, as well as leaving no room for fenders. A much better idea is to change to 700c wheels; this will allow the same brakes to be used, although if they are steel it might be a good idea to change to alloy, as they work better. The 700c's come in three different widths, and the medium width (28 mm) allows the use of both narrow and medium-width tires. The brake blocks, which are usually at full extension in their slots on 3-speeds, will have to be moved up a bit to fit the 700c rims.

If you're worried about banging up alloy wheels, you'll be pleased to know that the new alloy box-type rims are very strong, and being smaller than the 27¼-inch wheels that most 10-speeds come with, are even stronger because they are made of the same material and have a smaller diameter. The tires wear a little faster for the same reason.

Should you want the convenience of a quick-release hub on the front wheel so you can stop carrying two locks and can quickly load the bike into a car, the fork may have to be spread and/or the dropouts filed out to fit the thicker quick-release axle. This won't weaken a bike with brazed-on front drop-outs.

If you'd like to try wheel building this is a good place to start, because 3-speed wheels are built symmetrically and do not have to be dished like the rear wheel in a 10-speed.

If you have the bike store do this you might want to consider replacing your old hub with a new Sturmey-Archer 5-speed hub which will give you about the same range as an average 10-speed bike.

If riding a 10-speed has sort of spoiled you for your 3-speed because of the greater choice of gears on a derailleur bike, and you don't want the expense of changing to a 5-speed hub, you can improvise a 2-speed cluster. (There are specially designed clusters for 3-speed hubs, but they are hard to find.) A hybrid bike can be made by putting two gears on the hub; almost any derailleur will handle the larger chain if the difference in gears and the distance traversed are small; 16- to 22-teeth cogs are available. By reversing the dish and leaving out the spacer washer two sprockets can be put on. The chain must be joined by a chain tool, because a master link might hang up in the derailleur. Spacing washers may have to be used to spread the cage of the derailleur.

Almost any repair book can be referred to in maintaining a 3-speed, but a point often left out is that alignment is very important, perhaps even more important than lubrication, to the longevity of any internal hub.

How to Buy a Second Bike

John Krausz

The worst time to buy a bike is just before Christmas or during the cycling season in those parts of the country where cycling is seasonal. The store that might be willing to spend a lot of time with you and be willing to make a lot of adjustments in February, won't have the time in December or August. On the other hand, if you can wait until the end of school in a college town, you can pick up a real bargain in a second-hand bike that someone can't take home. And a bike you get at the end of a season gives you all winter to get in good working order.

Before you go shopping is the time to learn how a bike is supposed to operate. Not knowing how to work a certain type of bike puts you in a bad bargaining position, and possibly onto an unsafe machine. The same is true for not knowing how a bike is supposed to fit and what your position is supposed to be.

You're starting to think like a bike rider when you realize that you need more than one bike; most people who consider themselves cyclists have more than one—often many more. Even if you plan to ride the new bike almost exclusively, there is nothing sadder than not having a spare bike when you need one. The old bike is good for going to the bike store for parts, for riding around while you're thinking about how to fix the other one, and for lending to a visitor so you can go for a ride with them rather than sitting around talking and wishing you were out bike riding.

Two properly functioning machines will extend your riding greatly; you need both a zippy recreational bike and a rainy-day bike you can lock up on the street and not worry about while you're scouting a neighborhood or doing errands. "My dirt-road bike," "my transportation bike," "my shopping bike," are terms you hear bike riders use when they're describing their second or third machines.

There is another important reason to keep your first bike—with it you can search out distant bike stores, check out what they have, and see how they treat customers who come in for a small purchase. Salesmen will pressure you less and tell you more if you come in with a bike. They'll know that at least you don't need a bike to get you home from the store.

Two bikes hung up take little more space than one kept on the floor, and a trashmo bike often doesn't cost much more than the price of a good lock.

Unfortunately, the bicycle, which first gave us freedom to range when we were kids, is all tied up with ideas about childhood, which leads to thinking that people on bikes are just fooling around, or don't have the money for serious transportation. Feeling that bike riding is not a serious activity causes a lot of people to be very hesitant about buying a good bicycle—they don't want to spend a lot of money for a toy. But unless you plan to use it only for distances not much farther than you can walk anyway, a bicycle is not a toy. You are entrusting your life to that bicycle, so it should be built and put together with some care. People who have no compunction about spending money on ski equipment or hi-fi equipment begrudge every penny spent on a bike, yet for about the price of a cheap color TV you can get a bike that's really a joy, and that's made well enough so that you can consider it a long-term investment.

There are many disposable bikes on the market, and everyone, no matter how small their budget, should stay away from them. Bicycles with solid forks, or without proper dropouts, where the tubing is flattened and slotted to receive the wheel, or where the dropouts have been tacked on with a spot-welder—you don't have to know much about bikes to see how crudely these are made. Some have stems you can't raise or replace, funny-looking narrow steel handlebars, hubs with seams showing, pedals without dustcaps and hence with no outer bearings that can be serviced—these are all signs of inferior machines. Usually sold in a discount-type store, such bikes are known to cyclists as "toy-store bikes." There are people who would return a floor lamp made as crudely as some of these machines, but will still put their bodies on bad bikes because they don't know better. Most of these bicycles aren't meant for anything but occasional use.

Since about three-quarters of the bikes sold in America are not sold in bike stores, it doesn't make sense to leave the subject with only a slight warning. Not only is a cheap bike less fun to ride, the alignment of the frame is a matter of chance; it is seldom that everything will line up, and adjustment and maintenance are difficult on second-rate parts.

Bikes sold by reputable chain or department stores more often have standard parts and better-quality equipment, but a medium level of mechanical skill is required to assemble and put such machines into adjustment. Because they're either delivered knocked-down or are assembled by stockroom personnel, they may prove to be expensive bargains if your neighborhood bike store is not willing or able to repair or service them. There is also the danger that the bike inside the box will not be as well made as the floor sample.

The best place to buy a bike is a friendly bike store. The more the people there know about bikes, the less you have to know. They will make sure that you get a bike that fits you and your needs, or they can make the necessary changes to do this.

When you buy a bike in a bike store, you're also buying the guarantee and the future servicing of the bike. Cables stretch and parts will need adjustment and tightening after a bike has been ridden about fifty miles, and again after about four hundred. If you buy your bike in a reputable store they will do the first adjustment free and at least show you how to do the second one yourself.

Alloy cranks have to be tightened periodically as the bike is broken in. Loose cranks can totally disable a bike in no time flat, so buy a crankset tool at the same time as the bike, and have someone in the store demonstrate how to use it.

Get the service agreement and the guarantee spelled out on the bill of sale. You'll need the bill of sale if you want to insure the bike or take it out of the country.

Bike riders love to gossip about bike stores. This is a very good way to find out who handles what, what kind of service you can expect, who builds good wheels, and who takes the time to find solutions to tricky problems. If you want to know, ask the bike riders. You can recognize them by one or more of the following signs: bike clothes, especially shoes and worn bike gloves, toeclips, and their never letting their good bike out of their sight.

If you get good service from a local store, you should give them first crack at selling you a new bike before going farther afield. A bike bought forty miles away for a fifteen percent saving may not seem such a buy when it needs servicing.

When most people talk about buying a bike, they are talking about buying a "ten-speed." But when you're buying a bike, what you are buying is a bicycle frame with a lot of components that have been assembled to make a "complete" machine. (Very few of even the largest manufacturers make every bicycle component.) So the first rule is to buy the best frame you can get that's your size because it's the only thing that can't be changed.

Men's frames are made as small as 19 inches without a bent top tube (though it's hard to find one smaller than 21), and as large as 27 inches. The measurements refer to the length of the seat tube. Increments are as big as two inches in some models, as small as one centimeter (about two-fifths of an inch) in others. Bottom bracket heights vary, as does

Photograph by John Krausz

how much clearance is considered necessary for the top tube, so it's hard to translate frame size into inseam length, but it's approximately nine inches less than the distance from crotch to floor. The best guarantee of getting a frame that fits is still straddling it; wear the shoes you intend to ride in, and make sure the bike's tires are inflated properly.

The important thing to remember when buying a bike is that you're buying a frame with a set of preselected components, and the ones that are important to your fitting on the bicycle comfortably are the ones that should be easiest for the store to change—seat, stem, handlebar type and width, gearing, gear-shift mechanism, brake handles, and pedals. If you have wide feet you might prefer two-sided touring pedals to racing pedals, if you have small hands, you might want to exchange standard bike handles for the junior size.

Certain small changes may make the whole work better for you. Finding out if these changes are possible will often tell you a lot about the bike you're interested in, and may help you decide whether or not to buy it. Two machines with nearly identical equipment may have different chain sets, for example. If you find you can change the chainwheels on one and not on the other, this will help you make up your mind if you're considering the bike for touring. Some imported bikes come with nonstandard equipment that is not readily available. The time to find these things out is before you buy the bike.

Sometimes the strongest selling point on a bike might be the reason to reject it. For instance, the

new narrow high-pressure tires and rims (90 pounds as opposed to the standard 70) are a poor choice if you are heavy or have to ride on rough roads. Two things you'll be sure to regret are buying too much bike—too extreme a racing bike, for instance—or buying a bike that's too big for you. It's better to get a bike your size or even a trifle too small than be uncomfortable on a bike that's too big. Bicycles come in such luscious colors that you may need a little extra time to examine your motives. Buying a bike shouldn't be an impulse purchase—sleep on it. It's better to lose a small deposit or miss out on the bike altogether than to buy something you'll be unhappy with later.

Buying a Secondhand Bike

Decide what you need and get some idea of comparative cost new. Watch the ads on bulletin boards and in the shopping papers. Place your own notice—there are many more deserted bikes in basements and garages than new ones in the bike stores. Ask around. Go to garage sales and police auctions. Don't be afraid of bidding against the dealers; you can usually outbid them because they are looking for something that can be marked up later.

Bike stores are a good place to get secondhand bikes; their sources include last year's rental fleet, trade-ins, bikes brought in for repair and never picked up, and police auctions.

If you're in the market for something more than basic transportation, the best way to start is by asking other bike riders. One of the things that amazes newcomers about bicycling is the amount of horse-trading that goes on among enthusiasts. Conversations like the following are quite common:

"I hear that you bought Larry's Paramount."

"Yeah, he needed the money so he could get Steve's old Masi track bike from Jim, who's getting that new frame."

One of the best reasons for belonging to a bike club is that the club often acts as an informal marketplace. It's possible to put together an entire machine from parts bought one by one from fellow members. You may also never have to actually own any of the specialized tools to make this possible; they can usually be borrowed from friends.

A bike race, besides being exciting, is a place you can see super bikes and get the opportunity to ask about available machines. Don't be shy. The bike that was just given as a prize may be up for sale before it leaves the grandstand.

Prices vary locally. In some cases it's a buyer's market because some bikes are hard to sell—very small ones, very large ones, tandems, or anything people in the area don't think is practical. On the other hand, prices may be just plain crazy! Someone running a garage sale may have heard the person down the block got $75.00 for a bike, so he prices his junk accordingly. You may even be asked for more than the bike's original price. But if a bike is about ten years old it might be worth it, because they were made better then and prices have more than doubled since.

Last year's models may sell for one-half to three-quarters of their original price, but there is no "Blue Book" of bike prices and no one could possibly know all the brands on the market.

Be sure to get the price before you start looking at the bike!

Look for seams in the fork, the hubs, and the tubes of the frame—these are characteristics of toy-store bikes. If it's a bad idea to buy one new, it's an even worse idea to buy one secondhand.

Just because a bike has a famous tube maker's sticker on it don't think the bike is necessarily made of that tubing. It used to be possible to buy these stickers through mail order firms that advertised in the bike magazines. A bike made with really good tubing should ring like crystal somewhere on the frame. This place may be hard to find because the ringing may be damped by the presence of cable clamps, bosses, down-tube shifters, pump clamps, water-bottle cages, or an overtightened seat post.

Sight down the frame for straightness and see if both wheels are in the same plane. If they aren't, forget the bike. Check the tubes of the bike near the front for signs of a crash. If they are bent or the paint is crazed, forget about this one also, unless the parts themselves are worth the money.

On bikes with steel cranks slip the chain and rotate the cranks, holding a crank firmly in each hand, and see if you can find a bumpy spot. This is called brinelling and is caused by trying to extract the cotter pin without supporting the bottom bracket. Hammering has caused the ball bearing to make a dent in the bearing surface which will be felt with every pedal rotation. It is a serious defect, as it cannot be repaired.

Bent chainwheels on a 10-speed are dangerous, as the chain can get caught between them, and stop the bike short. A bent steel chainwheel can be straightened, an alloy one must be replaced.

Look for signs of wear on the chainwheel. A really worn chainwheel will need to be replaced, along with the chain and the cluster.

Check to see if the cranks run parallel to the frame and if the pedals are at right angles to the cranks. It is a truism about bicycles that you can get used to almost anything. But the bent crank that the previous owner had gotten used to can send you to the orthopedist.

Grab both sides of the chain with the left hand, and with the right hand try to pull the chain off the chainwheel. A worn chain will pull away more than three-eighths of an inch.

Look at the fork to see if it's bent. If it's only bent a little it may not have to be replaced.

A neglected bike that has never really been serviced often needs a new headset. Turn the handlebar and feel for a tight spot or a sudden release of pressure.

Bent handlebars can be straightened, but don't try to do it on the bike; compression in the stem may cause the bars to crack.

Spin each wheel in both directions and check for irregularities by using the brake blocks for a guide. Hops are more serious than wobbles, and rims with bad hops or dents will need to be replaced.

Defects such as these (or a bent-in derailleur) can be used as bargaining points or as reasons to forget the bike.

Sometimes a bike has been "cleaned up for sale." If so, check the headset and the chain because if these are tight the bike can be made to run even if everything else is almost worn out.

Almost any secondhand bike will need some work done on it. Some things should be checked out and replaced as a matter of course, such as worn brake shoes or twisted and frayed cables.

One thing you may have to count on is replacing the seat: No one with any sense will sell a bike with a seat he is comfortable on. And many old 3-speeds have seats with collapsed springs on one side.

It is often said that one of the best things about buying a secondhand bike is that you can try it before you buy it. So take along an adjustable wrench to see if you can move the seat post to the right height—often it has been overtightened. A small can of spray lubricant and a rag are useful for getting dirt and grease off the wheels and allowing the cables to run freely, and checking for rust. If the bike has steel rims, make sure that the rust is just on the surface. You should also check for more than surface rust inside the fork.

Don't get on any bike until you have assured yourself that the handlebars, brakes, seat, and wheels are on tight. Then try to walk the bike holding onto it by the seat. You should be able to steer from the seat if the headset is in good shape. You can check front-end alignment by riding the bike no-hands. Try the brakes while riding slowly to know how much pressure you need to stop once you've wound the bike up. Shake the cranks back and forth to see if they are loose and be sure to tighten them before you ride the bike for any length of time.

A bike that is in good condition sounds good when you ride it, and the parts have a good feel when you work them. Bearings which are not visible are really the parts of the bike you ride on more than the tires and should move freely in the direction traveled. Proper adjustment has to be arrived at by feel, and is a compromise between side-by-side tightness and free movement. This is only possible if the bearing surface is in good condition. Too loose or too tight a setting produces sawing, which causes scoring of the bearing surface. The headset, bottom bracket, pedals, and hubs all run on bearings and should be checked for scoring or brinelling by rotating firmly to see if there are jerks and starts that indicate rough spots. Every place this happens is a demerit against the bike, and suggests the part has to be replaced.

When bargaining find out if there are any extras that come with the bike. Baskets, racks, pumps, tools, extra tires and wheels will sometimes be thrown in or sold for a nominal fee if you remind the seller that they exist. If the bike looks as if it originally had fenders or a chain guard, ask for them.

Get some record of the purchase—the original papers (if possible), your cancelled check, or a signed witnessed receipt.

MAINTENANCE

"There are two ways you can get exercise out of a bicycle: You can 'overhaul' it, or you can ride it. On the whole, I am not sure that man who takes his pleasure overhauling does not get the best of the bargain. He is independent of the weather and the wind; the state of the roads troubles him not. Give him a screw-hammer, a bundle of rags, an oil can, and something to sit down upon, and he is happy for the day. He has to put up with certain disadvantages, of course; there is no joy without alloy. He himself always looks like a tinker, and his machine always suggests the idea that, having stolen it, he has tried to disguise it; but as he rarely goes beyond the first milestone with it, this, perhaps does not much matter. The mistake some people make is in thinking that you can get both forms of sport out of the same machine. This is impossible; no machine will stand the double strain. You must make up your mind whether you are going to be an 'overhauler' or a rider. Personally, I prefer to ride, therefore I take care to have near me nothing that can tempt me to overhaul. When anything happens to my machine I wheel it to the nearest repair shop. If I am too far from the town or village, I sit down by the roadside and wait till a cart comes along. My chief danger, I find, is the wandering overhauler. The sight of a broken-down machine is to the overhauler as a wayside corpse to a crow; he swoops down on it with a friendly yell of triumph."

Jerome K. Jerome, Three Men on a Bummel, *1900*

The Case for Hands-on Experience

Darryl Skrabak

If you are uninitiated to the mechanical arts, you might have found perusing the average repair

Darryl Skrabak is a bicycle advocate and president of the San Francisco Bicycle Coalition. He has been an instructor at many bike repair clinics.

manual beyond you. Despite efforts of manual writers to fashion instructions that will make working on your bike utterly straightforward, you may find that manuals simply fail to communicate.

If you are among those who experienced such failure—or based on experiences with other how-to literature, expect to—be assured that you enjoy considerable company. Many would-be mechanics pore over the manuals, yet remain hopelessly puzzled. Others find the manuals clear enough, but obstreperous parts prevent carrying out the instructions. The crushing blow comes to the would-be novice bike maintainer, when he learns from the manuals that bicycles are built with at least three separate standards – and that not only are parts not interchangeable, but country of origin of the bicycle does not assure that it's made to that country's standards!

Those of you for whom manuals are digestible, may proceed directly to listing at the end of this piece.

Much routine bicycle maintenance demands no more aptitude than required to string beads. Bicycles are not called simple machines for nothing. All the parts are pretty much open to easy investigation. There is little that is devious about bicycle construction.

Why, then, are the manuals difficult for you to understand?

Based on my own experience with bikes, and with people who go to bicycle repair clinics, I think there are two reasons.

1. You lack experience. You've never worked on bikes before.

2. You've never *seen* anyone actually perform the operations described in manuals.

That the first reason may not be received kindly is not unexpected. The manuals are supposed to serve as guides for the inexperienced, right? If you were experienced in bike work, you'd not need a manual to show you how.

However, first experiences at anything are usually the most difficult ones. First experiences at mechanics are no exception. The first time you get down to cases with your bike, tools and parts may come to hand awkwardly. Dealing with them and at the same time attempting to figure out what the book is saying, which involves translating images conjured by abstract print and two-dimensional graphics into something that applies to those suddenly alien bicycle bits and pieces facing you—well, the combination defeats some very good minds.

The second reason points up an instructional difficulty of books. Even a coherent text and step-by-step photos or drawings can fail to

transmit some essential learning that is best communicated by the actual witnessing of events. Maybe it works because when you've seen someone else do it, you *know* it can be done. If you've only read about it in a book, sometimes you're not quite convinced.

So, one way to learn about bicycle work is to hang around the backs of bicycle shops, observing. However, not all shop owners will tolerate this. Neither will all mechanics, many of whom become testy when being watched.

What to do then? Attend a bicycle repair course. Most are run so that you not only receive instruction, you take your bike along and work on it, too. When you get stuck, the instructor is on hand to help you. And back home, when you attempt things on your own, you'll find you understand that once-incomprehensible manual. And even if you can't or don't want to fix it, you know what's likely to be wrong.

Bicycle repair courses are usually offered somewhere in metropolitan areas. But they are not so prevalent as they might be. Bike shops, park and recreation departments, adult education, and alternative education operations are likely sponsors.

If a search uncovers no course, you might try to instigate one. Apply to a bicycle club. Local shops can direct you to those in your area. All clubs have some members who are expert mechanics capable of providing excellent instruction. Usually they can be prevailed upon to share their skills.

A couple of final comments: Learning how to work on your bike does not mean you sever relations with your local bike shop. The shop is still your source for parts and (we hope) much friendly advice. When you locate a shop where you have good rapport, cultivate it. In doing your own work, a good shop is an ally to be greatly valued.

You may prefer to have your shop do the big jobs for you. Even then you will be better off having acquired repair skills. You will communicate what's wrong and what you want done more effectively with shop mechanics, and will understand them when they describe problems and solutions. You may

have a greater appreciation for their efforts, too.

Lastly, even if learning bike maintenance does not come easily to you, it is a worthwhile endeavor. If you like bikes, probably you find a certain appeal in the independence they offer. On a bike, your transport is the result of your own efforts, and that's nice. However, you can go right back to feeling terribly dependent and inconsequential if your bike breaks down, and there you are, overcome by unmastered technology again.

It needn't be that way. Most on-road breakdowns won't happen if you do your own work. Becoming informed about repair will make you alert to pending failures. You'll catch them before they occur.

And when a breakdown does occur, likely you'll be equal to it. You can fix your bike and be on your way. Learning to do your own work, then, allows your bicycle to make good on an intrinsic promise: to be one of the few technologies that, while it serves you, will not simultaneously victimize you.

Repair Manuals

Most manuals are pretty good. They cover the material. Which is best for you depends on how the style appeals. Some people like photos. Some prefer line drawings. Some like straight-ahead writing, others the breezy *Complete Idiot* approach Tom Cuthbertson borrowed from John Muir (that's Muir the Volkswagen mechanic, not the naturalist).

So try to buy your manual from a bookstore or bike shop that offers a good selection. Take a few minutes to look through them. Choose one whose approach you find compatible and informative.

This is not to say manuals don't differ in content. They do. Mostly they differ in comprehensiveness.

Most manuals are reasonably comprehensive guides. *Richard's Bicycle Book* and *Anybody's Bike Book* are bestsellers in this category. These are good manuals for those who get along with mechanics and how-to literature. They, and similar books, are the only manuals most amateur mechanics will ever need.

But for some readers, comprehensiveness contributes to incomprehensibility. If you are in this category, try *How To Fix Your Bicycle* by Helen Garvy. This brief volume has a succinct, stripped-to-the-basics approach. It may be hard to find. Bike shops handling it report much positive feedback. Customers stymied by other manuals are delighted with Garvy's, because they can understand it.

At the opposite pole is the *Schwinn Service Manual.* It covers everything in great detail—too much detail for most amateurs. It is expensive: about fifty dollars. Your Schwinn dealer may be able to order a set—it comes in two volumes—or he may not. Availability is uncertain. The Schwinn manual is best left to the bike shops, which might have reason to afford it and to actually use it. Almost as complete as the Schwinn manual is *Glenn's Complete Bicycle Manual.* This is often the only manual mechanically-talented people have or need. It starts with assembling a crated bike, and covers every maintenance problem including over-

hauling 3-speed internal hubs.

There are some other manuals that, while not rightly repair manuals, nevertheless can make working on bikes easier. These are any of several mail-order bike parts catalogs; and a singular work known as *Sutherland's Handbook for Bicycle Mechanics.*

Sutherland's is not a manual in the ordinary sense; it is a reference. It consists of listings of various bicycle parts produced by various manufacturers, assembled in a manner as concise and coherent as can be managed. It tells which parts will fit with which other parts, and which won't, and why. It is rather like a dictionary for mechanicking.

Sutherland's is utterly dull stuff until one gets into working on bikes, at which time it becomes fascinating. Invaluable for the enthusiast who builds bikes from parts. Wonderful gift for bike freaks. For those already possessing a good repair manual, *Sutherland's* is a worthy addition to the library.

Anyone who works on bikes ought to have on hand one or more mail-order catalogs. These are full of wares and ordering advice. They tell you about goods you might otherwise not know are available. They are full of prices. This last is especially handy information. For many of us, cost is an important consideration. Because catalogs often employ a good-better-best approach, they can offer a good deal of information about what more money buys in various categories of components. Sometimes more money buys product improvements. Sometimes it buys mostly more prestige. Some catalogs are very good about pointing out the difference.

How to Repair a Flat

Mel Shleifer

Drawings by Barbara Remington

The repair most often made is to a flat tire. It's probably more than ninety percent if you commute or ride frequently in an urban area. Many years ago I only rode weekends and feared to venture beyond an open gas station air pump. This was because I didn't know what you're about to learn.

The best way to tackle any repair problem is with proper tools and knowledge. First the tools: 1. Tire irons; 2. Patches; 3. Glue; 4. Rub-

ber-cement thinner; 5. Scraper or sandpaper; 6. Toothpick or paper-clip "flag"; 7. Means of wheel removal; 8. Spare inner tube; 9. Small cloth or sponge; 10. Pump. These will be described in detail later.

Finding a Leak

When you have a flat, try to stop immediately. Quickly locate the approximate spot on the wheel where you hear a hiss. Turn bike upside down with something to protect the saddle from getting scuffed on the road (a piece of cardboard, a rag, etc.). If you located where the air is escaping, fine. If not, examine the tire for a nail or glass. This done,

use tire irons to lift only as much of the tire as you need to pull out the inner tube at the location of glass or air hiss. If neither was found, pull out the entire tube, pump it up as much as you can. The wheel is still on the frame. On the rear wheel, take the tube out on the side away from the chain. If you have quick-release brakes, release them for more clearance for tire and tube.

To locate what may be a pinhole, put the tube near your face and pass each section past your ear or your upper lip to hear or feel the air escaping. Put the flag into the hole if you can find it. Sometimes a large hole won't allow you to blow up the tube, 251

Mel Shleifer *is a long-time everyday cyclist and has taught many repair courses at the American Youth Hostel in New York City.*

so close off sections by folding the tube, and explore section by section. If you still can't find the leak, now remove the wheel for putting on spare inner tube. Continue reading at "Reassembling tire and tube."

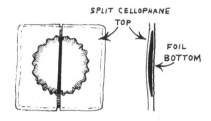

SPLIT CELLOPHANE
TOP
FOIL BOTTOM

Patching the Tube

With sponge or small rag, wipe tube area near flag free of dirt. Next use scraper to rough the area about patch size. Try to keep all surfaces being glued and patched clean and free of fingerprints after scraping. If you handle the tube with greasy hands, the patch probably won't stick. It also won't stick to a wet tube; in rain you may as well forget patching; use a spare.

Take a patch. If it has a protective top covering, like the Rema, fold it to widen cellophane split. Partially peel back protective material on contact side. Apply rubber cement to tube, then quickly peel off foil and stick down the patch. The flag is in place after cleaning with scraper and pulled out as patch is applied, so that the patch is centered on the hole. Press the patch on firmly all over between fingers. Remove cellophane from top of Rema-type patch. If edges look as if they blend into tube, good. If not, add a little glue around the edge.

If you're sure that's the only hole, prepare to refit tube into tire. If not, blow it up and look for more leaks. Sometimes a leak occurs from under a patch. If that's a "pinhole"-size leak, put another patch over the leak if the patch looks flush. If it has a raised edge, you may have to strip it off and repatch the area, cleaning traces of the previous patch off it.

Sometimes you get a slow leak and it can't be detected even with a bubble test; that usually means a patch is detaching at high pressure but remaining attached at low pressure. You should blow a tube like this up beyond the initial bulge stage and hang it up for a few days. Eventually the bad patch reveals itself.

You can do this to a good tube also, just to find out how long it holds air.

Every "mysterious" flat has a cause. Once I had a series of them caused by a wire strand imbedded in the casing. It was found by careful flexing and looking in the suspected area.

A wheel can also cause flats. It pays to check that the spoke nipples have smooth, unburred tops and that no spokes extend above them. Where the rim is welded or joined, file off any rough spots that might touch the tube.

Reassembling Tire and Tube

After searching the tire casing for flat causers, hold the wheel vertical, notice and clear out any debris at the bottom of the tire. Once I didn't and I had another flat immediately—some glass had dropped in.

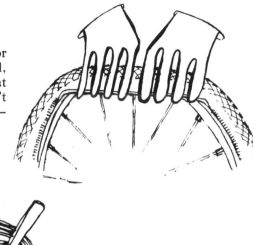

Put the tube in valve first; with your hands put the tire bead back onto the rim. Toward the end more force may be needed, so use the eight-finger pull-up. If that doesn't work, then—careful not to inflict a puncture—use tire irons to raise the tire bead over the rim.

Ideally, the valve should be perpendicular to the rim. If it isn't, before inflating the tire, with wheel on the bike, roll the bike forward or backward a few wheel revolutions while leaning on the bike. This causes a differential motion of tube relative to rim, the valve will lean from one side to the other. That's also why the valve leans when you ride a flat.

Pumping Up the Tire

Finally, blow up the tire to pressure stamped on sidewall; given a choice, use the highest, because that's the easiest rolling.

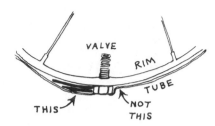

VALVE
RIM
TUBE
THIS
NOT THIS

Lean the bike against a wall with the valve at the top, so that you don't have to stoop too low. You should be kneeling, not bent at the waist. The left hand has a firm grip on the pump to brace against force

applied. The right hand is pushing the handle with the palm and pulling back with the fingers. This prevents bending the piston rod, as is possible with a firm grip on the handle.

Preventing Flats

Inspect a new wheel to see that no spokes extend above the rim, and smooth any rough edges. Now and then inspect the tire threads. If you see imbedded debris, dig it out before it penetrates the inner tube. If you ride through a patch of glass, wipe the tire clean as soon as it's safe to. Naturally, a great deal of glass can be avoided by not hugging the side of the road. Some people use tiresavers, others thorn-proof tubes. Rinsing off some of the grime from wheels and inner tubes doesn't hurt.

Choosing Tools

Tire irons are shaped like spoon handles. You should not be able to bend them. The part contacting the tire should not have any rough or sharp spots. If it does, file it smooth. If you have no file, take a stone and rub the point until smooth.

Patches come in various types. Many years ago I bought them in a kit which had a tube of glue, patches, and top scraper. I never used up the contents because after a while the glue or the patches dried out. You usually found this out on a ride when the stores were closed.

I discovered Rema patches were used by gas stations. Their advantages are long shelf life due to protective foil and cellophane; and tapered edges. The latter allows one patch to be piled on top of another indefinitely, something you can't do with a patch that isn't tapered. Remas are available in various diameters from about three quarters of an inch to several inches for auto-tractor use; they come bulk-packed thirty or a hundred to a box. I like the No. 0 (about one-inch diameter). I use from fifty to a hundred a year. When I get them home I put them into a seal-top jar so they will stay fresh.

Bike stores sell Rema kits consisting of some miniature, round, and oblong patches, tube of rubber cement, sandpaper or scraper, replacement rubber for Wood's valve. In bulk they're available from "tire rebuilder suppliers" in the Yellow Pages. I take at least six to twelve patches when I ride, even for a one-day outing.

When using these patches be sure to follow *all* the directions on the box. Before peeling off foil, prefolding patch with cellophane outside of fold will spread cellophane split and make it easier to peel. After application, be sure to peel off the cellophane on top, as this allows the patch to stick properly by allowing solvent evaporation.

Glue. The rubber cement must be almost watery. If it's thick, it means the solvent has evaporated and the patches will not stick. I carry a four-fluid ounce brush-top can of rubber cement in my kit all the time. An opened tube dries out fast. I add rubber-cement thinner to the can from time to time. To extend cement, dried pieces of rubber cement can be thrown in. I've been using the same can for more than five years.

Rubber-cement thinner is part of your home base. Add a bit to the glue as needed; if you add too much it'll evaporate anyway. With practice you'll use the correct amount. It's available in art or stationery stores, in pint metal cans.

The scraper is a piece of serrated flat metal usually supplied with a kit; or sandpaper may be supplied. I use a scraper from a Rema kit, it's small and flat. Its purpose is to rough the area of the puncture to aid in cleaning the rubber surface.

APPLY FORCE IN THIS DIRECTION ONLY

A *"flag"* is nothing other than a rounded-point toothpick or paper-clip, which is put into the puncture to prevent losing the place.

Wheel-remover. Either quick release or a wrench for nuts. I use nuts with serrated washers on both of my wheels. They're dependable, and I can't justify the extra cost of quick-release skewers on the basis of weight or time saved. If you're carrying an adjustable wrench for other uses, where's the weight saving? *I do not recommend wing nuts* because if you break the wings off while trying to loosen the wheel, where are you? I've come across an aluminum wing nut, something I'm saving for someone I don't like.

The adjustable wrench should be a 6-inch (or 8-inch if you're weak) with a brand name on it and drop

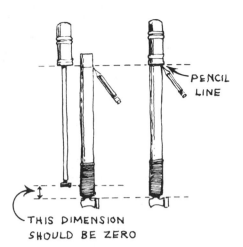

PENCIL LINE

THIS DIMENSION SHOULD BE ZERO

forged (so stamped). The adjustable jaw should close flush and parallel to the fixed jaw and have minimum wiggle. When applying force to wrench, position the wrench and your hand so that when the nut suddenly gives, your hand doesn't get skinned or impacted. Be sure adjustable jaw is tight on nut to avoid rounded corners.

Spare inner tube for when it's raining, cold, the leak can't be found immediately or is too difficult to patch. Depending on trip duration and weather, one or more should be carried.

The cloth or sponge is to wipe the tube clean prior to patching process.

Pump. Most pumps are good after their defects have been corrected. If you already own one without major dents we'll repair it. If you're out to buy one I'll tell you how to judge them.

All pumps are basically alike, except some fit Schraeder valves (the common automotive size) and others are made for Presta valves (the narrower European standard). In either case, the smaller the diameter of the barrel the less force you need to apply. The magnitude of this force is proportional to the diameter squared. This is a law of physics that can't be violated by any brand of sales pitch.

The next important point is that the piston should reach the barrel bottom at the end of the stroke. That way the full charge of air is delivered to the tire; if the piston does not go to the bottom then there is residual compressed air in the pump, which expands; only at the point where this air is at atmospheric pressure will the pump take in more air. This means you're pumping in less 253

PUMP DIAGRAM WITH PISTON ROD REPAIR

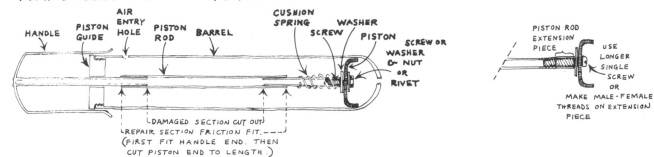

HANDLE • PISTON GUIDE • AIR ENTRY HOLE • PISTON ROD • BARREL • CUSHION SPRING • SCREW • WASHER • PISTON • SCREW OR WASHER & NUT OR RIVET

DAMAGED SECTION CUT OUT
REPAIR SECTION FRICTION FIT.
(FIRST FIT HANDLE END. THEN CUT PISTON END TO LENGTH.)

PISTON ROD EXTENSION PIECE — USE LONGER SINGLE SCREW OR MAKE MALE-FEMALE THREADS ON EXTENSION PIECE

air per stroke, and you're wasting energy by compressing air that's expanding again with each stroke.

To check how far the piston travels in the barrel, push the handle of the pump all the way to the end of the stroke, then draw a pencil line on the barrel by the end of the handle. Next remove the piston from the barrel by detaching the piston guide. Note the position of the piston relative to the end of the barrel. If you're buying a pump, reject it if there is more than a half inch of difference. If you own the pump and are handy, make a piston rod extension to reduce this space.

Another way to test a pump is to put your finger over the air-exit hole and pump. If you feel no pressure, there's a leak. It may consist of a loose screw holding the piston, in which case you tighten it. If there's a rivet you'll have to figure out how to tighten it. I avoid riveted piston pumps. A piston leather too small for the diameter of the barrel can also cause a leak; replace it with a larger piston leather. Putting neatsfoot-oil on leather pistons helps them work more smoothly and seal better. A plastic piston would not seal at below 30 degrees Fahrenheit; I changed it for a leather one and had no more problems.

When the piston has too good a seal you can't get a full charge of fresh air into the barrel; it feels as if you're trying to evacuate the chamber on the return stroke. The solution is to make a tiny hole at the top of the barrel; when the piston passes it, air enters to fill up the barrel. Before making such a hole, measure carefully; once done, you can't correct any mistake you made. Smooth any burrs on the barrel inside of the hole.

Every pump must have a connection to the tire. I prefer a thumb-lock connection because it is self locking, and on a Schraeder valve the valve

pin is depressed so you don't fight the spring. Never cut the spring off a Schraeder valve because this spring aids in sealing the valve. I probably would use a thumb-lock connection on a Presta valve also; I don't like having to hold the pump against the valve while I'm pumping. I prefer to grip the barrel firmly with one hand while pumping with the other.

If you use a screw-on hose con-

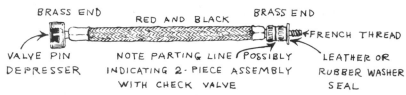

BRASS END • RED AND BLACK • BRASS END • FRENCH THREAD
VALVE PIN DEPRESSER • NOTE PARTING LINE POSSIBLY INDICATING 2-PIECE ASSEMBLY WITH CHECK VALVE • LEATHER OR RUBBER WASHER SEAL

nection, realize: 1. There are two different threads for hoses, a French one and a British one. Make sure your hose thread matches your pump thread; 2. Hoses come with or without valve-pin depressors. On Schraeder valves get one with a pin depressor. To avoid leaks, be sure you're using the washer seal where it connects to the pump; 3. Depressor-pin hoses must have check valves in them to prevent a backflow of air when attached to the valve. These valves can be placed at pump end or tire end. To minimize the dead space between tire and piston they should be at pump end; 4. Hoses rupture eventually at high pressure, and you have to be very fast when you unscrew them or you lose a lot of air.

Photograph by Paul Boyer

Component Wear

Donald Taylor

Many of the working surfaces on a bike wear in an irregular fashion. Because a component must be discarded when only one part has reached its wear limit, it is advantageous to spread the wear over all the working surface. By applying a "rotation" policy, the useful life of components can be greatly extended.

Tires

A tire is discarded either when the tread is worn or when the rubber is dried out and cracked. The rear tire, because it carries more weight and transmits pedaling power, wears faster than the front. Quite often the front tire will dry out and crack long before its tread is worn out. The overall life of a pair of tires can therefore be extended by swapping them when the rear is half-worn. By similar logic, it is useful to rotate the sidewall in contact with a dynamo–this wear rate can be higher than tread wear.

Chainwheel

Chainwheel teeth suffer heavy wear at the positions corresponding to the points of maximum pedaling force on each of the cranks.

By rotating the position of the chainwheel on the crank arms, fresh teeth can be brought into play. To go a step further, the chainwheel can be reversed on the crank, since the teeth wear only on the forward pulling edge; but this alters the chainline and spoils the appearance.

Derailleur

Both the teeth and the bearings on the upper derailleur pulley wear more quickly than on the lower, because the sideways chain force when gear changing is borne by the upper. Wear in the upper pulley contributes to sloppiness and jumping in the gear change, and the pulleys should be swapped when the upper one becomes worn.

Bottom Bracket

The bracket axle wears more heavily on certain parts of the bearing circumference, corresponding, like the chainwheel, to maximum pedaling forces. Cotterless cranks can be fixed in turn on each of four positions on the squared taper, to spread the wear. The axle has to be marked with a blob of paint before taking the cranks off.

Pedals

The spindle bearing surface wears unevenly because it always remains in the same position relative to the crank (i.e. relative to the direction of the forces). Placing a thin washer, half a thread pitch thick (0.025''), between spindle and crank rotates the spindle 180° to a new position.

Brakes

The brake lever pivots and stirrup bearing surfaces will develop sloppiness on the more used brake. Again, the most worn parts can be exchanged to where they have least effect, i.e. the lesser used brake. In the case of sidepulls, one caliper arm of the front stirrup eventually develops a bend under the forward pull of the wheel when braking. The rear wheel tends to push the stirrup arm in the opposite direction; switching front to rear will tend to straighten the bend (you can, of course, straighten it carefully with wrenches.) Brake blocks usually wear unevenly, but interchanging these can bring problems with squealing, which occurs when the block surface is at an angle to the rim.

Take care when fitting brake shoes that the closed end is toward the front of the bike, to prevent the wheel pulling the blocks out. At a more advanced level of maintenance, when respoking a pair of alloy wheels, it is worth switching rims if the rim's braking surface is noticeably eroded.

Headset

The headset bearing surfaces develop indentations (called "brinelling") in a characteristic pattern. This results in a feeling of the steering sticking in intermediate positions as a ball bearing drops into a pair of dents. The problem can sometimes, but not always, be temporarily alleviated by rotating the bearing race on the fork crown by about 90°, so that the indentations can only line up in a rarely encountered handlebar position.

Chain

The chain wears asymmetrically because it is being bent round both the chainwheel and cog in one direction only, so the link pins wear faster on one side. This can lead to a bewildering phenomenon when a chain on a single speed bike is put back after cleaning–the chain is apparently too short, and the split links will not reach each other, despite there being no alteration of the rear wheel position in the fork ends. The explanation is this: The effective length of the chain increases with link pin wear–if the chain is replaced bent round the chainwheel in the opposite direction, fresh relatively unworn pivot surfaces are brought into play, effectively tightening up the chain.

The Bicycle as an Instrument for Change

Stuart Wilson

Stuart Wilson, professor of engineering at Oxford University, is best known to American cyclists for his March, 1974 Scientific American *article, the first in modern times to treat the bicycle as a topic of serious study. His abiding interest in the promotion of the bicycle as an energy-efficient form of transportation is shown in the following paper, presented in Stockholm on August 28, 1979 at a symposium on Transport Technology and Social Change.*

Bicycle technology can be characterized as technology of human scale. It is a triumph of ergonomics, of matching the machine to the person, using the right muscles, in the right motion, at the right speed, and then transmitting and using the power efficiently. The obvious need to make the best use of the limited power available–compared to an engine–led to quite remarkable advances in the way of lightness and efficiency, both in construction and mechanism.

The lightweight, tubular-steel frame is a most elegant piece of construction, and one that was not copied by structural engineers until thirty years later. Tubular steel furniture did not originate at the Bauhaus in the 1920's, but with Richard Starley in the 1870's. The need for strong but light steel tubing led to advances both in high-strength steel alloys, to methods of forming them into tapered sections and to butted tubes, i.e. thicker in the wall toward each end. The brazed lug frame construction evolved in the 1880's still holds the field over welded joints, because brazing can be carried out at a lower temperature, thus preserving the full strength of the steel.

The manufacture of the steel lugs is a complex matter and one which was brilliantly solved by the Raleigh Cycle Co. in 1901, when they developed a method of making the bottom bracket from sheet steel. This is but one example of how bicycle technology stimulated production engineer-ing–bicycles were being made by the millions before Henry Ford made his first car.

Further examples of innovation include the development of ball bearings, involving both the metallurgical and grinding aspects, and Hans Renold's invention of the bush roller chain, which has proved so successful in other forms of power transmission. Again, the requirements of the chain for long life under adverse conditions stimulated considerable advances in metallurgy, lubrication, and production engineering. As is well known, the pneumatic tire was reinvented for the bicycle by Dunlop, and this has led to an enormous rubber industry. Even the bicycle's requirement for an effective lighting system led to the growth of the firm of Joseph Lucas to a large industrial enterprise, via automobile electrics.

But the major social effect of the bicycle was due to its lighting of a time bomb–the motor car. Daimler and Benz produced their first motor vehicles about 1885, the year that saw the appearance of the Rover Safety bicycle, the true progenitor of the modern bicycle. All these early car manufacturers were bicycle makers first, and the technology of the car owes much to the bicycle. Some twenty-five years or so were to pass before the motor car began to have a major impact on society, and in Europe not until after World War I did it come to dominate our lives to an ever-increasing extent.

Even the airplane owes much to the bicycle–the Wright brothers were bicycle makers who adapted the lightweight and efficient technology to conquer the air, with all the social effects we now know.

But quite apart from these mainly technical changes, the bicycle has been a factor in profound social changes. At first it was merely a novelty, an upper-class craze; then cycling became a competitive sport, still for a minority. But gradually the bicycle came to be seen as a liberating factor, enabling men and even women to travel greater distances than on foot and without the complications of keeping a horse or even a horse and carriage. The rise of the bicycle in popular esteem is well illustrated in the *Penguin Book of the Bicycle,* by Roderick Watson and Martin Gray, both lecturers in English literature at Stirling University in Scotland. They give extensive quotations from the literature of the 1890's and 1900's to show how quickly the bicycle entered popular culture.

This new-found freedom of travel had two notable social consequences; women acquired a much greater mobility at the same time that education for women began to blossom with the foundation of "women's lib." On the other hand the bicycle enabled men to breed in the next village, thus mixing up the genes and helping to rid the countryside of the village idiot, the product of too much inbreeding.

The Cyclists Touring Club was founded in England in 1898 and had a profound effect on improving roads and other facilities for cyclists. Soon, ambitious cyclists were penetrating to every corner of Europe and beyond. Between 1894 and 1897 three Englishmen cycled round the world and wrote a book, *Round the World on a Wheel,* about their experiences. What a different world it was, only eighty years or so ago. In Russia, Iran, and China, travelers of any sort were unwelcome, and even food was difficult to come by, let alone accomodation; yet in India, Japan, and the United States, the bicycle was already well known and the travelers were greeted by members of cycling clubs! One cannot deduce that the bicycle was the cause of such contrasts, but certainly it has been, on the whole, a civilizing influence.

Not that it has always been an instrument of peace; military bicycles were used in all wars from the Boer War of 1898 on, often with the greatest effect. The Japanese invasion of Malaysia and capture of Singapore were mainly due to their speed of advance on bicycles, while the Vietnamese war was, to a large extent, a duel between the bicycle carrying supplies on the Ho Chi Minh trail and the helicopter supplying the American troops. The bicycle won.

But it is the peaceful use of pedal power which is chiefly in evidence in India, China, and Indonesia—the bicycle, the cycle ricksha, and the bicycle-wheeled handcart and wheelbarrow. This successful use of bicycle technology is easily explained; it is because it is technology on a human scale, ergonomically sound, lightweight and efficient, both structurally and mechanically. Hence it tends to solve problems rather than create them, unlike the motor car, an example of technology on an inhuman scale, which tends to cause problems wherever it is in large-scale use.

With the growing problems of energy shortages (particularly oil), unemployment, and in the less developed countries, poverty and food shortage, bicycle technology has much to offer. Apart from bicycles, rickshas, etc., for transport—in rich and poor countries—there are many stationary applications for pedal power: cultivation by means of a two-man pedal-driven winch, water pumping, threshing, winnowing, and grinding grain. It is significant that pedal-driven corn grinders are in demand both in the United States and in Africa. Bicycle technology knows no bounds. Pedal-driven grain mills are being developed in the United Kingdom by the Tropical Products Institute and in the United States by Rodale Resources, Inc. In Sweden an ingenious pedal-driven winch, the Spider, has been evolved to enable the operator to pedal vertically up and down the side of a building.

These remind us that the profound changes that the bicycle has helped to bring about are not just a matter of past history. The bicycle is still just as much an instrument of change as it has been for the last hundred years and bicycle technology may well in the next hundred years assume an even more important role in society than it has in the past. This will be thanks to its essential virtues of technology on a human scale, lightness, and supreme efficiency in making the best use of that most available and enduring form of energy—muscle power.

Obstacles to Human-Powered Transport

David Gordon Wilson

David Gordon Wilson also contributed "Calories and Power." The following is reprinted from Technology Review, *copyright 1979 by the Alumni Association of the Massachusetts Institute of Technology, where Doctor Wilson is a member of the faculty.*

Today's multi-speed bicycle is a miracle of lightness, efficiency, and convenience: Why isn't it used more? Daily trips of appropriate length are extremely common in the United States today: Over half of all Americans' trips are less than five miles long, and about thirty per cent of our gasoline is consumed on trips of three miles or less. Except where climate or terrain is extreme, such distances are well suited to the modern bicycle. Factors that have kept the bicycle's popularity low in the United States include the following.

The competition. The automobile is a superbly designed, versatile, robust, easily controlled vehicle that can transport people and belongings with no effort, in luxurious comfort, at any reasonable speed, over great distances, and at a low price.

Economics. We have chosen, through acts of commission and omission, to subsidize the automobile—including highway systems and fuel—very heavily. Thus, the perceived cost of automobile travel is erroneously low. Real costs are enormous: The general taxpayer and homeowner foot the bill for roads, police protection, the disruption of travel and living patterns, air, water, and noise pollution, and for other adverse consequences of our dependence on automobiles.

Here at the Massachusetts Institute of Technology, for example, we provide very expensive, guarded parking garages for staff who live in suburban communities, but offer minimal facilities for safe bicycle parking. I have calculated, with some sadness, that my desire to live close enough to M.I.T. to be able to bicycle there comfortably makes me the equivalent of $10,000 per year poorer in apparent income because of the necessarily higher real-estate taxes and poorer services of a central city. "No good deed goes unpunished." The answer: Charge automobile drivers with the full costs of their activities. Then more would bicycle.

The hostile nature of the highway. Most of our older roads were upgraded and paved in response to the lobbying of bicyclists in the 1890's. As automobiles took over, the highway became hostile to nonmotorized travel. Today's bicyclist must travel as near to the right of the road as possible, where motoring revellers throw beer bottles, cans, and all sorts of trash and debris; where the doors of parked cars are vigorously snapped open by drivers usually—but not always—oblivious of the danger to passing bicyclists; where sewer gratings are often set inches below or above the road surface, like a trap set and waiting to catch a bicycle wheel and break the neck of the unwary; where potholes go unrepaired and gravel, stones, and piles of sand go unswept. And, perhaps worst of all, the cyclist on a road exactly two lanes wide must either hold ground and be a nuisance to drivers and perhaps a target for their vehicles or be continually dismounting and jumping out of the way.

The answer is not separate bicycle paths, which are too expensive for urban areas, never wide enough, and usually shared by pedestrians and parked trucks. The best answer, where it can be implemented, is a half lane to the right of the automobile travel lanes on regular roads (obviously not on high-speed superhighways). In many places such a half lane can be provided at little cost by reducing existing extra-wide lanes to a narrower standard width.

Thieves. We have better bicycle locks nowadays, but a determined professional thief is still hard to stop. Yet, until recently, even the U.S. Department of Transportation failed to provide secure parking facilities for its Washington cyclist employees and prohibited them from bringing their machines into their offices. When one has had five or six expensive, personalized bicycles stolen (I have) because of the lack of secure storage facilities coupled with public apathy at the sight of thieves at work, one's enthusiasm for saving energy and the environment can be diminished.

Attackers. Bicyclists have long known the punches, bottles, and oral brickbats thrown from passing cars. I was once lassoed on Massachusetts Avenue by a sportsman in the back seat of a convertible. The noose fortunately fell across my shoulder rather than around my neck. The editor of this article once narrowly escaped being struck by the door of a moving car opened to achieve that end, the act punctuated, incredibly, with an obscenity. It is quite conceivable that a fair proportion of bicyclists' deaths on our roads are homicides. Joggers are now learning to experience similar attention.

Bicycle design deficiencies. The bicycle itself is a delightful vehicle, but one with shortcomings, which include the following.

Safety provisions: Bicycles are not as safe as they should be. An over-the-handlebars fall can all too easily result in a fractured skull and/or a broken neck, in addition to severe facial injuries.

Brakes: generally poor when wet.

Weather protection: none.

Luggage capacity: little or none built-in.

Wind resistance: ignored by designers, even though this is where most of the rider's energy is dissipated.

Discomfort: Long-distance riders on today's "ten-speed" bicycles commonly suffer nerve damage in the areas which share the support: hands, feet and crotch. The recumbent bicycle eliminates these discomforts, but has yet to win popularity in the re-emerging human-powered transport market.

Recumbent bicycles aren't new. The first modern recumbent in the United States was made by a "Mr. Brown" and taken to Britain in 1901, where it was received with derision although acknowledged to perform rather well. Then in France during the 1930's, an unknown rider on a recumbent *Velocar* proceeded to break speed records and even to beat the world cycling champion in one-to-one contests. The response? The International Cycling Union met in consternation and announced that the Velocar "was not a bicycle" and had therefore not broken any bicycling records. It was summarily banned from further competition.

Unfortunately, recumbent bicycles designed for racing are not suitable for commuting with briefcase or shopping bag down Main Street. However, they are on the cutting edge of development and point to the way in which bicycles can be modified to make them more efficient, more comfortable, and safer.

I became interested in the safety potential of recumbents after reading about the deaths of several prominent bicyclists, including racing champions, in head-first accidents with conventional bicycles. After building a prototype, rather to my surprise I found that the recumbent configuration was not only vastly safer from this danger, but that it was also much kinder to the human frame, could carry luggage more conveniently, and had less wind resistance. In addition, it could also be easily fitted with streamlining that would provide weather protection; more effective brakes could be fitted without risk of inducing more head injuries because in a panic stop the rider tends to be deposited feet-first on the ground.

The Future of the Bicycle

Fred DeLong

The human-powered vehicle is a blood brother of highly sophisticated spacecraft. Its horizons are virtually unlimited. Useful for distant exploration, it can likewise be used for daily workhorse projects. But its performance depends, with its limited power supply, on obtaining the very highest return for the energy expended.

Space-age technology can be utilized effectively in the construction of our vehicle. The structure can be made of the same exotic materials, which combine maximum strength and stiffness with a minimum of weight. Boron-fiber reinforced aluminum 6061 alloy, heat treated to maximum strength after bonding, has been developed for use in the NASA space shuttle. It also makes extremely light but incredibly stiff bicycle frames. Power applied to the pedals is conveyed with minimum loss due to deflection under load, while the light weight makes acceleration and hill climbing easier.

The shape of this structure can be changed drastically to better suit the human power plant, and to transfer power from it to the point of use.

The characteristics of the engine itself must be studied in more depth to let it realize its maximum potential. What speed and duration of movement, what muscle stress are most effective? With a common source of oxygen and fuel-transporting fluid, will there be any gain in efficiency if arms as well as legs generate power?

At the lower end of the scale, the sturdy 1- or 3-speed gives us an inexpensive vehicle with a rather long life. If we just change tires and other relatively low-cost parts as they get worn, we can keep a bicycle in use for scores of years with not much care.

At the higher end, we have bicycles made with exotic materials or modes of construction that can cost twenty times as much. So our forecasts must be tempered by the costs for increasingly small improvements in performance. Of course, such bikes are rare now. With increased demand and increased production, the differential for highest quality equipment will lessen.

At this point, let us not hold out the promise that human power will in the future attain all the advantages of its more expensive counterparts. Moreover, we probably wouldn't really want it to. Our extra effort brings with it a physical and mental strengthening, so that life is fuller. And this more economical means of transport (the most expensive bike is still cheaper than the cheapest car) allows disposable income to be used for items that might otherwise be shelved.

Servicing Improvements

The use of high-precision antifriction bearings in all moving parts – hubs, bottom brackets (crank hangers), and pedals – is increasing. Even the headset design is being improved. High-capacity, long-life roller bearings give higher load and road-impact capacity.

These and even conventional cup-and-cone bearings have had their life extended by improved methods of sealing out dirt, moisture, and grit. This will be extended to better sealing of other sources of grit and water entry – such as the headset, handlebar stem, seat pillar, and openings for cables and for release of gases during frame manufacture.

Greater use of long-life plastics further improve weight, durability, and weather resistance of other components.

The freewheel and derailleur have in the past been sources of excessive maintenance time and cost. Freewheels

Fred De Long *is in a particularly good position to see what trends and innovations are happening from his vantage point as technical editor of* Bicycling *magazine. He took these photographs of the Muscar. He has reported on visibility earlier in this book.*

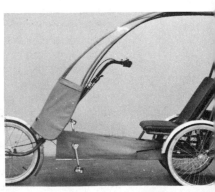

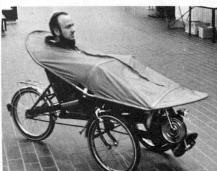

Bryan Allen flies MIT Chrysalis at Bedford Airport. MIT photo by Calvin Campbell, News Office, MIT

are being developed with improved sealing against outside elements, and are being designed to be removed rapidly, so spokes can be replaced easily and without the use of heavy tools.

Spokes generally fail at the bend where they enter the hub flange. Hub flanges that can be used with straight spokes will greatly lengthen spoke life, collect less dirt, be easier to keep clean, and permit closer approach of sprocket to hub flange.

Freewheels built into hubs permit nearly symmetrical wheels.

The combination of these developments will lead to wheels that are stronger and require less service.

While bicycle chains have given good service, new models will last longer and stay cleaner because less water and grit will enter, less lubricant will escape.

International safety and dimensional standards will be established. Servicing problems caused by the wide variety in component parts—their dimensions, form and threading—have made it hard to replace worn components. Those shops which did specialize in servicing, and the distributors who supplied them, had to stock sets of parts to fit whatever type of bicycle came along. This meant thousands of dollars tied up in parts, in storage space, in ordering and stocking costs.

Cutting Air Resistance

Because air resistance is the dominant force to be overcome by the rider's power plant, small reductions can have a considerable effect on performance and endurance. Just pushing harder won't help. If you work twice as hard you can only keep it up a tenth as long.

The cyclist's body is a major source of air resistance, but the bicycle also contributes with brakes, brake handles, cables, cranks, pedals, and baggage. Streamlining the bicycle and its rider is made more difficult because of their low speed compared to the wind itself. And it assumes the wind is coming directly at you, but crosswinds can make streamlining ineffective or even harmful.

The recumbent vehicle, when properly designed with the rider's legs extended forward slightly below the seat, has shown some distinct advantages over the conventional riding position. The erect body position gives good visibility, increased lung capacity, yet frontal area is reduced, which results in less fatigue and good hill-climbing potential. Foot pressure on pedals is resisted by the backrest in Dr. David Gordon Wilson's Avatar design (built by FOMAC Inc., in Wilmington, Massachusetts). The front wheel is 16 x 1 3/8-inches, the rear wheel a standard 27 x 1 1/4-inches, with 10 to 21 speed derailleur gearing, baggage space behind the rider, flag and reflectors for visibility.

The low center of gravity and low body position make for improved stability, and in case of brake failure, one or both legs can be lowered to slow forward speed. In case of a fall, the legs can be lowered to break the fall. Actual unplanned falls from this vehicle at speeds up to 30 miles per hour have caused little injury to the rider. A forward pitch over onto the head—common on the conventional 10-speed—is virtually impossible because of the extended wheelbase. Ample luggage capacity behind the rider's seat makes it good for commuting. Steering controls are located at the hip level, thus there is nothing to be struck in case of impact.

Super Portables

Another emerging trend is lightweight bicycles that can take up a tiny amount of space when not in use, so they can be loaded easily in the trunk of a car, carried onto public transport, and stored in minimal space in home or at destination.

Super Stable

For stability, there is considerable interest in the tricycle. A previous disadvantage of the dual rear-wheel driven trike has been the weight and complication of shifting gears, and the need for a differential to permit turning corners.

To overcome these disadvantages, several groups are working on tricycles with linked-steering front wheels, and a single rear drive wheel.

Even more advantageous, however, is a tricycle that will bank on turns like a bicycle. This is being worked on in England by Frank R. Whitt and by Dr. J.K. Cannell, and also in Japan. A successful model has been developed by Robert Bloom.

Weather Protection

Professor Paul Schoendorf, of the German Engineering University of Cologne, feels that while the human-powered vehicles meet a great need in urban transportation, only a spartan minority who are indifferent to inclement weather will make constant use of them. He and his students have been developing stable vehicles with room for groceries, clothes, or books—and permanent or folding weather protection—in both touring and sport models.

These "Muscars" have been extensively tested in traffic. They are easy to handle, easy to park, and have good visibility. The ones with foldable enclosures are light enough to carry up a flight of stairs. When open, the covering, combined with the rider's muscular effort, gives adequate protection from moderate cold. It has sufficient gearing and lighting to be used in hilly terrain and at night. Sprint performance may not be as exciting as on a stripped-down racer; however, the "Muscar" and "Muscabrio" solve many everyday commuting problems.

Conclusion

These developments will not replace the highly efficient lightweight conventional bicycle, but will widen the man-powered vehicle's sphere of usefulness.

A Look at Future Design

Alex Moulton, C.B.E.

The interest in the bicycle throughout its long history has never been greater than now. It is not difficult to see why this should be so. The recent worldwide awareness of the need to conserve natural resources has focused attention on personal mobility by that most efficient of vehicles, the bicycle. Also considerations of antipollution and the benefit to health of regular exercise point to the desirability of cycling. To shift the balance from eighty percent of travel by passenger car and one percent by bicycle in terms of passenger mile, as it is in Britain for instance, perhaps requires the provision of more segregated ways reserved for cyclists in urban areas rather than improvement of the bicycle itself.

However, the design of the bicycle will always continue to fascinate the engineer and the user. Unlike most other devices used by man, every component of the bicycle is exposed to his critical gaze. But I believe the scope for radical change is more limited than fantasy may suggest. This is due to ergonomic restraints imposed by the rider's needs for control, visibility, and power generation by rotating cranks. The "classic" position with the forward leaning of the trunk seems to me to be fundamentally right ergonomically. Of course this excludes the great reduction in frontal area which the prone or recumbent position permits.

The exciting annual speed contests initiated by Professor Chester Kyle show what advances in speed are possible by the drastic reduction in air drag. So I believe that we shall see developments in the fairing of the bicycle and rider while still retaining the classic riding position. The obvious restraint in the extent of fairing is the maintenance of control under gusts from passing traffic. The use of smaller wheels of sixteen to twenty-four inches in diameter (pioneered in the Moulton adult unisex machine introduced in 1962) helps this problem.

The search for further weight reduction in a vehicle is always meritorious, but the bicycle, which can carry a payload of some eight times its own weight, is already very efficient structurally. The weight control of the rider is perhaps the most important line of future development! Moreover, as the rider essentially produces power at very low rotational speeds, the alternating thrusts are high, and it is imperative that the frame should be stiff to avoid losses that are not recoverable. It is likely, therefore, that steel will

Dr. Alex Moulton *is the designer of the Moulton bicycle that began the modern trend toward small-wheel urban transit. He is continuing to develop this design, and is shown with a folding version of it.*

Dr. Moulton *with his 1975 Moulton bicycle. Photograph courtesy of Dr. Alex Moulton.*

remain the dominant contender for the choice of material for the frame structure against the alternative possibilities of light alloy and carbon fiber.

By the same argument, I cannot imagine a more appropriate means of transmission than a chain and sprocket mechanism, with development being directed toward lesser pitch and narrower width chains better able to withstand the environment, and more refined derailleurs.

Puncture-free alternatives to the pneumatic rubber tire as currently evolved from the invention of J.B. Dunlop, which precipitated the cycle revolution, will always attract the endeavors of inventors. However, we must not lose sight of the efficient way in which the narrow section, high-pressure tires perform the essential functions of low rolling resistance with adequate road grip. Certainly, improved tread life would be welcome.

In conclusion, I look forward to the further evolution of the bicycle, in which I hope to play a part. But I do not foresee radical changes in form. It is already a highly evolved device eminently suitable both as low-cost basic transport for people and goods in Third World countries, as well as being, in its more refined versions, a superb recreational and mobility machine for increasing use in developed countries. We must also remember that the vested interest and international competition in component manufacture will ensure improvement in this important aspect of the bicycle.

Different Spokes

Sandra Sims-Martin

Photographs by Sandra Sims-Martin

Still air accounts for up to eighty percent of the resistance to motion on a moving cycle (one study says up to ninety percent). The greater the speed, the higher the percentage, because power expenditure to overcome air drag goes up as the cube of speed. Therefore, it is apparent that, at satisfying cruising speeds, most of a cyclist's energy is used simply pushing through an unending wall of air.

Current interest in streamlined human-powered vehicles began in 1974 when Dr. Chester Kyle and a group of his mechanical engineering students at California State College at Long Beach began a project to test the rolling resistance of various bicycle tires and ended up with a project to determine efficiency of streamlining at cycling speeds. Dr. Kyle built a known wing shape out of aluminum and sailcloth, turned it vertically over a standard racing cycle, installed Olympic cyclist Ron Skarin, and broke four records: 200 meters, 44.69 mph; 500 meters, 42.62 mph; 1,000 meters, 41.2 mph; and one mile, 40.63 mph.

Earlier attempts to reduce drag through design and streamlining were attempted in the 1930's. The machines were successful and broke some records, but further interest was effectively discouraged when the International Cycling Federation banned radical design bicycles from sanctioned competition for unfair advantage. In 1975 the International Human Powered Vehicle Association was formed to sanction records, organize competitions, and encourage experiment.

Annually, in Ontario, California, the International Human Powered Speed

Sandra Sims-Martin *was contributing editor of* Bike World, *specializing in radical design bicycles. She regularly rides a recumbent and is part-owner of both the 1979 singles record vehicle and the 1978 IHPSC road-race winner.*

Championship dramatically demonstrates that air drag is the major limiting factor to human-powered speed. A mere six years ago, after a century of bicycle development, but before IHPSC, the fastest speed for a 200-meter sprint unaided by motor pacing, gravity, or tail wind was 42.2 mph. The 1980 record for a single rider was 56.55 mph set on a streamlined tricycle.

Streamliners have little in common with standard bicycles except the means of applying and transferring power. Most are not bicycles, but tricycles, or quadracycles. Inside the streamlining shells, they have little in common with each other. Each is a one-of-a-kind design limited only by the restriction against the use of any stored energy. Frames range from old bicycles cut up and welded back together, to aluminum tubing with handmade, two-piece lugs, bonded by resin. Fairings are made of anything from cardboard to Kevlar. Gears go up to almost 200 inches and are pushed by grandfathers and nationally ranked racers. Categories of division are based on number of riders and rider position.

In each class there are three general positions: standard, prone (head first), and supine (feet first). Both prone and supine are referred to as recumbents.

Recumbents dominate both classes. Although they didn't take over in the multiple class until 1978, it is notable that with the same number of riders, a supine vehicle exceeded the previous champion's speed by 4.5 mph. The success of the recumbents is a function of reduced drag through reduced frontal area and lower profile. Cyclists take advantage of the same thing when they draft or drop low on the bars into a "racer's crouch."

Using prone position is the easiest way to get a super low profile. The rider can be placed very low to the ground and still use rotary cranks. For instance, a triple prone may be only twenty-five inches high. Even lower machines can be (and have been) built using a recumbent position in conjunction with linear drive. However, there seems to be an inherent power waste at the end of each stroke on a linear drive. The problem has yet to be totally overcome and all of the fastest machines to date use rotary cranks.

The streamlining shells with the lowest drag are those that are loosely termed laminar flow shells. All streamlining is an attempt to pass through the air, disturbing it as little as possible. Simplistically, air flows in layers around a moving object and the boundary layer is responsible for drag. All boundary layers begin laminar (layered) then sooner or later become turbulent or separate from the object. Laminar flow shells have precise coordinates which determine a shape which is calculated to keep the boundary layer laminar to a given point. Thus they have the potential for greatly reduced drag and correspondingly higher speeds.

In 1979, three multiple rider vehicles broke 55 mph in the 200-meter sprint, with a spread of only 0.07 second between them. Only one, the fastest, did not have a laminar flow shell, but it had three riders while the others made do with two riders.

The record setters are made for speed. All practical design considerations are entirely secondary. Another segment of the IHPVA emphasizes practical application to general purpose cycling. In 1978 a road race and a one-hour time trial were added to the IHPSC to encourage development of more practical streamlined vehicles.

The hour event is run on a two-and-a-half-mile oval with wide sweeping curves. The road race is approximately 19 miles; seven times around a 2.7-mile (approx.) circuit. It has one long straightaway followed by a series of serpentine curves through the infield of the speedway. Multiples and singles compete against each other in both races. Unlimited class competition is a poor gauge of anything other than the speed of the winner. But when trends appear, they can be an indication of future direction. Supine bicycles may become an alternative design for general cycling. By general cycling I mean applicable to city streets and mountain passes as well as country lanes and bike paths, as opposed to designs aimed at specific groups within limited situations, such as the adult tricycle.

Supines have established themselves as favorites in the longer distance events. The IHPVA also organizes smaller criterium races throughout the year, including one where radical design streamliners, streamlined standard bicycles, partially streamlined standards, and totally unstreamlined racing bicycles competed against each other. Streamlined supines have dominated these events.

Both winners of the IHPSC road race use their supines (without streamlining) as their regular bicycles. Fred Tatch and John Thomas' Manuped, the 1979 and 1980 road race winner, features hand cranks in addition to foot cranks. Naturally, it is a front-wheel drive. The front wheel is not directly driven by the cranks. The cranks drive chainwheels which transfer power to a jack shaft that drives the front wheel by means of a chain.

Since the pedals are on the front wheel, both arms and legs are used in steering, and correct phasing between them is necessary. It's a learned skill and takes some practice, but is no more difficult than learning to ride a bicycle in the first place. The brakes are activated by backpedaling the hand cranks.

There are conflicting reports as to

Ron Skarin riding a bicycle enclosed by a full fairing designed by Dr. Chester Kyle. Photograph courtesy Fred De Long

Prototype of the Manuped, hand and foot cranked

whether hand cranking adds power in aerobic situations. There are conflicting reports on every aspect of the human-powered vehicles. Since the IHPVA created such a flurry of experiment, every person with access to accurate testing equipment has run tests. The results vary greatly not only with each other but with tests that had previously been used as standard reference. The current situation is total confusion.

Gardner Martin, Nathan Dean, and I all ride unstreamlined versions of the supine that won the first IHPSC road race. At 45.01 mph for 200 meters (with streamlining), it is also the fastest single-rider, supine vehicle. Although we are all converts from standard-position bicycles, we no longer own any standards and use our supines exclusively. We have each logged several thousand miles in varying terrains from Washington, D.C., to Washington state.

Martin uses his for daily transportation, commuting ten miles round trip through rolling hills, as well as longer pleasure trips on weekends. The only tour the bike has had was made by a

friend who took it approximately 400 miles down the California coastal highway in three and a half days.

Our Easy Racer is basically a stretched out, lowered bicycle. It has a triangulated frame with cross braces for strength and twist resistance. The frame telescopes to ensure a perfect fit. The front wheel is placed in front of the pedals in order to maintain direct steering while gaining the lowest possible profile which is still easily visible to traffic. The components are all normal bicycle components.

Supine bicycles are not new. Like streamliners, they've been around since the 1930's. Like streamliners, interest lagged when they were barred from competition. They're not likely to replace the diamond frame. But they could become a viable alternative. Supines have some obvious advantages. The lower profile reduces drag. Lowered center of gravity increases stability and allows use of the feet as stabilizers. They have some obvious disadvantages, too. They're generally heavier. There's no way to get off the seat and "stand

Gardner Martin and Nathan Dean's "Orca," which won the first IHPSC road race

to almost nothing and remaining un-affected by side blasts. Is such a vehicle possible? If we knew that, chasing after it wouldn't be so much fun.

The possibilities of reduced drag design as applied to human power are just beginning to be explored. Its future is anybody's guess. Here are some of the predictions:

Jack Lambie, co-founder IHPVA: "A vehicle with three or more riders might well exceed 90 mph."

Dr. Chester Kyle, co-founder IHPVA: "A completely stream-lined, stable platform vehicle that a so-so cyclist can average 35 mph in."

Paul Van Valkenburgh, twice singles record holder: "We will see a cyclist pedal a stream-lined shell from San Francisco to Los Angeles in one day."

Dr. Paul MacCready, official timer IHPSC and creator of the Gos-samer Albatross: "The value is in getting a perspective on what humans can do; in finding out how little power you can get by on; in directing thinking into the general area."

Sandra Sims-Martin: "We could have a choice of bicycles like we now have a choice of auto-mobiles. After all, pickup trucks don't suit everybody."

Gardner Martin and Nathan Dean on their favorite bikes

on" the pedals. It's not a case of dia-mond frame versus supine. It's merely personal preference. If supines become commercially available, they should at-tract a segment of the general popula-tion that is not attracted to bicycles now.

Supines also have the potential to develop into practical human-powered vehicles. Such a vehicle could provide weather protection for the rider and a couple of bags of groceries, be able to keep pace with city traffic without undue effort, and be stable in a cross-wind. This is admittedly a very long view. Design considerations of the streamlining alone are staggering. The shell must be high enough off the ground to maneuver a hairpin turn. It must have a floor to be efficient, so the vehicle itself must be a stable platform or the rider has to be able to get his feet on the ground through or around the floor. It must allow a large volume of air to pass inside for ventilation. It must permit full play of the wheels. It must not interfere with the rider's rear vision. It should not break in a crash. It must do all these things while reducing drag

END PAGES

The Cycling Race   Jacques Faizant

To the races already known on the globe, one must add the cycling race.

The cycling race has its own language, rituals, laws, and customs; its passwords, celebrations, costume, etiquette, and philosophy. These rarely correspond to those of the rest of the world.

No other athlete is looked upon by his contemporaries with such a mixture of circumspect astonishment and discreet commiseration. It seems completely normal for boxers to break each other's jaws, soccer players their shins, rugbymen their collarbones, and skiers all those and everything else. But let a cyclist say he enjoys spending ten or fifteen hours seated on a saddle, or climbing Mount Ventoux in the heat of summer, and you will see these kind folks struck by the stupor that gives so much expression to the eyes of a white hen when, perchance, it has hatched a blue duck.

I have to admit that the fate of the cyclist does not, at first glance, seem so enviable. Whipped by the wind, drenched by the rain, lashed by sleet, burned by sun, the cyclist, perched on a thin strip of hard leather, turns his legs for hours to push forward an unstable machine with which he even sometimes is unreasonable enough to climb mountains that are steeper than should be permitted.

Spectators may well ask themselves what masochism pushes a cyclist to such mortifications.

It is as difficult to explain this as to explain why one is in love with someone who is apparently ugly. To love biking madly, one has to do a lot of it. To do a lot of it, one has to train. To train, one needs willpower. To have such willpower, one has to love biking.

This cycle, as you see, is vicious.

But however pitiable the cyclist may appear to you, don't be sorry for him – envy him. He has discovered that flying carpets and seven-league boots really exist, as well as the serum of long life.

The cyclist is not, as some people believe, a fallen automobilist. He is a miraculously healed pedestrian.

Jacques Faizant, Albina et la bicyclette, *1968*

Translated from the French by Vera van der Reis Krausz

Teaching Bike Riding the Non-Strenuous Way

Vera van der Reis Krausz

The old "support and shove" method is dangerous for the learner and hard work for the teacher. It also has little to do with the realities of bike riding. When teaching, it is useful to know what steps a learner must follow.

It's hard to learn many new things at once; two new ideas are as many as most people can manage at a time. Each step must be practiced until it is second nature, because a rider must concentrate on traffic and not mechanics when on the road. A teenager can learn to balance in an afternoon, but it may take adults several sessions.

Most people are afraid of falling and of being laughed at, so scout out a place away from traffic and observers – such as a parking lot or playground on a Sunday. Use a 3-speed or coaster-brake bike that's low enough to place both feet flat on the ground while sitting on the seat. A folder with quick-release seat bolt is ideal.

1. Sit on the seat and push forward with your feet, then lift them, like on a hobby horse. This way you can learn to steer, use hand brakes, and keep your balance without fear of falling. Make turns, ride straight lines, and brake when a friend yells "Halt!" or "Brake!" After some practice on a flat surface, find a slight incline, then one a bit steeper. See how long you can ride and steer with feet lifted. This stage must not be rushed and is sufficient for an adult's first or second try.

2. You travel farthest when the pedal is a little past top center – about 1:30 or 2 o'clock. Pushing off from this position gives you plenty of time to bring your other foot up and place it on 265

the second pedal. As you push down with one pedal the other comes up. If you have footbrakes, practice pedaling backward to stop. Do it gently – learn to slow down by applying a bit of pressure, then stop by increasing it.

Only practice pedaling at this low height for a little while. It is bad for your knees to ride with the seat low enough for your feet to touch the ground, but a half-hour shouldn't hurt.

3. Raise the seat two inches. This still permits you to touch the ground with the ball of your foot. Repeat all the maneuvers listed in step 1.

4. Look at your bike from the side. When the pedal is at its lowest point it is only about four inches from the ground. This means when one foot is on it, the other can easily reach the ground also.

5. Stand with one foot on each side of the frame. Grasp the handlebars with both hands. Get the pedal to be mounted forward, in the fat part of the stroke – at about 2 o'clock. Place your foot on the raised pedal. Put your weight on it. Straightening your leg as you push down will lift your whole body, so it's easy to lower yourself onto the seat and get the second pedal and pedal off.

6. Dismounting. Slow the bike by braking gently. Place all your weight on the pedal at the bottom of the stroke as in step 4. Pull your body forward out of the saddle. Brake until you have almost stopped. Put your free leg on the ground. Now the other one. Practice steps 5 and 6 until you can do them quickly and smoothly.

7. Absolutely essential: Place the seat at the correct height, leg extended but not locked. Mount, steer, turn, brake, dismount.

8. You don't know how to steer well enough to be safe on the road unless you can ride a straight line about a foot wide. The acid test is staying within the foot-wide strip between parked-car spaces. You can simulate this with a row of soft-drink cups or by drawing lines with chalk.

9. Practice looking over your shoul-der without swerving more than three inches. Practice taking your left hand off the handlebars for turn signals (same as motorists': straight out for left turn, straight up for right turn, down for slowing or stopping).

10. Practice moving back on the seat and feathering the brakes.

11. Practice taking turns with the pedals level or the pedal that's inside the turn raised so it doesn't hit the ground.

12. You're ready for an outing. Obey traffic laws. Ride straight, look over your shoulder and signal before you change your line, don't drift into the curb. When going up a hill, pull the handlebars gently toward you for extra power.

13. Practice in a traffic-free area when learning to use any new equipment – toeclips, gear changers, dropped handlebars (reaching the brakes will be different).

Cycling Rejuvenates — Sex and Bicycling

Rokuro Koike, M.D.

Rokuro Koike, M.D., professor of urology at the Kyorin University School of Medicine in Tokyo, wrote us the following:

I have been commuting by bicycle since 1971, but initially could not commute every day because of fatigue.

Since 1977 I commute by bicycle every day (over 40 km) except for holidays and very rainy days. Since that time, I have noticed my rejuvenation and strength of sexual vigor as shown in Tables 1 and 2.

It is generally said that one hour of sport daily, consuming about 300 calories, is best for health. But I believe that one hour of sport twice every day is better. I also believe that one hour twice a day is better than two hours once a day.

I have not found a report about any other sport that rejuvenated and strengthened sexual vigor. I speculated on two possible causes:

(1) The bicycle saddle serves to stimulate Cowper's glands, which have a vital function in the process of erection. I believe that lifting the hips up out of the saddle as often as possible is better than continuous sitting on the saddle. A two-hour massage of the Cowper's glands and the prostate every day is bad, because they will be congested too much. I believe that prostatitis might be caused by continuously sitting on the saddle. Frequent short massage is good, but continuous long massage is bad.

Table 1
Standard frequency of sexual intercourse according to age (Kinsey)

Years old	26-30	31-35	36-40	41-50	51-
Frequency/ week	2-4	2-3	2	1-2	1

Table 2
My own frequency of sexual intercourse according to age.

Years old	29-35		36-40	41-50	51-52	53-
Frequency/ week	2-3		2	1-2	1	2-3

(2) I believe it is important to recover completely to strengthen sexual function, because semen is chiefly synthesized after complete recovery. Long-time training is necessary to recover completely from one hour's cycling within about eight hours. For me, it took six years commuting by bicycle before I could recover completely within about eight hours after one hour bicycling. During the previous six years I could not commute by bicycle every day, because over eleven hours of rest were needed for complete recovery. At present, I suffer slight fatigue after one hour of cycling. After complete recovery, I feel my strength of sexual vigor. For example, my strength of sexual vigor increases after 3 A.M., when I had come home by bicycle at 7 P.M.

266

Profession: Cyclist

Bertil Lundquist

This is a designation which not many people other than racing cyclists can use, but Mr. Malte Nilsson of Trelleborg, Sweden, can. His annual 32,000 miles never make the headlines of newspapers or magazines, though we ordinary cyclists in Sweden have reason to be grateful to Malte, for it is he who contributes largely to the improving quality of our tires.

Malte takes over where laboratories and test-rooms finish. He rides 195 kilometres daily, five days per week, all the year round. Every pedal turn is in service to science. His correct job description is tire-tester and he is employed by Trelleborgs Gummifabrik, Sweden's only manufacturer of cycle tires.

The best way of testing a tire is of course to let it roll on streets and tracks. There it will be exposed to all the stresses that a tire will suffer during its lifespan. At about seven o'clock every weekday morning Malte starts his job. Seven to eight hours later he is back in his home in Trelleborg having ridden from Trelleborg to Sveldala—Staffanstorp—Dalby—Sodra Sandby—Hardeberga—Lund and back again. The rest of the working day is used for keeping his bike in trim.

He has virtually a complete repairer's workshop on the cycle rack when he rides, though he does not often need to use it. Malte thinks that cycles are of a much better quality nowadays than before. He ought to know–he has worn many out over the years. It is more than twenty-five years since he started work as a tire-tester and now he has about three years left before his retirement. Malte explains how he got the job: "I had worked in a foundry before and was looking for a similar job in Trelleborg. But someone asked me if I wanted to take over the tire-testing. I did it with great pleasure, as I have never liked to work indoors."

Twenty-five years in the saddle has endowed Malte with good health. His face is smooth and rosy like a child's, and he has never been ill during his years as a cyclist. Just once he was run down and had to stay at home for a fortnight.

What does Malte do in his spare time? He says he rides quite a lot! He owns a car but thinks it is better left in the garage. You will not be surprised to hear his answer to the question about what he will do when he has retired. "Ride on! As long as I live!"

—*Reprinted by permission from* International Cycling Guide 1980, *published by A.S. Barnes and Company, Inc. and the Tantivy Press of London.*

Our Own Bookshelf

John Krausz

Bikes and Riders by James Wagenvoord (Van Nostrand Reinhold, 1972) is a really nice book, currently out of print but with a new edition in the works. Chapters include "The Founders," "The Golden Years," and "The Military-Industrial Bike Rider Complex" that explains how H.G. Wells got mixed up in the bicycle war between its exponents and the British War Department. A long story illustrated with Wagenvoord's photographs chronicles a season with the Metros, a racing club that trained in New York's Central Park.

Wagenvoord dug deep and found beautiful graphics and photographs, and was even able to quote from William Saroyan's *The Bike Rider in Beverly Hills* (a book that I have been hunting for years): "The thing about my bicycles that I want to remember is the way I rode them, what I thought while I rode them, and the music that came to me."

I wish I had done this book.

Seamus McGonagle's *The Bicycle in Life, Love, War, and Literature* (A.S. Barnes and Company, 1969) has been out of print for over ten years but can be obtained from bookdealers for about the published price, and is worth looking for. McGonagle is terrifyingly eloquent but hasn't much self control. He tells the story about the man with many illegitimate children who, when asked by the priest to explain himself, says, "Well, you see, I have a bicycle."

McConagle tells a lot of nice stories and wins hands down the contest for the best short history of the bicycle, covering an amazing amount of ground.

Had I been able to trace Mr. McConagle's whereabouts I would have asked to reprint "Bomb Their Bikes," an essay on the military use of bicycles. The piece starts by quoting Senator Fulbright in 1967 when, after hearing Harrison Salisbury tell how the Viet Cong hauled all their supplies into South Vietnam by bicycle, and that without bicycles North Vietnam would have to get out of the war, Fulbright remarked, "Why not concentrate on bicycles instead of bridges?"

Anybody's Bike Book and *Bike Tripping* (Ten Speed Press, 1971 and 1972 respectively), both written by Tom Cuthbertson and illustrated with Rick Morrall's drawings and zany cartoons, were put together before the bike boom and have been selling ever since. These books are like trusted friends; you forget just how much there is to them.

Anybody's, "an original manual of bicycle repairs" (if you can ride it you can fix it), has clear simple directions and nice freehand exploded views and drawings. I'd recommend it to just about anybody. *Anybody's* has sold 650,000 copies and was completely revised in 1979.

Bike Tripping is something else. Besides containing perhaps the best simple article ever written about bicycle frames (by Albert Eisentraut, the dean of American frame builders), the book starts with a chapter on learning to ride. It is a great introduction to many areas of the sport, and is an ideal present for someone you're trying to get interested in biking.

It's filled with sound advice: Watch it on the country roads, people go there to get drunk and take potshots . . . wear bright clothing during the hunting season . . . how to use two-by-fours to pack a lot of bikes into a truck or a U-haul trailer . . . which way and how hard the wind blows in different parts of this country throughout the year (we thought that information so useful you'll find it in our touring section).

Besides publishing the Cuthbertson books, Ten Speed Press has also reprinted Andrew Ritchie's *King of the Road* (1975), an illustrated history of cycling. This is not just another version of "how the bicycle came up the river from Stoke Podges," but offers both technical and social history. It is illustrated with several hundred beautiful vintage photographs and drawings which make clear not only the evolution of the machine but also the huge impact the bicycle has had on the way we live.

Just as Stuart Wilson's *Scientific American* article was the first piece on the subject printed in a major magazine in almost three generations, and the Whitt and Wilson *Bicycling Science* was the first serious book to treat it in this century, Archibald Sharp's *Bicycles and Tricycles* almost had the last word on the subject.

Published in 1896, we all owe a debt to MIT Press for reprinting it in 1977, *Bicycles and Tricycles* was the authoritative text for anyone interested in the problems of bicycle engineering. As David Gordon Wilson says in his introduction, "Sharp's definitive work on bicycles and tricycles marked and helped bring about the end of an exciting period in mechanical engineering." It was Sharp's intent to show that much of the experimentation being done demonstrated, as he said, "utter ignorance of the science," and he wanted his book to convince the makers to stop producing "mechanical monstrosities."

The book has 550 illustrations, about half of which are technical and the rest of which show machines and components. Spokeless disk wheels, recumbent bicycles, and anatomical saddles had already been tried by then and Sharp describes these and other things in clear and sometimes merciless terms.

Anyone, however ill equipped to deal with the more technical parts, can find enjoyment in the tone of the text and the insight that can be gained from Sharp's lucid mind. It is one of the rare books on technology that qualify as literature. Certainly those who intend to invent or design bicycles should expose themselves to Sharp's criticism. Though you may get lost at times in a sea of mathematics, the opening remarks of each chapter will often bring about a new level of understanding. There are passages I would like to quote but won't for fear of casting ridicule on some present-day exponents of some ideas of which he was scornful or that he thought dangerously silly.

Also published by MIT Press is *Bicycling Science, Ergonomics and Mechanics,* by Frank Rowland Whitt and David Gordon Wilson, paperback, 1976. Starting with the power needed for land locomotion, then progressing to human power generation, it explains how bicyclists keep cool and answers such questions as is the bicycle or the roller skate more efficient, should one walk or pedal uphill. It then goes into the problems of bicycle physics: drag coefficients, riding position and wind resistance, the advantages and disadvantages of small-wheeled bicycles.

This is the first book on bicycle science since Sharp's *Bicycles and Tricycles,* and in spite of its formidable title and enough math to perhaps scare you off, it's very readable. This is a book to be savored, dipped into, referred to. Whitt and Wilson have done the impossible . . . their book is every bit as interesting and informative as Sharp's.

The Guinness Book of Bicycling by Jean Durry (English edition, 1977, Blandford Press, distributed in the United States by Sterling Publishing Co.), skilfully translated from the French by J.B. Watley, a British cycling journalist, is a really beautiful book. Buy it for the coffee-table book it looks like and feast your eyes on beautiful machines and scenery, on exciting racing and picturesque touring photographs. Then read the text and find out that Durry's fifteen years experience as an amateur racing cyclist help him provide a wealth of information on many aspects of cycling, painted on a larger canvas than his *La veridique histoire des geants de la route.* The book has excellent archive photographs and drawings in black and white, plus stunning color photographs.

The Bicycle Builder's Bible by Jack Wiley (TAB Books, 1980). What makes this book different is Jack Wiley sharing his experience building specialist bikes—bronco bikes, double-deckers, artistic cycles,—transforming a child's tricycle into a penny-farthing . . . and he gives tips on how to ride them.

There's also a long chapter on unicycles, plus a hundred-page maintenance guide.

This book has the ring of truth. When discussing homemade tandems (made by joining two bicycles), Wylie says, "Of all the homemade tandems I have seen, and this includes quite a number, only a few are equal to or better than a typical used manufactured utility tandem." I know this is true, so when Wylie describes two methods of taking standard bikes and making it possible to fold them, he can probably be trusted.

The final chapter, "Generating Power With a Bicycle," includes designs for bicycle-powered grinders and pumps, plus pedal-driven winches, borehole pumps, and log splitters. It also shows how to build and use a bicycle generator to make your own power.

Jack Wylie doesn't despise cheap bikes. He shows how to fix them and how to turn them into something else.

The Penguin Book of the Bicycle, by Roderick Watson and Martin Gray, published in England in 1978, has now been released in the United States. It's like a college survey course on the bicycle, including social and technical history, a lot of really nice photographs, and a visit to the industry ranging from a full discussion of Raleigh, the General Motors of bicycle manufacturers, to an interview with custom builder David Moulton, who now builds bikes in New Jersey.

Watson and Gray like other books that I like, such as Daniel Behrman's *The Man Who Loved Bicycles (Memoirs of an Autophobe),* and their sixty-page chapter on cycle sport is a better introduction to the varied types of racing than many books on the subject. They also give a very good presentation of the technical aspects of bicycles.

The authors include the essential quote from Ivan Illich that makes it clear where the "velorution" people are coming from. There is also a description of the long battle between the Cyclists Touring Club and the British bureaucracy over the Rear Lamp Law passed because of the blackouts during World War I. The CTC felt that the burden of safety should be on the overcoming/passing vehicle, and that cyclists should not be held liable for damages caused to them by their not using extraordinary means to protect themselves.

This book has it all; it is the best general book about bicycling since James Wagenvoord's *Bikes and Riders.*

Yes, Those Were the Days!

Rex Coley

We found this essay on the joys of getting that first good bike absolutely irresistible. This is perhaps Rex Coley's three-thousandth essay on bicycling, so it's hard to have a favorite. He is touring editor of the British weekly, Cycling, *and has written many books under the name of "Ragged Staff."*

These days it is seldom a postman bangs loudly to secure attention, but when I was given a more or less grateful farewell by an army dispersal unit in the early months of 1920 I had an ear cocked for the postman's summons. Very simple: To arrive sooner or later would be a warrant authorizing payment of war gratuity or whatever was the official name; can't be sure after all this time.

The five years taken out of my life were made tolerably comfortable by the thought that burned ever strongly, that the first civilian money I received when November 11, 1918 brought great news to everyone, would go on the purchase of a bicycle.

I was one of the lucky ones to get a job when the war finished, a twenty-minute bus ride from my lodgings, and a plan had to be put into operation right away. By eight o'clock on this snowy March morning I had popped a note into the door of a local bike shop giving him the news that the gratuity had arrived, and would he add a Sturmey-Archer gear to the machine I long had had my eyes on, the highest-priced in the place, thirteen pounds with a 3-speed hub gear. (The derailleur was not to shake British faith in S.A. for several years yet.)

My note added, "I'll call for the bike soon after one o'clock. I'll go the whole way, so please fit a cyclometer." There was no need to ask about inflator or small tool bag – they came as "standard equipment."

Lunch hour arrived – who wanted food today? Not I, and I fairly leapt off the bus to burst into the cycle emporium.

Everything was ready, and the manager was dusting the handlebars and framework till everything fairly shone.

"Most expensive machine I've ever had in the shop," confessed the delighted manager. "I thought it too dear for a cash transaction, and was ready with the hire-purchase form! I share your pleasure that the gratuity came along at last."

He went on: "I can see from your expression and the way your legs are wriggling, you can't wait to get mounted, but I advise you to take things easily at first. Five years without cycling, unless you count an occasional heavy shoving of an army tank-like bike, is a long time,

and you really should take it in easy stages. You have the best saddle made, the Brooks B90, and you can't get better tires anywhere. I know you are only about twenty-one or twenty-two and very fit, but again I urge you to go slowly."

Then the businessman took over. "Weather is bad right now; let me sell you a decent-size cape, and waterproof hat, what we call a sou'wester. And leggings are a good purchase. Front mudguard extension would be money well spent, too."

I listened to the voice of experience, then came that heavenly moment I had waited for since 1915.

No trouble at all; not even a wobble as I fairly sprang on to the luxurious B90, confirming what I've often heard: Once you have ridden a bicycle you never lose the knack, even if there is a period of fifty years between your pedaling.

Up a steep Woolwich hill, low gear acting perfectly. I felt so robust that I was inclined to stay on the 96-inch gear, but harkening to what the shop manager had urged, I was sensible.

Into Charlton village in a matter of minutes (weather was clearing rapidly) to receive a whole barrage of "Oohs" and "Ahhs" from envious workmates. They kept saying between gasps for breath: "What a beauty!" "Best bike in south London, I bet," and "Any hope of borrowing it this weekend?" No hope at all, was my firm assurance.

The forthcoming Sunday brought a cold but sunny day, but the ride was a disappointment.

Workmate Harry Smith, who had quite a decent machine, expressed his astonishment that I had never visited Brighton in my life, and said such a serious omission must be remedied as quickly as possible.

My idea was to enjoy cycling lazily along the front, then sprawl on a bench to take in the soothing plash-plash of the incoming tide, but that wasn't Mr. Smith's idea at all. He was a billiards fanatic, and although I could swing a pretty nifty cue myself when called upon, I was far from a dedicated player. I followed Harry S. reluctantly into a basement pool room and we got started.

When Smithy had won twelve games and me three I suggested calling it a day, but I was given a glare at uttering such heresy.

"Look," I said, "the sun is blazing outside, and I didn't expect this ride to Brighton was to end in a billiards beano. Come on, let's go!"

I got my way, but Mr. S. was quite sulky. Five miles out of town he demanded more alcoholic refreshment, and intimated the ride to Woolwich would be taken in short, easy stages, with regular stops for the imbibing of a glass or two of "light ales."

That finished our joint ride, and the friendship, if it comes to that. Gladly I parted company with the man who had urged me so persistently to accompany him on a bicycle ride to Brighton, and rode on much relieved.

Nonstop to Crawley and a hearty snack at Tom Smith's (where else?), then into Surrey without further pause, ending in the gracious county of Kent, pleased that I had registered 104 miles on the cyclometer.

Good for a first ride, I told myself, and everybody who would listen.

On principle I don't object to work, but never have I grudged time spent on getting a living as I did during the first few weeks of post-war bicycle ownership. In those unfeeling days it was quite usual for Saturday morning attendance, in offices as well as shops, and I seldom threw an itching leg over the well-prized B90 till 1:30 at the earliest on Saturdays.

In the early 1920's I still had a home of sorts in north Birmingham, and visited it whenever the rather high (by the standards then prevailing) rail fare could be met.

Now in possession of a magic carpet, trains could be forgotten, and the trip, south London to north Birmingham, became quite frequent. One hundred and twenty-six miles each way (I couldn't imagine riding without the cheery tick-tick of a cyclometer) and not once did I have a puncture or suffer similar annoyances, and caping up was never necessary. I had better say again that during the year 1921 no rain fell on Britain for well over six months!

Now in 1978 I find a great longing with appropriate enthusiasm to do this out-and-home cycle ride; out through the night, back next morning. Brain working well, also wrists, but my shocked body exclaims, "What me?" No matter; much smaller ambitions are still my happy lot.

Later, when areas far north of the river were explored, well-meaning friend suggested taking train aid over dull, congested areas, to which I, with the arrogance of youth, replied with scorn, "No fear! I'm riding every inch of the way on this super bicycle. Taking the train part way – what a soppy idea!"

In 1922 I met a "fellow" enthusiast, a girl who had yet to taste the exhilaration of a "real" bicycle. We bought two models exactly alike, made by the notable Swift firm (she was thought daring by riding a man's bike), then, most happily, a sparkling – and it certainly did sparkle – d.g. tandem, derailleur-geared and costing every penny of fourteen pounds!

Yet nothing can dim the thrill and continued happiness of the truly "posh" bicycle bought in 1920 with the modest war gratuity. For some little time ahead cyclists remained "Kings of the Road."

The Wheelmen — America's Antique Bicycle Association

Robert T. McNair

Bob McNair's shows on bicycling history are always well-attended because he is so knowledgeable and articulate. No one can resist watching him and other Wheelmen ride the lovingly restored high-wheelers and lady-front tandems he brings along. Bob founded the Wheelmen, who publish an excellent magazine and can be reached by writing Lola Forsyth, 15633 Dixon Road, Dundee, MI 48131.

Robert McNair *sounding the call.*

American bikers were slow in organizing to preserve biking history. The antique auto clubs were in full swing by 1940 when their classics were only thirty years obsolete, and the Carriage Association rolled off in the early sixties when carriages were out of date by fifty years. But somehow eighty years slipped past from the demise of the high wheeler till the founding of The Wheelmen in 1967. We are dedicated to the preservation of America's bicycling heritage through collecting, restoring, and riding the bicycles, and researching and publishing bicycle history. Our members have done well, considering their eighty-year hind start, but there is still ample opportunity for others to join in the project. There are only six hundred Wheelmen from coast to coast compared to thousands of carriage collectors and hundreds of thousands of auto collectors.

The Wheelmen organization is unique among the collector clubs for its total authenticity. Having the "wheels" *correct* in their black enamel and nickel plate is only the

Photograph courtesy of Robert McNair

beginning with us. Our national head is the "commander," and each state is headed by a "captain." Our letterhead and our magazine cover both exude nostalgia. Our members wear clothing suitable to the machines they are riding. Since they usually ride high wheelers, our members come in snug corduroy breeches with brass buttons at the knee, knee socks, and cap as prescribed by their state captain. These uniforms are copied from the few originals that have survived. In the old days each club had its own color combination; now it is by state, and in major events you may spot the contingents from each state by uniforms as well as by the pennant. On tour the host captain leads with his bugler on his left, and the others fall in by twos.

Parades are more formal, with prescribed riding positions and a practiced series of formations and exhibitions. It is not a *bunch* of old bicycles. It is a single parade entry.

Another unique feature was designed to keep us from becoming a rocking chair society and to recapture that old spirit of adventure by reviving the traditions of riding the big wheels. The constitution provides that those completing an "official high-wheeler tour" of ten miles will be eligible to vote. Others have all the privileges, even to becoming commander, but do not vote. This novel rule has worked wonderfully well. Members enjoy riding the tours so much that they go time and time again. They really love riding their machines. The tour has become the biggest single event of a meet. On Labor Day of 1979 more than a hundred Wheelmen completed a century run at Mackinac Island in Michigan. That's one hundred miles on a high wheeler between sunup and sundown. Wheelmen are not athletes; they just have that old-fashioned spirit.

The club magazine carries articles of permanent interest, some technical details for the restorers, a lot on the social history side, and accounts of famous personalities of bicycling. National and state newsletters carry current news, event notices, and want ads. These can help you find a brake lever for your Columbia ordinary, or a correct hub for your Rambler tandem. They also include listings of parts and bicycles for swap or sale. As members find new treasures, their surplus bikes are offered first to other members.

In days of old, women did not ride high wheelers. How could they with all those petticoats? Having won their liberation in the Gay Nineties they now insist on riding high wheelers. They ride with us in the same bicycle uniforms as the men. Note that these are not just costumes, they are the practical attire for the sport. The ladies have their chance to show off bicycle dresses when they ride the big tricycles of the eighties or the lady-front tandems of the nineties.

Where will the Wheelmen go from here? So far the emphasis has been on the big wheels of the eighties. They are exciting to ride, they thrill the onlookers and they are, frankly, easier to restore since they have steel rims and hard-rubber tires. I would hazard a guess that there are 5,000 originals in America today, and that our members may have a third of them. We hope you will find others and bring them into the fold. It is hard to believe that the current price of a high-wheeler is less than the original cost times the inflation factor!

A swing to the classic safeties of the Gay Nineties becomes increasingly important. That truly was the golden era. The cycles were excellent. Twenty-five pounds was the average weight of a bike and more than half of the bikes had cotterless cranks. The bearings were silky smooth and the workmanship superb. We could not afford such excellence today. There must be tens of thousands still hidden away. You can spot them by their wooden rims, fixed wheels, and block chains—and do look closely for special quality features. Prices are a fifth as much as a high wheeler or less. Bargains! The tandems are particularly interesting, the quaint lady-front models with double steering, the double men thoroughbreds, and the three-to-seven man multi-tandems used for pacing on the race tracks. These cycles deserve good homes with people who will cherish and restore them. Whatever you find, show it to a Wheelman before you start restoring. Wheelmen members have become the experts on bone shakers, high wheelers, tandems and Gay Nineties safeties.

The Classic Collectable Bicycle

Leon Dixon

Leon Dixon is in love with classics, those balloon-tired darlings everyone rode during the thirties and forties. He lectures on the subject at bicycle shows, is writing a book about them, and conducts a forum for the exchange of information and parts in his Classic Bicycle and Whizzer News, *P.O. Box 765, Huntington Beach, CA 92648.*

Until very recent times the classic bicycle has been ignored, reviled, and subjected to all manner of indignities by those who couldn't understand it. Classics were little more than oddities—bizarre dinosaurs unworthy of note in the thinking of the sophisticated, modern cyclist. In fact, were it not for the dogged efforts of a handful of "Peter Pan" enthusiasts, the history of American bicycles since 1920 would have been lost, perhaps for all time. Bicycle manufacturers for the most part simply closed the door on the classic era once public attention was fixed on lightweights and 10-speeds. From that point on, it was as if classic bicycles never existed.

Somewhere along the way Americans became convinced that "lightweight" and "good" meant the same thing—the lighter the better and, of course, every bike should be light. If you're 97 years old or if you're delivering 200 pounds of newspapers you'll still hunch down over racing handlebars and perch on a seat which resembles a vinyl-covered two-by-four—

just like everyone else! This is what the logic seemed to say. The most common reaction of a 10-speed-oriented person is to run over and lift a balloon bike to check out how much it weighs. The practice is tantamount to concern over what kind of gas mileage a 1934 12-cylinder Packard might get.

Collectors tend to present a snooty image to some noncollectors, but in the case of classic versus antique, the classic collector was the outsider. If lightweight enthusiasts thumbed their noses at a classic and the poor devil who wanted fenders on his bike, there was little consolation to be offered by the antique collector. Turn-of-the-century bicycles have long had a great following, but their collectors seldom cared for anything made past the very early 1900's.

Enter the classic bicycle enthusiast into this scenario. This poor fellow would walk into a place with a high-wheeler stuck in the window, ask for historical or restoration information on a classic, and draw blank stares. Nor were the handful of American companies who had made classic bikes any help. Few of these would take time to answer strange requests like what color a 1935 Colson should be painted.

Historical books on bicycles tend to lead up to the 1930's and then skip right into the late 1960's, and that has rendered such works useless in regard to classics. Strangely enough, in the entire time that bicycle history has been written, probably not more than two or three such books have shown even a single photo of a classic.

What did American bicycle manufacturers make during the period roughly from 1920 to 1965? The answer is bicycle classics.

What were these mysterious classics? Think back to the bicycle you rode as a child—seen any like it lately? Chances are you rode some kind of single-tube, balloon, or middleweight tire bike, and most of these represent the classic era in bicycles.

Today it would be extremely difficult to economically reproduce some of the old, elaborate paint jobs (some of which were two or three tones *with* pinstriping) or the beautiful metal work and chrome once commonplace on bicycles. A deluxe bike from, say, the 1930's might have to retail for close to $1,000 with modern prices for labor and materials. Anyone who has ever inspected one of the old Lobdell-Emery rims

(no longer made) is in awe about the fact that rim welds are invisible—and about the gleaming chrome with the indestructible finish.

As with the old hot rodders and vintage car collectors of the 1950's and 1960's, a certain amount of competition exists between the beach cruiser crowd and collectors over the very limited supply of parts and bikes. Oftentimes very rare or very nice, original bikes have been cut up into beach cruisers—much to the dismay of the collector. Of course, these days no one would dare cut up an original condition Model T Ford to make a hot rod. Hopefully, as bicycle people and the general public become increasingly aware of classic collector's items, original bikes won't be subjected to destructive customizing jobs. Currently, competition is hot over such items as horn tanks and spring forks with great attention focused on Schwinn, Roadmaster, and Murray Ohio brands. We are talking about a finite number of bikes and parts that are being sought in ever-increasing demand by ever-expanding groups within the hobby. Predictably, prices are already on the rise as supplies of the high-demand items diminish.

Motorizing kits were always a part of the classic bicycle and as such are fast becoming another popular and nostalgic spinoff. Such brands as Whizzer, Marmon, Monark Super-Twin, and others have a large and enthusiastic following, especially in the case of the Whizzer. Devoted fans of this brand have already established an annual gathering and show fondly referred to as the "Whizz-In." Fans from all parts of the country attend the show to exchange notes and swap parts. In light of the present developments in energy, the vintage motorized bicycles (actually forerunners of the modern-day mopeds) are eminently practical as well as collectable. Whizzers, for instance, got more than a hundred miles per gallon of gas and offered the flexibility of pedaling for short distances. The present popularity of the moped is witness to the pioneer trail blazed by motorized classic bicycles.

It seems clear that classic bicycles are here to stay. The hobby (as well as its offshoots) is in its infancy, but promises to become one of the biggest things ever to hit the bicycle world. Every day, more and more people who have had the foresight to hold onto classic parts and bikes become aware of renewed interest. Thankfully, the trend of hauling old stuff to the dump is slowing down. We can now safely say that the wonderful designs and marvelous craftsmanship of classic bicycles will not be forgotten.

The Universal Gear-Speed-Cadence Chart

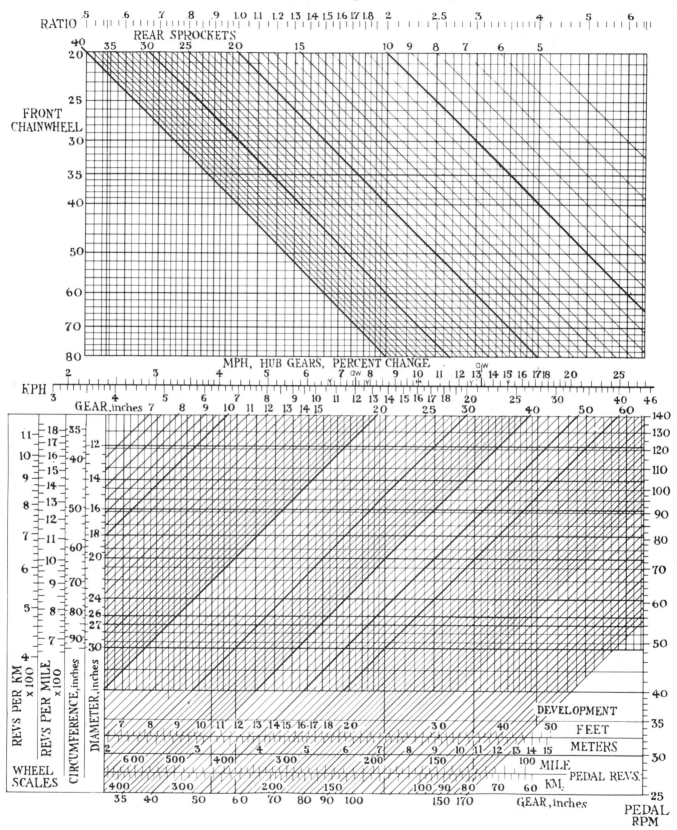

THE UNIVERSAL GEAR CADENCE SPEED CHART

Designed for THE BICYCLING BOOK, ©1981 by Mel Shleifer

The giant, the man on the high-wheeler, and the cyclist pushing a 120-inch gear all go the same distance with one complete revolution of the pedals or one stride forward with each foot. We can say that they are all in the same gear because having a gear of 120 is the same as having a driving wheel 10 feet high or having a stride of 31 feet.

Cadence is how many times you push the pedals around in a minute (pedal rpm). A gear half as large pedaled twice as fast produces the same speed and distance traveled. This and other relationships are shown graphically on the chart on the preceding page. John Krausz

THE UNIVERSAL GEAR-SPEED-CADENCE CHART

On the top part of the graph the diagonal lines stand for rear sprockets, the horizontal lines stand for chainwheels; the entire top part of the chart is devoted to figuring this ratio.

To figure gear, the number of teeth in the chainwheel (front sprocket) is divided by the number of teeth in the rear, or driving, sprocket, and multiplied by the diameter of the driving wheel. In the example shown, the diagonal sprocket line 20 crosses the horizontal chainwheel line 28, and the rear sprocket line 35 crosses 49 on the same vertical ratio line, because they are the same ratio (1.4). Ratios may be read off the uppermost scale.

The vertical ratio line is then followed down to the bottom part of the chart until it crosses the horizontal wheel-size line, which is read from the left, and in this case is 30 inches. The gear is 42, or about 38 with a 27-inch wheel. For decimal gear values such as 37.8 to be meaningful, the *true* diameter of the wheel must be found for the individual bicycle by measuring the distance traveled per revolution. Some of the variables are: size of the tire, air pressure, and the weight of the rider. To the

left of the lower part of the chart are Wheel Scales for more exact measurements.

The relationship between gear and distance traveled in feet/meters is called the "development," and can be read directly by following the diagonal gear line at the bottom of the chart (i.e., a gear of 100 takes about 200 pedal revolutions to cover a mile, a gear of 50 takes about 400). Meters traveled is the European way of calibrating gear tables.

To calculate speed, the diagonal gear line is followed until it crosses the pedal rpm line, which is read from the right. You have picked up a ratio line which is now followed up to the center scale, which reads directly in miles/kilometers per hour. In our example the 42-inch gear at 80 pedal rpms is 10 miles per hour.

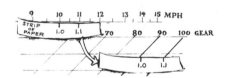

The narrow center scale labeled "MPH, Hub Gear, Percent Change" can be used to figure the range of hub gears or to put together a freewheel with a fixed percentage difference by calibrating a piece of paper. In the example shown, the calibration 10 is used to show 100 percent, and 11 is used to show 110 percent. The 1 and the 1.1 show that there is a ten percent difference between 90 and 100 inch gears. Since the chart is symmetrical, this calibration (or any other) can be used against any scale on it. On the same scale below the calibration 10 is the letter "h," which represents direct drive for most 3-speeds. The "aw" represents the highs and lows; the little letter "v" the high and low gears for a 5-speed internal hub. This scale is used the same as the percentage change scale.

To calculate something that appears on the graph but is not calibrated, you have to do a simple mathematical conversion. For example, to find a speed at 160 rpm's, the answer would have to be read off the 80 rpm scale and doubled; to find 20 you have to look up 40 and divide by two.

Designed for *The Bicycling Book* by Mel Shleifer. Copyright © 1981.

Index